BROWN BOOK

BROW

WAR AND NAZI CRI

PUBLISHER:
NATIONAL COUNCIL OF THE NATIONAL FRONT
OF DEMOCRATIC GERMANY
DOCUMENTATION CENTRE OF THE
STATE ARCHIVES ADMINISTRATION
OF THE GERMAN DEMOCRATIC REPUBLIC

N BOOK

NALS IN WEST GERMANY

STATE

ECONOMY

ADMINISTRATION

ARMY

JUSTICE

SCIENCE

VERLAG ZEIT IM BILD

Contents

PREFACE TO THE ENGLISH EDITION

On 2 July 1965 Professor Albert Norden, member of the Political Bureau of the Central Committee of the Socialist Unity Party of Germany and member of the presidium of the National Council of the National Front of Democratic Germany, submitted to the world public the Brown Book *War and Nazi Criminals in West Germany* at an international press conference of the National Council of the National Front of Democratic Germany and the Committee of Anti-Fascist Resistance Fighters of the GDR.

Already once before, in 1933, German anti-fascists – with active international support – published a Brown Book at a time when many people in Germany and abroad did not yet perceive the dangers arising from Hitler's seizure of power. In Paris they published that famous Brown Book which revealed the first crimes of the Hitler fascists. Professor Norden explained at the international press conference: *"It appeared after the Reichstag had been set on fire and its flames were illuminating the terror already raging in Germany and condemned the nazi backers of the Reichstag conflagration and their war plans. Today we are publishing this Brown Book before the German imperialists realize their plans"* in order to warn in time of the attempt once again entirely to destroy democracy and begin a new war.

This Brown Book appears on German soil, in the German Democratic Republic, proving that this anti-fascist and anti-imperialist German state is aware of its national mission to do everything possible to assure that war shall never again start from German soil.

The acute danger to peace arising from the rule of such war and nazi criminals in the Bonn state increases from day to day because this state incessantly uses its economic, political and especially military potentials for the preparation of the third world war.

"Nor is it of any use to console oneself about the fact that the nazi murderers of yesterday again exercise power in the Bonn state by saying that they 'are but a few thousand people' and 'that they will die out one day in any case'. Firstly, these few thousand dominate fifty million people and the strongest army in Western Europe, and secondly they have long since educated tens of thousands of successors as leading élite of their militarist state in the same evil spirit which made themselves become criminals", Professor Norden declared.

The Brown Book proves with names and facts how the leading section of the Hitler Reich has again become the leading section of the Bonn state. It proves that the forces behind the aggressive, revanchist Bonn policy must not only be punished for their crimes of yesterday but must also be pushed away from the levers of power because they are preparing new crimes.

When twenty years ago, in July-August 1945, the heads of government of the leading powers of the anti-Hitler coalition met in Cecilienhof Palace in Postdam the instruction of the peoples who had suffered so much, and of the German people, too, was that once and for all the lessons must be learned from two world wars and those forces which are guilty of the mass murder of peoples and which made thousands of millions in profits from the blood and suffering of millions must be deprived of power forever and eliminated. The Potsdam Agreement which was signed on 2 August 1945 took account of this demand of the peoples.

This Brown Book on war and nazi criminals in West Germany therefore belongs in the hands of every person to whom peace is dear and who loves justice. For this reason the editors join in expressing the hope which was formulated by Professor Norden, who is one of the authors of the historic first Brown Book of 1933, with these words:

"May this Brown Book help to spread the truth about West German conditions everywhere, for the light of truth breaks through the obscure twilight in which the Bonn conspirators wrap themselves in order once again to bring night over Europe."

The Editors

INTRODUCTION

In May 1965 was the 20th anniversary of the liberation of mankind from the horrors of war and fascist barbarism.

The self-sacrificing struggle of the peoples united in the anti-Hitler coalition, of whom the Soviet Union carried the main burden, ended with the utter defeat of the fascist aggressor, with the total collapse of a system which, through a chain of raids and military attacks, through a rule of terror and lawlessness, through mass murder and the perpetration of the worst war crimes, had become guilty of the death of 55 million people.

The term "war crimes and nazi crimes" had become synonymous with murder of the peoples, barbarism and sadism, and the governments of the anti-Hitler coalition expressed the feelings and demands of the whole peace-loving world when they stated in the Crimea Declaration:

"It is our unyielding resolve to destroy German militarism and national socialism, and to see that Germany can never again disturb the peace of the world. We are determined to bring all war criminals to trial and make sure that they are punished forthwith . . ."

The GDR made the aims of the anti-fascist resistance movement and the anti-Hitler coalition as laid down in the Potsdam Agreement, the basic principle underlying its actions. Those forces which prepared the Second World War and plunged Europe into war and abject misery were removed from all sectors of public life. This was as much in the interests of peace and security for the peoples of the neighbouring countries as it was in the interests of the German people.

The GDR fulfilled its obligations to the German people and the peoples of the world and condemned and justly punished the perpetrators of all war and nazi crimes. In the period from May 1945 to December 1964 in the Soviet occupation zone and in the GDR a total of

16,572 persons were charged with participation in crimes against peace and humanity and for war crimes. Of these

12,807 were found guilty, and

1,578 were acquitted. The prosecution of

2,187 was suspended because of absence, death

or due to Amnesty Order No. 43/48 of 18 March 1948 by the Soviet Military

Administration because conviction was not likely to result in a sentence of more than one year in prison.

Of the 12,807 persons found guilty 118 were sentenced to death, 231 to life imprisonment and 5,088 to imprisonment of more than three years.

Twenty years after the liberation from fascism, 20 years after the beginning of the trials of the major war criminals by the Nuremberg Tribunal of the Peoples, the world is nevertheless confronted with the fact that today in West Germany many thousands who were responsible for nazi and war crimes, are not only unpunished, but are in fact now occupying leading positions in the economy, the government, the Bundeswehr and police forces, in the educational system, as well as in leading publishing houses and in the mass media. The West German government, completely ignoring the just demands of all peoples, treating the Potsdam Agreement and the Nuremberg administration of justice with contempt, almost entirely stopped the prosecution of war criminals shortly after the establishment of the Federal Republic and promoted the main perpetrators of the worst nazi crimes and those who are behind them to government offices of decisive importance.

The illegal taking-over of laws of the Bonn state by West Berlin, which does not belong to the Federal Republic and is known to lie on the territory of the GDR, has led to the result that here, too, seriously incriminated fascists were re-employed in high positions in administration, justice and police. It is mainly these forces which, as supports of the Bonn rulers, strive for a constant aggravation of the situation in collaboration with the espionage headquarters and subversive groups through provocations at the GDR state frontier, kidnapping and other terrorist acts and try to thwart all efforts for negotiations of the government of the GDR to normalize conditions in the special territory of West Berlin.

Although after 1945 by far the greater part of nazi and war criminals had fled to the western occupation zones, in the West German Federal Republic, which in respect of population is three times the size of the GDR, only 12,457 persons had been charged with committing war crimes up to January 1964. By March 1965 the courts of the Federal Republic had legally convicted only 5,234 persons. In over 7,000 cases either a verdict of not guilty was returned, or the prosecution was withdrawn, or the trial was not even begun. In those cases, however, where a conviction resulted, the sentences as a general rule had no relation to the crimes committed. Of the 5,234 convicted nazi criminals and mass-murderers only 80 received the maximum penalty (9 sentenced to death, 71 to life imprisonment).

If in the last years – after a long interval – a few trials of nazi mass-murderers are again taking place in the Federal Republic, then the following must be stated: Firstly, they take place only in cases where the revelations of the GDR and the pressure of international public opinion leave the West German judiciary no other choice. Secondly, they are almost exclusively directed against the lower ranks of the SS and concentration camp murderers, whereas the high-ranking "desk" murderers and their supporters are spared. Thirdly and finally, the outcome of these trials are hair-raisingly light sentences; even Eichmann accomplices such as SS Führers Hunsche and Krumey, who participated in the deportation and slaughter of many hundreds of thousands of Hungarian Jews, were declared not guilty or given token sentences in Frankfurt-on-Main in 1964. These trials thus do not alter the fact that West Germany today is a veritable paradise for nazi and war criminals.

This Brown Book contains – as a first and as still incomplete statement – the names of over 1,900 heavily incriminated former leading nazi officials and war criminals who today either hold key positions in the West German government or economic apparatus, or else receive high pensions for their "valuable services" in the "Third Reich".

The Brown Book proves that of the number of supporters of the Hitler dictatorship, initiators and exploiters of the persecution of Jews, organizers and commanders of the attacks against almost every country in Europe and proven murderers of anti-fascists and resistance fighters, who are again at work in West Germany today . . .

21 are ministers and state secretaries of the Federal Republic;

100 are generals and admirals of the Bundeswehr;

828 are high judicial officials, public prosecutors and judges;

245 are leading officials of the Foreign Office, the Bonn embassies and consulates;

297 are high officers of the Police Force and the Office for the Protection of the Constitution.

And this is only the initial list.

Experts of the barbaric terror administration of the occupied eastern districts like Karl Friedrich Vialon are state secretaries. Murder generals like General Trettner command the Bundeswehr. Nazi hanging judges, who sentenced hundreds of people to death, control the judiciary. Even the highest representative of the Federal Republic, in the person of Heinrich Lübke, is a man who, in the realization of the most secret armament plans of the top nazi leadership and in the capacity of construction manager of the Göring-Himmler-Speer Jäger staff became involved in and responsible for the murder of several hundred concentration camp prisoners.

This Brown Book contains exclusively the names of such persons who really are seriously incriminated through their leading role in the preparation and perpetration of nazi crimes and acts of aggression, and who either participated in the mass slaughter directly, or on whose orders it was carried out, or who were the intellectual originators. In this connection it deliberately refrains from listing even such far from innocent persons as the West German head of government,

Ludwig Erhard, or the CSU chairman Franz Josef Strauss, although one actively supported the nazi regime as an economic expert and adviser to the nazi-Gauleiter Bürckel in the Saar district; and the other as a national socialist training officer.

Naturally the Brown Book does not contain any names of nominal members of the NSDAP (nazi party). The GDR has always clearly distinguished between the millions of former rank and file members of the nazi organizations, who were themselves misled and duped, and the odious group of supporters, initiators and profiteers of the nazi crimes. We do not intend to blame anybody who once made a political mistake and has since recognized his error and embarked on a new road – particularly not 20 years afterwards.

Finally, it must be pointed out that the Bonn government appointed the above listed nazi criminals to their offices, not in any lack of information about their past, but, on the contrary, with full knowledge of it. The Brown Book contains precise evidence on the number of years the incriminating information has been known to Bonn about some of the relevant persons.

The GDR has always considered it to be its right and duty to inform public opinion about the dangerous developments in West Germany and to make its own contribution to overcoming the past in the whole of Germany. Since 1955 the GDR, at numerous press conferences, named a total of 1,310 former jurists of the special nazi courts who have been restored to office and dignity in West Germany. Since 1959, after they had resisted and dodged acceptance for years, the West German justice officials were finally handed 1,580 files of death sentences which present active members of the West German judiciary had passed during their service in the nazi period. Further, 4,000 documents, personnel records, etc., pertaining to other nazi and war criminals were handed over or sent. At 113 trials of nazi and war criminals in West Germany, the GDR gave legal assistance with documents, witnesses and experts to aid in the establishment of all the facts and the uncovering of the truth.

Thus, the reason for the lack of prosecution and the reinstatement of nazi and war criminals is not that the Bonn authorities do not know of the incriminating documents or have no access to them. Neither is the lack of prosecution and the reinstatement of the nazi and war criminals an accident. Rather, it is a part of the policy of the Bonn government, which aspires to a revision of the outcome of the Second World War, and for a change in its frontiers. The last reason for the reinstatement of nazi and war criminals is that in the West German state the same fateful forces of the armaments industry control the government and the economy which raised Hitler to power, prepared the Second World War and today strain for revenge and retaliation for their defeat, and plan a renewed attack on the frontiers of neighbouring states. Because these forces today attempt to conduct the same disastrous policy as in the period of fascism they utilize the services of the same fascist gangsters. Because the social roots of fascism, the concentration of power in the hands of the armament monopolies, were not eliminated in West Germany, the nazi criminals were rehabilitated.

That is why the infamous 131st law has made it the duty of the West German authorities since 1951 to reinstate former nazi officials on all administrative levels.

That is why Bonn already on 8 May 1960 excluded the bulk of nazi and war criminals from prosecution on the grounds that all "manslaughter" crimes come under the statute of limitations.

That is why the federal government made the decision to apply the statute of limitations from 8 May 1965, to cease prosecution of even the worst nazi mass murderers, which was only forestalled by an international protest movement.

That is, finally, the reason for the decision of the Bonn Bundestag of 25 March 1965, in spite of world protest, to merely postpone for four years the application of the statute of limitations and to prepare an amnesty law for "those who acted on orders".

The persons responsible for the fascist crimes are today the main springs of the Bonn revanchist policy.

The persons responsible for the fascist crimes are today preparing and practicing the Emergency Laws, which for the purpose of aggression abroad are to destroy all democratic rights within the country.

The persons responsible for the nazi crimes today demand the right to be consulted and control over atomic weapons, to be able to drag other countries into new war adventures against the GDR and other socialist countries.

The persons responsible for the fascist war crimes are today unleashing a wave of nationalism and chauvinism in the Federal Republic, in order to condition the population for these plans.

The Brown Book proves that hundreds of nazi and war criminals, whose participation in the mean and bloody crimes is known and established through documentary evidence, are not made answerable in the Federal Republic. Hundreds of war and nazi criminals occupy leading positions in the state administration and in the social life of West Germany. The rule of these forces in Bonn, which have not learned anything from the past, represents a danger to world peace. These forces of neo-nazism and revenge work today, with the support of American imperialism, towards the realization of their aim to plunge the world into an atomic war which is in the interests of a small group of armament tycoons and militarists. The fight for the just punishment of all nazi and war criminals, for the removal of former leading fascists from leading positions in the West German state apparatus is therefore inseparable from the struggle for peace and the easing of world tension. Whoever is concerned with peace and security demands, along with all democratic and anti-fascist forces the world over:

Recognition of the international principle that the statute of limitations is not applicable to nazi and war crimes and must not be applied by the Bonn government!

Just punishment for all nazi and war criminals according to the gravity of their crimes!

Exclusion of all the guilty forces of the past from leading positions in the political and economic life of the West German Federal Republic!

An end to the Bonn policy of demanding a revision of frontiers, emergency laws and atomic war preparations!

In West-Germany, too, the liberation from fascism and militarism, which was begun on 8 May 1945, but has been reversed there, must finally be completed.

ARMAMENT MONOPOLIES AGAIN IN POWER

The Bosses and Beneficiaries of the Hitler Regime:

The German people were cheated of many decades of a happy life. Again and again they were driven into the vicious circle of boom – crisis – war. Two devastating wars in which 65 million people met their death have started from German soil in the last 50 years.

Who brought such evil to the world? Who bears the main responsibility for these millionfold crimes?

This evil results from the conquest-mad German imperialism. The armament monopolies and the big banks – IG-Farben, Flick, Thyssen, AEG, Siemens, Krupp, Haniel, the Deutsche Bank, the Dresdner Bank, the Commerz-Bank and others decisively determined the policy of the Hitler regime and are primarily responsible for the war and nazi crimes.

HELPED HITLER TO POWER

The nazi movement received contributions from the rulers of the banks and trusts amounting to millions to finance their election campaigns and for the suppression of the working class movement and all democratic forces by fascist terrorist gangs. As repayment, the tycoons expected profitable armament contracts from Hitler.

Long before 1933 the armament monopolies were paving the way for the Hitler dictatorship. Emil Kirdorf, the founder and for many years head of the Rhine-Westphalia Coal Syndicate wrote on 31 January 1934 in the *Preussische Zeitung:*

"I met the Führer for the first time in 1927 ... recognizing that only the policy of Adolf Hitler could lead to our goal, I put myself completely at the service of his movement, beginning with that time. Shortly after the Munich talks, as a result of a pamphlet written by the Führer which I distributed, several meetings took place between the Führer and leading personalities from industry in which Adolf Hitler formulated his ideas in a brief and clear cut form."

The outcome of the agreement with Hitler was: The coal syndicate allocated to the nazi party five pfennigs for every ton of coal sold. These payments gave the Hitler party, already before 1933, 6,150,000 RM (Reichsmarks) a year from the coal syndicate alone!

The great interest that the trust rulers displayed in the establishment of the fascist dictatorship, also manifested itself at the meeting of Hitler and the Rhine and Ruhr industrialists which took place at the Industrialists' Club in Düsseldorf on 27 January 1932. Fritz Thyssen wrote about this meeting in his book ... *Ich bezahlte Hitler* (I Paid Hitler), which was published in 1941:

"... practically, I established the connection between Hitler and the important industrialists of Rhine-Westphalia. It is generally known that on 27 January 1932 – a year before he came to power – Adolf Hitler made a 2-1/2 hour speech in the Industrialists' Club in Düsseldorf. This speech made a deep impression on the assembled industrialists, and as a result, a number of substantial donations began to flow from the sources of the heavy industries into the funds of the NSDAP ... In the last years before the seizure of power the large industrial associations provided funds continuously."

When the KPD (Communist Party of Germany) won a victory in the Reichstag elections on 6 November 1932 (about six million votes), and the NSDAP lost two million votes, Schacht wrote on 12 November 1932 to Hitler:

"I am in no doubt that the present development can have but one end, and that is that you become Reich Chancellor. It seems that our efforts to get signatures for this from the country's economic circles have not been quite in vain ..." (Prozess gegen die Hauptkriegsverbrecher vor dem Internationalen Militärgerichtshof Nürnberg – Trial of the Main War Criminals before the Nuremberg International Military Court, 42 volumes, Nuremberg, 1947–49, Vol. 1, page 196, referred to henceforth as IMT)

In similarly worded letters several big industrialists and bankers demanded in the same month that the then acting Reich President Hindenburg name Hitler as chancellor. (See Table 1, German Central Archives, Potsdam, under Office of the Reich President, File No. 47)

After the big monopolies had brought Hitler to power even more funds were made available to the nazi party and its organizations. Under the name "Adolf Hitler Donation of the German Economy" (see Table 2, Archive of the Nationally-Owned Film Factory in Wolfen) the capitalist enterprises, on the initiative of the big trusts – especially Krupp, IG-Farben, Flick and Thyssen, etc., – made available to the nazi party from 1933 to 1945 over 60 million RM a year. The Dresdner Bank alone paid in 1934 over 120,000 RM to the nazi party. (See Table 2, Archive of the Deutsche Notenbank, Dresden, Statement: Dresdner Bank)

Besides the payments to the Hitler Donation Fund, the armament monopolies made large financial contributions to the SS and other organs of the nazi terror apparatus.

Friedrich Flick was among the most ardent of the money donors and supporters of the nazi party. Along with steady payments to the so-called Circle of Friends of Himmler – annually over 100,000 RM – Flick paid large sums to the "Adolf Hitler Donation Fund" and to all local organizations of the nazi party. The Steel Works in Riesa, which belonged to his trust, for example, transferred over 34,000 RM to the local SA and SS units from 24 February 1933 until the end of 1934. After the signing of the Munich Agreement on 30 September 1938 the chairman of the board of IG-Farben, Hermann Schmitz, secured further substantial financial aid for Hitler.

"Being so deeply impressed, my Führer, by your achievement of bringing the Sudetenland home to the Reich the IG-Farben Industry Joint-Stock Company puts at your disposal for use in the Sudeten German area a sum of half a million Reichsmarks." (Nuremberg Trial, Case VI, Trial of Carl Krauch and other Representatives of the IG-Farben Trust, Document NI 2795, henceforth referred to as NG, IG-Farben Trial, see Table 3)

Altogether the IG-Farben trust – (without subsidiary companies) put over 84 million RM at the disposal of the Hitler clique in the years from 1933 to 1945.

The influence of the armament monopolies, however, was by no means limited to monetary donations to the nazi regime. It was crowned by the close personal connection of the monopoly and bank officials with the fascist state. Representatives of the most powerful trusts could be found in all central government offices. They occupied key positions.

Thus, Carl Krauch, the chairman of the IG-Farbenindustrie AG was simultaneously the "general agent for special questions of chemical production" and head of the "Reich Office for Economic Development". In this function he was the practical state commander over the entire chemical industry of Hitler Germany. Leading IG directors also had functions in the fascist power apparatus. For example, in the German Labour Front (Christian Schneider), in the Foreign Office (von Maltzan), in the Ministry for the East (Felix Prentzel), in the OKW Inland Defence (Christian Schneider main defence representative of IG-Farben), in the Ministry for Armaments (Ambros, Bütefisch and Wurster), in the Reichs-Bank (Schmitz), in the Reich Group Industry (Schmitz), in the Ministry for Economic Affairs (E. R. Fischer), in the Committee for Africa and the Soviet Union (W. R. Mann as chairman), in the Special Committee for South-East Europe and Hungary (Ilgner and Reithinger as chairman), in the War Economy Headquarters Thomas (Krüger and von der Heyde.).

In addition there was a large number of medium and lower IG-Farben employees who saw to the interests of the mammoth concern in the various government and party offices as well as in the occupied countries where they were attached to the military commanders and Reich commissars. (cf. NG, IG-Farben Trial, Document book of the prosecution, No. 62, pp. 253 ff.)

ENRICHED THEMSELVES THROUGH THE "ARYANIZATION"

The most influential trust enterprises committed jointly with the Hitler clique the terrible crime of the "Aryanization" of Germany. The so-called Aryanization of Jewish craft shops, businesses and enterprises, was utilized to usurp the personal property of the Jewish population. Who could carry out the "Aryanization", and get rich in this manner, was decided by the monopoly bosses. They retained the lion's share for themselves. For the Jewish citizen this meant the withdrawal of all basis for existence, the theft of his last possessions, isolation from the whole of public life, being drawn into forced labour and later centralization in ghettos and complete annihilation.

The Mannesmann Trust, for instance, "Aryanized" the eight metalworking factories of the Wolf, Netter and Jacobi Firm and other enterprises. Krupp used the persecution of Jews in order to acquire shipping lines. Friedrich Flick stole the enterprises Rawack and Guenfeld AG, Berlin and the Lübeck AG, Blast Furnace Works.

The main initiators of the appropriation of Jewish property were the big banks, which regularly informed their regular customers from the circle of armament monopolies about property confiscations of the "Enemies of the State" and the so-called "Non-Aryans". (See Table 4, Deutsches Zentralarchiv, Potsdam, under Deutsche Länderbank No. 196) Long before the infamous crystal night of 9 November 1938 – this pogrom was the preamble to the persecution on the largest possible scale – the Deutsche Bank had obtained precise knowledge of property values, in order to immediately participate in the major action against Jewish property. (See Table 5, Deutsches Zentralarchiv, Potsdam, under De-Di Bank No. 261)

The fascist state apparatus and the trusts worked hand in hand. The Nuremberg Racial Laws, which Globke, who was later state secretary in the Bonn government, helped to draft and comment on, were further broadened by the decree on the utilization of Jewish property of 4 December 1938 (Reichsgesetzblatt I, p. 1709) as the result of an intervention by Friedrich Flick. This enabled Flick to substantially enrich himself at the expense of the subsequently Aryanized Ignaz-Petschek-Trust brown coal mines.

THE WAR OF AGGRESSION IS PREPARED

In January 1944 Gustav Krupp von Bohlen und Halbach confirmed in a speech that the German armament monopolies had started, immediately after the lost First World War, to create the economic prerequisites for a new slaughter of the peoples. Krupp declared:

"It is the great merit of the entire German military economy that in those bad years it did not remain inactive, even if, for understandable reasons, its activities were hidden from the public. In years of quiet work the scientific and practical prerequisites were created so that the German Wehrmacht could resume work without loss of time and experiences at the given hour . . . Only due to this work of the German enterprises, which was shrouded in silence . . . was it possible immediately after 1933 to find speedy solutions to the new tasks of rearming, could the many new problems be mastered . . ." (IMT, Vol. 1, pp. 203–204)

After Hitler had been brought to power the big industrialists began with the direct orientation towards aggressive war. From the monopolies experts were sent to the government armament bodies. Here, together with the military, they fashioned their aggressive plans in the interests of their companies.

"The War Economy Staff attached to the High Command of the Wehrmacht", for example, was headed by Colonel Thomas, a member of the board of the Rheinmetal-Borsig trust. This "Wehrwirtschaftsstab" was the government instrument for the preparation of "total war", as well as the looting and transportation to the Reich of industrial plants, raw materials and foodstuffs from the occupied countries.

Carl Krauch, member of the board of IG-Farbenindustrie AG, became "general agent for special questions of chemical production" and head of the "Reich Office for Economic Development". Head of the special committee "Chemical War Materials" under the auspices of the "Appointee for the four-year-plan", Göring, was Otto Ambros, member of the board of the IG-Farbenindustrie AG, who also held office as head of the "Main Committee for Powder and Explosives" in the Armaments Ministry. The representatives of the monopolies directly participated in the preparation and organization of the war of aggression in these positions.

The head of the War Economy Staff, Colonel Thomas, had already in 1940 participated in the drafting of the "Barbarossa Plan". A file note on talks with his collaborators which he held on 28 February 1941 in preparation of the envisaged attack on the Soviet Union reports as follows:

"The main task of the organization will consist in the seizure of raw materials and in the taking over of all important enterprises. For the latter task it would be expedient to make use of reliable persons from the German concerns right from the start, as only with the aid of their experiences from the beginning can successful work be accomplished." (IMT. Vol. XXVII, Doc. 1317 – PS, pp. 170 ff.)

At the beginning of 1935 IG-Farben created its own "Intermediary Office W" (Wehrmacht), which had to prepare the economic side of the war and the mobilization plans jointly with the "War Economy Staff of the Supreme Wehrmacht Command". All IG directors were informed, as long ago as 1935, that this "Intermediary Office W" had to carry out the following tasks:

"... the central working out of the mobilization plans, plans for the change-over of production and the strategic moving of the production places, questions of raw materials, stockpiling, transport, securing or moving of labour power." (Archive of the Nationally-Owned Electrochemical Complex in Bitterfeld, Document of 28 August 1935)

Already on 23 October 1935 the IG "Intermediary Office W" informed the trust management about the war economy apparatus and its working in case of war.

The armament industrialists decisively influenced the aims of the predatory fascist war of extermination. For example, before Hitler Germany had concluded the (for France) ignominious cease-fire agreement with the French Vichy government at Compiegne, IG-Farben had already started to plan the taking over of the chemical industry of the whole of Europe. On 21 June 1940 von Schnitzler, the chairman of the commercial committee, invited a select circle to a conference in Frankfurt-on-Main. And even before the fascist war machine had occupied the whole of Europe *"... the designated order of all European interests concerning the chemical sector which was to be incorporated in the future peace treaty"* was discussed here and decisions adopted on the chemical industries not only of countries at war with Hitler Germany, but also of allied and neutral countries.

IG-Farben also provided fascism with appropriate war aims for the attack on Great Britain. Already in the plan "Operation Sea-lion" it was laid down which English industries would be taken over by IG-Farben after the completion of military operations.

On 8 August 1945 von Schnitzler was forced to admit that

"Through this course of action IG took on a great responsibility and gave, in the chemistry sector, substantial and even decisive aid for Hitler's foreign policy which led to war and the ruination of Germany. Therefore, I must come to the conclusion that the IG is largely responsible for the policies of Hitler." (NG, IG-Farben Trial, Doc. NI 5196)

The demand of IG-Farben was clear: A Europe completely under Hitler Germany and, in the sector of chemical production, under IG-Farben.

Krupp, Flick, Thyssen, Siemens, AEG and other trusts demanded the leadership in coal, steel and the electrical industry of Europe.

PLUNDERED FOREIGN PEOPLES

The imperialist war and the opportunity it gave to push themselves into a good position at the expense of the European peoples freed the armaments industrialists from their last inhibitions. In the summer of 1942, when the Hitler fascists believed victory over the peoples to be within their grasp, Propaganda Minister Goebbels said triumphantly that Hitler Germany did not conduct war for fine ideals but for material things. They were after the Ukrainian grain, coal and ore and Caucasian oil. Hitler Germany would push itself into a good position in the Ukraine, in the Kuban region and in the Caucasus.

Before, however, the fascist Wehrmacht had conquered the regions designated for robbery, the armaments industry was already presenting its special claims. In a letter from the economic policy department of IG-Farben of 15 July 1940 to the manager of the trust, Otto, the IG defence-appointee of the "Office Berlin NW 7" asked the directors to name addresses of patenting offices, construction offices, research institutes, etc., which should be confiscated for the IG after the victory over Britain. Particularly far-reaching plans were developed by the armament monopolies with regard to the plundering of the Soviet Union. It is characteristic that already a few days after the attack on the Soviet Union, IG-Farben brought forward a complete list of all Soviet chemical plants that were to be incorporated into its sphere of power. And AEG was not far behind. For the robbery of the Soviet Union it established a special company, the "AEG Ostlandwerk, G.m.b.H.".

From a document classified as "trop-secret" from the economic policy department of IG-Farben of 17 January 1945 about the "Position of the German-Hungarian Economic Relations", it transpires that the monopoly rulers, even in the face of total defeat, were still feverishly endeavouring to steal industrial plants and economically valuable goods for German imperialism. (See Table 6, German Central Archives, Potsdam, under IG-Farben, No. 1080)

DRAGGED OFF TO SERVE AS SLAVE LABOUR

Over 20 million people from almost all countries of Europe were dragged by the fascists into Hitler Germany as slave labour – hundreds of thousands of them were tortured, beaten to death, shot and gassed. The overwhelming evidence about the unlimited exploitation and oppression of foreign forced labourers by the German trusts forced the International Military Tribunal in Nuremberg to the conclusion: *"The dragging off to slave-labour possibly was the greatest and most terrible slave enterprise in human history."* (IMT, Vol. 2, p. 164)

For the appalling crimes of the mass deportations of millions of people the Reichstatthalter Fritz Saukel, Gauleiter and general in the SS, "general agent for the employment of labour", was put on trial in Nuremberg as one of the main war criminals – where he was sentenced to death. The armament industrialists, however, who enriched themselves beyond measure through this "use" of forced labour, went scot free.

In many factories the greater part of the labour force was made up of forced labourers. For instance, the percentage of foreign workers, concentration camp prisoners and prisoners of war in the Mitteldeutschen Stahlwerken (Flick trust) was 52 per cent of the entire staff. In the AEG-Hennigsdorf it was even 61 per cent. The Krupp "Family Enterprise" exploited a total of 97,952 foreign civilian workers, prisoners of war and concentration camp prisoners in its factories. In violation of Article 13 of the Geneva Convention many prisoners of war were forced into slave-labour in the armament industry.

In all large factories there were similar conditions in regard to the murderous exploitation methods and the impossible living conditions of deported persons and prisoners of war. In his statement under oath before the Nuremberg Tribunal, Dr. W. Jäger described the condition of French prisoners of war in the factories of war criminal Krupp:

"The French prisoner of war camp in the Nöggerathstrasse was destroyed in an air raid and the inmates were kept for almost half a year in dog kennels, lavatories and baking ovens. The dog kennels were 1 metre high, 3 metres long and 2 metres wide. Five men slept in each kennel. The prisoners had to crawl on all fours into these kennels. There were no tables, chairs or cupboards in this camp. Neither were there sufficient blankets. There was no water in the whole camp. Medical examinations which took place had to be undertaken in the open." (IMT, Vol. III, p. 497)

Of the foreign forced labour the Soviet and Polish people were exposed to the worst discrimination. Like all Jewish people, they too were forced to wear a discriminating badge.

The attitude of the armament industrialists, that the Slav peoples represented only an "inferior race", and that they could be exploited even far more than those from the West European countries, is especially expressed in the following order issued by IG-Farben:

"Russian women can be put, without hesitation, to performing men's work, as in any case any considerations or safety regulations with regard to work times or conditions are out of place." (Archives of the Nationally-Owned Film Factory in Wolfen, under IG-Farben)

After the defeat of the Hitler troops before Moscow in December 1941 the cry of the trust rulers for manpower became ever louder. The German imperialists began to think of how better to exploit the labour power of the Soviet people, especially the prisoners of war.

A memorandum of 20 February 1942 of Ministerial Director Dr. Mansfield of the Ministry of Labour states:

"The present difficulties with regard to the employment of labour would not have risen if one had decided in good time to make extensive use of Russian prisoners of war; 3.9 million Russians were available. There are now only 1.1 million left." (Evidence documents for the trial courts of the British Zone, 15 May 1946, Doc. No. 84)

About the effects of the cruel exploitation of Soviet people in the Krupp works Dr. W. Jäger testified under oath in Nuremberg:

"The supply plan provided for a small quantity of meat per week. But only meat unfit for human consumption could be used for this purpose; this was either meat from tubercular horses or otherwise contaminated meat . . . Typhus was also widely spread among these workers. Lice, the carrier of this disease, along with innumerable fleas, bedbugs and other vermin plagued the inmates of these camps. As a result of the filthy conditions in these camps almost all the workers from the East had skin diseases. The inadequate nourishment caused cases of oedema, nephritis and Shighekruse." (IMT, Vol. III, p. 495)

With what bestial methods foreign forced labour was worked to death by the armament industrialists is expressed in the punitive systems that they practised. The Graetz trust developed and practised during the Second World War its own factory punitive system, which made it possible to exploit the forced labour and the Jews to the point of total physical exhaustion. The following punishments were provided by this trust, whose 'manager', Erich Graetz, was promoted to "military economic leader" by Hitler and on whose board of directors the Deutsche Bank was represented:

"Exercises after work, relegation to a punitive group after work, loss of lunch for up to three days, confinement in darkness on bread and water without sleeping facilities. Refusal of medical care." (Archive of the Nationally-Owned Works for Signal and Safety Techniques, Berlin-Treptow; under Graetz trust)

The armament industrialists often used floggings to subdue their foreign forced labourers. In addition, these workers were subjected to the *". . . constant supervision of the Gestapo and SS, and if they attempted to leave their job they were transferred to educational or concentration camps."* (IMT. Vol. I. p. 276)

The Hescho concern in Hermsdorf/Thuringia, 53 per cent of whose labour force was foreign forced labour, constantly handed German and foreign workers to the Gestapo to keep "peace in the factory" and break all resistance. The armament industrialists feared the solidarity of German workers with the foreign workers. In factory announcements they threatened German workers with heavy penalties, in many instances even with the death penalty. (See Table 7, Archive of the Nationally-Owned Galvanik, Leipzig, under Langbein Pfanhauser Werke AG, and archive of the Nationally-Owned Ceramic Works, Hermsdorf, under Hescho-Konzern)

Neither did the big industrialists hesitate to deport children to Hitler Germany to exploit them for armament production. Because the fascist regime excluded Polish and Russian children from all child protection laws, child labour became one of the most profitable businesses. Many trusts demanded to be supplied with children and had them on their labour lists with details of their work obligations. The Hescho trust, for instance, which was very closely connected with the

AEG and Siemens, employed children eight years of age. They were given an hourly wage of eleven pfennigs. (See Table 8, Archive of the Nationally-Owned Ceramic Works, Hermsdorf, under Hescho-Konzern) In this way the net profit of the Hescho trust could be increased from 774,000 RM in 1938 to 10.4 million RM in 1942.

Many children, who were dragged to Germany with their mothers or even separately from their parents, became the victims of the German trust rulers. They died as a result of the inhuman exploitation and ill-treatment.

"BLESSED FRIENDSHIP" WITH THE SS

An especially close relationship existed between the German armament industrialists and the SS, which was pronounced by the Allied Military Tribunal in Nuremberg to be a "criminal organization". The "Circle of Friends of the Reichsführer SS", Himmler, which was created on their initiative, for instance, united representatives of the following trusts, among others:

Siemens-Schuckert-Werke AG
IG-Farbenindustrie AG
Mitteldeutsche Stahlwerke (Flick-Konzern)
Wintershall AG
Vereinigte Stahlwerke AG
Portland-Zement AG
Braunkohle-Benzin AG Berlin
Robert-Bosch-Konzern Stuttgart
Rheinmetall Borsig
Ilseder Hütte
Deutsch-amerikanische Petroleum-Gesellschaft
Hamburg-Amerika Linie
Norddeutscher Lloyd, Bremen
Deutsche-Continental-Gas-Gesellschaft, Dessau
Deutsche Bank
Dresdner Bank
Commerz- und Privatbank AG, Berlin
Bankhaus Stein

The trusts and banks joined together in the "Circle of Friends" provided the SS annually with one million RM for "special tasks". They supported this criminal organization in the building of its extermination camps and in the extermination of the politically and racially persecuted people.

By means of this "Circle of Friends", which met once a month under the leadership of Himmler for "informal talks", the bank and trust rulers secured control and a close insight into the most secret spheres of the Hitler dictatorship. The cooperation between the armament monopolies and the SS was characterized by former SS General Karl Wolff in his sworn evidence as follows:

"The relations between Himmler and the members of the 'Circle of Friends', as long as I participated in the meetings of the Circle of Friends, was so good that Himmler frequently took the gentlemen along to familiarize them with the work and problems of the SS and to show them what their donations were used for. I believe it was 1937 that Himmler took the members of the Circle of Friends to view his Allach porcelain factory and the Dachau concentration camp." (NG, IG-Farben Trial, Document Book of the Prosecution No. 91, pp. 23–24)

The trust rulers could not emphasize strongly enough that their *"friendship with the SS is a blessing"* (IG-Farben board member Otto Ambros in a letter), to which they added laudingly, that the wishes of the monopolies were fully satisfied by the SS.

Large enterprises began to organize Gestapo jails for their own use. In a letter from the AEG Apparatewerke Treptow, of 14 September 1944 it is stated among other things:

"With the agreement of Herr Commissar Refeldt we have set up two rooms in the Johannisthal camp to unburden the Secret State Police (Gestapo). One is for women, one for men – they are required for educational purposes for our foreign labour force." (Archive of the Nationally-Owned Electrical Apparatus Works, Berlin-Treptow, under AEG-Konzern)

The large enterprises even established their own works "education camps" during the war years, which were very much like the concentration camps. In the directors' meeting of the IG-Farben in Ludwigshafen on 5 June 1943, the following was stated about the organization of the firm's own "Education Camp":

"In agreement with the Gestapo, during this week a works education camp, so far only for working members of foreign nationalities, has been put into operation. From this measure, judging from the experience of other factories, we hope to obtain an effective stoppage of breaches of works discipline." (Archive of the Nationally-Owned Film Factory, Wolfen, under IG-Farben)

The armaments monopolies were not even satisfied with the Gestapo terror against the forced labourers. Thus the IG-Farben Works in Auschwitz (!) complained about the too "slack" attitude of the Gestapo and demanded the implementation of sharper measures.

EXTERMINATION THROUGH WORK

A memorandum of the IG-Farben about talks of the Gestapo with directors of the Berlin works on 9 February 1942 proves that the monopoly rulers were informed of all details of the coming Gestapo measures already within a few days of the infamous Wannsee Conference. (At the conference of 20 January 1942 in Berlin-Wannsee, leading fascists – among them Eichmann who was executed in Jerusalem in 1962 and Globke's superior, State Secretary Stuckart, who was convicted at Nuremberg – adopted the so-called final solution of the Jewish question, that is, the murder of eleven million Jews.)

The systematic extermination of children, women and old people began in Treblinka, Belcec and Auschwitz. The most powerful monopolies immediately participated in this criminal business. They invented and practised the method – 'Extermination through Work'. In the immediate vicinity of the extermination camps they built huge factories. Here the Jews were driven to work, without pay, given the worst food possible and under completely inadequate sanitary conditions.

The Auschwitz concentration camp commandant Rudolf Höss, in his sworn statement (NG, IG-Farben Trial, NI 034) named the monopolies – IG-Farben, Siemens and Halske, Krupp, Daimler-Benz and Henschel among others – which exploited concentration camp prisoners in the most inhuman way and on a large scale. IG-Farben played an especially shameful role in the exploitation of Jewish prisoners. It gave the SS money and building materials to enlarge the Auschwitz concentration camp, to make it the largest mass-extermination camp. The trust rulers wanted to accommodate masses of concentration camp prisoners in Auschwitz, to be able to constantly replace those exterminated through work with a new labour force.

As a rule prisoners able to work were destroyed by IG-Farben within a period of three to six months. After which the victims were caused by the monopoly rulers to be pushed out, as unfit for work, into the gas chambers of the SS.

But the German monopolies, particularly IG-Farben, made a profit even from the dying. They were murdered with the poison gas "Zyklon B", which had been developed in the laboratories of IG-Farben.

The "final solution" brought the pharmaceutical monopolies further profitable possibilities. To avoid high costs and lengthy pharmacological research, they used little tried or untried medical preparations on the prisoners. For this purpose IG-Farben sent huge quantities of medicaments to the concentration camp doctors. These experiments led to the excruciating deaths of many prisoners.

WAR PROFITS – MILLIONS OF PROFIT

The armament program of the Hitler government and the imperialist predatory war brought the large monopolies enormous profits over the years from 1933 to 1945. Thus, for instance, board report of the Elbtalwerk (EAG), Heidenau, and its branch works of 30 December 1943 (a subsidiary of the Mansfield trust) states:

"To begin with the turnover, looking back on the previous periods since the beginning of the war:

Total turnover	*1939*	*5,246,000 RM*	*Total staff*	*648*
"	*1940*	*6,463,000 RM*	*"*	*747*
"	*1941*	*8,382,000 RM*	*"*	*1,000*
"	*1942*	*13,414,000 RM*	*"*	*1,434*
"	*1943 some*	*27,000,000 RM*	*"*	*2,581*

"With an average turnover of 3 million a month, which we hope to carry on under any circumstances, at the present rate of orders, we shall be fully occupied for 2 to 2-1/2 years." (Archives of the Nationally-Owned Elbthalwerk, Heidenau, under Electrizitäts AG)

IG-Farben showed the following profits from 1932 to 1943:

Development of profits of IG-Farben in million Reichsmarks:

1932	1937	1939	1943
48	231	363	822

(Based on calculations of the Committee for the Study of Social Conditions and Their Changes in West Germany.)

Annual turnover of IG-Farben in million RM:

1933	1938	1939	1943
894.3	1,645.4	1,988.0	3,115.6

The share capital of IG-Farben increased from 720 million RM in 1938 to 1,400 million RM by 1942. The reserves shown in the balance sheets rose from 292.3 million to 440.2 million RM.

The Siemens trust, like most other large enterprises, held secret its turnover in the war years; alone from 1933 to 1938 through its participation in the armament the turnover rose from 329 million to 964 million RM. The shown reserves rose from 204.7 million at the end of 1938 to 280.3 million RM at the end of 1942. The share capital in this period rose from 227.1 to 640 million RM.

The armament of Hitler Germany also secured enormous profits for the Krupp concern. According to the statement of the US chief prosecutor Jackson in the Nuremberg trials of the chief war criminals in the years from 1935 to 1941 the officially listed, but in reality much higher profits, after taxes, presents and reserves, almost doubled; they rose from 57 million to 111 million RM.

The Mannesmann trust increased its turnover from 88.7 million in 1933 to 466 million RM in 1943. The profits, which can be calculated from the published balance sheets, after all deductions, increased in the same period from 11.3 million to 83.6 million RM.

The balance of the AEG trust rose in the war years from 598 million to 1.2 thousand million RM.

A similar situation existed with regard to other enterprises.

The misfortune that was brought over Germany and the other countries by the Hitler regime of the armament monopolies and big banks is immeasurable. It was fortunate for mankind, fortunate particularly for the German people, that the armies of the anti-Hitler coalition – above all the troops of the Soviet army – liberated Germany from the fascist rule of terror. Unanimously the peoples demanded just punishment for all those guilty of crimes against peace and against humanity.

This determined demand forced the western allies also to extend the prosecution to some of the armament tycoons, to whom the verdict of the International Military Tribunal primarily applies.

"The dictatorship, behind which these people tried to hide, was of their own making. Driven by the desire to create a position of power for themselves, they inaugurated this system, from which they received their orders. The continuance of this system was dependent on their constant support." (IMT, Vol. XIX, p. 515)

The Potsdam Agreement also contained the demand to eliminate the concentration of power of German monopoly capital. It was provided that:

"At the earliest practicable date, the German economy shall be decentralized for the purpose of eliminating the present excessive concentration of economic powers as exemplified in particular by monopolistic arrangements." (Das Potsdamer Abkommen und andere Dokumente – The Potsdam Agreement and Other Documents, Kongress-Verlag, Berlin, 1950, p. 18)

The verdict of the nations was unambiguous and clear:

The monopoly tycoons, who decisively determined the policy of the Hitler regime and are mainly responsible for the war and nazi crimes must be deprived of power and punished. That is the most important prerequisite for the development of Germany into a unified, peaceful and democratic state, the most important prerequisite that a war will never again start from German soil.

Again in Power

Since then 20 years have passed. What happened to the bosses and beneficiaries of the Hitler regime? Were they deprived of power and punished? And has there been an end put to the urge for the conquest of other countries, to domination over other peoples, to national hatred and aggression for all time in Germany, in the heart of Europe?

"In the German Democratic Republic, that is, where the working people have the say, we have consistently developed the principles of the anti-Hitler coalition

for the shaping of German post-war conditions. We have drawn the conclusions from the Second World War in all their implications. Prussian-German militarism, scourge of the Germans and scourge of other peoples, was torn up by the roots. The ground was cut from under any desires for conquests, for loot and robbery, for the territories of other peoples.

"We consider revanchism as a crime to be prosecuted by the courts. We have punished and deprived the war and nazi criminals of power. We have not a single factory, no enterprise, no offices, not a single piece of land which serves the interests of war and the armament profiteers. Whoever tries to instigate here against other peoples or advocates war is considered to be an enemy of the people.

"The basic demands of the German working class movement are those most human ideas of the German humanists: peace, social and cultural progress, international cooperation and understanding among peoples, are the foundation of the state doctrine of the German Democratic Republic." (From the Manifesto to the German People and to the Peoples and Governments of the World which was unanimously adopted by the Volkskammer, Neues Deutschland, Berlin, 6 May 1965)

94 MEN CONTROL THE ECONOMY

In West Germany the judgment of the peoples to deprive the monopoly tycoons of power was not carried out. The decisions of the Potsdam agreement were broken, particularly under the protective rule of the American occupation forces. The monopolies – the concerns, cartels, trusts – remained intact.

After the separate currency reform in West Germany in 1948 most trusts were able to exchange their Reichsmark shares (which were enormously increased through war profiteering) very favourably into new DM (German mark) shares. Thus, to give one example, the share-holders of the Vereinigte Stahlwerke, particularly the Thyssen family, obtained for an old share of a nominal value of 1,000 RM a new share of a nominal value of over 3,000 DM. If one adds the reserves, then the total capital of this enterprise rose from 731.5 million RM in 1938 to 3,655.3 million DM now; in spite of the "separating out" of its 18 successor enterprises in the Bonn state it succeeded through its war profits to grow almost five-fold.

IG-Farben could also fully realize its war profits. The Badische Anilin- und Sodafabrik AG, Ludwigshafen (BASF) – one of the three successor companies of IG-Farben – paid out a dividend of 18 per cent in 1963 and had a disclosed profit of 144 million DM.

The Farbwerke Hoechst paid 139 million and the Farbenfabriken Bayer 150 million marks to their shareholders.

The profits which can be calculated from the balance sheets according to the information of the German Economic Institute only for the three big basic enterprise groups of IG-Farben, came to 1,782 million marks in 1963. This shows that the same trust rulers who grabbed thousands of millions under Hitler today also put thousands of millions in profits into their pockets.

The influence and the power of these trust rulers has reached such a degree that the West German pro-government bourgeois weekly, *Christ und Welt* speaks of "The complete power of the hundred men", which, they say, is fraught with social explosive.

"Added together there are 94 men who in the combined functions of administration or board membership in essence control the West German economy. As a group they are responsible to nobody but themselves . . ." (Christ und Welt, Stuttgart, 4 September 1964)

If one asks who these men are and what their names are one gets a frightening answer: for the greater part they are the same persons as before 1945, yes, they are the same war criminals, who, according to the judgment of the peoples, should have been removed from power and punished.

Only a few of the armament industrialists were convicted by the American military court and given mild sentences. They did not even have to serve their time in jail thanks to the intervention of the Bonn government. Today those chiefly responsible for the nazi and war crimes, the IG-Farben directors, Flick, Krupp and other armament industrialists are among the most powerful people in West Germany. From the employers' associations headed by them they determine decisively the revanchist and aggressive internal and external policies of the Bonn state. Without their consent no important decision is made by the West German government.

Thirty-eight top associations are united in the Federal Association of German Industries (BDI), the successor organization of the fascist Reich Association of German Industries. About 400 special organizations belong to them. The president of the BDI is Fritz Berg, an owner of a medium-sized enterprise in Westphalia, who lent his name in 1949 to camouflage the then already completed restoration of the armament monopolies. Among the vice-presidents are: Wilhelm Alexander Menne, member of the executive borad of the Farbwerke Hoechst AG (IG-Farben), Otto A. Friedrich, chairman of the executive board of the Phoenix-Gummiwerke AG and member of the board of directors of the Benzin Petroleum GmbH and Hans-Günther Sohl, chairman of the board of the August-Thyssen-Hütte AG and director of the Deutsche Bank.

The Federal Association of German Employers (BDA) unites 55 'social-political' top specialist and national associations, to which belong over 850 employers' associations of industry, trade, the banks, insurance, transport and others.

Hitler's defence economy leader H. C. Paulsen, a former prominent member of the fascist armaments industry, representative of the Deutsche Bank and general director of the Aluminiumindustrie Singen AG, was the chairman from 1953 to 1964. His successor is the IG-Farben representative and retired Atomic Minister Siegfried Balke. Of the 22 members of the presidium of the association alone 14 represent enterprises which were declared criminal after the second world war.

The aims of these associations are accordingly the same as 50 years ago. The armament economy, in other words the preparation for war, has already been organized by them officially since 1955. The 1955–56 BDI business report states on page 178:

"In the conviction that it is necessary and according to present requirements to connect the bearers of the armament potential as early as possible with all defence economy problems so as not to lose the expert knowledge of the industry, it has put its defence economy apparatus at the disposal of the appropriate departments and gives them valuable information on which to base their decisions."

AGAIN IN THE ARMAMENT BUSINESS

The enquiries of the German Economic Institute of Berlin (DWI Reports No. 9/1963 and No. 2/1964) showed that at the end of 1964 already 109 West German enterprises were participating directly in armaments production. This group of enterprises also includes the Rheinstahl-Konzern affiliated to the IG-Farben group, which today is one of the steel works most intensively engaged in armaments production.

The production of chemical warfare materials, explosives and special fuel (jet and rocket fuels) is the domain of the successor to the nazi war criminal IG-Farben (BASF, Bayer and Hoechst), the Flick-Konzern (Dynamit Nobel AG) and the Krupp-Konzern (Wasag-Chemie AG and Nitrochemie GmbH.)

The IG-Farben successor company Farbenfabriken Bayer AG, Leverkusen, closely cooperates with American firms and military authorities in research and production in the field of chemical warfare agents. In accordance with international agreements, in particular with the Geneva Convention on chemical warfare agents, West Germany is not allowed to produce chemical warfare agents. The Bayer AG evades the obligations of international law by transferring the major part of its activities in this field to the territory of the USA, especially since the USA has not ratified the Geneva Convention on poison gases. For this purpose the Farbenfabriken Bayer AG founded in 1951 an American subsidiary company, the "Chemagro Corporation", in Kansas City, Missouri. This company has access to the great experience of its parent company in the course of two world wars, and is now supplying the US army with poison gases.

The "Chemagro Corporation" also employs, along with American specialists,

German specialists and closely cooperates with the "US Army Chemical Corps", thus directly influencing the chemical strategy of the American army. In this way the West German Bayer AG directly contributes to the chemical warfare of the USA against the Vietnamese people. Apart from the financial advantages the Bayer AG has from the sale of patents and licences to the USA the practical application of poison gases gives it the advantage of testing its theoretical discoveries.

Under the guidance of specialists Dr. Schrader and Dr. Wirth Bayer is also engaged in research, testing and developing chemical warfare agents in West Germany under the cloak of plant protection and combating insects. In the Bayer AG laboratories in Wuppertal-Elberfeld and the Biological Institute in Leverkusen phosphides are being tested under heavy secrecy. These phosphides produce a strong poisonous effect on the nervous system of warm-blooded beings. At present the insecticide and herbicide plants of the Bayer AG are already in such a position as to produce chemical warfare agents that, with regard to their effectiveness, greatly surpass the ill-famed Zyklon B. The switching-over to poison gas production will take one day at the most. (See also *France Nouvelle*, Paris, 30 June 1965)

Within the sphere of the Flick trust, as of 31 December 1962, there are 15 joint stock companies, 89 companies with limited liability and six companies with other legal forms, which together represent a capital of 993.3 million marks and have a turnover of about 7,500 million marks a year.

Nine of the most important enterprises of the Flick trust are devoted almost solely to armament production. Among other things they supply motor vehicles, diesel engines and tank motors, tanks, infantry arms, munitions, explosives and rocket boosters to the Bundeswehr.

The Flick trust has state concessions for the most important uranium deposits in West Germany, which are being mined with increasing intensity for war purposes. These deposits are considered to be the raw material basis for the West German state's own planned atomic armament.

When in June 1965 the AEG armaments trust in Frankfurt-on-Main and General Electric, one of the USA's largest atomic weapon producers, established the KRT Kernreaktorteile (atomic reactor parts) GmbH in Gross Welzheim, the armaments economy collaboration between the USA and Bonn was greatly strengthened. The AEG war crime trust which already collaborates with General Electric in the production of plutonium, a basic material for the making of atomic weapons, has a 55-per-cent participation in the new company.

According to the situation on 31 December 1962 24 joint stock companies, 72 limited liability companies and seven companies with other legal forms with a capital of 632.8 million marks belong to the Krupp trust. Their annual turnover amounts to about 5,900 million marks.

Four important enterprises of the trust are directly engaged in armament production. The trust supplies the mirror-antennae for the NATO radar system, rocket fuel and explosives and participates in the aircraft building program of the Star-Fighter and the Transall-C-160.

CHIEF INSTIGATORS OF REVANCHISM

The West German monopolies are not satisfied with their war profits and their current armament profits. For years they have continued to list their "eastern assets" in their business reports. In the annual reports, the executives of the IG successor companies say *"That the liquidation will only become possible after reunification."*

The West German trusts are anxious to regain possession of some thousand enterprises in the GDR, the People's Republic of Poland, the Czechoslovak Socialist Republic and the Soviet Union. That is why the armaments tycoons stand behind the revanchist associations, whose leaders are their catspaws. They also finance these revanchist organizations and have a decisive influence on the policy of the Kuratorium "Unteilbares Deutschland" (Committee for an Indivisible Germany), as well as on all ministries and other organizations which exclusively serve revanchism.

Revanchist leader and Federal Minister Seebohm, for instance, is an old friend of IG-Farben. His family was in charge of the incorporation of the Czechoslovak chemical industry into IG-Farben.

Siegfried Balke, a representative of IG-Farben, is also a member of the Kuratorium "Unteilbares Deutschland" in his capacity as president of the Federal Society of the Employer Associations. He there represents the interests of IG-Farben and of other armament trusts, whose aim it is to unleash an atomic war of revenge against the GDR and the socialist countries.

In the IG-Farben trial before the American court in Nuremberg, the charges against the leading employees of the IG-Farben trust were the planning, preparation, starting and leading of aggressive wars against other countries; looting and robbery, enslavement and mass murder; membership in the SS, joint planning and conspiracy. The crimes have not yet been atoned for, those chiefly responsible of the IG-Farben, however, are today to be found in the most influential positions of the West German chemical industry.

Ambros Otto **FRIEND AND PROMOTER OF THE SS**

today: Influential member of many boards of directors of the big chemical and other trusts, for example, Scholven-Chemie AG, Gelsenkirchen Buer; Feldmühle Papier- und Zellstoffwerke AG, Düsseldorf, Telefunken GmbH, West Berlin.

Professor Otto Ambros was a member of the executive board of the technical and chemical committee of the IG-Farbenindustrie AG. He was one of the prominent war economy leaders of the fascist state. Along with his leading functions in the IG he also acted as special representative for research and development attached to the Göring "Appointees for the four-year plan". There he was the leader of the "Chemical Weapons" special committee and of the "Powder and Explosives" main committee at the Armaments Ministry.

As a Buna specialist Ambros was chiefly responsible for the building of the fourth Buna factory of the IG-Farben at Auschwitz. He selected the site which he thought most suitable for the barbaric exploitation of the concentration camp prisoners and foreign forced labourers. On the occasion of the inauguration session of the Auschwitz works, Ambros sealed the close cooperation of the factory management with the administration of the concentration camp. In a letter he referred to the "new friendship with the SS", which caused the death of at least 370,000 victims in the Buna Auschwitz works and its auxiliary plants alone, as "a great blessing".

Ambros had several meetings with concentration camp commandant Höss, coordinated the close collaboration with the SS and inspected the Auschwitz concentration camp. He allocated extensive financial aid and building materials to the concentration camp administration, which made possible its expansion into the largest mass extermination camp.

As chief factory manager and member of the technical committee, Ambros confirmed the credit requirements for the building of IG-Farben's own concentration camp in Monowitz and the construction of jail and Gestapo buildings on the grounds of the Buna Auschwitz works. He received all the correspondence of the Auschwitz works. Ambros was informed about the inhuman working and living conditions of the prisoners for whom IG-Farben was responsible. He knew of the use of prisoners in the IG auxiliary plants around Auschwitz, he knew of the trade with the private possessions of the Jews who were murdered in the gas chambers in the Buna works. He travelled to Himmler and arranged with him to make even greater use of prisoners. Ambros himself admitted in Nuremberg under oath (NG, IG-Farben Trial, NI 9542) that he knew as long ago as spring 1942 about the burning of prisoners.

Ambros was also involved in the pillaging of foreign peoples. As member of the executive board and the technical committee he was jointly responsible for

TABLE 1

296

20. November 1932

Ew. Exzellenz,

Hochzuverehrender Herr Reichspräsident,

Gleich Eurer Exzellenz durchdrungen von heisser Liebe zum deutschen Volk und Vaterland, haben die Unterzeichneten die grundsätzliche Wandlung, die Eure Exzellenz in der Führung der Staatsgeschäfte angebahnt haben, mit Hoffnung begrüsst. Mit Eurer Exzellenz bejahen wir die Notwendigkeit einer vom parlamentarischen Parteiwesen unabhängigeren Regierung, wie sie in dem von Eurer Exzellenz formulierten Gedanken eines Präsidialkabinetts zum Ausdruck kommt.

Der Ausgang der Reichstagswahl vom 6. November d. J. hat gezeigt, daß das [illegible]

[illegible]

Umgestaltung des Reichskabinetts in einer Weise erfolgen möge, die die grösstmögliche Volkskraft hinter das Kabinett bringt.

Wir bekennen uns frei von jeder engen parteipolitischen Einstellung. Wir erkennen in der nationalen Bewegung, die durch unser Volk geht, den verheissungsvollen Beginn einer Zeit, die durch Überwindung des Klassengegensatzes die unerläßliche Grundlage für einen Wiederaufstieg der deutschen Wirtschaft erst schafft. Wir wissen, daß dieser Aufstieg noch viele Opfer erfordert. Wir glauben, dass diese Opfer nur dann willig gebracht werden können, wenn die grösste Gruppe dieser nationalen Bewegung führend an der Regierung beteiligt wird.

Die Uebertragung der verantwortlichen Leitung eines mit den besten sachlichen und persönlichen Kräften ausgestatteten Präsidialkabinetts an den Führer der grössten nationalen Gruppe wird die Schlacken und Fehler, die jeder Massenbewegung notgedrungen anhaften, ausmerzen und Millionen Menschen, die heute abseits stehen, zu bejahender Kraft mitreissen.

In vollem Vertrauen zu Eurer Exzellenz Weisheit und Eurer Exzellenz Gefühl der Volksverbundenheit begrüssen wir Euer Exzellenz

mit grösster Ehrerbietung

Fritz Thyssen

Berlin, den 1. Juni 1933.

Adolf Hitler-Spende der deutschen Wirtschaft

I.

Um die zahlreichen Einzelsammlungen der verschiedensten Stellen und Verbände der NSDAP abzulösen, ist unter dem Namen „Adolf Hitler-Spende der deutschen Wirtschaft" eine zentrale Sammlung aller Zweige der deutschen Wirtschaft ins Leben gerufen. Die Leitung der Spende liegt in den Händen eines Kuratoriums, das sich aus Vertretern der beteiligten Wirtschaftszweige zusammensetzt. Den Vorsitz des Kuratoriums hat Herr Dr. Krupp von Bohlen und Halbach (Anschrift: Berlin W 35, Königin-Augusta-Straße 28, Reichsverband der Deutschen Industrie) übernommen.

Die Wirtschaftszweige haben sich verpflichtet, innerhalb eines Jahres, und zwar in der Zeit vom 1. Juni 1933 bis zum 31. Mai 1934, einen bestimmten Betrag in einer für sie jeweils zweckmäßigen Form aufzubringen und die gesammelten Gelder an das Kuratorium abzuführen.

Der Reichsverband der Deutschen Industrie und die Vereinigung der Deutschen Arbeitgeberverbände **fordern die ihnen angeschlossenen Verbände und Firmen auf, mit allen ihnen zur Verfügung stehenden Mitteln** diese Sammlung **zu unterstützen. Wir erwarten die tatkräftige Mitarbeit aller** unserer Organisationen und aller Unternehmungen und den persönlichen Einsatz ihrer Führer. Es gilt, schnell und großzügig zu handeln, die Durchführung einfach und **sparsam zu gestalten** und alle **bürokratischen Hemmungen zu vermeiden.**

Bereits laufende Sonderabmachungen sind in die allgemeine Sammlung einzufügen.

7. Alle Fragen und Zuschriften sind an die Geschäftsführung der Industriesammlung zu richten. Abdrucke dieses Rundschreibens stehen auf Anforderung in beliebiger Menge zur Verfügung.

Für den Reichsverband der Deutschen Industrie

gez. Krupp von Bohlen und Halbach.

Für die Vereinigung der Deutschen Arbeitgeberverbände

gez. Köttgen.

Duplikat!

Adolf-Hitler-Spende der deutschen Wirtschaft

Bescheinigung

D Nr. 086867

Dresdner Bank

Berlin

ist an der »Adolf-Hitler-Spende der deutschen Wirtschaft« mit einem Betrag von

- - - - - - - -einhundertzwanzigtausend - - - - Reichsmark beteiligt.

Berlin, im Juni 1934

Das Kuratorium

Sammlungen bei dem Inhaber dieser Bescheinigung sind allen Angehörigen, Dienststellen und Einrichtungen der NSDAP von der Parteileitung der NSDAP verboten, wenn der Inhaber der Bescheinigung die entsprechenden Zahlungsbelege (siehe Sammlungsverbot) vorlegen kann.

Verbindungsstab der N.S.D.A.P. Berlin

Reichsdruckerei, Berlin

TABLE 2

C o p i e

DOCUMENT No. NI - 8795

Z.A.- Buero - 1. Okt. 1938.

T e l e g r a m m

30. September 1938.

An den Fuehrer und Reichskanzler Adolf H i t l e r

B e r l i n

Unter dem Eindruck der von Ihnen mein Fuehrer erreichten Heimkehr Sudetendeutschlands ins Reich stellt Ihnen die I.G.Farbenindustrie Aktiengesellschaft zur Verwendung fuer das sudetendeutsche Gebiet einen Betrag von einer halben Million Reichsmark zur Verfuegung.

Hermann S c h m i t z

Herrn Geheimrat Schmitz

Herrn Dr. Ilgner

Direktionsabteilung

Z.A.- Buero, Frankfurt a.M.

Z oryginałem zgodny

Jan Sehn

/Tom I.G.d.°51, k. 26 akt procesu w sprawie I.G. Farbenindustrie/.-

ABLE 3

Wirtschaftsgruppe Privates Bankgewerbe
— Centralverband des Deutschen Bank- und Bankiergewerbes —

Kurzanschrift: Bankiercentrale

Postscheckkonto Berlin 86 070

Herrn Pelm
Herrn Bruns

BERLIN NW 7, den 31. August 1939
Dorotheenstr. 4
Fernruf: 16 55 81

Manuskript nur für die Mitglieder!

Rundschreiben Nr. 154
(Im Anschluß an Rundschr. Nr. 151)

Streng vertraulich!

Betrifft: **Wichtige Einzelmitteilungen.**

1. Vermögensbeschlagnahmen
   a) unter Aberkennung der deutschen Staatsangehörigkeit
   b) auf Grund von Steuersteckbriefen.
2. Sonderdrucke und Vordrucke.

3.—4. Verlustmeldungen.

An unsere Mitglieder!

1. Vermögensbeschlagnahmen (Nr. 154 v. 31. August 1939)

a) unter Aberkennung der deutschen Staatsangehörigkeit

Der Reichsminister des Innern hat im Einvernehmen mit dem Reichsminister des Auswärtigen durch Bekanntmachung vom 24. August 1939 (Deutscher Reichsanzeiger Nr. 198 vom 28. August 1939) die nachstehend aufgeführten Personen gemäß § 2 des Gesetzes über den Widerruf von Einbürgerungen und die Aberkennung der deutschen Staatsangehörigkeit vom 14. Juli 1933 (RGBl. I S. 480) der deutschen Staatsangehörigkeit für verlustig erklärt und die **Beschlagnahme ihres Vermögens** verfügt:

1. **Adler**, Eugen, geb. 2. 7. 1892 in Speyer,
2. **Adler**, Fanny Flora geb. Brandt, geb. 17. 8. 1894 in Odenheim,
3. **Adler**, Alfred, geb. 28. 12. 1922 in Künzelsau,
4. **Adler**, Ruth Dina, geb. 13. 8. 1924 in Künzelsau,
5. **Becker**, Ludwig Eugen, geb. 7. 12. 1898 in Kaiserslautern,
6. **Becker**, Elisabetha Editha Helene geb. Huber, geb. 5. 7. 1905 in Homburg/Saar,
7. **Benario**, Paula geb. Mannheimer, geb. 4. 9. 1901 in Bütthard (BA. Ochsenfurt),
8. **Benario**, Walter Max, geb. 3. 8. 1924 in Stuttgart,
9. **Benjamin-Rasmussen**, Helmut Detlef, geb. 31. 1. 1915 in Hamburg,
10. **Berg**, Ernst, geb. 14. 5. 1886 in Obrigheim, Rheinpfalz,
11. **Berg**, Aloisia geb. Träger, geb. 9. 9. 1885 in München,
12. **Chrzanowski**, Paul Sally, geb. 16. 1. 1884 in Lessen (Kr. Graudenz),
13. **Cohn**, Leopold Israel, geb. 10. 5. 1878 in Duderstadt-Eichsfeld,
14. **Contwig** (früher Cohn), Kurt, geb. 16. 10. 1890 in Culmsee (Kr. Graudenz),
15. **Contwig**, Frieda Lina geb. Eckardt, geb. 14. 1. 1900 in Plauen i. V.,
16. **Dahl**, Karl Israel, geb. 3. 5. 1890 in Bielefeld (RB. Minden),
17. **Dahl**, Margarete geb. Weil, geb. 2. 2. 1897 in Krefeld (RB. Düsseldorf),
18. **Dahl**, Elisabeth, geb. 12. 5. 1923 in Krefeld,
19. **Dahl**, Berta, geb. 28. 7. 1926 in Krefeld,
20. **Berenberg**, Martha Louise Sara geb. Warburg, geb. 12. 3. 1879 in Hamburg,
21. **Dessauer**, Hellmuth Israel, geb. 24. 9. 1900 in Heringen (Kr. Hersfeld),
22. **Dessauer**, Paula geb. Baumgart, geb. 7. 10. 1899 in Völkershausen/Rhön,
23. **Dessauer**, Gerhard, geb. 7. 1. 1927 in Heringen (Kr. Hersfeld),
24. **Eckmann**, Marcus gen. Max, geb. 16. 1. 1866 in Schmalkalden,
25. **Eckmann**, Agnes Gretchen geb. Rosenbaum, geb. 7. 4. 1875 in Hamburg,
26. **Eckmann**, Walter Hans, geb. 13. 3. 1900 in Hamburg,

6100

TABLE 4

DEUTSCHE BANK

Vorstand

S. 5/38

Berlin, den 14. Januar 1938

An die

Direktionen unserer Filialen (Kopfstellen)

Umwandlung nichtarischer Firmen

Wir haben uns in letzter Zeit wiederholt mit Ihnen über die Behandlung unserer nichtarischen Engagements unterhalten und Ihnen erst vor einigen Tagen mitgeteilt, wie wir die künftige Entwicklung dieser Firmen beurteilen. Wir hörten darauf von Ihnen, dass Sie in dauernder Fühlungnahme mit diesen Unternehmen stehen und sich auf deren Wunsch bei der Arisierung zur Verfügung gestellt bzw. die Absicht haben, dies zu tun.

Da wir bisher nur einen Ueberblick über diejenigen nichtarischen Firmen Ihres Filialbezirks erhielten, die zu Ihren debitorischen Kunden zählen, dagegen nur wenig über Ihre nichtarische kreditorische Kundschaft unterrichtet sind, bitten wir Sie, uns eine weitere Aufstellung Ihrer nichtarischen debitorischen und kreditorischen Kundschaft und zwar derjenigen, die für die Arisierung in Frage kommt, zu übermitteln. Hierbei interessiert uns im einzelnen, wieweit der Arisierungsprozess des betreffenden Unternehmens gediehen ist und wieweit Sie selbst hierbei mitwirken. Der Zweck dieser Aufstellung soll für uns sein, hier im Hause zu überlegen, ob wir Sie in Anbetracht der täglich bei uns eingehenden zahlreichen Anfragen und der hierbei entstehenden Uebersicht bei Ihren Bemühungen unterstützen können, wobei wir selbstverständlich Wert darauf legen, dass die unmittelbaren Verhandlungen auch in Zukunft von Ihnen geführt werden.

Die ganze Angelegenheit muss vorsichtig und mit Ueberlegung behandelt werden und erfordert viel Geschick, damit nicht durch taktisch unrichtige Behandlung Verärgerungen und Verstimmungen ausgelöst werden, die, wie wir schon erfahren mussten, zu Folgerungen bezüglich des Geschäftsverkehrs geführt haben; das muss natürlich vermieden werden.

- 2 -

TABLE 5

Uhl

Geheim! 1

1. Dies ist ein Staatsgeheimnis im Sinne des § 88 RStGB.
2. Weitergabe nur verschlossen, bei Postbeförderung als „Einschreiben".
3. Aufbewahrung unter Verantwortung des Empfängers unter gesichertem Verschluß.

.FARBENINDUSTRIE AKTIENGESELLSCHAFT
WIRTSCHAFTSPOLITISCHE ABTEILUNG

Berlin NW 7, den 17.1.1945
Unter den Linden 78

S/J. 21/21

45 Exemplare

rn Geheimrat Dr. Schmitz	Heidelberg
rn Direktor Dr. Jlgner	Berlin NW 7
rn Direktor Dr. von Schnitzler	Frankfurt/Main
rn Direktor Haefliger	Berlin NW 7
rn Generalkonsul Wilhelm R. Mann	Waitzacker/Weilheim
rn Direktor Dr. Oster	Berlin NW 7
rn Direktor Otto	Berlin SO 36
rn Kommerzienrat Waibel	Frankfurt/Main
rn Direktor van Beek	Premnitz/Westhavelland
rn Direktor Bergwardt	Frankfurt/Main
rn Direktor Dr. Grobel	Homberg Bez. Kassel
rn Direktor von Heider	Frankfurt/Main
rn Direktor Dr. Kugler	Frankfurt/Main
rn Direktor Uhl	Berlin SO 36
rn Direktor Dr. Anderhub Kalle & Co. Aktiengesellschaft	Wiesbaden-Biebrich
rn Direktor Hanser Stickstoffsyndikat G.m.b.H.	Berlin-Schöneberg
rn Generaldirektor Prof. Dr. Paul Müller, D.A.G.	Troisdorf/ Bez. Köln

G. Berlin NW 7 nach internem Verteiler

---

gar n / Stand der deutsch-ungarischen Wirtschaftsbeziehungen

---

grund verschiedener Besprechungen, die wir in den letzten Tagen mit lichen Stellen hatten, können wir Ihnen über den Stand der deutsch-garischen Wirtschaftsbeziehungen folgende streng vertrauliche Angaben hen:

Räumung und Verlagerung ungarischer Industrie-Anlagen und Wirtschaftsgüter.

Die durch die Kriegsentwicklung entstandene Notwendigkeit, ungarische Industrie-Anlagen und Wirtschaftsgüter vor dem Zugriff des Feindes zu retten, hat das Problem der Räumung dieser Anlagen und Güter und ihrer Verlagerung ins Reich in den Vordergrund aller zwischen Deutschland und Ungarn schwebenden Probleme gerückt. Die notwendigen Aktionen laufen bekanntlich bereits seit längerer Zeit. Um die mit der Räumung und Verlagerung zusammenhängenden Arbeiten zu systematisieren und die sich aus dieser Überführung ungarischer Industrie-Kapazitäten ergebenden wirtschaftspolitischen und finanziellen Konsequenzen soweit wie möglich klar zu stellen, wurden in der Zeit vom 4. bis 6. Januar Verhandlungen zwischen der deutschen und ungarischen Regierung gepflogen, deren Ergebnis in einem "Abkommen über die

- 2 -

TABLE 6

Bekanntmachung

Betreff:
Ostarbeiter!

Beim Einsatz der in einigen Tagen bei uns eintreffenden Ostarbeiter ist von unserer Gefolgschaft auf das allerstrengste zu beachten, dass jeder, nicht durch den Arbeitseinsatz bedingte Umgang mit den Ostarbeitern untersagt ist!

Verstösse gegen diese Anweisung werden auf das allerhärteste, sogar mit dem Tode bestraft!

Wir erwarten von unserer Gefolgschaft die notwendige Disziplin und hoffen, dass keiner unserer Männer und Frauen von den genannten Strafen betroffen wird.

Leipzig, 3.7.42
BI Sz./30

abzunehmen: 30.7.42

Langbein-Pfanhauser Werke
Aktiengesellschaft

Hermsdorf-Schomburg-Isolatoren-Gesellschaft
Hermsdorf/Thür.

Mitteilung

Abzulegen unter Akten:

an Herrn: Dir. Petzsch
~~Abteilung:~~

Betrifft Gegenstand:

Aktion 20.Februar 1943

von Abteilung: Lohnbüro

am: 17.5.43 durch: Schl./Schf.

Erledigungsvermerk

Auf Grund vorstehender Aktion wurden am 19.3.43 die nachstehend namentlich aufgeführten deutschen Gefolgschaftsmitglieder:

Richard Bergner
Walter Knappe
Willi Tischendorf
Kurt Voigt I

sowie 18 Ostarbeiter und 2 Ostarbeiterinnen und am 9.4.43

Walter Bärwolf
Heinrich Degethoff
Walter Trömmler

ferner 2 Ostarbeiter und 3 Ostarbeiterinnen durch die Gestapo in Weimar ~~verhaftet.~~ fortgenommen.

Hermsdorf-Schomburg-Isolatoren-Gesellschaft
ZWEIGNIEDERLASSUNG DER PORZELLANFABRIK KAHLA
Personal- u. Lohn-Abteilung.

G 103 c — L/0183

ABLE 7

21.12.1943

R./Sch.

An das Gauarbeitsamt Mitteldeutschland
Erfurt

Dem hiesigen Betriebe ist eine polnische Arbeiterin mit 2 Kindern im Alter von 8 und 11 Jahren zugewiesen worden. Die Kinder werden im hiesigen Betriebe mit beschäftigt und erhalten als Entgelt einen Stundenlohn von 11 Rpf., verdienen also durchschnittlich in der Woche RM.5,00
Da sich die Kinder in einem volksschulpflichtigen Alter befinden, entsteht die Frage, ob die Kinder nach § 74 b A.V.A.V.G. versicherungsfrei sind.
Ich bitte Sie mir Ihre Ansicht hierüber mitzuteilen.

Der Leiter der Betriebskrankenkasse
der Hermsdorf-Schomburg-[illegible]-Gesellschaft
Zweigniederlassung der [illegible]

2074

Personal-Karte Nr.	Werk-Nr.	Mamaj	Vorname: Nina	Staatsangehörigkeit: Weißrussin

geb. am	5.4.33
zu	Medwedino
Kreis	Weleika
Wohnort	Hdf.
Straße	Ostlager
led., verh., verw., gesch., getr.	led.
Ehegatte	
1.–6. Kind (Name, geb. am)	
Lohnentwicklung: Stunden-Lohn / festgesetzt am	-.11
erlernter Beruf nach Arbeitsbuch	
Arbeitsbuch Nr.	A 230/Ju/2869
Berufsgruppe	23
Berufsart	24
beschäftigt in Abtlg.	Kond. II
als	Armaturenabkratzerin
Eintritt (Tag, Monat, Jahr)	29. 6. 44
Austritt (Tag, Monat, Jahr)	12. 4. 1945
Grund des Austritts	
Umstellung (am, nach Abtlg., als)	31.7.44, Kond. I, [illegible]
Besonderes	

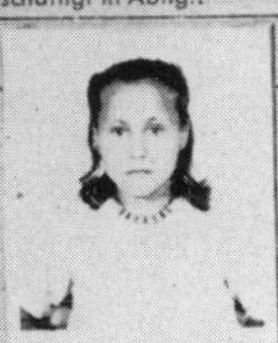

3845

17.7.44 Ak Lag

NSDAP Kriegsbeschädigt

957

Personal-Karte Nr.	Werk-Nr.	Kusnezow	Vorname: Peter	Staatsangehörigkeit: Russe

geb. am	10.1.34
zu	Wertgusowa
Kreis	Leningrad
Wohnort	Hdf.
Straße	Ostlager
led., verh., verw., gesch., getr.	led.
Ehegatte	
1.–6. Kind (Name, geb. am)	
Lohnentwicklung: Std.-Lohn / festges. am	-.16⁵
erl. Beruf nach Arbeitsbuch	
Arbeitsbuch Nr.	A 230/Ju/2807
Berufsgruppe	23
Berufsart	24
beschäftigt in Abtlg.	Kond. II
als	Armaturenabkratzer
Eintritt (Tag, Mon., Jahr)	29. 6. 44
Austritt (Tag, Mon., Jahr)	5 März 45
Grund des Austritts	A.A. gemeldet Muna
Umstellung (am, nach Abtlg., als)	31.7.44, Kond. I, [illegible]
Besonderes	

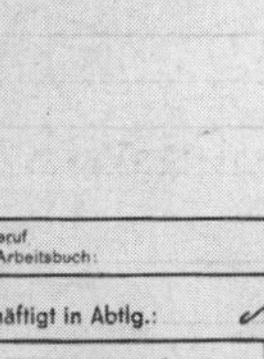

3850

17.7.44 Ak Lag

the incorporation of the Polish, Czech and French chemical industry into the sphere of control of IG-Farben.

For these "services" the fascists decorated him with the "Knight's Cross to the War Service Cross".

Ambros, who was sentenced by the American Military Tribunal in Nuremberg as a war criminal, was soon released as a result of the intervention of the Bonn government, because he was indispensable as an armaments expert for the task of remilitarizing West Germany.

Bütefisch Heinrich OF EQUAL RANK WITH THE AUSCHWITZ COMMANDANT

today: *As member of the board of the Federally-owned Ruhrchemie AG and of other large chemical enterprises, he is an important economy expert of the Bonn government. During the "Week of Brotherhood" in March 1964, which the Bonn government organizes every year, allegedly to especially commemorate the Jewish victims of nazi barbarism, Bütefisch was decorated by West German Federal President Lübke. He received the "Great Service Cross of the Order of Merit of the Federal Republic of Germany". Only after Professor Jürgen Kuczynsky from the GDR, as expert witness in the Frankfurt Auschwitz trial proved the decisive guilt of Bütefisch in the slaughter of many thousands of Jewish people, and after massive protests at home and abroad, was the decoration withdrawn on 25 March 1964.*

Engineer Heinrich Bütefisch belonged to IG-Farben's most influential representatives in the fascist state. He was a member of the executive board and of the technical committee, vice-chairman of the Sparte 1 of the IG-Farben (Chemicals, Explosives and Synthetics). Bütefisch represented IG-Farben on numerous boards of foreign and German works in matters pertaining to the chemical and mining industries.

In the fascist state apparatus he acted as associate of the chief appointee for chemical production and as production organizer for oil in the fascist armament ministry.

As SS Obersturmbannführer Bütefisch had the same rank as concentration camp commandant Höss, and in this capacity he represented IG-Farben in the "Circle of Friends of the Reichsführer SS". In this capacity also, he made all the fundamental arrangements with SS Obergruppenführer Wolff about conditions for the use of Auschwitz prisoners at the plant, for which he was the chief responsible officer, namely in the synthesis part of the Auschwitz branch of IG-Farben. For instance, it was their decision to fix the price for skilled prisoners at 4 RM and for unskilled at 3 RM (see Table 9).

As the responsible officer for the synthesis part of the IG-Works, Bütefisch visited Auschwitz several times. He was informed about all matters pertaining to the Auschwitz works. In his declaration under oath (NG, IG-Farben Trial, NI 4182) he confirmed that he had personally approved the program for the establishing of IG's own concentration camp in Monowitz and had then passed it on. He also was informed about the extensive financial and material support of the Auschwitz concentration camp administration by IG.

Hitler promoted him in 1939 to the rank of "War Economy Leader" and later decorated him with the Knight's Cross to the War Service Cross.

In the Nuremberg war crimes trial of the American Military Tribunal against IG-Farben he was only sentenced to 6 years imprisonment, of which he only served a part because of the recommendations of the Bonn government, which required his services as an armament expert for the federally-owned Ruhrchemie AG.

Dürrfeld Walther DIRECTOR OF THE AUSCHWITZ MURDER ENTERPRISE

today: *Member of the executive board of the Scholven-Chemie AG (IG-Farben trust) and holder of many boards and advisory council mandates.*

Engineer Walther Dürrfeld was a director of IG-Farben before 1945. He was responsible for the Auschwitz building project. He was one of the negotiators of IG-Farben who participated in the main talks with SS Obergruppenführer Wolff on the mass utilization of prisoners in the Auschwitz works in Berlin in spring 1941.

All details on the employment of concentration camp prisoners and cooperation with the SS in Auschwitz, were settled by Dürrfeld with camp commandant Höss (see Table 8). He met him frequently, visited him in the concentration camp and had friendly relations with his family. The first agreements with the concentration camp commandant he made as early as 27 March 1941 in Auschwitz.

IG's own concentration camp Monowitz was established on Dürrfeld's initiative. IG was responsible for the food, accommodation and working conditions of the prisoners. Through his constant insistence with the SS to be permitted to get rid of weak prisoners and only to employ strong and healthy ones, Dürrfeld is largely responsible for the systematic selections in the Monowitz concentration camp. The prisoners who were separated out at these selections were immediately murdered in the gas chambers of Birkenau.

Dürrfeld himself was present in the Monowitz camp, where according to the statements of former prisoners some 1,000 to 2,000 prisoners were selected for the gas chambers. Dürrfeld is also partially responsible for the 3–4 weekly selections in the Monowitz sickbay. He ordered SS Drs. Entress and Wirtz to keep the numbers in the sickbay down at a conference in the spring of 1943. In the appalling living conditions of the camp this demand could be met only through systematic "selections".

Dürrfeld was responsible for the destruction of lives at Monowitz as director of IG-Farben. The reports of the fluctuation of the prisoners reached him daily. Prisoners employed in the concentration camp office confirmed that the card index of the dead prisoners in the Monowitz concentration camp and the outlying camp in 1945 contained about 370,000 cards. On orders of Dürrfeld IG-Farben in Auschwitz conducted an extensive trade with the articles of clothing and other items of the murdered prisoners.

In the Nuremberg IG-Farben trial, the main defendant Dürrfeld was sentenced to only eight years' imprisonment. The federal government having intervened, he had to serve only a small part of his time.

Abs Hermann

WORKED SOVIET CHILDREN TO DEATH

today: General manager, chairman of the board of the Deutsche Bank, chairman of the board of directors of the IG-Farben successor trust Badische Anilin- und Soda-fabrik AG, vice-president of the Deutsche Bundesbahn, vice-chairman of the administrative council of Kreditbank for Reconstruction, chairman of over 40 boards of various enterprises, experienced representative of many employer associations and other organizations in West Germany. Is considered to be "Bonn's uncrowned Minister of Finance".

In the enterprises in which Dr. h. c. Hermann Abs was a member of the board of directors before 1945 – Abs was then director of the Deutsche Bank – foreign forced labour was exploited particularly mercilessly. To what extent the torture of human beings was taken in these enterprises is illustrated by the treatment of Soviet and Polish children who were killed there through forced labour conditions. Even the camp doctor, Dr. Römer of the Vereinigte Glanzstoff-Fabrik AG, Wuppertal-Elberfeld, Werk Elsterberg, protested resolutely against the further employment of a 10-year-old undernourished girl because, he wrote, her continuous occupation would mean child murder. Hermann Abs, the chairman of the board of this enterprise, was not interested in how many children perished. His main concern was that the profits could be increased through child labour.

"Abs was the spiritual rector of the infamous Deutsche Bank, which combined an unusual concentration of economic power with active participation in the criminal policies of the nazi regime. The Deutsche Bank of Hermann Abs acted as a top institution of the German government and served the economic pene-

tration of the satellite countries and the occupied countries of Europe ... Abs used all his energies to extend the rule of Germany over Europe." (OMGUS-Office of Military Government of the USA. Report of November 1946, pp. 2, 5, 51, 171 and 172; in Einheit Berlin, 1951, No. 17, pp. 1235–36)

After the Second World War Hermann Abs was sentenced in absentia in Yugoslavia to 15 years at hard labour. He has not served his sentence. As esteemed "financial adviser" under British-American protection, he was able already in 1950 to carry out official government tasks, and as a member of the economic-technical commission of the Schumann Plan Commission, again carry out state tasks officially on an international level.

In the following years he dedicated himself, as head of the largest West German monopoly bank, to the task of restoring German finance capital and he is considered to be the uncrowned West German minister of finance. For example, when the West German delegation came to the London Debt Conference in 1951–52, it was not led by the West German finance minister but by Hermann Abs.

This war criminal was already in 1953 decorated in the Federal Republic and received the highest award of West Germany – The Great Federal Service Cross with star, for his activity in restoring and consolidating the power of German finance capital.

The Franco regime also decorated Hermann Abs with a high ranking decoration in 1960 for his "services" on behalf of fascist Spain.

Flick Friedrich

COMMISSIONED BY GÖRING

today: *One of the most influential monopolists of German imperialism who was able to expand his power considerably after the fascist predatory war. Flick today again plays a leading part in the war production of West Germany. At the right time he managed to secure state licences for the most important uranium ore deposits in West Germany so as not to miss the business of a planned West German atomic armament.*

Already decades ago Friedrich Flick had accumulated a huge fortune through unbridled speculation and at the expense of the German people. He always supported the most reactionary circles of German politicians with large monetary contributions. Already in November 1932 Flick transferred to the "Special Himmler Fund" an advance payment of 100,000 RM "for special purposes". At the same time he signed, along with the big German industrialists and bankers, a letter to Hindenburg demanding that Hitler be named chancellor.

As "Göring's commissioner", as Flick called himself, he enriched himself beyond measure in the fascists' "Aryanization" drive. During the Second World

War he took over many enterprises into "trustee administration" in the occupied countries. In a letter to Göring of 1 November 1940 he requested a substantial part of the iron industry of Lorraine, which Göring readily handed over.

Flick also participated in the exploitation of the Ukrainian Steel Mills, as the Flick representative Hüttner named this robbery in the Soviet Union. In the enterprises of the Flick trust over 40,000 foreign forced labourers, concentration camp prisoners and prisoners of war were used.

The millions which he gained in the inflation after the First World War turned to thousands of millions in the second. As war economy leader and member of Himmler's "Circle of Friends" he conducted his dirty business in the blood of the peoples.

After the end of the war Flick was accused of having committed crimes against humanity and war crimes as an exploiter of slave labour. In 1947 he was sentenced to seven years in prison. During his imprisonment, however, he was permitted to conduct board meetings! Already on 3 February 1951 Flick was released on the intervention of the Bonn government.

Alfried Krupp

SYMBOL OF THE WAR ECONOMY

today: *He belongs to the front rank of the powerful German trusts. With over 104 enterprises which have an enormous production program he attains an annual turnover of almost six thousand million marks. A substantial portion of it comes from armament.*

Alfried Krupp von Bohlen und Halbach has participated in the total management of the Krupp armament works since 1937. As chairman of the board, and later as sole proprietor of the giant trust he has a substantial part in the development and strengthening of the fascist war economy. His role was described by the chief prosecutor of the United States of America at the International Court as follows:

"Krupp von Bohlen – like Alfried – lent his name, his prestige and his financial support to bring the nazi party, with its clearly recognizable program of unleashing a new war, to power in Germany ... After the war had started, for which both Krupps, Gustav von Bohlen as well as Alfried, are directly responsible, they led German industry, violating international agreements and international law. They employed forced labour, dragged and forced into Germany from almost all countries occupied by Germany ... There is more than sufficient evidence that these workers in Krupp's care and in Krupp's service were undernourished and overworked, misused and inhumanly treated." (IMT, Vol. I, pp. 148–9)

The American chief prosecutor got to the heart of the truth when he said that *"the Krupp trust is the symbol and beneficiary of the infamous forces which threatened the peace of Europe".*

Already in the first five years of the fascist armament drive Krupp could book a net profit of 500 million RM. In the fifth year of the war, 1944, his war criminal family had an accountable profit of over 110 million RM – gathered from the exploitation of 250,000 people who were put to work in the 81 Krupp factories, and of which tens of thousands perished as prisoners in the trust's own concentration camps.

Not only in Krupp's own concentration camps were thousands worked to death; Krupp also profited from the Auschwitz mass extermination camp. This can be seen from a letter of the Friedrich Krupp AG of 8 September 1942 to IG-Farben. The letter, which is addressed to war criminal Dürrfeld of the IG-Farben trust says, among other things:

"With the request to treat confidentially we inform you that our firm is preparing to commence the production in Auschwitz of important parts for the armed forces on premises and with labour supplied by the SS..." (Archive of the Nationally-Owned Buna Works, under IG-Farben-Konzern).

In the trial before the military Tribunal in Nuremberg in 1948 Krupp was sentenced to twelve years imprisonment and confiscation of his entire property. Already in 1951, at the request of the Adenauer government, however, he was released and the order for the confiscation of his property was rescinded. The Bonn government had already chosen the Krupp trust as the cornerstone of its rearmament.

Stooges of the Monopoly Rulers

The closest associates of the war crime trusts of the fascist state and economic apparatus took over high government functions in the Bonn state.

Lübke Heinrich CONCENTRATION CAMP BUILDING MANAGER

today: ***President of the Federal Republic.***

For many years it was possible for Dr. Lübke to present himself to the West German people as a victim of the nazi regime, until in the year 1964 the GDR was able to prove on the basis of original documents of the former Gestapo office in Stettin that Heinrich Lübke was a trusted collaborator of the Gestapo at least since 1940 – which was made public at an international press conference. As assistant manager of the "Schlempp Building Group" which at the beginning of the war was an armament building staff of the chief building inspector for the Reich capital, and later came under the national socialist Armaments Minister Speer, within the so-called "Jäger Staff" – Lübke participated in the building of the "Special Gestapo camp in Peenemünde". He threatened to transfer unwilling workers to that place. The Gestapo office added *"that in the further dealing with this occurrence . . . special reference can be made to Lübke"* (see Table 10).

In 1934 Lübke became, for the first time, a beneficiary of the Hitler regime due to a fascist law on the suspension of prosecution in certain circumstances. A criminal court in Berlin decided to suspend criminal proceedings against Lübke and his accomplices for *"embezzlement, removal of documents and other fraudulent actions"*. At the same time it was clearly stated that the *"proceedings had neither shown their innocence nor had it demonstrated that there is not a well-founded suspicion against them"*. (See Table 11 Mecklenburg Provincial Archive under Mecklenburg State Ministry, Siedlungsgesellschaft Bauernland AG, p. 47)

Since that time Lübke was one of those who supported fascism up to the unconditional surrender – unconditionally.

As organizer of top secret and most important war production, Lübke decisively participated in the mass use of concentration camp prisoners. As deputy manager of the Schlempp building group he worked to build the production sites of the ill-famed V-weapons. In the Peenemünde area he personally supervised 40 building sites! In 1944 Lübke was assigned to build the Leau concentration camp, an annex to the Buchenwald concentration camp. It was an especially important and highly secret task. To counter the devastating losses of the nazi Luftwaffe in spring 1944 a so-called Jägerstab was formed. It was given the task by the war criminal Speer of shifting war production plants of the aircraft industry from the bombed-out or endangered premises into subterranean production premises and to get production to a peak level at all costs. The "Schlempp building group" with its deputy manager Lübke, was also assigned to this group.

For this purpose Lübke, in his capacity as top building manager of the Schlempp group, requisitioned 2,000 concentration camp prisoners from Buchenwald. They had to carry out the heaviest cement and transport work underground in two shifts of twelve hours each in Peissen near Bernburg. The first prisoners were housed in tents at the end of August 1944. The dreadful conditions brought on an epidemic of dysentery. Many prisoners died. For the following prisoners a concentration camp 400 metres underground was prepared. Five hundred people vegetated there under the most dreadful conditions. At a conference on the grounds of the Leau concentration camp at the beginning of September 1944, which Lübke chaired, it was stated with satisfaction that "the work now shows visible progress on the whole front" (see Table 12, Archive of the Nationally-Owned Kaliwerk Bernburg, under Kali-Werk Friedenshall). In the minutes of this conference the firm referred to – ATG Leipzig – belonged to war criminal Flick.

The many original documents on the activity of the Lübke staff in Leau clearly prove that Lübke was responsible for implementing the Jäger program through using the slave labour of the concentration camp prisoners, war prisoners and the forced labourers of other countries. Lübke approved of the murderous conditions of work and existence which caused the death of hundreds of Poles, French, Italians, Soviet citizens and Germans. Up to now the names of 267 persons, exclusively political prisoners, are known from the register of the dead of Buchenwald concentration camp for whose death Lübke is largely responsible. They include 174 Poles, 58 French, 5 Soviet citizens and 18 Italians.

Westrick Ludger "TESTED" WAR ECONOMY LEADER

today: *Federal minister and leader of the Office of the Federal Chancellery, successor of the murderer of Jews Globke (who has been sentenced to hard labour for life in the GDR). Ludger Westrick surpasses most of the federal ministers in power not only because he works from the background of his key position as head of the Office of the Federal Chancellery but mainly because he has always been in the service of the industrial and bank magnates of imperialist Germany.*

Shortly before fascism came to power Dr. Westrick was acting as sales manager for the Vereinigte Stahlwerke-Konzern in South East Europa. This made him one of Krupp's men, who was one of the most influential supporters of the fascists and later himself a war criminal.

After 1933 Westrick became general director of the Vereinigte Aluminiumwerke AG Berlin (VAW), which belonged to the Vereinigte Industriewerke (VIAG), with which position he took over the management of the fascist armament, above all, for the Luftwaffe a very important industry. In the following period Westrick was prominent in the at first secret, and later open, war preparations. Particularly as he was a member of no less than 27 boards of directors or executive bodies, for example, in the Vereinigte Industriewerke AG, Berlin, Reichskreditgesellschaft AG Berlin and Vereinigte Deutsche Metallwerke AG, Frankfurt-on-Main (see Table 13, Deutsches Zentralarchiv Potsdam, under Reichswirtschaftsministerium, File No. 11 709). For these "services" Westrick was named by Hitler as a war economy leader and became a member of the 10-man industrial advisory council for the development of air force appliances under Göring.

In November 1941 Westrick wrote with feeling in the newspaper *Der Deutsche Volkswirt*: *"As long as the fanfares of war are still resounding, the German light metal industry has only one task and one aim, towards which all measures are and must be directed: Germany's final victory!"*

Shortly after this Westrick participated at a conference called by Göring's deputy Field Marshal General Milch, to discuss the partition of the European spheres of interest between the various interested German aluminium industrialists. In negotiations with representatives of France and Hungary in 1941–42 he demanded that the raw material deposits be completely subjugated to the interests of German imperialism.

The most brutal treatment was shown by Westrick to the foreign forced labourers and prisoners of war in the VAW trust which he led. During the war they constituted over 75 per cent of the entire labour force of the VAW works. As can be seen from a letter of the camp doctor of the Lauta works of the VAW of 28 August 1942 children of 13 years of age and foreign women from 60 to 62 years of age were forced to work there. They suffered from chronic diseases and were exposed to the most inhuman living and working conditions.

Uncounted human lives were lost as a result of this terror. As can be seen from the death certificates in Lauta hundreds of deaths were registered there. As cause of death, along with the cynical formulations of "general debility", the following are listed: suicide by letting oneself be run over by the works railway, fractured skull, tuberculosis and other infectious and malnutritional diseases. The death certificate of a French forced labourer carries the following explanation under "cause of death": *"shot by a gendarme official for resisting"*. People from almost all European nations are represented in the register of deaths (see Table 14, Death Register of the Registrar's Office of the town of Lauta). The Lauta works is only one of many aluminium works for which Westrick was responsible.

After 1945 war criminal Westrick was immediately reemployed as economic leader by the monopolies. Already in 1951 the armament trusts launched him into the office of state secretary in the Federal Ministry of Economic Affairs. In 1963 Westrick became Globke's successor in the Bonn Federal Chancellory.

Blessing Karl

HIMMLER'S FRIEND

today: President of the German Federal Bank.

Before 1945 Karl Blessing belonged to the infamous "Circle of Friends" of Himmler and was named war economy leader by Hitler. In 1933 he was working in the Deutsche Reichsbank from where he switched in 1934 as chief expert into the service of the fascist economic ministry. In 1937 he became a member of the directorium of the Reichsbank and later was a member of the even closer advisory council of the Deutsche Reichsbank. In this confidential office Blessing participated decisively in the financing, preparation and completion of the armament and war preparations.

With his aid Schacht established, as long ago as May 1933 in his capacity as president of the Reichsbank, with the participation of the Reichsbank and the armament firms of Krupp, Siemens, Rheinmetall and Deutsche Werke the Metallurgical Research GmbH (Mefo) in Berlin. It was a cover firm to camouflage the then still secret armament.

Due to the high position Blessing at the time had close ties with IG-Farben. IG-Farben wrote about Blessing to a South African firm: *"He is a leading personality in the Economic Ministry and one of Schacht's closest collaborators"* with which they pointed out what an important role Blessing played in the nazi state.

Blessing was counstantly called for consultations with leading fascist counselling groups, as in the talks with Göring about the "incorporation of Austria" on 11 March 1938. On the agenda of this conference, at which Blessing was present in his capacity as expert on Austrian affairs of the Reichsbank administration, was also the question of the Aryanization policy in Austria. At another meeting, which Göring considered to be most important in the framework of the four-year plan, Blessing reported on the question of mineral oil supplies in the "A-case". In December 1939, under the chairmanship of General Thomas, there was a consultation on armament with the Wehrmacht high command. Blessing participated in the discussion on questions of transport and about the securing of raw materials and bragged that he was personally involved in organizing a reliable system of supervision.

In January 1944 the manager of the planning office of the Chief Appointee for Armament Tasks charged the Dresdner Bank with *"... the constant observation and testing of the economic conditions in Sweden, research on specific trade policies and information about foreign personalities", etc.* The Dresdner Bank was further instructed: *"The constant contact with you and the cooperation in details will be effected through Herr Director Karl Blessing, Continentale Oel AG, who has on my orders undertaken the coordination and evaluation of the reports and suggestions of the individual officers."* (NG, Case XI, File No. 422, Doc. NI 2031)

Blessing not only actively participated in the pillaging and enslaving of occupied countries, he also helped to prepare planned acts of aggression against neutral countries.

After the end of the war Blessing, who was interned for a short time only, was received by the West German monopolists with open arms and already in 1957 they launched him into the office of president of the Federal Bank.

Vialon Karl Friedrich today:

THE BOOK-KEEPER OF THE SS MURDERERS

State secretary of the Bonn Federal Ministry for Economic Cooperation which coordinates all problems arising from the Bonn neo-colonial policies. Prior to that: ministerial director in the Federal Chancellery and adviser to Adenauer on economic and financial matters.

Karl Friedrich Vialon began his career with the fascist administration of justice. He was a provincial court counsellor at the high court of Karlsruhe. Then he changed over to the Reichs Ministry of Finance. At the beginning of the Second World War he helped as senior government counsellor to rob the occupied regions of Alsace. After passing this "test" he became government director and head of the finance department of the Reich Commissariat for the Eastern Regions in Riga. Here he left an indelible mark, which convicts him of the worst crimes.

In his area of activities, in the Esthonian, Latvian, Lithuanian and White Russian areas, the so-called final solution was carried out to perfection with the leading participation of Vialon. Hardly a single Jewish citizen escaped with his life. According to statements in the "Einsatz-Gruppen" (action group) trial in Nuremberg in 1947–48 in the Esthonian, Latvian and Lithuanian districts alone 118,430 Jewish people were murdered. Added to this is almost half a million from the White Russian district. Vialon was concerned with robbing these victims. He collected the property and personal effects of the murdered Jews and made them available for the fascist regime so that they could be utilized in perpetration of further murders.

On 16 March 1943 Vialon instructed the general commissar of Minsk in a secret document on the *"Delivery of Jewish property confiscated by the police"* to see that *"the pay offices of the commander of the security police and the SD"* should deliver the confiscated valuables and moneys to the official treasuries of the general commissars. Already on 2 May 1943 Vialon was reprimanding the commanding officer of the Ostland security service and security police that *"the announced delivery of confiscated properties valued at over one million Reichsmarks ... had not been paid in yet"*. He demanded to know when the delivery *"to his main pay office could be expected"*. (Central archives of the Latvian SSR, Riga, under Reich Commissariat for the Eastern Regions, see also Table 15)

Vialon not only organized the theft of Jewish property, he also participated in the "final solution of the Jewish question". On 31 July 1943 he ordered: *"The management of the concentration camp to be erected is, in accordance with my wishes, to be carried out by the general commissar of Riga ... The financial gain must, as previously, be paid into my treasury."* (See Table 16)

In April 1942 he allowed no less than 25,000 RM to the commander of Ostland security police and security service to break the resistance of the Latvian, Esthonian and White Russian population to the fascist rule of force and to drive together new work slaves, or as he called it, in order to combat the gangs. The "commander" had applied to Vialon for this sum for the *"additional catering for the auxiliary forces employed in fighting ... gangs"*. These terror actions against the resistance fighters, who were fighting to free their country meant displacement, evacuation of the population as forced labour, the burning of villages and public executions. Vialon not only knew of the murder of Soviet resistance fighters, he organized it as manager of the finance department with his budgetary means.

In 1963, Vialon, against his better knowledge, committed perjury when he testified as a witness in the trial of the SS mass murderer Hausser: *"I deny emphatically that I had any knowledge about the extermination of Jews."*

Despite new incriminating evidence and the documents published years ago Vialon continues to serve as state secretary.

Hettlage Karl-Maria

SS HAUPTSTURMFÜHRER AND ARMAMENT EXPERT

today: *Member of the High Authority of the Montan Union, prior to that, state secretary in the Federal Finance Ministry.*

Professor Dr. Karl-Maria Hettlage advanced in 1934 to city treasurer of Berlin. In the following years his sole ambition was to aid the fascist armament by means of a rigorous collection of taxes. In August 1935 he gave the instruction "that the tax laws must be interpreted according to the national socialist world outlook". Previously he had announced that *"the security of the nation must be re-established on the might of its arms, which is the work of the Führer and the purpose of all our endeavours"*. In this period Hettlage became SS Hauptsturmführer (SS No. 276 909) and close collaborator of Speer, who was convicted by the Nuremberg Military Tribunal as a war criminal. Speer later took Hettlage into his Ministry of Armament and War Production.

In a sworn statement before the Nuremberg Military Tribunal, the later executed SS Obergruppenführer and head of the SS chief economic administrative office, Pohl, answering the question, with whom he was in personal contact during his period in office, also named Hettlage and said: *"Dr. Hettlage from the Commerz Bank was Speer's finance man."*

That was a fact; Hettlage became, on the suggestion of Speer, a member of the board of directors of the Montanindustrie GmbH. On 31 March 1942 this mammoth enterprise had a trusteeship over 52 firms with 122 enterprises and

3,000 million RM trustee administered investment capital, i.e., looted investments; it had a staff of 178,970 workers, office employees, prisoners of war and forced labourers. Another member of the board was war criminal Flick.

In May 1943 a consultation on Swiss-German economic negotiations was held. In the course of this consultation, Hettlage declared *"that the order transfer to Switzerland constitutes a too small percentage of the total German armament volume, to warrant forcing it by pressure, which could lead to difficulties with Italy . . . Under these circumstances it seems appropriate to consider as pressure, in case of need, the use of an embargo on Swiss exports and following that the preventing of Swiss imports (through transport)." (Deutsches Zentralarchiv Potsdam)*

In autumn 1943 there was a meeting of the inter-ministerial committee for Italian affairs. Hettlage participated along with the "desk murderer" Globke. In this consultation they both distinguished themselves with chauvinist speeches.

In April 1944 Hettlage issued, representing the war criminal Speer, a decree on the switching over of production in factories and workshops, in which he says: *". . . I have ordered the cessation of production which is not urgently required for the continuation of the war, and the subsequent shifting of freed workers to more urgent war production."* (ibid.)

To the last minute Hettlage exerted himself for the continuation and support of the total war and propagated the fascist "final victory". After he had "disappeared" for a short time in 1945 in West Germany, the monopoly representatives let him advance again to ministerial director in 1956. A short time later Hettlage imparted his experiences from the nazi period as state secretary for the financing of the armament program.

Nazi Armament Experts – Rulers in Bonn

List of outstanding armament experts and war economy leaders of the Hitler regime who today have influential positions in the Bonn state.

Abs, Dr. Hermann

before 1945: member of the board of the Deutsche Bank, Berlin; Böhmische Union-Bank, Prague; chairman of the board of directors of the Deutsche Überseeische Bank, Berlin; Schlesische Bergwerks- und Hütten Aktiengesellschaft (mining and metallurgical company), Beuthen; Vereinigte Glanzstoff-Fabriken AG (artificial silk factories), Elberfeld-Wuppertal, etc.; deputy chairman of the board of directors of Generalbank Luxemburg AG, Luxemburg; Deutsch-Asiatische Bank, Shanghai-Berlin, etc.; member of the board of directors of Deutsche Solvay-Werke AG, Bernburg; IG-Farbenindustrie AG, Frankfurt-on-Main, and in many other companies

after 1945: sentenced as war criminal, but employed as "financial adviser" by the British-American occupation authorities; chairman of the Deutsche Bank AG, Frankfurt-on-Main; honorary chairman of the board of directors of the Deutsche Überseeische Bank, Hamburg-West Berlin; chairman of the board of directors of BASF Badische Anilin-Soda-Fabrik AG, Ludwigshafen-on-Rhine; Daimler Benz Aktiengesellschaft Stuttgart; Vereinigte Glanzstoff-Fabriken Aktiengesellschaft, Wuppertal-Elberfeld and further enterprises; chairman of the administrative council of the Kreditanstalt für Wiederaufbau (credit institute for reconstruction), Frankfurt-on-Main, Deutsche Bundesbahn (railway), etc.

Achter, Wilhelm
before 1945: war economy leader
after 1945: general manager of the Gladbacher-Wollindustrie AG, formerly L. Josten, Mönchengladbach (Henkel trust), vice-president of the Union of Textile Industry Employers

Albert, Dr.-Ing. Werner
before 1945: war economy leader
after 1945: member of the executive board of the Kronprinz AG, Solingen (Mannesmann trust)

Ambros, Dr. Otto
before 1945: war economy leader; member of the executive board of IG-Farbenindustrie AG, Frankfurt-on-Main; member of the technical committee; responsible for the entire Buna sector of IG-Farben; works manager of IG-Farbenindustrie AG, Auschwitz Works (until 1942); acting business-manager of the Buna-Werke GmbH, Schkopau; head of special commission C (chemical warfare); awarded the Knight's Cross to the War Service Cross
after 1945: sentenced as war criminal by the American Military Tribunal in the Nuremberg IG-Farben trial; deputy chairman of the board of directors of the Süddeutsche Kalkstickstoff-Werke AG (lime nitrogen works), Trostberg; member of the board of directors of the Telefunken-AG, West Berlin; Vereinigte Industrie-Unternehmungen AG (VIAG), Bonn and Brunswick; Bergwerksgesellschaft Hibernia AG (mining), Herne; Scholven-Chemie AG, Gelsenkirchen; administrative counsellor of the Berliner Handelsgesellschaft (BHG), West Berlin/Frankfurt-on-Main

Andreae, Christoph
before 1945: war economy leader; leader of a special sub-group of the economic group for mechanical engineering and the Rhineland Chamber of Labour
after 1945: owner of the August Hoenig fire-fighting equipment factory and filigree steel construction, Cologne-Nippes; chairman of the Committee of Industrial Protection of the BDI, the air-raid protection community of the top associations of industrial economy; decorated with the Distinguished Service Cross of the Order of Merit of the Federal Republic of Germany

Bergemann, Dr. Günter
before 1945: ministerial director in the Reich Ministry of Economics, authoritative participation in the plundering of the occupied countries of France, Norway and Yugoslavia
after 1945: his name is on Yugoslav war criminal list No. 56/51, retired state secretary in the Federal Ministry of Transport, business manager of the Margarine-Union GmbH, Hamburg (Unilever trust), member of the business management of the West German Unilever Group

Berning, Alfred
before 1945: war economy leader; head of special sub-group shoe and leather industriy machines of the engineering economic group; head of special sub-group iron and hardware industry of the materials refining economic group
after 1945: proprietor of the firm Gustav Rafflenbeul, Schwelm/Westphalia and Frankenberg/Eder, and the Alfred Berning Motorenbau, Schwelm/Westphalia

Biedenkopf, Wilhelm
before 1945: director of the IG-Farbenindustrie AG, Frankfurt-on-Main, party to the millionfold crimes in Auschwitz (Oswiecim)
after 1945: member of the executive board of DECHEMA Deutsche Gesellschaft für chemisches Apparatewesen (chemical apparatus), Frankfurt-on-Main, Dynamit Nobel AG, Troisdorf (Flick trust), labour ring of the Employers' Association of the West German Chemical Industry e. V., Wiesbaden

Birrenbach, Dr. Kurt
before 1945: representative abroad of Krupp, sent to Buenos Aires in 1939 with credentials from IG-Farben where he met and worked with the confidential people and the staff of the fascist "fifth column"; 1933 NSDAP and SA
after 1945: chairman of the board of directors of the August Thyssen-Hütte AG, Duisburg/Hamborn, Thyssen Gesellschaft für Beteiligung GmbH (holding company), Düsseldorf; deputy chairman of the board of trustees of the Fritz-Thyssen-Stiftung, Cologne; central advisory council of the Dresdner Bank; member of the Joint Session of the European Coal and Steel Community;

European Parliament; special ambassador of the Bonn government for the taking up of diplomatic relations with Israel; member of the Bundestag; CDU Bundestag candidate 1965

Blessing, Karl

before 1945: general associate in the Reich Ministry of Economcs; Reichsbank director; member of the "Circle of Friends of the Reichsführer SS"; business-manager of the Margarine-Verkaufsunion GmbH, Berlin (Unilever trust); member of the executive board of the Aktiengesellschaft für Fettindustrie, Vienna; Continentale Oel AG, Berlin; chairman of the board of directors of the "Nordsee" Deutsche Hochseefischerei AG, Wesermünde, and of other board of directors; member of the closer advisory council of the Reichsbank
after 1945: president of the Deutsche Bundesbank; German governor in the International Monetary Fund, Washington; member of the administrative council of the Bank for International Settlements, Basel; member of the executive board of the Margarine-Union AG, Hamburg (Unilever trust)

Blohm, Rudolf

before 1945: Personally liable partner of Blohm & Voss, Hamburg; leader of the main department for war-ships of the Reich Ministry of Armaments and War Production
after 1945: his name is on the American list of war criminals; chairman of the board of directors of the Blohm and Voss AG, Hamburg

Boden, Dr. Hans Constantin

before 1945: war economy leader, executive board of AEG Berlin, member of the board of directors of the AEG-Union, Vienna and of further trusts
after 1945: Boden was head of the AEG trust from 1956 to 1962; several times he took part in international negotiations on behalf of the Bonn government; honorary chairman of the board of directors of the Allgemeine Elektricitäts-Gesellschaft (AEG), West Berlin/Frankfurt-on-Main; chairman of the board of directors of the Kernreaktor Finanzierungsgesellschaft mbH, Frankfurt-on-Main; member of board of directors of other companies of the AEG trust and of the Mannesmann-AG, Düsseldorf, Dresdner Bank AG, Frankfurt-on-Main; chairman of the foreign trade committee of the Federal Association of German Industry; honorary president of the International Chamber of Commerce, Paris; member of the foreign trade advisory council of the Federal Ministry of Economics and the advisory council for development aid; decorated with the Distinguished Service Cross with star and shoulder ribbon of the Federal Republic of Germany

Boeder, Dr. Erich

before 1945: war economy leader
after 1945: member of the board of directors of the Hafen-Dampfschiffahrt AG, Hamburg; member of the Hamburg citizenry 1957; until 1957 deputy chairman of the board of the Deutsche Shell AG, charged by the Bonn government with coordinating the power policy for the Federal Republic within the EEC, adviser of the West German mineral oil industry of the OEEC and the Federal Ministry of Economics in the oil committee of the OEEC, Paris, chairman of the provincial committee of the CDU on economic policy, decorated with the Distinguished Service Cross of the Order of Merit of the Federal Republic of Germany

Bütefisch, Dr. Heinrich

before 1945: member of the executive board of the IG-Farbenindustrie AG, Frankfurt-on-Main; member of the technical committee; business manager of the Ammoniakwerkes (ammonia) Merseburg GmbH, Leuna-Werke; responsible for the Leuna part of the IG-Farbenindustrie AG, Auschwitz Works; member of the executive board of the Braunkohle-Benzin AG (lignite-petrol), Berlin, and other enterprises at home and abroad; member of the "Circle of Friends of the Reichsführer SS"; decorated with the war service medal 1st and 2nd class and the Knight's Cross to the war service medal
after 1945: accused in the Nuremberg IG-Farben trial, chairman of the board of directors of the Kohle-Öl-Chemie GmbH, Gelsenkirchen; board of directors of the Ruhrchemie AG, Oberhausen-Holten; leader of the technical expert committee of the International Convention of the nitrogen industry

Burkart, Dr. jur., Dr. rer. pol. Odilo

before 1945: general commissioner of the Friedrich Flick KG, Berlin
after 1945: his name was on the American list of war criminals; chairman of the executive board of the Eisenwerk-Gesellschaft Maximilianshütte AG, Sulzbach-Rosenberg (Flick trust)

Claussen, Dr. Wilhelm

before 1945: leader of the economic policy department of the IG-Farbenindustrie AG, Frankfurt-on-Main; senior military ad-

ministrative counsellor with the general representative for the economy in Serbia, directed the economic exploitation of the country and organized a system of slave labour
after 1945: state secretary in the Federal Ministry of Labour and Social Order; decorated with the Distinguished Service Cross with star and shoulder ribbon of the Federal Republic of Germany

Dahlgrün, Dr. Hans-Georg
before 1945: senior government counsellor with the head of civil administration in occupied Lorraine, worked directly with Globke, the expert of that time for Lorraine, Alsace and Luxemburg in the Reich Ministry of the Interior
after 1945: vice-chairman and member of the central bank council of the Deutsche Bundesbank; president of the Provincial Central Bank in Rhineland- Palatinate; retired minister of finance of Rhineland/Palatinate

Dahlgrün, Rolf
before 1945: justiciary of the Phoenix-Gummiwerke AG; member of various committees of the motor-car industry; participant in secret talks on the exploitation of occupied countries and the employment of forced labourers; appointed vice-district master of the hunt by Göring; 1933 NSDAP (No. 2957575), BNSDJ (No. 49050)
after 1945: Federal Minister of Finance; member of the federal executive of the FDP; FDP Bundestag candidate in 1965

Dichgans, Hans
before 1945: ministerial counsellor with the Reich Commissariat for the fixing of prices and leader of a labour staff with the Reich minister for armaments and war production
after 1945: chief business-manager, later managing member of the board of the Wirtschaftsvereinigung Eisen- und Stahlindustrie, Düsseldorf; member of the Bundestag and member of the finance committee of the Bundestag; CDU Bundestag candidate in 1965

Dinkelbach, Dr. h. c. Heinrich
before 1945: member of the executive board of the Vereinigte Stahlwerke AG, Düsseldorf
after 1945: his name was on the American list of war criminals, member of the board of directors of the Rheinische Stahlwerke, Essen; decorated with the star to the Distinguished Service Cross of the Order of Merit of the Federal Republic of Germany

Dörge, Friedrich
before 1945: war economy leader, member of the provincial committee of the head office of the Dresdner Bank, Berlin, chairman of armament committee III, Berlin
after 1945: business manager of the Mauser-Messzeug GmbH, Oberndorf, member of the executive board of the Employers' Association of the Metal Industry (1963)

Dürrfeld, Dr.-Ing. Walther
before 1945: chief engineer of the IG-Farbenindustrie AG, Leuna works; works manager of the IG-Farbenindustrie AG, Auschwitz Works (from 1943), district commissioner for Upper Silesia of the chemical industry economy group
after 1945: was accused as war criminal in the Nuremberg IG-Farben trial, member of the executive board of the Scholven-Chemie AG, Gelsenkirchen-Buer, board of directors: Phenolchemie GmbH, Gladbeck i. W., Friesecke & Höpfner GmbH, Erlangen

Eisfeld, Dr. Kurt
before 1945: responsible chemist of the IG-Farbenindustrie AG, Auschwitz Works; practised there clandestine trade with the valuables of the murdered persons
after 1945: member of the executive board of the Dynamit Nobel AG, Troisdorf (Flick trust); chairman of the board of directors of the Chemische Werke GmbH, Witten-on-Ruhr (Flick trust)

Eychmüller, Karl
before 1945: war economy leader, vice-chairman of the economic group of the metal industry, Berlin
after 1945: managing director, chairman of the managing committee of the Wieland-Werke AG, Ulm (Donau); honorary senator of the Technical College of Stuttgart and the University of Tübingen, decorated with the Distinguished Service Cross of the Federal Republic of Germany

Fahr, Dr.-Ing. Otto
before 1945: war economy leader, special group leader in the engineering economic group, leading colloborator in the special branch of iron and metal of the Reich leadership of the German Labour Front (DAF)
after 1945: chairman of the board of directors of the Maschinenfabrik Fahr AG, Gottmadingen (big shareholder of the Fahr family and in the Klöckner trust); deputy chairman of the advisory council of the Deutsche Bank, Württemberg district; board

of directors: Daimler-Benz AG, Stuttgart (Flick trust); Württembergische Metallwarenfabrik, Geislingen (Röchling trust); member of the committee for international relations of the Federal Association of German Industry (BDI); decorated with the Distinguished Service Cross of the Order of Merit of the Federal Republic of Germany

Faust, Max
before 1945: deputy works manager and superintendent of construction of the IG-Farbenindustrie AG, Auschwitz Works; jointly responsible for the extermination of 370,000 concentration camp prisoners through slave labour
after 1945: employee of Keram-Chemie, Siershahn/Westerwald

Fieseler, Gerhard
before 1945: war economy leader
after 1945: business manager of the Gerhard Fieseler Werke GmbH, Königstein (Taunus)

Fischer, Dr. Ernst Rudolf
before 1945: war economy leader, director of the IG-Farbenindustrie AG, Frankfurt-on-Main, vice business manager of the Ammoniak-Werk Merseburg GmbH, Leuna works; vice-chairman of the board of directors of the Oberschlesische Hydrierwerke AG, Blechhammer/Upper Silesia; leader of the fuel industry economic group Berlin; head of the mineral oil department in the Reich Ministry of Economics, and in the Reich Ministry of Armaments and War Production; chairman of the administrative council of the Kontinentale Öl AG, Berlin; member of the administrative council of the Dynamit Nobel AG, Pressburg/Slovakia
after 1945: chairman of the executive board of the Dynamit Nobel AG, Troisdorf, for many years; chairman of the board of directors of the Dynamit Nobel Genschow GmbH, Cologne; Chemische Werke Witten GmbH; Mitteldeutsche Sprengstoffwerke GmbH (explosives), Langelsheim; advisory council of the Deutsche Bank for Cologne/Aachen/Siegen

Fischer-Dieskau, Joachim
before 1945: war economy leader, ministerial counsellor in the Reich Ministry of Labour
after 1945: vice-chairman of the board of directors of the Wohnungs-AG, Salzgitter, Salzgitter-Lebenstedt; functions in further enterprises and bodies of the building and housing industry; co-authoer of the comments to the 1st and 2nd housing law and the federal rent law; decorated with the Distinguished Service Cross of the Federal Republic of Germany

Flick, Dr.-Ing. h. c., Dr. rer. pol. h. c. Friedrich
before 1945: war economy leader, personally liable partner of the Friedrich Flick KG, Düsseldorf; chairman of the board of directors of the Anhaltische Kohlenwerke, Berlin, Eisenwerk-Gesellschaft Maximilianhütte, Sulzbach-Rosenberg-Hütte, Essener Steinkohlenbergwerke AG, Essen, Harpener Bergbau AG, Dortmund, Mitteldeutsche Stahlwerke AG, Riesa-on-Elbe, Sächsische Gusstahl-Werke Döhlen AG, Freital, etc.; vice-chairman of the board of directors of the Linke-Hoffmann-Werke AG, Breslau, Waggon- und Maschinenfabrik AG, formerly Busch, Bautzen, etc.; member of the board of directors of the Allgemeine Elektrizitäts-Gesellschaft, Berlin, Allianz Versicherungs AG, Berlin, ATG Allgemeine Transportanlagen GmbH, Leipzig, Dresdner Bank, Berlin, Dynamit AG, formerly Alfred Nobel & Co., Hamburg, Vereinigte Stahlwerke AG, Düsseldorf, advisory council of the Reichsbank, Berlin
after 1945: principal defendant in the Nuremburg Flick trial; sentenced for war crimes, crimes against humanity and exploitation of slave labourers; personally liable partner and general manager of the Friedrich Flick Kommanditgesellschaft, Düsseldorf; chairman of the board of directors of the Dynamit-Aktien-Gesellschaft, formerly Alfred Nobel & Co., Troisdorf; shareholder or member of managing boards of many other enterprieses

Frank-Fahle, Dr. Guenther
before 1945: director of the IG-Farbenindustrie AG, Agency W. (Wehrmacht); managing clerk of the Ammoniakwerke Merseburg GmbH, Leuna; liaison man of IG-Farben with American chemical companies
after 1945: managing associate of the Deutsche Commerz GmbH, Frankfurt-on-Main, manager of the Continentale Commerz GmbH, Frankfurt-on-Main; advisory council of the Deutsche Bank AG

Frauendorfer, Dr. Max
before 1945: long-time member of the NSDAP and SS, member of the staff of Reichsführer SS Himmler, head of the office for the regular building of the NSDAP, chief department head of the Reich legal office,

president of the main labour department of the Generalgouvernement; here chiefly responsible for the deportation of hundreds of thousands of Polish citizens
after 1945: director of the Allianz Lebensversicherungs-AG, Stuttgart (life insurance); Allianz Versicherungs-AG, West Berlin/Munich

Fremerey, Gustav

before 1945: government director in the Reich Ministry of Economics, was responsible for military economic planning and took an active part in armament and war preparations
after 1945: president of the Federal Office for Trade and Industry which deals, among other things, with the registration and permission to be in possession of military weapons, and for development aid and the investigation of economic concentration

Freudenberg, Dr. h.c. Richard

before 1945: war economy leader, member of the board of directors of the Deutsche Bank, Berlin
after 1945: associate of the firm of Freudenberg & Co. KG, Weinheim; member of the board of directors of the Farbenfabriken Bayer AG, Leverkusen (IG-Farben group); Deutsche Bank AG; member of the board of the Union of German Industry and Trade (DIHT) in Bonn; president of the Chamber of Industry and Commerce in Mannheim; presidial member of the Federal Union of German Industry; member of the Bundestag from 1949 to 1953; decorated with the Distinguished Service Cross of the Federal Republic of Germany

Frydag, Karl

before 1945: war economy leader, head of the central committee for aircraft construction of the Reich minister for armament and war production
after 1945: for many years presiding business manager in the Federal Association of the German Air Navigation Industry e. v., Bad Godesberg, member of the board of directors of the Henschel-Flugzeugwerke, Kassel

Gajewski, Dr. Dr. h.c. Fritz

before 1945: war economy leader; member of the executive board of the IG-Farbenindustrie AG, Frankfurt-on-Main; director of section III of the IG-Farben (photographicial accessories, synthetic materials, artifical silk); vice-chairman of the board of directors of the Deutsche Celluloid-Fabrik AG, Eilenburg, Dynamit AG, Troisdorf; administrative council of the Dynamit Nobel AG, Pressburg/Slovakia; special group leader of the chemical industry economic group; took part in secret negotiations with the Wehrmacht on chemical war production; shares responsibility for the exploitation of concentration camp prisoners as slave labourers
after 1945: accused in the Nuremberg IG-Farben trial; member of the board of directors of the Chemie-Verwaltungs-AG, Frankfurt-on-Main; Chemische Werke Hüls AG, Marl, Recklinghausen region; honorary chairman of the board of directors of the Dynamit Nobel AG, Troisdorf (Flick trust); IG-Farbenindustrie AG in liquidation, Frankfurt-on-Main; decorated with the Distinguished Service Cross of the Order of Merit of the Federal Republic of Germany

Gattineau, Dr. Heinrich

before 1945: director of the IG-Farbenindustrie AG, Frankfurt-on-Main; head of the national economic and economic-political departments of the IG; works manager of the Dynamit Nobel AG, Pressburg, and the Donau Chemie AG, Vienna; friend of Himmler and Göring; SS Standartenführer
after 1945: accused in the Nuremberg IG-Farben trial; member of the managerial board of the Wasag-Chemie AG, Essen (Krupp trust), the Guano-Werke AG, Hamburg (Krupp and Quandt trust); member of the board of directors of the Mitteldeutsche Sprengstoffwerke GmbH, Langelsheim, and other enterprises; advisory council of the Dresdner Bank AG, Düsseldorf

Goetz, Carl

before 1945: chairman of the board of directors of the Dresdner Bank, Berlin
after 1945: his name was on the American list of war criminals, honorary chairman of the board of directors of the Dresdner Bank AG, Frankfurt-on-Main; decorated with the Dinstinguished Service Cross of the Order of Merit with star of the Federal Republic of Germany

Goldschmidt, Dr. Bernhard

before 1945: war economy leader, chairman of the board of directors of the Th. Goldschmidt AG, Essen
after 1945: his name was on the American list of war criminals; honorary president of the board of directors of the Th. Goldschmidt AG, Essen; decorated with the Distinguished Service Cross of the Order of Merit of the Federal Republic of Germany

Gräbner, Dr. Georg
before 1945: war economy leader, head of the Reich office for wood
after 1945: business manager of the Association of Wood Dealers, Hanover, Association of Wood Dealers, Lower Saxony and Bremen e. V., Hanover

Graetz, Erich
before 1945: war economy leader; chairman of the managing committee and works manager of the Ehrich and Graetz AG, Berlin; dominant participation in the exploitation of forced labour
after 1945: factory-owner, co-partner of the Graetz KG (limited partnership) Altona/Westphalia; member of the managing committee of Graetz AG, Hamburg (1963)

Haver, Kurt
before 1945: war economy leader
after 1945: chairman of the managing committee of the Sales Association for Tar Products AG; chairman of the management of the Ruhr Coal Consultation GmbH, Essen; chairman of the board of directors of the Westfälische Transport AG, Dortmund (Hoesch and Hoogovens trust); board of directors of the Essener Steinkohlenwerke AG, Essen (Mannesmann trust)

Hettlage, Professor Dr. Karl
before 1945: SS Hauptsturmführer; treasurer of the town of Berlin; general expert in the Reich Ministry for Armament and War Production; managerial board of the Commerzbank AG, Hamburg/Berlin; chairman of the board of directors of the Hansa-Bank, Riga, the Verwertungsgesellschaft für Montanindustrie GmbH and other boards; member of the Academy of German Law; professor of jurisprudence
after 1945: state secretary in the Federal Ministry of Economic Cooperation; vice-chairman of the board of directors of the Vereinigte Elektrizitäts- und Bergwerks AG, Hamburg/Bonn; member of the board of directors of the Vereinigte Industrie-Unternehmungen AG (VIAG), Bonn, Volkswagenwerk AG, Wolfsburg, Kernreaktor Bau- und Betriebsgesellschaft mbH, Karlsruhe, etc.; Professor of public law at Mainz University

Heyne, Dr. Hans
before 1945: war economy leader; member of the executive board and commissioner-general of the AEG Berlin; chairman of the board of directors of AEG; leader of the main committee for aircraft equipment with the Reich minister of armament and war production; member of the industrial council for the development of aircraft devices; Heyne received for his "services" to the fascist Luftwaffe the Knight's Cross to the War Service Cross
after 1945: chairman of the board of directors of AEG (Allgemeine Elektricitäts-Gesellschaft, West Berlin/Frankfurt-on-Main; Telefunken AG, West Berlin (AEG trust) (AEG and Telefunken are, because of their participation in the Starfighter program and the Hawk missile construction considerably involved in the armament of West Germany), Olympia-Werke AG, Wilhelmshaven (AEG trust), Osram GmbH, Munich/West Berlin (AEG, Siemens, General Electric Co); member of the board of directors of other AEG companies; member of the board of directors of the Deutsche Bank AG; decorated with the Distinguished Service Cross with star of the Order of Merit of the Federal Republic of Germany

Hinsel, Dr.-Ing. Paul
before 1945: war economy leader
after 1945: member of the executive board in the Union of the Bavarian Metal-Working Industry, honorary senator of the University of Economics and the Social Sciences in Erlangen-Nuremberg

Hinz, Dr.-Ing. Fritz
before 1945: war economy leader, works manager of Henschel und Sohn GmbH, Kassel, member of the board of directors of the Oberschlesische Lokomotivwerke AG, Kattowitz (Katowice), Steana Motrica Bucharest, Wiener Locomotiv-Fabriks-AG, Vienna
after 1945: personally liable partner of the Hessische Metallwerk Imfeld & Co., Kassel; honorary president of the Vereinigung Deutscher Lokomotivfabriken, Frankfurt-on-Main; decorated with the Distinguished Service Cross of the Federal Republic of Germany

Holtz, Wolfgang
before 1945: ministerial director in the Reich Ministry of Economics, worked closely with the coal and steel companies
after 1945: ministerial director and head of the defence economy department in the Bonn war ministry, board of directors of the Monopol-Bergwerks GmbH, Kamen (Flick trust)

Hopf, Volkmar
before 1945: district president in Pomerania, responsible there for the depor-

tation of anti-fascists to concentration camps, district prefect in Czechoslovakia, persecuted Czech patriots
after 1945: retired state secretary of the Federal Ministry of Defence (forced to resign because of the Spiegel affair); president of the federal auditing office; chairman of the board of directors of the Industrieverwaltungsgesellschaft mbH, Bad Godesberg; Deutsche Revisions- und Treuhand AG, West Berlin/Frankfurt-on-Main, AG für Wirtschaftsprüfung West Berlin/Düsseldorf

Hunke, Professor Dr. Heinrich

before 1945: war economy leader, president of the publicity council of the German economy, ministerial director and head of the foreign department in the Reich Ministry of National Enlightenment and Propaganda, chief lecturer of the official party control commission in the Reich Ministry of National Enlightenment and Propaganda, etc.
after 1945: ministerial director in the Lower Saxony Ministry of Finance, head of department II – property and financial aid –; chairman of the board of directors of Niedersächsische Zahlenlotto GmbH, Hanover; Fussball Toto GmbH, Hanover; deputy chairman of the board of directors of Niedersächsische Heimstätte GmbH, Hanover, etc.

Jähne, Dr.-Ing. h.c. Friedrich

before 1945: war economy leader; member of the executive board of the IG-Farbenindustrie AG, Frankfurt-on-Main, member of its technical and finance committee; chairman of the technical commission of the IG; member of several IG boards of directors; member of the big advisory board of the Reich group industry
after 1945: defendant in the Nuremberg IG-Farben trial, condemned to a prison sentence of many years, honorary chairman of the board of directors of the Farbwerke Hoechst AG, Frankfurt-on-Main, Hoechst (IG-Farben group); chairman of the board of directors of the Adolf Messer GmbH, Frankfurt-on-Main; decorated with the Distinguished Service Cross with star of the Order of Merit of the Federal Republic of Germany

Kaletsch, Konrad

before 1945: war economy leader; general agent of the Friedrich Flick KG, Düsseldorf; executive board of the Mitteldeutsche Stahlwerke AG, Riesa; vice-chairman of the board of directors of the Eisenwerk-Gesellschaft Maximilianhütte; member of the board of directors of many concerns
after 1945: accused in the Nuremberg Flick trial; personally liable partner of the Friedrich Flick KG, Düsseldorf; business-manager of the Mitteldeutsche Stahlwerke GmbH, West Berlin, Verwaltungsgesellschaft für Steinkohlenbergbau und Hüttenbetrieb mbH (hard coal mining and metallurgical works), Düsseldorf; member of the board of directors of Daimler-Benz AG, Stuttgart/Untertürkheim, Dynamit Nobel AG, Troisdorf, and Süd-Chemie AG, Munich, Eisenwerk-Gesellschaft Maximilianshütte mbH, Sulzbach-Rosenberg; decorated with the Distinguished Service Cross of the Order of Merit of the Federal Republic of Germany

Keyserlingk, Wedig, Freiherr von

before 1945: war economy leader
after 1945: business manager of the Deuta-Werke, formally Deutsche Tachometerwerke GmbH, Bergisch-Gladbach

Kiehn, Fritz

before 1945: war economy leader; member of the board of directors of the Deutsche Effekten- und Wechselbank, Frankfurt-on-Main, Berlin; NSU-Werke AG, Nekkarsulm; advisory council of the Reich Chamber of Economics, Berlin
after 1945: associate and business-manager of the Efka-Werke Fritz Kiehn GmbH, Trossingen/Württemberg

Knieriem, Dr. August von

before 1945: member of the executive board of the IG-Farbenindustrie AG, Frankfurt-on-Main; head of its legal committee (head lawyer); member of the central and labour committee of IG-Farben; member of the board of directors of Anorgana GmbH, Frankfurt-on-Main (poison gas works of IG-Farben)
after 1945: defendant in the Nuremberg IG-Farben trial, for many years chairman of the board of directors of the IG-Farbenindustrie AG in liquidation, Frankfurt-on-Main

Knott, Dr. Carl

before 1945: war economy leader, member of the executive board of the Siemens-Schuckert-Werke AG, Berlin-Siemensstadt
after 1945: for many years chairman of the managing committee of the Siemens-Schuckert-Werke AG, West Berlin/Erlangen; as representative of the Siemens trust member of several bodies of atomic economy and research; presidial member of the Ger-

man Atomic Commission, Bonn; member of the Bavarian Atomic Commission, Munich; advisory council for nuclear power of the Ministry of Economics of Baden-Württemberg; chairman of the managerial committee of the Rationalization Board of the German Economy (RKW), Frankfurt-on-Main; member of the administrative council of the Siemens Industrie Electrica S.A., Madrid; honorary doctor, honorary freeman and honorary senator of the University of Erlangen; decorated with the Distinguished Service Cross with star of the Order of Merit of the Federal Republic of Germany

Könecke, Dr. Dr.-Ing. h.c. Fritz

before 1945: war economy leader; chairman of the executive board of the Continental Gummi-Werke AG, Hanover; chairman of an armament committee
after 1945: his name was on the American list of war criminals; chairman of the board of directors of Holzindustrie Bruchsal GmbH, Bruchsal; decorated with the Distinguished Service Cross with star of the Order of Merit of the Federal Republic of Germany

Kreibich, Dr. Emil

before 1945: war economy leader; member of the board of directors of the Deutsche Bank, Berlin; president of the Chamber of Industry and Commerce of Reichenberg; head of the department of foreign trade for the Sudetenland, Reichenberg
after 1945: proprietor of the firm Wegena Dr. Kreibich KG, West Berlin and Hamburg

Krupp von Bohlen und Halbach, Dr.-Ing. h.c., Dr. rer. pol. h.c. Alfried

before 1945: war economy leader; member of the armament council, executive board of the Friedrich Krupp AG, Essen (until 1943); proprietor of Friedrich Krupp, Essen (from 1943); member of the presidium of the Reichsvereinigung Kohle
after 1945: main defendant in the Nuremberg Krupp trial; as war criminal sentenced to twelve years imprisonment and confiscation of his entire property in 1948 by the American Military Tribunal; since 1951 at the instigation of the Bonn government again owner of the Friedrich Krupp firm, Essen; chairman of the board of directors of the Weser Aktien-Gesellschaft, Bremen; Siepmann Werke AG, Belecke/Möhne; member of the board of directors of the Dresdner Bank AG, Frankfurt-on-Main

Küppenbender, Dr.-Ing. h.c. Heinrich

before 1945: war economy leader; member of the executive board of Zeiss-Ikon AG, Dresden; works manager of the Zeiss-Werke, Jena; received the Knight's Cross to the War Service Cross with Swords for "special services" for the fascist war production; terrorized thousands of foreign forced labourers
after 1945: executive board member of the Zeiss Konzern, Oberkachen, illegally formed by him misusing the name of Carl Zeiss; chairman of the board of directors of the Voigtländer AG, Brunswick, Zeiss-Ikon AG, Stuttgart, and others; decorated with the Distinguished Service Cross of the Order of Merit of the Federal Republic of Germany

Kugler, Hans

before 1945: director of the joint sales agency of the IG-Farbenindustrie AG, Frankfurt-on-Main; member of the South-East Europe committee of IG-Farben; primary responsibility in the occupation and plundering of the French chemical industry; commissioner of the Reich Ministry of Economics for the Aussig-Falkenau Werke in Czechoslovakia
after 1945: defendant in the Nuremberg IG-Farben trial, sentenced to imprisonment; member of the managing board of the Casella-Farbwerke Mainkur AG, Frankfurt-on-Main, Riedel de Haen AG, Seelze near Hanover; member of the central committee of the Federation of the Chemical Industry e.V., Frankfurt-on-Main

Lautz, Julius von

before 1945: senior government counsellor in the Reich Ministry of Economics, military department, participated in the war preparation and warfare of the fascists in the field of economics
after 1945: Minister of Justice of the Saarland, provincial chairman of the CDU (Christian Democratic Union) Saarland, member of the mediation committee of the Bundestag and the Bundesrat

Loew, Gottfried

before 1945: war economy leader, assistant general manager and works manager of the Lemwerder works of the "Weser" Flugzeugbau GmbH, Bremen
after 1945: business-manager of the Vereinigte Flugtechnische Werke GmbH, Bremen (Krupp, United Aircraft Corporation)

Lübke, Dr. h.c. Heinrich
before 1945: director of a settlement company, dismissed without notice for fraud; deputy leader of the Schlempp building staff; confidential agent of the Gestapo, directed the construction of the Leau concentration camp as branch of the Buchenwald concentration camp in 1944; responsible for the death of hundreds of Poles, Frenchmen, Italians, Soviet citizens and Germans through slave labour
after 1945: president of the Federal Republic of Germany; earlier federal minister of food, agriculture and forestry, minister of agriculture of North Rhine-Westphalia

Lüdinghausen-Wolff, Reinhold, Freiherr von
before 1945: member of the executive board of the Böhmische Escompte-Bank, Prague; vice-chairman of the administrative council of the Skoda works in Pilsen; president of the Ungarische Blechemballagenwerke AG, Györ
after 1945: his name was on the American list of war criminals; director of the Dresdner Bank AG, Hanover; chairman of the board of directors of the Sichel-Werke AG, Hanover-Limmer; member of other boards of directors

Mahle, Hermann
before 1945: war economy leader
after 1945: limited partner of the Mahle KG, Stuttgart-Bad Cannstadt; associate of the Mahle-Werke GmbH, Fellbach near Stuttgart, and other family enterprises; advisory council of the Deutsche Bank AG; honorary senator of the Technical College of Stuttgart

Malaisé, Dr. Gerhart von
before 1945: war economy leader
after 1945: member of the managing committee of the Hamburg Elektrizitätswerke AG, Hamburg; chairman of the board of directors of the Deutsche Porenbeton GmbH, Hamburg; member of the Hamburg provincial committee of the Commerzbank AG

Martini, Dr. Herbert
before 1945: ministerial director and Reich commissar at the Berlin exchange, participation in the Aryanization of various banks, expert for war and armament financing in the Reich Ministry of Economics
after 1945: deputy of the German adviser for the Marshal Plan; member of the executive board of the Kreditanstalt für den Wiederaufbau, Frankfurt-on-Main; member of the board of directors of the Deutsche Effekten- und Wechselbank, Frankfurt-on-Main, Industriekreditbank AG, Düsseldorf, Hoesch-Aktiengesellschaft, Dortmund, Hugo Stinnes AG, Düsseldorf, etc., administrative council of the European Investment Bank, Brussels, etc.

Mauterer, Dr.-Ing. h.c. Arthur
before 1945: member of the executive board of the Dortmund Union Brückenbau AG (bridge construction), Dortmund; leader of the main committee for steel and iron construction with the Reich minister for armament and war production
after 1945: his name was on the American list of war criminals; member of the executive board of Rheinstahl-Union, Maschinen- und Stahlbau AG, Düsseldorf

ter Meer, Dr. Dr. Ing. h.c. Fritz
before 1945: war economy leader; member of the executive board and one of the big shareholders of the IG-Farbenindustrie AG, Frankfurt-on-Main; member of its central committee; business-manager of the Buna-Werke GmbH, Schkopau; member of numerous supervisory bodies in IG-Farben enterprises, subsidiary companies and affiliations at home and abroad; commissioner for Italy of the Reich minister for armament and war production; chiefly responsible for IG-Farben crimes in Auschwitz; had a leading share in the incorporation of the chemical industry of the occupied countries
after 1945: main incriminated defendant in the IG-Farben trial in Nuremberg, condemned to a prison sentence of many years; honorary chairman of the board of directors and the managing committee of the Farbenfabriken Bayer AG, Leverkusen

Merck, Dr. Dr. rer. nat. h.c. Karl
before 1945: war economy leader, copartner and works manager of the E. Merck Chemische Fabrik, Darmstadt
after 1945: associate of the Emanuel Merck private firm, Darmstadt, member of the board of directors of the Gothaer Lebensversicherungs AG, Göttingen; honorary member of several employers' associations of the chemical industry; decorated with the Distinguished Service Cross of the Order of Merit of the Federal Republic of Germany

Merker, Dr.-Ing. Otto
before 1945: war economy leader; vice-chairman of the executive board of the Klöckner-Humboldt-Deutz AG, Cologne-Deutz; head of the central shipbuilding committee of the Reich Ministry of Armament and War Production

after 1945: member of boards of directors of various companies of the Rheinstahl trust at home and abroad; member of the executive board of the central union of the metal industrial employers' associations e.V., Cologne; advisory council of the Deutsche Bank AG; decorated with the Distinguished Service Cross of the Order of Merit of the Federal Republic of Germany

Messerschmitt, Prof. Dr.-Ing. h.c. Willy

before 1945: war economy leader; bearer of the fascist title "Pioneer of Labour"; member of the executive board of the Messerschmitt AG, Augsburg; shares responsibility for the forced labour of prisoners of the Dachau concentration camp
after 1945: his name was on the American list of war criminals; advisory council of the Bankhaus Aufhäuser; vice-chairman of the board of directors of the Messerschmitt AG, Augsburg, advisory council of the Bundesverband der Deutschen Luft- und Raumfahrtindustrie e.V. (aviation and space travel association), Düsseldorf; decorated with the Bavarian Service Medal, the Grand Cross of the Order of Merit of Spanish aviation (for his share in the development of a Spanish jet-fighter after the end of the war, awarded by the Franco regime in 1954)

Michel, Dr. Elmar

before 1945: ministerial director in the Reich Ministry of Economics, general expert for raw material questions; took an authoritative part in the economic preparation and carrying through of the fascist aggression, especially against the West European countries; military administrative chief with the military commander in France during the Second World War; co-initiator of measures for the plundering, exploitation, enslavement and deportation of the French population
after 1945: ministerial director in the Federal Ministry of Economics (retired), chairman of the executive board of the Salamander AG, Kornwestheim/Württemberg; chairman of the board of directors of the Cornelius Heyl AG, Worms/Rhine; member of the board of directors of the Victoria-Versicherung, Lebensversicherungs AG, West Berlin, Satorius-Werke AG, Göttingen, and others; chairman of the working group for defence economic questions of the German Union of Industry and Commerce, Bonn

Mittelstrass, Dr. Fritz

before 1945: defence commissioner and confidential agent of the Gestapo in the Reich Ministry of Armament and War Production, previously active in the Reich Ministry of Economics
after 1945: ministerial counsellor in the Federal Ministry of Economics, head of the department on basic political-economic questions of civil and military defence; had a part in working out the emergency legislation in the economic field which is planned and in part already sanctioned by the Bonn Bundestag

Möhlenbeck, Wilhelm

before 1945: war economy leader, head of the special group of the leather producing industry, chairman of the central association of the German Leather Industry Berlin
after 1945: Proprietor of the Wilhelm Möhlenbeck Firm KG, Wolfenhausen/Taunus

Nallinger, Prof. Dr.-Ing. h.c. Fritz

before 1945: war economy leader
after 1945: member of the executive board and chief engineer of the Daimler-Benz AG, Stuttgart/Untertürkheim; vice-chairman of the board of directors of the Auto-Union, Düsseldorf; member of the German Atomic Commission and the advisory aviation council with the federal minister of transport; decorated with the Distinguished Service Cross with star of the Order of Merit of the Federal Republic of Germany

Neef, Fritz

before 1945: political economist in the Reich Ministry of Economics sharing the responsibility for the economic measures of total war
after 1945: state secretary of the Federal Ministry of Economics, responsible for the Europe department

Oehme, Adolf

before 1945: war economy leader
after 1945: for many years member of the executive board of the firm Voigtländer AG, Brunswick

Pierburg, Dr.-Ing. h.c., Dr. h.c. Alfred

before 1945: war economy leader
after 1945: general business-manager and limited partner of the Deutsche Vergaser GmbH & Co. KG. Neuss (Rhine), A. Pierburg, Auto und Luftfahrt-Gerätebau KG, Neuss (Rhine), Deutsche Vergaser Gesellschaft (KG), West Berlin; limited partner of Bankhaus C.G. Trinkaus, Düsseldorf; member of the executive board of the Union of the Automobile Industry e.V., Frankfurt-on-Main

Pohle, Dr. Wolfgang
before 1945: director and commissioner-general of the Mannesmann AG, closest associate of general director Zangen
after 1945: took over the defence of the accused trust rulers Krupp and Flick in the Nuremberg trial and pleaded for the rehabilitation of the big industrialists; business-manager and personally liable partner of the Friedrich Flick KG, Düsseldorf; chairman of the board of directors of the ICT International Computers and Tabulators GmbH, Düsseldorf; chairman of the standing committee for German-Spanish economic cooperation; chairman or member of various committees of the BDI and the DIHT and the steel and iron economic union; member of the Bundestag from 1953 to 1957; CDU parliamentary group; CDU Bundestag candidate in 1965

Prentzel, Dr. Felix-Alexander
before 1945: head clerk of the IG-Farbenindustrie AG, Frankfurt-on-Main, leading associate of the political economic department and branch leader of the direction department of IG-Farben; collaborator in the Reich Office for Economic Development
after 1945: ministerial director in the Federal Ministry of Economics, responsible for the splitting up of the IG-Farben group, chairman of the executive board of the Deutsche Gold- und Silber-Scheideanstalt, formerly Roessler (Degussa), Frankfurt-on-Main; member of the board of directors of Metallgesellschaft, Frankfurt-on-Main, Farbwerke Hoechst, Frankfurt-on-Main, etc.; member of the directorial commission for the utilization of atomic energy at the OEEC, of the administrative council of the Institute for Developing Countries; vice-president of the Union of the Chemical Industry

Reuleaux, Dr.-Ing., Dr.-Ing. h.c. Otto
before 1945: war economy leader
after 1945: for many years chairman of the managing board of the Kali Chemie Engelhard-Katalysatoren GmbH, Hanover; chairman of the money, credit and currency committee of the Federal Union of German Industry, Cologne; member of the board of directors in the Solvay trust; chairman of the advisory council of the Deutsche Bank, Hanover; member of the board of directors of the Gerling-Konzern Lebensversicherungs-AG, Cologne; decorated with the Distinguished Service Cross with star of the Order of Merit of the Federal Republic of Germany

Reuter, Dr. Franz
before 1945: war economy leader
after 1945: member of the board of directors of the Hütten- und Bergwerke Rheinhausen AG, Rheinhausen (Krupp trust), Kronprinz AG, Solingen-Ohligs (Mannesmann trust); member of the advisory council of the federal ministry for the economic possessions of the federation, editor of the periodical Der Volkswirt (The Political Economist), the demagogic organ of the enterprisers; chairman of the economic committee of the FDP

Rienäcker, Waldemar
before 1945: war economy leader, regional office leader in the Office of Technology of Lower Silesia, Schlesische Electrizitäts- und Gas AG, Gleiwitz, member of the Licensing Office for Securities on the Silesian Exchange in Breslau
after 1945: chairman of the board of directors of the Rheingau-Elektrizitätswerk AG, Eltville, member of the board of directors of the Elektrizitäts AG, formerly Lahmeyer & Co., Frankfurt-on-Main; advisory council of the Dresdner Bank, Hesse

Rinn, Hans
before 1945: director of the Dresdner Bank, Berlin; had an authoritative part in the so-called Aryanization especially of Dutch-Jewish property
after 1945: member of the executive board of the Dresdner Bank AG, West Berlin; chairman of the board of directors of the Prix-Werke AG, Hamburg, and six other stock companies; deputy chairman of the board of directors of the Bank für Handel und Industrie AG, West Berlin, Deutsche Hypothekenbank, Bremen, and others

Rohland, Dr.-Ing. Walter
before 1945: war economy leader; head of the main committee for armoured vehicles with the Reich minister for armament and war production; business-manager of the industrial council of the supreme command of the army; member of the executive board of the Vereinigte Stahlwerke AG, Düsseldorf
after 1945: his name was on the American list of war criminals; co-owner of the Stahlwerk Mannheim AG, Mannheim-Rheinau, and member of the boards of directors of the Thyssen trust; advisory council of the Bergische Stahlindustrie, Remscheid

Rothe, Dr. Leo S.
before 1945: chairman of the executive board of the Junkers Flugzeug- und Motorenwerke AG, Dessau
after 1945: his name was on the Ameri-

can list of war criminals; for many years in the executive board of the Klöckner-Humboldt-Deutz AG, Cologne-Deutz; member of many boards of directors; honorary president of the Federal Union of the German Aviation and Space Industry e.V., Bad Godesberg; member of the managing board of the BDI

Sander, Hermann

before 1945: war economy leader; manager of the Carlshütte-Maschinen- und Stahlbau GmbH, Waldenburg-Altwasser/Silesia; vice-chairman of the board of directors of the "Glückauf" AG for brown coal utilization, Lichtenau, Liegnitz district
after 1945: member of managing board of the Firma Ehrhardt und Sehmer Maschinenfabrik AG, Saarbrücken; presidial member of the Union of Iron and Metallurgical Industry of the Saarland

Saur, Karl-Otto

before 1945: senior department head and office manager in the Reich Ministry for Armament and War Production; chief of staff of the "Jägerstab" and deputy head of the armament staff; in Hitler's testament he was designated successor to Speer
after 1945: head of a technical bureau in München-Pullach, participated in West German rocket production

Schattenberg, Horst-Henner

before 1945: deputy police president of Koblenz, senior government counsellor in the Reich Ministry of the Interior, department head with the Reich governor in Posen
after 1945: ministerial counsellor in the Federal Ministry of Economics, head of the welfare and emergency department, participated in the working out of the emergency legislation in the field of economics

Schirner, Karl

before 1945: war economy leader; chairman of the managing board of the Deutsche Erdöl AG, Berlin; member of the board of directors of the Deutsche Bank, Berlin; Continentale Oel AG, Berlin, 1933–1939 chairman of the managing board of the Vereinigte Aluminiumwerke Berlin and the Vereinigte Industrie-Unternehmungen AG, Berlin
after 1945: chairman of the board of directors of the Vereinigte Aluminium-Werke AG, Bonn; vice-chairman of the board of directors of the Deutsche Erdöl AG (DEA), Hamburg, Vereinigte Industrie-Unternehmungen AG (VIAG), Bonn, Ilseder Hütte AG, Peine, member of the board of directors of Braunschweigische Kohlen-Bergwerke, Helmstedt, Farbwerke Hoechst AG, Frankfurt-on-Main; decorated with the Distinguished Service Cross with star of the Federal Republic of Germany

Schlosser, Hermann

before 1945: chairman of the executive committee of the Deutsche Gold- und Silber-Scheideanstalt, formerly Roessler (Degussa), Frankfurt-on-Main; production commissioner for the chemical industry of the Reich minister for armament and war production
after 1945: his name was on the American list of war criminals; honorary chairman of the board of directors of Degussa, Frankfurt-on-Main; decorated with the Distinguished Service Cross of the Federal Republic of Germany

Schmid-Lossberg, Heinz

before 1945: war economy leader, business-manager of the armaments office in the Reich Ministry for Armament and War Production
after 1945: chief representative of the Berliner Handels-Gesellschaft, West Berlin/Frankfurt-on-Main, member of the executive committee of the Berliner Handelsbank AG, West Berlin; chairman of the board of directors of the Frankfurter Kredit-Bank GmbH, Frankfurt-on-Main, the Berliner AG für Vermögensverwaltung, West Berlin; vice-chairman of the board of directors of the Kabelwerke Wilhelminenhof AG, West Berlin, Neckermann Versand KG, Frankfurt-on-Main, and others

Schneider, Dr. Christian

before 1945: war economy leader; member of the executive board of the IG-Farbenindustrie AG, Frankfurt-on-Main; chief defence commissioner and general manager of IG-Farben; works manager of the Ammoniakwerke Merseburg GmbH, Leuna-Werke
after 1945: accused in the Nuremberg IG-Farben trial; member of the board of directors of the Süddeutsche Kalkstickstoff-Werke AG, Trostberg, Rheinauer Holzhydrolyse GmbH, Mannheim (chief shareholder of the IG-Farben group and Vereinigte Industrie-Unternehmungen Aktiengesellschaft)

Scholz, Dr.-Ing. h.c. William

before 1945: war economy leader
after 1945: member of the board of directors of Deutsche Werft AG, Hamburg (AEG and Haniel trust), Germanische Lloyd,

Hamburg, Hamburgische Schiffbau-Versicherungsanstalt; executive board of the Nuclear Energy Study Society, Hamburg; advisory council of the Deutsche Bank, Hamburg/Schleswig-Holstein; special committee "nuclear power for ships" of the German Atomic Commission, Bonn; decorated with the Distinguished Service Cross of the Order of Merit of the Federal Republic of Germany

Schulze-Fielitz, Günter

before 1945: state secretary in the Reich Ministry for Armament and War Production, deputy to Speer, general inspector for water and energy
after 1945: retired government architect; member of the executive board of the Hochtief AG für Hoch- und Tiefbauten, Essen; advisory council of the Deutsche Bank, Essen/Dortmund/Duisburg

Schwede, Walter

before 1945: member of the managing board of the Vereinigte Stahlwerke AG, Düsseldorf
after 1945: his name was on the American list of war criminals; honorary chairman of the board of directors of the Handelsunion AG (Thyssen trust), Düsseldorf; decorated with the Distinguished Service Cross of the Order of Merit of the Federal Republic of Germany

Siemens, Hermann von

before 1945: chairman of the board of directors of the Siemens & Halske AG, Berlin
after 1945: his name was on the American list of war criminals; board of directors of the Siemens & Halske AG, West Berlin/Munich; decorated with the Distinguished Service Cross with star and shoulder ribbon of the Federal Republic of Germany

Ter-Nedden, Dr. Wilhelm

before 1945: ministerial counsellor, "Eastern specialist" in the Reich Ministry of Economics, later active in the Reich Ministry for the Occupied Eastern Territories as assistant head of the Economic Staff East, main group W, participated in the plundering of the occupied countries
after 1945: ministerial director in the Federal Ministry of Transport, head of the department for general transport policy and economic transport questions

Thalau, Prof. Dr.-Ing. Karl

before 1945: war economy leader
after 1945: business manager of Ernst Heinkel Flugzeugbau (aircraft construction) GmbH, Speyer and Munich; deputy chairman of the board of directors of Junkers Flugzeug- und Motorenwerke AG, Munich

Thiedemann, Richard

before 1945: war economy leader, director of Junkers Flugzeug- und Motorenwerke AG, Dessau
after 1945: for many years member of the managing board of the Henschel Flugzeugwerke AG, Kassel, now member of the board of directors

Tix, Dr.-Ing. h.c. Arthur

before 1945: member of the executive committee of the Bochum Verein für Guss-Stahlfabrikation AG, Bochum; head of the main weapons committee with the Reich minister for armament and war production; member of the industrial council of the supreme command of the army; decorated with the Knight's Cross to the War Service Cross
after 1945: his name was on the American list of war criminals; managing board of the Bochum Verein für Guss-Stahlfabrikation AG (Krupp trust), Bochum; decorated with the Distinguished Service Cross of the Federal Republic of Germany

Tüngeler, Johannes

before 1945: Reich bank counsellor in the Reich Ministry of Economics, counter-intelligence agent, liaison man to the Gestapo and the Security Service (SD)
after 1945: bank director and member of the board of directors of the Deutsche Bundesbank and the Zentralbank, Frankfurt-on-Main

Vialon, Prof. Dr. Karl

before 1945: provincial court counsellor in the Superior Provincial Court in Karlsruhe; senior government counsellor in the Reich Ministry of Finance; participated in plundering occupied Alsace; government director and head of the finance department of the Reich commissariat for the eastern countries in Riga, participated in the "final solution of the Jewish question" not only through the theft of Jewish property and the belongings of murdered persons, but as head of the finance department also organized the setting up of concentration camps and the carrying through of terror actions against the Latvian, Esthonian and Byelorussian population
after 1945: state secretary in the Federal Ministry for Economic Cooperation; before ministerial director in the Office of the Federal Chancellor and Adenauer's adviser on economic and financial questions

Vits, Dr. Dr. h.c. Ernst Hellmuth
before 1945: war economy leader; chairman of the board of managers and works manager of the Vereinigte Glanzstoff-Fabriken AG (synthetic fibres), Wuppertal/Elberfeld, Österreichische Glanzstoff-Fabriken AG, St. Pölten, Glanzstoff-Fabrik Lobositz AG (Sudetenland); member of the board of directors of the Algemeene Kunstzijde Unic, Arnhem/Holland
after 1945: chairman of the managing board of the Vereinigte Glanzstoff-Fabriken AG, Wuppertal/Elberfeld (AKU trust), and others; member of the board of directors in various companies of the trust and of the Deutsche Erdöl AG (DEA), Hamburg, Zellstoffabrik Waldhof, Mannheim, Hamburg-Amerika-Linie, Hamburg, chairman of the Stifterverband für die Deutsche Wissenschaft, Präsidium Deutsche Forschungsgemeinschaft, advisory council of the Fritz-Thyssen-Stiftung; decorated with the Distinguished Service Cross with star of the Federal Republic of Germany

Voith, Dr.-Ing. h.c., Dr. rer. pol. h.c. Hanns
before 1945: war economy leader
after 1945: business-manager of the firm J. M. Voith GmbH, Heidenheim (Brenz); decorated with the Distinguished Service Cross with star of the Order of Merit of the Federal Republic of Germany

Wagner, Alfons
before 1945: war economy leader; chairman of the managing board of the Vereinigte Oberschlesische Hüttenwerke AG, Gleiwitz; chairman of the advisory council of the Schlesische Montan GmbH, Breslau; advisory council of the Deutsche Bank, Berlin
after 1945: his name was on the Polish list of war criminals No. 10/185; chairman of the board of directors of the Warsteiner Eisenwerke AG, Warstein; member of the board of directors of the Eisenwerk-Gesellschaft Maximilianshütte mbH, Sulzbach-Rosenberg (Flick trust), Gerling Konzern Lebensversicherungs-AG, Cologne, and others; decorated with the Distinguished Service Cross of the Federal Republic of Germany

Waldschmidt, Herbert
before 1945: war economy leader
after 1945: business-manager of the Knorr-Bremse GmbH, Munich; member of the managing board of the Knorr-Bremse KG, Munich, Motoren-Werke Mannheim AG, Mannheim

Walz, Hans
before 1945: war economy leader; SS Hauptsturmführer; member of the "Circle of Friends of the Reichsführer SS", business-manager of the Robert Bosch GmbH, Stuttgart
after 1945: his name was on the American list of war criminals; honorary chairman of the Bosch house; decorated with the Distinguished Service Cross with star of the Order of Merit of the Federal Republic of Germany

Weiss, Bernhard
before 1945: commissioner general of the Friedrich Flick KG, Berlin
after 1945: his name was on the American list of war criminals; business-manager of the Siemag Siegener Maschinenbau GmbH, Dahlbusch, vice-president of the Bundesverband der Deutschen Industrie e. V., Cologne

Werner, William
before 1945: war economy leader; manager, director and business-manager of Auto-Union AG, Chemnitz; chairman of the technical committee of the Vehicle Building Industry Economic Group, Berlin; Reich Committee for Increased Output
after 1945: for many years business-manager and technological head of Auto-Union GmbH, Düsseldorf-Ingolstadt; member of the board of directors of Zweirad-Union AG, Nuremberg (1963)

Westrick, Dr. Ludger
before 1945: war economy leader; chairman of the executive board of the Vereinigte Aluminiumwerke, Berlin; in its works prisoners of war and foreign forced labourers chiefly worked who were ground to death by the hundred under the most inhuman working and living conditions; member of the managing board of Innwerk AG, Munich; chairman of the board of directors of E. F. Ohle's Erben AG, Breslau, Rheinische Blattmetall AG, Grevenbroich, Vereinigte Wiener Metallwerke AG, Vienna, and others; member of the industrial council for the development of air weapons
after 1945: federal minister and head of the Office of the Federal Chancellor; before state secretary in the Federal Ministry of Economics; chairman of the board of directors of Bergwerksgesellschaft Hibernia AG, Herne, Vereinigte Industrie-Unternehmungen AG, Bonn, Innwerk AG, Töging (Inn), Vereinigte Aluminium-Werke AG, Bonn, and others; decorated with the Distinguished Service Cross with star and

shoulder ribbon of the Federal Republic of Germany

Weydenhammer, Dr. Rudolf

before 1945: war economy leader; general director and chairman of the managing board of Österreichische Magnesit AG, Munich; vice-president of Forsikringsaktienelskabet Nordeuropa, Copenhagen, Nippon Magnesium Metals Company Ltd., Konau/Japan, Riunione Adriatica di security; managerial council, Vienna-Trieste; member of the board of directors; American Magnesium Metals Corporation, Pittsburgh, Pa.; representative of the Reich protector in Bohemia and Moravia
after 1945: president and director of Oberrheinische Handels-AG, Zürich, honorary senator of the University of Munich

Wieland, Dr. Walter

before 1945: war economy leader, on the advisory council of the Deutsche Bank, Berlin
after 1945: vice-chairman of the board of directors of Omnipetrol GmbH for oil refining, Hamburg, Deutsch-Überseeische Petroleum AG, Hamburg; member of the board of directors of the Bayerische Rohrhandelsgesellschaft Munich, IG-Farbenindustrie in liquidation, Frankfurt-on-Main

Winnacker, Prof. Dr.-Ing. Karl

before 1945: director of IG-Farbenindustrie AG, Farbwerk Hoechst, Frankfurt-on-Main/Hoechst
after 1945: chairman of the managing board of Farbwerke Hoechst AG, Frankfurt-on-Main; member of the board of directors in various companies of the IG-Farben group; on the board of directors of Demag AG, Duisburg, Degussa, Deutsche Gold- und Silber-Scheideanstalt, formerly Roessler, Frankfurt-on-Main; chairman of DECHEMA, Deutsche Gesellschaft für chemisches Apparatewesen e. V., Frankfurt-on-Main; vice-president of the Union of the Chemical Industry; chairman of the board of directors of the Gesellschaft für Kernforschung (nuclear research) mbH, Karlsruhe; vice-chairman of the board of directors of the Dresdner Bank, vice-chairman of the German Atomic Commission; decorated with the Distinguished Service Cross with star and shoulder ribbon of the Federal Republic of Germany

Wisselmann, Heinrich

before 1945: war economy leader; general director of the Preussische Bergwerks- und Hütten-AG, Berlin; head of the mining group, Berlin; advisory committee of the Deutsche Reichsbank Berlin and the Reich Industrial Group, Berlin
after 1945: chairman of the board of directors of the Eisenwerk Weserhütte AG, Bad Oynhausen (Otto Wolff trust); vice-chairman of the board of directors of the Vereinigte Kaliwerke Salzdetfurth AG, Hanover (Salzdetfurth trust, Werhahn group); on the board of directors of the Mansfeld AG für Bergbau und Hüttenbetrieb, Hanover (Salzdetfurth trust), Klöckner-Werke AG, Duisburg, and others; decorated with the Distinguished Service Cross of the Federal Republic of Germany

Witzleben, Dr. Wolf-Dietrich von

before 1945: war economy leader; member of the managing board of Siemens- und Halske AG, Berlin, chief of personnel of the Siemens trust
after 1945: for many years vice-chairman of the board of directors of the Siemens-Schuckert-Werke AG, West Berlin/Erlangen; honorary president of the Society for the Promotion of Young Entrepreneurs, Cologne (1963)

Wurster, Prof. Dr.-Ing. Carl

before 1945: war economy leader; member of the managing board of the IG-Farbenindustrie AG, Frankfurt-on-Main; leader of the Betriebsgemeinschaft Oberrhein of the IG-Farben; member of the administrative council of the Deutsche Gesellschaft für Schädlingsbekämpfung mbH (DEGESCH) (pest control), Frankfurt-on-Main (which produced Zyklon B gas with which millions of people were gassed); decorated with the Knight's Cross to the War Service Cross
after 1945: defendant in the Nuremberg IG-Farben trial; chairman of the managing board of the Badische Anilin- und Soda-Fabrik AG, Ludwigshafen/Rhine; chairman of the board of directors of BASF Badische Anilin- und Soda-Fabrik AG, Ludwigshafen; member of the board of directors of the Deutsche Gold- und Silberscheideanstalt, Frankfurt-on-Main, Deutsche Bank AG, Frankfurt-on-Main, Buna-Werke Hüls GmbH, Marl, Vereinigte Glanzstoff-Fabriken AG, Wuppertal-Elberfeld; member of the managing board of the Stifterverband für die Deutsche Wissenschaft; presidium of the Union of the Chemical Industry; member of the Kuratorium der Stiftung Volkswagenwerk; decorated with the Distinguished Service Cross with star and shoulder ribbon of the Federal Republic of Germany and other distinctions

Zangen, Dr. h.c. Wilhelm

before 1945: war economy leader; general director of the Mannesmann trust; member of the armament council and head of the main Wehrmacht committee at the Reich Ministry for Armament and War Production; head of the Reich Industrial Group; praised by Hitler and Göring as an "outstanding leader personality"; was especially responsible for the plundering of foreign industry; member of the SS and NSDAP, Aryanized various firms

after 1945: on the American list of war criminals; chairman of the board of directors of the Mannesmann AG, Düsseldorf; vice-chairman of the board of directors of the Demag AG, Duisburg; member of the board of directors of Deutsche Bank, Salzdetfurth AG, Hanover, Wasag-Chemie AG, Essen (Krupp trust); decorated with the Distinguished Service Cross with star of the Federal Republic of Germany

GESTAPO, SS AND SD IN STATE AND ECONOMIC LIFE

Millionfold Murderers

The Bonn decision to apply the statute of limitations to nazi criminals also includes crimes committed by members of the Gestapo, SS and SD (security service). These organizations in themselves have become in all countries the symbol of nazi and war crimes. They were the main means by which German fascism tried to maintain its rule of terror and to realize its criminal aims.

If their initial tasks were to brutally subjugate the German people, to exterminate the anti-fascist and democratic forces in Germany through concentration camps and the guillotine, then at a later stage their sphere of activities was extended when the predatory fascist war was unleashed. Gestapo, SS and SD were the principal organizations which tried to inaugurate the "New Order in Europe" in temporarily occupied countries by dragging millions of human beings into the concentration camps, by carrying out mass-shootings, executions of prisoners of war and exterminating entire national groups.

Buchenwald, Sachsenhausen, Ravensbrück, Auschwitz, Maidanek, Treblinka, Sobibor, Bergen-Belsen, Amersfort, Oradour, Lidice, Marzabotto, Putten, Minsk, Kiev and other places of unimaginable sufferings are inseparably connected with the terms Gestapo, SS and SD.

Eleven million people were killed in the nazi concentration camps alone. The total number of women, men and children who were murdered by members of the Gestapo, SS and SD could not be established to this day. Even 20 years after the war new execution places are still being found and laid bare.

In the so-called action-group trial (case IX) the American Military Tribunal spoke of horrifying violations of international law, of crimes of unheard-of brutality and inconceivable cruelty. Neither the imagination nor human language suffice to comprehend these barbaric crimes.

Were these crimes against humanity then isolated acts and excesses committed by individual members or units of these organizations? The "Reichsführer SS and the Chief of the German Police", Himmler, declared in his speech of 4 October 1943 in Posen before the national socialist leader-corps:

"How the Russians fare, how the Czechs fare does not interest me in the least, what these peoples possess in the way of good blood of our kind we will take,

even if we have to take their children by force when necessary and bring them up in Germany. But whether the other peoples live in prosperity or perish from hunger, that interests me only in so far as we need them as slaves for our culture, otherwise I am not concerned with it. Whether 10,000 Russian women collapse from exhaustion when they build a tank trench interests me only to the extent that I want to have the tank trench made for Germany . . . Most of you will know what it is like when 100 corpses are heaped together, when five hundred corpses are piled up or a thousand. To have gone through that – and with the exception of human weaknesses – to have remained decent, that made us hard. This is a page of the glory of our history that has never been written and that will never be written . . ." (IMT, Vol. XXIX, p. 144)

THE NUREMBERG ACCUSATIONS

The overwhelming evidence available at the Nuremberg trials caused the International Military Tribunal to designate the Gestapo, SS and SD in their totality as criminal organizations. In justifying the decision the International Court cited the following as the main crimes committed by these organizations:

Cruelty and murders in the concentration camps
Persecution and extermination of the Jews
Terror, arrests and massacres in the occupied areas
Shootings of hostages
Ill-treatment and murder of prisoners-of-war and war-crimes of all kinds
Mass deportations and implementation of the forced labour program

Article 10 of the statute of the International Military Tribunal states:

"If a group or an organization has been declared by the Court to be of a criminal character, then the competent national authorities of each signatory has the right to bring persons to trial before a national, military or occupation court for membership in such criminal organization. In this case the criminal character of the group or organization is considered proven and will not be questioned." (IMT, Vol. I, p. 13)

In violation of all obligations under international law the initiators and persons mainly responsible for the crimes of these terror organizations have been appointed to leading positions in state and economic life. "Specialists" of the Gestapo, SS and SD created the so-called "protection of the constitution" for the suppression of the democratic and progressive forces in West Germany. "Specialists" of the Gestapo, SS and SD are in influential positions in the West German police force; they are continuing today to pursue their criminal activities in the Gehlen secret service and in the special units of the Bundeswehr.

The Gestapo commissars and SS Sturmbannführers appear before court, not as defendants but as witnesses for the defence. Retired State Secretary Dr. Globke, commentator of the Anti-Jewish Laws, was called to give expert testimony for the fascist race legislation in the Treblinka trial. The former "War administrator in France" and "Reich appointee" in nazi-occupied Denmark, Dr. Werner Best, today legal adviser of the Hugo Stinnes trust was called to Frankfurt-on-Main as an "expert" war criminal in the Auschwitz trial.

Further "witnesses of the defence" appearing in the witness-box in this or in other war criminal trials are:

Emil Finnberg, SS Sturmbannführer
today: lawyer in Hamburg

Dr. Kurt Niesling, SS investigating magistrate and court officer in Krakow
today: lawyer in Wiesbaden

Walter Entrich, gendarmerie captain in the Ukraine
today: police inspector in Neuhaus, Paderborn region

Dr. Kurt Uhlenbroock, SS Sturmbannführer and doctor in the Auschwitz (Oswiecim) concentration camp
today: physician in Hamburg

Helmut Bartsch, SS Hauptsturmführer and member of an investigating commission in Auschwitz (Oswiecim)
today: police inspector in Krefeld

Dr. Johannes Thümmler, SS Obersturmbannführer and head of the Chemnitz and Kattowitz (Katowice) central Gestapo offices
today: leading employee of a precision mechanical-optical works in Oberkochen

Joseph Schreieder, SS Obersturmbannführer and criminal director in occupied Holland
today: senior government counsellor in Munich

Günther Burmeister, SS Standartenführer and office head of the central SS court
today: senior provincial court counsellor in Schleswig

Dr. Hans Lauffs, SS Hauptsturmführer and SS judge
today: ministerial counsellor in Bonn

Hans Zentgraf, SS Obersturmbannführer and head of an SS and police court in Riga
today: lawyer in Aachen

Willy Osthues, SS Hauptsturmführer and judge at the SS and police court in Krakow
today: lawyer in Munich

Gustav Adolf Nosske (Düsseldorf), SS Obersturmbannführer and head of the Düsseldorf central Gestapo office

Albert Hartl (Braunschweig), SS Sturmbannführer, SS judge and group leader in the Reich Security Main Office

Friedrich Dern (Offenbach), SS Standartenführer and leader of the "Reichsführerbegleitbataillon" (Reich leader accompanying battalion)

Dr. Richard Wendler (Munich), governor of Krakow

Dr. Horst Barth, SS Obersturmbannführer and head of the criminal investigation department in Krakow

Globke, Best, Streckenbach, concentration camp doctors, SS storm troop leaders and SS judges as well as other "dignitaries" of fascist Germany are called upon in unlimited number by the SS counsels for the defence to prove that the fascist legislation was correct and legal and that the carrying out of the orders of the Reich Security Main Office was therefore an obvious duty and that consequently the accused SS and Gestapo murderers must be acquitted of all charges.

And here is the official attitude of the West German government: In the Bundestag debate on the application of the statute of limitations to nazi and war crimes the former Bonn minister of justice stated that one must gradually get used to the possibility of having to live under one roof with murderers. Minister of Justice Bucher was forced to resign by a world wide protest; but that this is not just his private opinion is shown in the following sections.

THE REICH SECURITY MAIN OFFICE

As a result of an order from Himmler on 27 September 1939 the central offices of the security police and the SD (security service), the main office of the security police, the main office of the Reichsführer SS, the office of the secret state police (Gestapo) and the Reich criminal police office were united in the Reich Security Main Office-Reichssicherheitshauptamt (RSHA).

This apparatus employed thousands of full-time and tens of thousands of part-time "freelance" operators. They decided on life and death in Hitler's and Himmler's sphere of power partly on instructions and partly on their own. With the RSHA a new institution of the "Führer-Might" was formed, which had almost unlimited power in the fascist state which served the interests of the monopolies. The institution had governmental as well as party jurisdiction.

Among the main tasks of the RSHA was also the "final solution of the Jewish question". On orders of the RSHA through the "action groups" alone two million and in the fascist concentration camps a further four million Jews were murdered. In addition, all executive measures within and outside Germany – from the sending to concentration camps, the dragging into forced labour from abroad, the organization of ghettoes, the torture and degradation of anti-fascists up to the euthanasia and other crimes – are part of the account of the RSHA, its leading officials and the greatest part of its employees.

THE CRIME IN THE VELODROME D'HIVER

They are responsible for the murder of 4,051 Jewish children who were arrested with their parents – altogether some 7,000 people in July 1942 in a wave of arrests in Paris. In the courtyard of the Velodrome d'Hiver, a big cycle racing track, they were imprisoned for five days without any food. Drinking water was available only from a water hydrant in the street. Women had to give birth to children under these conditions. Thirty people died immediately and many lost their reason.

On the 5th day the parents were dragged from their children and transported away. They perished in the gas chambers of the Auschwitz concentration camp. Although the French government tried to get permission for the placing of the remaining 4,051 children in children's homes, the RSHA decided to gas the children also. Without any care they were piled in bunches of 300 and 400 into waggons and transported to their death.

In spite of the verdict of Nuremberg that the criminals of the Reichssicherheitshauptamt should be punished wherever they appeared, most of these criminals, even the office heads, were not indicted. But precisely they were the direct organizers of the murders, out of their ranks came the leaders of the so-called action groups.

ACTION GROUPS IN OPERATION

These groups were formed on the basis of an agreement between the RSHA, the supreme command of the Wehrmacht (OKW) and the supreme army command (OKH). The agreement provided that the appropriate army groups or armies had to have a representative of the chief of the security police and the SD attached to it who had mobile units in the form of an "action group" at his disposal. The "action groups" were in turn organized into "action commandos" and "special commandos".

Under the pretext of the political security of the conquered areas in the occupied as well as in the rear areas of the Wehrmacht the "action groups" were supposed to ruthlessly liquidate all resistance to national socialism, not only present resistance but resistance in the past and the future. Entire classes and groups of people were to be killed, without investigation, compassion or remorse. The women were to be murdered together with their menfolk, and the children were to be executed, because otherwise they would grow up to be enemies of national socialism and might even harbour the wish to revenge the deaths of their parents." (NG, Case IX, p. 32)

These tasks, which corresponded to an "order from the Führer", the "action groups" carried out with the greatest possible precision. They went through the occupied territories, and hunted Jews, communists, partisans, political functionaries, mental defectives and "racially inferior" persons. The victims were shot, beaten to death, hanged where they were found. Hundreds and thousands of bodies filled the mass graves. Populations of entire villages and hamlets were herded together, murdered or dragged into Germany as forced labour. The farmsteads were burned down.

How these dreadful scenes were enacted is shown from the description of a German construction engineer who had the following experience on the Dubno airport on 5 October 1942, which he described under oath before the Nuremberg Court.

"... an old woman with snow-white hair held the one-year-old child in her arms and sung to it and tickled it. The child shrieked with delight. The married couple looked on with tears in their eyes. The father held a boy of about ten years of age by the hand and talked quietly to him. The boy fought back his tears. The father pointed to heaven, stroked his head and seemed to explain something. Then the SS man at the ditch called something to his comrade. He separated about 20 persons from the rest and ordered them to go behind the earth mound. The family, whom I just mentioned was among them. I remember exactly, how a slim, black-haired girl pointed to herself as she passed me closely and said: '23 years old'.

"I went around the earth mound and stood in front of a huge grave. Closely pushed together, the people were lying on top of each other in such a way that only their heads could be seen. From almost all heads blood was running over the shoulders. Some of those shot still moved. Some lifted their arms and their heads, to show that they were still alive. The grave was already three quarters filled. I estimated that there were already about a thousand people in it. I looked for the rifleman. He was an SS man who sat at the narrow end of the grave, with his feet dangling in the grave, on his knees was an automatic pistol and he was smoking a cigarette. The completely naked people went down steps which were dug into the clay soil of the side of the pit and slid over the heads of the ones who were lying in it up to the spot which the SS man indicated. They laid down in front of the dead and wounded people, some stroked the still living and spoke quietly

to them. Then I heard a series of shots. I turned back to the ditch and saw how the bodies convulsed or the heads already lay still on the bodies in front of them. Blood ran from their necks.

"I was surprised that I was not sent away, but I saw that two or three postal officials in uniform were also standing nearby. The next group was already approaching, went down into the pit, lined up next to the previous victims and was shot. As I went back around the earth mound, I noticed a newly arrived transport of people. This time there were some sick and feeble ones among them. An old, emaciated woman, with dreadfully thin legs was being undressed by other already naked people, while two others supported her. The woman was seemingly paralysed. The naked people carried the woman around the earth mound. I went away with Moennikes (a building labourer) and drove back to Dubno in the car.

"The next morning when I was again at the building site, I saw about 30 naked people near the pit; they were lying about 30 to 50 metres away from it. Some were still alive and looked ahead with set eyes and did not seem to feel the morning frost nor did they pay any attention to the workers of my firm who were standing around. A girl of about 20 spoke to me and begged me for clothes and help in escaping. But we already heard the noise of a rapidly approaching car, and I saw that it was the SS commando. I withdrew to my building site. Ten minutes later we heard shots near the pit. The corpses had been placed by the still living Jews into the pit, they themselves had to lie on top, to be also shot in the neck." (Gerald Reitlinger, Die Endlösung – The Final Solution, Colloquium-Verlag, West Berlin, p. 231 ff.)

That is what the "political safeguarding" of the occupied areas meant. The actions of the action groups had nothing in common with military warfare. There were atrocious mass murders of innocent men, women and children.

Of the action groups the groups A to D must be especially mentioned. Each of them had a strength of from 800 to 1,200 men and consisted of members of the general SS, the Gestapo, the SD, the regular police and the armed SS. The armed SS and the regular police force were represented with some 47 per cent and thus formed the greater part of the detachments.

Of these several thousands of criminals in the "action group" trial of 1947–48 only 24 leading representatives were accused:

6 SS Generals,
5 SS Standartenführer,
6 SS Obersturmbannführer,
4 SS Sturmbannführer and
3 SS officers of lower rank.

Fourteen death sentences were passed on 24 accused of which only four were confirmed. All the others, who were sentenced to long terms of imprisonment,

were pardoned already in 1951 and for the most part released from imprisonment. They include:
the leader of "Action commando" la, SS Standartenführer Sandberger;
the leader of "Action commando" 7a, SS Sturmbannführer Steimle;
the leader of "Action commando" 7b, SS Sturmbannführer Ott;
the leader of "Action commando" 6, SS Sturmbannführer Biberstein;
the leader of "Action group" D, SS Standartenführer Seibert;
the leader of "Special commando" 11b, SS Obersturmbannführer Schubert;
the leader of "Action commando" 4b, SS Sturmbannführer Haensch.

The greater part of these bestial murderers today live unmolested in West Germany or abroad. Only under the most extreme public pressure have proceedings been introduced in a few individual cases.

THE TERROR REGIME OF THE GESTAPO

A no less criminal role within the Reich Security Main Office was played by the Secret State Police (Gestapo) and the security service (SD). The Gestapo was formed from the Prussian Secret State Police Office and the political police of the provinces of the German Reich. When Himmler became chief of police in 1936 he formed the security police from the Gestapo and the criminal police. Together with the SD he placed it under the command of the SS leader Heydrich. The order of Himmler on 27 September 1939 to join these forces in the Reichssicherheitshauptamt was by then only a formality.

Gestapo and SD participated directly in the preparation and the carrying on of the Second World War through their brutal operations against the revolutionary working class and other democratic forces. It was also the Gestapo and the SD which created "fifth columns" in countries which were to be overrun by the fascist war machine and (especially in Czechoslovakia and Austria) paved the way for the later occupation.

Even the "external reasons" for starting the Second World War, the attack on the Gleiwitz radio station, was organized by the Gestapo. The faked attack was under the direct management of Gestapo chief Müller. SS Sturmbannführer Naujocks, who was given the job of carrying out this assignment, still lives in Hamburg. Although his crime is known to the West German judiciary, nothing has been done to apprehend him.

Inside Germany the Gestapo created a regime of terror of which there is no equal in the world. Tens of thousands of communists and social democrats, Christian workers, Jews and progressive intellectuals were arrested. Their tortures began in the Gestapo jails. One of the most infamous was the one in Berlin in the Prinz Albert Strasse 8. Here the Gestapo staged veritable blood baths to force statements from its prisoners. Those who survived the tortures were dragged into concentration camps.

The Gestapo alone had the jurisdiction to send persons to concentration camps. Its members had got themselves into these murder holes of fascism and are responsible for the painful deaths of many hundreds of thousands of prisoners. The Gestapo was named a criminal organization by the Nuremberg Military Tribunal. The resulting obligation to sentence incriminated members of the Gestapo and SD, was, however, not carried out in West Germany despite the fact that these crimes were of a cruelty that cannot be surpassed and of an extent that cannot be fully assessed.

"The Gestapo and SD were used for purposes which, according to the statute, were criminal; they included the persecution and extermination of the Jews, cruelties and murders in the concentration camps, excesses in the administration of occupied areas, the carrying out of the forced labour program and the ill treatment and murder of prisoners-of-war ... In the case of the Gestapo the Court includes in this definition all executive and administrative officers of Office IV of the RSHA or those who were concerned with Gestapo affairs in other departments of the RSHA, as well as all local Gestapo officials who served in or outside Germany." (IMT, Vol. I, 1947, p. 300)

The circle of persons belonging to the SD was also precisely fixed in Nuremberg:

"As to the SD, the Court includes offices III, VI and VII of the RSHA and all other members of the SD, including the local representatives and agents irrespective of whether they were working in an unpaid capacity or not, and irrespective of whether they were nominally members of the SS or not." (Ibid., p. 301)

THE DISCIPLINARY POLICE – A GANG OF SADISTS

The so-called disciplinary police was closely linked with the SS. This was shown by the fact that the Reichsführer SS already in 1936 was also "Chief of the German Police".

Along with him other SS leaders, like Heydrich, Kaltenbrunner and Daluege took over leading positions in the police apparatus. At the same time high police officers like Otto Winkelmann were taken over into the SS.

With its military style police divisions, regiments and battalions the disciplinary police force was involved in numerous crimes like the SS. For example police battalion No. 11 from Kaunas (Lithuania) made the town of Sluzk "free of Jews" within two days on 27 and 28 October 1942. A report to the general commissar of Minsk states about this "action".

"Concerning the execution of this operation I must to my deep regret emphasize

that it bordered on sadism. The town itself during the operation presented a terrible picture. With indescribable brutality... the Jewish people, but also including White Ruthenians, were dragged out of their flats and driven together. Everywhere in town shots resounded, and in the streets were piles of corpses of the Jews . . . Apart from the fact that the Jewish people, among them the artisans, were extremely brutally manhandled before the eyes of the White Ruthenian people, the Ruthenian people were also ill treated with rubber truncheons and rifle butts."

The following documents show the terror employed by the 15th Police regiment:

"O. U. 22 September 1942

Operation order for the extermination of settlements

1). Battalion destroys on 23 September 1942 in the area north-east of Mokrany gang-infested settlements of Borki, Zablocie and Borysowka.
Company Nürnberg destroys Kortelisy.

2). The following forces are deployed:
9th company – without the Frohn platoon – with attached gendarme troop (motorized) 16 for Borysowka,
10th company and $^1/_7$ of the headquarters guard and 3 drivers for Borki.
11th company with the Frohn platoon and 14 men Pzkw/10 for Zablocie

3). The companies – without reinforcements – arrive on 22 September before 18.00 hours in the settlements:
9th co. on foot to Dywin,
10th and 11th cos. with their own lorry to the western exit of Mokrany.

4). Reinforcements to be brought up:
a) Gendarme platoon (motorized) 16 reports on 22 September before 18.00 hours to the company leader of the 9th co. in Dywin before the building of the district farmers.
b) $^1/_7$ headquarters guard, 3 drivers, Frohn platoon and 14 men Pzkw/10 report on 22 September before 18.00 hours to the 11th co. at Mokrany.
c) Battalion reserve: Remainder of the gendarme troop (motorized) 15 and 4 signalmen.

5). Commencement of the operation: 23 September 1942 5.30 hours. By 4.35 hours the settlements are encircled (outer sealing).

6). Carrying out of the "action" in accordance with my orders at the officers' briefing on 21 September 1942.

7). Securing of cattle, agricultural implements, harvest stores and other equipment according to my oral orders.

8). For transport of the goods mentioned in 7) the companies will put together a convoy of horse-drawn wagons and bring them into the vicinity of the action. (verbally ahead) . . .

signed Holling"

(SZAOR of the USSR, Fund 7,021, list 148, file 3, p. 20)

"O. U. Kobryn 22 September 1942
From the war diary of the 3rd battalion of police regiment 15.

"The operation 'triangle' is temporarily postponed. The battalion receives the order to move with its attached units and the added platoon of gendarmes 16 (motorized) and to destroy the settlements to the north and north-east of Mokrany, Borki, Zablocie and Borysowka, which it has been established are gang-support-places. The 9th company with gendarme platoon 16 reaches Dywin in the evening; the 10th and 11th companies reach Mokrany. At each support point a group remains behind. The battalion fighting position is established in Mokrany."

"O. U. Kobryn 23 September 1942

"Battalion fighting position Mokrany. The action begins with the surrounding of the settlements, which is completed in the early hours of the morning. At dawn the inhabitants are collected and checked by the SD. After selection of absolutely reliable families according to orders in Borysowka 119 men, women and children are shot. After that the cattle, implements and grain are safeguarded." (op. cit., File 4, p. 193)

This and similar examples can be given about all police formations which were let loose in the temporary fascist occupied areas.

CORDIALLY WELCOME IN THE BONN STATE

Thousands of these criminals, mostly known by name and heavily incriminated by irrefutable evidence (primarily by documents which the DGR submitted to world public opinion and made available to the competent West German authorities), live unmolested in West Germany. Moreover, the members of the SS and police force which are living in West Germany, were given the opportunity to organize in the so-called "traditional associations".

Already in 1951 the SS organizations, camouflaged as a "Social Aid Society" (HIAG = Hilfsgemeinschaft auf Gegenseitigkeit ehemaliger Angehöriger der Waffen SS = Mutual Aid Society of Former Members of the Armed SS) were established.

A year later there were already 75 local SS associations and the number grew in the following years to 80. Over 40 other "SS traditional associations" exist besides the HIAG, camouflaged as "search service associations" of the Red Cross. The leaders of these organizations are without exception persons who participated in crimes against humanity.

On 29 June 1961 the Bonn Bundestag decided that all members of the former SS Readiness Troop who had been in the service of Himmler and Hitler for longer than ten years on 8 May 1945 have a right to be provided for. This decision opened the road into the West German government service to many thousands of Jew murderers and concentration camp henchmen.

Himmler's Departmental Chiefs and Special Agents

According to an estimate of the former deputy chief prosecutor of the USA at the Nuremberg chief war criminal trial, Dr. Robert Kempner, about 10,000 SS and nazi criminals still live in West Germany undisturbed and unmolested. The Bonn government forces the West German population to live under one roof even with the professional hangmen of the Reich Security Main Office. The following are but a few examples.

Best Werner MURDERED DANISH PATRIOTS

today: Leading position as economic legal adviser to the Hugo Stinnes trust (Mülheim/Ruhr) and expert in the West German Foreign Office

Dr. Best joined the NSDAP already on 1 November 1930 (No. 341 338). In 1931 he was one of the co-authors of the infamous "Boxheim documents". This "governmental proclamation" which was written by the fascist leaders in the Boxheim Estate (Hesse) already indicated the murderous terror of the years 1933–1945. It provided that all anti-fascists who were against a nazi government should receive the death penalty.

His co-authorship of this document was of course the best recommendation for his criminal career, which Best continued in 1934 with his entry into the SD of the "Reichsführer SS". Best was highly esteemed there as a "police legal expert" who created a considerable part of the "legal" bases for the brutal actions of the SD against the German people, especially against the working class, as well as against other peoples who were attacked by Hitler fascism. As chief of Department I of the RSHA (up to 1940) and as war-administration chief with the military commander in France and finally (1942) as "Reich commissioner in Denmark", he could apply his "theory" in practice. On his orders on 30 December 1943 the editor Christian Damm, on 4 January 1944, the well-known poet Kaj Munk and in August 1944 the engineer Snog Christensen were murdered.

For these and other crimes Best was sentenced to death in Denmark, but was shortly afterwards pardoned on the intervention of the Bonn government and finally released.

Streckenbach Bruno — BEST'S WORTHY SUCCESSOR

today: Commercial employee in Hamburg

In the person of Bruno Streckenbach Best found a worthy successor for the chief of Department I of the Reichssicherheitshauptamt. Streckenbach, SS Gruppenführer and lieutenant general in the police force, was already before 1933 a member of the NSDAP (No. 489 972) and of the SS (No. 14 713). Best called him from Poland to Berlin. In Poland he was responsible for the "pacification" by the SS and the police force and had distinguished himself in his efforts on behalf of the "Germanization policy" and most of all in the extermination of the representatives of the Polish intelligentsia.

In the RSHA he continued to rave against the "members of the eastern peoples". On 5 November 1942 he sent an express letter to all Sipo (security police) and SD offices about the "criminal law procedures against Poles and members of the eastern peoples". In accordance with it the regular court procedures should be dropped and they should be handed directly to the hangmen.

For his crimes, above all as "commander of the 19th Latvian SS grenadier division" he was sentenced in the Soviet Union to hard labour for life and was later handed back to the Federal Republic as a criminal who had not come under any amnesty. In contradiction to the undertaking to keep him in jail the Bonn government freed him.

Six Franz — HEAD OF THE "MOSCOW ADVANCE COMMANDO"

today: Advertising manager of the Porsche-Diesel-Motorenbau GmbH, Friedrichshafen, a subsidiary of the Mannesmann AG, agent with "special experience" at the "Federal Intelligence Service" (along with 4,000 other SS officers and SD informers).

Dr. Six found his way into the NSDAP as long ago as 1930 (No. 245 670) and in 1935 he joined the SS (No. 107 480). Already on 20 April 1935 he became head of Department II in the main security office of the Reichsführung SS, later head of Department II and Department VII of the Reich Security Main Office which developed out of it. With this he had all prerequisites for head of the "Moscow Advance Commando". This position he took over in 1941.

In the course of the Action Group trial (case IX), where he was one of the 24 defendants, it was established, among other things, that Six and his accomplices were guilty of crimes against humanity, war crimes and membership in criminal organizations. They are responsible for the deaths of over one million people. (Cf. NG, Case IX, p. 27)

As head of the "Moscow Advance Commando" Six arrived in Smolensk on 25 July 1941. He stayed there till the end of August 1941 and returned to Berlin. This commando should – according to Six' statement before the allied tribunal – immediately on the arrival of German troops in Moscow, safeguard the archives and documents. It is, however, a fact *that the "Moscow Advance Commando" during the time that it stood under the leadership of Six was used for the liquidation of people and that moreover the safeguarding of documents in Russia was not undertaken for economic or cultural reasons, but with the intention of obtaining lists of communist functionaries, who would themselves have become candidates for "liquidation"*. (Ibid., p. 161)

On 9 November 1941 Six was promoted to SS Oberführer for special services in the eastern operations of the security police.

On 10 April 1948 Six was sentenced by an American military court in Nuremberg to 20 years in prison but on 31 January 1951 his sentence was reduced to ten years by the high commissioner John McCloy and by the supreme commander of US forces in Europe, General Thomas Handy. A short time afterwards he was released before his time was up.

Jost Heinz DEMANDED A MOBILE GAS CHAMBER

today: *Represents West German concerns as an independent economic legal expert.*

Jost is among the oldest members of the NSDAP. (Entry date: 1 February 1928, membership No. 75946). In 1933 he joined the police service and in 1934 he was already leading the defence office in the security main office of the Reichsführer SS. From 1938 to 1942 he was head of department VI of the Reich Security Main Office. Jost managed to get to the rank of SS brigade leader and major general in the police force. In 1939 he participated in the crimes against the Polish people. With wide experience as an executioner he commanded in 1942 Action Group A against the Soviet Union and was at the same time commander of the Sipo and the SD in Riga. It was proved that "Action Group A" had committed thousands of murders. Alone during his period in office over one thousand people were killed. On 15 June 1942 Jost requested *"a mobile gas chamber and hoses for three available gas cars for action in White Ruthenia"*. (NG, Case IX, p. 150)

Sentenced by an American military tribunal in 1948 to life imprisonment, his sentence was commuted to ten years in 1951, and a short time afterwards he was released.

Bilfinger Rudolf SPECIALIST IN THE "FINAL SOLUTION OF THE JEWISH QUESTION"

today: *Until recently superior administrative court counsellor in the administrative court of Baden-Württemberg in Mannheim. Owing to the pressure of public opinion he had to be suspended from duty in March 1965 and pensioned in June 1965.*

Dr. Bilfinger, SS Obersturmbannführer and deputy head of department II in the RSHA took part at all principal discussions about the "final solution of the Jewish question". In March 1942, at a follow-up meeting of the infamous "Wannsee conference" – which took place at Eichmann's office IV B 4 – the compulsory sterilization of the so-called half breeds of the 1st degree was discussed. *"It was certainly not meant to let the half breeds live for a long period as a third little race"* – it is reported in the minutes of this meeting. (Robert M.W. Kempner, *Eichmann und Komplicen* – Eichmann and Accomplices, Europa-Verlag, Zürich-Stuttgart-Vienna, 1961, p. 170)

On 27 October 1942 a further meeting took place in the same office, where the details of the sterilization of "half breeds of the 1st degree" were laid down. According to that children with one Jewish parent were given the "choice" of either being sterilized or going to a concentration camp.

Bilfinger also did outstanding work in the pillaging of Jewish property. He worked out a "legal basis" for this. On 14 May 1942 he sent a circular to various nazi ministries, the higher SS and police officers, the SD leading offices and others in which he decreed that: *"Jews, who along with German citizenship also have a foreign citizenship lose the German citizenship . . . along with their property . . . which falls to the Reich."* (Ibid., p. 257)

The documents which convict Bilfinger of these and other serious crimes have been offerred to the West German government by the government authorities of the GDR over a period of years. But Bonn showed no interest in these documents.

Thus this blood-stained jurist was able to work up to March 1965 as a senior administrative court counsellor. The pressure of public opinion which was based on the GDR evidence material finally became so strong that Bilfinger was suspended. He is one of those "desk murderers" who up to this day have not had to account for their crimes.

Hermann Krumey ORDERED "SPECIAL TREATMENT" FOR THE CHILDREN OF LIDICE

today: *After a scandalous verdict in Frankfurt-on-Main again proprietor of a chemist's shop established with government credit in Korbach/Hesse.*

Hermann Krumey managed to advance to the rank of SS Obersturmbannführer in the Reich Security Main Office. Directly after the attack of the Hitler fascists on Poland in November 1939 he was entrusted with the management of the "Resettlement Centre, Lodz Branch". Krumey organized the forced displacement and annihilation of 12,000 Jewish people from this area alone. In summer 1942 he caused 88 children who had been dragged to Lodz from Lidice to be sent to a concentration camp. Here they were murdered.

In March 1944 Eichmann gave him the task of deporting all Jews living in Hungary. In close collaboration with Eichmann's legal adviser in department IV of the RSHA, Otto Hunsche, Krumey organized the transportation of 400,000 men, women and children to the extermination camps. At Auschwitz no less than 300,000 of these unfortunate people were murdered within a few months.

Krumey was the initiator of the exchange business "blood against goods"; he offered the intermediary Joel Brand the lives of one million Jews in exchange for the delivery of 10,000 lorries from abroad. Krumey pressed for the speedier conclusion of the negotiations with the argument: *"Each day costs 12,000 human lives!"*

These and other facts were known to the Frankfurt court when it gave its verdict in February 1965 after a trial that had lasted nine months. Krumey was sentenced to five years at hard labour which was nearly covered by his detention during trial, which lasted four years and nine months and therefore the sentence was almost equivalent to acquittal.

When Krumey was arrested he not only lived as an honourable businessman, but even belonged to the local legislative body in Korbach as a member of the BHE.

Hunsche Otto EICHMANN'S "LEGAL ADVISER"

today: *Lawyer in Datteln/Westphalia.*

In recognition of his services as the "legal adviser" to the deportation expert in Department IV B 4 of the RSHA, SS Hauptsturmführer Dr. Otto Hunsche was awarded the title of government counsellor. Among the numerous crimes in which Hunsche took part with a decisive influence, there is his participation in the murder of 1,200 Hungarian Jews from the Kistarosa concentration camp.

As member of the staff of Eichmann, Hunsche accompanied SS Obersturmbannführer Krumey at the beginning of 1944 to Hungary. Their task was to drive all the Jews together in the shortest possible time for transporting to the extermination camps. Up to the entry of Soviet troops in Budapest 400,000 Jewish people were dragged off, of which the greater part were painfully murdered in the Auschwitz concentration camp.

Only when survivors made charges and supplied evidence was Hunsche brought before the court and sentenced in April 1962 to five years at hard labour for "assisting in the murder of 600 people". Even this sentence was too high for Hunsche, however. As an "experienced lawyer" he was able to have the verdict rescinded and a new trial began.

In April 1964 the second trial began before the Frankfurt-on-Main Assizes; it resulted in his acquittal and gave him a chance to practice law again.

Thümmler Johannes

GESTAPO CHIEF IN CHEMNITZ AND KATTOWITZ

today: Leading employee of an enterprise in Oberkochen ("Carl Zeiss Foundation").

SS Obersturmbannführer and senior government counsellor in the RSHA, Dr. Thümmler belonged already before 1933 to the NSDAP (No. 1 425 547). In the SS he had membership No. 323 711. After the establishment of the Hitler dictatorship he at first acted in the police headquarters of Dresden and in the prefecture of Schwarzenberg. Here he was so successful in the ruthless pursuit and suppression of the opponents of the terror regime, that he was promoted to chief of the state police administration in Dresden and Chemnitz.

During the Second World War he decided as Gestapo chief at Kattowitz (Katowice) over the life and death of Polish people, who on his instructions were put into the Auschwitz concentration camp with the notation to give them "special treatment" because "in any case a death sentence" was to be expected.

For a lengthy period he was also leader of action commando 16 and of action group E which perpetrated mass crimes in southeastern Europe.

In November 1964 the former Gestapo chief was given the opportunity to appear at the Frankfurt-on-Main Auschwitz trial as a "witness for the defence".

The appearance of Thümmler as witness for the defence caused the GDR legal authorities to hand over documents about the crimes he had committed to the West German judiciary. Prosecution, however, has not been commenced to this day, although Thümmler had to admit during his testimony that he was court martial president in several hundred cases. Thümmler declared that during these trials some 60 per cent were sentenced to death, and the remaining 40 per cent to concentration camps.

Lammerding Heinz

SS HANGMAN IN ORADOUR AND TULLE

today: *Engineer and building contractor in Düsseldorf. Leading role in the SS organization HIAG.*

Lammerding, who early joined the NSDAP (No. 722 395) and the SS (No. 247 062), was promoted to the rank of SS Oberführer and general of the armed SS by Himmler. Among others he commanded the infamous SS tank division "Das Reich".

The progress of this SS division through the areas occupied by the Hitler army is marked by gallows and mass graves. On 10 June 1944 the SS hordes attacked the French settlement of Oradour; 548 inhabitants were driven into the church and there, on orders from Lammerding, they were bestially murdered. The peaceful settlement was then levelled to the ground.

In order to break the growing resistance of the French people against the fascist occupation using any means possible SS commander Lammerding ordered the public hanging of 120 French civilians in Tulle.

For these and other crimes committed in France Lammerding was sentenced by a court in Bordeaux to death in absentia. After he had first lived in Wiesbaden under the assumed name of Braune, he settled in Düsseldorf as building contractor under his own name.

Requests for extradiction to France directed to the West German judiciary were not granted.

Wolff Karl

HIMMLER'S ADJUTANT

today: *Wolff was arrested in his villa on Starnberg lake 17 years after the end of the war and sentenced for the murder of 300,000 Jews to 15 years at hard labour – for each murder 30 minutes of imprisonment.*

SS Obergruppenführer and general of the Waffen-SS (armed SS) Karl Wolff was "chief of the personal staff of the Reichsführer SS" and "Liaison officer of the Reichsführer with the Führer". Armed with all special powers Wolff had a leading part in the so-called "final solution of the Jewish question". He bore the

Dü.

Leuna-Werke, den 30. März 1941. Gs.

172

Lu

Besuchsbericht.

Besprechung mit dem Lagerkommandanten des Konzentrationslagers bei Auschwitz am 27.3.41, nachm. 15 Uhr.

Anwesend: Sturmbannführer Hoeß, Lagerkommandant,
Sturmbannführer Kraus, Leiter der Verwaltung der Konzentrationslager, Oranienburg,
Hauptsturmführer Burböck, Dezernent für den Häftlingseinsatz, Berlin-Lichterfelde,
und einige Obersturmführer und Sturmführer als Dezernenten für die besprochenen Sonderfragen.

Obering. Faust, Lu/Dyhernfurth,
Dipl.-Ing. Flöter, Lu/Dyhernfurth,
Ing. Murr, Lu,
Dr. Dürrfeld, Leuna.

Zweck der Besprechung:

Nach der vorbereitenden Besprechung, die in Berlin am Donnerstag, den 20. März, zwischen Dir. Dr. Bütefisch und Obergruppenführer Wolf unter Anwesenheit der Oberführer Glücks - Oranienburg (Inspekteur der Konzentrationslager) und Lörner - Berlin (Inspekteur für den Häftlingseinsatz) stattfand, sollten nunmehr die Einzelheiten über die Art der Hilfe, die das Konzentrationslager bei dem Bau des Werkes übernehmen kann, besprochen werden.

Allgemeines:

Es soll zusammenfassend vorausgeschickt werden, daß die Besprechung in einem außerordentlich sachlichen und doch sehr herzlichen Ton vonstatten ging. Es war in allen Fragen eine volle Bereitschaft festzustellen, nach Kräften beim Bau des Werkes von seiten des Konzentrationslagers Hilfestellung zu leisten. An die Besprechung schloß sich eine eingehende Besichtigung des Lagers mit allen seinen Einrichtungen und Werkstätten.

Verabredungen:

1.) Von Herrn Faust werden für das laufende Jahr etwa 1 000 Hilfskräfte und Fachkräfte - soweit sie vorhanden sind - gefordert. Diese Zahl kann das Lager ohne weitere Vorbereitungen stellen.

2.) Für das nächste Jahr wird ein Bedarf von etwa 3 000 Häftlingen angekündigt. Diese Zahl wird das KL stellen können, wenn die nötigen Unterkünfte in dem Lager zur Vermehrung der bisherigen Häftlingszahl von 8 000 geschaffen worden sind. Das Lager ist z.Zt. im Bau weiterer Unterkünfte, ist jedoch gehemmt durch den Mangel an Moniereisen für die Böden und Decken. Wir übernehmen es, zu prüfen, dem Lager zu einer schnelleren Beschaffung (Kennziffer und Lieferfrage) zu verhelfen.

3.) Eine weitere Gestellung von Arbeitskräften über die gesamte Zahl hinaus ist durchaus möglich, da das Lager für die Zahl von etwa 30 000 Häftlingen vergrößert werden soll. Maßgebend für das Tempo ist die Beschaffung des Eisens und die Beschaffung der nötigen Zahl von Kappos. Diese Kappos (Poliere und sonstige fachlich geschulten Kräfte) werden aus den Berufsverbrechern ausgesucht und sollen von anderen KL nach Auschwitz überführt werden. Diese Aktionen sind im Gange.

193

4.) Für die Heranführung der Häftlinge an die Baustelle wird ein direkter Weg über die Sola südlich von Auschwitz nach dem Werksgelände vorgeschlagen. Das KL baut hierzu eine Brücke. Über dieselbe Trasse soll ein Feldbahngleis gelegt werden, so daß die Häftlinge im Feldbahnzug nach der Baustelle und zurück befördert werden können. Um die Beschaffung der notwendigen Gleise kümmern sich beide Parteien.

5.) Die Arbeitszeit richtet sich nach der Jahreszeit und kann mit 10 - 11 Stunden im Sommer, im Winter mit mindestens 9 Stunden angenommen werden. Die Leistung wird auf 75 % eines normalen deutschen Arbeiters geschätzt. Für die Häftlinge soll pro Hilfsarbeiter und Tag 3 RM, pro Facharbeiter und Tag 4 RM gezahlt werden. In diesen Kosten ist alles einbegriffen, Transport, Verpflegung u.s.w. Über diese Kosten hinaus fallen keinerlei Unkosten für uns für die Häftlinge an, es sei denn, daß zum Ansporn dann und wann kleine Vergütungen (Zigaretten u.s.w.) gegeben werden.

6.) Eine gleichzeitige Beschäftigung von Kriegsgefangenen ist zum mindesten im laufenden Jahr untunlich, insbesondere deswegen, weil die geforderte Zahl von Kräften durch das Lager restlos gedeckt werden kann.

Zusammenfassung:

Die gesamte Verhandlung wurde in herzlichem Einvernehmen geführt, wobei von beiden Seiten der Wunsch herausgestellt wurde, sich gegenseitig jede mögliche Hilfe angedeihen zu lassen. So z.B. stellte der Lagerkommandant für den Notfall alle im Lager vorhandenen Kräfte, Lagerarzt, Krankenauto, gegebenenfalls auch Transportmittel, zur Verfügung, bis die Baustelle eingelaufen ist. Es wurde verabredet, bei neuauftretenden Fragen eine ähnliche Besprechung zu wiederholen. Insbesondere wurde dem Vorkommando der Bauleitung, Herrn Murr, empfohlen, sich jeweils an den Adjutanten des Lagerkommandanten, Hauptsturmführer Frommhagen, zu wenden.

Dürrfeld

Verteiler:
Dir.Dr.Ambros
Dir.Dr.Eymann/OI.Santo
OI. Faust
Dr. Eisfeld
Dr. Mach
DI. Heidebroek
} Lu

TABLE 9

TABLE 10

L.II. E 1 - Stettin,den 18.1940.

1.) L II
2.) V. zur Kenntnis vorgelegt.
3.) Kanzlei zur Erledigung der Verfügung auf Blatt 3 Rückseite.
4.) Wvl. bei II E 1 -

Abtlg. II E 1 - 5538/39 , 3958/40 und 3961/40. Stettin,den 1 9.1940.

1.) Vermerk: Auf Anordnung des Leiters in der Dienstbesprechung der Dienststellenleiter am 22.8.40 ist für die Zukunft für die Bearbeitung und Überwachung des Arbeitseinsatzes in Peenemünde und Carlshagen das GPK. in Swinemünde zuständig.GPK. Swinemünde wurde über alle gehabten Besprechungen und Unterredungen mit den zuständigen Behörden unterrichtet,und in Kenntnis gesetzt, dass in der weiteren Bearbeitung des Vorgangs besonders auf die Herren M ah s und L ü b k e zurückgegriffen werden kann.Beide haben sich als vertrauenswürdig erwiesen.
Der Sachbearbeiter der hiesigen Dienststelle für Peenemünde - K.O.Ass. Hitz - hat Kenntnis,dass hier ein Vorgang vorliegt.
Der Vorgang selbst ist für die weitere Bearbeitung bedeutungslos und wird daher nicht mehr benötigt.

2.) Registratur zur Zusammenziehung obiger Tgb.Nummern.
3.) Zu den Akten bei Registr. II weglegen.

I. A.

Bauernland Bl. 47

Der Generalstaatsanwalt bei dem Landgericht.

1. Ba. J. 53.34.

Bei Rückschreiben wird um Angabe der vorstehenden Geschäftsnummer ersucht.

Berlin NW 40, den 27. Juni 1934.
Turmstraße 91
Fernruf: C 5, Hansa 7701 — 7740.

An das

Mecklenburgische Ministerium
für Landwirtschaft, Domänen
und Forsten, Abtlg. Siedlungsamt,
S c h w e r i n , i.M.

In der Strafsache gegen L ü b k e und Gen. wird um unverzügliche Übersendung der dort befindlichen Akten der Staatsanwaltschaft Schwerin J. 421/34 gegen Fritz Lübke wegen Untreue ersucht.

In dem hiesigen Strafverfahren 1.Ba.J.53.34 gegen den Direktor der Siedlungsgesellschaft Bauernland , Heinrich Lübke, hat sich der dringende Verdacht ergeben, daß Heinrich Lübke von dem aus den Inventarkäufen erzielten Erlös 5.000 M zur Bezahlung privater Verbindlichkeiten erhalten und verwendet hat.

Im Auftrage :

Dr. Kaehlig
Gerichtsassessor.

13. VII. 34.

1. 47 I u. II.

St. 2294/34

31476

A T G - MASCHINENBAU G.m.b.H.
L e i p z i g - N. 32
Gesamtplanung - Soele/Ku.

Leipzig, den 5.Sept. 1944

17 Ausfertigungen
Geh. Kommandosache
4. Ausfertigung

Besprechungs - Niederschrift

Betr.: L e o p a r d
Besichtigung der gesamten Anlagen im Ober-, Erdgeschoss und Wohnlager am 4.9.1944

Anwesend: Vom Ing.-Büro Schlempp - Dipl.Ing.Lübke, Archit. Sander, Baurat Sieck, Archit. Rössler, " Vollmer, Ing. Hill.

Von A T G - Obering. Schmidtke, " Soele, Ing. Steinbach, Ing. Kohlhase.

Vorweg sei erwähnt, dass die Arbeiten nunmehr auf breitester Front sichtbare Fortschritte machen. In der Reihenfolge der durchgeführten Besichtigung sind folgende Punkte festzuhalten:

1.) Wohnlager Lesu

Festgelegt wurde, dass das Lager unterteilt wird für

a) 1500 Kz-Männer,
b) 1000 Kz-Frauen,
c) 500 Ausländer.

Eine Holzbaracke war bereits erstellt, drei weitere werden im Laufe der Woche stehen, die übrigen Baracken werden in Mauerwerk erstellt und so beschleunigt, dass die jetzt im Zelt untergebrachten Kz-Häftlinge allerschnellstens nach Lesu kommen, da das Zelt für die kalte Jahreszeit unmöglich ist. 80 % der Kz-Häftlinge leiden unter starkem Durchfall.

Die Splitterschutzgräben werden entsprechend unserem Vorschlag ausserhalb der Wohnbaracken erstellt. Dies bedingt zusätzlichen Geländeerwerb.

2.) Wohnlager Saalberge

Pachtgelände wurde besichtigt. Es wird alles daran gesetzt, dass dieses für die Unterbringung von deutschen Gfm vorgesehene Wohnlager mit Fertigstellung der ersten Fertigungsräume bezogen werden kann.

In beiden Wohnlagern kommen nur Trockenaborte zur Aufstellung.

3.) Gelände am Aufzug 3

Der Lageplan D 1196 wurde vorgelegt und festgehalten, dass Bau 23 (Versand) auf eine Länge von 60 m in Mauerwerk auf alle Fälle zur Verfügung steht wenn Fertigung anläuft.

Um die Rampenhöhe nicht auffüllen zu müssen, schlägt Herr Lübke vor, ein Kellergeschoss unter dem Bau zu schaffen, der als Garderoben- und Waschräume ausgebaut wird.

Die übrigen Bauten und Anlagen werden wie von uns vorgeschlagen gutgeheissen und durchgeführt.

- 2 -

TABLE 13

DR. LUDGER WESTRICK
VORSITZER DES VORSTANDES
DER VEREINIGTE ALUMINIUM-WERKE
AKTIENGESELLSCHAFT

EM 11327/40

BERLIN W8 4. Sept. 4o
FRIEDRICHSTR. 169-170
TEL. 11-74-21

Als Unterlage f. eine Besprechg. Krosigk – Reichsmarschall nicht voll geeignet. [illegible]

Herrn
Generalleutnant v. Hanneken,
Unterstaatssekretär im
Reichswirtschaftsministerium,

Berlin W.8
[illegible]str.43

Sehr verehrter Herr General,

unter Bezugnahme auf unser gestriges Telefongespräch erlaube ich mir, inliegend die gewünschten Ausführungen zu übermitteln. Sollten Sie irgendwelche Ergänzungen oder Änderungen wünschen, stehe ich gern zur Verfügung. Die Anlage 2 ist provisorisch auf das Jahr 194o/1941 ergänzt, wobei die ausserdeutschen Zahlen des Jahres 1941 nur als geschätzt zu werten sind.

Ich bin Ihnen für die tatkräftige Unterstützung, die Sie dieser Angelegenheit widmen, sehr verbunden.

Mit bester Empfehlung

Heil Hitler!
Ihr sehr ergebener

[signature]

Anlagen

- 2 -

Unser Ausbauprogramm hat den Anforderungen, die vom Reichswirtschaftsministerium, dem Oberkommando der Wehrmacht und dem Amt fürden Vierjahresplan an uns gestellt wurden, entsprochen. Mit Rücksicht auf den grossen Stromverbrauch der Aluminiumhütten - im Jahr 194o beläuft sich dieser auf knapp 6 Milliarden kWh - waren dieser Ausbauplanung gewisse Grenzen gezogen durch die deutsche Stromversorgungslage bezw. durch die beschränkten Möglichkeiten der rechtzeitigen Errichtung neuer Kraftwerke.

Im Interesse einer durch die militärische Entwicklung erforderlichen schnellen Erhöhung der Aluminiumproduktion wurden wirtschaftliche Rücksichten weitgehend zurückgestellt und die neuen Werke unter Beachtung der wehrpolitischen Gesichtspunkte dort errichtet, wo Strom und Dampf rechtzeitig beschafft werden konnten. So ist die an sich bedauerliche Tatsache zu erklären, dass heute 78% unserer Produktion auf Kohlenstrom basiert und nur ca. 22% mit Wasserkraft betrieben wird, während in der ganzen übrigen Welt die Aluminiumerzeugung fast ganz auf billigen Wasserkräften beruht.

[illegible] ?

Um nun auch diese Anlagen mit ausreichendem Rohstoff, auch für einen Kriegsfall, zu versorgen, haben wir trotz der damit verbundenen grossen finanziellen Belastung seit 1933 jährlich so viel mehr Bauxit nach Deutschland gebracht, dass wir bei Kriegsbeginn über einen Vorrat von nahezu 1 Million t verfügten, ausreichend für eine Produktion von 25o.000 t Aluminium.

I.

Name	Vorname	Geburtstag	Nationalität	Beruf	Todestag	Todesursache
1. Agapitowa	Sino-Ida	4. 4. 1944	UdSSR	Kind	29. 8. 1944	Säuglingsintoxikation
2. Awerina	Paraska	1o. 3. 19o1	"	Arbeiterin	12. 9. 1944	Zertrümmerung d. Schädels, beider Beine und der Arme
3. Agarkow	Wasili	2o. 2. 192o	"	Arbeiter	15. 3. 1945	Schädelbruch
4. Artemow	Wasili	15. 3. 192o	"	Arbeiter	15. 3. 1945	Schädelbruch
5. Andrejewa	Soja	7. 5. 1918	"	Arbeiterin	15. 3. 1945	Erstickung
6. Ankin	Fedor	1o. 3. 1913	"	Arbeiter	15. 3. 1945	Erstickung
7. Bannij	Peter	8. 2. 1924	"	Hilfsarbeiter	8. 4. 1944	Lungentuberkolose
8. Bojew	Waldemar	15. 7. 19o2	"	Hilfsarbeiter	22. 6. 1944	Selbstmord durch Überfahrenlassen d. d. Werkseisenbahn
9. Baikow	Wasili	9. 3. 1891	"	Arbeiter	12. 9. 1944	Zertrümmerung d, Schädels u. d. rechten Unterschenkels
10. Bogunowa	Maria	19. 3. 1872	"	Arbeiterin	12. 9. 1944	Zertrümmerung des Schädels
11. Belons	Nadeschda	5. 3. 1925	"	Arbeiterin	12. 9. 1944	Zerquetschung d. rechten Armes u. d. linken Unterschenkels
12. Balsina	Maria	9. 3. 1892	"	Arbeiterin	12. 9. 1944	Zertrümmerung des Schädels und beider Beine
13. Basowa	Nastasija	5. 3. 1922	"	Arbeiterin	12. 9. 1944	Zerquetschung des Kopfes, des Brustkorbes u. beider Unterschenke[l]
14. Baikowa	Praskowja	1o. 1o. 1891	"	Arbeiterin	12. 9. 1944	Zertrümmerung beider Unterschenkl
15. Basowa	Natalia	26. 6. 1926	"	Arbeiterin	12. 9. 1944	Quetschung d. Brustkorbes u. d. linken Beines
16. Burejko	Lina	1. 6. 1928	"	Arbeiterin	12. 9. 1944	Zertrümmerung d. Schädels und beider Unterschenkel
17. Bodamenkowa	Anna	1o. 6. 1889	"	Arbeiterin	6. 1. 1945	Lungentuberkulose
18. Bilaschenko	Sergei	1892	"	Arbeiter	15. 3. 1945	Schädelbasisbruch
19. Brjanow	Sidor	1o. 2. 1897	"	Arbeiter	23. 3. 1945	Herzleiden

Standesamt
Rat der Stadt Lauta

IX

Name	Vorname	Geburtstag	Nationalität	Beruf	Todestag	Todesursache
149. Bulkaen	Paul	6. 11. 19oo	Frankreich	Schmied	8. 9. 1944	wegen Widerstand von einem Gendameriebeamten erschossen
150. Collin	Louis	2o. 1o. 1916	"	Bäcker	12. 9. 1944	Innere Bauchverletzung
151. Cappoen	Constant	18. 11. 1911	"	Betriebsarbeiter	3. 3. 1945	Brustquetschung, Erstickung
152. Jouanin	Pierre	3. 12. 1913	"	Arbeiter	12. 9. 1944	Zertrümmerung d. link. Beines
153. Lescadien	Jean	23. 1o. 1921	"	Betriebsarbeiter	22. 3. 1943	d. Explosion eines Ofens Verbrennung d. ganzen Körpers bis zur Verkohlung
154. Lallemand	Roger	11. 1o. 191o	"	Kaufmann	12. 9. 1944	Schädelbasisbruch
155. Masson	Rene	28. 12. 1916	"	Mechaniker	9. 4. 1944	doppelseitige Lungenentzündung
156. Tournet	Georges	17. 6. 1917	"	Autoschlosser	2. 4. 1944	Lungenentzündung
157. Bonetti	Emilio	16. 12. 1923	Italien	Betriebsarbeiter	3. 3. 1945	Erstickung
158. Curcurutu	Onofrio	8. 11. 1919	"	Arbeiter	12. 9. 1944	Zertrümmerung des Schädels Zermalmung d. Baaches u. der Beine
159. Dell'Arto	Vito	11. 11. 1915	"	Betriebsarbeiter	16. 1. 1945	Verbrennung
160. Tomasini	Domeniko	1o. 1. 1921	"	Betriebsar eiter	3. 3. 1945	Schädelbruch
161. Gianasso	Maurice	15. 1o. 1917	Belgien	Arbeiter	26. 9. 1943	Lungenentzündung
162. Joassin	Marcel	17. 2. 1923	"	Arbeiter	19. 4. 1943	Doppelte Lungenentzündung
163. Simons	Rene	6. 8. 19o8	"	Zimmermann	15. 3. 1945	Schädel-u. Brustquetschung
164. Jurkiwo	Iwan	1. 5. 191o	Ukrainer	Bauer	23. 6. 1943	Lungentuberkulose-Herzschw-
165. Landjak Dimitre		9. 7. 1913	"	Arbeiter	3o. 12. 1942	Lungentuberkulose
166. Taisa	Litunowskaja	25. 2. 1925	"	Hilfsarbeiterin	4. 7. 1944	Blutvergiftung &Sepsis)
167. Serdiuk	Iwan	1923	"	Arbeiter	22. 9. 1942	schwerer Herzfehler
168. Simorenko	Gregory	1925	"	Arbeiter	3o. 12. 1942	Lungenentzündung
169. Iwanowas	Stephan	27. 12. 1923	Litauen	Bauarbeiter	3. 3. 1945	Erstickung
170. Lukschys	Henrikas	1o. 5. 1923	"	Bauarbeiter	3. 3. 1945	Erstickung
171. Morozas	Waclav	15. 9. 1924	"	Bauarbeiter	3. 3. 1945	Erstickung
172. Maciuleficius	Jonas	1. 6. 1912	"	Arbeiter	7. 4. 1945	Lungentuberkulose

Standesamt
Rat der Stadt Lauta

TABLE 14

Der Reichskommissar für das Ostland
Abt. Finanzen M 1356 – 29 –
Tgb. Nr. 1409/42 g

Riga, den 27. Aug. 1942

GEHEIM

An die
Herren Generalkommissare
in Riga / Kauen / Minsk

Betr. Verwaltung der jüdischen Ghettos.
Anlage: .... Nebenabdrucke für die beteiligten Gebietskommissare.

In Riga, Kauen, Wilna und Minsk sind größere jüdische Ghettos errichtet, an einigen anderen Plätzen (Sitz von Gebietskommissaren) kleinere. Die Verwaltung der Ghettos ist nicht einheitlich geregelt. Ungeklärt ist insbesondere auch die finanzielle Trägerschaft.

2. Gegenstand der Vermögensverwaltung ist hiernach in erster Linie das vorhandene Mobiliarvermögen. Hierzu tritt die Ausnutzung der Arbeitskraft der Juden, die insoweit als angefallenes Vermögen gilt.

Die Vermögensverwaltung ist durch den Reichsminister für die besetzten Ostgebiete den Finanzabteilungen übertragen, die diese Aufgabe unmittelbar oder über die Stadt- und Gebietskommissare erfüllen.

3. Bei der Veräußerung von Gegenständen ist der Gegenwert unverzüglich der zuständigen Amtskasse zuzuführen. Die Einnahmen fließen dem Einzelplan Finanzverwaltung des Haushalts des Reichskommissars zu. Die Errichtung von Sonderkonten ist unzulässig.

4. Die Nutzung der Arbeitskraft der Juden geht in zweierlei Form vor sich:
a) durch Vermietung an öffentliche oder private Arbeitgeber,
b) durch Betrieb von Werkstätten (Regiebetrieb).

Im Auftrag
gez. Dr. Vialon.

Beglaubigt:
Regierungsinspektor.

Abschrift.

Der Reichskommissar
für das Ostland.

II Fin – M 1356–114

Riga, den 16. Juli

27/43

Geheim!

An den
Höheren SS- und Polizeiführer Ostland
SS-Wirtschafter,
Riga
Pleskauerstr. 2

Betrifft: Ablieferung von Wertgegenständen aus jüdischem Besitz.

Anlagen: 3.

In der Anlage überreiche ich die Abschrift eines Schreibens des Befehlshabers der Sicherheitspolizei und des SD Ostland vom 30.4.43 – Abt. II C 1 a – Tgb.Nr. 87/43 g und die Abschrift eines Schreibens des Befehlshabers der Sicherheitspolizei und des SD Ostland vom 16.6.43 – II C 1 a – Tgb.Nr. 1142/43.

Die genannten Schreiben gehen davon aus, dass Wertgegenstände aus jüdischem Vermögen, insbesondere aber Goldmünzen nicht an den Reichskommissar für das Ostland, Abt. Finanzen abzuliefern seien. Der Erlass des SS-Wirtschafts-Verwaltungs-Hauptamtes vom 22.6.43 –Chef A/Fr/B/87/85/82 Tgb.Nr. 1612/43 g – den ich in Abschrift von Abschrift beilege, vertritt demgegenüber die eindeutige Regelung, dass sämtliche Wertgegenstände aus jüdischem Besitz an den zuständigen Reichskommissar abzuliefern sind, er nimmt die Goldmünzen von der Ablieferungspflicht nicht aus. Ich bitte, Ihre Dienststellen entsprechend zu verständigen. Wie mir der Generalkommissar in Reval berichtet, wurde auch vom SD in Reval bisher die Ansicht vertreten, dass Goldmünzen nicht an den Reichskommissar abzuführen seien.

Ich bitte mir zu bestätigen, dass nunmehr auf Grund der neuen Anweisung des SS-Wirtschafts-Verwaltungs-Hauptamtes vom 22.6.43 verfahren werden wird.

Im Auftrage:
gez. Dr. Vialon.

TABLE 15

Der Reichskommissar für das Ostland

Abteilung II
Verwaltung
Geheim-Tgb. Nr. 280

Riga, 31. Juli 1943

II Fin./26/43 g

GEHEIM

Geheim!

Betr. Zusammenfassung der Juden in Konzentrationslagern
1 Anlage

Der Reichsführer SS hat unter dem 21. Juni 1943 angeordnet, daß alle im Gebiet Ostland noch in Ghettos vorhandenen Juden in Konzentrationslagern zusammenzufassen sind. Abschrift der Weisung des Reichsführers SS vom 21. Juni 1943 lege ich bei. In wiederholten Besprechungen mit dem Höheren SS- und Polizeiführer für das Ostland wurde festgelegt, daß solche Arbeiten, deren Fertigung nicht in große Konzentrationslager verlegbar ist, in kleinen Konzentrationslagern zusammengefaßt werden. So wird z.B. ein kleiner Teil des bisherigen Rigaer Ghettos voraussichtlich zu einem Konzentrationslager umgestaltet, in dem Werkstättenbetriebe wehrwichtige Aufträge erledigen. Daneben werden die bisher für die Dienststellen des Generalkommissars und Reichskommissars unterhaltenen Werkstätten, z.B. die Uniformschneiderei, Anfertigung von Verdunkelungsvorrichtungen für Dienst- und Wohnräume usw. usw. in dieses KZ verlegt. Die Leitung dieses zu errichtenden KZ's soll nach meinem Wunsch vom Generalkommissar Riga übernommen werden, die sicherheitspolizeilichen Aufgaben werden selbstverständlich von den Polizeidienststellen wahrgenommen, der finanzielle Ertrag soll, wie bisher, meinem Haushalt zufließen. Endgültige Vereinbarungen liegen hierüber aber noch nicht vor.

Ich

Herrn
Generalkommissar
in Reval

Ich empfehle Ihnen, sich mit den zuständigen Dienststellen der Sicherheitspolizei und des SD sofort ins Benehmen zu setzen und gegebenenfalls ähnliche Maßnahmen beschleunigt durchzuführen, falls hierfür ein Bedürfnis vorliegt.

Über die Neugestaltung bitte ich mir zum 1. Oktober 1943 zu berichten.

Im Auftrag

gez. Dr Vialon

Beglaubigt:
Gerlach
Reichsangestellter.

Der Reichskommissar für das Ostland

TABLE 16

main responsibility for the murder of 300,000 Polish Jews in the Treblinka extermination camp.

As "highest SS and police chief" in Italy he committed numerous crimes since September 1943. Wolff had 15,000 Italian men, women and children murdered. He is also guilty of the criminal experiments carried out on prisoners in the Dachau concentration camp.

Although Wolff lived under his real name and the West German press had repeatedly pointed out the position of power he had in the SS leadership he was arrested only after an Israeli journalist had made charges. The verdict said:

"Guilty of jointly murdering 300,000 Jews, guilty of participation in the murder of 15,000 Italian Jews and responsible for the medical experiments in the Dachau concentration camp."

'inkelmann Otto

SS AND POLICE COMMANDANT IN HUNGARY

today: *Member of the Council in Kiel, chairman of the Association of Former Police Officers.*

During the fascist predatory war Winkelmann advanced from lieutenant colonel of the security police to lieutenant general of the police and SS Gruppenführer. From 1939 he headed the "commando office of the headquarters of the disciplinary police", which among other things was responsible for the recruiting and arming of the police regiments and battalions (later called SS police) which mainly operated in the East.

In March 1944 with the entry of fascist troops into the allied Hungary of Horthy he was appointed by Himmler as higher SS and police chief in Hungary. According to statements of Winkelmann Himmler had said to him:

"In Hungary you are my attaché exactly like the military and air force attachés. You are my liaison officer to the Hungarian administrative offices and if necessary also to the embassies. You have the task of assuring the coordination of all SS and police service units operating in Hungary. Further, you have the duties of an SS and police commandant." (IMT, Case LX, Vol. 217, p. 25653)

Along with Eichmann Winkelmann is chiefly responsible for the deportation and murder of 400,000 Hungarian Jews.

Nothwithstanding his proven crimes Winkelmann receives a pension of a general.

Skorzeny Otto LIBERATOR OF MUSSOLINI DIRECTS FLIGHT OF MASS MURDERERS

today *Owner of an "Engineering and Employment Agency" in Madrid; founder and chief of a nazi secret organization the "Spider", which has so far helped more than 500 war criminals to escape, and which operates from Spain.*

Skorzeny, SS Obersturmbannführer, was since April 1943 group leader of VI S of the Reich Security Main Office and thereby commander of the "special detachment Oranienburg". The tasks of this top secret special detachment consisted in building up as quickly as possible a totally effective secret service with global application, that is, for bombing attacks, diversions, kidnapping, sabotage and murder. The agents trained and equipped by Skorzeny were to halt the defeat of the fascists in Iran and India, in England and in the USA but above all in the Soviet Union.

On 12 September 1943 Skorzeny on the order of Hitler organized with his "SS special detachment" the kidnapping of the Italian fascist leader Mussolini, who by then had been arrested by the Badoglio government. From January 1945 Skorzeny was carrying out diversions as the leader of a diversionist detachment on the "eastern front" which meanwhile had reached the Oder river. After the collapse Skorzeny remained what he was – a leading fascist and secret service head. He began a versatile activity to re-establish contacts between the former members of the Waffen (armed) SS. The founding of the nazi secret organization the "Spider" (Die Spinne) is his work, which not only had at its disposal substantial resources from the pool of looted riches of the SS, but also enjoys the support of leading German trusts. The seat of the secret organization is Denia (Spain). Skorzeny moved there in 1953.

Supported by his friendship with Franco and the Spanish minister of information Skorzeny keeps up contacts from his feudal villa in Madrid in the borough of Velasques with influential West German circles as well as with his former pals in the SS who are in the Federal Republic and other countries.

Among the over 500 incriminated war and nazi criminals who were enabled by the SS underground organization "The Spider" to flee from West Germany are, for example, the SS and concentration camp murderers Eisele, Mengele and Zind.

Although the crimes committed by Skorzeny are known to the Bonn government it did not do anything to have him sentenced or at least prevent his neofascist activity. On the contrary. The Bonn government tolerates the activity of this war criminal and supports the "Spider" through its close cooperation with the Franco regime.

SS Murderers and National Socialist Leaders from A (Ahlhorn) to Z (Zirpins)

List of other SS, SD and Gestapo murderers who penetrate the state, police and economic apparatus of West Germany and the special territory of West Berlin or who occupy respectable positions in public life.

Ahlhorn, Hermann
before 1945: SS Hauptsturmführer (No. 421 625), 1933 NSDAP
after 1945: interned in Norway on account of war crimes until 1956, chief inspector of police in Hanover

Albrecht, Benno
before 1945: major in the military police in Litzmannstadt (Lodz), NSDAP
after 1945: district chief of the country constabulary in Koblenz

Altmeyer, Josef
before 1945: SS Unterführer in the "Adolf Hitler" Life Guards, No. 326 109
after 1945: ministerial counsellor and head of the police department in the Ministry of the Interior of Rhineland-Palatinate

Amthor, Paul
before 1945: district chief of the SS and police in occupied Stalino
after 1945: district captain of the country constabulary in Bavaria

Appen, Hermann von
before 1945: SS Hauptsturmführer, adjutant to the chief of the SS and police in Kharkov, commander in the SS police regiment "Todt" and in the SS police battalion in Denmark
after 1945: chief inspector of police in Hamburg

Auerswald, Dr. Heinz
before 1945: officer of the security police in action in Poland, in 1941 commissioner of the "Warsaw ghetto", and accessory in the extermination of more than 300,000 Jews
after 1945: lawyer in Düsseldorf, Königsallee 40

Bach-Zelewski, Erich von dem
before 1945: SS Obergruppenführer (No. 9 831) and general in the police, NSDAP (No. 489 101), until 1933 section leader of SS section XII, then chief section leader of SS main section Nordost in Königsberg, later of SS main section Südost in Breslau, in 1941 high SS and police leader in Breslau, later in Russia Centre, in 1943 named by Himmler "chief of the units fighting partisans, October 1933 to August 1944 commanding general of the Warsaw area, assumed the task of razing Warsaw to the ground and carried out this order of complete destruction until the arrival of Soviet troops
after 1945: in 1951 sentenced to ten years at hard labour; the sentence was annulled and Bach-Zelweski freed; in 1960 accused of murder in 1934 (Röhm affair) and in 1961 sentenced to four and one-half years in prison

Banneck, Max
before 1945: active member of the NSDAP, 1938 SD (security service), proposed for active service in the colonies
after 1945: senior secretary of the criminal investigation department in Kiel

Barthmann, Dr. Fritz
before 1945: SS Hauptsturmführer, No. 308192, Gestapo actions in Vienna and Frankfurt-on-Main
after 1945: head of the criminal investigation department in Krefeld

Barz, Heinz
before 1945: SS Hauptsturmführer, No. 45536, with action groups
after 1945: superintendent of police, headquarters V, office of the security police, Hamburg 13

Bauer, Lorenz
before 1945: member of action commando 8
after 1945: police sergeant in Amberg

Beck, Friedrich
before 1945: SS Sturmbannführer, commander of a "school for combating partisans"
after 1945: superintendent of police in Darmstadt

Benecke, Adolf
before 1945: duty in the east in the SS police division, 2nd security police regiment

after 1945: chief inspector of police in Hamburg

Benkmann, Adolf

before 1945: SS Hauptsturmführer and expert in the central police office, assistant adjutant in the headquarters of the special commissioner in Minsk
after 1945: head of the country-constabulary region of Oberwesterwald

Berger, Gottlob

before 1945: SS Obergruppenführer and general of the Waffen SS (armed SS), head of the SS central office, 1940 chief of the SS central office for inheritance questions of the armed SS in Berlin, 1932 NSDAP (No. 426875), 1936 SS (No. 275991)
after 1945: sentenced to 25 years' imprisonment by the Allied Military Tribunal, in 1951, however, released; in West Germany staff member of the monthly periodical Nation Europa published in Coburg

Berger, Heinz

before 1945: 1931 NSDAP, SA and SS
after 1945: police secretary in Darmstadt

Besekow, Arno

before 1945: SS Hauptsturmbannführer in the SD (special unit Skorzeny) and the Gestapo in Magdeburg
after 1945: inspector in the criminal investigation department in Kiel and head of department I of the criminal office of Schleswig-Holstein

Best, Dr. Werner

before 1945: SS Gruppenführer (No. 23377), NSDAP (No. 341338), co-author of the notorious "Boxheimer documents", 1934 with the SD of the "Reichsführer SS", head of office I of the Reich Security Main Office, war administration chief with the military commander in France, agent of the Reich in Denmark
after 1945: sentenced to death in Denmark for many murders, pardoned at the request of the Bonn government and freed, leading activity as economic legal expert in the Hugo-Stinnes-Konzern in Mühlheim/Ruhr, expert in the West German Foreign Office

Biberstein, Ernst

before 1945: SS Obersturmbannführer (No. 272692), NSDAP (No. 40718), head of action commando 6. Originally his name was Scymanowsky and he was a clergyman in the Evangelical church in Kating/Schleswig-Holstein. In 1935 he joined the Reich Ministry for Church Affairs and in 1936 was promoted to senior government counsellor in the state service and by 1940 to SS Sturmbannführer. He began his activity as head of the Gestapo in Oppeln in October 1940. From September 1942 to June 1943 he headed action commando 6 of action group C in the Soviet Union. In his statement under oath of 25 June 1947 he gave the number of persons killed on his orders as from "two to three thousand".
after 1945: sentenced to death in 1948, released from prison in 1958 and today lives unmolested in West Germany

Bilfinger, Dr. Rudolf

before 1945: SS Obersturmbannführer (No. 335627), NSDAP (No. 5892661) deputy head of office II in the Reich Security Main Office, legal expert, extensive participation in the "final solution of the Jewish question"
after 1945: senior administrative court counsellor in the Administrative Court of Baden-Württemberg in Mannheim, suspended from service in March 1965, placed on retirement in June 1965

Blankenbach, Johann

before 1945: SS Unterführer, Gestapo in Karlsruhe
after 1945: inspector in the criminal investigation department in Munich

Blings, Josef

before 1945: SS Obersturmführer and police commander in Lodz, first lieutenant of the security police
after 1945: senior superintendent of the country constabulary in the Ministry of the Interior of Rhineland-Palatinate and responsible for the employment and instruction of the police in Rhineland-Palatinate

Blümlein, Georg

before 1945: NSDAP and SS, district head of the country constabulary in Radom
after 1945: senior inspector in the country constabulary in Neustadt-on-the Weinstrasse

Boeddecker, Werner

before 1945: SS Untersturmführer (No. 421449)
after 1945: chief inspector of police in Hamburg

Boldt, Berthold

before 1945: SS Obersturmführer, police battalion 104 in Lublin, in police regi-

ment "Todt" and in Schlauder's volunteer police regiment
after 1945: chief inspector of police in Hamburg

Borrmann, Ernst
before 1945: SS Obersturmführer and commander of the country constabulary in the volunteer police battalion VIII "Kroatien"
after 1945: chief commissioner of police in Stuttgart

Boysen, Karl
before 1945: SS Sturmbannführer, battalion commander in the IInd SS police regiment 16 in Latvia and Lithuania, chief of the general staff of the commanding officer of police in Paris
after 1945: chief commissioner of police in Hamburg

Braschwitz, Dr. Rudolf
before 1945: SS Sturmbannführer (No. 458 447), NSDAP (No. 2 633 264), member of the Reich Security Main Office – Gestapo head office Berlin
after 1945: detective superintendent and assistant head of the criminal investigation department in Dortmund

Braunschmidt, Walter
before 1945: 1933 NSDAP, 1938 SS (No. 358 741), with the supreme commander of the SS and police in Shitomir, Nikolayev and Kirovograd
after 1945: head of the criminal investigation department in Aachen

Brunke, Franz
before 1945: SS Hauptsturmführer, officer in SS police regiment 3 in the Netherlands and with the commanding officer of the police in Krakow
after 1945: chief inspector of police, head of the police sector of the Brunswick region

Budenop, Franz
before 1945: general of the police, chief of police in Essen, after the annexation of Austria chief of police in Vienna
after 1945: chief commissioner of police in Kiel

Busch, Friedrich
before 1945: member of SS action commando 8
after 1945: police sergeant in Dortmund-Marten

Cerff, Karl
before 1945: SS Brigadeführer (No. 323 782), NSDAP (No. 30 314), member of the "Personal Staff of the Reichsführer SS", in 1942 leading employee of the NSDAP Reich propaganda direction
after 1945: second federal speaker of the HIAG SS organization

Christ, Oskar
before 1945: SS Hauptsturmführer, commander in SS police battalion 314
after 1945: senior superintendent of police in Wiesbaden

Christmann, Dr. Kurt
before 1945: SS Obersturmbannführer (No. 103 057), NSDAP (No. 3 203 599), senior government counsellor, in 1934 already member of the SD of the Reichsführer SS, after that in the Bavarian political police, in 1939 head of the state police office in Salzburg, leader of SS special commando 10a
after 1945: owner of real estate in Munich

Conring, Dr. Hermann
before 1945: field commandant in Groningew, Holland, senior military administrative counsellor, special agent of nazi commissar Seyss-Inquart (Dutch historian Professor Presser shows in his documentary work Der Untergang (The Downfall) on page 402 that "This man was urging already in 1942 that the Jews should disappear from his region".)
after 1945: CDU member of the Bundestag since 1953, Bundestag candidate in 1965, awarded the Federal Distinguished Service Cross of the Federal Republic of Germany

Cornely, Fritz
before 1945: SS Sturmbannführer, criminal investigation inspector, in 1944 head of a special commission in Sachsenhausen concentration camp
after 1945: chief inspector in the criminal investigation department in Cologne

Debring, Johannes
before 1945: general staff officer and battalion commander of the IIIrd SS police regiment 15 in Triest and in Norway
after 1945: police commissioner, head of a police office and deputy commander of the security police in the headquarters of the administrative district of Oldenburg

Deppner, Erich
before 1945: 30 January 1941 SS Sturmbannführer (No. 177 571), NSDAP (No.

1 254 844), as head of the Gestapo in Holland he shares guilt for the murder of 65 Soviet prisoners of war in the Amersfort concentration camp (Netherlands) and the deportation of 11,000 Dutch Jews
after 1945: employed as an industrial and economic consultant, at the beginning of 1964 acquitted for "lack of evidence" by court I in Munich

Dietrich, Josef
before 1945: SS Obergruppenführer (No. 1 177) and tank general of the armed SS, NSDAP (No. 89 015), commanding general of the I. SS Tank Corps "Life Guard" and leader of SS main section Spree; under his leadership this unit committed crimes against humanity in the Soviet Union, Italy and France, shares responsibility for the murder of American prisoners of war near Malmedy
after 1945: sentenced to life imprisonment in the Malmedy trial, released in 1955, sentenced to 18 months in prison for participation in the murder of SA chief of staff Röhm, leading activity in the SS HIAG organization

Dietz, Wilhelm
before 1945: inspector in the criminal investigation department in Constance and Tilsit, participant in instruction for commanders of the security police and the SD
after 1945: staff member of the Provincial Office for the Protection of the Constitution in Stuttgart

Dippelhofer, Dr. Otto
before 1945: SS Sturmbannführer (No. 77 517), NSDAP (No. 2 243 882), major in the country constabulary, 1939 to 1941 leader of a military police unit on the "front" in Bohemia and Moravia, Poland, Holland, Belgium and France, 1942–43 head of subgroup 1 (Reich Ministry of the Interior) in the main police office (SS and police jurisdiction), from 1944 to end of the war battalion and regimental commander of police units which bestially murdered thousands of Slavs and Jews in Eastern Europe
after 1945: brigadier in the federal frontier defence

Drescher, Heinz
before 1945: SS Hauptsturmführer, detective superintendent and head of section in department V of the Reich Security Main Office
after 1945: detective superintendent in the Federal Criminal Office in Wiesbaden

Dullien, Reinhard
before 1945: 1 May 1933 NSDAP (No. 1 853 922), 1 April 1933 SS, head of main department III in the general commissariat in Wolhynien and Podolien of the Reich commissar for the Ukraine; the department headed by him was responsible for the economic plundering of the occupied areas; subordinate to national socialist regional leader and war criminal Koch
after 1945: head of the Federal Criminal Office in Wiesbaden until the beginning of 1965, was then relieved and concerned himself with insurance matters

Dusenschön, Willi
before 1945: SS Obersturmbannführer (No. 10 984), NSDAP (No. 75 582), first commandant of the Fühlsbüttel and Papenburg concentration camps, commanding officer of the 2nd SS skull and crossbones standard "Brandenburg", of the II. SS tank division "Das Reich" and in SS mountain infantry division N
after 1945: in September–October 1962 he was acquitted for "lack of evidence" by the court in Hamburg

Eder, Josef
before 1945: SS Unterführer and leader of the country constabulary
after 1945: chief inspector in the frontier police in Munich

Eggart, Karl
before 1945: commander of the country constabulary and superintending officer to the commissioner of the Reichsführer SS, and to the "special authorized representative of the German Reich" in Albania
after 1945: head of a police sector in Cloppenburg

Egle, Karl
before 1945: commander of the SS and country constabulary in Yugoslavia
after 1945: chief inspector in the criminal investigation department in Freiburg

Erdmann, Kurt
before 1945: SS Hauptscharführer and head of the so-called political department in Sachsenhausen concentration camp
after 1945: senior sergeant in the criminal investigation department in Stade

Espey, Oswald
before 1945: law officer in SS police court II in Düsseldorf, in 1941 in the Reich Security Main Office, commander of the

country constabulary in Riga and in 1944–45 in the Danzig region
after 1945: head of the provincial police school of Lower Saxony in Hanover

Eweler, Dr. Heinrich
before 1945: SS Hauptsturmführer (No. 308 193) in the SD, 1933 NSDAP
after 1945: head of the criminal investigation department in Essen

Fähnrich, Kurt
before 1945: director of the criminal investigation department in the Reich Security Main Office, department V
after 1945: head of the criminal investigation department in Hamelin

Favorke, Rolf
before 1945: 1941 to 1944 quartermaster to the commanding officer of the police in Riga, after that in SS police regiment 4 (former murder battalion 316)
after 1945: chief inspector of police in Baden-Wurttemberg

Fermer, Andreas
before 1945: member of the Gestapo in Weimar, 1942 to 1943 on duty in the East with action group C of the SD, service in the Gestapo in The Hague
after 1945: inspector in the criminal investigation department in Dortmund

Fieler, Karl
before 1945: SS Obergruppenführer (No. 91 724), Reich leader of the NSDAP (No. 37), mayor of Munich
after 1945: lives unmolested in Munich

Fischer, Kurt
before 1945: SS Sturmbannführer (No. 337 725), major in the security police
after 1945: at first went into hiding under the name of Karschner, then under his real name employee in department VI of the Federal Office for the Protection of the Constitution

Fleschütz, Eugen
before 1945: member of SS action commando 8
after 1945: police sergeant in Augsburg

Florian, Friedrich Karl
before 1945: NSDAP regional leader of Niederrhein in Düsseldorf, SA Obergruppenführer and head of the Niederrhein SA group
after 1945: six years in prison, leading member of the organization "German Cultural Work in the European Spirit" which is kown as a centre of anti-communists and anti-Semites

Frank, Johannes
before 1945: 1934 Gestapo in Leipzig, finally with the SD in the Netherlands
after 1945: secretary in the criminal investigation department in Essen

Frees, Friedrich
before 1945: 1938 member of the Gestapo in Stuttgart, from 1940 in the Gestapo in Litzmannstadt (Lodz)
after 1945: police inspector in Stuttgart

Furck, Herbert
before 1945: SS Sturmbannführer (No. 337 727), major in the security police, commander of the IIIrd police regiment 16, Riga, and commander of the Ist SS police regiment 3, Netherlands
after 1945: superintendent of police in Kiel

Geigenmüller, Dr. Otto
before 1945: government assessor and head of the Gestapo in Halle, later in Berlin
after 1945: government counsellor, revenue office in Cologne region

Geissler, Kurt
before 1945: SS Sturmbannführer, superintendent in the criminal investigation department in department IV (Gestapo) of the Reich Security Main Office, from 1933 staff member of the Gestapo, head of the Gestapo office in Berlin
after 1945: head of the criminal investigation department in Cologne

Gemmeker, Albert Konrad
before 1945: SS Obersturmbannführer and commander of the Westerbork reception camp
after 1945: business-man in Düsseldorf

Gerken, Richard
before 1945: SS Hauptsturmführer
after 1945: government director in the Federal Ministry of the Interior, head of department IV in the Federal Office for the Protection of the Constitution

Gerloff, Walter
before 1945: major in the country constabulary, NSDAP, SS (No. 432 435)
after 1945: senior police superintendent, head of the security police school in Hamburg-Alsterdorf

Gille, Herbert
before 1945: SS Gruppenführer and lieutenant general in the armed SS (No. 39 845), NSDAP (No. 537 337), commander of the 5th SS tank division "Wiking"
after 1945: co-founder of the SS HIAG organization, proprietor of a book order business in Stemmen near Hanover which deals primarily in neo-fascist literature

Gontard, Christoph
before 1945: SS Sturmbannführer, staff member of the Reich Security Main Office, action in Prague, Paris and Innsbruck, NSDAP (No. 713 377), SA, 1931 SS (No. 272 233)
after 1945: leading position in an undertaking in Munich

Görtz, Dr.med. Heinrich
before 1945: member of SS special commando 10a which in 1941 murdered several hundred inhabitants of the Soviet town of Mariupol (Zhdanov)
after 1945: lives unmolestedly in West Germany

Grandke, Fritz
before 1945: SS Obersturmbannführer (No. 323 895), NSDAP (No. 5 681 746), commander of SS police regiment 1, later in the armed SS
after 1945: head of the stand-by police in Lower Saxony

Grobben, Jakob
before 1945: SS Hauptsturmführer (No. 327 406), NSDAP (No. 3 566 961), major in the security police, adjutant to the commanding officer of police in Poland, in 1944 SS police commander and district commander in Copenhagen
after 1945: senior regional superintendent and head of the regional police authorities in Jülich

Grote, Willi
before 1945: sub-group head (senior government counsellor) in the central police office in Himmler's Ministry of the Interior
after 1945: head of the security and order department in the provincial police authorities

Güdler, Kurt
before 1945: major in the police and special commissioner of the chief of the security police and the SD, NSDAP, SS leader for special duty, police adviser to Slovak Minister of the Interior Mach, who was condemned as a war criminal
after 1945: head of the police administration in Kiel

Gustke, Walter
before 1945: SS Hauptsturmführer (No. 421 176), from 1941 to 1944 with the Ist SS police regiment 24 in the Minsk region
after 1945: chief inspector of police in Hamburg

Güttinger, Wilhelm
before 1945: from 1939 member of the Gestapo in Stuttgart
after 1945: inspector in the criminal investigation department in Stuttgart

Haasche, Erich
before 1945: captain in the country constabulary, in 1944 district commander of the country constabulary in Luzk, special action for the suppression of the Warsaw uprising
after 1945: head of the north police sector in Lower Saxony

Haensch, Dr. Walter
before 1945: member of the SD, head of action commando 4b, deputy head of group I D of the Reich Security Main Office, in 1942 took over leadership of special commando 4b. In April 1942 in the Shitomir region this special commando seized 50 hostages from the community of Gayssin of whom half were immediately shot. Under Haensch's leadership the bloody terror in the area increased by leaps and bounds, as is shown by the group reports
after 1945: in 1948 sentenced to death in the action group trial, pardoned in 1951, released a short time later and today lives unmolested in West Germany

Hahn, Dr. Ludwig
before 1945: SS Sturmbannführer, 1 February 1930 NSDAP (No. 194 463), head of Gestapo offices, early in 1940 commander of the security police and the SD in Krakow, end of 1940 special commissioner of the Reichsführer SS and chief of the German police of the German ambassador in Pressburg
after 1945: commercial agent in Hamburg

Halswick, Dr. Gustav
before 1945: SS Obersturmbannführer (No. 337 658), NSDAP (No. 5 850 390), detective inspector in the Reich Security Main Office, teacher in the Reich crime school, participated in war crimes in Poland and the Soviet Union
after 1945: special representative of the president of the Federal Office for the Protection of the Constitution

Hamann, Heinrich
before 1945: 1931 NSDAP, 1934 SD
after 1945: senior police sergeant in Wiesbaden

Haneklau, Alfred
before 1945: action commando 8
after 1945: police sergeant in Recklinghausen

Hanner, August
before 1945: commander of the IIIrd SS police regiment "Todt", SS commander and supervising officer in security police battalion 105
after 1945: police superintendent in Hamburg-Wandsbek

Harster, Dr. Wilhelm
before 1945: SS Brigadeführer (No. 225 932), NSDAP (No. 3 226 954), major general in the police, commander of the security police and SD in North and Central Italy (Verona) and later in Holland; took part in the murder of innocent people; shares responsibility for the deportation of 11,000 Dutch Jews
after 1945: sentenced in Holland in 1947 to twelve years in prison; released in 1953 on the intervention of the Bonn government and immediately installed in the Bavarian Ministry of the Interior as a senior government counsellor; retired in 1963

Haxler, Franz
before 1945: SS Gruppenführer in the Reich Security Main Office (No. 64 697), NSDAP (No. 754 133), state secretary in the Reich Ministry of Economics and assistant head of the military administration east
after 1945: head of an export and import limited partnership in Munich

Heissmeyer, August
before 1945: SS Obergruppenführer (No. 4 370), NSDAP (No. 21 573), general of the armed SS and the police, chief of the central office of the SD in the Reichsführung SS, inspector of the national-political educational establishments
after 1945: sentenced to 18 months' imprisonment for having lived under the fictitious name of "Stuckebrode", amnestied in 1949, director of a coca-cola plant in West Germany

Hellersen, Heinrich
before 1945: 1933 NSDAP and SS (No. 78 005), proposed by the SD for active service in the colonies
after 1945: senior secretary in the criminal investigation department in Darmstadt

Hellmuth, Dr. Otto
before 1945: NSDAP regional leader, in 1927 in Unterfranken and later in Mainfranken; government president; 1919 in the "Wurzburg" people's defence regiment against the Bavarian workers' government; took part in Hitler's march on Koberg in 1922
after 1945: condemned to death by an American military court for having shot an American flyer; sentence commuted to 20 years and released from Landsberg prison in 1955; received an imprisonment indemnity of over 5,000 marks; practices as a dentist in Reutlingen

Hermann, Günther
before 1945: SS Obersturmbannführer in the Reich Security Main Office (No. 267 283), NSDAP (No. 2 475 252), head of Gestapo offices in Kiel and Brünn, staff member in the headquarters of the "chief of the security police and SD" in Austria, leader of SS action commando in Troppau and Prague and of action commandos 4b and 12 in the Soviet Union
after 1945: lives unmolestedly in West Germany (see Table 17)

Herrmann, Gustav
before 1945: SS Hauptsturmführer (No. 487 520)
after 1945: chief inspector of police in Leer

Hersmann, Dr. Werner
before 1945: SS Sturmbannführer (No. 9 416), major in the security police, 1930 NSDAP (No. 298 662), 1941 commander of security police in occupied Esthonia, 1942 officer in action group D, action commando 11b
after 1945: after having undergone a short term of imprisonment Hersmann lives as a mechanical engineer in West Germany

Herz, Hermann
before 1945: SS Hauptsturmführer (No. 211 028), detective superintendent in the Reich Security Main Office, NSDAP (No. 4 340 641)
after 1945: detective superintendent in Stuttgart

Hierl, Josef
before 1945: SS Hauptsturmführer and commander of the country constabulary in Croatia
after 1945: police inspector in Wiesbaden

Hochgräbe, Hans-Joachim
before 1945: SS Hauptsturmführer and detective superintendent in the Reich Security Main Office
after 1945: acting head of the criminal investigation department in Duisburg

Hödel, Ludwig
before 1945: SS Untersturmführer, 1941 "combating partisans", captain in the Ist police regiment 3
after 1945: bailiff of the police in Rosenheim, leader of the commando of the Bavarian frontier police

Hölfling, Wilfried
before 1945: captain of the country constabulary and SS Sturmbannführer
after 1945: chief inspector of police in Wuppertal

Hörath, Siegfried
before 1945: SS Hauptsturmführer (No. 419 861) and captain in the security police, officer in an SS police division
after 1945: chief inspector of police in Düsseldorf

Hofer, Franz
before 1945: NSDAP regional leader in Tirol and Vorarlberg, Reich governor; participated in the murder of from 600 to 700 Austrian Jews and shares responsibility for the murder of 30,000 persons
after 1945: wanted in Austria since 1945 for murder; was arrested by the American occupation authorities; was able to flee in 1948; returned to Mülheim/Ruhr under a false name; lives there again under his own name as an independent businessman and declared in a UPI interview: "I was, am and shall remain a national socialist"

Hoffelder, Johann
before 1945: district commander of the SS and police
after 1945: bailiff of the country constabulary in Kaiserslautern

Hoffmann, Dr. Max
before 1945: SS Sturmbannführer, (No. 340 711), NSDAP (No. 1 496 604), government counsellor and expert in department II B/1 of the Reich Security Main Office
after 1945: senior police inspector in Wiesbaden (see Table 18)

Holzbecher, Helmut
before 1945: SS Obersturmführer, police battalion 215 in Norway and SS police regiment 26 in the USSR and Poland
after 1945: chief inspector of police in Hamburg

Horn, Dr. Rudolf
before 1945: SS Sturmbannführer (No. 353 366), government counsellor and detective superintendent in the Reich Security Main Office, 1933 NSDAP (No. 462 825)
after 1945: head of the provincial office of the criminal investigation department in Aurich

Hucko, Wilhelm
before 1945: SS Sturmbannführer, (No. 375 079) in the Reich Security Main Office, NSDAP (No. 3 512 041)
after 1945: deputy head of the criminal investigation department in Cologne

Hudy, Wilhelm
before 1945: member of the Gestapo in Karlsbad (Karlovy Vary), SS leader
after 1945: police inspector in police headquarters in Hanover

Hüttemann, Peter
before 1945: SS Hauptsturmführer to the commanding officer of the security police and the SD in France
after 1945: president of military administration district III in Düsseldorf (for the province of North Rhine-Westphalia)

Hunsche, Dr. Otto
before 1945: SS Hauptsturmführer in the Reich Security Main Office, office IV B 4 (Jewish questions – Eichmann); "legal adviser" to Eichmann
after 1945: lawyer in Datteln/Westphalia

Huppenkothen, Walter
before 1945: SS Standartenführer (No. 126 785), group leader in office IV/E (Gestapo) of the Reich Security Main Office, commander of the security police and SD in Krakow and Lublin, NSDAP (No. 1 950 150)
after 1945: In 1951, 1952, 1955 and 1956 he underwent trial accused of having participated in the murder of Hitler's espionage chief, Canaris, and other participants of the conspiracy of 20 July 1944; after having been acquitted he lives unmolested in Mannheim as an insurance employee

Jost, Heinz
before 1945: SS Brigadeführer (No. 36 243) and major general in the police, 1 February 1928 NSDAP (No. 75 946), head of office VI of the Reich Security Main Office, head of action group A, commander of the security police and SD "Ostland" in Riga
after 1945: 1948 sentenced to life imprisonment by an American military court; 1951 sentence commuted to ten years, a short time later he was released, independent economic jurist

Kammer, Heribert
before 1945: SS Sturmbannführer (No. 205 196), SS and police official in Danzig, chief of police, NSDAP (No. 501 681)
after 1945: head of the police station in Herford

Kaufmann, Dr. Heinz
before 1945: SS Obersturmbannführer (No. 358 719), NSDAP (No. 824 859), staff member of the Gestapo office in Saxony, from 1938 Gestapo office in Dresden
after 1945: In 1948 preliminary proceedings were instituted against him which ended with his being sentenced to 14 months' imprisonment, which was regarded as being fulfilled by his period of internment.

Kaufmann, Karl
before 1945: SS Obergruppenführer (No. 119 495), 1921 NSDAP (No. 95), Reich commissioner for military district X and for sea-navigation, Gauleiter (district leader) of the NSDAP and Reich governor in Hamburg
after 1945: he lives in Hamburg as a business-man

Kehrer, Walter
before 1945: member of special commando 10a, SS leader
after 1945: lives unmolested in West Germany

Keunecke, Dr.
before 1945: SS Sturmbannführer in the Reich Security Main Office
after 1945: detective superintendent and acting head of the criminal investigation department in Essen

Kiehne, Helmut
before 1945: first lieutenant in the security police and officer in police cavalry detachment II to the commanding officer of the disciplinary police in the Ukraine; engaged in "combating gangs"
after 1945: 1956 delivered to the West German government as a war criminal, immediately re-engaged as a chief inspector of police in the Hamburg police service, head of the mounted police and police dog department

Kiehne, Karl
before 1945: SS Sturmbannführer (No. 375 136), detective inspector in the Reich Security Main Office, NSDAP (No. 5 528 055)
after 1945: senior police superintendent and head of the criminal investigation department in Cologne

Kocks, Herbert
before 1945: SS Hauptsturmführer in the IInd SS police regiment 24 and volunteer police regiment I in Croatia
after 1945: superintendent of police, head of the police office in Delmenhorst

Köllner, Fritz
before 1945: staff member of the Reich Security Main Office; took part in the deportation of Jews into the Theresienstadt concentration camp
after 1945: senior government counsellor in the Ministry of the Interior in Bavaria

Konitzki, Gerhard
before 1945: member of SS action commando 8
after 1945: police official in Essen

Koppe, Wilhelm
before 1945: SS Obergruppenführer (No. 25 955) and general of the armed SS, NSDAP (No. 305 584), state secretary and higher commander of the SS and police in occupied Poland, responsible for the extermination of 350,000 Polish Jews, 1,500 mental patients in East Prussia, 20,000 people in the Chelmno concentration camp suffering from tuberculosis, and 80 Polish resistance fighters in Dachau concentration camp

after 1945: with the knowledge of West German authorities he lived under the fictitious name of "Lohmann" in Bonn until 1960, director of a branch office of the Sarotti firm for a long time.

Kordts, Helmut

before 1945: SS Hauptsturmführer
after 1945: chief inspector of police in Hamburg

Kosching, Maximilian

before 1945: from 1938 in the Gestapo in Trier, 1931 SA, later SS
after 1945: head of the police station in Oberlahnstein-Niederlahnstein

Kraiker, Hermann

before 1945: member of SS action commando 8
after 1945: police sergeant in Wattenscheid

Kraiker, Hermann

before 1945: SS Sturmbannführer (No. 354185), NSDAP (No. 1545743), major in the security police, commander of battalions in the SS police regiment Gieseke and in the ill-famed battle group of SS Obergruppenführer Prützmann (see Table 19)
after 1945: in a managerial position in the police administration in Bochum

Krüger, Bernhard

before 1945: SS Sturmbannführer (No. 15249) in the Reich Security Main Office, NSDAP (No. 528739); Krüger was chief of the central forgery office of section F in department VI of the Reich Security Main Office and provided for the equipment of agents of the SD with forged identity papers and counterfeit foreign bank-notes; he was responsible for the murder of prisoners of Sachsenhausen concentration camp who were forced to do this forging
after 1945: Standard-Elektrik-Lorenz AG; only in March 1964 were preliminary proceedings instituted against him in the Provincial Court of Göttingen

Krumey, Hermann

before 1945: SS Obersturmbannführer (No. 310441) in the Reich Security Main Office,co-worker of Eichmann in the department on Jewish questions
after 1945: proprietor of a drug store in Korbach/Hesse

Lammerding, Heinz

before 1945: SS Oberführer (No. 247062), general in the armed SS, commander of SS tank division "Das Reich", NSDAP (No. 722395)
after 1945: building contractor in Düsseldorf, leading position in the HIAG SS organization

Lauterbacher, Hartmann

before 1945: SS Obergruppenführer (No. 382406), NSDAP (No. 86837), district leader of Hanover-Süd, Brunswick; took part in the deportation of Jews to mass extermination in the ghettos; sending antifascists to concentration camp, mass shooting of Soviet prisoners of war on the Seelhorster cemetery; sent children and aged people to the front with panzer fists and senselessly sacrificed them
after 1945: after having remained in hiding for years he again re-entered public life in Munich officially in 1956 and since then has conducted a lucrative business with the firm "Laboratory-Industrial Projecting – Foreign Trade Agent"

Lindner, Kurt

before 1945: SS Hauptsturmführer (No. 310260), instructor at the school for leadership training of the SD
after 1945: head of the criminal investigation department in Duisburg

Lischka, Kurt

before 1945: SS Obersturmbannführer (No. 195590) Reich Security Main Office, NSDAP (No. 4583185); on orders of Himmler he was in charge of the "inquiry" against the Hitler opponents of 20 July 1944
after 1945: managing clerk in a big establishment in Cologne

Lorenz, Werner

before 1945: SS Obergruppenführer (No. 6636) and general in the police, NSDAP (No. 397994), head of the Folk German Liaison Office, authorized representative of the NSDAP commissioner for foreign policy questions
after 1945: lives unmolested in West Germany; he has close relations with the head of the Springer press trust, in Hamburg

Ludwig, Dr. Wilhelm

before 1945: SS Obersturmführer (No. 307478), officer of the 87th SS standard in Innsbruck
after 1945: government director, head of department V in the Federal Office for the Protection of the Constitution in Cologne

Lütgering, Hans
before 1945: adjutant in police battalion I/1 in Prague and in police regiment South of action group south of the SD
after 1945: chief inspector of police, head of a police sector in Luneburg

Marbach, Hubert
before 1945: adjutant and company commander in action groups of the Reich Security Main Office, e. g., in SS police regiment 2
after 1945: head of the provincial police school in Bonn

Meier, Paulus
before 1945: battalion commander of the 9th police battalion, which was ill-famed as a result of its mass murders, and of the IInd SS police regiment 14, major in the police
after 1945: police superintendent in Bonn

Mengele, Dr. Josef
before 1945: SS Hauptsturmführer, SS camp physician in Buchenwald and Auschwitz (Oswiecim); in these concentration camps he took an active part in selections and medical experiments
after 1945: after having lived unmolestedly in West Germany for many years he was able to evade punishment by flight to a South American country

Menke, Dr. Josef
before 1945: SS Sturmbannführer (No. 351096), government counsellor, staff member in the central office of the security police, later Reich Security Main Office, 1933 NSDAP (No. 3152619)
after 1945: senior detective superintendent and head of the criminal investigation department in Dortmund

Merveldt, Gisbert, Graf von
before 1945: major in the security police and officer with the commanding officer of disciplinary police in Ukraine in Luzk, supporter of the SA and SS
after 1945: head of the provincial police school of Rhineland-Palatinate

Messer, Hermann
before 1945: district captain of the country constabulary, member of action commando Kharkov of the country constabulary, finally district commander of the SS and police in Geissin, 1 May 1933 NSDAP
after 1945: chief inspector of police in the police administration of Stuttgart

Methfessel, Fritz
before 1945: SS leader and Gestapo official, mistreated allied airmen during the war
after 1945: sentenced to two years' penal servitude by the American Military Court, nevertheless he is head of the criminal investigation department in Grewen

Metschullat, Herbert
before 1945: SS Obersturmführer, IInd SS police regiment 10
after 1945: chief inspector of police in Hamburg

Miethe, Erhard
before 1945: on duty in the east as a captain in the security police
after 1945: head of the provincial police commissariat in Reutlingen

Müller, Balduin
before 1945: staff member to the SS district commander of police in Litzmannstadt (Lodz), NSDAP, SS (No. 344999)
after 1945: police sergeant in Düsseldorf

Müller, Eugen
before 1945: district captain of the country constabulary, detachment commander of the country constabulary in the Ilkenau region, administrative district of Kattowitz (Katowice), 1943 appointed to the sphere of the "higher commander of the SS and police Russia-South and Ukraine"
after 1945: head of the provincial police commissariat in Freudenstadt, chief inspector of police

Nägele, Friedrich
before 1945: SS Sturmbannführer, 1922–1923 NSDAP, re-joined on 1 May 1937 (No. 5021878), 1942 district commander of the SS and police in Caucasia (Piatigorsk), 1944 adjutant in the staff of the police commander of the foreland of the Alps zone of operations
after 1945: leading official in the police headquarters of Stuttgart

Neher, Konstantin
before 1945: captain in the country constabulary and head of an action commando in the east, 1944 member of the 30th infantry division of the armed SS
after 1945: chief inspector of police, head of the provincial police regional commissariat in Ehingen (Wurttemberg)

Noack, Egon
before 1945: engaged in the area of responsibility of the Reich Security Main Office, member of an action group
after 1945: chief inspector of the criminal investigation department in Kiel

Obstfelder, Kurt
before 1945: leader of a commando of the military police
after 1945: sentenced to 15 years' penal servitude for war crimes committed among the civilian population of the USSR, chief of police in Hanover

Ochs, Dr. Josef
before 1945: inspector of the criminal investigation department in the Reich Security Main Office, SS Obersturmführer
after 1945: detective superintendent in the Federal Criminal Office

Odewald, Walter
before 1945: SS Sturmbannführer (No. 323731), from 1937 in the operations staff of the SD in Paris and later in Prague
after 1945: senior government counsellor in the Provincial Office for the Protection of the Constitution in Lower Saxony

Oehl, Gerhard
before 1945: SA Obersturmführer, part-time officer to the commander of the country constabulary in Simferopol/Crimea and head of the country constabulary prefecture on the Adriatic coast
after 1945: senior police sergeant in Stuttgart

Olbrich, Erhard
before 1945: SS Obersturmbannführer (No. 337745), NSDAP (No. 579317), chief of staff to the commanding officer of disciplinary police, SS General Daluege, organizer of the fascist terror in occupied Hungary
after 1945: major in the police headquarters of Mannheim

Opitz, Paul
before 1945: SS Sturmbannführer (No. 332024), detective superintendent and senior government counsellor in department IV/E 1 (Gestapo) of the Reich Security Main Office
after 1945: staff member in the Federal Office for the Protection of the Constitution in Cologne

Ottersbach, Dr. Arnold
before 1945: government director, expert on defence of the Reich and official of the Reich Defence Commissioner competent for military district VI in Munich, NSDAP (No. 5410609)
after 1945: deputy head of the provincial police authorities in Munster

Papenkort, Willi
before 1945: SS Sturmbannführer (No. 313915), NSDAP (No. 206471), major in the security police, shares guilt for the shooting of Jews in the Soviet Union
after 1945: captain of police in Essen (see Table 19)

Paulat, Bodo
before 1945: first lieutenant in the security police, service in the ill-famed police battalion 215, which among others was stationed in Norway in March 1941
after 1945: chief inspector of police and head of the police sector of Bad Gandersheim

Peiper, Joachim
before 1945: SS Obersturmbannführer (No. 132496), member of the armed SS with the same rank, responsible for the burning of Boves in Italy which he ordered as commander of a tank regiment of the SS tank division "Adolf Hitler Life Guards", and for the murder of 71 unarmed American prisoners of war south-east of Malmedy in December 1944
after 1945: sentenced to death by an American military court, later commuted to 25 years' penal servitude and released in 1956; employed in the Porsche plants, last employed as advertising manager of a Volkswagen car dealer in Reutlingen

Poethke, Herbert
before 1945: SS Hauptsturmführer and first lieutenant in the security police, 1941 with an action commando in the east
after 1945: chief inspector of police in Mönchen-Gladbach

Pötke, Karl
before 1945: captain in the security police and SS commander seconded for special duty, commander of the IInd SS police regiment 16 and regimental commander in the group SS police east
after 1945: police superintendent and head of commando Ia of the security police in Hamburg

Preckel, Erich
before 1945: SS Sturmbannführer (No. 342786) in the Reich Security Main Of-

fice, department IV (Gestapo), NSDAP (No. 1947373)
after 1945: head of the criminal investigation department in Opladen

Priller, Franz

before 1945: leader of a commando of the SD in the district of Radom, branch office Kielce, member of the NSDAP and SS, employed in the so-called SS relief work in Dachau concentration camp, commissioner of the SD in the annexation of Austria and staff member of the Gestapo in Oppeln
after 1945: leader of a commando of the Bavarian frontier police

Pruss, Hans

before 1945: SS Sturmbannführer (No. 450691), 1 May 1933 NSDAP (No. 2955038), major in the security police, orderly officer in an SS police division
after 1945: senior superintendent of police and representative of the commander of the security police with the government president in Hildesheim, head of the police station in Hildesheim

Puchta, Adolf

before 1945: SS Sturmbannführer (No. 107193), NSDAP (No. 3469510), before 1933 leading position in the SA, 1931 Reich leadership school of the SA, Reich Security Main Office, Gestapo in Czechoslovakia, leader of an action commando in Norway, later in the Soviet Union
after 1945: expert in the Provincial Office for the Protection of the Constitution in Bavaria, leading member of the revanchist "Witikobund"

Rabe, Karl-Hermann

before 1945: SS Obersturmbannführer (No. 54628), NSDAP (No. 259544) leader of action commando 7b which murdered 4,000 men, women and children
after 1945: only now have preliminary proceedings been instituted against him (see Table 20)

Radtke, Albert

before 1945: employee of the SD espionage apparatus
after 1945: vice-president of the Federal Office for the Protection of the Constitution

Rapp, Dr. Albert

before 1945: SS Standartenführer (No. 280341), NSDAP (No. 774433), government counsellor and staff member of the SD, leader of action commando 7c of action group B which murdered 3,000 Jews in the Soviet Union, inspector of the security police and the SD in military district XI in Brunswick, 1944 Reich Security Main Office, department VI, head of group C
after 1945: only in 1965 were proceedings instituted against Rapp

Reinefarth, Heinz

before 1945: SS Brigadeführer (No. 56634) and major general in the police, NSDAP (No. 1268933), head of SS main section "Warthe" and higher SS and police official in military district XXI (Warthe), 1933 "legal adviser" of SS section XII, whose leader was von dem Bach-Zelewski; shares responsibility for the murders and destruction of Warsaw, especially in putting down the uprising in the Warsaw ghetto and "liquidating" the ghetto
after 1945: until 1964 mayor of Westerland/Sylt, member of the Schleswig-Holstein provincial diet; Polish requests for his extradition have been repeatedly refused by the Bonn government

Reinhard, Hellmuth

before 1945: SS Sturmbannführer (No. 121174) in the Reich Security Main Office, NSDAP (No. 2382157); as a leading staff member in the Gestapo office in Oslo he was responsible for the deportation and death of 690 Norwegian Jews
after 1945: under his former name of Patschke he was editor, chief editor and finally manager of a publishing house in Baden-Baden; arrested in December 1964

Remold, Josef

before 1945: regimental commander and district commander of the SS and police
after 1945: chief of the Bavarian standby police

Reuscher, Dr. Fedor

before 1945: senior government counsellor, district president in Königsberg, deputy to the general commissioner for White Ruthenia, Gauleiter (regional leader) Kube, representative of the district president of Litzmannstadt (Lodz)
after 1945: Federal Ministry of the Interior, head of department III

Rheindorf, Konrad

before 1945: lieutenant colonel, general staff officer in the headquarters of SS police regiment 26, 1943 district commander of the SS and police in Krakow and Lublin
after 1945: acting head of the provincial police administration in Swabia

Riedel, Fritz

before 1945: SS Hauptsturmführer, commander of the military police in Latvia
after 1945: inspector in the criminal investigation department in Munich

Riese, Werner

before 1945: tactics officer in several SS action groups, major in the police
after 1945: chief inspector of police in Hamburg

Rippich, Dr. Fridrich

before 1945: SS Sturmbannführer (No. 185093), NSDAP (No. 2586731), government counsellor in the Reich Ministry of the Interior, district president for Sieratz region in the government Litzmannstadt (Lodz); responsible for sending persons to concentration camp
after 1945: in hiding in Argentina; 1954 employed in the Federal Ministry of the Interior on the grounds of a decree by the then Minister of the Interior Schröder on the employment of former SS people; today head of the special staff for "psychological defence" in the "civil population defence" department

Röhl, Friedrich

before 1945: last captain in the country constabulary, commanding officer of the disciplinary police, from January 1943 in the Federation of the East (BdO) in Riga, NSDAP
after 1945: police official, deputy head of the provincial police school in Rhineland-Palatinate

Rösch, Heinrich

before 1945: district captain in the country constabulary, 1941 active as a regional commander of the country constabulary in Grodno, Bialystok district, 1943 with the commander of the disciplinary police in Marseille, 1944 in the constabulary action department in Thorn
after 1945: head of the country constabulary in the region of Pirmasens, since August 1964 retired

Rohlfs, Willi

before 1945: captain in the country constabulary, 1942 raged in the Soviet Union in police regiment 17
after 1945: chief inspector of police, head of the Wesermünde police sector in Bremerhaven

Rosendahl, Johannes

before 1945: SS Hauptsturmführer, captain in the country constabulary
after 1945: chief inspector of police and head of the police sector of the rural region of Lüchow-Dannenberg (see Table 20)

Rottach, Josef

before 1945: SS Sturmbannführer (No. 263095), SS troop drill grounds "Kurmark", NSDAP (No. 4458951)
after 1945: senior police sergeant in Speyer

Rutz, Horst

before 1945: SS Hauptsturmführer in Ukrainian security police battalion 61 and in securitiy police regiment 57, SS district police leader
after 1945: chief inspector of police in Hamburg

Sandberger, Dr. Martin

before 1945: SS Standartenführer (No. 272495), NSDAP (No. 774980), deputy head of a section in department I/E of the Reich Security Main Office, leader of action commando 1a of action group A, in December 1941 commander of the security police and SD in Esthonia
after 1945: 1948 sentenced to death, later pardoned and released

Schäfer, Eugen

before 1945: member of the Gestapo in Meissen and of action groups of the SD
after 1945: chief inspector in the criminal investigation department in Cuxhaven

Schäfer, Johannes Robert

before 1945: SS Untersturmführer in the Reich Security Main Office, head office of the criminal investigation department in Cologne
after 1945: inspector in the criminal investigation department in Wiesbaden

Schaefer, Dr. Oswald

before 1945: SS Obersturmbannführer (No. 272488), NSDAP (No. 1772081), detective inspector, head of the Gestapo head office in Munich and successor of Wiebens in the direction of action commando 9 which murdered 6,500 men, women and children
after 1945: Schaefer has up to now not been punished for these crimes

Schatteburg, Wolfgang

before 1945: SS Hauptsturmführer (No. 311870), captain in the security police, part-time associate judge of SS and police

court III in Prague, district commander of the SS and police in the Ukraine
after 1945: chief inspector of police in Hamburg

Schaub, Julius
before 1945: SS Obergruppenführer (No. 7), NSDAP (No. 81), Hitler's adjutant, member of the NSDAP from 1923 and of the SS
after 1945: druggist in West Germany, 1949 acquitted of the charge of complicity in murder for "lack of evidence"

Scheffler, Herbert
before 1945: intelligence officer in the Reich Security Main Office, 1941 with the commissioner of the Reichsführer SS for the establishment of SS and police bases in the new areas in the east
after 1945: police superintendent in Hiltrup

Schindhelm, Hans Gerhard
before 1945: SS Obersturmbannführer (No. 353 427), NSDAP (No. 2 452 706); after Bradfisch and Richter he took over the command of action commando 8 in Mogilev
after 1945: In July 1961 the trial of Dr. Otto Bradfisch, head of action commando 8, took place. He was sentenced to 10 years' penal servitude for complicity in the murder of 15,000 people; Schindhelm remained unmolested

Schliefke, Waldemar
before 1945: member of SS action commandos
after 1945: sentenced to death for war crimes, later commuted to 25 years' deprivation of liberty, 1953 released before the completion of the sentence, chief inspector of police in Hof

Schloemp, Georg
before 1945: SS Untersturmführer (No. 424 361), first lieutenant in the military police
after 1945: chief inspector of police in police headquarters in Hamburg

Schloer, Hans Karl
before 1945: SS Obersturmführer, adjutant of the sector commander "Reichswerke Hermann Göring"
after 1945: chief inspector and acting head of police headquarters in Neumünster

Schmidle, Adolf
before 1945: major in the police, staff officer to the "higher commander of the SS and police" in Hanover, NSDAP
after 1945: police superintendent in Düsseldorf

Scholz, Herbert
before 1945: SS Sturmbannführer (No. 308 265), NSDAP (No. 2 840 674), major in the security police, district commander of the SS and police in Norway and The Hague
after 1945: chief of police in Augsburg

Schrübbers, Hubert
before 1945: public prosecutor in the prosecutor general's office in Hamm/Westphalia; dealt primarily with charges of high treason against progressive forces and gave high prison sentences
after 1945: president of the Federal Office for the Protection of the Constitution

Schüler, Walter
before 1945: officer in action commandos of the SD in Poland
after 1945: condemned by the Polish Military Court, 1953 released, inspector of police in Ansbach

Schuler, Anton
before 1945: SS Sturmbannführer (No. 87 344), NSDAP (No. 1 232 958), major in the security police, 1935 graduated from the SS Junker school in Brunswick
after 1945: chief inspector of police, head of the provincial police regional commissariat in Wolfach in South Baden

Schulz, Erwin
before 1945: SS Brigadeführer (No. 107 484), NSDAP (No. 2 902 238), major general in the police, head of department I in the Reich Security Main Office, 1941 leader of SS action commando 5 of action group C
after 1945: commercial employee in Bremen

Schulze, Albert
before 1945: member of the SS standard "Adolf Hitler" Life Guards and of the guard force in Sachsenhausen concentration camp; active in the combating of partisans within an SS brigade
after 1945: government official in the administrative office of the Hessian provincial police in Wiesbaden

Schwerdt, Otto
before 1945: SS Obersturmführer, from 1942 member of the "special formation Friedenthal"; in December 1943 he went to

Copenhagen; organized the terror against the Danish resistance movement, carried out the murder of Danish patriots, among others of Kaj Munk, which was ordered by SS Obergruppenführer Dr. Best (cf. Dr. Best, page 78)
after 1945: after a trial in Copenhagen in 1948 he went into hiding in West Germany

Seibert, Willi
before 1945: SS Standartenführer (No. 272 375), NSDAP (No. 1 886 112), acting head of department III of the Reich Security Main Office, leader of action group D in the Soviet Union
after 1945: sentenced to death, later amnestied and released in 1955

Settels, Franz
before 1945: SS Sturmbannführer (No. 353 365) in the central office of the SD, Gestapo, NSDAP (No. 4 189 335)
after 1945: head of the criminal investigation department in Leverkusen

Siemens, Karl-Heinz
before 1945: SS Obersturmführer in the "Adolf Hitler Leibstandarte"; participated in this unit's notorious crimes
after 1945: first lived under the name of Dr. Kaiser in West Germany and is now under his own name senior government counsellor in department III of the Federal Office for the Protection of the Constitution

Siemers, Otto
before 1945: captain in the security police and adjutant to the chief of police in occupied Posen (Poznan)
after 1945: police superintendent and leader of the central radio patrol car station in Hamburg

Sinnhuber, Fritz
before 1945: SS Sturmbannführer (No. 393 357) in the central office of the disciplinary police in Berlin, SS legal officer
after 1945: deputy head of the police school in Schleswig-Holstein

Six, Professor Dr. Franz
before 1945: SS Oberführer (No. 107 480), NSDAP since 1930 (No. 245 670), 1935 head of department II in the security main office of the Reichsführer SS, later department VII of the Reich Security Main Office, 1941 head of the front action commando Moscow
after 1945: 1948 sentenced to 20 years in prison by an American military court, 1951 commuted to 10 years, released soon afterwards; advertising manager of the Porsche-Diesel-Motorenbau-GmbH, Friedrichshafen; agent of the federal intelligence service

Skorzeny, Otto
before 1945: SS Obersturmbannführer (No. 295 979), NSDAP (No. 1 083 671), Reich Security Main Office department VI, head of group S, commander of the "Oranienburg special unit", head of a diversionist group on the eastern front
after 1945: proprietor of an engineering and real estate office in Madrid; founder and head of secret nazi organization "die Spinne" (the Spider)

Smeets, Wilhelm
before 1945: member of Gestapo offices in Cologne and Klagenfurt, participant in a course of instruction at the SS school for leadership training, 1926 NSDAP, 1931 SS
after 1945: senior regional director and head of the regional police authorities in Kleve

Staake, Hermann
before 1945: SS Hauptsturmführer
after 1945: chief inspector of police in Hamburg

Stadie, Paul
before 1945: SS Obersturmführer, first lieutenant in the security police, active as a military policeman during the war
after 1945: chief inspector of police in police headquarters in Hamburg

Steeger, Christian
before 1945: group commander in police regiment 27 and in the IIIrd SS police regiment 15
after 1945: senior police sergeant in Linz

Steimle, Eugen Karl
before 1945: SS Obersturmbannführer (No. 272 575), staff member in department IV/B (Gestapo) of the Reich Security Main Office, NSDAP (No. 1 075 555), commander of the main sector of the SD in Stuttgart, 1941 leader of action commando 7a of action group B, 1942 leader of action commando 4a of action group C
after 1945: sentenced to death, 1951 amnestied and released soon afterwards

Steiner, Felix Martin
before 1945: SS Obergruppenführer and general in the armed SS (No. 253 351), NSDAP (No. 4 264 295), commander of SS tank divisions and corps in the Soviet Union and the SA
after 1945: co-founder of the SS organization HIAG

Stieler, Adam
before 1945: member of the Gestapo in Liegnitz and an action commando of the disciplinary police in Lublin
after 1945: senior regional director and head of the regional police authorities in Monschau

Stratmann, Johannes
before 1945: captain in the country constabulary and commander of a motorized military police detachment in the Soviet Union
after 1945: chief inspector of police in the Norden region in Lower Saxony

Streckenbach, Bruno
before 1945: SS Gruppenführer and lieutenant general in the police (No. 14 713), NSDAP (No. 489 972), head of department I of the Reich Security Main Office, commander of the 19th Lettish SS grenadier division, commander of the 8th SS cavalry division
after 1945: sentenced to life imprisonment in the Soviet Union for his crimes, transferred to the Federal Republic as a non-amnestied war criminal, was immediately freed; commercial employee in Hamburg

Strübing, Johann
before 1945: SS Hauptsturmführer in department IV (Gestapo) of the Reich Security Main Office; took part in mistreating and torturing anti-fascist prisoners
after 1945: employee of the Federal Office for the Protection of the Constitution; employed as informer against upstanding West German trade unionists

Terrée, Werner
before 1945: lieutenant in the security police, 1944 officer in the IInd SS police regiment 2 in Bialystok
after 1945: chief inspector of police, head of sector in the Osnabrück region

Tezlaff, Otto
before 1945: candidate member of an SS squadron, 1939 received into the Gestapo in Stuttgart
after 1945: sergeant in the criminal investigation department in the provincial criminal investigation authorities in Lower Saxony

Thümmler, Dr. Johannes
before 1945: SS Obersturmbannführer (No. 323 711), NSDAP (No. 1 425 547) senior government counsellor in the Reich Security Main Office, head of the Gestapo main offices in Dresden, Chemnitz and Kattowitz, head of action commando 16 of action group E in South-East Europe
after 1945: leading employee of an optical works in Oberkochen (Zeiss foundation), defence witness in the Auschwitz trial

Toyka, Dr. Rudolf
before 1945: government counsellor to the Reich governor in Posen (Poznan), liaison man to the Gestapo and SD, later security commissioner with the generalgouverneur
after 1945: ministerial director in the Federal Ministry of the Interior and head of the sub-department for "public and administrative law", directed the action against the news magazine Der Spiegel; as a result had to be released from this function from 1 August 1964; entered the trial against the Association of Victims of Nazism (VVN) as representative of the Federal Ministry of the Interior; actively engaged in drafting the emergency legislation

Trimborn, Kurt
before 1945: SS Obersturmführer (No. 2 558), NSDAP (No. 175 815), as leader of a special commando in Krasnodar took part in the murder of 214 children in a Soviet children's home
after 1945: lives unmolested in Wuppertal

Trossmann, Hans
before 1945: 1940 to 1945 with Reich commissioner for price fixing, 1942 ghetto administration of Litzmannstadt (Lodz) and promoted to senior government counsellor for his activity there
after 1945: since 1947 leading activity in the CSU, since 1953 director of the West German Bundestag

Ulrich, Fritz
before 1945: 1933 staff member of the Gestapo, 1939 in the SD in Linz
after 1945: administrative director in the provincial criminal investigation department in Lower Saxony

Unger, Walter
before 1945: training officer in police battalion Recklinghausen, the later murder battalion 316, 1943 in SS police regiment Griese
after 1945: police superintendent in Cologne

Volkmann, Heinz
before 1945: head of the Gestapo office in Elbing
after 1945: chief inspector in the criminal investigation department of the political police in Stuttgart

Voss, Ludwig
before 1945: until 1939 SD in Magdeburg, later member of the secret field police
after 1945: inspector in the criminal investigation department in Luneburg

Wachtendong, Walter
before 1945: member of action commando 8
after 1945: police officer in Recklinghausen

Wagner, Wilhelm
before 1945: SS Hauptsturmführer, as a staff member of the Gestapo office in Oslo jointly responsible for the crimes committed against 690 Jewish citizens
after 1945: lives unmolested in Bonn

Waldbillig, Hermann
before 1945: head of the department for Jewish questions in the Gestapo office in Düsseldorf, 1930 NSDAP
after 1945: chief inspector of police in Cologne

Weber, Fritz
before 1945: SS Sturmbannführer in the Reich Security Main Office, 1933 NSDAP
after 1945: director of the criminal investigation department in the Ministry of the Interior of North Rhine-Westphalia

Wehner, Dr. Bernhard
before 1945: SS Hauptsturmführer and detective inspector in department V of the Reich Security Main Office; participated in the killing of Soviet prisoners of war in Buchenwald concentration camp
after 1945: head of the criminal investigation department in Düsseldorf

Weigold, Hermann
before 1945: SS Hauptsturmführer to the district commander of the SS and police in the Netherlands
after 1945: inspector of police in Stuttgart

Weinreich, Hermann
before 1945: 1932 SS
after 1945: inspector of police in Hamburg

Wendt, Erich
before 1945: SS Hauptsturmführer and company commander in volunteer police regiment 2
after 1945: chief inspector of police in Essen

Wenzel, Erich
before 1945: as member of the SS participated in the shooting of Jews in Shitomir in 1942
after 1945: secretary in the criminal investigation department in Essen

Wicke, Oswin
before 1945: leader of SS action commandos
after 1945: police superintendent in the provincial police authorities in Hanover, condemned as a war criminal in the Soviet Union

Wiebens, Wilhelm
before 1945: SS Obersturmbannführer in the Reich Security Main Office (No. 16 617), NSDAP (No. 546 524), leader of action commando 9 in Witebsk
after 1945: lives unmolestedly in West Germany

Wilhelm, Georg
before 1945: SS and country constabulary Unterführer, member of the SA and the NSDAP from 1929
after 1945: senior police sergeant in Kassel

Winkelmann, Otto
before 1945: SS Gruppenführer (No. 308 238) and lieutenant general in the police, NSDAP (No. 1 373 131), head of the commando office of the headquarters of the disciplinary police, higher SS and police leader in Hungary
after 1945: councillor in Kiel, president of the Association of Former Police Officers; receives a general's pension of more than 1,700 marks

Wittmann, Max
before 1945: SS Hauptsturmführer (No. 309 825), district commander of the SS and police in Litzmannstadt (Lodz)

after 1945: chief inspector of police in Hamburg

Wohlauf, Julius
before 1945: SS Hauptsturmführer and company commander in Krakow, 1943 IInd SS police regiment 7, Oslo
after 1945: chief inspector of police in Hamburg

Wolff, Karl
before 1945: SS Obergruppenführer (No. 14 235) and general in the armed SS, NSDAP (No. 695 131), "chief of the personal staff of the Reichsführer SS", highest SS and police leader in Italy, liaison officer of the Reichsführer SS with the "Führer"
after 1945: until 1962 living on a general's pension on Starnberger See; sentenced to 15 years in prison in 1964 for the murder of more than 300,000 Jews

Wollschina, Wilhelm
before 1945: SS Hauptsturmführer, captain in the security police, 1931 NSDAP (No. 793 715), among other things active in Brünn and Tabor
after 1945: chief inspector of police and chief of police in Offenbach

Wurbs, Alfred
before 1945: SS officer in the SD, member of action commando of the security police in Kristiansand, Norway; involved in arranging the transport of Norwegian Jews to the annihilation camps
after 1945: until 1956 employed under "cover names" in the Federal Office for the Protection of the Constitution with the knowledge of the federal government; now works there under his real name as group leader in central department V

Zapf, Willi
before 1945: member of the SS guard unit in Sachsenhausen and Auschwitz (Oswiecim) concentration camps
after 1945: official in the administrative office of the Hessian provincial police in Wiesbaden

Zech-Nenntwich, Hans-Walter
before 1945: SS Obersturmführer
after 1945: for complicity in the murder of Polish Jews sentenced to four years' in prison in April 1964

Zietlow, Fritz
before 1945: SS Hauptsturmführer in department VI of the Reich Security Main Office, editor and government counsellor in the Ministry of Propaganda, NSDAP (No. 36 519), SS (No. 6 126)
after 1945: editor and correspondent in Hamburg-Volksdorf

Zipfel, Fritz
before 1945: SS leader, 1929 NSDAP, 1932 SS
after 1945: police inspector and head of a precinct in Freiburg

Zirpins, Dr. Walter
before 1945: SS Sturmbannführer (No. 342 009), head of the criminal investigation department in department IV (Gestapo) of the Reich Security Main Office, action in the "final solution of the Jewish question" in Warsaw and Litzmannstadt (Lodz)
after 1945: senior government counsellor and head of the provincial criminal police in Lower Saxony

Members of the Gestapo, SD and SS in the West Berlin Police Force

Altmann, Johannes
before 1945: secretary in the criminal investigation department in department IV A 3 of the Reich Security Main Office, 1 May 1933 NSDAP (No. 2 579 426)
after 1945: carries on the same official function as secretary in the criminal investigation department

Anton, Max
before 1945: 1933 Gestapo head office in Berlin
after 1945: secretary in the criminal investigation department

Birr, Franz
before 1945: SS Hauptsturmführer, first lieutenant in the security police and company commander of the fascist disciplinary police in Graudenz
after 1945: chief inspector of police

Boosfeld, Walter
before 1945: SS Obersturmführer (No. 254 223), adjutant to the commander of the

SS and police in Dnepropetrovsk, later in the police guard battalion in Denmark, leader in the SS "Oberbayern" death head standarte in the Dachau concentration camp
after 1945: platoon leader in the action commando of the police inspectorate of West Berlin-Steglitz (see Table 21)

Burkhardt, Martin
before 1945: member of the Gestapo head office in Berlin, 1943 to 1945 in Norway
after 1945: secretary in the criminal investigation department

Durek, Josef
before 1945: member of the Gestapo head office in Berlin
after 1945: police employee

Ebel, Rudolf
before 1945: member of the SS, senior assistant in the criminal investigation department in the Gestapo head office in Berlin
after 1945: police employee

Feussner, Konrad
before 1945: senior government inspector and chief police inspector in department IV/C 2 of the Reich Security Main Office, 1933 from police headquarters to the Gestapo (Gestapo head office in Berlin)
after 1945: senior government inspector in the police service

Gabriel, Kurt
before 1945: police assistant in the Gestapo head office in Berlin
after 1945: government inspector

Gehrmann, Kurt
before 1945: commander of the Ist SS police regiment 4, among other things participated in the persecution of Jews
after 1945: sentenced to 25 years in prison by the Soviet Military Court, 1955 handed over to the West Berlin authorities for the purpose of the completion of his sentence; there, however, he was engaged as an inspector in the West Berlin police

Götsche, Ernst
before 1945: SS Obersturmführer in an SS police division
after 1945: police inspector

Graurock, Wilhelm
before 1945: SS Hauptsturmführer; committed war crimes in the Soviet Union, Croatia and Denmark
after 1945: chief inspector in the headquarters of the West Berlin security police

Gross, Gerhard
before 1945: SS Sturmbannführer, commander in the 4th SS police panzer grenadier division, SS (No. 422 185)
after 1945: leader of squadron north of the traffic police

Günther, Johannes
before 1945: senior assistant in the criminal investigation department of the Gestapo head office in Berlin
after 1945: secretary in the criminal investigation department

Haak, Wilhelm
before 1945: crime secretary in department IV/A 4 of the Reich Security Main Office
after 1945: secretary in the criminal investigation department

Hartmann, Willi
before 1945: company chief and battalion commander of SS police regiment 15, action against Jews in the Soviet Union, 1944 head of the IInd battalion which was subordinate to the SS units of SS Brigadeführer Zimmermann in Italy
after 1945: chief inspector of police in the West Berlin security police

Hayn, Wilhelm (former name Wojtecki)
before 1945: secretary in the criminal investigation department and SS Untersturmführer in the Reich Security Main Office from 1937 to 1945
after 1945: senior secretary in the criminal investigation department

Helbing, Willi
before 1945: member of the Gestapo
after 1945: police inspector

Herden, August
before 1945: police secretary in department IV/E 2 of the Reich Security Main Office
after 1945: official in the criminal investigation department

Heublein, Adolf
before 1945: member of the Gestapo
after 1945: inspector in the criminal investigation department

Hild, Hermann
before 1945: SS Hauptsturmführer of the armed SS (No. 326 677)

after 1945: inspector of police in the police inspectorate of West Berlin-Tempelhof

Holzhäuser, Walter
before 1945: member of the Reich Security Main Office and assistant in the criminal investigation department of the Gestapo
after 1945: senior secretary in the criminal investigation department

Huhn, Kurt
before 1945: 1943 captain and company chief of SS police regiment 14, adjutant to the commanding officer of the disciplinary police in Croatia; participated in crimes against Poles, Jews and Yugoslavs
after 1945: senior police superintendent, group commander for the US sector of West Berlin

Jaeger, Augustinus
before 1945: SS Untersturmführer and senior secretary of police in the Gestapo head office in Berlin
after 1945: senior police secretary

Johanningmeier, Wilhelm
before 1945: SS Obersturmbannführer (No. 313 901), major in the security police, member of the military police, commander of the IIIrd police regiment 9 in the Soviet Union, NSDAP (No. 1 169 368)
after 1945: inspector of police, precinct superintendent of the police inspectorate of West Berlin-Tiergarten

Jungnickel, Helmut
before 1945: senior police secretary in department IV/C 2 of the Reich Security Main Office, temporarily engaged in the police of Litzmannstadt (Lodz)
after 1945: police secretary

Kamptz, Imanuel von
before 1945: volunteer in the armed SS, captain in the security police
after 1945: inspector of police, confidential agent of the inspectorate of West Berlin-Kreuzberg

Kania, Josef
before 1945: member of the Gestapo
after 1945: secretary in the criminal investigation department

Kirsch, Georg
before 1945: SS Hauptsturmführer and captain of the security police, member of the SS "Prinz Eugen" volunteer division which participated in crimes against Yugoslav citizens
after 1945: commander of the action commando of the inspectorate of Wilmersdorf

Kleist-Bornstedt, Artur von
before 1945: SS Sturmbannführer (No. 340 713), major in the security police, staff of SS main sector in Fulda-Werra
after 1945: inspector of police, head of police precinct 122

Kohlmorgen, Hans-Joachim
before 1945: SS Obersturmführer, head of a country constabulary prefecture; participated in mass shootings of the civilian population in Mosyr and surroundings (USSR)
after 1945: senior police superintendent in the inspectorate of West Berlin-Charlottenburg

Kramer, Otto
before 1945: member of the SS, action commando III in Croatia
after 1945: secretary in the criminal investigation department

Krumholz, Kurt
before 1945: SS Sturmbannführer (No. 493 015), NSDAP (No. 4 313 349), staff leader to the higher commander of the SS and police in Hungary
after 1945: leader of the action commando of the police inspectorate of West Berlin-Charlottenburg

Mehl, Gerhard
before 1945: secretary in the criminal investigation department in the Gestapo, 1 May 1933 NSDAP
after 1945: senior secretary in the criminal investigation department

Menzel, Hubert
before 1945: member of action commando 8
after 1945: police sergeant in West Berlin-Spandau

Nawrot, Hans
before 1945: member of the Gestapo
after 1945: official in the criminal investigation department

Neumann, Kurt
before 1945: member of the SD and Gestapo head offices in Berlin and Königsberg

after 1945: secretary in the criminal investigation department

Paetzold, Erich

before 1945: member of SS police regiment 4, took part in the so-called "combating of gangs" (partisans), major in the security police
after 1945: member of the West Berlin police

Paulie, Reinhold

before 1945: member of the Gestapo
after 1945: senior assistant in the criminal investigation department

Remer, Willi

before 1945: SS Obersturmführer in department IV/C 4 of the Reich Security Main Office
after 1945: chief police inspector

Rossbach, Hermann

before 1945: member of the 1st SS brigade
after 1945: secretary in the criminal investigation department

Samuel, Hermann

before 1945: police inspector and SS Hauptsturmführer in the Reich Security Main Office, last in department IV/F 5, deputy section head
after 1945: police inspector

Schild, Karl

before 1945: member of the Gestapo head office in Berlin, secretary in the criminal investigation department
after 1945: police secretary

Schimkat, Hellmut

before 1945: first lieutenant in the security police and SS Hauptsturmführer (No. 46052)
after 1945: police inspector

Schulz, Karl

before 1945: SS Hauptsturmführer in the Führer's escort detachment
after 1945: leader of the action commando of the inspectorate of West Berlin-Tiergarten

Sommer, Ferdinand

before 1945: senior assistant in the criminal investigation department in department IV/A 1 of the Reich Security Main Office
after 1945: secretary in the criminal investigation department

Sperber, Paul

before 1945: SS Untersturmführer, member of the SD
after 1945: member of the West Berlin police

Stubbe, Erwin

before 1945: 1934 joined the Gestapo, finally chief police inspector in the Gestapo office in Berlin
after 1945: chief police inspector

Togotzes, Werner

before 1945: SS Hauptsturmführer, central office of the SD
after 1945: head of the section north of the criminal investigation department

Uhden, Johannes

before 1945: SS Untersturmführer, first lieutenant of the security police, member of an SS police division
after 1945: inspector of police, deputy head of the action commando of the security police in West Berlin-Tiergarten

Wassenberg, Hans

before 1945: SS Sturmbannführer in department IV/K 1 of the Reich Security Main Office (No. 280100), NSDAP (No. 1772317)
after 1945: police official

Werner, Hans-Ulrich

before 1945: August 1944 first staff officer to the SS and police commander in Upper Italy centre, responsible for the planning of the actions of the country constabulary and the police commandos against the civilian population
after 1945: senior police superintendent, deputy head of the Hiltrup police institute, now commander of the West Berlin security police

Wittek, Josef

before 1945: assistant in the criminal investigation department in the Gestapo head office in Berlin
after 1945: assistant in the criminal investigation department

RE-ESTABLISHMENT OF JUSTICE BY TERROR

Bonn Justice Is Based on Nazi Injustice

The legal system was also one of the "Third Reich's" inhuman instruments of terror. It helped to prepare the way for the reactionary fascist suppression at home and its aggressive policy abroad. When the nazi dictatorship had been established the judiciary began by persecuting Hitler's opponents from all social classes and of all creeds. The decrees and laws issued in 1933–34 gave the nazi lawyers a welcome pretext for suppressing with much bloodshed all opposition to the tyranny. Let us recall such legislative hotchpotch as

the "Decree concerning treason against the German people and treasonable activities" of 28 February 1933,

the "Decree on the acceleration of proceedings concerned with high treason" of 18 March 1933,

the "Decree on defence against treacherous attacks on the government of the national uprising" (i. e. National Socialist seizure of power) of 21 March 1933,

the "Decree on the formation of special courts" of 21 March 1933,

the "Decree on the competence of the special courts" of 6 May 1933,

the "Law on the pronouncement and execution of the death sentence" of 29 May 1933,

the "Law for defence against political atrocities" of 4 April 1933,

the "Law for the guarantee of judicial peace" of 13 October 1933,

the "Law on the amendment of regulations concerning penal law and criminal procedure" of 24 April 1934,

the "Law against malicious gossip" of 20 December 1934, and

the "Law against dangerous habitual criminals, Measures for security and improvement" of 24 November 1933.

THE AUTHOR IS A MINISTERIAL DIRECTOR IN BONN

The man who at that time contributed decisively to the creation of these murder laws, Government Counsellor in the nazi Ministry of Justice Dr. Josef Schafheutle, today makes use of his experience as ministerial director in the Federal

Ministry of Justice. He commented triumphantly in his concoction: *"The most important change is the sharpening of penalties"*. (*Die Strafgesetznovellen von 1933 und 1934* – Amendments to the Penal Laws of 1933 and 1934, Berlin 1934, p. 137)

Schafheutle was to be proven right: thousands of German anti-fascists were imprisoned on the basis of these laws, carried off to concentration camps, delivered up to the hangman or tortured to death in the Gestapo cellars.

With the aid of the "Decree on the formation of special courts" and of the "Law on the amendment of regulations concerning penal law and criminal procedure" a complete network of special courts for terrorizing the population was set up in Germany in the form of the notorious people's courts and special courts.

Even before, or immediately after, fascist Germany's occupation of the neighbouring states, new laws of terror against the German population and the oppressed peoples were created which served, without exception, the nazi aims of destroying dissenters, other peoples and races. They were such laws as

the "Decree on wrong-doers against the people" of 5 September 1939,

the "Decree concerning special war-time penal laws" of 17 August 1938,

the "Decree on violent criminals" of 5 December 1939,

the "Decree of the Reich Protector in Bohemia and Moravia against acts of sabotage" of 26 August 1939,

the "Law on the change of instructions for general penal procedures, military penal procedures and the penal code" of 16 September 1939,

the "Decree on the administration of criminal law against Poles and Jews" of 4 December 1941,

the "Decree of the military commander in Belgium and Northern France" of 13 June 1940,

the "Edict on the exercise of the jurisdiction of the Wehrmacht in Denmark against persons of non-German nationality" of 1 August 1940,

the "Decree on the prohibition of political parties in Norway" of 25 September 1940,

the "Decree on the prohibition of activity in favour of the Norwegian royal family" of 7 October 1940,

the "Decree of the Reich Commissar of the occupied Norwegian territories on the state of civil emergency" of 31 July 1941,

the "Undercover decree" of 7 December 1942, etc.

These coercive and terror laws were largely "legal" foundations for the activities of the nazi emergency jurisdiction. This consisted of:

the special courts, which, after the "Decree on the formation of special courts" of 21 March 1933, were created in every superior provincial court district in Germany, the "People's Court", which – as has already been mentioned – came into existence on the basis of Schafheutle's "Amendments to the penal laws",

the military courts which were re-introduced by the Hitler government's law of 12 May 1933,

the Reich Military Court, the highest court of the Wehrmacht, which began its activities on 26 June 1936 and the infamous "summary courts of justice" which were set up during the war by the "Decree of the Reich Minister of Justice" by "Order of the Führer".

The special courts aimed firstly at silencing all opposition to Hitler, so that, by "grave-yard peace" at home, aggression abroad could be prepared. The accused were deprived of practically all their rights.

The Reich Court confirmed this characteristic of the special courts in a verdict of 9 November 1938 – reference number S T 537/38 – where it states that the special courts are *"courts which exist beyond the public jurisdiction, not only in name but also in their nature"*. Wolfgang Idel, today provincial court director in Düsseldorf wrote in his dissertation *Die Sondergerichte für politische Strafsachen* (The Special Courts for Political Criminal Cases), Freiburg, 1935, on page 36, that the task of these courts consisted in,

"completely exterminating all opponents of the Third Reich, particularly communists and social democrats".

In their dissertations Robert Fuchs *Die Sondergerichtsbarkeit in Deutschland* (The Special Jurisdiction in Germany), Tübingen, 1937, and Adolf Schlesinger *Die Entwicklung der deutschen Gerichtsorganisation seit 1879* (The Development of the German Judicial System since 1879), Jena, 1938, came to similar conclusions.

From the duties of these courts of terror it can be seen that the judges and public prosecutors were the most trustworthy and ruthless fascists.

After Hitler Germany had invaded the neighbouring states, special courts were established in almost all occupied countries thus violating the Hague Agreement on Land Warfare. They carried out, by means of the "administration of juristice", Hitler's and Himmler's extermination orders. The most horrible balance is shown by the nazi special courts in Poland. On the basis of the infamous Decree on penal law in Poland, thousands of Polish citizens were sent to the scaffold, simply for recognizing Poland as their own nation, for opposing the policy of starvation or because they were branded as "worthless lives" on the directives laid down by Globke's register of the population.

The special courts, which were first created to pass judgement on political "offences", pronounced death sentences, under conditions of total war both in Germany and in the occupied states, for insignificant offences, for example, minor thefts of food, which would go unpunished in civilized countries and would be regarded as a case of pilfering.

The People's Court was formed in 1934 and was at first responsible for cases of high treason. The structure of the people's courts clearly reveals that it was an important constituent of the system of special courts in the fascist state. It reveals quite clearly that the members of the People's Court were appointed by Hitler personally and the remaining employees of the People's Court by the Reich minister of justice. In addition to the professional judges, representatives of the nazi party and the fascist Wehrmacht were present at every session as "special judges".

The people's court was made particularly notorious under the presidency of the bloodthirsty lawyer, Freisler, and by proceedings against such upright Germans as Lieselotte Hermann, Judith Auer, Werner Seelenbinder, Anton Saefkow, Franz Jacob, Hilde and Hans Coppi, Georg Schumann, Bernhard Bästlein, Adam Kuckhoff as well as the Czechoslovakian patriot and journalist Julius Fučik. The proceedings against those who took part in the officers' revolt of 20 July 1944 before the People's Court also attracted the attention of the world to this supreme criminal court.

The martial jurisdiction of the nazi Wehrmacht was a special legal system similar to the fascist special courts and the People's Court. It was introduced at almost the same time as the special courts. From 26 June 1936 the Reich Military Court served as the supreme court of the Wehrmacht. The re-introduction of military courts in times of peace proves among other things that the nazis were preparing for a war against the European peoples from the very first day of their rule in 1933; for the military courts were created to safeguard the army of invasion against all "demoralizing" ideas of democracy and peace. This is emphasized even more by the fact that the "Decree on military criminal procedure in war and during special operations" and the notorious 'Decree on the special penal law in war and during special operations" were issued as early as 17 August 1938.

During the war Hitler's military courts also assumed the role of special courts for the civilian population in some occupied states like Holland, Belgium, France, Norway and Denmark. They vented their fury in Czechoslovakia and Poland too until the special courts for civilians were set up.

80,000 DEATH SENTENCES

The then state secretary in the nazi Ministry of Justice, Dr. Roland Freisler, introduced this darkest chapter in the history of German legal administration on 24 October 1939 at a conference of the presidents of the special courts and official experts in cases coming up before special courts, with these words:

"He (the legislator – author) moulds the procedure of administering the penal

law into a sword, to be handled with superiority, in the hand of the judge ... moreover he (the legislator – author), wherever it is at all required, makes it permissible to exceed the general framework of penalties, which was previously accepted as appropriate, often to the extent of pronouncing the death sentence ... The legislator does this and continues to do so." In the same breath he came to the statement: *"The decisive factor is, however, that the observance of the penal law does so! That it wants to, is obvious. That it does so, however, is decisive."*

They did it. They fulfilled with the utmost precision their task as *"summary courts of the home front"* – as nazi Minister of Justice Thierack called the special courts in a letter of 5 July 1943 to the presidents of the superior provincial courts and public prosecutors. Their horrifying balance according to statistics, which are not complete: about 50,000 death sentences. In addition there are more than 25,000 other death sentences from the military courts. This does not include the sentences of the Reich Military Court. (Convictions according to the criminal statistics of the DKW (Supreme Command of the Wehrmacht) HR 6 – III d and IV c for the period from 26 August 1939 to November – December 1944 for the army and up to and including the second quarter 1944 for the airforce and navy).

Since the ruthlessness of the military courts and the summary courts reached its peak during the last months of the war, the number of death sentences pronounced by the military courts – without the Reich Military Court – can be safely estimated at at least 30,000. Thus the total number of death sentences amounts to at least 80,000.

The jurists who cooperated in the nazi emergency jurisdiction either directly by "creating laws" or indirectly by "administering justice" are implicated in the fact that

the Hitler dictatorship was able to become established and last for twelve years;

aggression abroad could be prepared for by aggression at home;

Hitler's occupation regime could be built up and remained in existence until the very last;

the laws characterized as criminal in the Nuremberg lawyer trials came into being and were put into practice;

in many cases even the inhuman penalties of the nazi terror laws were exceeded;

tens of thousands of people fighting for their nation or for their lives were simply murdered.

They exclusively served injustice and inhumanity, whether they pronounced judgements in Germany against Germans or against those doing forced labour who, moreover, were exposed to the most dire distress or whether they were active at the front against German soldiers or in the occupied states against the population which was deprived of its rights, humiliated and pillaged.

PURIFICATION OF JUSTICE – A BINDING DUTY

In the Nuremberg trial of jurists the American court came to this conclusion:

"The essence of the accusation in this case is that the laws, Hitler's decrees and the draconic, corrupt and depraved national socialist legal system, as such, represent in themselves war crimes and crimes against humanity and that participation in issuing and carrying out these laws implies criminal complicity ... The accusation, in short, is that of conscious participation in a system of cruelty and injustice, spread over the whole country and organized by the government, in violation of the laws of war and the laws of humanity, committed in the name of justice and of the authority of the Ministry of Justice and with the aid of the courts. The murderer's dagger was concealed beneath the robe of the jurist. (Das Nürnberger Juristenurteil – The Judgement in the Nuremberg Jurists' Trial – Allgemeiner Teil, Hamburg, 1948, p. 42)

Therefore the Allied Control Council decreed in article IV of its law no. 4 of 30 October 1945 on the basis of the Potsdam Agreement:

"For the purpose of transforming the German legal system, all previous members of the nazi party who took an active part in its activities, and all other persons who were directly involved in the methods of punishment of the Hitler regime must be deprived of their office as judges and public prosecutors and may not be re-admitted to such offices."

On the basis of democratic international law the United Nations Economic and Social Council (ECOSOC) adopted the following resolution on 28 July 1965:

1. All states are called upon to continue their efforts to ensure that, in accordance with international law and national legislation, those criminals responsible for war crimes and crimes against humanity are to be traced, seized and punished appropriately by the competent courts. They should cooperate for this purpose, especially by making available all documents they have on such crimes.
2. All states concerned which have not yet joined the Convention on the prevention and punishment of crimes of genocide of 9 December 1948 are called upon to do so as soon as possible.

THE GDR ESTABLISHED ORDER

In the German Democratic Republic these obligations were fulfilled. Jurists who were active members of the NSDAP and participated in the legislation or jurisdiction of the "Third Reich" were removed at once from the judicial system in

1945. Their place was taken by anti-fascist lawyers, members of the resistance, workers, peasants and office employees. There is not one judge or public prosecutor in the GDR who belonged to the NSDAP.

Jurists who took part in the terror sentences were justly punished, as was, for example, the previous public prosecutor in the special court in Leipzig, Dr. Dr. Anger, who was proved to have been involved in a judicial murder in 1945. Having served a long term of imprisonment in the GDR he was welcomed in West Germany and employed as public prosecutor in Essen. Even a criminal lawyer like the previous assessor of the special court in Posen (Poznan), Johannes Breier, who had succeeded in disappearing as keeper of the archives in a factory did not escape his punishment. When documents concerning his participation in death sentences were discovered the district court at Schwerin sentenced him to eight years' imprisonment.

His still more heavily incriminated superiors in the nazi special court in Posen (Poznan), Bömmels and Hucklenbroich, on the other hand became duly installed jurists in West Germany, Bömmels as senate president in Saarbrücken and Hucklenbroich as provincial court director in Wuppertal. Today they receive high pensions and they have avoided criminal procedures up till now. Their accomplice, Dr. Jungmann, formerly public prosecutor in the special court in Posen, is still in office as public prosecutor in Essen.

The legal administration of the GDR, which was completely rebuilt on the basis of humanist German legal traditions, punished and expiated all nazi and war crimes as a matter of course.

COMPREHENSIVE LEGAL AID

The GDR has always regarded it as its right and duty to point to the dangerous development in West Germany and to demand that the past be consistently overcome. It gave legal aid in 113 trials of nazi and war criminals in West Germany. It supplied West German judicial authorities with innumerable preliminary inquiries, e. g. the Bernburg region alone made available material against 78 persons in 1948. In the Auschwitz trial in Frankfurt-on-Main, the greatest West German post-war trial of nazi and war criminals, the GDR is represented by the representative of the co-plaintiffs, Professor Dr. Kaul.

A further 1,580 death sentences in which lawyers working in West Germany collaborated were handed over to the West German legal authorities and 4,000 documents on other nazi or war crimes handed over or sent.

Finally the GDR has named, at numerous press conferences since 1955, a total of 1,310 former jurists previously belonging to the nazi emergency courts, who are again in office in West Germany.

What happened to the guilty nazi jurists in West Germany?
Were they removed from office?
Were they justly punished?

BONN PROTECTS THE MURDERERS

Contrary to official announcements of the Federal Ministry of Justice, more than 800 jurists of the nazi emergency courts are still practising in West Germany. Not one of the nazi lawyers, some charged with over 100 death sentences, were brought to trial. These "administrators of justice", who without exception served inhumanity, injustice and aggression have, up to now, again reached the highest positions in the West German state and judicial system.

Even nazi and war criminals legally sentenced by states of the anti-Hitler coalition were employed by Bonn in full knowledge of their past. Thus, for exemple, Dr. Leonhard Drach was promoted public prosecutor in Frankenthal in 1956 and later senior public prosecutor although as a nazi public prosecutor in courts martial and special courts in occupied Luxemburg he had requested many death sentences which had been complied with. After 1945 Drach was sentenced in Luxemburg to 20 and 15 years in prison for his crimes.

Former public prosecutor Josef Wienecke at a special court in Luxemburg who after 1945 was sentenced to ten years imprisonment in absentia because he did not return from a leave on parole became public prosecutor in Koblenz in 1953. Later he was promoted first public prosecutor although his past was known.

The former employee of the nazi administration of justice Dr. Otto Bauknecht who was sentenced to four years in prison after the liberation of Luxemburg was also installed in office in West Germany in 1956, first as provincial court president in Kreuznach. Today young jurists have to prove their qualification for the West German juridical service in the first and second state examination before him who is now president of the juridical examination office.

Even the chairman of the special court in Luxemburg Adolf Raderschall – sentenced to death in absentia – as a provincial court director retired, serves in Rhineland-Palatinate as a lower court counsellor and is now an old-age pensioner with a pension exceeding many times those of his victims. Drach, Wienecke and Bauknecht have not yet been removed from their offices up to this day despite protests from Luxemburg. (Data from *Der Spiegel*, Hamburg, 5 May 1965 and 3 February 1965 and *Die Welt*, Hamburg, 15 July 1965)

Dr. Kurt Bellmann, hanging judge in Prague who was sentenced to life imprisonment in Czechoslovakia and delivered to the Federal Republic as a non-amnestied person became provincial court director in Hanover. Bellmann was responsible for 110 proved death sentences against Czechoslovak citizens. Today he receives a monthly pension of more than 2,000 marks as remuneration for his murders.

The effects of the Bonn policy of protecting and promoting nazi and war criminals and the identification of Bonn with the "Third Reich" are clearly reflected in the Schlegelberger family.

The father, Dr. Franz Schlegelberger, was acting minister of justice in the Hitler government in 1941–42. During his period in office and with his approval the organs of justice killed thousands of German and foreign opponents of the Hitler war. Jews who were sentenced to imprisonment by the courts were executed on the order of Schlegelberger. The notorious "undercover decree" which provided for the imprisonment of all Hitler opponents without an arrest warrant was worked out by him, too. During his period in office the "criminal law decree against Poles" was issued, which instructed all special courts to pass death sentences for the slightest offences. He himself proposed that half-Jews be sterilized or deported.

Schlegelberger was sentenced to life imprisonment for his crimes in the Nuremberg jurists' trial. But today Bonn remunerates his blood guilt with a monthly pension of 1,450 marks.

His son Hartwig sentenced German soldiers to death as senior staff judge of the nazi navy and participated in their execution in the Brandenburg prison. (See Table 22)

Today Dr. Hartwig Schlegelberger as minister of the interior of Schleswig-Holstein sees to it that this province is a paradise for war criminals. His special care is devoted to the preparation of the emergency dictatorship. On the occasion of an official visit of Danish Prime Minister Krag Hartwig Schlegelberger tried in a fascist manner to force upon him the involvement of Denmark in his emergency plans. Prime Minister Krag reacted upon this encroachment on the sovereignty of his country by "ignoring" Schlegelberger's statements. (*Süddeutsche Zeitung*, Stuttgart, 26–27 June 1965)

The second son of the leading blood jurist of Hitler Germany, Günther Schlegelberger, earlier served in the Ribbentrop Foreign Office. He, of all persons, was named ambassador to Saigon by the Erhard government, where he is one of the wire-pullers for the support and extension of the barbaric war of invasion of the USA as official representative of the Federal Republic.

THE WAGES OF CRIME

All seriously incriminated nazi jurists who had to retire from their offices after revelations of the GDR, Czechoslovakia, the People's Republic of Poland, France, and the protests of democratic forces throughout the world received high pensions from the day of their retirement, pensions which exceed by far the indemnifications of their victims.

These wages of crime were legally fixed by paragraph 116 of the West German judges law of 8 September 1961. According to it those hanging judges who retired receive full pensions even before reaching the retirement age. All those who did not abandon their sphere of influence voluntarily by 30 June 1962 were to be retired from office without payment according to a Bundestag decision of 14 June 1961. But up to the present day no case has become known in which one of the seriously incriminated nazi jurists was removed from his position without reward and by force. This means that Bonn even disregarded its own mild regulations in order to protect the murderers in judges' robes. The following seriously incriminated jurists, among others, had to retire from office and receive pensions of from 1,300 up to 2,000 marks:

Name of jurist	Pensioned in	Number of death sentences proved by the GDR or Czechoslovakia
1	2	3
Dr. Bruchhaus before 1945: public prosecutor in the "People's Court" after 1945: public prosecutor in Wuppertal	May 1961	33
Dr. Bömmels before 1945: provincial court director in the special court in Posen (Poznan) after 1945: senate president in the Superior Provincial Court in Saarbrücken	September 1961	44
Dannegger, Dr. Johannes before 1945: provincial court counsellor in the special court, Prague after 1945: senior judge in Wiedenbrück	May 1961	29
Fränkel, Wolfgang before 1945: deputy Reich prosecutor in the Reich Court in Leipzig 1962: federal prosecutor general	July 1962	50
Eisele, Dr. Walter before 1945: lower court counsellor and senate president in the special court, Prague, Czechoslovak war criminal list No. A-38/65 after 1945: superior provincial court counsellor in Stuttgart	July 1962	32
Heine before 1945: lower court counsellor in the special court, Prague after 1945: lower court counsellor in Duisburg	May 1961	46
Dr. Hucklenbroich before 1945: provincial court counsellor in the special court, Posen (Poznan) after 1945: provincial court director in Wuppertal	March 1961	63

Name of jurist	Pensioned in	Number of death sentences proved by the GDR or Czechoslovakia
1	2	3
Jaager before 1945: public prosecutor in the special court, Vienna, and accuser in the "People's Court" after 1945: first public prosecutor in the Superior Provincial Court in Schleswig	August 1959	13
Dr. Lenhardt before 1945: provincial court director, accuser in the "People's Court" after 1945: senior public prosecutor in Neustadt on the Weinstrasse	June 1960	24
Ludwig, Dr. Franz before 1945: senior public prosecutor in the special court, Prague after 1945: public prosecutor in Düsseldorf	March 1961	77
Michalowski before 1945: provincial court counsellor in the special court, Bromberg (Bydgosccz) Polish war criminal list No. III/18 after 1945: lower court counsellor in Mönchen-Gladbach	March 1963	58
Dr. Mohs before 1945: provincial court counsellor in the special court, Hohensalza (Inowraclaw) after 1945: provincial court counsellor in Frankenthal	January 1961	81
Dr. Reimers before 1945: supreme court counsellor, judge in the special court, Berlin and in the "People's Court" after 1945: provincial court counsellor in Ravensburg	January 1963	124
Weiss, Klaus before 1945: provincial court director in the special court, Zichenau (Ciechanov) after 1945: provincial court counsellor in Oldenburg	May 1962	127
von Zeschau before 1945: provincial court counsellor, accuser in the "People's Court" after 1945: provincial court counsellor in Nuremberg	December 1962	18
von Zeynek, Dr. Wolfgang before 1945: public prosecutor in the special court, Prague after 1945: provincial court counsellor in Nuremberg	December 1962	112

The preliminary inquiries which had to be introduced by reason of charges by the Association of Anti-fascist Resistance Fighters of Czechoslovakia or West German citizens were stopped by the West German courts. This happened, for example, in the case of the former deputy Reich prosecutor, Fränkel. This nazi lawyer was prosecutor general in West Germany in 1962!

The Superior Provincial Court in Karlsruhe said, on 3 September 1964, on discontinuing the preliminary proceedings, *"the possibility of proof . . . that the accused ever doubted the validity of the regulations mentioned, let alone recognized their invalidity, during the war . . . is lacking"*. Fränkel who was charged by the GDR with 50 murders is granted *"inconclusive evidence"* in this decision *"which excludes proof of intent"*.

This implies nothing less than sanctioning the crimes of the robed murderers and vindicating the nazi regime.

The reason for this ingenious argumentation becomes obvious when one knows the role which these servants of injustice were to play in West Germany. They stood in the first rank in the setting up of a special political justice, in the working out of new arbitrary laws and finally in the preparation of a military dictatorship.

HITLER'S SPECIAL COURTS AS EXAMPLE

Dr. Ernst Kanter, former judge in the Reich Court, chief judge in occupied Denmark and general judge of the nazi Wehrmacht, had an authoritative share in the construction of the special justice of West Germany on the model of the nazi special courts. Kanter was shown to have committed the most serious crimes by the GDR and Danish citizens and authorities.

Bonn installed him as highest judge of political attitudes as senate president of the third penal senate of the Federal Supreme Court. Here he examined the nazi jurists active in his sphere. On 26 November 1957 he wrote to the *Deutsche Volkszeitung* in Düsseldorf that *"it could be stated without more ado that reproaches which could be the occasion for penal or disciplinary punishments can not be justified"*.

Under his supervision a whole network of political special courts came into existence. As the nazis had a special court in every superior provincial court district a special political court now exists in every superior provincial court district in West Germany. One of the most notorious jurists of these special political courts was Public Prosecutor Ottersbach in Lüneburg who won his laurels as public prosecutor in the special court, Kattowitz (Katowice). (See page 135 and Table 23)

200,000 POLITICAL PROCEEDINGS

The juridical basis for the reintroduction of the political attitude justice is the first criminal change law (lightning law) of 30 August 1951. This law was worked out by the already mentioned former government counsellor in the nazi

Ministry of Justice and present ministerial director in the Federal Ministry of Justice, Dr. Josef Schafheutle. He took his "experiences" from his terror laws of 1933 on the basis of which the notorious People's Court and the nazi special courts came into existence; they delivered tens of thousands of citizens of almost all European countries to the hangman. Since the coming into force of Schafheutle's lightning law in 1951 until the end of 1961, 200,000 political proceedings were carried through according to information of the 11th working session of the West German amnesty committee and the defending counsels in political criminal proceedings which affected 500,000 West German citizens.

Prominent representatives of the CDU/CSU have for years been demanding the reintroduction of the death penalty for political acts. Bundestag Vice-President Jaeger (CSU) demanded this already in 1957 (*Frau und Politik* – Women and Politics, Bonn, 15 December 1957), and no less a person than the then minister of justice Schäffer (CSU) wanted to introduce the death penalty for "high treason" in 1958. (*Neue Ruhr-Zeitung*, Essen, 14 June 1958) At a press conference on 25 June 1965 in Berlin Max Reimann, secretary of the Communist Party of Germany, revealed the alarming fact that the endeavours of the West German emergency politicians in the legal committee of the Bundestag – which always closely cooperated with Schafheutle in the preparation of laws hostile to the people – have already reached the stage of the bill on the reintroduction of the death penalty.

THE NEW PENAL CODE – A NAZI LAW

At the same time Schafheutle is responsible to the Federal Ministry of Justice for working out the draft of the penal code, which contains a number of increased penalties, for example, for "high treason", these sometimes corresponding in content or word for word with the definitions of 1933–34 which were formulated by him.

Besides Schafheutle, 23 well-known lawyers work or worked in the "Great Penal Law Commission". Sixteen of them had already held important judicial posts during the nazi dictatorship, among them

- *the former president of the Senate of the Federal Supreme Court, Dr. Kanter,*
- *the prosecutor general in 1962, Fränkel, who was charged with 50 murders by the GDR and now draws a monthly pension of at least 2,500 marks, and*
- *the former official expert for political crimes in the nazi Ministry of Justice, Dr. Wilkerling, today ministerial director in the Ministry of Justice of Lower Saxony.*

With the new draft of the penal code, the administration of justice with regard to political convictions, the proceedings against patriots, opponents of nuclear war and emergency legislation are to be intensified even more. Moreover, it directly serves Bonn's aggressive aims. The official explanation on paragraph 3 ("The German penal law applies to crimes which are committed within the country") states, for example:

"The country includes, concerning the present situation in international law, besides the regions which belong to the area where the penal code is in force (i.e., the Federal Republic) also those which lie beyond this area. This includes the Soviet occupation zone of Germany, the Soviet sector of Berlin and the remaining areas of the German Reich within the borders of 31 December 1937, which are at present under foreign administration."

The draft states further, that an introductory law must determine the penalties coming into force for crimes *"which are committed on German territory but beyond the area where the penal law is in force (i.e., Federal Republic)"*. However, it explicitly emphasizes: *"The draft, however, does not intend to determine these principles (for the transition period) in the penal code intended for long-term use."*

Thus it is openly stated what areas are to be annexed. Thus the West German penal code fully serves the armament monopolies and the Hitler generals whose sole aim is to have their revenge for the defeat in the Second World War.

The effect that the penal code has had, even before its acceptance, was shown by the arrest of the chief editor of the Deutschlandsender broadcasting station, Dr. Grasnick at the end of July 1962. Even Public Prosecutor, Loesdau had to admit that Dr. Grasnick was guilty of no crime within West German territory. He was arrested only on account of his activities in the GDR, he said.

SPECIALISTS IN DICTATORSHIP CREATED THE EMERGENCY LAWS

As in the case of the new penal code – intended as a part of a system based on emergency laws – Hitler's specialists in dictatorship were also authors of the emergency laws. Bonn's Minister of the Interior Höcherl is mainly responsible for the draft of the emergency laws, having served the Hitler dictatorship as public prosecutor in Regensburg on the basis of available testimony. In this position he demanded the death penalty for a Polish citizen, because of a love affair with a German girl shortly before the end of the war.

As the former chairman of the Bundestag's Commission on Justice – he is now defence delegate in the Bundestag – Matthias Hoogen (CDU/CSU) (Christian Democratic Union – Christian Social Union) pressed to get the dictatorship laws into force as quickly as possible. Hoogen was judge advocate with the nazi Luftwaffe and chief regimental judge with the "Kurlandarmee". (see p. 130 and

Table 24) Dr. Hans Globke, Adenauer's former state secretary, condemned to imprisonment for life in the GDR, also helped to draw up the drafts of the emergency laws. In addition to his ingenious murder directives against the Jewish population, Globke proved his "value" to the nazis by drafting the "law for removing the distress of the people and the country" of 1 June 1933 (Hitler's enabling act for Prussia).

The present ministerial director in the Bonn Ministry of the Interior and head of the "Constitution, Constitutional Law and Administration" department, Dr. Rudolf Toyka, is also one of the authors of the emergency laws. During the Second World War Toyka was a government counsellor with the "Reich governor" in Posen (Poznan), liaison man with the Gestapo and Himmler's Security Service.

Ministerial Counsellor Rippich is one of the emergency experts of the Ministry of the Interior. He gathered his experiences for this activity as SS leader under Himmler; he therefore thought it to be desirable to go into hiding in Argentina after 1945. In 1954 he was *"assigned to the Federal Ministry of the Interior ... on the basis of reliable recommendations"* as the *Hamburger Echo* noted on 18 November 1958.

In the Bonn Ministry of the Interior he organized the struggle against the democratic referendum action against the atomic armament of the Bundeswehr as head of the "psychological defence" special staff.

Dr. Stothfang, who worked as the head director of administration in the Federal Office for Labour Supply and Unemployment Insurance of the Federal Ministry of Labour until 1962, worked out the Emergency Service Act. Under Hitler he gained his spurs as ministerial counsellor to the notorious "Deputy for Labour Supply", Sauckel. In the Nuremberg trial nazi Gauleiter and SS General Sauckel, who organized the enforced deportation of hundreds of thousands of citizens from occupied countries and their employment in Germany as slave labourers, was sentenced to death.

Whoever knows these facts can no longer be surprised that the emergency laws have the same purpose as Hitler's dictatorship and forced labour laws – namely to secure the peace of the grave-yard at home so as to be able to realize aggressive political aims abroad. Nothing else could be expected from the lawgivers of fascist Germany, who serve the interests of the aggressive armament monopolies today, just as they did then.

CONCENTRATION CAMP MURDERER AND GESTAPO INFORMER GRANTS GENERAL AMNESTY

The fact that the West German judicial system is permeated with lawyers with blood on their hands and that they support Bonn's policy of aggression and its suppression of those holding other political beliefs is one of the reasons why there is no genuine prosecution of nazi and war criminals in West Germany.

Up to 1 January 1964 a total of 12,457 persons were charged with nazi crimes. But only 5,234 of them, i.e., 42 per cent, were sentenced. 3,872 of the accused, i.e. almost 1 in 3, were acquitted. The proceedings against 2,539 persons were discontinued. (Figures from *Die Verfolgung nationalsozialistischer Straftaten im Gebiet der Bundesrepublik Deutschland seit 1945* – The Prosecution of National Socialist Crimes in the Territory of the Federal Republic of Germany since 1945, Bonn, 1964)

The protection given by Bonn to the nazi and war criminals is particularly evident if one considers the degree of punishment of those condemned. West German Public Prosecutor Dr. Barbara Just-Dahlmann established:

"One mark per murder" or *"ten minutes of imprisonment per accused murder"*. (*Der Spiegel*, Hamburg, 1961, No. 51)

The so-called desk criminals, a stroke of whose pen wiped out the lives of hundreds of thousands of human beings, were excluded from any kind of prosecution from the very beginning.

Bonn's attempts to grant a general amnesty to all nazi and war criminals are as old as the Federal Republic itself. Already three months after its formation an act of amnesty ("Law on the granting of impunity") was adopted on 1 December 1949. These attempts reached their peak in the "Law on the calculation of the terms of limitation, which was announced on 13 April 1965 by the confidant of the Gestapo office at Stettin (Szczecin) and the murderer of the Leau concentration camp, Federal President Lübke.

Thereby the limitation of the time within which nazi murder and mass murder must be prosecuted is arbitrarily fixed for 31 December 1969. This statute violates all the norms of international law, which recognizes no statute of limitations for crimes against peace and humanity, no statute of limitations for war criminals. It is aimed against the will of the peoples, which is expressed in worldwide opposition to fascism, a will demanding just punishment for all war and nazi criminals.

This statute, which is contrary to international law, was drawn up – according to an announcement of the American press agency UPI on 18 March 1965 – by Hitler's lawgiver, Dr. Josef Schafheutle, who has already been named several times.

They Returned Bloody Verdicts

Berthold Wolfgang DEATH PENALTY FOR A LOVE AFFAIR

today: financial court counsellor in Hanover

Paul Berkheim, born on 10 August 1911, had to fight his way through life for years as a casual labourer. It was very difficult for him as a "half-Jew" to get a steady job during the regime of Globke's race laws. Eventually, in 1941, he succeeded, having had to adopt the second first name of Israel in accordance with Globke's name law, in finding employment as porter and occasional waiter. But after a short time he was again torn out of this situation – this time for ever.

Paul Berkheim had an "Aryan" girl-friend. According to Globke's "Law on the protection of the race" this was a crime, for according to his paragraphs 2 and 5, intercourse between Jews and "Aryans" was subject to penal servitude. In his commentary to paragraph 2 of the "Law for the protection of the race" Globke even wrote: *"They (the Nuremberg Laws – editor) force the half-caste, the bastard, to die out"*.

According to the verdict Paul Berkheim had *"committed three intentional crimes within a space of less than 5 years ... The assessment of the crime as a whole reveals that he is a dangerous habitual criminal."*

An original sentence of seven years imprisonment pronounced by the special court in Berlin was still not severe enough for the Reich Court. A plea of nullity was lodged. The case was taken to Berlin for a second trial.

At this second trial, which took place on 9 April 1943 before special court III in Berlin, the then public prosecutor, Dr. Berthold, acted as plaintiff. On his request Berkheim was *"condemned ... to death for contaminating the race in three instances"*. (Reference number: Sond. III I DKLs 35/42 – 783/42). The explanation for the verdict shows how little the nazi lawyers valued the life of a Jewish citizen. It says on this point, among other things: *"Bringing dishonour to the race is in itself a crime ... which is aimed against the stability of German nationhood ... wherever the German nation finds itself struggling for its ... future, threatened by world-wide Jewry ... The worthlessness of his personality ... makes any further toleration ... appear insufferable."*

This shameful verdict was already published four years ago by the Committee for German Unity in the document "Rewarded Murderers". Meanwhile a further five death sentences have been found on which Berthold worked. But to this day this murderer holds, completely unmolested, his high position as financial court counsellor in the Federal Republic. (See Table 25)

Dally **AN ATTEMPTED MURDER FRAME-UP**
Karl
today: provincial court director in Duisburg

Former nazi Judge Dally, now living in Duisburg and having advanced to provincial court director, condemned the Polish citizen Ignatz Lorenz to death for "attempted murder" on 5 November 1941 before the special court in Bromberg (Bydgoszcz). (Reference number: 6 SD Kls. 46/41)

A few days after the invasion of Poland by Hitler Germany, when some of the German minority, misused by the nazis as a 5th column, were committing wholesale acts of sabotage behind the lines of the Polish troops, Lorenz was supposed to have shot at a "Volksdeutsche" (i.e. folk German – persons of German origin living abroad) who was under arrest and accompanied by an armed Polish railway policeman. On the other hand, according to his evidence, Lorenz, who had met both of the persons by chance, had fired into the air when the man under arrest escaped. Neither the court nor the witnesses, who contradicted one another, could prove the contrary. Nevertheless the then nazi Judge Dally constructed from this a charge of attempted murder. He regarded as *"proven"* the charge that the accused had intended to kill with a base motive a *"defenceless German"*, whose crimes are shamefully kept secret in the verdict. Two years after the alleged crime he condemned him to death by the retrospective application of the nazi laws.

Dally also rejected the appeal for mercy. In the report of the attorney-general of 26 November 1941 in which mercy was refused it had to be admitted: *"That it could not be established whether Lorenz had shot at a fleeing German. However, the court has regarded as proven the charge that Lorenz fired at the man under arrest . . ."*

On 20 January 1942 the sentence was carried out by the executioner.

According to information which is as yet incomplete, Dally condemned 23 Polish citizens to death. Because of these crimes against humanity Dally was added to the list of war criminals by the Polish government. The GDR has been publishing documents signed by Dally since 1959. The West German Socialist Students' Union made indictments against him several years ago. Despite the great amount of conclusive evidence the public prosecutor stopped the preliminary proceedings begun against Dally in Duisburg on 16 August 1962 (Reference number: 14 Js 4 p 9/60). Dally still holds office today and can dispense "justice".

Dreher Eduard MORE SEVERE THAN THE SPECIAL COURT

today: ministerial director in the Federal Ministry of Justice, Bonn

At the proceedings of the special court at Innsbruck on 15 April 1942, Public Prosecutor Dr. Dreher demanded the death penalty for the Austrian pedlar Karoline Hauser. Frau Hauser had bought clothing coupons from a second-hand dealer who should have given them up for pulping. This meant that she could trade freely with clothing articles and underclothing, which had been rationed by the government in Austria since the nazi occupation. The special court did not accept Dreher's request. It condemned Frau Hauser to 15 years' imprisonment.

This did not satisfy Dreher. He wanted the death penalty at all events and moved a plea of nullity. The Reich Court then quashed the verdict and referred the matter once again to the special court at Innsbruck for a new decision. On 14 August 1942 Dreher again demanded the death penalty. This time too the special court turned down his proposal and sentenced her for a second time to 15 years' imprisonment. Dreher, however, succeeded in having her sent to a "work-house", i.e., a concentration camp, which in most cases meant the same as a death sentence. (Reference number: Kls. 37/42)

Another victim of Dreher's "legal conceptions" is the gardener Josef Knoflach against whom Dreher effected a death sentence from the Innsbruck special court because Knoflach had used a bicycle without authority and taken some foodstuffs, that is, the theft of food.

Dreher's name has already been mentioned in 1959 in the document *Wir klagen an* (We Accuse). This publication was sent to the Federal Ministry of Justice and to all important legal institutions. Yet not a hair of Dreher's head was hurt. On the contrary. After two representatives of the prosecutor general of the GDR in West Germany had handed over two death sentences in which Dreher had played a part, he was promoted – almost as a reward for his crimes – from ministerial counsellor to ministerial director.

As a coordination expert and reporter of the Great Penal Law Commission he had decisive influence on the draft of the Penal Code. Thus, for example, he wants to deprive the opponents of Bonn's policies of the right to vote:

"In my opinion, the statute proceeds from the principle that the citizen can, on the one hand, vote as he wants to, but that, on the other hand, he should vote as he thinks best for the benefit of the state. If, however, a citizen stabs, so to speak, the state in the back and thus proves that he is opposed to the well-being of the state, it might be quite sensible to deprive him of his right to vote." (Minutes of the Great Penal Law Commission, Vol. X, p. 253)

At the conference on "high treason" Dreher demanded that a crime endangering the state suffice as basic evidence: *"Actually I would have no scruples about letting a crime endangering the state suffice as basic evidence..."* (op.cit. p. 210). Dreher regards strike action as a forbidden *"means of coercing parliament"* (op.cit. p. 261)

The distorter of the law and enemy of democracy Dr. Dreher is the type of experienced nazi lawyer that the Bonn government, in the interests of its policies which are inimical to the interests of the people, does not want to relinquish.

Felmy Dr. THE GESTAPO WAS TOO MILD FOR HIM

today: public prosecutor in Oldenburg

As he did not want to leave his aged mother and had to support a sick sister as well, the miner, Franz Koslowski, born 3 September 1912 and without any previous convictions, asked the competent nazi occupation authorities not to deport him to Germany. The labour office promised to take his request into consideration. He would have to produce a certificate stating that he was fully employed in that district, within 24 hours. When he fulfilled this request he was described by one of the labour office officials as unwilling to work, seized by the collar and handed over to the police. According to statements made by the officials, a scuffle between the two of them ensued.

The Polish citizen was held under arrest for a few weeks by the Gestapo, and then released, however, as they considered the case, according to the verdict, *"not particularly serious"*.

Felmy, the public prosecutor at the special court at Graudenz (Grudziadz), held a different view. On 7 November 1941 he reported to the nazi Ministry of Justice: *"I first became acquainted with the case on 16 June 1941 through a telephone call from the lower court judge in Neumark (Dr. Babendreyer, today lower court counsellor in Lippstadt – editor), who did not consider the local political police station's handling of the case sufficient ... we must reckon with the death penalty."*

At the main proceedings of the special court at Graudenz on 4 December 1941 Felmy demanded the death penalty for the innocent Polish citizen. The court complied with his demand. Thereupon Franz Koslowski was executed on 28 January 1942. (See Table 23)

Felmy's name is on the Polish government's list of war criminals under number 80/192. Since February 1959 19 death sentences in which he was implicated have been published by the Committee of German Unity. Yet until now Bonn and the Ministry of Justice in Lower Saxony have not regarded this as a reason for removing Felmy from office and justly punishing him. Nor was any attention paid by the provincial Ministry of Justice to the indictment of the 1st Chairman of the VVN (Association of Victims of Nazism) of Lower Saxony, Ludwig Landwehr, on 2 May 1960.

Ganser Josef

SENTENCED TO DEATH FOR SHELTERING A CHILD

today: *senate president in the Federal Patent Court until April 1965*

"I protest to the utmost . . . against the verdict of 30 July 1943!" Thus wrote the nazi lawyer Dr. Ganser on 4 January 1944, when he gave his reasons for opposing a verdict acquitting the Polish woman, Anna Zwarycz.

Anna Zwarycz had adopted an 18-month-old Jewish child in October 1942 to save it from certain death in the nazi gas chambers. In the lower court on 30 July 1943 she was acquitted because she had *"kept the child openly and made known to everyone that it was Jewish"*. For Ganser, the senior government counsellor in the nazi Ministry of Justice and head of department III of the main department for justice in the "Generalgouvernement", Anna Zwarycz' humane action was a crime deserving death:

". . . This regulation makes it quite clear that its intention is to bind the Jews to certain places and moreover to deprive them of the possibility of staying anywhere other than these places. Therefore, any attempt to facilitate such a stay by granting shelter and food must be regarded . . . as giving refuge . . . It would be most unjust if one who granted shelter openly and audaciously should go unpunished, while one who does the same thing secretly incurs the death penalty. Therefore in the case at hand there can be no doubt that the accused gave refuge to a Jewish child."

Ganser achieved his inhuman aim. Anna Zwarycz was condemned to death on 3 March 1944. (See Table 26) As a result of Ganser's "protest to the utmost" a sentence of two years' imprisonment against the Polish physician Dr. Sigismund Walczynski was quashed and changed to a sentence of death. Ganser wrote:

"The sentence of two years' imprisonment passed on the accused Walczynski is quite inadequate. An abortion carried out on a German women signifies a weakening of the vitality of the German nation . . . In this case a sentence is required which completely exhausts the judicial framework of penalties . . ."

Thereupon Dr. Walczynski was condemned to death on 9 February 1943 by the German superior court at Krakow as "harmful to the German people".

In an interview with the Munich newspaper *Abendzeitung* Ganser made a first partial confession of his murder guilt. In April 1965 Ganser had to retired on pension because of the GDR's exposures. The reward for his crimes is a monthly pension of 2,400 marks.

Hoogen Mathias

HOLD-OUT POLICY IN TOTAL WAR

today: defence delegate of the Bundestag

Hoogen completed his "probation" for the post of defence delegate as a judge advocate in the fascist Luftwaffe and judge with the rank of colonel in the Kurlandarmee. In 1944 Hoogen was still giving murder orders in accordance with Hitler's policy of holding out to the very last. Thus on 24 April 1944 he demanded the death penalty for the German soldier Felix Stolz, the father of five children.

Stolz had succeeded for the time being in fleeing from one of the notorious convict fighting units. The doctor who carried out the medical inspection stated on 22 April 1944:

"As the exact circumstances of his desertion were still completely unknown a definite verdict on his mental condition at the time of committing the crime cannot be made with certainty ..."

Nevertheless Hoogen demanded the death sentence for "desertion" only two days later.

The arguments of the counsel for the defence, Lieutenant Ostermann, also failed to have any effect on Hoogen. The former expressed his attitude to the verdict once more in writing on 28 April 1944. Here he says:

"One must also take into consideration the fact that Stolz was in a convict unit for some time before his crime, whereby he was presumably weakened physically even more, also as a result of the poor nourishment (50 per cent of normal rations) ... for the reasons stated it seems fitting to change the sentence of death into a sentence of penal servitude."

Yet Felix Stolz was killed on 18 July 1944 in accordance with the wishes of Hoogen and the present superior provincial court counsellor in Düsseldorf, *Lefringhausen*, who gave the firing orders. (See Table 24)

After the defeat of fascism Hoogen quickly came back into favour in West Germany. In 1949 he became a delegate of the CDU to the Bundestag. In 1956 he had a leading part in suppressing the protest that the compulsory military service act was a violation of the constitution. Hoogen welcomed wholeheartedly the illegal prohibition of the KPD (Communist Party of Germany) and actively opposed the national referendum on equipping the Bundeswehr with nuclear weapons in 1958. As chairman of the judicial committee of the Bundestag Hoogen gained special "honours" by whitewashing Strauss, the former corrupt minister of war.

Hoogen, when he held this post, also prevented the judicial system from being purged of nazi hanging judges. He missed no opportunity of pressing to have the emergency laws passed. He wanted the dictatorship laws to go through the Bundestag as early as 1964.

In December 1964 the blood-guilty lawyer Hoogen was given the post of defence delegate in the Bundestag so he can completely build up the Bundeswehr and put the emergency laws, which he helped to work out, into practice against the population of West Germany.

Hüpers Dr. DEATH PENALTY FOR DEFENCE AND SELF-DEFENCE

today: chief public prosecutor in Oldenburg

When it became known on 7 September 1939 – seven days after the fascist invasion of Poland – in what was then Mönchsee and Dolenhain, that German paratroopers had been dropped in the area, several inhabitants tried to arm themselves in the emergency and defend their country. They searched the countryside for paratroopers and the farmsteads belonging to German settlers for weapons. In doing so they arrested two persons and took them to the station of the Polish national defence.

This was a case of a legal act of defence or self-defence against the aggressors and real violators of the peace and against the fifth column which was in league with them. Hüpers, however, the first public prosecutor at the special court at Hohensalza (Inowraclaw) demanded that the death sentence be passed on Eduard Beger, Stanislaw Koslowski and Jan Roszak on 9 September 1941 for *"severe breach of the peace"*. Three other Polish citizens were sentenced to five years' imprisonment for *"simple breach of the peace"*.

They were convicted, contrary to all legal principles, according to a law which had no validity for the accused on the day of the "crime". Hüpers expressed his attitude to a petition for mercy on 3 October 1941. In fascist jargon he said: *"... I consider a reprieve impossible. In the case of the condemned men Beger, Koslowski and Roszak, we are dealing with dangerous criminals ..., for whom, therefore, there can no longer be room in the community of the people."*

According to information known up to now, Hüpers had a part in 26 murder orders. Bonn has been informed of Hüper's crimes by GDR publications since at least 1959. The 1st Chairman of the VVN of Lower Saxony, Ludwig Landwehr, presented an indictment in November 1961. Yet it was not Hüpers who was punished but Ludwig Landwehr who was arrested in July 1962.

Krebs Heinrich DEATH PENALTY BECAUSE HE SOUGHT THE TRUTH

today: judge in the Federal Social Court

As early as four years ago the Committee on German Unity proved that the former judge in Stuttgart, specialist in cases of high treason, Dr. Heinrich Krebs, was one of Hitler's bloodstained lawyers who pronounced the death sentence for trivialities. As an official of the public prosecutor's office Krebs demanded the death sentence for the workman Heinrich Fehrentz of Heidelberg at the superior provincial court in Stuttgart on 26 October 1943. Fehrentz had sought the truth which the nazis withheld from the German people and had listened to various foreign radio broadcasts. He discussed the news with acquaintances. For Krebs this was a crime deserving death.

The fascist special decree forbidding listening to foreign broadcasting stations generally provided for sentences of imprisonment for such offences. But Krebs did not apply this decree during his prosecution. He demanded that he be condemned for "undermining the military potential" on the basis of the notorious "Decree on special war-time penal laws" and demanded the death penalty. He did not consider any possibilities of mitigating the sentence.

The death sentence against Heinrich Fehrentz was carried out. It had to be admitted in the verdict that he had said nothing but the truth: *"He told of the alleged successes of the Russians on the Eastern Front, declared that Russia had been invaded by Germany and was fighting in defence of its freedom."* (Reference number: OJs 115/43)

Krebs did not have to pronounce the death sentence even according to the unjust nazi laws – but he wanted to murder the nazi opponents who told the truth. (See Table 27)

Liebau Dr. DEATH PENALTY ON SUSPICION

today: chief district judge in Seesen

The former expert on special courts in the nazi Ministry of Justice and district judge at the special court in Posen (Poznan) confirmed the emergency courts' terror sentences by his signature many times. One of Liebau's comments on ten Czechoslovakian resistance fighters, condemned to death on 27 November 1942, stems from 9 April 1943. They were charged with having maintained contacts with the allied powers – Great Britain and the Soviet Union – and with having informed them of conditions in their own country. Liebau wrote:

00016

Lebenslauf.

Ich wurde am 15. 9. 1908 in Minden

15. II. 1935 zum Geheimen Staatspolizeiamt in Berlin zur probeweisen Beschäftigung einberufen, kam am 1. 5. 1935 als Stellvertreter des Leiters zur Staatspolizeistelle in Kiel und wurde des gleichen

Jahres zur Staatspolizeistelle Kassel, deren Leiter ich bis zu meiner im Sommer 1939 erfolgenden Versetzung nach Brünn war. – Seit dem 1. 7. 1938 bin ich Regierungsrat.

Während meiner Tätigkeit in Kassel war ich – ab 1. 11. 1937 – gleichzeitig Führer des S.D.-Abschnitts Kassel. – Im übrigen war ich zu den Einsätzen in Österreich [beim Stab des Chefs der Sicherheitspolizei und des SD.], im Sudetenland [als Führer des Einsatzkommandos Troppau] und in Böhmen und Mähren [als Führer des Einsatzkommandos Prag] abgeordnet.

Zur Zeit bin ich Leiter der Staatspolizeileitstelle Brünn.

Brünn, den 1.7.1940

Günther Herrmann

S.S.-Sturmbannführer.

TABLE 17

Bewerbung um Verwendung in der Sicherheitspolizei und im SD für die Kolonien.

Name: **H o f f m a n n**
Vorname: **Max,**
geboren am: **9.11.07** in: **Breslau**
ϟϟ-Dienstrang: **ϟϟ-Sturmbannführer**
Pol.-Dienststellung: **Regierungsrat**
Dienststelle: **Inspekteur der Sicherheitspolizei und des SD**
Bei Abordnung auch Heimatdienststelle: **Reichssicherheitshauptamt, Amt IV.**
Wohnung (Ort, Strasse): **Berlin-Zehlendorf, Planettastr. 4.**

Familienstand (led., verh., gesch.,verw.): **verheiratet**
Kinder (Zahl, Alter): **2 K., 3 Jahre und 7 Jahre.**
Schulbildung (Abschlussprüfung):
Abitur,

Berufsausbildung(vor Eintritt in Polizei oder SD):
Juristisches Studium, Gerichtsreferendar, Gerichtsassessor, Regierungsassessor,
Polizeiliche Prüfungen: (auch Sonderausbildung)
keine besonderen Prüfungen

Sprachkenntnisse (geläufig od.schulmässig):
schulmässig: französisch, englisch, russisch,
Technische Kenntnisse (Führerschein, Zeichnen, funktechn.Kenntnisse):
Führerschein III.Klasse, (früher III b).

- 6 -

Versichere dienstlich, dass ich die vorstehenden Fragen wahrheitsgemäss beantwortet habe.

Dr. Max Hoffmann
(Eigenhändige Unterschrift)

Der Chef der Ordnungspolizei

Berlin, den 5. ~~Sept.~~ Okt. 1944

Kdo II P 2a (3) Krai. VII 119

00253

Chef Kdo.	:	GenMaj.Flade i.V.
Kdo. II	:	Oberst Abeßer i.V.
Gr.-L.	:	Oberstlt. Hühne i.V.
U.Gr.L.	:	Oberstlt. Hühne
Sachb.	:	Hptm. Jaster i.V.

Betr.: Planmäßige **Ernennung des** ϟϟ-Hstufs.-u.Hptms.d.SchP.
Hermann K r a i k e r **zum** ϟϟ-Stubaf.u.Major d.SchP.

Zum jetzigen Dienstgrad ernannt mit Wirkung vom 1.8.1939

RDA.: 10.9.1939 **RRL.-Nr.:** 1008

I. **Personalangaben:**

a) **Name, Vorname** Kraiker, Hermann **geboren am** 12.8.1912
Familienstand verh. **Kinder** 3
NSDAP seit: 1.3.1933 **Glaubensricht.:** ggl.
ϟϟ seit: 1.6.1940

b) **Erklärung über Familienstand:**
Liegt vor. (bl. Heft Bl. 37).

c) **Nachweis über deutschblütige Abstammung des Offiziers und seiner Ehefrau:** Ist erbracht, bl.Heft Anh.Bl.13 und 14.

d) **Fronteinsatz (auch Luftkriegsgebiet):**
Osteinsatz - 2 J. 9 Mon. -
Ungarn (seit 31.7.1944)

e) **Verwendung ~~im jetzigen Dienstgrad~~:**
Als Lt. und Oblt.: 1937/39 Zugfhr., Adju., u.Lu.-Sachb.in Bochum.
Als Hptm: 1 J.1 Mon.Adju.u.Pers.-Sachb.i.Bochum u.Aussig, 10 Mon.Komp.-Fhr., Ausbildgs.-Batl.Recklinghausen, 1 J.5 Mon. 1938 Komp.-Fhr., Pol.Batl 316 (Osteinsatz), 1 J.2 Mon., Aufsichtsoffz.bei Schuma.-Batl.147-156(Oster[illegible] 2 Mon. Taktiklehrgang Waffenschule I, 2 Mon. Batl.-Fhr.ϟϟ-Pol.-Regt.Giesel[illegible]

f) **Politisches (ggf. Belastung und Bewährung):** Ab 31.7.44 Batls.-Fh[illegible] III/ϟϟ-Pol.in Ungarn.

./.

g) **Zustimmung der Parteikanzlei:**

h) **Kriegsauszeichnungen (Weltkrieg und jetziger Krieg):**
EK.II.Kl. (1941), EK.I. Kl. (1943), Ostmedaille (1943), Verwundetenabzeichen in schwarz (1944), Inf.Sturmabzeichen in Silber (1944), Tapferkeitsauszeichnung für Ostvölker I.Kl.in Silber (1944)

TABLE 19

Nationalsozialistische Deutsche Arbeiterpartei

002

Der Stellvertreter des Führers

Stab

München, den 4. September 1936.
Braunes Haus

III D - Kr -
2195/3435/36.

Der Chef der Ordnungspolizei
-7.SEP.1936

O.[illegible] P 2a Pa 62.

An den
Reichsführer SS
u.Chef der deutschen Polizei
im Reichsministerium des Innern
B e r l i n NW 7,
Unter den Linden 74.

Betrifft: Gesuch des Feldwebels Willi Papenkort, 3.Kom. Radf.Bat. 1, Tilsit um Rücküberführung in die Schutzpolizei und Zulassung zu der Offizierslaufbahn.

In der Anlage übersende ich Ihnen ein Gesuch des Feldwebels Willi Papenkort um Rücküberführung in die Schutzpolizei und Zulassung zu der Offizierslaufbahn. Papenkort war vom 1. März 1930 bis zu seiner Überführung in die Wehrmacht unter der Mitgliedsnummer 206 471 Mitglied der NSDAP. und hat sich gerade als Polizeibeamter auch in der Kampfzeit jederzeit rücksichtslos für die Bewegung eingesetzt. Das Gesuch wird von mir wärmstens befürwortet. Ich bitte Sie, nach Überprüfung der Angelegenheit mir kurz das Ergebnis zu berichten.

1 Anlage

Heil Hitler!

i. A.

[illegible]

TABLE 20

00014

Der Führer des SD-Leitabschnitts Prag
L

Prag-Bubentsch
Sachsenweg
Fernsprecher 77444

2. August 1940

B e u r t e i l u n g

Betr.: SS-Sturmbannführer Karl Hermann R a b e, geb. 11.6.1905 in Mühlhausen/Th., SS-Nr. 54 628

SS-Sturmbannführer R a b e ist seit dem 16. August 1939 beim SD-Leitabschnitt Prag tätig. Er bearbeitet hier in Personalunion mit der Dienststelle des Befehlshabers der Sicherheitspolizei und des SD in Böhmen und Mähren die gesamten Personalsachen einschliesslich des BV-Wesens völlig selbständig.

R a b e ist kompromissloser Nationalsozialist und alter SS-Führer. Er besitzt m.E. hervorragende Eignung für eine Verwendung im Kolonialdienst in leitender Stelle. Mir ist in charakterlicher, gesundheitlicher, sportlicher, militärischer oder fachlicher Hinsicht nichts bekannt, was gegen eine Verwendung des Sturmbannführer Rabe im Kolonialdienst geltend gemacht werden könnte.

SS-Obersturmbannführer

Der Reichsführer-SS und Chef der Deutschen Polizei im Reichsministerium des Innern

Berlin NW 7, den
Unter den Linden 74
Fernsprecher: Ortsverkehr 120034
Fernverkehr 120037

5. Juni 1943.

0-Kdo.g 2 (O/RV) Nr.78 II/43
Bitte in der Antwort vorstehendes Geschäftszeichen und Datum anzugeben.

023

Schnellbrief

Betr.: Einberufungen zur Feldgend. der Waffen-SS.

Jch bitte, den Oblt.d.Gend. Johannes R o s e n d a h l gemäß Erlaß vom 11.2.1942 – O-Kdo.I RV (2) 1 Nr.33/42 – zum 18.6.1943 zur Mob.Verwendung als Führer eines Feldgend.Trupps der Waffen-SS für SS-Kraftfahr-Ersatz-Abteilung in Weimar-Buchenwald einberufen zu lassen.

Oblt.R. ist vor seiner Abstellung über die H.Dv.275 zu belehren und darüber zu unterrichten, daß diese Vorschrift in vollem Umfange auch für die zur Feldgend. der Waffen-SS abgestellten Angehörigen der Ordn.Pol. maßgebend ist, insbesondere auch hinsichtlich der Einstufungen der Unterführer der Ordn.Pol. in die Waffen-SS entsprechend ihrem polizeilichen Dienstgrad.

Jm Auftrage
gez. F l a d e.

F.d.R.
Siekmann
Lt.d.SchP.d.Res.

An
den Herrn Regierungspräsidenten
in M e r s e b u r g.

Nachrichtlich:
An den Höheren SS- und Pol.-Führer Elbe
– Jnspekteur der Ordn.Pol. –
in D r e s d e n.

M/C.

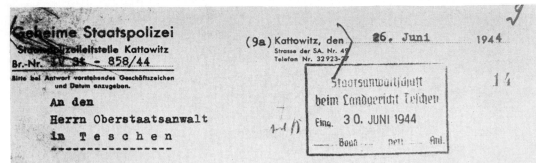

Geheime Staatspolizei
Staatspolizeileitstelle Kattowitz
Br.-Nr. IV 3a - 858/44
Bitte bei Antwort vorstehendes Geschäftszeichen und Datum anzugeben.

(9a) Kattowitz, den 26. Juni 1944
Strasse der SA. Nr. 49
Telefon Nr. 32923-27

9

Staatsanwaltschaft beim Landgericht Teschen
Eing. 30. JUNI 1944
.... Bd. ....Anl.

14

An den
Herrn Oberstaatsanwalt
in Teschen

Betrifft: Standgerichtssache gegen Stanislaus F i g w e r, geb. 5.4.1923 in Jaworzno.

Vorgang: Dort. Aktz.: VRs. 502/43.

Gegen den Strafgefangenen Stanislaus F i g w e r schwebt hier ein Standgerichtsverfahren wegen Vorbereitung zum Hochverrat. Er hat hier Todesstrafe zu erwarten.

Ich bitte, Figwer dem Standgericht bei der Staatspolizeileitstelle Kattowitz zu überstellen und ihn nach dem Konzentrationslager Auschwitz zu meiner Verfügung zu überführen. Den Tag der Überführung bitte ich mir mitzuteilen.

D.

VRs 502/43

TABLE 21

0256

Kdo. II

Berlin, den 20. Okt. 1944.

Betr.: Hptm. Boosfeld.

An

P 2a.

Wie GenLt. Göhrum heute in Gegenwart von Major Siegmund vortrug, bittet er darum, den Hptm. Boosfeld, der die SS-Werbung in Berlin auf die Beine gebracht hat und gute Verbindungen besitzt, etwa noch 8 Wochen in Berlin zu belassen, bevor er seine neue Dienststelle im Westen antritt.

Bitte um Vorlage Erlassentwurf.

I.V.

TABLA 22

Gericht der Wehrmachtkommandantur
B e r l i n
A.Z. B/S 14 p/u

Berlin NW 40, den 30.5.1944
Lehrter Str.58

9. Juni 1944

An den
Vorstand des Zuchthauses
B r a n d e n b u r g - Görden

Am Montag, den 12. Juni 1944 um 13.oo Uhr werden in der dortigen Anstalt die Todesurteile gegen

1.) den ehem. Gefreiten Alfred H a a s e,
geb. 13.7.1923 in Berlin-Weissensee, evangl.

2.) den ehem. Kanonier Friedrich M a l l a s c h i t z,
geb. 6.3.1921 in Blumau, Krs. Wiener-Neustadt

3.) den ehem. Obergefreiten Helmut R o s e,
geb. 25.3.1921 in Oberhausen

4.) den ehem. Schützen Günther B a a r s,
geb. 27.11.1921 in Brieg/Breslau, evangl.

5.) den ehem. Obertruppführer Wilhelm K l a p p r o t h,
geb. 24.6.1918 in Soest/Westfalen, evangl.

6.) den ehem. Scharführer Jgnatz W a l l n e r,
geb. 18.7.1897 in Fisching/Steiermark, r.kath.

mit dem Fallbeil vollstreckt.
Der Scharfrichter R ö t t g e r ist mit der Hinrichtung beauftragt.
Die Bekanntgabe an die Verurteilten erfolgt dort am gleichen Tage um 11.oo Uhr.
Mit der Leitung der Vollstreckung ist Oberleutnant Dr. Z e l l m a n n unter Zuziehung des Feldjustizinspektors K i l h o f beauftragt.
Die Verurteilten befinden sich im Wehrmachtuntersuchungsgefängnis Berlin-Tegel, Seidelstr.39.
Das Polizeipräsidium Berlin - Überführungsstelle - ist ersucht, die Verurteilten am 12.Juni 1944 vormittags nach dort zu überführen.
Um Annahme wird ersucht.
Es wird gebeten, den dortigen Anstaltsarzt zur Vollstreckung zur Verfügung zu stellen.

Oberkriegsgerichtsrat.

Gericht der Kriegsmarine
Berlin
J III 181/44

(1)Berlin-Charlottenburg, den 12.6.1944

14. Juni 1944

An
den Vorstand
des Zuchthauses Brandenburg-Görden.

Am 19. Juni 1944 um 13.00 Uhr wird in der dortigen Anstalt das Todesurteil gegen den Matrosen IV Horst H e n z e, geboren am 22.8.1924 in Berlin, Religion gottgläubig, mit Fallbeil vollstreckt.

Der Scharfrichter R ö t t g e r aus Berlin ist mit der Hinrichtung beauftragt worden. Die Bekanntgabe an den Verurteilten erfolgt dort am gleichen Tage um 11 Uhr.

Mit der Leitung der Vollstreckung ist Mar.Stabsrichter Dr. S c h l e g e l b e r g e r unter Zuziehung des Urkundsbeamten Marinejustizinspektor N o t h e l f e r beauftragt.

Der Verurteilte befindet sich im Wehrmachtuntersuchungsgefängnis Berlin, Zweigstelle Tegel, Seidelstr. 39.

Das Polizeipräsidium Berlin Überführungsstelle ist ersucht, den Verurteilten am 19. Juni 1944 vormittags nach dort zu überführen. Um Annahme wird ersucht.

Es wird gebeten, den dortigen Anstaltsarzt zur Vollstreckung zur Verfügung zu stellen.

Im Auftrage

Marinestabsrichter.

9 7

In Namen des Deutschen Volkes !

...e gegen

...derin Bronislawa C i e s i e l s k a, geb. Sluzalek ...owitz, Zeilenweg 18, geb. am 5.8.189. ebenda, verheiratet,

...ckereiinhaberin Ottilie W o j c i k i e w i c z, ... Sluzalek aus Sosnowitz, geb. am 8.2.1907 ebenda, verheiratet, ...,

wegen Kriegswirtschaftsverbrechens nach Ziff. I Abs. 3 der Polenstrafrechtsverordnung vom 4.12.1941, § 47 StGB.

Das Sondergericht I in Kattowitz hat in der Sitzung vom 23. 1942, an der teilgenommen haben:

Landgerichtsdirektor B u r k
als Vorsitzer,
Landgerichtsrat Dr. S c h m i d t,
Landgerichtsrat Baron T i e s e n h a u s e n
als beisitzende Richter,
Staatsanwalt O t t e r s b a c h
als Beamter der Staatsanwaltschaft,
Justizangestellter M a t t h i e s
als Urkundsbeamter der Geschäftsstelle,

...cht erkannt:

Die Angeklagten werden wegen Schädigung des Wohles des ...en Volkes, begangen durch Kriegswirtschaftsverbrechen, bei ...klagten Wojcikiewicz zugleich durch Preisüberschreitung, stra... Art. I Abs. 3 der Polenstrafrechtsverordnung zum T o d ...

...r bei der Angeklagten Ciesielska sichergestellten ... RM (achthundert Reichsmark) eingezogen.

...n des Verfahrens tragen die Angeklagt...

G r ü n d e

...er Oberstaatsanwalt als Leiter der Anklagebehörde bei dem Sondergericht.

...-Nr. 5 Sd KLs 68/41.

(In Eingaben ist obige Geschäfts-Nr. anzugeben.)

Graudenz, den 7. November 1941.

Fernruf Nr. 1123

Staatsanwaltschaft beim Oberlandesgericht Danzig
Eing.: 14. NOV. 1941
Bd. ...... Heft ...... Anlage 1

2

...den
...rn Reichsminister der Justiz
B e r l i n W 8
...helmstraße 65
...ch den
...rn Generalstaatsanwalt
D a n z i g
...garten 30/34.

...rifft:
...afverfahren gegen den ...en Franz Koslowski aus ...eltowo, Krs.Neumark, wegen ...brechens gegen Art.II, § ...bs.I der Verordnung über Einführung des Deut...en Strafrechts in den ...gegliederten Ostgebie... vom 6.6.40 (RGBl.I S. ...).

...äß § 7 der Mitteilungen.

...ichtsverfasser: Staatsanwalt Dr. Felmy.

...age: 1 Anklageschrift.

Die anliegende Abschrift der Anklage zum Sondergericht wird überreicht.

Der Vorfall ist mir erst durch eine telefonische Mitteilung des Amtsrichters in Neumark am 16. Juni 1941 bekannt geworden, der die Behandlung der Angelegenheit durch die hiesige Staatspolizeistelle nicht für ausreichend hielt. Aus den Akten ergibt sich, daß der Beschuldigte nach der Tat eine Woche in Neumark in Polizeigewahrsam saß, dann 3 Wochen im Internierungslager der Gestapo in Graudenz zubrachte und sodann wieder auf freien Fuß gesetzt wurde.

Es ist mit einem Todesurteil zu rechnen.

...05 E-K 17/41

(signature)

TABLE 23

TABLE 24

Feld - ober - gericht

. St. L. /19 44.

O.U., den 8. Januar 19 44

12

Haftbefehl

Der Gefr. Johann R o m a n n , 3.l. Flakersatz-Abteilung,

geb. am 22.2.1903 in Zoppot

ist in Untersuchungshaft zu nehmen. Er ist dringend verdächtig, in Italien im Juli 1943, in der Absicht , sich der Verpflichtung zum Dienste in der Wehrmacht dauernd zu entziehen, seine Truppe verlassen zu haben.

Der Gerichtsherr

Der Untersuchungsführer

Leutnant und Gerichtsoffizier

O s t e r m a n n
Oberleutnant
Ln.-Stelle A (o) 101/I, Riga-Spilve

89

Riga, den 28. April 1944.

Eing. 29. APR. 1944

S t e l l u n g n a h m e

Aus den aufgeführten Gründen, scheint es angebracht, die Todesstrafe in eine Zuchthausstrafe umzuwandeln. Falls St. die Möglichkeit dazu geboten würde, ist er bereit, seinen Fehltritt durch Einsatz vor dem Feind wettzumachen, was er schon vor dem Gericht betonte.

Ostermann

Erklärung des Soldaten Stolz

" Da ich zu Hause Familie und Kinder habe, bitte ich,mir Ge genheit zur Bewährung vor dem Feihde zu geben. "

"ich beabsichtige, ein Gnadengesuch einzureichen "

Felix Stolz

Oeffentliche Sitzung

30

Feldgerichts des Kommandierenden Generals und Befehlshabers im Feldluftgau XXVI

O.U., den 24. 4. 1944.

Beginn: 15, Uhr 35 Min.

K. St. L. 514 /1944

Gegenwärtig:

1. Ober-Kriegsgerichtsrat Thiel als Verhandlungsleiter
2. Hauptm. Prescher Lw./Bau Batl 126/IV
3. Ogfr. Gösseljohanns Flg.H.Komp. Riga-Spilve als Beisitzer
4. Lt. und Gerichtsoffizier Hoogen als Vertreter der Anklage
5. Uffz. Siegmund als Urkundsperson verpflichtet

In der Strafsache

gegen den Strafgefangenen Felix Stolz

von der 4./Feldstrafgefangenenabtl. 14

Feldpost-Nr. 02 177

z. Z. in Untersuchungshaft in der Kriegswehrmachthaftanstalt in Riga

geb. am 22. 2. 08 in Oliva

wegen Fahnenflucht

erschienen nach Aufruf der Sache:

1. der Angeklagte – vorgeführt –
2. Oblt. Ostermann, Ln.-Stelle Riga-Spilve als Verteidiger
3. ~~die geladenen Zeugen:~~

Feldgericht
des Kommandierenden Generals
und Befehlshabers im Feldluftgau XXVI

K.St.L. 514/44

O.U.,den 18.Juli 1944

97

N i e d e r s c h r i f t

über den Vollzug der Todesstrafe an dem Kanonier Felix S t o l z , Feldstrafgefangenenabteilung 14,

Anwesend waren:

1) Hauptmann Behrends, Komp.Führer der Ausb.u.Ers.Komp.z.b.V.1 – als leitender Offizier –
2) Kriegsgerichtsrat d.Lw. Lefringhausen, – als richterlicher Militärjustizbeamter –

Der Verurteilte starb sofort.
Der San.Offizier stellte den Tod um 04.03 Uhr fest.
Die Leiche wurde dem Beerdigungskommando der Ausb.u.Ers.-Komp. z.b.V.1 zwecks Beisetzung übergeben.

Lefringhausen
Kriegsgerichtsrat d.Lw.

Justizinspektor d.Lw.

"The sentence appears faultless ... In view of the facts of this case it is of no decisive significance that objectively no state secret has been betrayed ... Considerations for family and parents are not decisive in view of the extent of public interest involved."

Nine of the Czechoslovakian citizens were then executed on 3 May 1943. (Reference number: 12J 184/42g)

The death sentence against 35-year-old Franziska Angermeier – who was accused of arson – the special court could not establish any proof at all that she had committed the crime – also went through Liebau's hands. In his comment of 16 April 1943 he says: *"The factual and legal statements in the verdict are faultless. The accused was seen coming from the direction of the scene of the crime."* Liebau maintained that she was convicted for this reason and continues: "... above all the security of the German people ... demands that the death sentence be carried out."

Thereupon Franziska Angermeier was handed over to the executioner on 7 May 1943. (Reference number: 1 KLs SO 11/43)

This seriously incriminated nazi jurist was officially appointed by the Bonn state to continue his previous activity only with changed methods. Liebau became chief public prosecutor at the special court for political crimes in Lüneburg. Sometimes his indictments resemble those of the fascist special courts almost to the very wording. In an indictment of 4 August 1954 (Reference number: 26 JS 306/53) against two youths he says, for example: *"There is sufficient reason to suspect that both the accused also ... belonged to the illegal FDJ (Free German Youth – editor) after it had been prohibited."*

Liebau was removed from office only after the democratic element of the public brought this about by protest. But even then the West German judicial authorities did not want to be deprived of the guilty nazi lawyer. They quietly transferred him to the post of chief district judge in Seesen.

Meusel DEATH PENALTY FOR PROCURING FOOD

today: provincial court director in Göttingen

The cousins Drahomir and Miroslaus Holdrzyk, 22 and 21 years old, Czechoslovak citizens, were condemned to death for "crimes against the war economy" by the special court at Bielitz (Bielsko) on 27 May 1944. In the hearing of this case nazi Judge Meusel, before 1945 provincial court director in the special courts in Breslau (Wroclaw) and Bielitz was in the chair.

In view of the starvation rations for Czechs the young men had acquired, via middlemen, ration cards for food supplies. Nazi Judge Meusel and his hanging judge colleagues were agreed from the start that the two should be condemned to death "in the name of the German people".

The mayor of the town of Dombrau addressed the counsel for the defence for both the accused in a letter:

"The attitude of the local population to the fact that both Moldrzyks have been condemned to death is completely incomprehensible ... A petition for reprieve is recommended by me as head of the local government in Dombrau as well as because of the sentiment which prevails here against the severe sentence."

On 16 July the chief Reich prosecutor took sides with Meusel and refused to allow a plea of nullity.

According to information received up to now Meusel has been implicated in 22 death sentences.

Neidhard Friedrich DEATH PENALTY BECAUSE OF PATRIOTIC CONDUCT

today: government director in the Ministry of Justice of Baden-Württemberg

How "serious" the Bonn government is with its protestations of friendship towards the French people can be gathered from the Neidhard case. Although the appropriate government and judicial authorities in West Germany have known for years that Neidhard gave orders to have French citizens judicially murdered, he was even promoted – instead of being removed from office – in 1959 from senior government counsellor to government director.

A special sensation was aroused by the exposure of the Strasbourg *Humanité d'Alsace et de Lorraine* which reported on 17 February 1963: Through the verdict of the hanging judge Neidhard on 17 February 1943 13 young Frenchmen who opposed military service were murdered by a fascist firing-squad in the vicinity of the Struthof concentration camp.

On the questions put by the journalist Hellmut Rieber of Karlsruhe, Neidhard, the former district judge at the special court in Strasbourg still justified this butchery in February 1963: *"It was a proper court. The case is reviewed here. It was a legal verdict and, as far as I can remember, for murder."* In reality the young Frenchmen had tried to flee to Switzerland because they did not want to be misused for Hitler against their own people.

Yet this does not exhaust the blood on Neidhard's account by a long way. According to information discovered up to now five death sentences signed by him exist. On 26 November 1943 he condemned, among others, the two Alsatians Karl Ziller and Robert Eckert to death for alleged *"treasonable activities, preparations for high treason, aiding the enemy, abusing the Reich and listening to non-German broadcasting stations"*. (Reference number: So KLs 193/43)

Both the condemned had offered resistance to fascism. As an Alsatian Ziller had devoted himslef to several proclamations against the introduction of universal military service in occupied Alsace which was in violation of international law. Eckert had likewise written a proclamation against nazi rule. Neidhard passed the sentence on them because of their conduct, which was patriotic, democratic and in accordance with international law. The fascist wrote in the verdict: *"Whoever dares to lift his hand against the Reich has forfeited his life . . . Even if the actual damage caused was insignificant in any case. This alters nothing . . ."* (see Table 28)

Ottersbach Karl Heinz — DELIVERED JEWS TO THE GESTAPO

until early 1965 public prosecutor in Lüneburg

Ottersbach belongs to those guilty nazi lawyers who were reinstalled in the political service of Adenauer's judicial system because of their "experience". As the former public prosecutor at the special court of Kattowitz (Katowice) he gained particular honour, in the nazi sense of the word, by his close cooperation with the Gestapo.

On 26 April 1942 Ottersbach drew up an indictment against the Polish citizen Jakob Horowitz, born on 15 May 1896, from Chrzanow and the widow, Reisla Gutfreund, born on 28 December 1908, likewise from Chrzanow. Both citizens had to bear the second given name of Sara or Israel in accordance with Globke's race laws.

After the fascist occupation they were robbed of their existence. In order to earn a livelihood they managed to continue their scanty trade in textiles in their flat. As Jews were allotted almost no food at all – in 1941 they received only 184 calories a day, that is less than two rolls – they exchanged textiles for food.

Ottersbach, therefore, demanded that the remaining goods, which were hardly worth mentioning, should be confiscated and six and three years imprisonment in a concentration camp, which meant certain death for the Jews. Ottersbach's proposal with regards to Horowitz was confirmed by the verdict of the special court at Kattowitz on 10 September 1942. Yet the monster Ottersbach was not even satisfied with this. In his own handwriting he wrote a letter handing the Polish citizen Horowitz over to the "state police station" in Kattowitz. As for Frau Gutfreund there is only an entry in the reports to the effect that she was taken to Auschwitz concentration camp by the Gestapo on 15 April 1942. That this was also Ottersbach's work is revealed by an entry in a document of 10 August 1942 in which he wrote:

"I shall not read out the charge against Gutfreund during the main hearing."

Demanded the Death Penalty for Innocent Poles

On 9 July 1942 the shoemaker Vinzent Furmann, born on 31 March 1903, went before the special court at Kattowitz (Katowice). He was charged with possessing weapons. During the interrogations Furmann asserted his innocence. Then, however, he was so beaten up that he even had to be supported to be photographed. During such an "inquiry" a confession was wrung from him which lacked any foundation whatsoever. Even the verdict of the special court had to admit this:

"The accused could not be convicted on account of the testimony of witnesses during the main proceedings. The witness Polaczek, secretary of the criminal police, has confirmed that the accused was struck by the informer. Therefore, the admissions made by the accused at that time cannot be taken as a basis for the verdict."

However, Ottersbach still proposed the death penalty at the main hearing of the special court on 9 July 1942. He wanted the murder of an innocent person at all costs. When even the fascist special court had to acquit him, Ottersbach proposed handing Vinzent Furmann over to the Gestapo. As this arbitrary action of Ottersbach was too obvious, even the special court at Kattowitz, which otherwise passed a sentence of death without scruple, found itself forced to reject this proposal as well.

Devoid of All Human Feeling

"Herewith I, a thirteen-year-old child, apply, with a fervent entreaty, for the release of my only dear mother. We are seven very young children, my youngest brother is only three months old, I am helpless, as I have no money and I am too young to look after six brothers and sisters by myself . . . I am already ill myself.

"We are orphans without father or mother, as father has been away from us for months now and we have heard nothing of him."

These words were written by the daughter of Helene Michon, born 22 June 1907 and of Roman Michon on 16 June 1942 in an appeal for mercy which was handed on to the public prosecutor's office, i. e., Ottersbach. Both parents were in custody; the mother – until then unconvicted – because she had bought stolen poultry in order ro keep her family alive.

The Polish inhabitants for years received only one-third of the hunger rations of the population of Germany in 1945. The report reveals nothing else about the father.

Ottersbach demanded ten years' imprisonment in a concentration camp for

Helene Michon, which hardly any human being survived, during the main hearing on 29 May 1942. The special court pronounced a sentence of four years' imprisonment in a concentration camp. This victim of Ottersbach's was also taken to Auschwitz concentration camp on 16 December 1942. On 3 May 1943 the Gestapo informed the chief public prosecutor of the special court at Kattowitz (Katowice) that Frau Michon had "died" in Auschwitz concentration camp.

Ottersbach had the opportunity of saving the mother of the seven children. But he brought about the frightful tragedy of this Polish family.

In addition Ottersbach demanded the following sentences of death, according to information available up to now:

on 19 May 1942 for Eduard Rodak, born 22 May 1916, for participating in the illegal slaughtering of a cow;

on 23 July 1942 for Bronslawa Ciecielska, born on 5 August 1896 and for Ottilie Wojcikiewicz, born on 8 February 1907 for selling bread, being the proprietors of a bakery, to the needy population and for trying to cover the sales with forged bread coupons. Both of the last-named were executed on 14 August 1942 (See Table 23).

Despite this burden of guilt Ottersbach was reinstalled in the West German judicial system. What is more he was appointed to sit in judgement, in the special court for political crimes, against peace fighters and upright democrats.

The retired superior provincial court president, Dr. Richard Schmid of Stuttgart said of Ottersbach:

"This case is the worst of all and the one which allows least doubts and excuses. In my opinion the administration of justice in Lower Saxony should have immediately cancelled or opposed the oppointment of Public Prosecutor Ottersbach . . ." (Stern, Hamburg 7 June 1964)

Ottersbach immediately resumed his special court activity. He admitted this quite candidly in the illegal chief proceedings against Paul Butschek, a citizen of the GDR, on 13 May 1960, when he declared:

"You have learned nothing from your period of imprisonment between 1933 and 1945."

Ottersbach also declared that they would have to make an example of Hérr Butschek, whom he described as "an incorrigible communist functionary" and proposed eight months' imprisonment. Butschek had had discussions with colleagues from the DGB (German Trade Union Federation)!

On 14 June 1961 Ottersbach demanded 51 months' imprisonment for West German citizens Richard Brennig, retired district president, and Heinz Hilke, journalist, for having contributed to the "Association for the Protection of Democratic Rights". In a speech for the prosecution lasting seven hours the hanging judge propagated arming the Bundeswehr with nuclear weapons; he described a policy of negotiation as silly.

The GDR and the democratic citizens of West Germany had to fight for more than four years to have Ottersbach removed from his post. The minister of justice of Lower Saxony, von Nottbeck, who himself belonged to Hitler's 5th column in what was then Esthonia and after the invasion of Poland rushed through Hitler's economic policy in Poznan by force, kept protecting the blood-stained lawyer. Only in spring 1965 did he withdraw Ottersbach from the line of fire. But until now nothing has been done to bring him to judgement. On the contrary: He receives a high pension.

Ottersbach who had Polish citizens murdered can look back on a new burden of guilt. He helped to bring about, according to established evidence which is not yet complete, the condemnation of 21 patriots – mainly women, who worked in the labour community "Happy Holidays for All Children" – who received a total of 19 years imprisonment.

Rhode Werner

DEATH PENALTY AS "DETERRENT"

today: *government director in the Ministry of Justice of Schleswig-Holstein*

The Czech casual labourer Josef Tyburec had been trained as a switchman – so said the verdict of the special court at Prague (Praha) on 26 January 1945. On the demand of the public procecutor at the special court in Prague, Werner Rhode, the death sentence was passed because the accused had allegedly *"caused a collision on purpose and thus attempted sabotage"*. In this accident nobody was injured. Nevertheless the court maintained that this collision could only be atoned for with the highest penalty. The court therefore admitted that it had the possibility, even according to the nazi laws, of passing a milder sentence. As justification for the death penalty the "need for a deterrent" was invented and it added cynically: –

"even if the personal circumstances of the accused and his slight feeble – mindedness are taken into account".

Five years ago the Association of Anti-fascist Resistance Fighters of Czechoslovakia and the Socialist Student Union of West Germany made an indictment against Rhode. Rhode is on the Czech government's list of war criminals under the number A 38/88. At the beginning of August 1962 a spokesman of the Provincial Ministry of Justice of Schleswig-Holstein declared explicitly that they were informed of Rhode's arbitrary verdicts. The spokesman remarked cynically that his authorities had no intention, however, of calling Rhode to account.

One hundred ten death sentences for which Rhode applied have so far been discovered. Nevertheless the public prosecution at Kiel stopped the preliminary proceedings begun against Rhode on 8 December 1960 (Reference number: 2 Js 840/59). Rhode's "experience" as the lawyer of death are to be used in the service of the new penal code and the emergency dictatorship.

Schüle Erwin SENTENCED WAR CRIMINAL BECAME BONN'S NAZI "HUNTER"

today: *director of the Central Office for Clearing Up National Socialist Crimes of Violence*

"In 1933 I joined the SA and have been a member of the party since 1935." Thus wrote Erwin Schüle in his own handwriting in his personnel record on 3 September 1943 "in the field".

The role he played there is revealed by the fact that he was condemned to 25 years' forced labour in the Soviet Union as a war criminal. Schüle had belonged to the IC unit of the divisional staff of the 215th infantry division since March 1943, which had practised the scorched earth policy and that of starving the civilian population before Leningrad. Immediately before the end of the war he was still commanding one of the notorious special convict companies of the 253rd infantry division.

Bonn turned the past of the present chief public prosecutor to its own advantage by appointing him to the post of advocate responsible for the Central Office for Clearing Up Nazi Crimes, which was formed with a great deal of propaganda. From the very beginning the intention had been to give him the role of continning the policy pursued systematically by Bonn since the Federal Republic came into existence, of protecting nazi and war criminals under the cover of the central office. Indeed, since the central office came into being not one of the desk murderers, a stroke of whose pen sometimes meant the death of thousands and tens of thousands, has been tried in court.

When the Bonn government decided on 5 November 1964, contrary to the wishes of other peoples and to international law, to allow the nazi and war crimes to come under the statute of limitations in May 1965, Schüle also declared his support for limitation.

The West Berlin *Spandauer Volksblatt* wrote on 16 February 1965 on the Schüle case:

"Now there could be no objection if Herr Schüle devoted his valuable services to the Federal Republic as official expert of a land registry, even in a prominent official position. Nor would anyone hinder his career as an adviser to the railways or postal services. But the fact that the federal government is sending none other than the former SA man and NSDAP champion Schüle to Warsaw to clear

up nazi crimes is more than just an intolerable disregard for the feelings of all the peoples barbarously enslaved by the nazis. Is no one in a responsible post capable any more of drawing a line between that which is bad taste and that which is intolerable? (See Table 29)

A Fine-spun Network

Certainly no more examples are required to prove that the Bonn state is continuing the "Third Reich's" system of legal terror with slightly changed methods. Only one thing remains to be shown: How the network of nazi lawyers in West Germany was tightened up to insure its function and how well the roles were allotted in it.

THE SUPERIOR PROVINCIAL COURT DISTRICT OF HAMM

Hamm is one of the 18 superior provincial court districts of the Federal Republic. According to the 1964 legal handbook on *'The representatives and organs of the judicial authorities in the Federal Republic of Germany"*, page 126, this superior provincial court district comprises the government districts of Arnsberg, Detmold and Münster and of the Düsseldorf government district the towns Essen and Kettwig. There are ten provincial courts in it which are located in Arnsberg, Bielefeld, Bochum, Detmold, Dortmund, Essen, Hagen, Münster, Paderborn, Siegen. The legal administration of this district is responsible for 8,323,259 people.

TERRORIST JUDGES IN DORTMUND

In the criminal prosecution office in Dortmund there is Senior Public Prosecutor Pippert, formerly first public prosecutor in the special court, Vienna. As expert in the nazi Ministry of Justice he seconded the death sentence against the Greek citizens Nicolaus Mourtzeas and Johann Saridakis who had been forcibly brought to Germany. In his comment of 15 November 1944 he declared: "There are no objections to the judgment. The sentenced persons have unscrupulously misused the right of guests (!) which they enjoyed in Germany . . ." (AZ: 6 S KLs 65/44, 802)

Along with Pippert there is Otto-Wolfgang Schultze, former accuser in the special court Essen, in office as first public prosecutor. In addition there are Provincial Court Director Dr. Rudolf Becker, former senior military court counsellor of the Berlin Wehrmacht commandantura, former Military Court Counsellor Walter Philippi and former Senior Judge Fähndrich of the special court, Kattowitz (Katowice). Fähndrich, for example, on 3 December 1942 sentenced five Polish citizens to death in a procedure based on the "Poland criminal law decree". On 27 October 1944 he passed the same sentence against Wilhelm and Johann Wieczorek for so-called preparation of high treason.

Also in office in this town are the Lower Court Counsellors Bruntsch – former lower court counsellor in the Freiberg special court and specialist for high treason in the nazi Ministry of Justice – and Dr. Claus Büngener, also formerly at the Freiberg special court.

...IN BIELEFELD...

In Bielefeld which has only one fourth as many inhabitants as Dortmund the picture of the "purified justice" is still worse. There Senior Public Prosecutor Depenbrock was accuser at the special court of the same town already under Hitler. First Public Prosecutor Bellwinkel even was public prosecutor in the "People's Court". Bellwinkel passed the death sentence against the Erfurt chamber musician Ernst Fink, among others. The reason: Fink had cut up two pictures of the "Führer".

First Public Prosecutor Dr. Josef Glunz was public prosecutor at the Essen special court. His colleague of the same rank Hagmann and Public Prosecutor Hans Köhne were accusers in "racial disgrace matters" in Dortmund. Provincial Court Director Huber gathered his experience as provincial court counsellor in the Dortmund special court, Provincial Court Director Dr. Keil as military court counsellor, Provincial Court Director Dr. Kuhlmann as senior military judge, Chief Judge Strümpler as superior provincial court counsellor in the Bielefeld special court, Lower Court Counsellor Oldenburg in the same position at the Prenzlau special court. On 26 November 1943 Oldenburg sentenced the agricultural labourer Friedrich Wilhelm Bartelt to death because after an air-raid he had taken a few things worth about 15 Reich marks.

Of the Bielefeld provincial court counsellors, senior lower court judges and lower court counsellors who served their "Führer" in military and special courts only Provincial Court Counsellor Dr. Regis will be mentioned here. His name is on the international list of war criminals (No. 40/142). Even the notorious prisoners' camp at Oberems and the Bielefeld prison are directed by a former senior military judge, Government Director Dr. Bernd Holl.

...IN BOCHUM...

Bochum also belongs to the Hamm superior provincial court district. This coal and iron town is half as big as Dortmund but there are even more former military and special judges here than in Dortmund. With Senior Government Counsellor Heinz Esser a man was appointed chief of the prison and the remand prison who as first public prosecutor for political offences was active for the fascist occupants in the Czech-Bohemian district town of Leitmeritz (Litomerice).

Senior Public Prosecutor Dr. Hüntemann was also public prosecutor for political offences during the war in the Hamm Superior Provincial Court. His colleague Senior Public Prosecutor Schäper was accuser at the special court, Brünn (Brno). On 23 February 1944 alone he passed four death sentences for "favouring the enemy" – that means because of the favouring of Czechs by Czechs! Public Prosecutor Sernau was public prosecutor at the Dortmund special court, Provincial Court Director Dr. Boes provincial court counsellor in the Essen special court, Provincial Court Directors Hänert and Dr. Witzig military court counsellors. According to a sentence by Hänert Gerhard Wagner was shot as late as 6 March 1945. Two days before Hänert had sentenced him to death for "cowardness". Lower Court Counsellor Schmiedeberg was public prosecutor in the special court in Stettin (Szczecin) and Lower Court Counsellor Wallis was senior staff judge of the 8th division in Oppeln (Opole).

...IN MÜNSTER...

Let us have another look at another town of the Superior Provincial Court District of Hamm, Münster. Provincial Court Director Bödding who is in office there was provincial court counsellor at the Bielefeld special court in the Hitler state and Provincial Court Director Dr. Verspohl was senior staff judge of the 12th air force field division. On Verspohl's account of guilt there are death sentences against the Czechoslovak citizen Albert Michek and the Alsatian Heinrich Stenger who had been pressed into the fascist Wehrmacht in violation of international law. Senior Public Prosecutor Duhme was an accuser at the Bielefeld special court, Senior Administrative Court Counsellor Hönneckes was military court counsellor, Social Court Counsellor Dr. Kieler was senior lower court judge at the special court in Oppeln (Opole) and Senior Public Prosecutor Dr. Knippenberg was accuser at the Dortmund special court.

First Public Prosecutor Niemer, Senior Administrative Court Counsellor Dr. Roesler and Senior Administrative Court Counsellor Dr. Wildt were specialists on Polish criminal matters, Niemer as first public prosecutor in Hamm, the seat of the superior provincial court, Roesler as superior provincial court counsellor in Posen (Poznan), Wildt as public prosecutor in Kassel.

Public Prosecutor Rosendahl has passed several death sentences as accuser at the special court in Thorn (Torun) and First Public Prosecutor Schwarze at the Halle special court. His personnel file shows, for example, that in the war he was *"freed"* from military service *"to fulfil tasks of importance for the war"*. Schwarze became a member of the NSDAP on 1 May 1933, joined the SA, became a promoting member of the SS, legal adviser in the Sturmbann I/174 (storm troop), manager of the regional court of the NSDAP, regional chief for propaganda and training, chamber president of the regional party court, etc.

Dr. Diderichs, also public prosecutor in Münster, sentenced the young Alsatian Peter Schröder to death in the last weeks of the war as senior staff judge of the 8th tank division who had shot himself through the hand to withdraw from further senseless military service. Diderichs stated in the sentence of the court martial of the 8th tank division: *"As an Alsatian he does not want to fight for the German concern . . ."* Private Werner Grieser who was only 20 years old had to die on 19 March 1945 on the order of Diderichs.

. . . AND IN HAMM . . .

The administration of justice of the superior provincial courts is directive and binding for the juridical practice of the provincial and lower courts. The superior provincial court competent for Dortmund, Bielefeld, Bochum and Münster is that in Hamm.

In Hamm there are four senior public prosecutors in office who came out of the fascist criminal judiciary. They all would have had to be dismissed according to the laws issued by the Control Council. Senior Public Prosecutor Dr. Göke was accuser at the Bielefeld special court during the war, the other three raged in special courts behind the "eastern front": Stähler in Danzig (Gdansk) Wälzholz and Leading Senior Public Prosecutor Dr. Gugler in Breslau (Wroclaw).

Up to now over 30 death sentences have been found which were passed on Stähler's request, among them a number against women. Even in the last year of the war he effected six death sentences on a single day *"because of abetment to desertion"*. Among these sentenced persons there was also a woman. Many accused persons were declared to be "wrong-doers against the people" by him and delivered up to the hangman.

To the guiding accusers in Hamm there come such judges of the superior provincial court as Senate President Laube, former public prosecutor for political death sentences in the nazi Ministry of Justice and Dr. Rein, senior public prosecutor at the Dortmund special court already in the Hitler period. There are furthermore Superior Provincial Court President Dr. Rempe, former superior provincial court counsellor in the nazi Ministry of Justice, Senate President

Josef Schwarze, former provincial court counsellor in the nazi Ministry of Justice, Superior Provincial Court Counsellors Boenicke – formerly active in the department for political offences in the nazi Ministry of Justice – Lindemann, former provincial court counsellor in the Dortmund special court, and Helmut John, former military court counsellor of the 20th tank division, etc.

It is understandable that these leading nazi jurists use every opportunity to bring their old accomplices into positions in which they can again exercise their influence as unhinderedly as possible. This occurred also in the case of former Senior Staff Judge Dr. Siegfried Wehdeking, judge of the 999th prisoners' penal brigade. His personnel file says that Wehdeking *"made great efforts to capture the escapees"*. This military judge was given a post which enables him to work in the same spirit although in a somewhat different form as parson in the Werl prison. And Werl also belongs to the Hamm Superior Provincial Court District. Former Senior Public Prosecutor Dr. Theodor Grunau at the special court in Graudenz (Grudziadz) is today government director in the Hamm penal execution office. In December 1941 Grunau refused to pardon the Polish underground construction worker Franz Koslowski who was sentenced to death. Koslowski had asked the fascist occupation authorities not to deport him to Germany for enforced labour because he had to provide for his aged mother and ill sister.

In the last year several other former special and military judges have been discovered in the Hamm Superior Provincial Court District. Their names were published in November 1964 in the documentation of the National Council of the National Front of Democratic Germany entitled "Bonn Sanctions War Crimes". Is any more proof necessary that conditions are similar in the other superior provincial court districts of West Germany?

A FATAL OFFENCE

The bourgeois English journalist Sefton Delmer assessed this dangerous development in the *Daily Express* on 17 September 1957 as follows:

"Of all the offences against the allied plans which Dr. Konrad Adenauer sanctioned in the eight years which he has already been in power I think this re-employment of Hitler's terror judges is most fatal. For the constant danger exists that these men who once held the stirrups for a dictator will be ready to do so again!"

The International Federation of Resistance Fighters (FIR), Vienna, reached this conclusion in 1965:

"The fact that, almost twenty years after the capitulation of the 'Third Reich' the problem of nazi crimes has still not been solved in a satisfactory way, that it poisons international relations and represents a threat to the future, arises from

the fact that the German Federal Republic refuses to adapt the principles of its penal law and its practical application to those principles which are generally acknowledged in international law as well as by the jurisdiction of all civilized countries."

It is undisputed that the Bonn state always and in every respect kept its hands protectingly over the murderers in judges' robes.

Nazi Jurists Shape Bonn Justice

List of incriminated nazi jurists in the service of the Bonn state

Abbott, Josef born 28. 7. 1913
formerly: public prosecutor in the special court in Danzig (Gdansk)
today: first public prosecutor in Koblenz

Ahlborn, Alfred born 20. 12. 1906
formerly: provincial court counsellor in the nazi Ministry of Justice
today: lower court counsellor in Stuttgart

Aichinger, Rudolf born 13. 9. 1904
formerly: military court counsellor in 6th armoured army, senior field judge in the judicial office of the army command
today: lawyer in Weissenburg

Albani, Theodor born 3. 10. 1906
formerly: senior military judge
today: lower court director in Detmold

Albrecht, Paul born 12. 2. 1905
formerly: lower court counsellor in the special court, Duisburg
today: lower court counsellor in Mönchen-Gladbach

Albrecht, Dr. Rudolf born 5. 2. 1903
formerly: military court counsellor rearward areas 540 command, senior field judge in the high command of the 17th army
today: lawyer in Munich

Althanns, Dr. Moritz born 19. 11. 1907
formerly: public prosecutor in Leipa (Ceská Lipa)
today: provincial court director in Bamberg

Altherr, Anton born 26. 1. 1909
formerly: public prosecutor in Zweibrücken; 1933 SS; SD, operational group D
today: first public prosecutor in Kaiserslautern

Amedick, Dr. Ewald born 3. 2.1907
formerly: provincial court counsellor in Dortmund; took part in "racial disgrace" judgments
today: provincial court director in Paderborn

Anger, Dr. Dr. Erich born 1. 7. 1902
formerly: public prosecutor in the special court, Leipzig
today: first public prosecutor in Essen

Ankenbrand, Dr. Otto born 19. 2. 1907
formerly: lower court counsellor in the special court, Nuremberg-Fürth
today: lower court counsellor in Erlangen

Arland, Friedrich born 22. 8. 1904
formerly: public prosecutor in the special court, Prague (Praha)
today: lower court counsellor in Hamburg

Arndt, Professor Dr. Karl born 27. 2. 1904
formerly: supreme court counsellor, deputy group leader of the "Reich Protector" in Prague, SS 1933
today: superior provincial court president in Bremen, chief of the "reparation senate" in Bremen, chief of the international commission for reparation in Koblenz

Arndt, Hans-Dietrich born 22. 10. 1909
formerly: provincial court counsellor in Mainz, magistrate of "People's Court"
today: senate president in the Superior Provincial Court, Koblenz

Arnold, Dr. Heinrich born 1. 11. 1908
formerly: flying army judge, senior staff judge army A.O.K. 6 with the military commander in France and A.O.K. 14
today: lawyer in Memmingen

Augat, Kurt born 11. 8. 1901
formerly: military court counsellor in the 710th infantry division
today: provincial court counsellor in Kiel

Aumüller, Dr. Gustav born 27. 10. 1903
formerly: military court counsellor in 5th mountain division
today: provincial court director in Würzburg

Axt, Otto born 11. 2. 1904
formerly: military court counsellor in 182nd infantry division
today: lower court counsellor in Darmstadt

Babendreyer, Dr. born 6. 4. 1910
formerly: judge in Neumark, denounced Polish underground worker Franz Koslowski (see page 128)
today: lower court counsellor in Lippstadt

Bähr, Dr. Karl born 16. 9. 1906
formerly: lower court counsellor in the special courts in Celle and Hanover
today: lower court counsellor in Hanover

Bäumler, Dr. Josef born 7. 2. 1902
formerly: provincial court counsellor in the special court, Nuremburg
today: lower court director in Amberg

Baitinger, Gustav born 13. 9. 1908
formerly: public prosecutor in Stuttgart, joined NSDAP on 3 November 1931, head of a regional legal office of the NSDAP
today: lower court director in Ulm

Bakenhus, Heinz born 10. 5. 1904
formerly: military court counsellor in Supreme Field Command 393
today: provincial court director in Oldenburg

Bandel, Dr. Robert born 18. 2. 1908
formerly: public prosecutor in the "People's Court"
today: senior judge in Kehl

Barbier, Erich born 17. 12. 1908
formerly: army judge in 46th infantry division
today: provincial court director in Frankenthal

Baring, Eberhard born 23. 6. 1911
formerly: senior military judge
today: senate president of the provincial social court in Celle

Bartz, Dr. Hans born 1. 7. 1901
formerly: first public prosecutor in the special court, Frankenthal
today: senior public prosecutor in Hamburg

Bauknecht, Dr. Otto born 29. 11. 1902
formerly: provincial court counsellor in the special court Luxemburg; sentenced to four years imprisonment in Luxemburg
today: president of the Legal Examining Board in Mainz

Baumgartl, Anton born 30. 4. 1906
formerly: lower court counsellor in the Silberk court, in 1931 founding member of the Frontier Youth of the DNP, SS Sturmbannführer, SS judge in Warsaw
today: lower court counsellor in Regensburg

Becker, Dr. Heinrich born 15. 9. 1905
formerly: provincial court counsellor in the special court, Cologne, in 1944 in The Hague
today: provincial court president in Bonn

Becker, Dr. Rudolf born 28. 10. 1903
formerly: senior military court counsellor in the Wehrmacht Command, Berlin
today: provincial court director in Dortmund

Beer, Dr. Herbert born 8. 12. 1909
formerly: lower court counsellor in Pilsen (Plzn), legal adviser to the NSDAP
today: lower court counsellor in Arolsen

Behne, Heinrich born 12. 11. 1907
formerly: lower court counsellor in the nazi Ministry of Justice
today: senate president in the Provincial Social Court in Essen

Behr, Dr. Bernhard born 7. 7. 1900
formerly: provincial court counsellor in the special court, Hamburg
today: provincial court director in Hamburg

Behrendt, Dr. Herbert born 4. 10. 1907
formerly: lower court counsellor in the special court, Magdeburg
today: lower court counsellor in Gütersloh

Beinhorn, Hans-Joachim born 12. 5. 1910
formerly: senior military court counsellor Berlin Command
today: superior provincial court counsellor in Brunswick

Beismann, Dr. Ernst born 7. 9. 1906
formerly: military court counsellor in the 159th, 166th and 328th infantry divisions
today: provincial court counsellor in Paderborn

Bellebaum, Dr. born 9. 11. 1906
formerly: public prosecutor in the special court Kattowitz (Katowice)
today: senior public prosecutor in Duisburg

Bellwinkel born 1. 9. 1904
formerly: public prosecutor in the "People's Court"
today: first public prosecutor in Bielefeld

Benker, Hans born 11. 4. 1907
formerly: first public prosecutor in the special court, Nuremberg
today: provincial court counsellor in Schweinfurt

Berger, Dr. Hugo born 24. 9. 1897
formerly: military court counsellor, field command, 238th and 408th divisions
today: federal judge of 1st Senate of Federal Constitutional Court

Bergmann, Leo born 22. 7. 1907
formerly: provincial court counsellor in the special court, Königsberg (Kaliningrad)
today: provincial court director in Hamburg

Berlin, Fritz born 31. 5. 1914
formerly: military secret police
today: lower court counsellor in Bad Mergentheim

Berner, Ludwig born 1. 10. 1912
formerly: provincial court counsellor in the special court I, Prague (Praha)
today: senior public prosecutor in the Federal Court

Bernzen, Dr. Alphons born 24. 7. 1910
formerly: military court counsellor
today: public prosecutor in Lübeck, seconded to the federal service in 1964

Berthold, Dr. Wolfgang born 13. 6. 1911
formerly: public prosecutor in the special court, Berlin
today: fiscal court director in Hanover

Bertram, Wilhelm born August 1907
formerly: public prosecutor in the nazi Ministry of Justice
today: ministerial counsellor in Federal Ministry of Justice

Bessler, Otto born 2. 7. 1907
formerly: provincial court counsellor in the special court in Bromberg (Bydgoszcz)
today: lower court counsellor in Herford

Bessler, Dr. Johann born 29. 6. 1901
formerly: provincial court counsellor in the special court, Bamberg
today: superior provincial court counsellor in Bamberg

Beyer, Dr. Gerhard born 17. 5. 1903
formerly: provincial court director in the special court III, Berlin
today: superior provincial court counsellor in Frankfurt-on-Main

Beyer, Dr. Paul born 20. 11. 1904
formerly: military court counsellor in 178th infantry division, Liegnitz (Legnica)
today: lower court director in Nuremberg

Beyling, Günter born 2. 6. 1904
formerly: public prosecutor in the special court in Linz
today: public prosecutor in Hamburg

Bilfinger, Dr. Rudolf born 20. 5. 1903
formerly: SS Obersturmbannführer, 1934 Gestapo main office, Stuttgart, 1937 government counsellor in the central office of Heydrich's security police (see Table 29)
until July 1965: senior administrative counsellor in Mannheim

Blanck, Walter born 17. 6. 1905
formerly: military court counsellor in the 413th division
today: lower court counsellor in Traunstein

Blohm, Friedrich born 26. 5. 1906
formerly: public prosecutor in the special court, Hanover

t o d a y : senior public prosecutor in Hanover

Blumenhagen born 27. 8. 1907
f o r m e r l y : naval senior military court counsellor defence area Baltic Sea
t o d a y : provincial court counsellor in Oldenburg

Bock, Dr. Hans born 7. 2. 1903
f o r m e r l y : provincial court counsellor in the special court, Hamburg
t o d a y : federal judge in the Federal Court

Bock, Werner born 10. 9. 1903
f o r m e r l y : provincial court counsellor in the special court, Sankt Pölten
t o d a y : lower court counsellor in Oldenburg

Bockhorn, Fritz born 6. 10. 1905
f o r m e r l y : public prosecutor in the special court, Berlin
t o d a y : lower court in Kiel

Bockisch, Willi born 3. 8. 1904
f o r m e r l y : military court counsellor in 1st A.A. divison command
t o d a y : provincial court counsellor in Kiel

Bödding, Heinrich born 10.10.1904
f o r m e r l y : provincial court counsellor in the special court, Bielefeld
t o d a y : provincial court director in Münster

Böhm, Dr. Edgar born 18. 1. 1902
f o r m e r l y : provincial court counsellor in Leitmeritz (Litomerice)
t o d a y : lower court counsellor

Boehr, Dr. Günther born 5. 12. 1900
f o r m e r l y : military court counsellor in 346th infantry division
t o d a y : provincial court counsellor in Hanover

Böllinghaus, Friedrich born 26. 3. 1909
f o r m e r l y : military court counsellor in Luftgau II, Warsaw (Warszawa)
t o d a y : superior provincial court counsellor in Düsseldorf

Boenicke, Heinz born 18. 8. 1907
f o r m e r l y : lower court counsellor in the nazi Ministry of Justice, Department III, political cases
t o d a y : superior provincial court counsellor in Hamm

Börner born 24. 11. 1906
f o r m e r l y : lower court counsellor in the special court, Frankfurt-on-Main
t o d a y : lower court counsellor in Hochheim

Boes, Dr. Walter born 13. 2. 1904
f o r m e r l y : provincial court counsellor in the special court, Essen
t o d a y : provincial court director in Bochum

Böttger, Dr. Georg born 7. 7. 1902
f o r m e r l y : provincial court counsellor in the special court, Jena
t o d a y : lower court counsellor in Nieburg

Bogenrieder, Dr. Alfons born 3. 10. 1900
f o r m e r l y : first public prosecutor in the special court, Stuttgart
t o d a y : ministerial counsellor in Ministry of Justice, Baden-Württemberg

Bolley, Dr. born 27. 3. 1903
f o r m e r l y : public prosecutor in the special courts in Hagen and Dortmund
t o d a y : public prosecutor in Essen

Bollmann, Alfred born 9. 9. 1905
f o r m e r l y : senior military court counsellor in the field court of the commander of naval air corps, west
t o d a y : first public prosecutor in Lüneburg

Bonnekamp, Dr. Carl born 25. 9. 1913
f o r m e r l y : public prosecutor in the special court, Düsseldorf
t o d a y : senior public prosecutor in Düsseldorf

Bonnemann, Dr. Josef born 10. 3. 1900
f o r m e r l y : public prosecutor in the special court, Koblenz
u n t i l J u l y 1 9 6 5 : administrative court director in the Federal Disciplinary Chamber in Frankfurt-on-Main

Bordfeld, Dr. Ferdinand born 3. 2. 1908
f o r m e r l y : military court counsellor in 306th infantry division
t o d a y : senior judge in Königswinter

Borgmann, Eberhard born 17. 3. 1911
f o r m e r l y : military court counsellor in the supreme field command 399
t o d a y : public prosecutor in Osnabrück

Brandstetter, Dr. Elmar born 16. 4. 1908
formerly: senior military field judge army supreme command
today: federal prosecutor in the defence service senate of the Federal Disciplinary Court in Munich

Brandt, Walter born 1. 7. 1908
formerly: senior military court counsellor
today: lower court counsellor in Hameln

Brem, Walter born 13. 12. 1902
formerly: lower court counsellor in the special court, Nuremberg-Fürth
until August 1965: provincial court director in Fürth

Bretzfeld, Heinz
formerly: military court counsellor of the Luftwaffe in the execution department of the field courts of the commanding general and commander, Luftgau III, Berlin-Charlottenburg
today: lawyer in Rotenburg/Fulda

Brinz, Arnold born 19. 6. 1901
formerly: military court counsellor in field command 1019
today: lower court counsellor in Miesbach

Brunsch born 29. 4. 1909
formerly: lower court counsellor in the special court in Konitz (Chojnice) and Bromberg (Bydgoszcz)
today: lower court counsellor in Krefeld

Bruntsch born 3. 3. 1909
formerly: lower court counsellor in the special court, Freiberg, and expert on high-treason cases in the nazi Ministry of Justice
today: lower court counsellor in Dortmund

Buchholz, Herbert born 23. 11. 1905
formerly: military court counsellor in the 156th infantry division
today: provincial court director in Trier

Buck, Roland born 18. 6. 1903
formerly: navy senior staff judge, defence area Baltic Sea
today: lower court counsellor in Hamburg

Bücklein, Georg born 23. 2. 1907
formerly: lower court counsellor in special court III, Munich
today: superior provincial court counsellor in Munich

Bühler, Hanns born 16. 5. 1900
formerly: provincial court counsellor in the special court, Stuttgart
until August 1965: provincial court director in Heilbronn

Bülow, Professor Dr. Arthur born 17. 11. 1901
formerly: ministerial counsellor in the nazi Ministry of Justice; participant in the "Reich Party Congress" already in 1933
today: state secretary in the Federal Ministry of Justice

Bülow, Dr. Hennecke von born 23. 4. 1908
formerly: senior staff judge in 32nd and 72nd infantry divisions
today: government counsellor in penitentiary, Ziegenhain

Büngener, Dr. Claus born 19. 4. 1911
formerly: lower court counsellor in the special court, Freiberg
today: lower court counsellor in Dortmund

Bürger, Dr. Hans born 20. 9. 1908
formerly: public prosecutor in the special court, Linz
today: public prosecutor in Wuppertal

Buhl, Dr. Hans born 14. 1. 1907
formerly: provincial court counsellor in the special court, Danzig (Gdansk)
today: lower court director in Ansbach

Bujnoch, Dr. Leo born 19. 5. 1907
formerly: public prosecutor in the special court in Troppau (Opava); on Czechoslovak war criminal list A – 6/206
today: lower court counsellor in Kempten

Burchardt, Wolfgang born 9. 6. 1910
formerly: public prosecutor in the special court, Düsseldorf
today: senior public prosecutor in Düsseldorf

Buri, Eugen born 4. 11. 1911
formerly: provincial court counsellor in the nazi Ministry of Justice, Dept. III
today: administrative court president in Sigmaringen

Busch, Dr. Herbert born 19. 6. 1900
formerly: provincial court counsellor in Superior Provincial Court, Dresden, senate for high-treason cases

until July 1965: senate president in Neustadt an der Weinstrasse and member of the constitutional court of Rhineland/Palatinate

Bussert, Dr. Rudolf born 22. 9. 1905
formerly: military court counsellor in 462nd infantry division
today: lower court counsellor in Bielefeld

Butz, Hans born 6. 1. 1906
formerly: lower court counsellor in the special court in Danzig (Gdansk), joined the NSDAP in 1933, expert on questions of race and genealogy in Kulmsee
today: lower court counsellor in Goslar

Carmine, Dr. Erich born 24. 8. 1906
formerly: provincial court counsellor in Krumau (Ceský Krumow), magistrate in "People's Court"
today: lower court counsellor in Nuremberg

Carstensen, Dr. Otto born 11. 4. 1904
formerly: lower court counsellor in Ratzeburg, joined the NSDAP in 1931, chief district leader, head of Office for Legal Policy, deputy head, district law office and deputy district leader
today: superior provincial court counsellor in Schleswig

Chaluppa, Johannes born 29. 10. 1902
formerly: lower court counsellor in the special court, Kattowitz (Katowice)
today: labour court counsellor in Cologne

Christ, Dr. Wolfgang born 18. 7. 1900
formerly: corps judge of the head of the military administration, France
today: public prosecutor in Brunswick

Clauditz, Rudolf born 20. 1. 1899
formerly: senior military court counsellor in 461st infantry division
today: provincial court director in Hildesheim

Claussen, Kai born 1. 4. 1910
formerly: provincial court counsellor in the special court, Hamburg
today: senate president in superior provincial court, Hamburg

Clemens, Dr. Hermann born 27. 1. 1913
formerly: senior staff judge of the 182nd infantry division
today: lower court counsellor in Annweiler

Coenen, Dr. Hans-Wolf born 5. 11. 1907
formerly: senior military field judge in 16th and 31st infantry divisions
today: senate president in the provincial social court, Stuttgart

Collani, Hans-Joachim von born 13. 3. 1909
formerly: navy military court counsellor in minesweeper formations, east
today: provincial court counsellor in Lüneburg

Collet, Josef born 23. 7. 1903
formerly: provincial court counsellor in the special court, Saarbrücken
today: provincial court director in Saarbrücken

Cordier, Franz born 30. 7. 1905
formerly: public prosecutor in the special court, Kassel
today: senior public prosecutor, Frankfurt-on-Main, head of board of public prosecutors

Cünnen, Wilhelm born 12. 11. 1911
formerly: court assessor in the special court, Cologne
today: public prosecutor in Cologne

Czesla, Richard born 1. 12. 1903
formerly: lower court counsellor in the special court, Königsberg (Kaliningrad)
today: lower court counsellor in Pinneberg

Däubler, Helmut born 21. 1. 1904
formerly: superior provincial court counsellor in the nazi Ministry of Justice, Dept VII
today: senate president in Stuttgart

Dally, Karl born 14. 9. 1900
formerly: lower court counsellor in the special court, Bromberg (Bydgoszcz)
today: provincial court director in Duisburg

Dallinger, Dr. Wilhelm born July 1908
formerly: provincial court counsellor in the nazi Ministry of Justice
today: ministerial director in the Federal Ministry of Justice

Damman, Marcus born 8. 3. 1914
formerly: provincial court counsellor in the special court, Hamburg
today: superior provincial court counsellor in Hamburg

Dassler, Dr. Gerhard born 8. 11. 1905
formerly: provincial court counsellor and counsel for the prosecution in special court, Dresden
today: provincial court counsellor in Karlsruhe

Dede, Christian born 26. 8. 1906
formerly: public prosecutor in the special court, Weimar
today: provincial court director in Hanover

Dehns, Eduard born 8. 8. 1908
formerly: military court counsellor in the Luftwaffe
today: lower court counsellor in Ahrensburg

Depenbrock, Heinrich born 17. 12. 1905
formerly: public prosecutor in the special court, Bielefeld
today: senior public prosecutor in Bielefeld

Derks, Dr. Hermann born 25. 8. 1903
formerly: provincial court counsellor in the special court, Würzburg
today: provincial court director in Augsburg, appointed permanent representative of the provincial court president

Dettmer, Dr. Helmut born 9. 11. 1904
formerly: military court counsellor in 180th infantry division
today: lower court counsellor in Cuxhaven

Dewitz, Egmont von born 18. 10. 1907
formerly: military court counsellor in "Luftgau" III, Berlin
today: lower court counsellor in Cologne

Diderichs, Dr. Alexander born 17. 3. 1906
formerly: senior staff judge in 8th armoured division
today: public prosecutor in Münster

Dietrich, Dr. Hans born 31. 5. 1900
formerly: military court counsellor in the Berlin command
until August 1965: lower court counsellor in Frankfurt-on-Main

Dinckelacker, Helmut born 30. 11. 1906
formerly: lower court counsellor in the special court, Stuttgart
today: government director in the Ministry of Justice, Baden-Württemberg

Dittrich, Martin born 2. 8. 1910
formerly: public prosecutor in the special court, Breslau (Wrocław)
today: lower court counsellor in Giessen

Dobisch, Dr. Rudolf born 4. 8. 1904
formerly: government counsellor in Königinhof (Dvur Králové), member of "SdP", from 1938 SA Hauptsturmführer
today: administrative court counsellor in Münster

Döge, Dr. Hans born 29. 3. 1913
formerly: senior staff judge in 23rd army corps
today: government director in the Federal Disciplinary Court

Döllen, August von born 17. 8. 1899
formerly: senior staff judge in 180th division, Bremen
today: provincial court director in Oldenburg

Dölves, Heinrich born 28. 4. 1903
formerly: military court counsellor
today: senior judge in Wuppertal

Doerr, Dr. Karl born 3. 11. 1902
formerly: senior judge in special court, Darmstadt
today: provincial court director in Darmstadt

Doms, Dr. Wilhelm born 4. 6. 1911
formerly: senior staff judge in 36th infantry division
today: public prosecutor in Freiburg (Breisgau)

Dorer, Karl born 1. 6. 1909
formerly: public prosecutor in the special court, Stuttgart
today: senior public prosecutor in Stuttgart

Dossmann, Dr. Georg born 6. 12. 1906
formerly: provincial court counsellor in the special court, Strassburg (Strasbourg)
today: provincial court counsellor in Mannheim

Drach, Leonhard born 9. 3. 1903
formerly: first public prosecutor in the special court in Luxemburg; sentenced to 35 years imprisonment there in 1949
today: senior public prosecutor in Frankenthal

Dreher, Dr. Eduard born April 1907
formerly: first public prosecutor in the special court, Innsbruck
today: ministerial director in the Federal Ministry of Justice

Drews, Dr. Richard born 29. 3. 1901
formerly: provincial court counsellor in the special court, Dresden
today: provincial court counsellor in Hagen

Drinkuth, Dr. born 5. 1. 1897
formerly: military court counsellor of the field court in the Berlin command
today: lawyer in Bad Pyrmont

Dümler, Ludwig born 4. 3. 1909
formerly: senior government counsellor in the nazi Ministry of Justice
today: lower court counsellor in Hassfurt

Dürwanger, Karl born 23. 12. 1908
formerly: lower court counsellor in the special court, Brünn (Brno)
today: lower court counsellor in Nuremberg

Duhme born 4. 3. 1903
formerly: public prosecutor in the special court, Bielefeld
today: senior public prosecutor in Münster

Dyckmanns, Franz born 13. 6. 1905
formerly: military court counsellor in the Kaiserslautern command
today: lower court counsellor in Kaiserslautern

Ebersberg, Heinrich born July 1911
formerly: first public prosecutor in the nazi Ministry of Justice
today: ministerial counsellor in the Federal Ministry of Justice

Ebmeyer, Gottfried born 29. 12. 1906
formerly: provincial court counsellor in the special court, Bielefeld
today: senior judge in Bielefeld

Eckardt, Dr. Erich born 16. 7. 1900
formerly: senior military court counsellor with the commandant of Greater Paris, NSDAP, SS
today: superior provincial court counsellor in Hamburg

Eckert, Dr. Herbert born 15. 10. 1905
formerly: military court counsellor in 432nd infantry division
today: first public prosecutor in Oldenburg

Eder, Dr. Hugo born 18. 4. 1903
formerly: provincial court counsellor in the special court, Munich
today: supreme provincial court counsellor in Munich

Ehlers, Ernst born 16. 10. 1909
formerly: in 1938 head of main department II/22 in the Reich Security Main Office, in 1940 chief of state police office in Liegnitz (Legnica), in 1941 agent of chief of security police for Belgium and Northern France
today: administrative court counsellor in the administrative court of Schleswig Holstein

Eickhoff, Dr. Ernst-Wilhelm born 14. 2. 1907
formerly: senior military court counsellor at the High Command of the Army
today: ministerial counsellor in the North Rhine-Westphalian Ministry of Justice

Eigenwillig, Georg born 18. 8. 1909
formerly: senior military field judge OKH (high command of the army)
today: ministerial counsellor in the Federal Ministry of Defence

Eisenberg, Paul born 28. 12. 1909
formerly: military field judge in the 433rd and 463rd infantry divisions at Frankfurt-on-Oder
today: lower court counsellor in Lippstadt

Eisenblätter, Helmut born 5. 2. 1905
formerly: senior military court counsellor of the 9th AOK (Army High Comman), 1st, 87th and 173rd divisions
today: first public prosecutor in Frankfurt-on-Main

Elsenheimer, Georg born May 1903
formerly: lower court counsellor in the special court, Bamberg
today: ministerial counsellor in the Federal Ministry of Justice

Enkhaus, Rudolf born 14. 6. 1902
formerly: military court counsellor in the 168th infantry division
today: provincial court counsellor in Bückeburg

Erbel, Otto born 31. 5. 1908
formerly: provincial court counsellor in the special court, Aachen
today: federal judge of the Federal Court

Esser, Heinz born 20. 1. 1904
formerly: first public prosecutor for political cases in Leitmeritz (Litomerice)
today: senior government counsellor, head of the penitentiary and remand prison, Bochum

Fähndrich, Hans-Karl born 23. 1. 1901
formerly: senior judge in the special court, Kattowitz (Katowice)
today: lower court counsellor in Dortmund-Hörde

Fangmann, Dr. Arnold born 30. 3. 1901
formerly: senior military court counsellor of the 570th Supreme Field Headquarters and the High Command of the Army
today: provincial court president in Oldenburg

Fedder, Dr. Julius born 27. 2. 1900
formerly: lower court counsellor in the special court, Hamburg
today: provincial court director in Hamburg

Felmy, Dr. Heimfried born 16. 10. 1904
formerly: public prosecutor in the special court, Thorn (Torun) and Graudenz (Grudziadz), appears on the Polish list of war criminals No. 80/192
today: public prosecutor in Oldenburg

Filter born 30. 9. 1909
formerly: military court counsellor with the general of the Luftwaffe, North Norway
today: lower court counsellor in Lübeck

Fink, Ludwig born 2. 9. 1904
formerly: military court counsellor of the 407th infantry division
today: first public prosecutor in Kempten

Fleischmann, Dr. Rudolf born 1903
formerly: supreme court counsellor in the nazi Ministry of Justice
today: ministerial counsellor in the Federal Ministry of Justice

Fliessbach, Dr. Wilhelm born 4. 12. 1901
formerly: senior military court counsellor at the High Command of the Wehrmacht
today: federal judge in the Federal Fiscal Court

Foge, Dr. Wilhelm born 17. 8. 1906
formerly: public prosecutor in the legal department of the General Commissariat in Minsk
today: first public prosecutor in Kaiserslautern

Framheim, Dr. Otto born 12. 9. 1901
formerly: provincial court counsellor in the special court, Hamburg
today: provincial court director in Hamburg

Francke, Fritz born 11. 8. 1911
formerly: SS Unterscharführer, legal adviser to SS-Sturm II/36, lower court counsellor in Danzig (Gdansk)
today: provincial court counsellor in Nuremberg-Fürth

Frankenberg, Johannes born 7. 1. 1906
formerly: provincial court counsellor in Berlin, took part in "racial disgrace" sentences
today: lower court counsellor in Münnerstadt

Franz, Dr. Eugen born 25. 12. 1905
formerly: senior military court counsellor, senior military field judge of the 19th tank division
today: provincial court counsellor in Lübeck

Fraustein, Dr. W. born 17. 7. 1901
formerly: first public prosecutor in the special court, Posen (Poznan)
today: senior public prosecutor in Koblenz

Freyberg, Dr. Walter von born 2. 5. 1904
formerly: public prosecutor in the special court, Dresden
today: public prosecutor in Frankfurt-on-Main

Fricke, Dr. Andreas born 10. 11. 1903
formerly: lower court counsellor in Lobenstein, magistrate at the "People's Court"
today: provincial court counsellor in Brunswick

Friedrichs, Dr. Hans born 19. 1. 1910
formerly: public prosecutor at the Superior Provincial Court in Prague (Praha)
today: senior public prosecutor in Cologne

Fröhlich, Dr. Hans born 18. 6. 1905
formerly: public prosecutor in the special court, Munich
today: senior public prosecutor in Munich

Frühbrodt, Hermann born 28. 8. 1905
formerly: military court counsellor in the 401st infantry division
today: public prosecutor in Göttingen

Fürsen, J. N. born 13. 5. 1908
formerly: lower court counsellor and prosecutor in the special court, Kiel
today: provincial court director in Kiel

Fürstenhagen, Dr. Heinz-Otto born 30. 4. 1905
formerly: naval senior staff judge in the 9th security division
today: provincial court director in Hamburg

Full, Werner born 6. 3. 1914
formerly: public prosecutor for political cases at the Munich Superior Provincial Court
today: superior provincial court counsellor in Munich

Fuxius, Dr. Albert born 25. 7. 1907
formerly: military court counsellor of the 812th field headquarters
today: senior judge in Cologne

Gabrysch, Dr. Georg born 27. 9. 1904
formerly: public prosecutor in Maribor, SS Hauptsturmführer, appears on the Yugoslav list of war criminals No. A 16–1066
today: provincial court director in Hanover, at the Ministry of Justice of Lower Saxony

Gärtner, Hermann born 7. 3. 1907
formerly: public prosecutor in the special court, Essen
today: first public prosecutor in Essen

Ganser, Dr. Josef born 17. 8. 1901
formerly: senior government counsellor in the nazi Ministry of Justice
today: senate president in the Federal Patent Court, retired April 1965

Gatzschke, Alfred born 1. 12. 1905
formerly: lower court counsellor in the the 465th infantry division
today: lower court counsellor in Hanau

Gauger, Dr. Wilhelm born 16. 9. 1904
formerly: lower court counsellor in the special court, Stuttgart
today: senior public prosecutor in Tübingen

Geiger, Professor Dr. Willi born 22. 5. 1909
formerly: provincial court counsellor in the special court, Bamberg
today: judge in the Federal Constitutional Court

Geis, Walter born 28. 3. 1909
formerly: military court counsellor, headquarters of reserve unit 2-XVII, Linz
today: first public prosecutor in Giessen

Geppert, Johann born 10. 7. 1900
formerly: lower court counsellor in the special court, Leitmeritz (Litomerice)
today: lower court counsellor in Aachen

Gerard, Dr. Martin born 11. 8. 1905
formerly: provincial court counsellor in the special court, Mannheim
today: superior provincial court counsellor in Karlsruhe

Gerits, Dr. born 19. 12. 1906
formerly: provincial court counsellor in the special court, Cologne
today: provincial court director in Cologne

Gerlach, Dr. Bodo born 13. 2. 1908
formerly: public prosecutor in the special court, Oldenburg
today: first senior public prosecutor in Oldenburg

Geyer, Dr. Franz born 23. 3. 1905
formerly: military court counsellor in the 15th and 260th infantry divisions
today: senior social court counsellor in Nuremberg

Gichtel, Dr. Hermann born 12. 1. 1907
formerly: public prosecutor in the special court, Munich
today: supreme provincial court counsellor in Munich

Giese, Kurt born 16. 10. 1902
formerly: military court counsellor in the 13th field division of the Luftwaffe
today: provincial court counsellor in Lübeck

Giesecke, Dr. Hans-Werner born 3. 6. 1907
formerly: senior military field judge, LXVIII Army Corps, Greece
today: provincial court director in Frankfurt-on-Main

Gille, Dr. Wolfgang born 8. 11. 1901
formerly: military field judge in the 154th and 444th infantry divisions
today: federal judge in the Federal Disciplinary Court

Glasenapp, Günther von born 11. 10. 1913
formerly: senior staff judge in the Berlin command
today: public prosecutor in Detmold

Gleine, Wilhelm born 8. 9. 1900
formerly: lower court counsellor in the special court, Brünn (Brno)
today: lower court counsellor in Stuttgart

Gloge, Dr. Walter born 18. 8. 1904
formerly: military court counsellor in the Brescia I. 1016 command
today: lower court counsellor in Brunswick

Glund, Bruno born 13. 5. 1905
formerly: provincial court counsellor in the special court, Breslau (Wrocław)
today: provincial court counsellor in Kempten

Glunz, Dr. Josef born 4. 6. 1911
formerly: public prosecutor in the special court, Essen
today: first public prosecutor in Essen

Göke, Dr. Karl born 27. 6. 1907
formerly: public prosecutor in the special court, Bielefeld
today: senior public prosecutor in Hamm

Gösser, Helmut born 14. 10. 1909
formerly: lower court counsellor in the special court, Posen (Poznan)
today: lower court counsellor in Düsseldorf

Gonnermann, Dr. born 27. 9. 1905
formerly: public prosecutor in the Superior Provincial Court (high treason cases), Kassel
today: first public prosecutor in Frankfurt-on-Main

Gonnermann, Dr. Otto born 15. 2. 1908
formerly: 1935 member of the Gestapo, head of the government sub-department for police administration, Bromberg (Bydgoszcz), 1943 district president in Bydgoszcz
today: administrative court director in Darmstadt

Goose, Helmut born 19. 6. 1908
formerly: military court counsellor at the Danzig (Gdansk) command
today: lower court counsellor in Gifhorn

Gosewisch, Hans born 17. 5. 1902
formerly: provincial court counsellor in the special court, Kalisch (Kalisz)
today: provincial court director in Brunswick

Gräser, Dr. Hans born 10. 10. 1910
formerly: provincial court counsellor in the nazi Ministry of Justice
today: lower court director in Heidelberg

Graf, Dr. Ludwig born 17. 2. 1903
formerly: first public prosecutor in the special court, Munich
today: senate president in the Supreme Provincial Court

Gramm, Dr. Erich born 3. 5. 1906
formerly: ministerial counsellor in the nazi Ministry of Justice; promoting member of the SS
today: senate president in the superior provincial court in Hamburg, first chairman of the association of judges in Hamburg

Greger, Hubertus born 4. 9. 1907
formerly: military court counsellor in the 8th rifle division
today: lower court counsellor in Kassel

Grendel, Dr. Wilhelm born 14. 12. 1902
formerly: superior provincial court counsellor in the "People's Court"
today: superior provincial court counsellor in Celle

Griffel, Dr. Anton born 20. 4. 1903
formerly: first public prosecutor in the special court, Bamberg
today: supreme provincial court counsellor in Munich

Gröger, Karl born 20. 4. 1905
formerly: public prosecutor in the special court, Breslau (Wroclaw)
today: first public prosecutor in Memmingen

Grosch, Dr. Walter born 6. 3. 1906
formerly: provincial court counsellor in the special court, Mainz
today: provincial court counsellor in Frankenthal

Groskopff, Herbert born 29. 12. 1904
formerly: military court counsellor in the 190th infantry division
today: provincial court director in Oldenburg

Grotewold, Heinrich born 28. 9. 1900
formerly: senior staff judge in the 180th, 190th and 84th infantry divisions
today: lower court director in Soltau

Groth, Dr. Erich born 12. 3. 1904
formerly: public prosecutor for cases of high treason in the Superior Provincial Court in Hamburg
today: public prosecutor in Hamburg

Grüb, Dr. Josef born 18. 5. 1902
formerly: first public prosecutor for political cases in Nuremberg
today: senate president in the Superior Provincial Court in Munich

Gruhl, Gerhard born 11. 5. 1900
formerly: lower court counsellor in the special court, Kiel
today: lower court counsellor in Lübeck

Grunau, Dr. Theodor born 22. 12. 1902
formerly: senior public prosecutor in the special court, Celle
today: government director in the penal executory office, Hamm

Grunert, Friedrich born 12. 10. 1912
formerly: military court counsellor in the 4th armoured division
today: lower court counsellor in Kiel

Grussdorf, Joachim born 31. 5. 1907
formerly: military court counsellor in the 143rd infantry division
today: lower court counsellor in Göttingen

Günther, Karl born 4. 3. 1906
formerly: public prosecutor in the special court, Hamburg
today: provincial court counsellor in Hamburg

Güntner, Dr. Hans born 23. 4. 1906
formerly: public prosecutor in the special court, Eger (Cheb)
today: provincial labour court director in Tübingen

Gugler, Dr. Heinrich born 28. 8. 1906
formerly: public prosecutor in the special court, Breslau (Wroclaw)
today: leading senior public prosecutor in Hamm

Guntermann, Dr. Franz born 20. 1. 1908
formerly: public prosecutor in Munich and chief executory officer at executions
today: provincial court counsellor in Munich

Haase, Dr. Johannes born 1. 5. 1908
formerly: public prosecutor in the special court, Zichenau (Ciechanow)
today: public prosecutor in Hildesheim

Habben, Herbert born 30. 3. 1909
formerly: senior military field judge in the 6th infantry division, Bielefeld
today: public prosecutor in Hanover

Hachmeister, Dr. Karl born 8. 1. 1912
formerly: SS Führer and SS judge
today: lower court counsellor in Wolfsburg

Häfele, Dr. Karl born 28. 11. 1902
formerly: provincial court counsellor in the special court, Frankfurt-on-Main
today: provincial court director in Frankfurt-on-Main

Haferkorn, Dr. Alfred born 28. 4. 1903
formerly: superior provincial court counsellor in the special court, Dresden
today: senior judge in Korbach

Hagedorn, Richard born 1. 2. 1906
formerly: supreme military court counsellor in the 83rd infantry division
today: senior public prosecutor in Hamburg

Hagemann, Dr. Heinz born 9. 10. 1904
formerly: first public prosecutor in the special court, Celle
today: senior public prosecutor in Verden

Hagemeister, Heinrich born 1. 2. 1906
formerly: military court counsellor at an army high command
today: provincial court director in Itzehoe

Hagenbeck, Dr. Werner born 29. 3. 1903
formerly: military field judge at the 606th field headquarters

today: lower court counsellor in Düsseldorf

Hagens, Dr. Hans von born 10. 12. 1911
formerly: senior staff judge at the headquarters of the Wehrmacht, Berlin and in the 257th and 169th infantry divisions
today: provincial court counsellor in Verden/Aller

Hagmann, Heinz born 21. 6. 1907
formerly: assistant judge and prosecutor of the Ist Grand Criminal Court, Dortmund, took part in "racial disgrace" sentences
today: public prosecutor in Bielefeld

Haidinger, Dr. Oskar born 29. 3. 1908
formerly: provincial court counsellor in the special court, Litzmannstadt (Lodz)
today: senate president in the Federal Supreme Court

Haller, Dr. Walter born 5. 1. 1909
formerly: public prosecutor in the special court, Stuttgart
today: lower court director in Waiblingen

Hamaekers, Dr. Walter born 28. 11. 1904
formerly: public prosecutor in the special court, Kattowitz (Katowice)
today: public prosecutor in Wuppertal

Hammer, Dr. Hermann born 28. 8. 1906
formerly: provincial court counsellor in the special court, Stettin (Szczecin)
today: senior judge in Stadthagen

Hänert, Berthold born 5. 8. 1901
formerly: military field judge in the 14th and 174th divisions
today: provincial court director in Bochum

Härlin, Dr. Ernst born 5. 1. 1901
formerly: senior military court counsellor in the 15th infantry division
today: provincial court director in Stuttgart

Hannemann, Erich born 28. 2. 1907
formerly: senior military court counsellor in the 94th division and army high command 1
today: public prosecutor in Hamburg-Wandsbek

Harder, Dr. Erwin born 8. 11. 1903
formerly: provincial court counsellor in the special court in Hamburg
today: provincial court director in Hamburg

Harder, Dr. Herbert born 28. 1. 1907
formerly: senior staff judge in the 11th division, Allenstein
today: lower court counsellor in Hamburg

Hardrath, Dr. Günter born 17. 10. 1909
formerly: public prosecutor in the nazi Ministry of Justice
today: federal judge in the Federal Disciplinary Court

Harms, Adolf born 2. 3. 1900
formerly: provincial court counsellor in the special court, Oldenburg
today: provincial court director in Oldenburg

Harms, Dr. Alfred born 4. 9. 1905
formerly: military court counsellor in the 19th field division of the Luftwaffe
today: senate president in Celle

Hartinger, Josef born 14. 9. 1893
formerly: military court counsellor, headquarters LX
today: state secretary in the Bavarian Ministry of Justice

Hartke, Ernst born 12. 7. 1906
formerly: military court counsellor at the headquarters of Greater Paris
today: senior judge in Wetter-on-Ruhr

Hartmeyer, Dr. Wilhelm born 18. 5. 1912
formerly: provincial court counsellor at the special court, Essen
today: provincial court director in Essen

Heerhaber, Wilhelm born 23. 1. 1903
formerly: military field judge at the Wehrmacht command, Berlin
today: senior judge in Tecklenburg

Hegener, Wilhelm born 31. 12. 1906
formerly: lower court counsellor at the "People's Court" for cases of high treason
today: lower court counsellor in Salzkotten

Heinemann, Dr. Friedrich born 9. 6. 1904
formerly: military court counsellor in the 371st infantry division
today: provincial court director in Kassel

Heinke, Erhard born 13. 3. 1913
formerly: public prosecutor in the special court, Breslau (Wrocław)
today: provincial court director in Nuremberg-Fürth

Heinrichs, Fritz born 13. 5. 1904
formerly: first public prosecutor in the special court, Mainz
today: first public prosecutor in Darmstadt

Henke, Alfred born 13. 10. 1909
formerly: military court counsellor in the 190th infantry division
today: provincial court counsellor in Osnabrück

Hennecke, Kurt born 12. 7. 1905
formerly: public prosecutor in the special court, Prague (Praha)
today: senate president in the Provincial Social Court in Celle

Hennig, Dr. Martin born 1. 8. 1901
formerly: provincial court counsellor in the special court, Leipzig
today: lower court counsellor in Plettenberg

Hensel, Ernst born 22. 12. 1911
formerly: senior staff judge in the 9th armoured division
today: public prosecutor in Brunswick

Henseling, Dr. Jakob born 10. 1. 1913
formerly: lower court counsellor for political cases at the Superior Provincial Court, Kassel
today: provincial court director in Kassel

Herbert, Karl born 28. 2. 1904
formerly: military court counsellor at the Aachen command
today: senate president in the Superior Provincial Court in Koblenz

Hergt, Dr. Albert born 13. 1. 1901
formerly: provincial court counsellor in the special court, Frankfurt-on-Main
today: lower court counsellor in Wiesbaden

Herrnreiter, Dr. Ferdinand born 8. 3. 1907
formerly: public prosecutor in the "People's Court"
today: provincial court director in Augsburg

Herting, Dr. Hans born 25. 7. 1909
formerly: public prosecutor in the special court, Dessau
today: public prosecutor in Koblenz

Herzing, Wilhelm born 6. 1. 1903
formerly: public prosecutor in the special court, Würzburg
today: senior judge in Bad Neustadt-on-Saale

Herzog, Dr. Josef born April 1903
formerly: first public prosecutor in the Superior Provincial Court in Prague (Praha)
today: ministerial counsellor in the Federal Ministry of Justice

Herzog, Dr. Siegmund born 24. 5. 1910
formerly: military court counsellor in military district B/SW, France and field command Lissa (Leszno)
today: lower court counsellor in Osnabrück

Hey, Hubert born 10. 6. 1901
formerly: miltary court counsellor at the Wehrmacht High Command
today: leading ministerial counsellor in the North Rhine-Westphalian Ministry of Justice

Heyde, Waldemar born 12. 6. 1908
formerly: military field judge in the 404th division, Dresden and the 171st division, agent of the Gestapo
today: provincial court director in Stuttgart

Heyer, Dr. Kurt born 7. 6. 1908
formerly: military court counsellor
today: public prosecutor in Brunswick

Heyne, Heinz born 7. 5. 1903
formerly: judge at the special court, Radom
today: senate counsellor in the Federal Patent Court

Hezel, Dr. Friedrich born 12. 2. 1912
formerly: provincial court counsellor in the nazi Ministry of Justice
today: superior provincial court counsellor in Stuttgart

Hildebrand, Heinz born 4. 7. 1903
formerly: first public prosecutor for political cases in Lübeck
today: senior public prosecutor in Lübeck

Hildebrandt, Dr. Hans-Ulrich born 7. 1. 1909
formerly: provincial court counsellor in the special court, Stettin (Szczecin)
today: lower court counsellor in Castrop-Rauxel

Hille, Fritz born 4. 3. 1907
formerly: public prosecutor in the special court, Hanover
today: senior public prosecutor in Detmold

Hillenkamp, Ulrich born 5. 4. 1912
formerly: senior staff judge at the 17th Army High Command
today: lawyer in Viersen

Hillmann, Dr. Arno born 29. 11. 1909
formerly: senior military field judge at the Army High Command
today: senior public prosecutor in Stuttgart

Hillrichs born 21. 5. 1911
formerly: public prosecutor in the special court, Oldenburg
today: provincial court counsellor in Osnabrück

Hirmer, Dr. Hans born 31. 1. 1909
formerly: provincial court counsellor in the special court, Munich
today: lower court counsellor in Munich

Hirschbrich, Georg born 18. 9. 1902
formerly: military field judge at the Army High Command/HR
today: senior judge in Freising

Hodes, Dr. Fritz born 6. 2. 1908
formerly: military court counsellor in the 26th and 36th infantry divisions, employee of the nazi journal on military law
today: superior provincial court counsellor in Frankfurt-on-Main

Höfer, Dr. Gerhard born 26. 8. 1901
formerly: military field judge of the 17th engineering headquarters staff
today: lower court counsellor in Hanover

Höffler, Dr. Siegfried born 16. 2. 1909
formerly: public prosecutor in the special court, Berlin
today: first public prosecutor in Bremen

Höher, Dr. Konrad born 9. 5. 1905
formerly: public prosecutor in the special court, Aachen and in the "People's Court"
today: public prosecutor in Cologne

Höhn, Dr. Rudolf born 13. 10. 1908
formerly: public prosecutor in the special court, Würzburg
today: provincial court counsellor in Würzburg

Hönneckes, Dr. Heinrich born 31. 5. 1910
formerly: military court counsellor in the 20th division, Hamburg
today: senior administrative court counsellor in Munster

Hoffmann, Walter born 3. 6. 1909
formerly: senior staff judge in the 34th division, Koblenz
today: public prosecutor in Mainz

Hoffrichter, Otto born 1. 6. 1906
formerly: senior staff judge in the 246th infantry division
today: provincial court director in Waldshut

Holl, Dr. Bernd born 20. 12. 1907
formerly: senior military field judge
today: government director of the Oberems prison camp and Bielefeld prison

Holstein, Heinz born 2. 4. 1913
formerly: lower court counsellor in the special court in Jena
today: provincial court counsellor in Stuttgart

Holtzheimer, Dr. born 8. 2. 1908
formerly: lower court counsellor in the special court, Königsberg (Kaliningrad)
today: lower court director in Herzberg/Harz

Holz, Dr. Waldemar born 5. 11. 1904
formerly: lower court counsellor in the special court, Bielitz (Bielsko)
today: lower court director in Geislingen

Holzki, Alfred born 27. 11. 1911
formerly: military court counsellor in the 11th and 12th divisions, Allenstein
today: lower court counsellor in Kronach

Hoof, Dr. Rudolf born 12. 4. 1899
formerly: supreme court counsellor in the nazi Ministry of Justice

today: ministerial counsellor in the Hessian Ministry of Justice

Hoogen, Matthias born 25. 6. 1904
formerly: military court counsellor of the Luftwaffe and senior military judge of the Kurland army
today: defence commissioner of the Bundestag

Hornig, Erich born 29. 12. 1901
formerly: supreme court counsellor in the nazi Ministry of Justice, dept. VI
today: ministerial director in the Ministry of Justice of Lower Saxony

Huber, Ulrich born 7. 5. 1904
formerly: provincial court counsellor in the special court, Dortmund
today: provincial court director in Bielefeld

Hubernagel, Wilhelm born 8. 2. 1903
formerly: public prosecutor in the special court, Radom and Leitmeritz (Litomerice)
today: senior public prosecutor in Düsseldorf

Hübener, Ulrich born 15. 12. 1901
formerly: provincial court counsellor in the special court, Schwerin
today: provincial court counsellor in Hamburg

Hückstädt, Dr. Hermann born 31. 1. 1902
formerly: lower court counsellor in the special court, Kiel
today: provincial court director in Kiel

Hülle, Dr. Werner born 30. 4. 1903
formerly: chief judge
today: superior provincial court president in Oldenburg

Hüntemann, Dr. born 3. 1. 1904
formerly: public prosecutor for political cases at the Superior Provincial Court in Hamm
today: senior public prosecutor in Bochum

Hüpers, Dr. born 29. 10. 1904
formerly: public prosecutor in the special courts in Hohensalza (Inowraclaw) and Beuthen (Bytom)
today: first public prosecutor in Oldenburg

Humbert, Dr. Jürgen born 7. 1. 1908
formerly: public prosecutor in the special courts in Frankfurt-on-Oder, Litzmannstadt (Lodz) and Berlin
today: public prosecutor in Lübeck

Hunger, Horst born 4. 5. 1902
formerly: military court counsellor in the 463rd infantry division
today: federal judge in the Federal Social Court

Husslein, Dr. Otto born 25. 10. 1905
formerly: judge of a field court in Denmark
today: provincial court president in Deggendorf

Huyke, Dr. Wilhelm born 5. 9. 1900
formerly: senior staff judge, Fester Platz Borissow
today: superior provincial court counsellor in Oldenburg

Indra, Dr. Rudolf born 10. 3. 1901
formerly: lower court counsellor in Freiwaldau (Fryvaldov) magistrate at the "People's Court"
today: provincial court counsellor in Giessen

Itzen, Alwin born 4. 5. 1908
formerly: lower court counsellor in the special court, Oldenburg
today: lower court counsellor in Wilhelmshaven

Jacobs, Dr. Werner born 19. 5. 1907
formerly: senior staff judge in the 52nd and 428th infantry divisions
today: lower court director in Karlsruhe

Jaeger, Helmut born 20. 6. 1901
formerly: counsellor in the Public Prosecutor's Office at the "People's Court"
today: superior provincial court counsellor in Munich

Jagow, Clemens von born 14. 2. 1903
formerly: provincial court counsellor in the special court, Kiel
today: provincial court president in Lübeck

Jahn, Dr. Günter born 7. 9. 1901
formerly: military court counsellor at the 397th supreme field command, army high command 11
today: lower court director in Lüneburg

Jakob, Hermann born 4. 10. 1906
formerly: 15 July 1932 SS Oberscharführer, legal adviser to an SS regiment
today: provincial court counsellor in Augsburg

Jakubassa, Dr. Paul born 15. 2. 1900
formerly: senior military field judge in the 5th armoured division and the 432nd division

until July 1965: administrative court director in Arnsberg

Jancke, Helmut born 27. 6. 1907
formerly: provincial court counsellor in the special court, Posen (Poznan)
today: lower court counsellor in Herford

Janischowsky, Dr. Ewald born 13. 8. 1905
formerly: provincial court counsellor in the special court, Oppeln (Opole)
today: lower court counsellor in Hanover

Japes, Dr. born 10. 1. 1904
formerly: public prosecutor in the special court, Essen
today: senior public prosecutor in Siegen

Jarzina, Ludwig born 11. 2. 1902
formerly: lower court counsellor in the special court I, Berlin
today: lower court director in Hechingen

Jenniches, August born 7. 9. 1909
formerly: public prosecutor in the special court, Nuremberg
today: provincial court director in Nuremberg

Jeremias, Dr. Hans-Georg born 13. 2. 1902
formerly: military court counsellor 584th rear services command
today: senate president in Celle and member of the Lower Saxony State Court

Jessenberger, Dr. born 13. 12. 1905
formerly: lower court counsellor in the special court, Zichenau (Ciechanow)
today: administrative court director in Neustadt-on-Weinstrasse

John, Helmut born 7. 5. 1906
formerly: military court counsellor at the 582nd supreme field command
today: superior provincial court counsellor in Hamm

Johnn, Felix von born 27. 6. 1903
formerly: senior naval court counsellor
today: provincial social court counsellor in Schleswig

Jürgens, Ulrich born 15. 7. 1904
formerly: military court counsellor in the 174th division, Hanover
today: lower court counsellor in Lüdenscheid

Juncker, Heinz born 3. 2. 1907
formerly: lower court counsellor in the special court, Posen (Poznan)
today: lower court counsellor in Diez

Jung, Hans born 11. 7. 1904
formerly: public prosecutor in the special court, Brünn (Brno)
today: public prosecutor in Siegen

Jung, Dr. Herbert born 22. 5. 1903
formerly: superior provincial court counsellor in the special court, Kassel
today: superior provincial court counsellor in Frankfurt-on-Main

Junghanns-Konopka, Dr. Herbert born 20. 6. 1902
formerly: lower court counsellor in the special court I, Posen (Poznan)
today: lower court counsellor in Ballingen

Jungmann, Dr. Franz born 21. 5. 1905
formerly: public prosecutor in the special court, Posen (Poznan)
today: public prosecutor in Essen

Kammer, Dr. Erich born 9. 6. 1905
formerly: public prosecutor in the special court for Lorraine in Sulzbach
today: senate president in the Superior Provincial Court in Saarbrücken

Kannengiesser, Heinz born 9. 10. 1907
formerly: senior naval court counsellor
today: lower court counsellor in Bremerhaven

Karow, Karl born 13. 8. 1905
formerly: military court counsellor in the Berlin command
today: first public prosecutor in Hanau

Karpen, Dr. Werner born 2. 10. 1905
(formerly Karpinski)
formerly: public prosecutor for political cases in Danzig (Gdansk)
today: senior public prosecutor

Karrasch, Günter born 16. 11. 1911
formerly: senior staff judge in the 8th and 14th divisions
today: lower court counsellor in Oberhausen

Kaulbach, Günter born 26. 5. 1904
formerly: supreme court counsellor in the nazi Ministry of Justice
today: vice-president of the Superior Pro-

vincial Court in Karlsruhe and member of the 1st Senate of the Supreme Restitution Court in Rastatt

Kaune, Dr. Bernhard born 12. 10. 1906
formerly: senior military field judge in the 1st armoured division and the Greater Paris command
today: senate president in the Provincial Social Court in Stuttgart

Kayser, Alexander born 16. 4. 1903
formerly: military court counsellor in the Wehrmacht-WR High Command
today: senate president in Celle

Keidel, Theodor born 9. 12. 1902
formerly: senior public prosecutor for political cases at the Superior Provincial Court in Munich I
today: supreme provincial court counsellor in Munich

Keil, Dr. Werner born 1. 7. 1900
formerly: military court counsellor in the Berlin command
until August 1965: provincial court director in Bielefeld

Keisel, Heinrich born 24. 9. 1908
formerly: public prosecutor in the special court, Munich
today: senior public prosecutor in Munich

Keller, Otfried born 28. 4. 1911
formerly: senior staff judge in the 26th division, Cologne
today: provincial court president in Marburg

Kemper, Dr. Heinz born 22. 9. 1913
formerly: judge in the special court, Aachen
today: administrative court director in Koblenz, Chamber of Trier

Keppel, Otto born 1. 12. 1908
formerly: senior military field judge in the 12th, 32nd and 218th infantry divisions
today: public prosecutor in Darmstadt

Kessel, Franz born 21. 8. 1908
formerly: provincial court counsellor in the special court, Aachen
today: superior provincial court counsellor in Cologne

Kettnacker, Hans born 17. 7. 1905
formerly: military court counsellor in the 465th infantry division
today: senior judge in Stuttgart

Keutgen, Dr. Hans born 12. 6. 1912
formerly: judge in the special court, Aachen
today: provincial court director in Aachen

Keyser, Dr. Werner born 26. 5. 1904
formerly: public prosecutor for political cases at the Superior Provincial Court in Dresden
today: first public prosecutor in Kassel

Kieckbusch, Günther born 6. 11. 1909
formerly: Hauptsturmführer in the armed SS, counsel for the prosecution and chairman of an SS and police court, official in charge of the execution of sentences and cases of reprieve in the central office of the SS Court
today: counsellor of justice in Philippsburg

Kieler, Dr. Herbert born 18. 1. 1905
formerly: senior judge in the special court, Oppeln (Opole)
today: social court counsellor in Munster

Kinnen, Peter born 22. 5. 1902
formerly: senior staff judge in the 102nd and 526th infantry divisions
today: lower court counsellor in Solingen

Klein, Karl born 27. 8. 1904
formerly: military court counsellor in the 156th infantry division
today: federal judge in the Federal Administrative Court

Kleinknecht, Otto born 12. 6. 1901
formerly: public prosecutor in the special court, Stuttgart
today: senior judge in Marbach

Kleiss, Bruno born 8. 2. 1914
formerly: military court counsellor
today: senior public presecutor in Oldenburg

Klemp, Dr. Max born 7. 12. 1897
formerly: senior military court counsellor, commanding officer of the Supply District Centre and of the 285th security division
today: provincial court counsellor in Stade

Klenner, Willibald born 19. 6. 1908
formerly: senior staff judge in Norway
today: provincial court director in Stuttgart

Klier, Dr. Walter born 17. 7. 1908
formerly: public prosecutor for political cases in Leitmeritz (Litomerice)
today: lower court counsellor in Regensburg

Knackstedt, Karl born 11. 1. 1905
formerly: military court counsellor in the 158th division
today: provincial court director in Brunswick

Knippenberg, Dr. born 13. 4. 1904
formerly: public prosecutor in the special court, Dortmund
today: senior public prosecutor in Munster

Knobloch, Gottfried born 17. 10. 1911
formerly: public prosecutor in the special court, Kattowitz (Katowice)
today: first public prosecutor in Frankfurt-on-Main

Knop, Walter born 17. 8. 1906
formerly: superior provincial court counsellor in Brunswick, member of the NSDAP from 1926, member of the Reichstag of the "Third Reich", Supreme Party Court
today: lower court counsellor in Seesen

Knossalla, Dr. Arnold born 5. 8. 1902
formerly: public prosecutor in the special court, Breslau (Wrocław)
today: provincial court director in Wiesbaden

Kobel, Otto born 13. 6. 1912
formerly: senior staff judge in the 156th infantry division and 158th reserve division
today: provincial court counsellor in Hamburg

Koch, Adalbert born 14. 10. 1910
formerly: senior staff judge in the 61st and 141st infantry divisions and army high command 9
today: lawyer in Bünde, Westphalia

Koebel, Dr. Ulrich born 19. 6. 1901
formerly: lower court counsellor, senate for cases of high treason, Stuttgart
today: senate president at the Superior Provincial Court in Stuttgart

Köhne, Hans born 18. 10. 1902
formerly: public prosecutor in Dortmund, also responsible for arbitrary sentences against Jews
today: public prosecutor in Bielefeld

König, Fritz born 27. 8. 1905
formerly: senior staff judge in the 173rd and 271st infantry divisions
today: lower court counsellor in Brunswick

Kolb, Dr. Karl born 12. 1. 1903
formerly: first public prosecutor in the special court, Kalisch (Kalisz)
today: senior public prosecutor in Würzburg

Kori, Manfred born 24. 1. 1906
formerly: lower court counsellor and prosecutor in the special court in Leoben
today: provincial court counsellor in Nuremberg

Kornhuber, Dr. Helmut born 15. 10. 1900
formerly: provincial court director in the special court, Königsberg (Kaliningrad)
today: superior provincial court counsellor in Schleswig

Kraemer, Dr. Leo born 18. 9. 1901
formerly: public prosecutor in the "People's Court"
today: senior public prosecutor in Cologne

Krah, Bernhard born 9. 7. 1912
formerly: court officer in the court martial of the artillery, Dept. 75
today: provincial court counsellor in Bonn

Krapp, Dr. Philipp born 7. 8. 1906
formerly: lower court counsellor in the special court, Mährisch Ostrau (Moravska Ostrava)
today: superior provincial court counsellor in Bamberg

Krautwig, Dr. Carl born 5. 11. 1904
formerly: senior military field judge in the 20th armoured division and LXXXI army command
today: state secretary in the Ministry for All-German Affairs

Krebs, Dr. Heinrich born 6. 1. 1910
formerly: lower court counsellor in the senate for cases of high treason, Stuttgart
today: federal judge in the Federal Social Court

Krekel, Adolf
formerly: public prosecutor in the special court, Kattowitz (Katowice)
today: lawyer in Cologne-Klettenberg

Kress, Dr. Gustav born 17. 9. 1902
formerly: military court counsellor in the 413th infantry division
today: senior judge in Schwabach

Kristl, Dr. Karl born 1. 7. 1910
formerly: assistant judge in the chamber for political crimes of the Provincial Court in Eger (Cheb)
today: provincial court director in Nuremberg-Fürth

Krohn, Hans-Martin born 18. 1. 1904
formerly: military court counsellor in the 190th division
today: senate president in the Superior Provincial Court of Schleswig

Krüger, Ulrich born 24. 12. 1907
formerly: public prosecutor in the special court, Frankfurt-on-Main
today: senior public prosecutor in Frankfurt-on-Main, permanent deputy of the Prosecutor General

Krüger, Walter born 23, 11. 1905
formerly: senior military field judge in the 1st infantry division
today: lower court director in Lübeck

Kruss, Dr. Jakob born 12. 8. 1902
formerly: provincial court counsellor in the nazi Ministry of Justice, Dept. III for political cases
today: provincial court director in Krefeld

Kubasch, Theodor born 9. 7. 1902
formerly: superior provincial court counsellor in Luxemburg, chief office administrator in the Moselland legal district office
today: senior judge in Rheinbach

Kühn, Max born 10. 9. 1902
formerly: provincial court counsellor in the special court, Cologne
today: provincial court director in Cologne

Kühn, Dr. Fritz born 13. 3. 1906
formerly: public prosecutor in the special court, Nuremberg
today: senior public prosecutor in Nuremberg-Fürth

Kuhlmann, Dr. Fritz born 5. 11. 1905
formerly: senior military field judge in the 6th division, Bielefeld
today: provincial court director in Bielefeld

Kuhn, Horst born 16. 1. 1910
formerly: public prosecutor in the special court, Königsberg (Kaliningrad)
today: first public prosecutor in Frankfurt-on-Main

Kümmel, Fritz born 5. 6. 1908
formerly: senior staff judge in the 227th infantry division
today: public prosecutor in Mönchen-Gladbach

Künnecke, Erich born 18. 2. 1906
formerly: military field court counsellor in the 190th infantry division
today: lower court counsellor in Lüneburg

Küster born 26. 1. 1901
formerly: lower court counsellor in the special court, Aachen
today: lower court counsellor in Düren

Kuhnert born 4. 5. 1910
formerly: provincial court counsellor in the special court, Aachen
today: senior public prosecutor in Essen

Kuhr, Erich born 8. 8. 1910
formerly: senior staff judge in the Frontier Headquarters, Wedel
today: public prosecutor in Giessen

Kulemann, Dr. Johannes born 7. 2. 1899
formerly: military court counsellor in the 560th field headquarters
today: lower court counsellor in Hamburg

Kummer, Georg born 4. 8. 1900
formerly: lower court counsellor in the special court, Hagen
today: lower court counsellor in Bielefeld

Kurze, Paul born 14. 11. 1901
formerly: supreme court counsellor in the nazi Ministry of Justice, Werewolf, SA Sturmführer

today: social court counsellor in Brunswick

Kutschmann, Dr. Hans Werner born 10. 1. 1908
formerly: public prosecutor in the nazi Ministry of Justice, Dept. III, for political cases
today: superior provincial court counsellor in Celle

Lampen, Dr. Gregor born 22. 12. 1905
formerly: army judge in the 82nd infantry division
today: lower court counsellor in Lingen

Landwehr, Wilhelm born 1. 7. 1903
formerly: senior military court counsellor in the 5th tank division
today: senior public prosecutor in Hanover

Lange, Hans-Ulrich born 27. 1. 1911
formerly: public prosecutor in the special court, Troppau (Opava)
today: federal judge in the Federal Disciplinary Court

Last, Hans born 29. 4. 1909
formerly: military court counsellor in the 670th supreme field headquarters
today: lower court counsellor in Ansbach

Laube born 5. 5. 1908
formerly: public prosecutor in the nazi Ministry of Justice, Dept. IV for political cases
today: senate president in Hamm

Laudes, Josef born 15. 4. 1904
formerly: provincial court counsellor in the special court, Wuppertal
today: lower court counsellor in Solingen

Lay, Werner born 1. 2. 1906
formerly: first public prosecutor in Mannheim; SS Obersturmführer
today: superior provincial court counsellor in Karlsruhe

Lefringhausen, Paul born 8. 10. 1900
formerly: military court counsellor in Field Luftgau (air force district) XXVI
today: superior provincial court counsellor in Düsseldorf

Lehnhoff, Günther born 31. 7. 1911
formerly: public prosecutor in the special court, Danzig (Gdansk)
today: senior public prosecutor in Düsseldorf

Leick, Waldemar born 25. 1. 1900
formerly: adviser to a corps headquarters in the Ukraine
today: vice-president of the Superior Administrative Court in Schleswig-Holstein

Leiterer, Dr. Richard born 8. 2. 1902
formerly: head of the Gestapo head-office in Magdeburg, SS Obersturmbannführer in the security service of the NSDAP Reich leadership
today: administrative court counsellor in the Schleswig-Holstein Administrative Court

Lenski, Dr. Konrad born 13. 6. 1901
formerly: military court counsellor in the Reich Military Court and the 6th Field Military Court
today: provincial court director in Lüneburg

Lerch, Dr. Christoph born 2. 3. 1902
formerly: military court counsellor in the 464th infantry division
today: senior judge in Duderstadt

Leverenz, Dr. Bernhard born 15. 2. 1909
formerly: naval senior staff judge
today: Minister of Justice in Schleswig-Holstein (also see section: The Intellectual Fathers of Genocide again Poison Public Opinion)

Liebau, Dr. born 15. 11. 1905
formerly: lower court counsellor in the special court, Posen (Poznan), official in charge of special courts in the nazi Ministry of Justice
today: senior judge in Seesen

Liebich, Johannes born 5. 8. 1908
formerly: public prosecutor in the special court, Kattowitz (Katowice)
today: public prosecutor in Kaiserslautern

Lind, Dr. Helmut born 1. 12. 1913
formerly: senior staff judge in army high command 14, 4th mountain division, SA
today: social court counsellor in Giessen

Lindemann born 23. 6. 1900
formerly: provincial court counsellor in the special court, Dortmund
today: superior provincial court counsellor in Hamm

Lindscheid born 7. 12. 1908
formerly: lower court counsellor in the special court, Dortmund
today: lower court counsellor in Hagen

Linsenhoff, Karl born 22. 9. 1901
formerly: senior military court counsellor high command of the 4th Armoured Army
today: provincial court counsellor in Oldenburg

Lipps, Dr. Herbert born 30. 7. 1911
formerly: provincial court counsellor in the special court, Posen (Poznan)
today: lower court counsellor in Weiden

Littek, Richard born 5. 11. 1901
formerly: senior staff judge in the 291st infantry division, High Command of the Army/HR
today: lower court director in Hamburg

Löde, Dr. Helmut born 14. 9. 1906
formerly: public prosecutor in the special court, Dessau
today: public prosecutor in Hanover

Löllke, Ernst born 19. 7. 1905
formerly: public prosecutor in the special court, Rostock
today: public prosecutor in Hamburg

Lörtz, Johann born 23. 3. 1905
formerly: military court counsellor in the 344th infantry division
today: senate president in Karlsruhe

Lösch, Dr. born 12. 2. 1905
formerly: lower court counsellor and prosecutor in the special court, Weimar
today: lower court counsellor in Zeven

Lösch, Alwin born 12. 2. 1904
formerly: military court counsellor in the 339th infantry division
today: lower court director in Offenbach

Löscher, Dr. Otto born 15. 6. 1910
formerly: provincial court counsellor in the nazi Ministry of Justice, Dept. III
today: federal judge in the Federal Court

Lohner, Dr. Otto born 23. 7. 1912
formerly: senior staff judge, special tasks (Lorraine and Luxemburg, penal camp Papenburg, brigade 999, and others)
today: lawyer in Mayen

Lohrey, Heinrich born 13. 9. 1909
formerly: lower court counsellor in the special court, Mannheim
today: provincial court director in Mannheim

Looft, Walter born 14. 11. 1905
formerly: worked with the "Reichskommissar" in Vienna from 1938 to 1940, in 1941 with the Reich representative in Posen (Poznan) and in 1943 employed in Hitler's private chancellory
today: administrative court director in the Schleswig-Holstein Administrative Court

Lorenz, Dr. Hans-Helmut born 18. 4. 1913
formerly: military court counsellor in the Berlin command
today: lawyer in Hamburg-Wandsbek

Lorenzen, Dr. born 14. 2. 1909
formerly: lower court counsellor in the nazi Ministry of Justice, Dept. III
today: superior provincial court counsellor in Schleswig

Ludolph, Dr. born 21. 4. 1904
formerly: first public prosecutor in the special court, Danzig (Gdansk)
today: public prosecutor in Brunswick

Ludwig, Heinz born 12. 11. 1905
formerly: lower court counsellor in special court II, Hohensalza (Inowraclaw)
today: lower court counsellor in Stuttgart-Bad Cannstadt

Lüders, Dr. Hans born 27. 3. 1906
formerly: public prosecutor in the special court, Brunswick
today: superior provincial court counsellor in Brunswick

Lüning, Richard, born 18. 9. 1910
formerly: public prosecutor in the special court, Celle
today: superior provincial court counsellor in Celle

Luther, Dr. born 26. 2. 1909
formerly: provincial court counsellor in the special court, Frankfurt-on-Main
today: provincial court counsellor in Limburg

Mäth, Albert born 23. 5. 1911
formerly: provincial court counsellor in the special court, Zichenau (Ciechanow)
today: lower court director in Kiel

Mahlke, Karl born 5. 4. 1899
formerly: military field court counsellor in the 85th infantry division
today: lower court counsellor in Ratzeburg

Maisenhälder, Dr. Alois born 18. 8. 1910
formerly: lower court counsellor in the special court, Stuttgart
today: superior provincial court counsellor in Stuttgart

Malessa, Johannes born 25. 5. 1911
formerly: senior staff judge in the 76th infantry division
today: provincial social court counsellor in Schleswig

Manchot, Dr. Karl born 25. 3. 1906
formerly: public prosecutor in the special court, Munich
today: provincial court director in Munich

Martens, Dr. Hans-Hermann born 24. 2. 1904
formerly: military court counsellor in the 411th special duty division
today: senate president in the Provincial Social Court in Celle

Martens, Jakob born 7. 5. 1905
formerly: 1932 NSDAP, chairman of an NSDAP regional court, local group leader of the NSDAP, 1938 assistant adviser in the nazi Ministry of the Interior, 1940 war administrative counsellor at the High Command of the Army (OKH) in Holland
today: administrative court director in the Schleswig-Holstein Administrative Court

Martens, Kurt born 3. 4. 1910
formerly: provincial court counsellor in the special court, Kiel
today: provincial court director in Kiel

Martin born 6. 2. 1906
formerly: provincial court counsellor in the special court, Jena and Weimar
today: lower court director in Bitburg

Marx, Dr. Gerhard born 16. 12. 1906
formerly: public prosecutor in the special court, Aachen
today: lower court director in Eschweiler

Mattern, Dr. Friedrich born 6. 11. 1908
formerly: provincial court counsellor in the special court, Brünn (Brno)
today: federal judge in the Federal Court

Matthiessen, Heinrich born 10. 12. 1906
formerly: public prosecutor in the special court, Posen (Poznan)
today: public prosecutor in Kiel

Mayer, Dr. Josef born 25. 6. 1905
formerly: lower court counsellor in the special court, Nuremberg
today: provincial court director in Nuremberg

Mayer, Karl Bernhard born 28. 5. 1905
formerly: public prosecutor in the special court, Darmstadt
today: public prosecutor in Giessen

Meier-Branecke, Dr. Hans born 4. 7. 1900
formerly: supreme military court counsellor, chief judge in the Army Supreme Command
today: senate president at the Brunswick Superior Provincial Court

Meinardus, Dr. born 28. 5. 1904
formerly: public prosecutor in the special court, Koblenz
today: first public prosecutor in Trier

Meiser, Fritz born 1. 1. 1914
formerly: naval assistant judge
today: government director in the Bavarian Ministry of Justice

Mellwitz, Artur born 19. 2. 1909
formerly: lower court counsellor in the special court, Naumburg
today: federal judge in the Federal Social Court

Mende, Gerhard born 20. 6. 1901
formerly: provincial court counsellor in the special court, Breslau (Wrocław)
today: provincial court director in Arnsberg

Menger, Dr. Georg born 12. 8. 1903
formerly: military court counsellor in the 413th infantry division
today: senior judge in Mellrichstadt

Mennecke born 1. 1. 1901
formerly: public prosecutor in the special court, Zweibrücken
today: provincial court counsellor in Landau

Merz, Dr. Helmut born 10. 9. 1911
formerly: public prosecutor in Landau/Palatinate, SS Hauptsturmführer
today: superior provincial court counsellor in Neustadt-on-Weinstrasse

Metten, Dr. A. born 16. 4. 1902
formerly: Reich public prosecutor for political cases in the Reich Court
today: senior public prosecutor in Essen

Metz, Dr. born 22. 12. 1908
formerly: public prosecutor in the nazi Ministry of Justice, Dept. III, for political cases
today: superior provincial court counsellor in Neustadt-on-Weinstrasse

Meusel, Johannes born 30. 7. 1900
formerly: provincial court counsellor in the special court, Breslau (Wrocław)
today: provincial court director in Göttingen

Meusel, Dr. Gotthold born 23. 4. 1905
formerly: military court counsellor
today: senate president in the Superior Provincial Court in Nuremberg

Mewes, Dr. Günther born 6. 12. 1908
formerly: senior military court counsellor in the 2nd and 29th armoured divisions
today: provincial court counsellor in Marburg

Mey, Werner
formerly: military court counsellor, senior staff judge in the High Command of the Army South
today: senate president in the Superior Provincial Court in Bremen

Meyer, Friedrich born 17. 8. 1905
formerly: public prosecutor in the special court, Erfurt
today: senior public prosecutor in Münster

Meyer, Hans born 25. 5. 1904
formerly: military field court counsellor in the 444th security division, NSDAP, political leader
today: provincial court director in Brunswick

Meyer-Hentschel, Dr. Gerhard born 9. 9. 1911
formerly: military court counsellor in the 409th division
today: president of the Superior Administrative Court in Koblenz and member of the Constitutional Court of Rhineland-Palatinate

Meynen, Hermann born 21. 8. 1898
formerly: provincial court counsellor in the special court, Kiel
today: superior provincial court counsellor in Schleswig

Mezger, Hans-Robert born 22. 7. 1904
formerly: military court counsellor in the 293rd infantry division
today: federal judge in the Federal Court

Misera, Dr. Alfons born 6. 12. 1900
formerly: public prosecutor in the special court, Berlin
today: senior social court counsellor in Augsburg

Mittelbach, Dr. Jürgen born 19. 9. 1903
formerly: public prosecutor at the special court in Berlin
today: superior provincial court counsellor in Cologne

Möhl, Dr. Wolfgang born 23. 5. 1905
formerly: provincial court director in the special court, Leslau (Wloclawek)
today: senior public prosecutor at the Supreme Provincial Court in Munich

Moeker, Dr. A. born 30. 10. 1908
formerly: public prosecutor for political cases in Kattowitz (Katowice)
today: public prosecutor in Mönchen-Gladbach

Möller, Wilhelm born 19. 8. 1904
formerly: senior military field judge in the 1st Armoured Army High Command
today: senior judge in Oldenburg

Mohns, Gerhard born 7. 6. 1910
formerly: public prosecutor in the special court, Berlin
today: senior public prosecutor in Celle

Mollenhauer, Werner born 14. 9. 1905
formerly: first public prosecutor in the special court, Königsberg (Kaliningrad)
today: provincial court counsellor in Hanover

Morschbach, Dr. Josef born 3. 5. 1905
formerly: public prosecutor in the special court, Cologne
today: senior public prosecutor in Mainz

Mühlenfels, Willy von born 27. 9. 1905
formerly: provincial court counsellor in the special court, Mannheim and Karlsruhe
today: provincial court president in Baden-Baden

Mühlhaus, Dr. Hermann born 8. 3. 1903
formerly: military court counsellor in the 264th infantry division
today: supreme provincial court counsellor in Munich

Müller, Dr. Hanswerner born 7. 7. 1899
formerly: superior provincial court counsellor in the nazi Ministry of Justice
today: federal judge in the Federal Administrative Court, Berlin

Müller, Dr. Helmut born 18. 12. 1906
formerly: 1939–42 senior government counsellor, finally permanent representative of the chief of police in Gdansk, 1942 SS Sturmbannführer, chief of police in Gdynia
today: administrative court counsellor in the Schleswig-Holstein Administrative Court

Müller, Kurt born 19. 8. 1905
formerly: senior military judge in the 6th, 196th, 70th, 463rd, and 172nd divisions, Berlin command
today: provincial court director in Hagen

Müller, Robert born 26. 5. 1909
formerly: public prosecutor in the special court, Freiburg
today: lower court director in Freiburg

Müller, Dr. Walter born 21. 10. 1901
formerly: supreme military court counsellor in France
today: provincial court director in Stuttgart

Münich, Dr. Alfred born 2. 9. 1906
formerly: military field court counsellor, member of NSDAP from 1933, in 1937 in the "People's Court", took part in many judgements against anti-fascists
today: senate president in the Superior Provincial Court in Munich

Münstermann, Dr. Wolfgang born 1898
formerly: chairman of the special court, Berlin, and judge in the "People's Court"
today: lawyer in Celle

Müntinga, Dr. Helmut born 4. 8. 1907
formerly: lower court counsellor in the special court, Kiel
today: senior judge in Bad Seegeberg

Mugler, Dr. Hans born 3. 11. 1904
formerly: military court counsellor in the 320th infantry division
today: supreme provincial court counsellor in Munich

Munzinger, Dr. born 9. 8. 1909
formerly: lower court counsellor in the special court, Mannheim
today: government president of Nordbaden

Nagel, Dr. Hellmuth born 28. 5. 1906
formerly: senior military field judge in the 62nd infantry division
today: superior provincial court counsellor in Munich

Nappe, Dr. Walter born 26. 11. 1908
formerly: lower court counsellor in the special court, Königsberg (Kaliningrad)
today: lower court counsellor in Kiel

Nebel, Dr. born 20. 9. 1904
formerly: senior military field judge in the Mailland (Milano) command
today: senate president in the Superior Provincial Court in Düsseldorf

Neidhard, Friedrich born 7. 9. 1907
formerly: lower court counsellor in the special court, Strassburg (Strasbourg)
today: government director in the Ministry of Justice, Baden-Württemberg

Nellessen, Dr. born 28. 11. 1900
formerly: senior public prosecutor in the special court, Bielitz (Bielsko)
today: senior public prosecutor in Aachen

Neuberger, Erich born 8. 2. 1910
formerly: lower court counsellor in Bromberg (Bydgoszcz), SS Sturmbannführer, SS court main office
today: public prosecutor in Saarbrücken

Neumaier, Dr. Alois born 17. 6. 1901
formerly: provincial court counsellor in the special court, Munich
today: supreme provincial court counsellor in Munich

Neuroth, Hans-Heinrich born 19. 11. 1908
formerly: senior military field judge in the Berlin command, army judge in the tank army high command and Saarland
today: lower court counsellor in Schlüchtern

Nickels, Dr. Peter born 17. 3. 1903
formerly: public prosecutor in the special court, Hamburg
today: lower court director in Hamburg

Niemer born 30. 1. 1902
formerly: first public prosecutor for political cases, Hamm
today: first public prosecutor in Münster

Niese, Hans born 18. 4. 1911
formerly: military judge in the 30th division, Lübeck
today: leading senior public prosecutor in Krefeld

Nieuhoff born 5. 10. 1900
formerly: provincial court counsellor in the special court, Hanover
today: lower court counsellor in Hanover

Nissen, Rudolf born 19. 6. 1911
formerly: military court counsellor
today: provincial court director in Hamburg

Nix, Josef born 30. 4. 1904
formerly: military court counsellor in division 409
today: senate president in Mainz

Noack born 12. 10. 1898
formerly: provincial court counsellor in the special court, Litzmannstadt (Lodz)
today: lower court counsellor in Schleswig

Nössler, Dr. Kuno born 27. 10. 1904
formerly: senior staff judge in the Central Court of the Army, Berlin-Charlottenburg
today: senior judge in Aachen

Normann, Hans-Henning von born 23. 2. 1903
formerly: ministerial counsellor to the Reich Marshal, agent for the four-year plan, Göring, head of Section 2, including "Jewish Affairs"
today: federal prosecutor in the Federal Administrative Court

Nürnberger, Dr. born 7. 7. 1912
formerly: lower court counsellor in the special court, Magdeburg
today: administrative court director in Arnsberg

Nüsslein, Dr. Andreas born 5. 3. 1909
formerly: public prosecutor in Brünn (Brno), on the list of war criminals No. A – 6/316
today: lower court director in Coburg

Nüsslein, Dr. Franz born 12. 10. 1908
formerly: senior public prosecutor with the "Reich Protector" in Prague (Praha)
today: consul-general in Barcelona

Oberländer, Dr. Alexander born 17. 5. 1906
formerly: senior military administrative counsellor; chief district leader in Thuringia
today: administrative court counsellor in Hanover

Ocker, Hermann born 17. 7. 1905
formerly: military court counsellor in the 71st infantry division
today: provincial court director in Hildesheim

Oellrich, Dr. Walter born 3. 3. 1903
formerly: public prosecutor in the special court, Hamburg
today: provincial court director in Hamburg

Oeser, Dr. Richard born 15. 10. 1905
formerly: public prosecutor in the special court, Munich
today: senior public prosecutor in Munich

Oesterreich, Hans born 20. 10. 1905
formerly: provincial court counsellor in the special court, Breslau (Wrocław)
today: first public prosecutor in Kassel

Ohm, Dr. K. born 4. 5. 1903
formerly: lower court counsellor in the special court, Hanover
today: superior provincial court counsellor in Celle

Oldenburg, Fritz born 4. 1. 1901
formerly: lower court counsellor in the special court, Prenzlau
today: lower court counsellor in Bielefeld

Oligmüller born 15. 5. 1912
formerly: public prosecutor in the special court, Essen
today: provincial court director in Essen

Oppe, Dr. born 2. 9. 1911
formerly: public prosecutor in the special court, Oppeln (Opole)
today: senior public prosecutor in Duisburg

Oppenhauser, Walter born 15. 12. 1904
formerly: military field court counsellor
today: provincial social court counsellor in the Saarland Provincial Social Court

Ortmann, Hans born 10. 4. 1903
formerly: senior staff judge in the 526th infantry division
today: lower court counsellor in Duisburg

Orzechowski, Dr. Wolfgang born 16. 6. 1904
formerly: public prosecutor in the special court, Breslau (Wrocław)
today: senior public prosecutor in Cologne

Oskierski, Wilhelm born 7. 8. 1904
formerly: military court counsellor in the 428th special duty division

t o d a y : provincial court counsellor in Krefeld

Ostermeier, Dr. Robert born 29. 5. 1903
f o r m e r l y : provincial court counsellor in the special court, Nuremberg-Fürth
t o d a y : provincial court director in Nuremberg-Fürth

Otter, Dr. born 7. 1. 1903
f o r m e r l y : army judge in Garrison Command 192
t o d a y : senior public prosecutor in Celle

Ottersbach, Karlheinz born 10. 6. 1912
f o r m e r l y : public prosecutor in the special court, Kattowitz (Katowice)
u n t i l s p r i n g 1 9 6 5 : public prosecutor in Lüneburg

Päth, Dr. Gerd born 23. 8. 1911
f o r m e r l y : public prosecutor in the special court, Hamburg
t o d a y : lower court counsellor in Hamburg

Passauer, Hans born 25. 5. 1909
f o r m e r l y : senior staff judge in the 12th division, Schwerin
t o d a y : public prosecutor in Itzehoe

Pecher, Dr. Otto born 29. 4. 1903
f o r m e r l y : provincial court counsellor in the special court, Cottbus
t o d a y : federal judge in the Federal Labour Court

Petersen, Dr. Harro born 22. 4. 1912
f o r m e r l y : public prosecutor for political cases, Kattowitz (Katowice)
t o d a y : provincial court director in Flensburg

Petzke, Dr. Hans born 30. 7. 1901
f o r m e r l y : senior military court counsellor
t o d a y : senior public prosecutor in Nuremberg

Pfenningsdorf born 27. 4. 1908
f o r m e r l y : lower court counsellor in the nazi Ministry of Justice, special court cases, Eastern Regions
t o d a y : provincial court counsellor in Bonn

Pfleiderer born 2. 2. 1912
f o r m e r l y : public prosecutor in the special courts Prague (Praha) and Brünn (Brno)
t o d a y : first public prosecutor in the Superior Provincial Court in Celle

Philippi, Walter born 8. 12. 1902
f o r m e r l y : military court counsellor, senior staff judge in the 176th infantry division
t o d a y : lower court counsellor in Dortmund

Pichon, Lothar born 5. 2. 1903
f o r m e r l y : lower court counsellor in the special court, Frankfurt-on-Oder
t o d a y : provincial court counsellor in Osnabrück

Piesker born 24 .5. 1904
f o r m e r l y : first public prosecutor in the special courts Celle and Hanover
t o d a y : superior provincial court counsellor in Celle

Pingel born 18. 5. 1907
f o r m e r l y : public prosecutor in the special court, Kiel
t o d a y : public prosecutor in Kiel

Pippert born 24. 5. 1904
f o r m e r l y : first public prosecutor in the special court, Vienna
t o d a y : senior public prosecutor in Dortmund

Plock, Dr. Gerhard born 17. 2. 1913
f o r m e r l y : senior staff judge in the 52nd and 166th infantry divisions and the 20th armoured division Pz. AOK 3
t o d a y : lawyer and notary in Dillenburg

Plönnies, Dr. Rudolf born 8. 9. 1908
f o r m e r l y : provincial court counsellor in the special court, Brünn (Brno)
t o d a y : lower court counsellor in Itzehoe

Plonner, Hermann born 1. 3. 1907
f o r m e r l y : lower court counsellor in the special court, Bielitz (Bielsko)
t o d a y : superior provincial court counsellor in Munich

Poddey, Traugott born 5. 10. 1904
f o r m e r l y : provincial court counsellor in the special court, Halle
t o d a y : senate president in the Provincial Social Court in Stuttgart

Pöhlmann, Heinrich born 31. 8. 1904
f o r m e r l y : public prosecutor in the special court, Saarbrücken
t o d a y : provincial court director in Bayreuth

Poersch, Dr. Lothar born 14. 10. 1906
formerly: senior military field judge in the 24th infantry division
today: lower court director in Selb

Pöschla, Dr. born 25. 3. 1900
formerly: military court counsellor in the Luftwaffe
today: first public prosecutor in Wuppertal

Pohlmann, Gert born 3. 10. 1901
formerly: provincial court counsellor in Berlin, 14 May 1923 NSDAP (No. 9664), golden badge of honour of the NSDAP, regional instructor
today: administrative court director in Stuttgart

Poos, Dr. born 13. 1. 1904
formerly: lower court counsellor in the special court, Celle
today: lower court counsellor in Hanover

Poppelbaum, Helmut born 22. 10. 1903
formerly: military court counsellor in the supreme command of the army and the 6th division, Bielefeld
today: provincial court director in Lüneburg

Preiser, Dr. born 23. 8. 1898
formerly: provincial court director in the nazi Ministry of Justice, Dept IV, section leader for political cases
today: superior provincial court counsellor in Brunswick

Priedigkeit, Georg born 29. 3. 1908
formerly: public prosecutor in the special court, Schneidemühl (Pila)
today: labour court counsellor in Hagen

Pröhl born 14. 10. 1905
formerly: provincial court counsellor in the special court, Magdeburg
today: provincial court counsellor in Frankfort-on-Main

Prüfer, Hans born 5. 11. 1903
formerly: lower court counsellor and counsel for the prosecution in the special court, Freiburg
today: senior legal counsellor in Mülheim

Quack, Rudolf born 7. 7. 1910
formerly: senior staff judge in the 17th, 18th, and 213th infantry divisions
today: provincial court director in Giessen

Raab, Dr. born 5. 1. 1910
formerly: lower court counsellor in the special court, Prague (Praha)
today: provincial court counsellor in Kleve

Raabe born 19. 6. 1898
formerly: military court counsellor in the 209th infantry division
until August 1965: senior judge in Uslar

Rabenau, Reinhard von born 12. 3. 1913
formerly: senior staff judge in the 3rd and 17th armoured divisions
today: provincial court counsellor in Düsseldorf

Raeder, Rudolf born 18. 8. 1904
formerly: public prosecutor in the special court, Düsseldorf
today: leading senior public prosecutor in Cologne

Rahn, Dr. Dietrich born 14. 4. 1914
formerly: military field court counsellor in the 463rd infantry division
today: senior public prosecutor in Frankfurt-on-Main

Ral, Dr. Franz born 3. 8. 1905
formerly: public prosecutor in the special court, Munich
today: administrative court director in Munich

Randebrock born 22. 1. 1904
formerly: provincial court counsellor in the Provincial Court, Essen ("racial disgrace cases")
today: provincial court director in Koblenz

Raschik, Dr. Friedrich born 30. 3. 1906
formerly: provincial court counsellor in the special court, Mährisch-Schönberg (Sumperk)
today: superior provincial court counsellor in Frankfurt-on-Main

Rathmayer, Otto born 15. 12. 1905
formerly: lower court counsellor, counsel for the prosecution in the "People's Court"
today: provincial court counsellor in Landshut

Rathske born 16. 9. 1903
formerly: public prosecutor in the special court, Düsseldorf
today: public prosecutor in Koblenz

Rausch, Dr. born 14. 9. 1909
formerly: provincial court counsellor in the special court, Magdeburg
today: superior provincial court counsellor in Celle

Rebmann, Dr. Gustav born 13. 5. 1904
formerly: public prosecutor in the special court, Berlin
today: senior public prosecutor in Düsseldorf

Reckmann, Dr. Hans born 21. 6. 1902
formerly: military court counsellor in the 526th infantry division
today: senior legal counsellor in Goch

Regis, Dr. Reinhold born 6. 1. 1904
formerly: superior provincial court counsellor, Jena, judge of summary jurisdiction
today: provincial court counsellor in Bielefeld

Rehbock, Dr. born 2. 9. 1898
formerly: supreme court counsellor in the special court, Berlin
today: provincial court director in Kiel

Reichelt, Dr. born 20. 1. 1904
formerly: public prosecutor in the "People's Court"
today: first public prosecutor in the Superior Provincial Court in Koblenz

Reil, Theodor born 20. 6. 1909
formerly: military court counsellor in the 404th infantry division
today: provincial social court counsellor in Stuttgart

Rein, Dr. Arthur born 6. 8. 1901
formerly: senior public prosecutor in the special court, Dortmund
today: senate president in Hamm

Reiners, Dr. Friedrich born 25. 3. 1904
formerly: army judge in the Central Army Court, Berlin-Charlottenburg
today: superior provincial court counsellor in Hamburg

Rempe, Dr. Heinrich born 24. 4. 1902
formerly: superior provincial court counsellor in the nazi Ministry of Justice, Dept III
today: superior provincial court president in Hamm

Renatus, Heinrich born 21. 10. 1902
formerly: military court counsellor and senior staff judge in the 464th infantry division
today: provincial social court counsellor in Munich

Retsch, Georg born 2. 2. 1901
formerly: senior staff judge in the 1st armored division
today: supreme provincial court counsellor in Munich

Reubold, Dr. Hans born 29. 9. 1900
formerly: first public prosecutor in the special court, Munich
today: provincial court president in Nuremberg-Fürth

Reusch, Dr. Werner born 23. 10. 1902
formerly: chief judge in the Army Supreme Command
today: senate president in the Superior Provincial Court in Frankfurt-on-Main

Reuter, Dr. Rudolf born 12. 6. 1905
formerly: public prosecutor in the special court, Prague (Praha), on Czechoslovak list of war criminals, No. A 38–87
today: leading senior public prosecutor in Wuppertal

Rheinen, Dr. Fritz born 14. 6. 1905
formerly: military court counsellor in the 176th infantry division
today: provincial court director in Duisburg

Rhode, Werner born 1. 2. 1913
formerly: public prosecutor in the special court, Prague (Praha), Czechoslovak war criminal list No. A 38–88
today: government director in the Ministry of Justice, Schleswig-Holstein

Richert born 18. 12. 1898
formerly: lower court counsellor in the special court, Elbing (Elblag)
today: lower court counsellor in Flensburg

Rieder born 11. 3. 1903
formerly: senior military court counsellor in the Wehrmacht Command, Berlin
today: provincial court president in Zweibrücken (see Table 30)

Riemann, Kurt born 17. 7. 1913
formerly: military court counsellor
today: provincial court director in Hanover

Riepenhausen, Ernst born 23. 8. 1903
formerly: provincial court counsellor in the special court, Leslau (Wloclawek), on Polish list of war criminals
today: superior provincial court counsellor in Bamberg

Rietmeyer, Dr. Otto born 10. 1. 1909
formerly: public prosecutor in the special court, Cologne
today: senior judge in Lindlar

Rimelin, Dr. Renatus born 12. 4. 1909
formerly: public prosecutor in the special court, Stuttgart
today: superior provincial court counsellor in Stuttgart

Rittinger, Dr. Josef born 10. 3. 1906
formerly: military court counsellor in the 17th army, Passau
today: senior judge in Eichstädt

Rochlitz, Dr. Viktor born 16. 3. 1914
formerly: associate judge, counsel for the prosecution in the special court, Strassburg (Strasbourg)
today: provincial court counsellor in Heidelberg

Rodominski, Herbert born 15. 11. 1912
formerly: judge in the special court, Hamburg
today: lower court counsellor in Hamburg-Harburg

Roemer born August 1902
formerly: first public prosecutor in the special court, Munich
today: ministerial director in the Federal Ministry of Justice

Römer, Josef born 29. 3. 1914
formerly: counsel for the prosecution in the special court, Wuppertal
today: ministerial counsellor in the Ministry of Justice, North Rhine-Westphalia

Roesler, Dr. Karl born 18. 6. 1903
formerly: superior provincial court counsellor for political cases in Posen (Poznań)
today: superior administrative court counsellor in Münster

Rössiger born 9. 10. 1911
formerly: divisional judge
today: senior judge in Vlotho

Rogalla, Hans born 24. 2. 1901
formerly: public prosecutor in the special court, Stettin (Szczecin)
today: first public prosecutor in Verden

Rogge born 15. 8. 1901
formerly: provincial court counsellor in the special court, Kiel
today: provincial court director in Flensburg

Roggenkamp, Dr. Kurt born 31. 10. 1906
formerly: military court counsellor in the 384th infantry division
today: lower court director in Hamburg-Blankenese

Romatzek, Wilhelm born 18. 12. 1905
formerly: lower court counsellor in the special court, Königsberg (Kaliningrad)
today: lower court counsellor in Königshofen im Grabfeld

Ronke, Professor Dr. Maximilian born 27. 11. 1904
formerly: superior provincial court counsellor in the special court, Prague (Praha)
today: provincial court director in Würzburg

Rosendahl born 7. 4. 1905
formerly: public prosecutor in the special court, Thorn (Toruń)
today: public prosecutor in Münster

Ross born 31. 5. 1908
formerly: provincial court counsellor in the nazi Ministry of Justice
today: lower court counsellor in Düsseldorf

Rostock, Heinrich born 22. 7. 1904
formerly: military court counsellor in the 409th infantry division
today: lower court counsellor in Eschwege

Rothe, Dr. Gerhard born 29. 8. 1906
formerly: provincial court counsellor in the special court, Naumburg
today: federal judge in the Federal Court

Ruepprecht, Dr. Hans-Ulrich, Freiherr von born 9. 7. 1911
formerly: provincial court counsellor in Ravensburg, magistrate of the "People's Court"
today: superior provincial court counsellor in Stuttgart

Ruff, Wilhelm born 11. 9. 1912
formerly: senior staff judge in the 9th infantry division
today: lower court counsellor in Stuttgart

Saage, Dr. born July 1907
formerly: supreme court counsellor in the nazi Ministry of Justice
today: ministerial director in the Federal Ministry of Justice

Sand, Hermann born 1. 7. 1907
formerly: provincial court counsellor in the special court, Munich
today: superior provincial court counsellor in Munich

Sandrock, Dr. Heinz born 18. 2. 1902
formerly: provincial court counsellor and public prosecutor for political cases in the Reich Court
today: superior provincial court counsellor in Frankfurt-on-Main

Sauer, Valentin born 27. 12. 1901
formerly: military court counsellor in the 409th infantry division
today: provincial court counsellor in Marburg

Sauter, Philipp born 6. 7. 1903
formerly: military court counsellor in the 362nd infantry division
today: lower court counsellor in Eberbach/Karlsruhe

Schade, Dr. Dr. Hans born 10. 9. 1901
formerly: supreme court counsellor in the nazi Ministry of Justice
today: senate president in the Federal Patent Court

Schäfer, Dr. Karl born 11. 12. 1899
formerly: superior provincial court counsellor in the nazi Ministry of Justice, Dept. III
today: senate president in Frankfurt-on-Main

Schäper, Theodor born 6. 11. 1901
formerly: first public secutor in the special court Brünn (Brno)
today: senior public prosecutor in Bochum

Schafheutle, Dr. Josef born March 1904
formerly: provincial court director in the nazi Ministry of Justice
today: ministerial director in the Federal Ministry of Justice

Schattenberg, Dr. Ulrich born 11. 2. 1906
formerly: chief naval court counsellor, according to his own statements took part in missions of the fascist navy in Spain to supply the fascists with arms, ammunition and foodstuffs
today: first public prosecutor in Lübeck

Schauergans born 15. 12. 1901
formerly: provincial court counsellor in the special court, Aachen
today: lower court counsellor in Aachen

Scheer, Willy born 29. 11. 1904
formerly: military court counsellor with the 213th security division
today: lower court counsellor in Celle

Scherer, Dr. Werner
formerly: military court counsellor at the High Command of the Wehrmacht
today: senate president at the Federal Disciplinary Court

Schicht, Dr. Wolfgang born 10. 10. 1908
formerly: military court counsellor
today: first public prosecutor in Stuttgart

Schiedt, Dr. Robert born 1. 9. 1911
formerly: public prosecutor in the special court, Munich
today: superior provincial court counsellor in Munich

Schiffner born 23. 7. 1910
formerly: public prosecutor in the special court, Elbing (Elblag)
today :public prosecutor in Lüneburg

Schikowsky, Dr. born 16. 9. 1902
formerly: provincial court counsellor in the special court, Königsberg (Kaliningrad)
today: lower court counsellor in Peine

Schilgen, Dr. Walter born 28. 6. 1900
formerly: superior provincial court counsellor for political cases in Kattowitz (Katowice)
today: federal judge in the Federal Labour Court

Schlaefke, Wilhelm born 2. 3. 1902
formerly: senior military court counsellor in the 12th infantry division
today: public prosecutor in Hamburg

Schlegelberger, Dr. Hartwig born 9. 11. 1913
formerly: naval senior staff judge
today: minister of the interior in Schleswig-Holstein (see Table 30)

Schlichting, Dr. Erich born 12. 5. 1897
formerly: senior military court counsellor in the Reich Military Court and the Sofia command
until August 1965: senate president in the Superior Provincial Court in Schleswig

Schlinke, Kurt born 19. 12. 1899
formerly: lower court counsellor in Zörbig, court officer of the Wehrmacht prison at Torgau
today: lower court counsellor in Hildesheim

Schlüter, Dr. Erich born 29. 5. 1903
formerly: senior military court counsellor in the High Command of the Army/HR
today: provincial court president in Ansbach

Schmidt, Kurt born 23. 9. 1904
formerly: lower court counsellor in the special court, Hohensalza (Inowraclaw)
today: lower court counsellor in Hoya

Schmiedeberg, Heinz born 9. 10. 1908
formerly: public prosecutor in the special court, Stettin (Szczecin)
today: lower court counsellor in Bochum

Schmitt, Dr. Josef born 22. 8. 1905
formerly: military court counsellor in field headquarters 672
today: lower court counsellor in Dachau

Schmitt, Walter born 13. 7. 1905
formerly: army judge of the 1st mountain division, Munich, the 7th and the 467th divisions, Munich, the army command Lanz of the Berlin command Army Group E XXII AK
today: lawyer in Landau

Schmitt-Winter, Albert born 23. 2. 1903
formerly: military court counsellor
today: senior public prosecutor in Saarbrücken

Schmitz, Dr. Erich born 25. 7. 1905
formerly: military court counsellor in the 467th infantry division
today: provincial court director in Munich

Schmole, Dr. born 29. 6. 1900
formerly: provincial court counsellor in the special court, Dresden
today: provincial court counsellor in Hanover

Schöllgen, Dr. born 10. 8. 1901
formerly: senior judge in the special court, Wuppertal
today: provincial court director in Mönchen-Gladbach

Schoene, Josef born 9. 1. 1903
formerly: lower court counsellor in the special court, Essen
today: provincial court director in Essen

Schoengarth, Dr. Hans-Otto born 29. 8. 1905
formerly: public prosecutor in the special court, Breslau (Wroclaw)
today: lower court counsellor in Hagen

Scholz, Heinrich born 22. 9. 1904
formerly: senior military court counsellor in the Königsberg (Kaliningrad) command XXVI AK
today: leading senior public prosecutor in Hamburg

Schoppmann, Dr. born 17. 10. 1910
formerly: public prosecutor in the special court, Elbing (Elblag)
today: provincial court director in Bremen

Schorn, Joachim born 9. 8. 1903
formerly: military court counsellor in the 201st security division
today: lower court director in Osnabruck

Schrader, Karl-Heinz born 27. 10. 1909
formerly: provincial court counsellor in the special court, Essen
today: senior judge in Plettenburg

Schreiber, Georg born 19. 3. 1898
formerly: provincial court director in Berlin, 1 December 1932 NSDAP, president of the party regional court, naval court counsellor
today: lower court counsellor in Kiel

Schreiber, Theodor born 22. 12. 1905
formerly: military court counsellor in the 173rd infantry division
today: provincial court counsellor in Passau

Schreitmüller, Dr. Adolf born 8. 11. 1902
formerly: provincial court counsellor in the special court, Stuttgart, and in the "People's Court"
today: provincial court director in Stuttgart

Schroiff born 10. 8. 1908
formerly: public prosecutor in the special court, Breslau (Wroclaw)

today: first senior public prosecutor in Stade

Schubert, Dr. Franz born 4. 10. 1910
formerly: provincial court counsellor in the special court, Troppau (Opava)
today: provincial court counsellor in Traunstein

Schubert, Dr. Johannes born 18. 8. 1905
formerly: military court counsellor in the 408th division
today: lower court director in Gifhorn

Schubert, Johannes born 13. 8. 1908
formerly: public prosecutor in the special court, Oppeln (Opole)
today: senior public prosecutor in Karlsruhe

Schubert, Wolfgang born 1. 8. 1908
formerly: public prosecutor in the special court, Kattowitz (Katowice)
today: lower court counsellor in Friesoythe

Schüle, Erwin born 2. 7. 1913
formerly: assistant adjutant IC of ID 215, leader of the special penal company ID 253; sentenced to 25 years forced labour in the Soviet Union
today: senior public prosecutor, head of the central office for the clearing up of national socialist crimes

Schürmann, Wolfgang born 18. 8. 1913
formerly: senior staff judge in the 153rd division, Potsdam and the 75th infantry division
today: public prosecutor in Hildesheim

Schultz, Johannes born 24. 11. 1902
formerly: provincial court counsellor in Berlin; ministerial counsellor in the nazi Ministry of Finance; SA Oberscharführer, Sturm 31/9
today: ministerial director in the Lower Saxony Ministry of Justice

Schultze, Otto-Wolfgang born 10. 1. 1905
formerly: public prosecutor in the special court, Essen
today: first public prosecutor in Dortmund

Schulze, Friedrich born 11. 2. 1903
formerly: provincial court counsellor in the special court, Halle-on-Saale
today: lower court counsellor in Gronau

Schumacher, Dr. Franz born 28. 6. 1907
formerly: senior military field judge in the 34th division, Koblenz
today: senior public prosecutor in Limburg

Schutte, Dr. Eberhard born 22. 6. 1900
formerly: lower court counsellor in the special court, Litzmannstadt (Lodz)
until August 1965: lower court counsellor in Wuppertal

Schwaller, Dr. Karl von born 5. 10. 1903
formerly: public prosecutor in the special court, Brünn (Brno)
today: lower court counsellor in Augsburg

Schwarze, Johannes born 25. 10. 1902
formerly: public prosecutor in the special court, Halle-on-Saale
today: first public prosecutor in Münster

Schwarze, Josef born 20. 11. 1910
formerly: provincial court counsellor in the nazi Ministry of Justice
today: senate president in the Superior Provincial Court in Hamm

Schwedes, Dr. Franz born 4. 6. 1904
formerly: military court counsellor in the field headquarters 520
today: lower court counsellor in Kassel

Schweichel, Dr. born 23. 8. 1906
formerly: military court counsellor in the 95th infantry division
today: senior public prosecutor in Cologne

Schweling, Otto born 4. 3. 1904
formerly: senior military court counsellor in the Luftwaffe Court and judge in Italy
today: senior public prosecutor in the Federal Court

Seibert, Dr. Claus born 4. 6. 1902
formerly: military court counsellor in the 463rd infantry division
today: federal judge in the Federal Court

Seiffert, Dr. Werner born 8. 10 1902
formerly: supreme court counsellor in the nazi Ministry of Justice
today: lower court director in Stuttgart

Seither, Dr. Karl born 29. 1. 1901
formerly: first public prosecutor in Regensburg and member of a court-martial
today: supreme provincial court counsellor in Munich

Semmler, Jakob born 10. 1. 1903
formerly: provincial court counsellor in the special court, Frankenthal
today: senior public prosecutor in Zweibrücken

Sernau born 2. 1. 1904
formerly: public prosecutor in the special court, Dortmund
today: public prosecutor in Bochum

Seydewitz, von born 20. 6. 1908
formerly: provincial court counsellor in the special court, Petrikau
today: provincial court counsellor in Hanover

Siebers, Werner born 21. 11. 1907
formerly: senior military court counsellor in the 5th armoured division Oppeln (Opole) and the 177th division Brünn (Brno)
today: public prosecutor in Brunswick

Siedenburg, Walter born 2. 9. 1900
formerly: lower court counsellor in the special court, Oldenburg
today: provincial court counsellor in Oldenburg

Sielaff, Dr. born 10. 6. 1908
formerly: lower court counsellor in the special court, Mainz
today: lower court counsellor in Ludwigshafen

Sinn, Dr. Heinrich born 18. 12. 1903
formerly: senior staff judge in the 329th infantry division
today: senate president in the Superior Provincial Court in Stuttgart

Skok, Dr. Herbert born 18. 11. 1906
formerly: public prosecutor in the special court, Hamburg
today: senior public prosecutor in Hamburg

Sommer, Karl born 12. 11. 1904
formerly: first public prosecutor in the special court, Litzmannstadt (Lodz)
today: first public prosecutor in Düsseldorf

Sosna, Viktor born 2. 11. 1904
formerly: public prosecutor in the special court, Graz
today: public prosecutor in Oldenburg

Spehr born 28. 2. 1905
formerly: provincial court counsellor in the special court, Düsseldorf
today: provincial court counsellor in Düsseldorf

Spies, Gebhardt born 2. 6. 1905
formerly: provincial court counsellor in the special court, Brunswick
today: provincial court counsellor in Brunswick

Spillner, Dr. Herbert born 7. 9. 1909
formerly: public prosecutor in the special court, Dresden
today: social court director in Lübeck

Splett, Bruno born 18. 8. 1909
formerly: military court counsellor of the Luftwaffe, Norway
today: senate president in the Superior Provincial Court in Cologne

Splettstösser, Dr. Erich born 10. 3. 1908
formerly: public prosecutor in the special court, Prague (Praha)
today: public prosecutor in Hanover

Spreckelsen, Dr. von born December 1905
formerly: superior provincial court counsellor in the nazi Ministry of Justice
today: ministrial director in the Federal Ministry of Justice

Springorum born 5. 11. 1915
formerly: assistant judge in the special court, Thorn (Torun)
today: lower court counsellor in Kusel

Susemihl born 19. 10. 1904
formerly: public prosecutor in the special court, Hanover
today: first public prosecutor in Aurich

Staat, Dr. born 10. 9. 1907
formerly: public prosecutor for political cases in the Superior Provincial Court in Hamm
today: leading senior public prosecutor in Arnsberg

Stähler, Fritz born 6. 1. 1903
formerly: public prosecutor in the special court, Danzig (Gdansk)
today: senior public prosecutor in Hamm

Stamp, Wolfgang born 21. 12. 1910
formerly: member of a court martial
today: superior provincial court counsellor in Hamburg

Stangl, Dr. Walter born 21. 5. 1910
formerly: public prosecutor in the special court, Eger (Cheb)
today: public prosecutor in Bamberg

Stanglmair, Dr. Herrmann born 29. 5. 1910
formerly: military court counsellor in the 169th infantry division
today: supreme provincial court counsellor in Munich

Stanke, Georg born 6. 8. 1906
formerly: lower court counsellor in the special court, Kattowitz (Katowice)
today: lower court counsellor in Baden-Baden

Starck, von born 12. 10. 1904
formerly: provincial court counsellor in the nazi Ministry of Justice
today: provincial court director in Kiel

Staud, Dr. Hans born 19. 5. 1900
formerly: senior military court counsellor in the High Command of the Army/HR
until August 1965: senate president in Frankfurt-on-Main

Steckel, Kurt born 17. 7. 1901
formerly: public prosecutor in the special court, Königsberg (Kaliningrad)
until July 1965: provincial court director in Hamburg

Steffen, Dr. Erich born 20. 5. 1904
formerly: provincial court counsellor in the special court, Düsseldorf
today: provincial court director in Düsseldorf

Steffen, Hermann born 23. 10. 1902
formerly: military court counsellor, XII AK
today: lower court director in Bünde

Stein, vom born 9. 5. 1904
formerly: provincial court counsellor in the special court, Düsseldorf
today: senate president in the Superior Provincial Court in Düsseldorf

Steiner, Dr. Hans born 20. 10. 1900
formerly: lower court counsellor in the special court, Berlin
today: lower court counsellor in Düsseldorf

Steinke, Max born 7. 10. 1910
formerly: public prosecutor in the "People's Court"
today: senior judge in Singen

Steinle, Dr. Kurt born 1. 3. 1914
formerly: lower court counsellor in the special court, Munich
today: superior provincial court counsellor in Munich

Steinmayr, Dr. Hans born 16. 1. 1905
formerly: provincial court counsellor in the special court, Bamberg
today: provincial court counsellor in Schweinfurt

Stephan, Heinz born 3. 6. 1913
formerly: senior staff judge in the 408th and the 28th divisions Breslau
today: provincial court counsellor in Munich

Stöhr, Karl born 22. 2. 1905
formerly: government counsellor in Butzbach, 1933 up to 1937 SA Oberscharführer Sturm 4/29, thereafter SS
today: government director in the Nuremberg penitentiary

Stölzel, Ulrich born 2. 12. 1905
formerly: provincial court counsellor at the special court, Kassel
today: senate president in the Superior Provincial Court in Frankfurt-on-Main

Stolting II, Herman born March 1911
formerly: public prosecutor in the special court, Bromberg (Bydgoszcz)
today: lawyer in Frankfurt-on-Main

Stoppel, Dr. Adolf-Friedrich born 30. 10. 1901
formerly: military court counsellor in Luftgau II Warschau (Warszawa)
today: lower court counsellor in Witten

Stransky, Dr. Maximilian born 15. 9. 1910
formerly: public prosecutor for political cases in Troppau (Opava), No. A-6/365 on the list of war criminals of Czechoslovakia
today: provincial court counsellor in Kempten

Streller, Karl born 28. 10. 1907
formerly: public prosecutor in the special court, Brünn (Brno)
today: provincial court counsellor in Rottweil

Strödter, Dr. born 27. 5. 1909
formerly: lower court counsellor in the special court, Linz
today: lower court director in Wetzlar

Strohbach, Dr. Rudolf born 6. 1. 1913
formerly: army judge in the 391st infantry division
today: lawyer in Bremerhaven

Stromsky born 21. 12. 1909
formerly: military court counsellor in the 210th infantry division
today: senior judge in Oelde

Strümpler born 2. 10. 1901
formerly: superior provincial court counsellor in the special court, Bielefeld
today: senior judge in Bielefeld

Stuhldreer, Kunibert born 14. 7. 1904
formerly: provincial court counsellor in the special court, Breslau (Wroclaw)
today: lower court counsellor in Landshut

Stumpf, Dr. Hermann born 9. 10. 1912
formerly: assessor in the nazi Ministry of Justice, Dept. III
today: senate president in the Federal Labour Court

Stumpf, Richard born 4. 2. 1907
formerly: public prosecutor in the special court, Litzmannstadt (Lodz)
today: first public prosecutor in Nuremberg

Suckow, Harald born 16. 5. 1903
formerly: military field court counsellor in High Command 4 of the Tank Army
today: lower court counsellor in Dillingen-on-Danube

Szogs, Gerhard born 8. 7. 1908
formerly: senior staff judge in the 3rd division Frankfurt-on-Oder, field command 530
today: public prosecutor in Hanover

Tacke born 27. 5. 1907
formerly: public prosecutor in the special court, Frankfurt-on-Main
today: first public prosecutor in Frankfurt-on-Main

Talpa, Dr. Erich born 14. 1. 1904
formerly: lower court counsellor in the special court, Troppau (Opava)
today: senior public prosecutor in Ulm

Tank, Ernst born 17. 4. 1904
formerly: public prosecutor in the special court, Eger (Cheb)
today: senior government counsellor in Kiel, penitentiary

Tennigkeit born 27. 6. 1906
formerly: public prosecutor in the special court, Königsberg (Kaliningrad)
today: public prosecutor in Essen

Teufl, Dr. Max born 10. 2. 1902
formerly: provincial court counsellor in the special court, Zweibrücken
today: provincial court president in Koblenz

Thamm, Ernst born 25. 3. 1904
formerly: public prosecutor in the special court, Kiel
today: senior public prosecutor in Kiel

Thierbach, Ernst born 19. 1. 1902
formerly: provincial court counsellor in the special court, Berlin
today: senate president in Düsseldorf

Thomashoff born 7. 2. 1901
formerly: provincial court counsellor in the special court, Düsseldorf
today: provincial court director in Düsseldorf

Thomsen, Willy born 20. 9. 1906
formerly: lower court counsellor in the special court, Kiel
today: senate president in Schleswig

Thurmayr, Dr. Alois born 22. 1. 1909
formerly: lower court counsellor in the special court, Munich
today: lower court counsellor in Starnberg

Tiedtke, Dr. born 3. 6. 1908
formerly: provincial court counsellor in the special court, Berlin
today: provincial court counsellor in Arnsberg

Tillmann born 16. 4. 1905
formerly: public prosecutor and chief executory officer in the special court, Stettin (Szczecin)
today: public prosecutor in Kleve

Timmermann, Wennemar born 6. 7. 1906
formerly: public prosecutor in the special court, Celle
today: provincial court director in Hanover

Töpfer, Dr. Karl born 13. 8. 1903
formerly: provincial court counsellor in the special court, Schneidemühl (Pila)
today: lower court counsellor in Gladbeck

Beglaubigte Abschrift. 28

(Sond.III) 1 KLs. 35.42(783.43)

Im Namen des Deutschen Volkes!

S t r a f s a c h e

g e g e n

den Gelegenheitsarbeiter Paul Israel B e r k h e i m, geboren am 10. August 1911 in Berlin, z. Zt. in dieser Sache in Strafhaft im Zuchthaus Brandenburg - Görden, ledig, Jude, wegen Rassenschande.

Das Sondergericht III beim Landgericht Berlin hat in der Hauptverhandlung vom 9. April 1943, an der teilgenommen haben:

Landgerichtsdirektor Dr. Böhmert
als Vorsitzender,
Landgerichtsrat Herfurth,
Landgerichtsrat Schultz
als beisitzende Richter,
Staatsanwalt Dr. Berthold
als Beamter der Staatsanwaltschaft,
Justizangestellter Meyer
als Urkundsbeamter der Geschäftsstelle,

für Recht erkannt:

Der Angeklagte wird als gefährlicher Gewohnheitsverbrecher wegen Rassenschande in drei Fällen zum Tode, zum dauernden Verlust der Rechte aus den §§ 32 ff StGB und zu den Kosten des Verfahrens verurteilt.

G r ü n d e .

Der Angeklagte ist durch Urteil des Sondergerichts V bei dem Landgericht Berlin vom 26.9.1942 wegen Rassenschande in drei Fällen zu insgesamt 7 Jahren Zuchthaus und zum Verlust der Rechte aus den §§ 32 ff StGB auf 5 Jahre verurteilt worden. Auf die vom Oberreichsanwalt eingelegte Nichtigkeitsbeschwerde hin hat das Reichsgericht dieses Urteil am 18.2.1943 im Strafausspruch nebst den ihm insoweit zu Grunde liegenden Feststellungen aufgehoben und das Verfahren in diesem Umfang zu neuer Verhandlung und Entscheidung an das Sondergericht zurückverwiesen, weil nicht geprüft worden ist, ob die Voraussetzungen der §§ 20a Abs. 2, 42 e StGB und § 1 des Gesetzes zur Aenderung des Reichsstrafgesetzbuchs vom 4.9.1941 gegeben sind.

TABLE 25

11

(19) 2 OJs. 110/44(56/44)

Vertraulich!

U r t e i l !

Im Namen des Deutschen Volkes !

In der Strafsache
g e g e n

den Grubenlehrhäuer Max K y a s aus Gleiwitz III, Bischofstraße 53, geboren am 20. März 1895 in Makoschau, Krs. Kattowitz, katholisch, Reichsdeutscher, verheiratet, vorbestraft,

z.Zt. in der Haftanstalt in Beuthen OS.

wegen Zersetzung der Wehrkraft,

hat der 1. Strafsenat des Oberlandesgerichts Kattowitz in Beuthen OS. auf Grund der Hauptverhandlung vom 15. August 1944,

an der teilgenommen haben

Oberlandesgerichtspräsident D r e n d e l
als Vorsitzender,
Oberlandesgerichtsrat Dr. Z d r a l e k,
Oberlandesgerichtsrat B u r z l a f f
als beisitzende Richter,
Staatsanwalt Dr. Z i e n i c k e X
als Beamter der Staatsanwaltschaft,
Gerichtsreferendar J a n u s
als Urkundsbeamter der Geschäftsstelle,

für R e c h t e r k a n n t :

Der Angeklagte hat im Kreise von Arbeitskameraden immer wieder durch Schmähungen der deutschen Führung und deutscher Soldaten sowie durch zersetzende Bekrittelung militärischer Handlungen und Kriegsmaßnahmen wiederholten Mahnungen und Warnungen zum Trotz den Willen des Deutschen Volkes zur wehrhaften Selbstbehauptung zu lähmen gesucht.

Er wird deshalb mit dem Tode bestraft.

Die Ehrenrechte werden ihm aberkannt.

Hauptverhandlung am 3. März 1944 9 Uhr,
vor dem Deutschen Obergericht in Krakau
Stock, Zimmer 119

Geladen sind:
Angeklagte
Verteidiger
Zeugen
Sachverständige
Nebenkläger

Terminsvermerke:

Antrag
gegen
Todesstrafe [illegible]
[illegible]
[illegible] Abs. II [illegible]

Entscheidung
gegen
[illegible]

[illegible]

Hauptverhandlung am
vor de
Stock, Zimmer
3. [illegible] Uhr
Geladen sind:
Angeklagte
Verteidiger
Zeugen
Sachverständige
Nebenkläger

Terminsvermerke:

Antrag
gegen

gegen

Kanzlei
erhalten } 10.3.44 [illegible]
gefertigt
zu
ab
ab zu 11.3.44

Js 156/44
KLs 4/44

Regierung des Generalgouvernements
Hauptabteilung Justiz

Krakau, den 4. Januar 1944.

Ju Ber.S.296/43.

An das
Sondergericht beim Deutschen Gericht
in Lemberg.

Betrifft: Strafsache gegen Anna Zwarycz.
- 4 KLs 46/43 -

Gegen das Urteil vom 30. Juli 1943 erhebe ich gemäß § 32 der VO. über die deutsche Gerichtsbarkeit im Generalgouvernement vom 19. Februar 1940 (VBlGG. I S.57)

außerordentlichen Einspruch.

Als Gericht, das in der Sache von neuem zu entscheiden hat, bestimme ich gemäß § 8 der VO. zur Vereinfachung der Strafgerichtsbarkeit im Generalgouvernement vom 24. Oktober 1942 (VBlGG.S.667) das Deutsche Obergericht in Krakau.

Begründung:

Nach der Feststellung des Sondergerichts hat die Angeklagte im Oktober 1942 das damals 18 Monate alte Kind des Juden Hirsch-Mamut aus Brody bei sich aufgenommen und es bis Anfang April 1943 bei sich behalten und verpflegt, obwohl sich das jüdische Kind spätestens ab 1. Dezember 1942 in dem seit jener Zeit in Brody errichteten jüdischen Wohnbezirk hätte aufhalten müssen. Das Sondergericht hat dazu weiter festgestellt, daß die Angeklagte das Kind offen und für jedermann als jüdisches Kind erkenntlich bei sich gehabt und dies sogar noch kurz vor ihrer Festnahme einer bekannten Frau erzählt habe. In diesem Verhalten hat das Sondergericht kein

Voraussetzung für die Strafbarkeit des Unterschlupfgewährers die Erfüllung des äußeren Tatbestandes seitens des Juden genügt. Diese Voraussetzung ist im vorliegenden Falle gegeben, denn es handelt sich bei dem von der Angeklagten beherbergten Kinde um einen Juden, der einem gesetzlichen Verbote zuwider und ohne behördliche Ausnahmegenehmigung, also (objektiv) unbefugt außer-

... meine Rv. vom 10.[illegible] 1943, [illegible] 4/2-1/43).

In Vertretung
gez. Dr. Ganser.

TABLE 26

TABLE 27

Abschrift. 18. 26

Oberlandesgericht Stuttgart.

OJs 115/43. I.Strafsenat.

Haft!

Hochverratssache!

Im Namen des Deutschen Volkes!

U r t e i l .

In der Strafsache gegen

1.) den am 23.September 1923 in Nieder-Dyeutz (Lothr.) geborenen, in Heidelberg, Bahnhofstr.9 wohnhaften, ledigen Koch

Désiré H a m b u r g e r ,

2.) den am 26.Juni 1908 in Spiessen/Saargebiet geborenen, in Heidelberg, Dreikönigstr.15 wohnhaften, verheirateten Kraftfahrer

Heinrich Hermann F e h r e n t z ,

3.) den am 21.Juli 1920 in Straßburg i.E. geborenen, in Heidelberg, Hauptstraße 120 wohnhaften, ledigen Metzgergesellen

Eduard Arthur C l a u s s ,

4.) den am 1.Januar 1920 in Straßburg i.E. geborenen, in Heidelberg, Hauptstraße 120 wohnhaften, ledigen Metzger

Paul Robert K o e h l ,

5.) den am 6.November 1897 in Heidelberg geborenen, daselbst, Ziegelhäuserlandstr. 23 wohnhaften, verheirateten Hilfsarbeiter

Johann G a n z ,

6.) dessen Ehefrau, die am 11.April 1901 in Ziegelhausen Krs.Heidelberg geborene, in Heidelberg, Ziegelhäuserlandstr.23 wohnhafte Hausfrau

Maria G a n z geb.Werle,

7.) den am 4.Mai 1921 in Straßburg i.E. geborenen, in Heidelberg, Hauptstraße 105 wohnhaften, ledigen Konditor

Andreas E r t z ,

sämtliche bisher in Untersuchungshaft im Gerichtsgefängnis Heidelberg,

wegen Vorbereitung zum Hochverrat u.a.,

hat der I.Strafsenat des Oberlandesgerichts Stuttgart in der Sitzung vom 26.Oktober 1943 in Heidelberg, an welcher teilgenommen haben:

als Richter:

Senatspräsident Dr.Kiefer,

Oberlandesgerichtsrat Dr.Sick,

Oberlandesgerichtsrat Dr.Stuber,

als Beamter der Staatsanwaltschaft:

X Amtsgerichtsrat Dr.Krebs,

nach mündlicher Verhandlung für Recht erkannt:

I. Es werden verurteilt:

die Angeklagten Hamburger, Fehrentz, Clauss, Koehl und Johann Ganz je wegen fortgesetzten verbotenen Abhörens ausländischer Sender in Tateinheit mit fortgesetzter Verbreitung von staatsfeindlichen Nachrichten solcher Sender, die Angeklagten Hamburger, Fehrentz, Clauss und Koehl zugleich auch wegen Vorbereitung zum Hochverrat und Wehrkraftzersetzung,

der Angeklagte Ertz wegen teils versuchten, teils vollendeten verbotenen Abhörens ausländischer Sender,

die Angeklagte Maria Ganz wegen versuchten Abhörens ausländischer Sender und versuchten Verbreitens von Nachrichten solcher Sender, und zwar

Fehrentz

z u m T o d e ,

Johann Ganz zu der

Zuchthausstrafe von vier Jahren,

Hamburger und Clauss je zu der

Zuchthausstrafe von drei Jahren,

Koehl zu der

Zuchthausstrafe von zwei Jahren und sechs Monaten

ABSCHRIFT 30

30.KLs.193/43 Im Namen des deutschen Volkes!

U r t e i l

Strafsache gegen

1. den am 10. Februar 1900 in Buchsweiler geborenen, in Sufflenheim wohnhaften, verheirateten Angestellten beim Reichsluftschutzbund

   Karl Z i l l e r und

2. den am 18. November 1905 in Straßburg geborenen, in Bischweiler wohnhaften, verheirateten Angestellten

   Robert E c k e r t

wegen hochverräterischer Umtriebe, Vorbereitung zum Hochverrat, Feindbegünstigung, Beschimpfung des Reichs und Abhörens nichtdeutscher Sender.

Das Sondergericht beim Landgericht Straßburg (Elsaß) hat in der Sitzung vom 26. November 1943, an welcher teilgenommen haben:

Landgerichtspräsident Dr. Huber,
als Vorsitzender,
Landgerichtsrat Zander,
Landgerichtsrat Neidhard, X
als beisitzende Richter,
Oberstaatsanwalt Luger,
als Beamter der Staatsanwaltschaft,
Justizassistent Gilch,
als Urkundsbeamter der Geschäftsstelle,

für Recht erkannt:

Karl Ziller hat in den Jahren 1942 und 1943 in großem Umfange anonyme Hetzschriften verbreitet, in denen er die Einführung der Wehrpflicht im Elsaß bekämpfte und die elsässische Bevölkerung aufforderte, sich gegen die deutsche Führung im Elsaß zusammenzuschließen, ihr Widerstand zu leisten und für die Befreiung durch Frankreich zu arbeiten. Zur Unterstützung seiner Bestrebungen hat er sich auch an die englischen Konsulatsbehörden in der Schweiz gewandt. Robert Eckert hat im Jahre 1942 einen Aufruf gegen die Einführung der Wehrpflicht im Elsaß verfaßt und diesen an Ziller weitergegeben.

Die Angeklagten werden hierwegen zum Tode und zum dauernden Verlust der Ehrenrechte verurteilt.

Die Angeklagten haben die Kosten des Verfahrens zu tragen.

Oberstaatsanwalt
[be]im Landgericht
[Stra]ssburg (Elsass)

5 52a

Strassburg, den 20.Januar 1944.

So Kls. 193/43

[A]n den Herrn Reichsminister der Justiz
in **Berlin W 8**
Wilhelmstrasse 16

-7. FEB. 1944 -5FEB1944 IV g. 10a

[Str]afsache gegen Karl ZILLER, wegen landesverräterischer Feindbegünstigung und Wehrkraftzersetzung.

[Z]u meinem Gnadenbericht vom 3.Dezember 1943 -

Der Herr Chef der Zivilverwaltung im Elsass hat mit Erlass vom 5.Januar 1944 einen Gnadenerweis abgelehnt.

Die vom Sondergericht Strassburg mit Urteil vom 26.November 1943 gegen ZILLER ausgesprochene Todesstrafe wurde am 15.Januar 1944 um 5 Uhr lo Min.5o Sek. ohne Zwischenfall vollstreckt.

Die Leiche wurde der Anatomie Freiburg i.Br. zu Forschungszwecken überlassen.

Luger.

10a 5786 5786/43 439

TABLE 28

Erwin Schüle, Assessor
Stuttgart, am Tazzelwurm 17
z. Zt. Leutnant, F.P.N. 12207 D

Im Feld, den 3. Sept. 1943.

Lebenslauf.

Geboren am 2. Juli 1913 in Stuttgart-Bad Cannstatt als Sohn des Weingärtners Ernst Schüle und seiner Ehefrau Anna Maria geb. Österle. Mein Vater fiel im Jahre 1916 vor Verdun.

1921 trat ich in die Oberrealschule in Stuttgart-Bad Cannstatt ein und legte daselbst im Frühjahr 1933 die Reifeprüfung ab.

Nach abgeschlossenem Studium der Rechts- und Staatswissenschaften an den Universitäten Tübingen und Königsberg legte ich im Herbst 1937 meine erste juristische Staatsprüfung beim Oberlandesgericht in Stuttgart ab. Im Jahre 1933 trat ich der S.A. bei und bin seit 1935 Parteigenosse.

Am 1. Januar 1938 begann ich mit der Ableistung meines Vorbereitungsdienstes beim Amtsgericht in Waiblingen. Auch meinen weiteren Vorbereitungsdienst leistete ich im Bezirk des Landgerichts Stuttgart ab. Ende Dezember 1939 musste ich meinen Vorbereitungsdienst unterbrechen, da ich zum Heeresdienste einberufen wurde. Anlässlich eines Sonderurlaubs legte ich im Januar 1941 meine große juristische

TABLE 29

Der Reichsminister des Innern
Pol. I C (a) 1 a Nr. 1254/40

V/54

RP 3272/40

Präsidialkanzlei des Führers und Reichskanzlers
Eingeg. 13 MRZ 1940

Vorschlag zur Ernennung

des

Regierungsrats Dr. B i l f i n g e r zum Oberregierungsrat

in der Reichsbesoldungsgruppe A 2 oder der ihr entsprechenden Landesbesoldungsgruppe

Anlage: 1 mitgezeichnete Urkunde

"Der Stellvertreter des Führers hat Einwendungen gegen die Ernennung nicht erhoben"

Berlin, den 29. Februar 1940

An den
Herrn Staatsminister und Chef der Präsidialkanzlei
des Führers und Reichskanzlers
Berlin W 8
Voßstraße 1

I.V.
H. Himmler
248

(Dieser Raum ist der Präsidialkanzlei des Führers und Reichskanzlers vorbehalten)

Hierzu ist bei RP. 3400/40 verfügt:

Im Namen des Deutschen Volkes

ernenne ich
den obengenannten Beamten.
Die Ernennungsurkunde ist unter dem heutigen
Tage mit meiner faksimilierten Unterschrift auszufertigen.

Berlin, den 15. März 1940

Der Führer und Reichskanzler
gez. Adolf Hitler

Präsidialkanzlei Berlin, den 15. März 1940

Zu 1. Zu 1. 3. 4

1. Die unter obenstehender Orts- und Datumsangabe mit der faksimilierten Unterschrift des Führers und Reichskanzlers ausgefertigte Urkunde geht mit Anschreiben an die antragstellende Behörde zurück.
2. Zu den Akten

gez. Dr. Meissner

Prüfungsgang oder Nachweis der sonstigen Eignung	Tag des Eintritts in den Reichs- oder Landesdienst	Bisherige dienstliche Laufbahn	[illegible]
1 juristische Prüfung im Herbst 1929 mit der Note "3 a mitte" und die große Staatsprüfung im Herbst 32 ebenfalls mit der Note "3 a mitte" bestanden.	13.12.1929	Vom 13.12.29 bis 3.3.1932 Gerichtsreferendar im Bezirk des Oberlandesgerichts Stuttgart. Vom 1.4.33 – 5.1.34 Rechtsanwalt in Tübingen, Vom 8.1.34 bis 30.4.34 Gerichtsassessor beim Oberamt Balingen. Am 2.5.34 beim Württ. Politischen Landespolizeiamt (Staatspolizeileitstelle) in Stuttgart einberufen. Am 23.7.34 zum Regierungsassessor ernannt. Am 1.6.36 zum Regierungsrat ernannt. Am 1.4.37 endgültig in den Dienst der Geheimen Staatspolizei übernommen. Am 5.11.37 zum Hauptamt Sicherheitspolizei – S V 1 – versetzt.	a) ja b) durch Urkunden.

[illegible]	Militärverhältnis a) früher b) jetzt	a) Mitglied der NSDAP b) seit wann? c) Mitglieds-Nr. d) Ämter in der Partei	Welchen politischen Parteien und Verbänden hat der Beamte früher angehört und wie lange?	Hat der Beamte a) Logen b) vor dem 30. Januar 1933 ... angehört	Strafen	Bemerkungen
–	a) – b) Feldw. der Reserve	a) ja b) 1.5.37 c) 5 892661 d) SS-Hauptsturmf.	NSDAP bis Frühjahr 1923 bis zur Auflösung im Herbst 1929.	–	–	–

TABLE 30

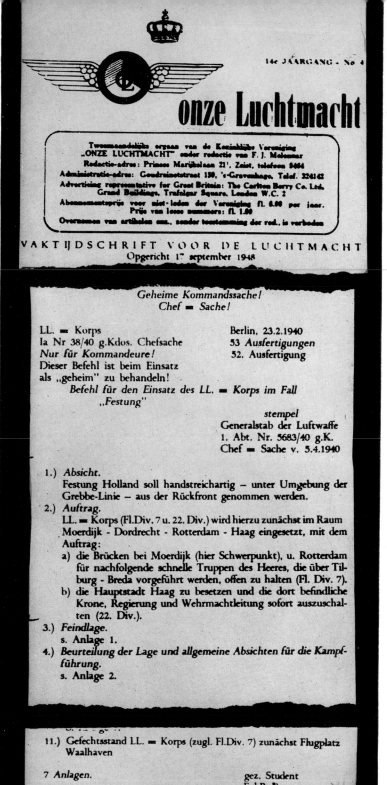

14e JAARGANG - No 4

onze Luchtmacht

Tweemaandelijks orgaan van de Koninklijke Vereniging
„ONZE LUCHTMACHT" onder redactie van F. J. Molenaar
Redactie-adres: Princes Marijkelaan 21', Zeist, telefoon 8464
Administratie-adres: Goudreinetstraat 150, 's-Gravenhage, Telef. 324142
Advertising representative for Great Britain: The Carlton Berry Co. Ltd.
Grand Buildings, Trafalgar Square, London W.C. 2
Abonnementsprijs voor niet-leden der Vereniging fl. 6.00 per jaar.
Prijs van losse nummers: fl. 1.00
Overnemen van artikelen enz., zonder toestemming der red., is verboden

VAKTIJDSCHRIFT VOOR DE LUCHTMACHT
Opgericht 1e september 1948

Geheime Kommandssache!
Chef = Sache!

LL. = Korps
Ia Nr 38/40 g.Kdos. Chefsache
Nur für Kommandeure!
Dieser Befehl ist beim Einsatz
als „geheim" zu behandeln!

Berlin, 23.2.1940
53 *Ausfertigungen*
52. Ausfertigung

Befehl für den Einsatz des LL. = Korps im Fall „Festung"

stempel
Generalstab der Luftwaffe
1. Abt. Nr. 5683/40 g.K.
Chef = Sache v. 5.4.1940

1.) *Absicht.*
Festung Holland soll handstreichartig – unter Umgebung der Grebbe-Linie – aus der Rückfront genommen werden.

2.) *Auftrag.*
LL. = Korps (Fl.Div. 7 u. 22. Div.) wird hierzu zunächst im Raum Moerdijk - Dordrecht - Rotterdam - Haag eingesetzt, mit dem Auftrag:
a) die Brücken bei Moerdijk (hier Schwerpunkt), u. Rotterdam für nachfolgende schnelle Truppen des Heeres, die über Tilburg - Breda vorgeführt werden, offen zu halten (Fl. Div. 7).
b) die Hauptstadt Haag zu besetzen und die dort befindliche Krone, Regierung und Wehrmachtleitung sofort auszuschalten (22. Div.).

3.) *Feindlage.*
s. Anlage 1.

4.) *Beurteilung der Lage und allgemeine Absichten für die Kampfführung.*
s. Anlage 2.

11.) Gefechtsstand LL. = Korps (zugl. Fl.Div. 7) zunächst Flugplatz Waalhaven

7 *Anlagen.*

gez. Student
F.d.R. [3])
Trettner.
Major d.G.

TABLE 31

Anlage 3.
zu I a Nr. 38/40 g. Kdos.
53 Ausfertigungen
52. Ausfertigung.

Einzelaufträge für Fl. Div. 7.

1.) *Gruppe Süd* (*verst. Fallsch. Jäg. Regt.* 1) - Führer Oberst Bräuer
I./Fallsch. Jäg. 1
II./Fallsch. „
14./Fallsch. „
Fallsch Nachr. Zug 7 (Teile)
1./Pi. 22
Div. Geschützbatt. 7
1. Zug Div. Flakbatt. 7 u. FS.-San. Halbkomp.
setzt sich - nach vorherigem Bombenangriff - handstreichartig in den Besitz der beiden Brücken bei Moerdijk, beseitigt sofort alle vorhandenen Sprengvorbereitungen u. nimmt diese Brücken fest in die Hand. Brücken müssen unbedingt gehalten worden, bis vorderste Teile des Heeres eintreffen.

Gleichzeitig ist eine besond...

Anlage 4.
zu Ia Nr 38/40 g. Kdos.
53 Ausfertigungen
52. Ausfertigung.

Sperrzone für eigenen Bombenwurf.

Zum Schutze der eigenen Erdtruppen werden folgende Gebiete für eigenen Bombenwurf gesperrt:

1.) *Ab* x + *45 Min. bis* x + *150 Min.* (Einsatz der Fallsch. Truppen) Landeplätze Katwijk, Ypenburg, Kijkduin, Waalhaven u. Brückenstellen bei Rotterdam u. Dordrecht in einem Umkreis von 3 km (ab Platzmitte bezw. Brückenmitte).
Brücken bei Moerdijk bis zu einer Entfernung von 5 km von beiden Brückenenden.

2.) *Ab* x + *150 Min.* (Einsatz u. Marschbewegung der Div.'n). Raum Katwijk aan Zee (einschl.) - Oegstgeest (einschl.) - Leiden (ausschl.) - Benthuizen (einschl.) - Moerkapelle (ausschl.) - Nieuwerkerk (ausschl.) - Kinderdijk (ausschl.) - Noord Maas (einschl.) - Merwede bis Eisenbahnbrücke (einschl.) - Hooge Zwaluwe (einschl.) - Zevenbergschenhoek (einschl.) - Klundert (ausschl.) - in gerader Linie nach Nordwesten bis Maassluis (ausschl.) - Monster (ausschl.).
Angriffe gegen Feindkräfte innerhalb dieser Sperrzone werden nur auf besondere Anforderung u. unter Verantwortung des LL.-Korps durchgeführt.

gez. Student.
F.d.R.
Trettner
Major d. G.

behälter zu bergen u. sicherzustellen, um eine baldige erneute Einsatzbereitschaft gewährleisten zu können.

gez. Student
F.d.R.
Trettner
Major d.G.

TABLE 32

Trabert, Dr. Rudolf born 21 1. 1904
formerly: provincial court counsellor in the special court, Munich
today: senior public prosecutor in the Superior Provincial Court in Munich

Tramm, Dr. Willy born 19. 2. 1901
formerly: public prosecutor for political cases in the nazi Ministry of Justice
today: lower court president in Düsseldorf

Traub, Kurt born 26. 6. 1904
formerly: provincial court counsellor in the special court, Litzmannstadt (Lodz)
today: senior public prosecutor in Stuttgart

Treichel, Werner born 15. 8. 1908
formerly: military field judge
today: senior judge in Schwarzenbeck

Trepte, Dr. Martin born 30. 7. 1912
formerly: lower court counsellor in the special court, Leipzig
today: provincial court counsellor in Koblenz

Troost, Dr. Sigismund born 23. 9. 1911
formerly: military court counsellor
today: social court counsellor in Duisburg

Tschofen, Franz born 22. 10. 1910
formerly: military court counsellor, Litzmannstadt (Lodz) headquarters
today: lower court counsellor in Traunstein

Uhlig born 26. 2. 1909
formerly: public prosecutor in the special courts in Freiberg and Königsberg (Kaliningrad)
today: public prosecutor in Düsseldorf

Uhse, Dirk born 24. 6. 1907
formerly: senior staff judge in the 3rd division, Frankfurt-on-Oder
today: lower court counsellor in Kassel

Ullrich, Dr. Hans born 17. 9. 1907
formerly: provincial court counsellor in the special court, Weimar
today: provincial court counsellor in Mosbach

Verres, Paul born 26. 4. 1903
formerly: public prosecutor in the special court, Frankfurt-on-Main
today: first public prosecutor in Wiesbaden

Verspohl, Dr. born 22. 7. 1908
formerly: senior staff judge in the 12th air force field division
today: provincial court director in Münster

Viergutz, Hans-Werner born 18. 7. 1908
formerly: senior staff judge in the 28th division, Breslau (Wrocław)
today: first public prosecutor in Ravensburg

Viertel, Lothar born 28. 5. 1910
formerly: military court counsellor in the 409th infantry division
today: lower court counsellor in Fulda

Vogel, Hans born 23. 6. 1906
formerly: public prosecutor in the special court, Hamburg
today: senior public prosecutor in Hamburg

Vogel, Dr. Hermann born 2. 2. 1904
formerly: provincial court counsellor in the special court, Hamburg
today: superior provincial court counsellor in Hamburg

Voigt, Dr. Erich born 12. 11. 1902
formerly: senior military court counsellor in the Berlin headquarters and in the High Command of the Army
today: lower court counsellor in Hanover

Voithenberg, Dr. Voith von born 29. 8. 1904
formerly: lower court counsellor in the special court, Bamberg
today: administrative court director in Bayreuth

Vollmar, Franz born 8. 3. 1906
formerly: public prosecutor in the nazi Ministry of Justice, Dept. III
today: senior judge in Sinsheim

Vollrath, Dr. born 10. 9. 1907
formerly: lower court counsellor in the special court, Dresden
today: lower court director in Bad Salzuflen

Vornbäumen, Dr. H. A. born 23. 6. 1903
formerly: public prosecutor in the Superior Provincial Court in Kassel (political cases)

today: senior public prosecutor in Frankfurt-on-Main

Vornweg born 5. 11. 1902
formerly: lower court counsellor in the special court, Bielefeld
today: senior judge in Meschede

Wälzholz, Ulrich born 27. 10. 1903
formerly: public prosecutor in the special court, Breslau (Wrocław)
today: senior public prosecutor in Hamm

Wagner, Dr. Hans-Hein born 31. 3. 1909
formerly: military court counsellor in the 4th and 413th armoured divisions
today: provincial court director in Aachen

Wagner, Dr. Walter born 31. 7. 1901
formerly: senior public prosecutor to the Prosecutor General of Posen (Poznan)
today: federal prosecutor in the Federal Court

Wahl, Ernst born 29. 11. 1903
formerly: judge in the special court II, Breslau (Wrocław)
today: lawyer and notary in Frankfurt-on-Main

Wallis, Gerhard born 25. 2. 1906
formerly: senior staff judge in the 8th division, Oppeln (Opole)
today: lower court counsellor in Bochum

Walter born 3. 3. 1903
formerly: provincial court counsellor in the special court, Kalisch (Kalisz)
today: provincial court counsellor in Mainz

Walther, Wolfgang born 7. 5. 1908
formerly: public prosecutor in Erfurt, SS Court Central Department, SS Sturmbannführer
today: government director in the Ministry of Justice in Baden-Württemberg

Weber, Dr. Erich born 9. 4. 1901
formerly: provincial court counsellor in the special court, Düsseldorf
today: provincial court counsellor in Duisburg

Weber, Kurt born 29. 10. 1907
formerly: judge in France, took part in executions in Alsace
today: federal judge in the Federal Court in Karlsruhe

Weber, Dr. Walter born 31. 10. 1902
formerly: military court counsellor in the 409th infantry division
today: lower court counsellor in Parsberg

Webermeier, Herbert born 4. 1. 1906
formerly: public prosecutor in Wuppertal, SS Untersturmführer in staff II/20
today: public prosecutor in Dortmund

Wehdeking, Dr. Siegfried born 18. 8. 1913
formerly: senior staff judge in penal brigade 999
today: parson in a prison in Werl

Wegert, Dr. Kurt born 15. 9. 1907
formerly: military court counsellor in the 4th tank army
today: superior provincial court counsellor in Munich

Wehner, Martin born 10. 11. 1906
formerly: senior staff judge in the 17th division, Nuremberg
today: lower court counsellor in Munich

Wehrmeister born 15. 10. 1902
formerly: lower court counsellor in the special court, Stettin (Szczecin)
today: lower court counsellor in Moers

Weiden, Dr. von der born 21. 11. 1905
formerly: provincial court counsellor in the special court, Aachen
today: lower court counsellor in Aachen

Weinelt, Dr. Wilhelm born 2. 6. 1904
formerly: provincial court counsellor in the special court, Prague (Praha)
today: lower court counsellor in Nuremberg

Weinerth, Dr. Dr. Kurt born 19. 2. 1902
formerly: senior military court counsellor
today: administrative court president in Neustadt-on-Weinstrasse

Weise born 15. 2. 1905
formerly: public prosecutor for political cases in the Superior Provincial Court in Dresden
today: public prosecutor in Duisburg

Weissenberger, Heribert born 10. 2. 1905
formerly: lower court counsellor in the special court, Bayreuth
today: lower court counsellor in Forchheim

Weitnauer, Dr. born July 1910
formerly: lower court counsellor in the nazi Ministry of Justice
today: ministrial counsellor in the Federal Ministry of Justice

Weitzel, Philipp born 26. 8. 1908
formerly: public prosecutor for political cases in Kassel
today: senior public prosecutor in Marburg

Wendel, Wilhelm born 26. 3. 1904
formerly: military court counsellor
today: senate president in the Superior Provincial Court in Munich

Wendik born 9. 3. 1904
formerly: lower court counsellor in the special court, Zichenau (Ciechanow)
today: lower court counsellor in Eschershausen

Wenzel, Dr. Friedrich-Karl born 4. 2. 1912
formerly: public prosecutor in the special courts in Hanover and Celle
today: public prosecutor in Göttingen

Wenzel, Kurt born 24. 10. 1904
formerly: provincial court counsellor in the special court, Frankfurt-on-Oder
today: lower court counsellor in Westerland

Werber, Karl born 18. 10. 1913
formerly: public prosecutor in the special court, Magdeburg
today: lower court counsellor in Gifhorn

Werner, Dr. Berthold born 20. 8. 1898
formerly: military court counsellor in the 71st, 182nd, 28th, and 433rd divisions and provincial court director in the special court, Vienna
today: lower court director in Siegen

Werther, Dr. Friedrich born 13. 8. 1903
formerly: military court counsellor in the 174th division, senior staff judge, supreme field command
today: provincial court counsellor in Düsseldorf

Westerburg, Dr. born 7. 4. 1907
formerly: public prosecutor in the special court, Bielefeld
today: first public prosecutor in Arnsberg

Wettengel, Dr. Alfred born 22. 3. 1903
formerly: provincial court counsellor in the special court, Eger (Cheb)
until June 1965: lower court counsellor in Heilbronn

Wickmann born 12. 12. 1901
formerly: public prosecutor in the special court, Aachen
today: senior public prosecutor in Aachen

Widera born 16. 2. 1905
formerly: public prosecutor in the special court, Breslau (Wrocław)
today: public prosecutor in Brunswick

Wiedemann, Dr. Viktor born 16. 10. 1905
formerly: military court counsellor in Supreme Field Command 379
today: senior public prosecutor in Munich

Wienecke, Josef born 8. 8. 1906
formerly: public prosecutor in the special court, Luxemburg, 1949 sentenced to ten years forced labour there
today: first public prosecutor in Koblenz

Wildt, Dr. Hans born 14. 7. 1908
formerly: public prosecutor for political cases in Kassel
today: superior administrative court counsellor in Münster

Wilkerling, Dr. Joachim born 5. 9. 1900
formerly: superior provincial court counsellor in the nazi Ministry of Justice
today: ministerial director in the Ministry of Justice of Lower Saxony

Will, Dr. Hermann born 23. 9. 1905
formerly: military court counsellor
today: provincial court director in Landshut

Willecke born 10. 6. 1910
formerly: public prosecutor in the special court, Vienna
today: public prosecutor in Kassel

Willer, Herbert born 10. 11. 1904
formerly: lower court counsellor in the special court, Frankfurt-on-Main
today: lower court director in Frankfurt-on-Main

Wimmer, Dr. Eberhard born 27. 6. 1903
formerly: senior judge in Pulsnitz, SS Oberscharführer, political officer of Sturmbann I/84

today: lower court counsellor in the lower court in Wuppertal

Winckhler, Dr. Hugo born 28. 8. 1913
formerly: lower court counsellor in Munich, SS Scharführer
today: superior provincial court counsellor in Munich

Wintermann
formerly: lower court counsellor in the special court, Oldenburg
today: lower court in Delmenhorst

Witt, Dr. Heinz born 1. 1. 1910
formerly: lower court counsellor in the special court, Rostock
today: lower court counsellor in Rheinberg

Witzig, Dr. Konrad born 24. 4. 1901
formerly: military court counsellor in the 106th infantry division
today: provincial court director in Bochum

Wodtke born 22. 12. 1908
formerly: senior military court counsellor in the 30th infantry division and in the Reich Military Court in Berlin
today: lower court director in Siegen

Wöstmann, Dr. born 26. 12. 1896
formerly: senior military court counsellor in the 191st division
today: provincial court director in Hildesheim

Wohnsdorf, Hans born 28. 2. 1905
formerly: military court counsellor in the 214th and 408th infantry divisions
today: provincial court counsellor in Hechingen

Woldt, Dr. Heinz born 3. 11. 1909
formerly: senior staff judge in the 20th infantry division
today: superior provincial court counsellor in Hamburg

Wolff, Paul born 9. 12. 1905
formerly: provincial court counsellor in the special court Oppeln (Opole)
today: lower court counsellor in Paderborn

Wolfrum, Dr. born 20. 9. 1907
formerly: provincial court counsellor in the special court, Kattowitz (Katowice)
today: provincial court director in Aachen

Woll, Albert born 16. 8. 1906
formerly: lower court counsellor in the special court, Mannheim
today: prosecutor general in the Superior Provincial Court in Karlsruhe

Wollschläger born 8. 8. 1909
formerly: assessor in the special court, Schwerin
today: lower court counsellor in Siegen

Wonhas, Dr. Paul born 6. 9. 1906
formerly: military field judge, FP.-No. 16 688
today: provincial court director in Munich

Wroblewski, Dr. born 28. 3. 1908
formerly: lower court counsellor in the special court, Litzmannstadt (Lodz)
today: superior administrative court counsellor in Lüneburg

Wünschmann, Dr. Walter born 7. 1. 1912
formerly: senior staff judge in the 2nd tank division
today: senior government counsellor in the Federal Disciplinary Court

Wulkow born 1. 7. 1908
formerly: public prosecutor in the special court, Reichenberg (Liberec)
today: senior public prosecutor in Neustadt-on-Weinstrasse

Zain, Dr. born 21. 2. 1904
formerly: provincial court counsellor in the special court, Koblenz
today: provincial court director in Cologne

Zaske, Dr. born 12. 1. 1903
formerly: lower court counsellor in the special court, Elbing (Elblag)
today: lower court counsellor in Northeim

Zaum, Dr. Hermann born 9. 8. 1903
formerly: lower court counsellor in the special court, Weimar
today: lower court director in Dinslaken

Zbikowski, Dr. born 21. 3. 1902
formerly: public prosecutor in the special court, Koblenz
today: public prosecutor in Bad Kreuznach

Zellmann, Dr. Walter born 19. 4. 1905
formerly: court officer in the Wehrmacht, Berlin command
today: superior administrative court counsellor in Münster (see Table 30)

Zienicke, Dr. Hans-Albrecht born 21. 2. 1906
formerly: public prosecutor in the special court, Bielitz (Bielsko)
today: administrative court director in Düsseldorf

Zimmer, Johannes born 2. 12. 1902
formerly: lower court counsellor in the special court I, Dresden
today: lower court counsellor in Tübingen

Zimmerath born 16. 8. 1908
formerly: public prosecutor in the special court, Aachen
today: first public prosecutor in Bonn

Zoller, Max born 21. 2. 1903
formerly: provincial court counsellor in the special court, Munich
today: superior provincial court counsellor in Munich

Nazi Jurists in West Berlin

List of incriminated nazi jurists in the justice apparatus of the special territory of West Berlin:

Creifelds, Dr. Carl born 3. 4. 1907
formerly: supreme court counsellor in the nazi Ministry of Justice
until July 1965: senate counsellor of justice

Fäder, Bernhard born 3. 4. 1902
formerly: lower court counsellor in the special court in Litzmannstadt (Lodz)
today: senior judge in Tempelhof-Kreuzberg

Höfer, Gerhard born 6. 2. 1911
formerly: military court counsellor 388th A.A. division
today: provincial court counsellor

Hübner, Fritz born 21. 5. 1900
formerly: senior military court counsellor at the Berlin Wehrmacht command
until July 1965: provincial court director

Imme, Arnold born 18. 1. 1907
formerly: public prosecutor in the special court in Berlin
today: senior public prosecutor in the supreme court

Kolb, Erich born 25. 12. 1902
formerly: first public prosecutor in the special court in Kalisch (Kalisz)
today: government director, head of the Tegel penitentiary

Kurtze, Helmut born 7. 7. 1907
formerly: provincial court counsellor in the nazi Ministry of Justice
today: provincial court director

Lell, Dr. Heinz Günter born 1. 8. 1904
formerly: public prosecutor in the "People's Court"
today: senior public prosecutor

Manske, Erich born 31. 8. 1906
formerly: lower court counsellor for political cases in the nazi Ministry of Justice
today: provincial court director

Rosga, Ernst born 21. 3. 1901
formerly: military court counsellor, supreme field command 548
today: supreme court counsellor in West Berlin

Schuppenies, Dr. Günter born 9. 6. 1908
formerly: senior staff judge in the army command, substitute troop IX
today: lower court counsellor in West Berlin-Charlottenburg

HITLER'S GENERAL STAFF COMMANDS THE BONN ARMY

The General Staff – Instrument of Aggression of German Imperialism

The Prussian-German General Staff has long played a disastrous role in planning and unleashing German imperialism's wars of aggression. It was, therefore, only logical that the reactionary officer corps offered the Hitler clique its sympathy even before 1933, undermined the republic and to a certain extent openly supported the nazi movement. The general officers agreed with the establishment of the fascist dictatorship to a large extent, because Hitler's aims were in accordance with their own aims of rearmament and preparation for a new war of aggression to gain revenge for defeat in the First World War.

Only four days after the assumption of power by the fascists at the beginning of February 1933, the leaders of the army and navy obtained Hitler's assurance that his government was prepared to realize the aggressive plans of the General Staff and his armament industrialists. In gratitude for this assurance the General Staff gave Hitler its unqualified support after the so-called Röhm-affair in 1934.

Reichswehr Minister Colonel General von Blomberg declared: *"If the government of the Reich should prove incapable of completely pacifying the tense situation alone, the president (Hindenburg – editor) would proclaim a state of martial law and transfer the control of state affairs to the army.* (J.W. Wheeler-Bennet: *Die Nemesis der Macht – Die deutsche Armee in der Politik 1918–45* – (The Nemesis of Power, The German Army in Politics 1918–45, Drosle-Verlag, Düsseldorf, 1954)

The General Staff also supported the fascists' aggressive foreign policy. When Germany withdrew from the League of Nations in 1933 and left the Conference on Disarmament in protest, the General Staff took measures to safeguard this step. Thus one of Blomberg's orders of 25 October 1933 says:

"The further development of the political situation abroad, which was created by Germany's declaration concerning its withdrawal from the League of Nations and its withdrawal from the Conference on Disarmament, may result in sanctions being applied against Germany . . . The government of the Reich intends to offer local armed resistance to any hostile actions without regard to the prospects of military success." (IMT, vol. XXXIV, p. 488)

SECRET ARMAMENT UNDER PROTESTATIONS OF PEACE

In their aims and methods the armament monopolies, the Hitler clique and the General Staff were therefore in agreement. Accordingly the General Staff undertook the task of building up the Reichswehr into a massive army with modern equipment for the planned acts of aggression. As early as 4 April 1933 the Reich Cabinet had decided, on the initiative of the General Staff, to form a "Reich Defence Council". On 22 May 1933 the first session took place. It was organized by the General Staff and presided over by its representatives, headed by the chief of the General Staff Lieutenant General Adam and the head of the section concerned with army organization, Colonel Keitel, as he then was. The fact that this so-called Reich Defence Council promoted the direct preparation for a new war of aggression is revealed by the reasons which Keitel gave on behalf of the General Staff. He declared:

"The war (1914–18 – editor) showed sufficiently well that the cooperation with the individual departments of the Reich before the war was not close enough. The consequences did not fail to appear ... The disadvantages of the previous system lie in the separate departments of the Reich working side by side in the sphere of RV (Reich defence). To avoid this mistake a central office has been created which is already dealing with the problems of defence, in the broadest sense, already during peace time." (IMT, vol. XXXVI, doc. 177–EC, p. 22)

The conclusion arrived at by Hitler Germany's General Staff from defeat in the First World War was that it was necessary to rearm even more intensively and to put the whole of the state machinery at the disposal of the preparations for the war of revenge in a more purposeful way.

Whereas the Hitler government and its diplomats talked on every opportunity of peace, equality, self-determination and disarmament, the General Staff increased rearmament according to plan. The whole of the German economy was adapted to the requirements of the future conduct of war although there was still peace. In this way the General Staff succeeded in putting an army, which was the strongest in numbers and the best equipped in the capitalist world, at the disposal of the bellicose German imperialists, and in rapidly increasing profits in the armament industry.

THE "BLITZKRIEG (LIGHTNING WAR) STRATEGY"

The General Staff's conception of military strategy was adapted to "Blitzkrieg" (lightning warfare). The foundation for this was the order given by Minister of War Blomberg on 2 May 1935:

"The enterprise must be carried out as a surprise attack at a moment's notice on receipt of the key-word "carry out training". The time for the mobilization of the forces involved is not available, they must be employed in peace-time formation and with peace-time equipment . . ." (IMT, vol. XXXIV, doc. 139–C, p. 485)

This "Blitzkrieg strategy" was put into practice in the Second World War.

The strategic ideas and the detailed plans for the occupation of Poland (Operation White), of Norway and Denmark (Operation – Weser Exercise), of France, Holland and Belgium (Operation Yellow), for the military occupation of Greece and Yugoslavia (Operation Marita) and for the invasion of the Soviet Union (Operation Barbarossa) all originated in the General Staff.

Among others the former first staff officer and future chief of army operations, Adolf Heusinger, participated extensively in working out these plans.

PAVED THE WAY FOR THE SS TO AUSCHWITZ, LIDICE AND ORADOUR

The German General Staff, however, did not just passively receive Hitler's orders and make plans for him but also fought for German imperialism and carried out its plans for gaining world dominion and for subjugating and exterminating other peoples and countries by colonialism.

The General Staff participated without scruples in organizing and staging those provocations and intrigues contrary to international law, with which the fascists prepared and began their invasions.

The German General Staff took an active part when the invasions had begun, in crimes against humanity and trod underfoot international law and the law of warfare. With its assistance and frequently under its direct control, numerous peoples were robbed of their national sovereignty and their physical extermination was begun.

The German General Staff adopted the fascist racial theory completely and participated in the extermination of the Jews.

With all its orders and decrees, which violated international law and the law of war, the General Staff organized the wholesale murder of hundreds of thousands of Soviet prisoners of war. But numerous Belgian, Dutch, Yugoslavian, Greek, Norwegian, French, British and American prisoners of war were also brutally maltreated and murdered.

Had the German General Staff not planned, organized and carried out the fascist invasions on the European peoples and without its close cooperation with the criminal SS, there would have been no million murders at Auschwitz, no bestial crimes at Oradour and Lidice.

ACCUSED IN NUREMBERG – TODAY AGAIN ACTIVE

After the defeat of Germany under Hitler, the leading politicians of the coalition against Hitler confirmed their agreement, which had already been made during the war, to wipe out German militarism and to destroy the foundations of its power for ever. The Postdam Agreement contains clear and unequivocal statements to this effect.

In the Nuremberg Trials the crimes of the General Staff and the Supreme Command of the Wehrmacht (OKW) were proved without doubt. In particular these are:

the preparation for, and realization of, the Second World War and numerous acts of aggression and attacks on other peoples;

the brutal violation of all the rules of international law and humanity in the course of the war;

the active role played by the OKW and the fascist Wehrmacht in the barbaric oppression of the peoples in the occupied areas;

the gross violation of all international agreements on the treatment of prisoners of war;

the active cooperation in plundering the temporarily occupied areas and in the forced deportation of millions of slave workers;

the close cooperation with the SS, SD, Gestapo and other criminal organizations.

In the territory of the GDR – faithful to the aims of the anti-Hitler coalition and of the Postdam Agreement – German imperialism and militarism, the scourge of the German and other peoples, were uprooted and eliminated. Thus the foundations for any urge for conquests, for the territory of other nations were destroyed. The desire for revenge is considered criminal.

War and nazi criminals were deprived of their power and punished. In the GDR there is no factory, no works, no office and no piece of land which serves the interests of war and armaments profiteers.

Peace, social and cultural progress, international cooperation and understanding among the peoples are the foundations of the state doctrine of the GDR.

The other German state, the so-called Federal Republic of Germany – created and developed with the aid of the imperialists of the western powers – is ruled by armament monopolies, militarists and chauvinists. This state is the continuation of the Hitler state.

The successor to the fascist General Staff, the leading staff of the Bundeswehr, has cold-bloodedly reckoned with an atomic war in its "forward strategy". The Hitler generals and the officers permeated by their spirit who command the West German army are grasping for nuclear means of mass destruction and have devised the criminal plan of laying a belt of atomic mines right through Germany.

West German imperialism has built up one of the most powerful armies in the capitalist camp. The spirit of this army is the revenge-seeking spirit of the big trusts, of Hitler's former war economy leaders, the Hitler generals and Hitler officers, who train and direct the Bundeswehr and poison the minds of West German youth.

In West Germany the past was not overcome, but the Potsdam Agreement systematically broken.

"EASTERN EXPERIENCES" ARE EXPLOITED

Immediately after the capitulation of the Hitler Wehrmacht the American occupation authorities took the former chief of the General Staff of the nazi Wehrmacht, Colonel General Franz Halder, into their pay. At the head of 120 former generals under Hitler, including Guderian, Manteuffel, Schwerin and others, he evaluated the military experiences of Hitler's predatory attacks and was even then working out the plans for remilitarizing the future Federal Republic.

Hitler General von Choltitz reported on the camp at Allendorf, in which he worked until 1947: *"Here there was a group of generals and staff officers who were writing military history on the instructions of the historical division . . . We had our own maps at our disposal, which were supplemented by those of the American staffs . . . In all 300 officers were in the camp."* (Dietrich von Choltitz, *Soldat unter Soldaten* – A Soldier among Soldiers, Europa-Verlag, Constance, Zürich, Vienna, 1951, p. 283 f)

The members of the fascist General Staff used their activity for the USA to work out their own plans undisturbed. After the creation of the separatist West German state the experts of this clique of members of the General Staff became the official advisers of the Bonn government.

THE CAMOUFLAGED WAR MINISTRY

The "Amt Blank" (Blank Office) was formed as the central office for carrying out the plans for remilitarization. In this camouflaged ministry of war the experts of the fascist General Staff occupied the key-positions from the very first day. Besides General Speidel, the head of army operations, General Heusinger, belonged, above all, to the most intimate and influential of Adenauer's staff officers. They gathered a group of military men about them who possessed all-round experience of illegal rearmament. This group included

General of the Tank Corps Hans Röltiger,
General of the Air-Force Josef Kammhuber,
Vice Admiral Friedrich Ruge,

Lieutenant General Max Pemsel

and also Hitler Generals Harlinghausen, Freiherr von Lüttwitz, Reinhardt, Rogge, Schimpf and others.

These military men took part, without exception, in that decisive meeting of the General Staff at which the fundamental document for the future rearmament of West Germany was drawn up in all its details. The present commanding officer of the NATO ground striking forces in Central Europe, Lieutenant General Graf von Kielmansegg reported on this in a lecture to the Officers' Training College at Sonthofen, a former nazi training school for political leaders:

"As the possibility of a genuine German military contribution became more and more apparent it became necessary to find an individual German conception of this in good time and before beginning any sort of negotiations. It is not a case, as one can read over and over again even today, of the Federal Republic having become involved in things without a conception."

As early as 1950 remilitarization, according to the plans of seriously incriminated Hitler generals, was pushed ahead on Adenauer's initiative. With the acceptance of West Germany in the aggressive NATO in 1955 the old war criminals and generals began to realize their plans, which had been worked out in all their details, for rebuilding a million-strong army of aggression.

As early as 16 June 1951 the British newspaper *Daily Express* wrote: *"The German General Staff, the ruthless machine which planned European Wars for one hundred years, is here again. The master-plan of the German General Staff is known to only a few allied circles. The French, remembering three German invasions in 70 years, are alarmed."*

LEADING POSITION IN NATO

The process of building up the Bonn Wehrmacht, which has now been more or less completed, was pushed ahead in all its decisive aspects by those who were formerly Hitler's staff officers. This applies both to the top leadership of the Bonn army and to the commanding posts in the lower units and in the sphere of authority of the "territorial defence".

Hitler's and Adenauer's staff officers created the personnel required for building up a new army by drawing the fascist staff officers back to the conference table. They organized and armed this army. And not only that. Under cover of integration they knew how, not to incorporate the Bundeswehr into NATO, but to incorporate NATO into the Bundeswehr. They used their economic and military strength to exert pressure on their NATO partners, established numerous military bases in other countries and occupied important positions of command in NATO.

The West German Federal Republic has developed into the strongest military power in NATO next to the USA. More and more openly Bonn demands henceforth that it should have nuclear weapons at its disposal, so that it can involve its NATO partners in its military adventure of carrying out it plans for revenge. The "forward strategy" which Bonn's staff officers put through at the NATO Council Conference in Ottawa in 1963 served this purpose as did the plan which resulted from it of laying a belt of atomic mines along the borders of the GDR and Czechoslovakia, which was presented by Hitler General Trettner at the NATO Council Conference in Paris on 15 December 1964.

The "forward strategy" is, to the greatest extent, in accordance with the aims of the militarists in Bonn: its principal points are the aggressive concentration of Bundeswehr and NATO troops right on the borders of the GDR and Czechoslovakia and the propagation of, and preparation for the "screened war". Contrary to stipulations made by NATO the leaders of the Bundeswehr demand the supply of nuclear warheads to commanders down to brigade level and the early – as early as possible – employment of tactical nuclear weapons and high-explosive nuclear mines in the event of war.

In order to chain their allies to themselves even more closely the militarists at Bonn are reaching out for further command positions in NATO. In doing so they are not least pursuing the aim of gaining considerable influence on NATO strategy and on the right to make decisions on the employment of nuclear weapons. The whole military potential of NATO is to be used to the advantage of the adventurist plans of the extreme circles in West Germany.

With the increase in the military importance of the Bundeswehr in NATO, the number of West German generals and officers in the NATO leadership and in positions of command has also increased. At the beginning of 1964 21 generals, 53 colonels and 242 staff officers and captains were working in NATO headquarters. Today more than a thousand West German military men, including 30 generals, are fighting for Bonn's conception of nuclear war in NATO.

Hitler Generals Went – Hitler Officers Came

The leadership of the Bundeswehr, i. e., the General Staff of the West German army, was "rejuvenated" in recent years. When worldwide protests forced a number of the "old" generals to resign, they went into "retirement" and are drawing good pensions from the state. This, however, does not at all mean that they have given up influencing the policy of revenge. On the contrary! They are working, now as before, as advisers to the federal government or to the provinces (Länder) and also as presidents of the largest associations of militarists, e. g., Speidel, Ruge, Kammhuber, Matzky.

The military men who were pensioned off were replaced by the "new leadership" of the Bundeswehr, trained and drilled by them. They were likewise Hitler's staff officers and commanders throughout, who received their training at the fascist General Staff or at officers' training colleges and distinguished themselves particularly during the fascist wars of aggression and for this reason were quickly promoted.

Of the present 189 generals and admirals in the Bundeswehr more than half are former officers of the General Staff of Hitler's Wehrmacht; the rest were officers in the fascist Wehrmacht without exception. All the generals in the Bundeswehr had a part, directly or indirectly, in preparing and carrying out acts of aggression. Among the present generals and admirals in the Bundeswehr there is not a single one who fought against the fascist state. On the contrary. For their oaths of loyalty a great number were appointed to high positions in the general staff or positions of command as late as 1944–45. Six of these military men were condemned to long terms of imprisonment for war crimes, including Maeder, Herzog, Rosenthal and Karpinski.

The past of the officers in the Bundeswehr, right down to the captains, is similar. And finally, the majority of the lieutenants and second lieutenants received their training after 1955 at the officers' training colleges directed by Hitler officers.

All the West German generals were Hitler officers – but not one of the generals of the National People's Army of the GDR were Hitler officers. The majority of them were active fighters against Hitler fascism and proved their fidelity to the working class in the struggle in defence of the Spanish Republic, in fascist concentration camps and prisons.

Trettner Heinz

A WAR CRIMINAL AT THE HEAD OF THE BUNDESWEHR

After Generals Heusinger and Foertsch a convicted war criminal stands once more at the head of the Bonn Bundeswehr – former Hitler General Heinz Trettner.

Trettner is one of those ruthless officers, who held out to the end, and were favourites of Hitler who shrank from no crime and were highly decorated for not doing so. His career – Trettner rose in the course of only seven years from captain to lieutenant general – can only be compared to that of a few of Himmler's favourites in the SS.

The Murderer of Guernica

Trettner was one of the first volunteers for the fascist "Condor Legion" which Hitler sent, in violation of international law, to support General Franco's military coup d'état against the young Spanish Republic. At first he entered the staff of the commander of the "Condor Legion", Major General Sperrle, as an adjutant. From March 1937 he was squadron leader of fighter squadron 88 which bombed the peaceful Basque country towns of Durango and Guernica on 31 March and 26 April 1937 respectively. These barbaric attacks were the beginning of the fascist terror raids against the civilian population, which were later continued against Warsaw, Rotterdam and Coventry. The result of these terror raids was smoking ruins and murdered civilians – in Durango 248, including 14 nuns and a priest, in Guernica 1,654 dead and 889 wounded.

Mathieu Corman gave an account of the destruction of the famous place of pilgrimage, Guernica in his book *Salud Camerada – cing mois sur la front d'Espagne* (Edition Tribord, Paris, 1937). Corman visited this town with correspondents Steer (Times) and Holmes (Reuter) and at the end of his account he accused: *"The low-lying clouds have taken on the colour of all the blood which will forever bear witness against Mola, Franco, Göring and all the others. Against those who ordered this horrible massacre, against those who carried it out and against those who approved it from afar!"*

The Destroyer of Rotterdam

At the beginning of 1938 Trettner continued his training for the General Staff at the Air Force Academy in Gatow and became senior staff officer (1a) of the 7th Air (paratroop) Division. This was that crack division of Göring which was destined to carry out special tasks within the Blitzkrieg strategy of the fascists. Trettner worked out the plans for this.

The first major assignment came on 10 May 1940 with the invasion, contrary to international law, of the Netherlands, Belgium and Luxemburg under the command of General Student and his chief of staff, Major Trettner. (See Table 31)

On the afternoon of 13 May the staff of the air landing corps demanded an attack on Rotterdam by strong bomber formations for the next day. The liaison officer of the 54th fighter squadron received a map with the targets which were to be *"destroyed by a carpet of bombs"*. (See Table 32)

After the bombardement of Rotterdam had been announced, the city commandant decided in the interests of the helpless population and the old city's historic buildings, to open negotiations on capitulation. They began on 14 May 1940 at 10.30 a. m. A cease-five had been agreed upon for the duration of the negotiations.

Trettner was fully informed about these events as his commanding officer. General Student took part in the negotiations on capitulation. Despite this the bombing of Rotterdam began at 3.0 p.m. "according to plan", as agreed and discussed with Trettner. *"In the middle of this cease-fire the German bombing raid struck like a huge, destructive thunder storm."* (R. Böhmler, *Fallschirmjäger* – Paratrooper, Verlag Hans-Hennig Podzun, Bad Nauheim, 1961)

874 people weres killed, more than 2,000 wounded and over 78,000 made homeless; 24,978 dwellings, 1,329 workshops, 2,320 shops, 31 factories, 10 hospitals, 24 churches, 62 schools and hundreds of other public and private buildings lay in ruins.

In this way Trettner had put into practice for the first time on a large scale what he himself had practised as a member of the "Condor Legion" in Spain. He proved his worth and was awarded the Knight's Cross by Hitler, on Göring's proposal, as he had *"prepared the deployment of troops in an exemplary way and, taking part in the operation himself, had taken command of the troops dropped and maintained communications"*.

Now Trettner planned and organized further operations for the paratroops – the attacks against Great Britain, Crete, Malta, the Soviet Union and, after the fall of the Mussolini government, against Rome, Monte Rotondo and Gran Sasso.

The Grave-digger of Florence

On 22 January 1944 the allies landed near Anzio-Nettuno to the South of Rome. The 4th paratroop division, set up in November 1943 and commanded by Trettner, was thrown into this area. When they were defeated the fascist troops left behind, on Trettner's orders, a dead zone of destroyed villages and towns, including Frosinone, Itri, Fondi, Velletri, Gaeta, Tivoli, Capua and Littoria. Horst Zabel from Dessau, who formerly belonged to the 4th paratroop division, declared on this:

"We retreated from Ardea via Albano, Rome, Bracchiano, Orvieta, Montepulciano, Perugia, Florence, Futa-Pass, Bologna and Castel St. Pietro ... In the retreat through Rome the city was open to plundering because of partisan activities ... As the retreat continued all strategically important targets and objects important for the supply of the population, such as waterworks, power plants, etc. were blown up to a depth of 20 kilometres behind the main battle line. The civilian population in the first 5 kilometres also had to leave the area without much food and retreat to the larger towns ... Many crimes were committed in carrying out these orders in the command area of the 4th paratroop division, which was commanded by Major General Trettner.

In mid-July 1944 the 4th paratroop division took over the Florence sector.

The conservative Florentine lawyer Gastano Casoni described this time in his diary:

"Saturday 22 July: The German forces in Florence now consist of line troops, i.e., paratroops and sappers. The paratroops have an even worse reputation than the SS. They really do behave like men who are just about to clear out and want to take as much booty with them as possible, leaving a broad track of destruction and grief behind them."

Although Florence had been declared an "open city" by Hitler himself, extensive preparations for dynamiting and measures for destroying the town were begun at the end of July by Trettner's supreme command. Residential areas with a population of 50,000 had to be cleared within 24 hours.

In the night of 3 to 4 August 1944 five bridges and many of the finest architectural monuments, including the Machiavelli House, the Towers of Givolaeni – Gheradini and Parte Guelfa, the Accianiuoli Palace and world-famous churches were blown up. The work of destruction continued when the city had been evacuated. A former member of the 4th paratroop division, Leutelt from Wernigerode, stated *"that artillery units of the 4th paratroop division had taken up position on the hills to the north of Florence and fired continuously on Florence"*.

Characteristic of the mad frenzy of Trettner's troops in the surroundings of Florence are the massacres which took place in the small town of Fiesole. Trettner had about 500 of its 2,000 inhabitants herded together and deported to dig trenches on the "Gothic Line". Many inhabitants were murdered. Pasquale Pucci, for example, was shot only for possessing an English dictionary. A similar crime was committed against three carabinieri who had left their quarters so as not to be forced to take part in reprisals against their own people. Although they were responsible to the Italian authorities, they were shot in the night of 12 August 1944 on the orders of Trettner's divisional staff.

The crimes in and around Florence were continued in Autumn 1944 in the Bologna region together with SS and police units in "mopping up" campaigns against partisans.

Trettner had meanwhile been awarded the laurel wreath and promoted to lieutenant general. On 1 May 1945 the supreme command of the German army in Italy offered to capitulate. But Trettner, the fascist general who believed in holding out to the end, continued the senseless struggle on his own. Many German soldiers, Italian civilians and members of the allied forces died for another four days.

He Grasps for Nuclear Weapons

This war criminal stands today at the head of the West German Bundeswehr, whose basic conception is that of the "forward strategy". To achieve this, Trettner is grasping for nuclear weapons, either in the form of a NATO nuclear force or of a belt of atomic mines. Trettner presented this criminal plan in the middle of December 1964 at the NATO Council Conference in Paris. UPI reported on 18 December 1964:

"From military circles it became known that the atomic mines are supposed to . . . give an early atomic warning. In this way they would fit into the conception of the forward strategy approved by NATO."

The *Frankfurter Allgemeine Zeitung* wrote on 22 December 1964:

"The plan was not made by the Inspector General of the Bundeswehr alone. Nevertheless one can still refer to a Trettner Plan since the Inspector General showed his responsibility by his signature."

And the *Vorwärts* declared on 23 December 1964:

"Apparently this proposal was made in the attempt to develop a new version of the aim of the leaders of the Bundeswehr to gain control of nuclear weapons."

Nuclear weapons in the hands of such an unscrupulous and warmongering nazi general, whose military career has proved that international law and the law of humanity mean nothing to him, is not only a danger to peace in Germany and in Europe, but to the world.

Kielmansegg Johann Adolf von

A NAZI AGGRESSION OFFICER COMMANDS NATO UNITS

After the war criminal Speidel, an officer is now at the head of NATO's land forces in Europe-Centre, who had a leading part in the Hitler invasions – General Johann Adolf von Kielmansegg.

Kielmansegg went through the school of the fascist General Staff. As 3rd staff officer (Ic) – defence – of the 1st tank division he took part in the invasion of Poland and as 2nd staff officer (1b) – relief – of the same division in that of France. Later he became 1st staff officer (Ia) – operations – of the 6th and 1st tank divisions, entered the operations section of the General Staff of the army under war criminal Heusinger and finally took over the 111th armoured regiment as colonel.

Kielmansegg wrote several articles on the first part of his career, his book *Panzer zwischen Warschau und Atlantik* (Tanks between Warsaw and the Atlantic) which was published in 1941 by *Die Wehrmacht* being a comprehensive description of his fascist convictions. (See Table 33)

Fanatical "Blitzkrieg" Fighter

On the first pages of his concoction he revealed that he *"had done nothing else for thirteen years but learn the art of war and study theoretically the different types of war"*. Now he could hardly wait for the war to begin at last: *"We held our breath when we heard the Führer's last ultimatum to Poland ... And we would not have been German soldiers if we had not hoped that Poland would reject it."*

Then the time had come:

"I light a cigarette – if it goes out, there will be a war. Two minutes later and the war begins. It is a strange and exciting feeling to experience, so consciously and so immediately, a historic moment the significance of which cannot be foreseen! 4.45 a.m.! ... The war has begun! ... But this war was going to be different from the world war. Not only the result would be different, there was no doubt about that, but in other ways too."

After the occupation of Poland Kielmansegg regretted that there was a pause in the fighting before further acts of aggression: *"We would have preferred to have carried on winning straight away ..."*

When nine months later the fascist war machine was set in motion in the West, he rejoiced: *"German military ability and organization had actually reached the point where it was only necessary to press the famous button to set things in motion."*

When the fascist armies of aggression arrivied at the North Cape, the Channel and the Bay of Biscay he was eager to be present at "the final victory" without fail.

"We are able to report that we have carried out the task which history, Germany and the Führer set us, to the end and we are able to report that we are prepared to carry out the task of conquering England, which alone stands between us and freedom, in exactly the same way."

"Forward over Graves!"

Death and destruction, burning towns and villages marked the path of the invading armies in Poland. The work of destruction was so thorough *"that you thought you were being burned even when driving through quickly."* Together with this the terror activities of the fascist occupation troops began against the civilian population. *"In this village of Polichno we also introduced, for the first time, a method of insuring an immediate curfew, which later became a regulation and stood the test very well. All the inhabitants of the village, who were late, were herded together in a big yard and locked up for the night ..."*

Kielmansegg lolled about in the official chair of the former president of Poland and said triumphantly:

"I sat in the seat of the head of a state which we had not only conquered by arms but which our victory completely erased from history, after it had tried to exist for twenty years contrary to the sense of history, having been brought to life artificially . . ."

When things "got underway at last" against Luxemburg, Belgium, the Netherlands and France, he rejoiced at the bombing of Sedan:

"This tremendous, overwhelming scene lasted for four hours . . . A wonderful picture unfolded before our very eyes. Behind burning Avancon which is still under fire from German artillery, the tanks crush all resistance in their path . . ."

Kielmansegg's motto was: *"'Advance over graves!' In this moment we can tell ourselves with justified pride and deep joy that we are on the point of making these words come true in a most wonderful way."*

Kielmansegg exulted in the intoxication of the fascist aggressor's victory after the capitulation of "France, the hereditary enemy": *"Not ten years ago the tricolour was still fluttering on the Ehrenbreitstein. That it would be only ten years less ten days from the day it was lowered there to the day when France, smashed and conquered, would sign the armistice in 1940 in the Bois de Compiègne, was certainly unforeseen by any of us on that 11 May."*

Driven by Racial Madness

Like a red thread the racial madness and the master race theory extend throughout Count Kielmansegg's concoction. Thus on page 61 in the jargon of *Der Stürmer* he wrote about a Polish village: *"The houses were caked with filth, the air could hardly be breathed. That was accounted for when one saw the inhabitants who were almost all Jews."*

He thought that in France *"an atmosphere of degeneration and depravity"* prevailed. He said it made *"the impression of a stagnating country"* and was *"a barren country"*. Therefore: *"'Space without a people' – France . . . 'a people without space' – Germany."*

Kielmansegg provided the formula for changing this situation on pages 246–47, where he described the occupation of the French town of Belfort: *"In the afternoon the Hotel de Ballon itself . . . is at last in our hands and so after 22 years becomes once more, and this time for good, the German 'Belchen'."*

In the General Staff as "Tank Specialist with Experience on the Eastern Front"

As 1st staff officer (Ia) of the 6th tank division of army group north, Kielmansegg invaded the Soviet Union. His aim was to capture Leningrad quickly. When this plan failed he gave order No. 50 to the division on 18 September 1941 which says in a demogogic way: *"The fate of Petersburg is sealed and only a question of time."* The watchword was: *"To do the utmost for Führer and fatherland until the final decision has been won and Germany's future made secure."*

At the beginning of 1944 Kielmansegg was appointed as 2nd staff officer in the operations division of the general staff of the army, his chief being the war criminal Heusinger, because of his "experience on the eastern front". There he assessed "reports on the situation", made them up into general reports and passed these on to the army groups as "a guide to actions".

Some of the "secret command matters" signed by Kielmansegg (see also Table 34) say:

"Position 3. 4. 44, 12.00 hours

I. France

... 80 inhabitants shot, 20 arrested ... several depots and houses destroyed, 24 terrorists shot, 107 arrested." (IMT, Doc. No. NOKW – 1557 CONT'D, p. 17)

"Position 4. 4. 44, 12.00 hours

I. France

Continuation of mopping up operations in the Dordogne Department, several depots and houses destroyed, 19 terrorists shot, captured material – motor vehicles and weapons." (IMT, Doc. No. NOKW – 1557 CONT'D, p. 19)

"Position 12. 7. 44, 06.00 hours ...

b) Serbia

In Banat 40 communists shot in retaliation." (IMT, Doc. No. NOKW – 1557 CONT'D, p. 34)

"I. France, Position 13. 7. 44, 06.00 hours ...
AOK I: 18 terrorists shot, great amount captured material ...
AOK 19: ... 15 terrorists shot ...
Mil. Com. F.: 156 terrorists shot." (IMT, Doc. No. NOKW – 1557 CONT'D, pp. 37–38)

His First Commandment – "Forward Strategy"

Under Heusinger and Speidel, Kielmansegg was one of Adenauer's chief military advisers and had a decisive part in the formation of Bonn's army of aggression. For him the first commandment is the "forward strategy" as is striving for control of nuclear weapons. As early as 6 January 1955 he wrote in a leading article in the *Welt*: *"Whoever accepts that the Federal Republic must be defended must demand that this defence begins on the border of the Zone, and, what's more, that it is operationally effective."*

Today this fascist officer who is guilty of acts of aggression commands all the NATO military forces between Hamburg and the Alps. This includes, beside West German, Dutch, Belgian, British, American and Canadian soldiers, those that belong to the great French nation, which was insulted and humiliated in a most base way by the chauvinist and race-fanatic, Kielmansegg, 25 years ago.

Heusinger Adolf FROM HITLER'S CHIEF PLANNER TO ADENAUER'S CHIEF PLANNER

Heusinger enlisted in the imperial army in 1915 as an ensign and took part in the war against France. After the First World War he was transferred to the Reichswehr and gained the special knowledge for his later activities in the General Staff as a lieutenant in the courses for leader assistants at the illegal military academy. In 1929 he entered the Ministry of Defence. In the "staff of the army command" the name used to camouflage the forbidden General Staff, he assisted in supplying the German imperialists with an army of great striking force.

Heusinger's career began with Hitler's seizure of power. From 1935 to 1937 he gathered "experience in troop leadership" as chief staff officer of the 11th division and was afterwards appointed 1st staff officer of the operations division of the supreme command of the army. Henceforth he helped to plan and decide all the military operations of the fascist Wehrmacht and gained the special confidence of Hitler. In 1940 he became chief of operations of the General Staff of the supreme command of the army and in 1943 acting chief of the General Staff of the army.

During his activity in the General Staff of the army and with Heusinger's active assistance and that of others, the plans for aggression against Czechoslovakia, Poland, Norway and Denmark, against Holland, Belgium, Luxemburg and France, against Greece and Yugoslavia, Africa, the Soviet Union, Egypt, Italy, Hungary, Rumania, England, Switzerland, Portugal and Spain were worked out – for the most part during peace-time.

On the basis of these invasion plans the various offensive operations of the fascist army were worked out in detail in many "secret command matters" under Heusinger's direction.

Thus, for example, in the "secret command matter" No. 4402/39 of the operations department of the general staff of the army of 7 October 1939, preparations were made for the invasion of Holland and Belgium. This document, signed by Heusinger, says:

"At the same time army group B has to make all the preparations, in accordance with special instructions, to move immediately into Dutch and Belgian territory, if the political situation should demand this. The order to March will be given by OKW (supreme command). Until then any violation of the borders of Dutch or Belgian territory is to be strictly avoided."

Heusinger also assisted the practical men in the conduct of the fascist war in the preparations for the invasion of Yugoslavia, which had the code-word "Marita". In a "secret command matter" to Yugoslavia of 27 March 1941 on a conference on the situation, in which Heusinger took part, it says:

"The Führer is determined, without the possible declarations of loyalty . . . to make all the preparations to destroy Yugoslavia's army and the organization of the state . . . it is a question of acting as quickly as possible . . . Politically it is particularly important that the blow is directed with ruthless force and that the destruction of the military forces is carried out in a lightning operation . . . In this connection the beginning of the Barbarossa operation must be postponed for four weeks." (H. A. Jacobsen, *1939–1945, Der zweite Weltkrieg in Chronik und Dokumenten* – 1939–1945, The Second World War in Chronicle and Documents, Wehr und Wissen, Verlagsgesellschaft, Darmstadt, p. 202)

Heusinger, however, did not only plan the fascist invasions but also directed the use of the fascist Wehrmacht against innocent women, children and old people in the invaded countries in the form of "combating gangs" and with the application of "scorched earth tactics".

Thus the operations department of the army, whose chief was Heusinger, had more than 100 hostages, including women, old people, children and young people, murdered in "retaliation" for an attack carried out on 28 August 1942 by Soviet partisans on the railway station at Slavnoye and the garrison of the fascist police and Gestapo stationed there. Telegram No. 11 027/42 ss from the operations department of the army to the supreme command of the army group says:

"The Führer demands measures of retaliation with the use of the most severe deterrent measures for the partisan attack on Slavnoye. Report on the measures taken."

Heusinger, an accessory to the attempt to blow up Hitler, was by no means shot or handed over to the hangman like all the others, even those remotely involved, but was personally received by Hitler and rehabilitated after his short term of imprisonment. Hitler declared, with reference to a "statement", written by Heusinger during his imprisonment:

"I have studied your statement written in prison. I am grateful to you for it." (A. Heusinger, Befehl im Widerstreit – Command in Conflict, Tübingen, p. 236)

In this memorandum on the "final victory" Heusinger recommended drafting 15 and 16-year-olds and all the older people up to the age of 60 as new cannon fodder. At the end of September 1944 Heusinger was "rehabilitated" – in the middle of October 1944 Hitler ordered the formation of the "Volkssturm" (home guard).

During his "captivity" Heusinger was the constant adviser of the Historical Division for War of the US Army, evaluated his "experience" and prepared himself, in this way, for future tasks.

After his release Hitler's favourite became Adenauer's favourite. Together with Speidel Heusinger became his adviser in military matters. Just as Heusinger was once indispensable to Hitler, he became so henceforth for Adenauer, too.

In 1950 he became official adviser to the federal government on "security questions" and an "employee" of the "Blank Department", the illegal ministry of war. Here he planned the formation of the new Wehrmacht and took part in all important conferences. In 1952 Heusinger became head of the military department in the "Blank Office".

"The hard years in the 'Blank Office' – years of selfless, controversial, uncertain waiting and preparatory work – which made great demands on all those concerned – were finally rewarded in 1955, when Germany's alliances made a new form of defence policy on a national basis within NATO possible, by the reconstruction of German military forces, in which Heusinger and Speidel had a leading part." (Das neue Journal, 26 February 1958)

In November 1953 Heusinger took on the permanent chairmanship in the Military Command Council of the Bundeswehr and became its first inspector general on 1 March 1957. From 1 April 1961 to 29 March 1964 this former acting chief of the General Staff of Hitler's army was chairman of the "Permanent Military Commission of NATO" in Washington and therefore practically its chief of staff. In this way the West German imperialists had occupied one of the most important posts in NATO for three years during which Heusinger exerted decisive influence on the strategic conception of NATO, prepared the attempt of Bonn's Hitler generals to gain control of nuclear weapons and helped to an increasing extent to launch West German generals into influential posts in NATO.

Like war criminal Speidel, his accomplice Heusinger did not retire after being pensioned. The leading party of the West German monopolies, the CDU/CSU (Christian Democratic Union/Christian Social Union), appointed him as their military adviser. In this position Heusinger today is once more working out the plans for total remilitarization under Adenauer, Erhard and Barzel as he did even during his "term of imprisonment" for Hitler. The realization of the nuclear "forward strategy", the pressing for nuclear weapons, the mobilization of masses and emergency laws are inextricably bound up with his work. The war criminal Heusinger was, and is, the military exponent and main advocate of the aggressive, unpatriotic policy of the Bonn state.

Speidel Hans WAR CRIMINAL AND MILITARY ADVISER TO THE BONN GOVERNMENT

Dr. Speidel has been in the service of German militarism since 1914. After the First World War he transferred to the Reichswehr, was trained as a leader's assistant (staff officer) and transferred in 1930 to the section France of the 3rd department of the illegal general staff. With Hitler's seizure of power in 1933 Speidel went to the German embassy in Paris as assistant to the military attaché and organized espionage against France there. Next he became head of the "Foreign Armies West" department in the General Staff of the army, in which he procured and evaluated the military data for the invasion of the West European countries and helped to work out the appropriate plans.

Speidel participated directly in preparing and carrying out the invasion of France as 1st staff officer of the IX Army Corps and of Army Group B. On 14 June 1940 he became chief of the General Staff, with the military command in Paris and on 1 August 1940 chief of the General Staff with the military command in France. As such he shares the guilt for the establishment of the cruel regime of terror in France and for numerous crimes against the French civilian population. Speidel summarized the results of these criminal activities in his reports on "mood and internal security" in which he gave information on the barbaric "measures of retaliation" against the French civilian population under his supervision. Thus in his report on the situation, written on 28 February 1942 to the war criminal Keitel, he says:

"The following measures of retaliation were ordered at the time of reporting: 100 communists and Jews were transferred to Compiègne to be deported to the East.

"In Rouen extensive raids were carried out on communists and Jews, leading to numerous arrests. In connection with these measures ... an order was given for the whole of the occupied area to arrest 1,000 communists and Jews. These have been made ready for deportation to the East."

In March 1942 Speidel went, first as chief of the general staff of the V Army Corps and later as chief of the general staff of the 8th Army, to the Soviet Union. There he continued his crimes on a wide scale. He was chiefly concerned with planning and putting into effect the "scorched earth tactics" which were carried out in his area in the most ruthless fashion. Whole landscapes were turned into dead zones.

In April 1944 Speidel, who had in the meanwhile been promoted to lieutenant general and awarded the Knight's Cross for his crimes in the Soviet Union, emerged once more in France – this time as head of the general staff of army group B, led by Rommel. Here he wanted to put into practice once more his "experience", gathered during the retreat of Hitler's defeated armies in the Soviet Union. So in August 1944 he passed on without scruples, and explicitly approved the order, according to which Paris was to be turned into a field of rubble.

Field Marshal Rommel was driven to commit suicide by the nazis in connection with 20 July 1944. His chief of staff and confidant Speidel remained unmolested because he was one of those who denounced Rommel to the Gestapo to save his own neck.

After 1945 Speidel settled in southern Germany as a "historian", until Adenauer appointed him and his accomplice Heusinger as his military advisers in 1950.

Speidel became the West German expert at the negotiations on "West Germany's contribution to defence" and chief delegate at the EEC negotiations. When this project failed because of the French National Assembly's veto Speidel was one of the main advocates of West Germany's acceptance in the aggressive NATO and one of the military leaders at the negotiations.

When West Germany had become a member of NATO and the Ministry of War was officially formed, Speidel became head of the "Military Forces Department". Even then, and immediately afterwards, as commander of NATO Land Forces Central Europe Speidel did his utmost to get the conception of the resurrected fascist general staff and its possibilities of influencing NATO accepted and to increase them.

On the occasion of Speidel's being given a pension on 31 March 1964 the militarist organ *Wehrkunde*, Munich, confirmed, in No. 4/1964:

"It was due to him that SHAPE's conceptions of defence changed decisively in the course of years, eventually leading to the formation of the "forward strategy" which draws the whole territory of the Federal Republic into the conception of a lasting defence."

Being pensioned, however, did not mean retirement for Speidel. Having put over the nuclear "forward strategy"' in NATO, he is henceforth the "special adviser of the Federal Republic on questions concerning NATO" and one of the main wirepullers in the attempt of the Bonn militarists to gain control of nuclear weapons, to carry out the preparations for total war and to establish a dictatorship built on emergency laws. His influence has not decreased but increased.

Rogge **PIRATE CAPTAIN AND MURDERER OF SOLDIERS**
Bernhard
today: military adviser in Schleswig-Holstein

After Rogge had served in the imperial navy in the First World War from 1915 to 1917, he joined the Reich navy in 1920 and became a specialist for the training of naval officers. Thus he was training leader on the sailing ship "Niobe" and in 1930 took over the command as cadet training officer on the cruiser "Emden". Afterwards he became military specialist in the inspection of the training service in Kiel and commander of the sailing school ships "Gorch Fock" and "Albert Leo Schlageter".

At the beginning of the fascist predatory war he was with the rank of captain commander of the armed merchant cruiser "Atlantis" with which he carried through pirate raids on all seas for nearly two years without any consideration for the rules of naval warfare. Under various camouflages and even under foreign colours Rogge captured and sank a total of 22 mechant ships with his armed merchant cruiser. Hitler awarded him the Knight's Cross and oak-leaves for it.

From 1942 to 1944 Rogge was chief of staff or inspector of the naval training service. When the fascist troops which were defeated in the Baltic Soviet republics swept back Rogge as vice admiral was appointed commander of the training unit of the navy which operated in the Baltic Sea as the "Rogge combat group". With his flagship, the heavy cruiser "Prinz Eugen", he mercilessly fired on Baltic and East Prussian towns. These operations extended and prolonged the senseless shedding of the blood of German soldiers and the sufferings of the tormented population in these areas.

When the rest of the Rogge warship units had arrived in Schleswig-Holstein, the demobilization of the Wehrmacht increased and the fascist leadership had already capitulated unconditionally, Rogge as "court president" confirmed at least four murder sentences against German members of the navy on 6 and 10 May 1945. Thus leading seamen Willi Albrecht, Karl-Heinz Freudenthal and Günther Källander were sentenced to death and executed on 6 May 1945. On 11 May 1945, that is, three days after the capitulation, seaman Christian Lüss was shot in the headquarters of the Hitler successor and war criminal Dönitz in Flensburg-Mürwik because had made "rebellious statements".

Although the relatives of the murdered men made constant efforts to clear up the fate of the seamen Rogge kept silent for twenty years and pretended to be an honourable man.

After being released from war imprisonment he became provisional district president of the rural district of Schleswig-Holstein. The appointment was made by the then senior president of Schleswig-Holstein, CDU politician and Adenauer friend Theodor Steltzer with the approval of the British military government. But soon he thought it better to disappear from public life for some time and submerge in West German industry until in 1957 he joined the Bundeswehr as rear admiral.

Up to his retirement on pension in March 1962 Rogge was commander in the 1st defence district for Schleswig-Holstein and Hamburg. Since then he has acted as adviser on "civil defence questions" of the Schleswig-Holstein provincial government.

Gericke Walter until 31 March 1965:

TRETTNER ACCOMPLICE FORMED THE BONN PARACHUTIST TROOPS

commander of the 1st air-borne division of the Bundeswehr

Gericke's military career began in 1929 at the arch reactionary Prussian police school in Brandenburg. As a member of the "General Göring Regiment" which came into existence out of the fascist Wecke police department the former First Lieutenant Gericke became an air force officer in 1935 and one of the first drillers and commanders of Göring's paratroopers. His main concern until the outbreak of the Second World War was: *"If only at last it would really become serious!"* (W. Gericke, *Fallschirmjäger hier und da* – Parachuists here and there, Schützen-Verlag, West Berlin, 1941, page 46)

After his participation in the attack of the fascist troops on Poland his first action as paratrooper took place during the occupation of Denmark for which Hitler's loyal staff officer Trettner worked out the plans. With Trettner he invaded Holland and landed as battalion commander in a paratroop storm regiment on Crete. No document could better show the criminal and anti-human attitude of this arch fascist than his own description of the attack on the Mediterranean island:

"Wait, you swine! And at the vineyard they get him. A concentric charge is thrown. Smoke and iron fragments whirl up. Finished. How the paratroopers hate the faces under the flat helmets! And they fire into them with a vengeance... I also have a mattress, 'without vermin', but no sheet; so the blue-white Greek flag which is found on a shelf must do..." (W. Gericke: Von Malemes bis Chania – From Malemes to Chania, Verlag Die Wehrmacht, Berlin, 1943, pp. 52ff.)

After quite a longe operation in the Soviet Union he came to Italy and carried out "special tasks" in the extermination of Italian freedom fighters in close co-operation with war criminal Trettner. As commander of a special fighting group he tried in vain to capture the Italian general staff that had fallen away from fascist Germany.

Gericke was several times ordered on special training tasks; thus as leading instructor at the Stendal paratrooper school, course instructor for company and battalion leaders at the ground fighting school of the air force in Mourmelon and La Courtine (France) and as head of the leadership school of the first parachute corps in Verona.

Gericke unscrupulously carried out every order of the fascist leadership. He finally drove soldiers and civilians into death on the Lower Rhine for his own glory as colonel and commander of the 11th parachute division. For this he received the highest fascist orders from Hitler.

The total defeat of German fascism and militarism was no reason for Gericke to give up his fascist way of thinking. In 1955 he continued his book series which he had begun in the nazi period to glorify the fascist paratroops under the title *Da gibt es kein Zurück* – There Is No Return.

As a "textile merchant" he devoted himself quite as eagerly especially to the gathering together of former parachutists. As editor of the information organ of the paratroop association called *Der deutsche Fallschirmjäger* he saw to the spreading of militarist ideas until he joined the Bundeswehr as one of the first paratroop officers of the former Hitler Wehrmacht.

In recognition of his merciless fighting method and fascist drilling methods Gericke was named commander of the parachute school of the Bundeswehr and trained paratroopers as he had under Hitler. As major general and commander of the 1st air-borne division he was placed on provisional retirement on 31 March 1965.

de Maizière Ulrich

CONFIDANT IN THE FÜHRER'S BUNKER

today: *inspector of the Bonn army, lieutenant general*

Ulrich de Maizière is an officer who went through the school of the fascist general staff. Having taken part in the invasion of Poland as regimental adjutant he went to the military school in Dresden to be trained for the general staff. Afterwards he became 1st orderly officer in the staff of Army Group C and during the invasion of the Soviet Union 2nd staff officer (1b) of the 18th motorized infantry division.

De Maizière evaluated his first "experiences on the Eastern Front" as expert adviser in the organization department of the general staff of the army in 1942–43 under the direction of the future Bundeswehr General Müller-Hillebrand. From 1 May 1943 he began, as 1st staff officer (1a) of the 10th armoured division, helping to put an end to the collapse, which was becoming evident, of the Army Group South in the Ukraine and in Rumania.

De Maizière enjoyed Hitler's special confidence and that of the leaders of the fascist Wehrmacht. As late as February 1945 he was called to the "Führer's bunker". There as lieutenant colonel and 1st staff officer (1a) of the operations department of the general staff of the army he reported regularly to Hitler on the situation and was concerned with the efficiency of Hitler's, Bormann's and Goebbels' isolated "command post".

Thus on the evening of 23 March 1945 he reported:

"Now extensive sections are already operating below, in so far as the installations above have not yet been repaired. For example, General Krebs, head of the operations department, works below. The equipment, therefore, which is here now, will function, even if the buildings above ground level are destroyed." (H. Heiber, *Lagebesprechungen im Führerhauptquartier* – Discussions on the Situation in the Führer's Headquarters, Deutscher Taschenbuchverlag GmbH, Munich, 1964)

As the final destruction of the last pockets of resistance in Berlin by the Soviet army approached, de Maizière was sent to Hitler's successor, Dönitz, who was in Schleswig-Holstein. There he was to keep the operations department of the general staff functioning and to support the war criminal Dönitz in his intrigues concerning separate negotiations with the allies, as 1st staff officer (1a) of the operations department.

After the total defeat of fascism and its war machine de Maizière was among those Hitler officers who were the first to recall the war criminals Heusinger and Speidel to the "Blank Office", the illegal ministry of war, to form a new army of aggression. From the start de Maizière has been one of the keenest advocates of Bonn's "forward strategy", nuclear armament and the emergency laws.

In *Wehrwissenschaftliche Rundschau,* West Berlin and Frankfurt-on-Main, No. 3/1964 he wrote *"that the 'forward defence' which is now being realized, was mainly due to constant German efforts . . . The demand for influence on the planning and distribution of nuclear weapons is another important step in this direction (i.e., the realization of the forward strategy – editor) . . ."*

Panitzki Werner

THE AIR WAR EXPERT

today: chief of Bonn's Luftwaffe, lieutenant general

Panitzki belonged to the nazi Luftwaffe's specialists on operations and was one of war criminal Göring's confidants. Having attended the air force academy he became 1st staff officer of air fleet 1 under war criminal Kesselring. As squadron captain in the "Edelweiss Squadron" Panitzki took part in the raids on Norway and France and in the terror attacks on England.

In 1942–43 Panitzki, as 1st staff officer, planned the operations of air fleet 3 and thus shares responsibility for the barbaric bombings of British towns. From autumn 1944 Göring appointed Panitzki as 1st staff officer of the operations department in his general staff.

In American captivity, in a "special camp for high-ranking officers" he concerned himself with the evaluation of "war historical experiences" and worked on the plans to remilitarize West Germany.

In 1952 he was appointed to the "Blank Office" by the Adenauer government. As head of the planning group of the Luftwaffe and member of Bonn's military command he reconstructed the new West German air force staff. In 1957 Panitzki was chief of staff in the command of the Bundeswehr under war criminal General Heusinger. Today he is, as inspector of Bonn's Luftwaffe, one of the most dangerous agitators among the leaders of the Bundeswehr, who have tried for years to get hold of nuclear weapons.

In September 1964 Panitzki again demanded long-range nuclear missiles for the Bundeswehr, for *"without missiles in sufficient quantity and with sufficient range the (West) German air force would not be able, in the long run, to fulfil the tasks which it has been set by NATO".* (*Frankfurter Allgemeine Zeitung,* 19 September 1964)

Zenker Karl-Adolf WITH HITLER AGAINST NORWAY, DENMARK AND HOLLAND

today: inspector of the Bonn Navy, vice admiral

Karl-Adolf Zenker is the third generation of Zenkers who served German imperialism as admirals, planned its predatory military attacks and had a decisive part in carrying them out. His grandfather was an imperial admiral and flag officer; his father was chief of the naval command of the Reichswehr and thus the predecessor of war criminal Raeder.

From 1939 to 1941 Karl-Adolf Zenker was 3rd naval staff officer in the staff of the naval group command west or north and worked there on the plans for the invasions of Denmark, Norway and the Netherlands and, in particular, on those for the conduct of mine warfare in the North Sea. After holding various commands at sea, Zenker was transferred to the operations department of the navy's supreme command as expert in January 1944 and was there one of the most faithful followers of Hitler, Raeder and Dönitz.

In July 1951 Zenker became naval expert and provisional head of the navy department in the "Blank Office" and in this position worked out and put into practice the plans for building up the Bonn navy. This planning is being carried out with the direct aim of committing aggression in the Baltic Sea area. As early as 1954 Zenker wrote: *"Even though the Baltic Sea is a sea of secondary importance it does nevertheless lead into the territory of a possible enemy and thus forms for him an open flank, on which he remains vulnerable."* (*Bulletin der Bundesregierung*, Bonn, 11 February 1954)

Not only in his aims but also in spirit, Zenker has remained the old aggressive fascist officer. He proved this at the first swearing in of recruits in the navy in Wilhelmshaven on 16 January 1956, when he characterized war criminals Dönitz and Raeder as models for the Bonn navy. Zenker said:

"Each of us old navy men, who served under the command of both admirals of the fleet, know that . . . there is no blemish on the person of our former commanders-in-chief. The first and exclusive question which arose for me and all my colleagues in Bonn was whether we should take up our work as long as our former commanders were kept under arrest. Only from the German viewpoint of the vitally necessary task of defending our common liberty is our disregard for the fates of our old comrades defensible. With the knowledge of the characters of our old commanders who always put responsibility and duty before self, I was sure that they would also approve of this conduct. I had the satisfaction of knowing that Admiral of the Fleet Raeder endorsed my attitude when he was released." (*Leinen los*, Bremen, No. 2, February 1956, p. 228)

Zenker not only extols war criminals Raeder and Dönitz in this speech but asks his ideal Raeder, after the event, for actual permission to join the Bundeswehr – permission from that Raeder who declared on the occasion of a commemoration of Hindenburg and Ludendorff in the first years of the "Third Reich":

"The German nation has adopted national socialism, born of the spirit of German soldiers at the front, as its philosophy and follows the symbols of it renaissance with both warm affection and fanatic passion. It experienced national socialism and did not suffer it as so many helpless critics abroad believe. This is the reason for the pure and relentless declaration of war against bolshevism and international Jewry, having had enough experience of their activities which have a destructive effect on nations, as we have felt in the case of our own nation." (*Blätter für deutsche und internationale Politik*, Cologne, No. 6, 20 June 1958)

And on 12 May 1944 Dönitz agitated in the same direction:

"What would have become of our homeland today if the Führer had not united us in national socialism! Split into parties, saturated with the decomposing poison of Jewry and vulnerable to this, since we lacked the defence of our present uncompromising philosophy, we would have long succumbed to the burden of this war and have been exposed to the ruthless extermination of our enemies." (op. cit.)

Maeder Hellmuth SENTENCED WAR CRIMINAL

today: head of the Troop Office of the Army, major general

Hellmuth Maeder, one of Hitler's generals and commander of the elite division "Greater Germany" was sentenced as a war criminal. As orderly officer of the 34th infantry division he took part in the invasion of Poland and, as battalion, regimental and division commander, on the attack on the Soviet Union. Under his command were for a time Lithuanian SS volunteer units. As the "commandant of Schaulen" he was awarded the Oak Leaves to his Knight's Cross by Hitler and promoted to major general. Then he attempted as commander of the armoured division "Grossdeutschland" (Greater Germany) to prolong the days of fascism.

Maeder is responsible for innumerable crimes committed by units under his charge and was sentenced to 25 years' imprisonment for them. As battalion commander in the 297th infantry division he took part in atrocities against Soviet citizens in 1941 and 1942. Against all the laws of war, international law and human rights the battalion commanded by Maeder raged especially in the areas temporarily occupied by the fascist troops in the first months after the invasion. A few examples prove with what brutality and cruelty this happened. Thus the soldiers of the Maeder battalion stole the property of the inhabitants of the village of Vvedenko, Chuguev region, at the end of October 1941. Later soldiers belonging to Maeder's battalion deported 20 Soviet citizens to Germany. In November 1941 a woman by the name of Tarussina was brutally beaten and finally murdered for resisting an attempt to rape her. The citizen Mishner was maltreated because he had tried to resist the plundering.

Maeder's soldiers also arrested Pastuchov, an inhabitant of the village of Vvedenko. He was suspected of belonging to the Communist Party. For 13 days he was kept in a cold cell and maltreated. On the 14th day he was placed on a red-hot stove. Then the fascists led him, with his hands bound together, through the village. In the village of Gavrilovka, in the Chuguev region, the inhabitants were also plundered by the soldiers belonging to Maeder's battalion.

This war criminal was given a post in the Bundeswehr, having been prematurely handed over to the West German authorities, and since 1960 has been head of one of the most important command posts in the Bonn army.

Übelhack Friedrich SCORCHED EARTH POLICY IN NORWAY

today: *commander of the "territorial army" which is exclusively under West German command, lieutenant general*

As staff officer of the fascist mountain troops Friedrich Übelhack had a leading part in almost all of the Wehrmacht's acts of aggression, beginning with the invasion of Poland and extending to the invasion of the Soviet Union.

On 10 December 1941 he went to Northern Finland as 1st staff officer (1a) of the XXXV (mountain) Army Corps and later became 1a of the 20th (mountain) Army and with the "Wehrmacht Command in Norway". There, when Finland had left the fascist bloc, he planned in particular the paratroop dropping operations "Birch Tree" and "Northern Lights". That was the long-prepared retreat from Northern Finland and Northern Norway and resulted in barbarous destruction in these areas.

On 21 October 1944 the nickel works and settlement at Kolosjoki and the town of Rovaniemi were completely destroyed and in Petsamo too *"the required work of destruction was carried out"*. The former commander of the 20th army, the condemned war criminal Rendulic, reported that his soldiers and officers were evacuating the population (about 40,000) from the area north of the Lyngenfjord to the south, where they were being handed over to the organs of the fascist "Reichskommissar", Terboven. In the "area set free" all dwellings and communications, the streets, bridges, ships and docks as well as whole towns, among others, Hammerfest, were completely destroyed.

After these acts of destruction Übelhack was promoted, on 1 January 1945, to colonel and appointed 1st staff officer of the Wehrmacht command in Norway. His tasks also included the suppression of the Norwegian resistance movement.

Since 1 May 1956 Übelhack has been in the Bundeswehr and has occupied a key position in the total remilitarization of West Germany since 1 April 1964.

Like war criminal Trettner he belongs to the clique of former general staff members who already in the Second World War were planners of death and the "scorched earth".

Gerlach Heinrich PRAISES THE FASCIST DICTATORSHIP

today: *commander of the Bonn fleet, vice admiral*

Before the fascist predatory war Heinrich Gerlach worked in the headquarters of the high command of the Navy under the direction of war criminal Raeder. As 2nd naval staff officer in the headquarters of the chief of torpedo-boats or destroyers Gerlach later took part in the invasions of Poland, Denmark, Norway and France. During the operation "Weser manoevre", the invasion of the northern states, he distinguished himself particularly during the fascist occupation of Narvik.

After this Gerlach became 1st navy staff officer of the operations department of the naval command and there he worked out, from June 1941 until December 1943, in an influential position, the plans for the future conduct of the fascists' war at sea. Having held various naval commands Gerlach was made a naval captain under war criminal Dönitz and appointed chief of staff with the Navy High Command as late as May 1945.

In May 1951 Gerlach published an article with the title "On the ethical foundations of a new Wehrmacht" in which he extols the fascist authoritarian principle and openly proclaims his fascist convictions. He wrote: "*All power proceeds from the people – in practice this does not mean that individual citizens exert an immediate influence on public matters. The mass of little people is absolutely incapable of making its own decisions and of acting independently. It wants to be governed.*"

And these are Gerlach's "teachings":

"*Now what is this new Germany, for which it is worth staking one's life, to look like? Naturally this new structure must and should be built on the foundations of the past, a principle which must be emphasized in the reconstruction of a Wehrmacht more than in any other connection ... If we wish to make use of these experiences it is first of all necessary to recognize national socialism and all the events of the Third Reich as a part of our German history. I make no secret of the fact that I do not consider everything that originated in the period of the Third Reich as an error which ought to be rejected simply for this reason*".

And these are his "conclusions":

"*Among all the mistakes that were made, much was nevertheless so exemplary, so appropriate to the conditions of the time and the character of the nation that it can be accepted as good for the future. In my opinion all these flaws were caused in a decisive way by the fact that Adolf Hitler unfortunately did not depend on the old leading class of our nation ... Just imagine: the first thousand supporters of a party leader, of the same mould as Hitler, mainly from the circles of the good old bourgeoisie, the church, the officers! I am convinced that with such a 'party' and these 'old party members' our history would have taken a completely different course.*"

This fascist today commands the Bonn fleet.

Thilo RAGED IN THE BALKANS
Karl-Wilh.
today: *commander of the 1st Mountain Division, major general*

One of Hitler's colonels and the former head of the operations department of the Command South, Karl-Wilhelm Thilo – vented his fury on the Balkans in a particularly cruel way. The path of his unit was marked by brutality and terror and by the shooting of completely innocent native civilians in masses.

In April 1943 the 1st Mountain Division coming from Bulgaria arrived in Yugoslavia. As early as 8 April the order was given to all units of the division concerning measures of retaliation against rebels. This order is signed by the division commander, Lieutenant General Stettner, and the 1st staff officer Thilo.

The order says:

"1 *Whoever is caught*

a) fighting with weapons in his possession

b) assisting rebels

c) carrying out acts of sabotage

is, on principle, to be shot or hanged on the spot.

Leaders, political commissars and couriers are to be handed over to Div./1c and to be shot after interrogation ...

5 *b) quotas for retaliation:*

50 prisoners to be shot for one German or Bulgarian killed,

25 prisoners to be shot for one German or Bulgarian wounded,

10 prisoners to be shot for one person otherwise under protection killed,

5 prisoners to be shot for one person otherwise under protection wounded,

up to 1,000 prisoners to be shot for any attack on objects under protection depending on the seriousness of the case ..." (*Nürnberger Prozesse* – NG, Case VII, Vol. 4, Doc. NOKW – 978)

The reports of the "Salminger Marching group" signed by Thilo give particulars on the shooting of hostages and on whole villages razed to the ground (see Table 31, NG, Case VII, Vol. 4, Doc. NOKW – 1032).

In addition Thilo also signed himself as responsible for the execution of Italian officers, as is clearly revealed in one of his reports to the XXII Army Corps of 9 October 1943. (see Table 34, NG, Case VII, Vol. 6, p. 1901)

Even today Thilo knows no scruples and boasts of his crimes:

"The intensification of partisan fighting makes it urgently necessary that we penetrate the hornet's nest, Montenegro, and destroy the crack units of the growing communist national army down to the roots. The regiments of the Edelweiss Division are passing through the Kopaonik Mountains to the west of the Niv, so as to reach the initial positions for Operation 'Black', – the Ibar Valley near Novi Pazar and Mitrovica. Where there are individual engagements with rebels,

the resistance is broken by a quick assault after the fashion of riflemen." (H. Lanz, Gebirgsjäger – Die I. Gebirgsjäger-Division 1935/45 – Mountain Riflemen – The 1st Mountain Rifle Division 1935–45, Bad Nauheim, 1945, p. 245)

Trautloft Johannes

THE MURDERER OF THE CHILDREN OF GETAFE

today: commanding general of the Luftwaffe Group South, lieutenant general

Johannes Trautloft was one of the first six fighter pilots that Hitler sent to Spain in July 1936 to support Franco's fascists and to try out his new murder weapons. As "volunteer" for the "Condor Legion" he fired machine-gun salvos like hail stones on defenceless Spanish children, women and old men or flew as fighter escort for fascist bomber squadrons. At that time the machines which turned the town of Badajoz into rubble with their bombs, used to take off from the aerodromes at Tablada and Seville. Trautloft described in the jargon of a trooper one of these operations on which he flew over the front at Talavera on 15 September 1936 on page 91 of his book *Als Jagdflieger in Spanien* (As a Fighter Pilot in Spain):

"We are allowed to fight and that suffices, that satisfies us completely. Here it would seem there are primeval instincts which have long been covered up, the instincts of the hunter suddenly breaking through again. We have found the way back to the beginnings of mankind, a promise that the age of our white race will last a long time yet. How philistine is the outcry that we have reverted to barbarism."

He extols the barbaric attack on the little village of Olalla in Toledo Province with the words:

"Flying low we fire our machine-gun bursts into the enemy, see how lorries, suddenly deprived of a driver, rush sideways and turn over. Human beings creep forth, many stagger, fall, lie still . . . Certainly nothing can give the soldier more satisfaction than the sight of the enemy in a confused, panic-stricken flight . . . Before flying back to Caceres we drink several glasses of light ale and then fly home with considerable dash." (op. cit. 75 f)

Trautloft also took part in the attack on Getafe on 30 October 1936 in which a hundred Spaniards were killed. Two-thirds of the village were completely destroyed, including the hospital and the school. Among the defenceless victims of this bombing there were 63 children. They were crushed by the rubble of their school which was hit, or blown to bits on the playground. This crime has been stigmatized throughout the world as the "massacre of the children of Getafe".

Infanticide Trautloft, however, wrote full of enthusiasm in his diary: *"The work accomplished today is tremendous."*

Further evidence that Trautloft is an arch-fascist is supplied on page 215 of his concoction:

"20 January – the commemoration of the foundation of the Reich. At 10.00 a.m. we begin. The commander gives a fairly long speech, sketches clearly the events since the seizure of power and reminds us that we also have our duty to fulfil. Next we listen to the Führer's speech in the great hall of the castle, hear the shouts of 'heil' which it produces and join in vigorously: 'Germany, Germany above all . . .'".

When his term in Spain came to an end he observed with regret:

"'I find it hard to part from the war. I murmur to myself. How strange! I'm supposed to fly home as though the war wasn't going on, as if it had ended. The soldier in me rebels, a bitter feeling mounts up within me. I manage to control it only with difficulty." (op. cit., p. 243)

As a reward for these inhuman crimes Trautloft received the Cross of Spain in Gold from Göring and became a lecturer and gave courses at the fascist school for fighter pilots in Bad Aibling. As a squadron-captain he took part in the invasion of Poland and as wing-commander of fighter squadron 51 in the aggression against France. From 1940 until 1943 he was squadron-leader and commanding officer of fighter squadron 54. As early as 27 July 1941 he received the Knight's Cross from Hitler for his operations during the invasion of the Soviet Union. Other stages in the further career of Trautloft, who had in the meantime been promoted to colonel, were inspector (East) of fighter planes, inspector of day-fighting units and commander of the 4th flying (training) division.

After 1945 this murderer devoted himself to the building of new militarist organizations. As one of the organizers of the first internal meeting of the traditional association of the "Condor Legion" he declared at Klopp castle in Bingen in 1956: *The effectiveness of the "Condor Legion" in Spain must be an example to young people in Federal Germany.*

Wichmann Heinz

TESTED IN THE "REICH COMMISSARIAT FOR THE EAST"

today: chief of the Personnel Department of the Bundeswehr, ministerial director

Heinz Wichmann was for a long time not only the chief of the Bundeswehr administration in Schleswig-Holstein, the Eldorado of nazi and war criminals, but also, as an active fascist, a close confidant of the present minister of war in Bonn, von Hassel. The *Taschenbuch für Wehrfragen 1960/1961* (Pocket-book of Defence Questions 1960–61) purposely conceals important facts and only contains the following information on his career up to 1945:

"1931 to 1934 judge and public prosecutor. From 1939 in branch of the Reich

Ministry of Economics (Defence Economy) in Hamburg and Kiel. In 1942 deputy head of the Agricultural Office of Schleswig-Holstein as senior government counsellor. From 1942 to end of war, served in Wehrmacht, wounded, final rank lieutenant and acting battery commander."

The fact is, however, as is revealed by the proposal that he be appointed senior government counsellor on 21 April 1942, that Wichmann joined the NSDAP (membership No. 2726400) on 2 November 1933 and belonged to the NSRB as cell leader. On 1 August 1940 he went to the "Reich Commissariat for the East" to Riga as personal assistant to the Reich commissioner.

The tasks of the "Reich Commissariat for the East" included among other things making reprisals on the population and working out secret "directives on the treatment of Jews in the area of the Reich Commissariat of the East" in close cooperation with the security police.

On 20 November 1941 the "General Commissioner in Riga", Dept. IIa reported to the "Reich Commissioner for the East": *"The plain in the whole of the general commissariat of Latvia is free of Jews."* (see Table 35, Latvian Central Archive in Riga, under Reichskommissar Ostland)

The then personal assistant Heinz Wichmann not only had exact knowledge of the crimes committed in this area but also had a direct part, as a close colleague of the "Reich Commissioner", Lohse, in preparing and carrying out the extermination of the Jews and other crimes. What Dr. Globke put down as the bureaucrat of death, in laws, decrees and commentaries, Wichmann put into practice during his stay in the "Reich Commissariat for the East". (see Table 35, Latvian Central Archive, Riga, under Reichskommissar Ostland)

Hitler General Staff Officers in Leading Posts of the Bundeswehr

Most of the Bundeswehr generals named in the following list held influential positions in the fascist general staff or had a leading part in the aggressions of German imperialism as commanders of "élite" units. In Bonn they are preparing new aggressions in decisive positions.

Aldinger, Hermann

before 1945: first lieutenant and commander of the first heavy anti-aircraft battery of the fascist "Condor Legion"; took part in defeating the liberation struggle of the Spanish people and in murdering defenceless women and children; at the last colonel and commander of an anti-aircraft regiment

after 1945: major general; general of the fighting units and superintendent of flying units in the Air Force Office

Baer, Bern von

before 1945: colonel, G.S.O., chief of the general staff of the Hermann Göring Armoured Airborne Corps, decorated with the Knight's Cross in January 1944 and the Oak-Leaves in February 1945

after 1945: major general; deputy commanding general of the 3rd Corps

Baudissin, Wolf Graf von

before 1945: major, G.S.O., third general staff officer (Ic) of the "German Africa Corps" after 1945: lieutenant general, deputy chief of staff and head of the planning and leading section of NATO headquarters in Europe (SHAPE), active in the "Blank Office" after 1951

Bennecke, Jürgen

before 1945: colonel, G.S.O., chief of staff to the commander-in-chief of the "Adriatic Coast" zone of operations, took part in the attacks on Poland, France and the Soviet Union
after 1945: major general, commander of the General Staff College of the Bundeswehr

Berger, Oskar Alfred

before 1945: colonel, G.S.O., chief of the general staff of the 24th Tank Corps, took part in the predatory war against the Soviet Union, sentenced war criminal
after 1945: brigadier, chief of staff and deputy chief of the Troop Office of the Army

Biesterfeld, Horst

before 1945: commander, department head of the Technical Intelligence Department of the Navy High Command, took part in the invasion of Norway
after 1945: commodore, head of a subdepartment of the Bundeswehr leading staff

Birnbacher, Carl-Heinz

before 1945: lieutenant commander, commander of the 1st speedboat flotilla and destroyer commander, received the Knight's Cross from Hitler on 17 June 1940
after 1945: commodore, commander of the east navy sector command

Burchardt, Heinz

before 1945: lieutenant colonel, adjutant to the chief of the Technical Intelligence Service of the Army High Command, took part in the attacks on Denmark, France and the Soviet Union
after 1945: brigadier

Butler, Peter von

before 1945: colonel, G.S.O., group leader in the operations department of the Army General Staff, took part especially in the aggressions against Poland and the Soviet Union
after 1945: major general, commander of the 12th tank division

Canstein, Rabahn Freiherr von

before 1945: colonel, G.S.O.
after 1945: brigadier, West German military representative at the US Army Headquarters in Europe

Carganico, Walter

before 1945: major, G.S.O., general staff officer (Ia) of the 86th Army Corps
after 1945: brigadier, superintendent of armoured forces in the Troop Office of the Army

Drews, Werner

before 1945: lieutenant colonel, G.S.O., chief of staff of a tank corps
after 1945: major general, commander of the 2nd armoured grenadier division

Ebeling, Werner

before 1945: lieutenant colonel, commander of the 154th grenadier regiment, received the Knight's Cross and Oak-leaves
after 1945: brigadier, commander of the 16th armoured grenadier brigade

Eckert, Dietmar

before 1945: counter intelligence officer of an infantry division of the Army Group North (Kurland), sentenced war criminal
after 1945: brigadier, commander of the 2nd Army Officers' College

Enneccerus, Walter

before 1945: lieutenant colonel, as commanding officer of a squadron of the 2nd dive-bomber wing he received the Knight's Cross already on 21 July 1940
after 1945: brigadier, chief of staff of the Air Force Office

Erdmann, Heinrich

before 1945: lieutenant commander, chief of staff of the speedboat commander
after 1945: commodore, commander of the North Sea Naval Forces

Erhardt, Wolfgang

before 1945: lieutenant commander, second-in-command of the "Michel" auxiliary cruiser, head of the naval bases in Malaya and the Singapore base
after 1945: commodore, commander of training ships

Ferber, Ernst

before 1945: colonel, G.S.O., head of a sub-section (chief-group) in the organizational department of the Army High Command
after 1945: major general, director of the planning group of the NATO Standing Group and chief of staff, became a member of the "Blank Office" already in 1951

Fischer, Kurt
before 1945: major, G.S.O., general staff officer of the anti-aircraft artillery
after 1945: brigadier, superintendent of anti-aircraft troops in the Air Force Office

Foertsch, Friedrich
before 1945: lieutenant general, chief of the general staff of the Kurland Army Group; took part in the attacks on Poland, France and the Soviet Union; decorated with the Knight's Cross; sentenced war criminal
after 1945: general, until the end of 1963 general inspector and chief of the leading staff of the Bundeswehr

Freiwald, Kurt
before 1945: captain in the navy, adjutant to the commander-in-chief of the navy, war criminal Raeder, commander of submarine No. 181
after 1945: commodore, commander of naval bases

Freyer, Joachim
before 1945: colonel, G.S.O., member of the staff of the inspector general of Armoured Forces (Guderian) as chief of the general staff of the 11th Army Corps, decorated with the Knight's Cross by Hitler in 1944
after 1945: major general, superintendent of the technical forces in the Troop Office of the Army, in the "Blank Office" since 1951

Freytag, Bernd Baron von Loringhoven
before 1945: major, G.S.O., adjutant to the last chief of the general staff of the army, General Krebs
after 1945: brigadier, commander of the 19th armoured infantry brigade

Gaedcke, Heinrich
before 1945: major general, chief of the general staff of a tank corps, army corps and army high command, took part in the attacks on France and the Soviet Union, Knight's Cross
after 1945: lieutenant general, commanding general of the 3rd Corps until 31 March 1965

Gartmayr, Georg
before 1945: colonel, G.S.O. (Ia) of the 6th mountain troops division and subsequent service in the Army High Command; took part in all aggressions of the fascist Wehrmacht
after 1945: major general, deputy head of the air and special operations department of NATO headquarters in Europe (SHAPE)

Gaudecker, Gerlach von
before 1945: colonel, commander of the 33rd armoured infantry regiment, received the Knight's Cross on 15 August 1944
after 1945: brigadier, commander of the Territorial Defence Staff in Koblenz

Gerber, Kurt
before 1945: lieutenant colonel, G.S.O., first general staff officer (Ia) of the 58th Army Corps, previously served in the Army High Command
after 1945: major general, commander of the 10th armoured infantry division, member of the "Blank Office" since 1951

Gericke, Walter
before 1945: colonel, commander of the 11th parachute division, received the Oak-leaves on 20 September 1944
after 1945: major general, until 31 March 1965 commander of the 1st airborne division, meanwhile retired

Gerlach, Heinrich
before 1945: captain in the navy, as admiralty staff officer he took part in the preparation and carrying through of the invasions of the Nordic countries; in May 1945 chief of staff of war criminal Dönitz, commander-in chief of the German navy
after 1945: vice admiral, commander of the fleet

Gieser, Kurt
before 1945: colonel, commander of rocket-launching unit 17, German Cross in Gold, took part in the predatory campaigns against Poland, France, Italy and the Soviet Union
after 1945: brigadier, until 31 March 1965 deputy commander of the 1st airborne division

Greiner, Hans
before 1945: colonel, chief of the general staff of the Bünau general command, took part in aggressions against Poland, France and the Soviet Union, German Cross in Gold
after 1945: brigadier, deputy commander of the 1st mountain troops division

Groeben, Peter von der
before 1945: major general, general staff officer (Ia) of the Centre Army Group, took part in the predatory campaigns on Poland, France and the Soviet Union
after 1945: lieutenant general, until 31 March 1964 deputy commander of the Baltic Sea Outlets NATO Command

Guderian, Heinz
before 1945: lieutenant colonel, G.S.O., general staff officer of the 116th tank division, received the Knight's Cross on 25 October 1944
after 1945: brigadier, commander of the 14th tank brigade

Haag, Werner
before 1945: colonel, adjutant of the 8th army
after 1945: major general, head of the personnel department in the Bonn war ministry

Härtel, Johannes
before 1945: colonel, G.S.O., staff officer of the chief of transport in the Army High Command
after 1945: major general, commander of the 4th armoured infantry division

Harlinghausen, Martin
before 1945: lieutenant general, commanding general of the 2nd Air Corps; decorated with highest fascist distinctions for his ruthless air warfare against France and Britain
after 1945: lieutenant general, until 31 December 1961 commanding general of the North Air Force Group in Münster

Heck, Walter
before 1945: lieutenant commander, member of the navy press department of the Navy High Command, teacher in the Mürwik Naval College
after 1945: commodore, deputy chief of the logistics department in the NATO headquarters in Europe (SHAPE)

Hempel, Dr. Adolf
before 1945: major, G.S.O., quartermaster of an anti-aircraft artillery corps, decorated with the Knight's Cross on 18 January 1943
after 1945: major general, commander of the 3rd air force division

Henning, Werner
before 1945: department head in the Air Force High Command; took part in terror raids against Britain as squadron captain
after 1945: brigadier, chief of the supply department of the Bundeswehr

Hepp, Leo
before 1945: colonel, G.S.O., chief of staff to the chief of the military intelligence service of the Army High Command
after 1945: lieutenant general, commanding general of the 2nd Corps

Herrmann, Paul
before 1945: major general, chief of the general staff of the 16th Army, took part in the attack on France and the Soviet Union
after 1945: major general, until 20 September 1961 commander in the 4th defence area, now military adviser to the Hessian provincial government

Herzog, Karl
before 1945: colonel, commander of the field engineering brigade, sentenced as war criminal for participation in the murder of Polish citizens in Warsaw, Knight's Cross
after 1945: major general, second-in-command of the 2nd Corps

Hess, Wilhelm
before 1945: colonel, G.S.O., senior quartermaster of the 20th mountain troops army in Finland and Scandinavia
after 1945: major general, commander in the 6th military district

Hetz, Karl
before 1945: lieutenant commander, 2nd admiralty staff officer with the commander of destroyer formations
after 1945: rear admiral, chief of staff and deputy inspector of the navy

Heusinger, Adolf
before 1945: lieutenant general, chief of the operations department of the Army General Staff, war criminal
after 1945: general, until 29 March 1964 chairman of the Standing Military Committee of NATO in Washington, now military adviser of the CDU

Hinkelbein, Claus
before 1945: lieutenant colonel, chief of the general staff of the Feldluftgaukommando (district air command) XIV, took part in the attacks on Poland, France and the Soviet Union, received the Knight's Cross on 19 June 1940

after 1945: brigadier, commander of the Internal Command School of the Bundeswehr

Hobe, Cord von

before 1945: colonel, G.S.O., commander of the 79th people's grenadier division and of the 212th division of the SS Army Corps Simon, as hold-out officer decorated with the Knight's Cross shortly before the capitulation
after 1945: lieutenant general, commander of NATO armed forces in Jutland and Schleswig-Holstein (COMLANDJUT)

Hoffmann, Werner-Eugen

before 1945: lieutenant colonel, G.S.O., senior quartermaster of the Air Force Command in Italy, later of the Reich Air Force Command
after 1945: lieutenant general, commanding general of the Air Force Command North

Hozzel, Paul Werner

before 1945: lieutenant colonel, commander of the 1st dive-bomber squadron, first general staff officer (Ia) of the 1st Air Force Command, received the Oak-leaves on 14 April 1943, sentenced war criminal
after 1945: brigadier, chief of staff of the Air Force Command South

Hrabak, Dietrich-Adolf

before 1945: colonel, commander of the 54th fighter squadron, one of the first German aerial fighters who was decorated with the Knight's Cross by Hitler on 21 October 1940, received the Oak-leaves on 25 November 1943
after 1945: brigadier, head of the operations department of the 2nd Allied Tactical Air Command

Jeschonnek, Gert

before 1945: lieutenant commander, admiralty staff officer in the operations department of the High Naval Warfare Command
after 1945: rear admiral, second-in-command of the NATO Baltic Sea Command

Jordan, Paul

before 1945: lieutenant colonel, G.S.O., chief of the general staff of the 5th Army Corps, took part in the attacks on Poland and the Soviet Union
after 1945: major general, general of the combat troops in the Troop Office of the Army

Kammhuber, Josef

before 1945: air force general, took part in the preparation and carrying through of the attacks of nazi Germany, closest intimate of Hitler and Göring. He ordered the bombardment of the German town of Freiburg-in-Breisgau in 1940 which served as a pretext to begin the total air war
after 1945: general, until 30 September 1962 inspector and chief of the leading staff of the air force

Karpinski, Peter

before 1945: major, G.S.O., in various general staff positions, sentenced as a war criminal
after 1945: brigadier, commander of the 24th tank brigade, previously personal adviser and adjutant of war criminals Heusinger and Foertsch, former general inspectors of the Bundeswehr

Keilig, Friedrich Wolfgang

before 1945: major, G.S.O., general staff officer (Id) of the F Army Group (South-east), first general staff officer (Ia) of the 6th tank division
after 1945: brigadier, head of sub-section VIII (military planning) of the Bundeswehr leading staff, 1951 to 1955 member of the central office of the Association of German Soldiers, now chairman of the German Federal Defence Union

Kemnade, Friedrich

before 1945: lieutenant commander, member of the Naval Warfare Command of the Navy High Command, received the Oak leaves on 27 May 1943
after 1945: commodore, head of the Navy department of the Bundeswehr General Staff College

Kielmansegg, Johann-Adolf von

before 1945: colonel, G.S.O., dogged militarist and Hitler adherent
after 1945: general, commander of the Central Europe NATO armed forces

Klemm, Helmut

before 1945: commander, head of a sub-division of the Navy High Command
after 1945: commodore, commander of the Bundeswehr Logistics College

Kleyser, Paul

before 1945: colonel, G.S.O., general staff officer of the army operations department of the Wehrmacht Supreme Command.

He was promoted colonel as late as 20 April 1945.
after 1945: brigadier, head of the Army department in the Bundeswehr General Staff College

Köstlin, Wolfgang

before 1945: major, G.S.O., general staff officer of the operations department of the Army General Staff, co-worker of Heusinger and Kielmansegg
after 1945: brigadier, head of the subdepartment "Internal Command" of the leading staff of the Bundeswehr

Krantz, Hans-Ulrich

before 1945: colonel, G. S. O., chief of the staff of the inspectorate for education and training of the Army General Staff, took part in the attacks on Poland, France and the Soviet Union
after 1945: major general, second-in-command of the 1st Corps

Kretschmer, Otto

before 1945: commander, notorious submarine commander of the fascist navy, decorated with the highest nazi distinctions
after 1945: commodore, chief of staff of the NATO Baltic Sea naval forces

Kuhlmey, Kurt

before 1945: colonel, commander of the 3rd combat group, received the Knight's Cross on 15 July 1942
after 1945: major general, commander of the 5th air force division

Kuhnke, Günther

before 1945: lieutenant commander, commander of the 33rd U-boat flotilla, received the Knight's Cross on 19 September 1940
after 1945: commodore, until May 1965 deputy commander-in-chief of the fleet

Kuntzen, Gustav-Adolf

before 1945: lieutenant colonel, G.S.O., general staff officer of an army group
after 1945: lieutenant general, deputy general inspector of the Bundeswehr

Laegeler, Hellmuth

before 1945: major general, under Himmler chief of the staff of the supplementary army, took part in the attacks on Poland and the predatory war against the Soviet Union
after 1945: major general, until 31 March 1962 commander of the General Staff College of the Bundeswehr, now adviser of the provincial government of Baden-Württemberg

Lechler, Otto

before 1945: lieutenant colonel, G.S.O., served in various general staff positions and took part in the attacks on Poland, France and the Soviet Union
after 1945: major general, commander in the 5th military district

Lemm, Heinz-Georg

before 1945: lieutenant colonel, commander of the 27th fusilier regiment, awarded highest fascist decorations and the Golden Badge of Honour of the HJ (Hitler Youth), took part in the attacks on Poland, France and the Soviet Union
after 1945: brigadier, commander of the 3rd Army Officers' School

Looschen, Hans

before 1945: commander, engineer in the staff of the commander-in-chief of U-boat training
after 1945: commodore, commander of the naval engineering command

Lorch, Anton

before 1945: colonel, commander of the 144th regiment of mountain troops, took part in the attacks on Poland and the Soviet Union, received the Knight's Cross on 15 June 1944
after 1945: brigadier, commander of 1st Combat Forces College

Lueder, Hans-Georg

before 1945: colonel, head of a subdivision and liaison officer of the inspector of tank forces in the Army High Command, adjutant of the 6th Army
after 1945: brigadier, commander of the 1st Army Officers' College

Lüttwitz, Smilo Freiherr von

before 1945: general of tank troops, chief of the 9th Army; Hitler awarded him the highest war distinctions for his participation in the fascist war of aggression
after 1945: lieutenant general, until January 1961 commanding general of the 3rd Corps

Maeder, Hellmuth

before 1945: major general, decorated with the highest fascist orders by Hitler, sentenced war criminal after 1945: major general, head of the Troop Office of the Army

Mahlke, Helmuth

before 1945: lieutenant colonel, G.S.O., commander of a dive-bomber wing, received the Knight's Cross on 16 July 1941
after 1945: commodore, commander of the naval air force

de Maizière, Ulrich

before 1945: lieutenant colonel, G.S.O., as Heusinger's co-worker he had an authoritative share in the working out of Hitler's war plans in the operations department of the Army General Staff
after 1945: lieutenant general, inspector and chief of the army leading staff

Markert, Arthur

before 1945: colonel, G.S.O., general staff officer of the staff of the German general staff chief of the 1st Italian Army, took part in war crimes in the Balkans
after 1945: major general, until 1 October 1964 deputy commanding general of the 3rd Corps

Matzky, Gerhard

before 1945: general of infantry, commander of the 16th Army Corps, decorated with the Knight's Cross for ruthless warfare in the Soviet Union
after 1945: lieutenant general, until 29 February 1960 commanding general of the 1st Corps, now president of the Association of German Soldiers

Meier-Welcker, Dr. Hans

before 1945: lieutenant colonel, G.S.O., chief of the general staff of the 31st Army Corps, German Cross in gold
after 1945: brigadier, until 30 September 1964 chief of the military history research office of the Bundeswehr

Meyer-Detring, Wilhelm

before 1945: colonel, G.S.O., first general staff officer (Ia) of the operations department of the army in the General Staff of the Wehrmacht Supreme Command
after 1945: lieutenant general, commanding general of the 1st Corps

Möller-Döling, Joachim

before 1945: colonel, G.S.O., chief of the general staff of the 72nd Army Corps, senior quartermaster of Army Group A
after 1945: brigadier in the Army Troop Office

Molinari, Karl-Theodor

before 1945: lieutenant colonel, commander of the 1st unit of the 36th tank regiment, decorated with the Knight's Cross on 15 November 1944
after 1945: brigadier, head of subgroup I (personnel, internal command) in the army leading staff, until June 1963 chairman of the German Bundeswehr Association

Moll, Josef

before 1945: colonel, G.S.O., first general staff officer of Army Group C
after 1945: major general, deputy inspector of the army

Müller, Christian

before 1945: colonel, G.S.O., chief of the general staff of the 4th tank army, took part in the invasion of the Soviet Union
after 1945: major general, until 30 September 1964 commander in the 2nd military area, now adviser for "defence questions" of the Lower Saxony provincial government

Müller-Hillebrand, Burkhardt

before 1945: major general, took part in the planning of the aggressions of the Hitler Wehrmacht as chief of the organizational department of the army general staff and in their implementation as general chief of staff of tank corps and tank armies
after 1945: lieutenant general, until 31 March 1965 deputy chief of staff for planning and basic questions in the NATO headquarters in Europe (SHAPE)

Neuss, Helmut

before 1945: commander, admiralty staff officer of the operations department of the Naval Warfare Command
after 1945: commodore, West German representative in the NATO Northern Europe sector (AFNORTH)

Obermaier, Albrecht

before 1945: lieutenant commander, admiralty staff officer in the naval operations department of the Wehrmacht Supreme Command
after 1945: commodore, commander of the central naval command

Panitzki, Werner

before 1945: colonel, G.S.O., took part in the attacks on Poland and terror attacks against British, French and Norwegian towns as staff officer of war criminal Kesselring after 1945: lieutenant general, inspector and chief of the leading staff of the air force

Pape, Günther
before 1945: major general, commander of the Feldherrnhalle tank division, decorated with the Oak-leaves by Hitler for his ruthless actions in the Soviet Union
after 1945: major general, commander of the 3rd Military District

Pemsel, Max-Josef
before 1945: lieutenant general, chief of the general staff of the 18th mountain army corps, took part in war crimes in Yugoslavia
after 1945: lieutenant general, until 19 September 1961 commanding general of the 2nd Corps

Philipp, Ernst
before 1945: colonel, tank officer in staff of the 8th Army and of Army Group South, received the Oak leaves on 30 September 1944
after 1945: brigadier, commander of the 2nd Combat Forces College

Plato, Anton-Detlef von
before 1945: colonel, G.S.O., chief of the general staff of the 4th tank corps, received the Knight's Cross on 19 August 1944
after 1945: brigadier, commander of the 1st armoured infantry division

Pöschl, Franz
before 1945: major, commander of the 143rd mountain-infantry regiment, decorated with the Knight's Cross on 6 March 1944, took part in the attacks on Greece, Italy and the Soviet Union
after 1945: brigadier, deputy commander of the 1st airborne division

Poser, Günter
before 1945: lieutenant (navy), commander of U-boat 202
after 1945': commodore, head of a subdepartment of the Leading Staff of the Bundeswehr

Prilipp, Wilhelm
before 1945: lieutenant colonel, groupleader Ib with the general of artillery in the Army High Command
after 1945: brigadier, artillery commander of the 3rd Corps

Reidel, Herbert
before 1945: lieutenant colonel, G.S.O., deputy group-leader for the command instructions of the tank troops in the staff instructions and training section of the Army General Staff
after 1945: major general, commander of the 7th armoured infantry division

Reinhardt, Hellmuth
before 1945: major general, shares responsibility for the brutal suppression of the Danish population as chief of the general staff of the Wehrmacht commander-in-chief in Denmark
after 1945: major general, until 30 September 1962 commander in the 5th Military District, now study-leader of the Evangelical Academy in Bad Boll and from 18 June 1965 chairman of the Military Science Society

Reischauer, Peter
before 1945: lieutenant commander, expert on naval warfare in the Navy High Command
after 1945: commodore, deputy head of the logistics department of Allied Forces Northern Europe

Rösing, Hans-Rudolf
before 1945: captain in the navy, commanding officer of U-boat Forces West, received the Knight's Cross on 29 August 1940
after 1945: rear admiral, commander-in-chief of the 1st Military District

Rogge, Bernhard
before 1945: vice admiral, inspector of the naval educational system, ill-famed pirate captain and murderer of soldiers, was decorated with the Oak-leaves on 12 March 1942
after 1945: rear admiral, until 31 March 1962 commander-in-chief of the 1st Military District, now adviser on "civil defence" to the provincial government of Schleswig-Holstein and the Senate of Hamburg

Rosenthal, Wilfried von
before 1945: colonel, G.S.O., chief of the general staff of the 10th Army Corps assigned to the 18th Army under the command of war criminal Foertsch in Latvia and Kurland, sentenced war criminal
after 1945: brigadier, deputy chief of staff for operations in Centag (Central Europe NATO Army Group)

Ruge, Friedrich
b e f o r e 1 9 4 5 : vice admiral, chief of the office for warship construction, one of the co-workers of war criminal Kesselring in Italy, took part in the attacks on Poland, Holland, Belgium, France and Denmark, decorated with the Knight's Cross as "commander-in-chief for security in the west"
a f t e r 1 9 4 5 : vice admiral, until August 1961 inspector and chief of the Naval High Command, now chairman of the "Association of Bundeswehr Reservists", until 17 June 1965 chairman of the Military Science Society

Schäfer, Heinrich
b e f o r e 1 9 4 5 : lieutenant colonel, G.S.O., first general staff officer (Ia) of Army Group South, German Cross in gold
a f t e r 1 9 4 5 : brigadier, inspector for education and training in the Army Troop Office

Schimpf, Dipl.-Ing. Richard
b e f o r e 1 9 4 5 : lieutenant general, commander of the 3rd parachute division, took a leading part in almost all raids of the fascist Wehrmacht, decorated with the Knight's Cross
a f t e r 1 9 4 5 : major general, until 26 June 1962 commander of the 3rd Military District

Schlichting, Friedrich Carl
b e f o r e 1 9 4 5 : major, G.S.O., volunteer in the "Condor Legion", commanding officer of a squadron of the 27th bomber wing, shot down in a terror raid on England in 1940
a f t e r 1 9 4 5 : major general, deputy inspector of the air force

Schnez, Albert
b e f o r e 1 9 4 5 : colonel, G.S.O., general of the transport system of the Army Group South (Italy)
a f t e r 1 9 4 5 : lieutenant general, commanding general of the 3rd Corps

Schultze, Hellmut
b e f o r e 1 9 4 5 : colonel, G.S.O, chief of the general staff of the 11th Army Corps
a f t e r 1 9 4 5 : major general, deputy chief of staff for intelligence of the AFCENT (Central Europe Allied Armed Forces of NATO)

Schwatlo-Gersterding, Joachim
b e f o r e 1 9 4 5 : major general, chief of the general staff of the 17th Army, took part in attacks on Poland, France and the Soviet Union, sentenced war criminal
a f t e r 1 9 4 5 : lieutenant general, until 31 March 1964 commander-in-chief of the "Territorial Defence Command"

Selmayr, Josef
b e f o r e 1 9 4 5 : colonel, G.S.O., first general staff officer of Army Group F (South-East Europe), took part in war crimes
a f t e r 1 9 4 5 : brigadier, until 31 March 1964 head of the "Security Office of the Bundeswehr" (MAD)

Sieber, Peter Wilhelm
b e f o r e 1 9 4 5 : lieutenant colonel, G.S.O., head of a sub-department of the Air Force High Command
a f t e r 1 9 4 5 : brigadier, second-in-command of the "Territorial Defence Command"

Sonnek, Hubert
b e f o r e 1 9 4 5 : lieutenant colonel, G.S.O., first general staff officer of the 49th mountain corps
a f t e r 1 9 4 5 : brigadier, commander of the 1st airborne division

Speidel, Dr. Hans
b e f o r e 1 9 4 5 : lieutenant general, chief of the general staff of Army Group B, war criminal
a f t e r 1 9 4 5 : general, until 31 March 1964 commander-in-chief of the Central Europe Armed Forces of NATO, now military adviser to the Bonn government

Steinhoff, Johannes
b e f o r e 1 9 4 5 : colonel, commander of the 77th pursuit group, decorated by Hitler with the highest fascist orders for his participation in the criminal air warfare
a f t e r 1 9 4 5 : major general, chief of staff and second-in-command of the NATO Central Europe Air Forces (AIRCENT)

Streib, Werner
b e f o r e 1 9 4 5 : lieutenant colonel, commander of a night pursuit squadron, received the highest fascist decorations
a f t e r 1 9 4 5 : brigadier, superintendent for training in the Air Force Office

Tempelhoff, Hans-Georg von
b e f o r e 1 9 4 5 : colonel, G.S.O., general staff officer of Army Group B, commander of the 28th rifle division, took part in the attacks on Poland, France and the Soviet Union, German Cross in gold
a f t e r 1 9 4 5 : major general, commander of the 3rd tank division

Thilo, Karl-Wilhelm
before 1945: colonel, G.S.O., took part in crimes against patriots in Yugoslavia, Albania and Greece
after 1945: major general, commander of the 1st mountain infantry division

Trautloft, Johannes
before 1945: colonel, shares responsibility for the murder of Spanish women and children as a member of the "Condor Legion" in 1936, decorated with the Knight's Cross on 27 June 1942
after 1945: lieutenant general, commanding general of the Air Force Group South

Trettner, Heinz
before 1945: lieutenant general, decorated with the highest war distinctions for his participation in the fascist attacks on Holland and Belgium, war criminal
after 1945: general, general inspector and chief of the Leading Staff of the Bundeswehr

Übelhack, Friedrich
before 1945: colonel, G.S.O., took part in almost all fascist invasions and especially in the suppression of the Norwegian people as first general staff officer (Ia)
after 1945: major general, commander-in-chief of the "Territorial Defence Command"

Vangerow, Kurt von
before 1945: major, G.S.O., head of a section in the staff of the artillery general in the Army High Command,
after 1945: brigadier, artillery commander of the 2nd Corps

Varnbüler, Ulrich Freiherr von und zu Hemmingen
before 1945: colonel, G.S.O., first general staff officer (Ia) of the 2nd tank army
after 1945: brigadier

Wätjen, Rudolf
before 1945: lieutenant colonel, head of a section of the inspection of the tank troops in the Army High Command, received the Knight's Cross on 18 April 1943
after 1945: brigadier, commander of tank brigade 21

Wagenknecht, Willi
before 1945: lieutenant colonel, head of a department of Reich Air Ministry personnel office
after 1945: brigadier, commander of the Air Force Officers' College

Wegener, Edward
before 1945: captain in the navy, first leading general staff officer in the Fleet Command, specialist for naval warfare operations
after 1945: vice admiral, until 31 March 1965 commander-in-chief of the NATO Baltic Sea Naval Forces, CDU Bundestag candidate in 1965

Wessel, Gerhard
before 1945: lieutenant colonel, G.S.O., head of section 1 of the "Foreign Armies East" department of the general staff of the Army High Command, leading counter-intelligence officer of the fascist Wehrmacht
after 1945: lieutenant general, West German representative in the NATO Military Committee in Washington, confidential agent of nazi General Gehlen, head of the federal intelligence service

Wichmann, Heinz
before 1945: personal adviser of war criminal Lohse, former Reich commissioner in the Reich Commissariat for the East in Riga, had a direct part in the preparation and carrying through of the extermination of Jews
after 1945: ministerial director, head of the personnel department of the Bonn war ministry

Wilcke, Hennig
before 1945: lieutenant colonel, G.S.O., first general staff officer (Ia) of the Air Force Command Atlantic, lecturer in the College of Air Warfare, German Cross in gold
after 1945: major general, commander-in-chief of the 2nd Military District

Zawadzki, Wolf von
before 1945: colonel, G.S.O., first general staff officer of the chief of the military mission in Bulgaria, shares responsibility for the suppression of the Bulgarian people, played a leading part in the persecution of all progressive forces there
after 1945: brigadier, chief of staff of the NATO Land Forces Jütland/Schleswig-Holstein

Zenker, Karl-Adolf
before 1945: commander, commander of destroyers, took part in the planning of attacks on Denmark, Norway and Holland
after 1945: vice admiral, inspector and chief of the Naval High Command

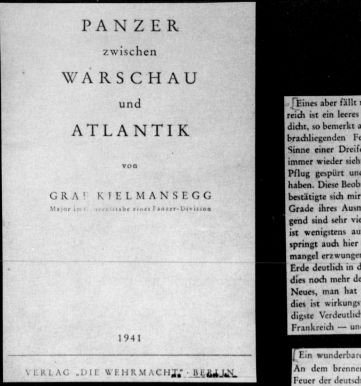

PANZER
zwischen
WARSCHAU
und
ATLANTIK

von

GRAF KIELMANSEGG

Major im Generalstabe einer Panzer-Division

1941

VERLAG „DIE WEHRMACHT" · BERLIN

[Es war uns allen klar, Deutschland machte sich bereit, den polnischen Übermut zu brechen, der bereits über die Grenze griff. Wir hielten den Atem an, als wir des Führers letztes Angebot an Polen hörten, eine Straße und eine Eisenbahnlinie! Und wir wären keine deutschen Soldaten gewesen, wenn wir nicht gewünscht hätten, daß Polen nicht annähme.]

[Ich saß auf dem Stuhl des Oberhauptes eines Staates, den wir nicht nur einfach militärisch besiegt hatten, sondern der durch unseren Sieg ausgelöscht war aus der Geschichte, entgegen deren Sinn er, künstlich ins Leben gerufen, zwanzig Jahre lang versucht hatte, zu existieren — obwohl die Geschichte bereits vor einhundertfünfzig Jahren ihr verdammendes Urteil über ihn gesprochen hatte.]

[Der Wehrmachtbericht über den Feldzug in Polen hatte mit den Worten geschlossen: „Das deutsche Volk kann wieder mit Stolz auf seine Wehrmacht blicken. Sie aber sieht mit sieghaftem Vertrauen ihren weiteren Aufgaben entgegen."

Das taten wir, weiß der Himmel! Voll Vertrauen und voll Ungeduld. Wir hätten am liebsten gleich „weitergesiegt", aber daß das nicht möglich war, wurde einem ja bei der geringsten Überlegung klar.]

[Eines aber fällt mir vor allem auf. Dieses blühende Frankreich ist ein leeres Land. Ist die Besiedlung schon nicht sehr dicht, so bemerkt auch der landwirtschaftliche Laie die vielen brachliegenden Felder, und zwar nicht brachliegend im Sinne einer Dreifelderwirtschaft. Nein, das, was man hier immer wieder sieht, sind Äcker, die seit vielen Jahren keinen Pflug gespürt und kein Getreidekorn mehr aufgenommen haben. Diese Beobachtung, die ich hier zum erstenmal mache, bestätigte sich mir dann eigentlich überall in Frankreich, im Grade ihres Ausmaßes nur wenig abgestuft. In dieser Gegend sind sehr viele Weiden, und der nicht beackerte Boden ist wenigstens auf diese Weise ausgenutzt, trotzdem aber springt auch hier schon die allerdings durch den Menschenmangel erzwungene „Großzügigkeit" in der Ausnutzung der Erde deutlich in die Augen. In anderen Teilen des Landes ist dies noch mehr der Fall. Diese Tatsache ist mir an sich nichts Neues, man hat davon gehört und darüber gelesen. Aber dies ist wirkungsvollster Anschauungsunterricht und lebendigste Verdeutlichung der Begriffe: „Raum ohne Volk" — Frankreich — und „Volk ohne Raum" — Deutschland.]

[Ein wunderbares Bild entwickelt sich vor unseren Augen. An dem brennenden Avancon vorbei, auf dem noch das Feuer der deutschen Artillerie liegt, walzen die Panzer jeden Widerstand vor sich nieder; über zweihundert sind es, auf engem Raum, dort, wo sie auf den Wegen fahren, den Kreideboden der Champagne zu dichten Staubwolken aufwirbelnd.]

[Wir können melden, daß wir den Auftrag, den die Geschichte, Deutschland und der Führer uns gestellt haben, durchführten bis zum letzten, und wir können melden, daß wir bereit sind, genau so den Auftrag durchzuführen, der als einziger noch zwischen uns und der Freiheit steht, die Vernichtung Englands.]

Keine Anerkennung aber kann uns stolzer machen als die des Führers, als er am 19. Juli in seiner großen Rede vor dem Reichstage sagte: „In diesem Kriege hat sich die deutsche Panzerwaffe in die Weltgeschichte eingeführt." Ein Teil dieser Panzerwaffe war die Division, die unter dem Zeichen deutschen Heldentums, unter dem Eichenblatt, kämpfte und siegte, in Polen und in Frankreich, an der Warthe und an der Weichsel, bei Sedan und in Flandern, an der Aisne und an der Marne, an der Grenze der Schweiz und bei Belfort,

meine Division.

TABLE 33

TABLE 34

-783 (7) Stempel: II
Geheime Kommandosache
91
Fernschreiben

Durch Geheimschreiber.

Kr.

Lageorientierung Stand 3.4., 12.00 Uhr.

1.) Frankreich.

Gen.Kdo. LXII.Res.Korps nach Draguignan (AOK 19) verlegt.

Von Transportzug 12.SS-Pz.Div. 0 Lille 2 Waren auf Mine gefahren. Zug anschliessend aus einem Dorf beschossen. Bei sofortiger Abwehr 80 Einwohner erschossen, 20 festgenommen.

Unternehmen gegen Terroristen im Department Dordogne. Mehrere Lager und Haeuser zerstoert, 24 Terroristen erschossen, 107 festgenommen.

OKH
Gen St d H Op.Abt.(II)
Nr. 3447/44 g.Kdos.

3.4.1944

I.A. u.i.V.

Nach Abgang:
MJ Chef Gen St = 3. Ausf.
Op.Abt. 'Ia, = 4. "
III, = 5. "
II). = 6. "

gez. Graf von Kielmansegg
Fuer die Richtigkeit:

gez. Frhr.v.Thesenhausen ?
Major i.G.

handschr.:
ab 3.4.44 Gerlach

Abendmeldung Marschgruppe Salminger
11.7.43 21.30 Uhr Init. Th.(Thilo)

1. Gr. Salminger sichert im befohlenen Raum von Pkt. 1120 (8 km nordostw. Leskovic) beiderseits der Vormarschstrasse nach Süden bis zu Brücke 4 km ostw. Mawrowuni.
Säuberungsaktion 1./Pz. 44 Rest des Aoos-Fl. nach Nordwesten vorstossend bis Tsarsova. Gelände und Ortschaft feindfrei. Ortschaft wurde niedergebrannt. 11./79 links des Aoos.-Fl. nach Nordwesten vorstossend, über Seja bis Drasowa. 60 männliche Zivilisten wurden dabei erschossen, die beiden Ortschaften niedergebrannt, wobei zahlreiche Munition, die in den Häusern versteckt war, in die Luft ging.

Abendmeldung Gruppe Salminger
12.7.43 20.00 Uhr Init. Th(Thilo)

1. 5 Zivilisten durch Sicherungsposten der 16./98 in Gegend Vreptska erschossen.
Aufklärung der 11. Battr. in Stärke eines Zuges nach Moliwdoskepastos und Wlachos stellte weitere Ortschaften als feindfrei fest.
In den Vormittagsstunden wurde Aufklärung der 9/98 in Aidonochori angeschossen. Daraufhin angesetzte Säuberungsaktion in Zugstärke hatte keine Feinberührung mehr. Aj Dimitrios und Aj Theodori (westl. und nordwestl. Aidonochori) wurden niedergebrannt.

"In der Anlage überreicht die Division die Listen der in Saranda erschossenen italienischen Offiziere.
Gleichzeitig wird ein Rücksack übergeben, in dem sich die Nachlasssachen dieser Offiziere befinden. Für die in Nr. 3, 4, 10, 18, 32, 33, 35, 36, 40 und 47 genannten Offiziere waren keine Nachlasssachen beigefügt..."+

+ Fall 7, Stenogramm Band VI, S.1900

Im Südostgeneralprozess hob der Anklagevertreter ausdrücklich die Tatsache hervor, dass dieser Bericht unterschrieben ist "Für das Divisionskommando; vom ersten Generalstabsoffizier" (vgl. ebenda).

Ständig gab Thilo dem XXII. Armeekorps Meldungen wie diese durch:
"... An 58 italienischen Offizieren wurde Führerbefehl Nr. 1 durchgeführt... Für das Divisionskommando, der erste Generalstabsoffizier."

182

A b s c h r i f t :

Durch Leg.Rat Schumburg
AUSWÄRTIGES AMT
83-26 19/1

Berlin, den 25. Januar 1939

Inhaltsangabe:

Die Judenfrage als Faktor der Außenpolitik im Jahre 1938.

1. Die deutsche Judenpolitik als Voraussetzung und Konsequenz der außenpolitischen Entschlüsse des Jahres 1938
2. Ziel der deutschen Judenpolitik: Auswanderung
3. Mittel, Wege und Ziel der jüdischen Auswanderung
4. Der ausgewanderte Jude als beste Propaganda für die deutsche Judenpolitik.

Es ist wohl kein Zufall, daß das Schicksalsjahr 1938 zugleich mit der Verwirklichung des großdeutschen Gedankens die Judenfrage ihrer Lösung nahegebracht hat. Denn die Judenpolitik war sowohl Voraussetzung wie Konsequenz der Ereignisse des Jahres 1938. Mehr vielleicht als die machtpolitische Gegnerschaft der ehemaligen Feindbundmächte des Weltkriegs hat das Vordringen jüdischen Einflusses und der zersetzenden jüdischen Geisteshaltung in Politik, Wirtschaft und Kultur die Kraft und den Willen des deutschen Volkes zum Wiederaufstieg gelähmt. Die Heilung dieser Krankheit des Volkskörpers war daher wohl eine der wichtigsten Voraussetzungen für die Kraftanstrengung, die im Jahre 1938 gegen den Willen einer Welt den Zusammenschluß des großdeutschen Reiches erzwang.

Die Notwendigkeit für eine radikale Lösung der Judenfrage ergab sich aber auch als Konsequenz der außenpolitischen Entwicklung, die zu den im Altreich lebenden

An
alle diplomatischen und berufskonsularischen Vertretungen im Ausland

---

Reichsführer SS
Chef des Sicherheitshauptamtes

186

II 112 o
C 41
H/Pi

13. März 1939

Geheim!

Geheim
S.D.O.A. Donau
Br. Nr. 691
Eing. 14. März 1939
mit 1 Anlagen

An den
SD-Führer des SS-O.A.
II 112

Betr.: "Die Judenfrage als Faktor der Außenpolitik im Jahre 1938"

Vorg.: Ohne

Anliegend wird ein zusammenfassender Bericht des Auswärtigen Amtes über die Bedeutung der Judenfrage für die Außenpolitik des Jahres 1938 zur Kenntnisnahme übersandt.

Es wird darauf hingewiesen, daß der Bericht zwar richtig eine radikale Lösung der Judenfrage durch die Auswanderung - wie sie hier schon seit Jahren verfolgt wird - vertritt, daß es jedoch im Augenblick noch nicht zweckmäßig sein kann, in allen europäischen und außereuropäischen Staaten die Judenfrage zu provozieren, da dies die Auswanderung der jetzt noch in Deutschland wohnhaften Juden stark behindern könnte. Unter Hinweis auf diesen Mangel in der Darstellung des Problems ist das Reichsministerium des Innern auch bereits auf schriftlichem Wege an das Auswärtige Amt herangetreten.

1 Anlage

Der Chef des Sicherheitshauptamtes
i.A.
Der Leiter der Zentralabteilung II 1
i.V. gez. E h r l i n g e r
SS-Obersturmbannführer.

f.d.R.
SS-Hstuf.

14 März 1939

SS-H'Stuf. Eichmann z. K.
2/3. 39.

TABLE 35

Der Chef der Sicherheitspolizei und des SD
-Kommandostab-

Berlin, den 11.IX.1942

Auswärtiges Amt
D II 1369 g
eing. 18 SEP 1942
Anl. (fach) Dopp. f. Eing.

Meldungen aus den besetzten Ostgebieten

Nr. 20

Der Befehlshaber
der Sicherheitspolizei und des SD
im Bereich des Militärbefehlshabers
in Frankreich

Paris, den 31. August 1943

Nr. IV E 44 - 245 g.Rs.

Geheim!

DEUTSCHE BOTSCHAFT PARIS
13 SEP 1943
Anl: Akz.

An die
Deutsche Botschaft
z.Hd.v.Herrn Gesandtschaftsrat Dr. GOSSMANN
P a r i s

Betr.: "A t t e n t i o n II" (hier: Finanz-Inspektor B a u m g a r t n e r).

Vorg.: Fernmündliche Unterredung zwischen Gesandtschaftsrat Dr.Gossmann und ⚡⚡-Stubaf.Hagen, vom 19.8.1943.

Anlg.: Ohne.

Seitens der Deutschen Botschaft wurde um eine schriftliche Stellungnahme über die Gründe gebeten, die zu der Festnahme des Finanz-Inspektors Wilfrid B a u m g a r t n e r Veranlassung gegeben haben.

Grundsätzlich darf ich dazu feststellen, daß die Liste "Attention II" unter Mitwirkung der deutschen Botschaft (Gesandter Schleier und Gesandter Dr.v.Rohde) zusammengestellt worden ist. Bei der Abstimmung wurde jede der für eine Festnahme in Betracht kommenden Personen durchgesprochen und in jedem Falle alle für und gegen eine Inhaftierung sprechenden Momente erörtert.

DER MILITÄRBEFEHLSHABER IN FRANKREICH
KOMMANDOSTAB ABT. Ic

PARIS, DEN 11.1.1943

Der Verbindungsoffizier
zur Deutschen Botschaft
Nr. 7/43

DEUTSCHE BOTSCHAFT PARIS
33100 * 12 JAN 1943
Anl: Akz. 110/43

Herrn
Legationssekretär von N o s t i t z

Durch Urteil des Feldkriegsgerichts der Feldkommandantur 748 vom 22.12.42 wurden wegen Freischärlerei, Feindbegünstigung u.a. verurteilt:

a) der Kupferschmied Edouard Hervé zum Tode
b) der Mechaniker Pierre Langlais zum Tode
c) der Mechaniker Maurice Fourrier zum Tode
d) der Schuhmacher Albert Leshommes zum Tode
e) der Arbeiter Joseph Poussin zum Tode
f) der Handelsangestellte Pierre Chalopin zu 1 Jahr Gefängn
g) der Eisenbahnarbeiter Jean Jaffrés zum Tode
h) der Eisenbahner Maurice Leost zum Tode
i) der Arbeiter Yves Bitous zum Tode
k) der Steinbruchpächter Ernest Moraux zum Tode
l) der Steinbruchpächter Louis Moraux zum Tode
m) der Angestellte Joseph Vaillant zum Tode
n) der Anstreicher Victor Fortin zum Tode
o) der Tapezierer Albert Gérard zum Tode
p) der Schlosser René Mirel zum Tode
q) der Elektriker Henri Bougeard zum Tode
r) der Geschäftsführer Yves Deniel zum Tode
s) der Eisenbahnarbeiter Pierre L'Hotellier zum Tode
t) der Eisenbahnarbeiter Georges Riandière zum Tode
u) der Eisenbahnarbeiter René Mobilet zum Tode
v) der Eisenbahnarbeiter Albert Martin zum Tode
w) der Heizungsmonteur Albert Deniel zum Tode
x) der Eisenbahner Leo Jaffré zum Tode
y) der Heizer Jean Bras zum Tode
z) der Zementarbeiter Jean Belliard zum Tode

aa)

179187

aa) der Metalldreher Henry Dero zum Tode
bb) der Eisenbahnangestellte Jean Dubois wurde freigesprochen.
Die Todesurteile wurden am 30.12.42 vollstreckt.
Das Urteil gegen Pierre Chalopin und Jean Dubois wurde aufgehoben.

2) Durch Urteil des Feldkriegsgerichts der Feldkommandantur 748 vom 26.12.42 wurde der Landwirt und Holzhauer Roger Michot wegen unbefugten Waffenbesitzes zum Tode verurteilt. Das Urteil wurde am 31.12.42 vollstreckt.

TABLE 36

Auswärtiges Amt

Nr. Pol II 5183 g

Es wird gebeten, dieses Geschäftszeichen und den Gegenstand bei weiteren Schreiben anzugeben.

Berlin W 8, den 22. Dezember 1944

Schnellbrief

In der am 4.ds.Mts. auf Grund einer Führerweisung an das internationale Komitee vom Roten Kreuz gerichteten Note hat die Reichsregierung zum Schutz der in französische Hände gefallenen Deutschen und der französischen Kollaborationisten in Frankreich Repressalien angedroht. Der Wortlaut unserer in der Presse veröffentlichten Note ist beigefügt.

Da mit dem Fall zu rechnen ist, daß mit den angekündigten Repressalien Ernst gemacht werden muss, erscheint es angezeigt, schon jetzt folgende Fragen zu klären:

1.) Bestände eine Möglichkeit, auf Grund des vorliegenden Belastungsmaterials gegen die in unseren Händen befindlichen gaullistischen Häftlinge Strafverfahren, die ähnlich wie die jetzigen Prozesse gegen die Kollaborationisten in Frankreich mit schweren Strafen enden müssten, einzuleiten, oder, wenn solche Verfahren auf Grund der Führerweisung vom Frühjahr ds.Js. eingestellt worden sind, sie wieder aufzunehmen ? Könnte eine Liste von solchen Personen angefertigt werden ?

2.)

An

das Reichsjustizministerium
das Oberkommando der Wehrmacht
Wehrmachtsrechtswesen,
Heeresstandortverwaltung Bereich R
Jüterbog
das Reichssicherheitshauptamt Abt.IV

– je besonders –

2

2.) Könnten die Fälle, in denen französische Schutzhäftlinge in Deutschland zum Tode verurteilt worden sind, und das Urteil vollstreckt worden ist, ohne dass bisher eine Bekanntgabe erfolgte, angegeben werden ? Es könnte daran gedacht werden, sie eventuell in solcher Form zu veröffentlichen, daß in Frankreich der Eindruck entsteht, als ob sie bereits das Ergebnis der unter Ziffer 1.) genannten Vergeltungsprozesse seien.

3.) Könnte eine Liste der französischen Schutzhäftlinge, die wegen Teilnahme an der Widerstandsbewegung oder wegen sonstiger feindseliger Betätigung gegen Deutschland durch deutsche Gerichte zum Tode verurteilt, dann aber von uns begnadigt worden sind, aufgestellt werden ? Würden Bedenken dagegen bestehen, angesichts des Mordterrors gegen die deutsch-freundlichen Franzosen in Frankreich die von uns ausgesprochenen Begnadigungen zu widerrufen ?

Ich darf hinzufügen, daß es erwünscht wäre, wenn die Listen in Stichworten kurze Angaben über die Personalien der betreffenden Franzosen enthalten würden, damit sich ersehen lässt, inwieweit es sich um Personen von einer gewissen politischen oder sozialen Bedeutung handelt.

Um beschleunigte Stellungnahme wird gebeten.

In Vertretung

[signature]

TABLE 37

Durchdruck.

Gesandter Dr. F. Grobba e.o. Pol VII 1189 GRs

pr. 4.9.42 Geheime Reichssache

Betr.: Sonderstab F bezw. "Deutsches Orientkorps".

68

General Felmy teilte mir über die Umwandlung des bisherigen Sonderstabes F in einen Korps-Verband, dessen Gliederung und bevorstehenden Einsatz vertraulich folgendes mit:

Der Sonderstab F werde in einen Korps-Verband umgewandelt, der voraussichtlich die Bezeichnung "Deutsches Orientkorps" führen werde. Dieses Korps werde aus folgenden Einheiten bestehen:

1 arabisches Bataillon (Deutsch-Arabische Lehrabteilung), Kommandeur: Hauptmann Schober,
- 1 Kompanie Araber aus Palästina, Syrien und dem Irak,
- 1 Kompanie Araber aus Nordafrika (ehemalige Mitglieder der französischen Legion an der Ostfront),
- 2 weitere Kompanien werden noch aufgestellt.

1 deutsches Bataillon, Kommandeur: Hauptmann Daumüller,

67

Das Korps wird etwa 6000 Mann zählen und vollständig motorisiert sein mit 1640 Fahrzeugen. Die Bewaffnung enthält die allermodernsten Modelle.

Dem Korps stehen zur Bewaffnung arabischer Freiwilliger und Überläufer Waffen für eine Division zur Verfügung.

Das Korps wird in Stalino zusammengestellt. Die einzelnen Verbände sind dorthin zurzeit unterwegs. Nach Einnahme von Tiflis wird das Korps nach dem Kaukasusgebiet verlegt. Es ist für den Einsatz durch Westiran nach dem Irak mit Richtung Basra vorgesehen.

Hiermit
über
Dg. Pol.
u. St. S.
bei Herrn Botschafter Ritter
vorgelegt.

Durchschlag an:
H. Ges. Ettel,
H. LR. Melchers.

Berlin, den 3. September 1942.

gez.: Grobba.

TABLE 38

6. August 2.

xxxxxxxxxxxxxx Zagreb

xxxxxxxxxxxx
Geh.Verm.f.Geh.Reichssachen
xxxxxxxxxxxxxxxxxxxxxx
xxxxxxxxxxxxxxxxxxxxxx

LR Picot
i.V.:VK Geiger

Betrifft: Dienststelle des Polizeiattachés

Auf Bericht vom 20. Juli - Pol 2
Nr. 2 - A 430/42 -

Zu 1.
Mit Abstellung ᛋᛋ-Hauptsturmführers Abromeid zum Polizeiattaché zwecks Durchführung Übersiedlung kroatischer Juden in Ostgebiete vom 1. August bis 30. September 1942 einverstanden.

Zu 2.
Abstellung ᛋᛋ-Obersturmführers Heinrich nach Agram zur Bearbeitung von Kirchenfragen wird nicht zugestimmt.

Reichssicherheitshauptamt wird über diese Entscheidung entsprechend unterrichtet werden.

Nach Abgang
Abt. Pers
D XII
D XII
Pol IV
z.Kts.

2) Wvl.im Referat (betr.Unterrichtung des RSHA)

Luther

Eingegangen am A. A. eing. 11.DE[redacted]

Nr.*) 122

10

Verzeichnis

der von dem Deutschen Konsulat in Apenrade am 10. Dezember 1940. mit†) der Post über Flensburg. an das Auswärtige Amt in Berlin abgesandten Berichte usw.

Datum	Tagebuchnummer	Kontrollnummer	Kurze Inhaltsangabe	An Abteilung gegeben (Nur von dem Hauptbüro bei Auswärtigen Amts auszufüllen)
9.12.	645		Betr. Verfügungsmittel	
9.12.	646		Reisekosten VK Dr. Lammer. 2 Schrb. Herrn VLR. Rödiger.	
9.12.	642		Gebührenüberweisungsliste November 1940. Anlagen zur Baubedarfsnachweisung.	
			1 Brief f.Reichssicherheitshauptamt	
			1 Brief für ABt. Deutschld.	
			1 Brief für den Herrn Chef der Sicherheitspolizei.	

Seitenrand (nicht beschreiben!)

*) Die Berichtsverzeichnisse, die als Unterlagen für die Verteilung und Kontrolle der Berichte dienen, sind mit jährlich fortlaufenden Nummern zu versehen, damit das Ausbleiben einer Sendung bei dem Hauptbüro des Auswärtigen Amts sofort an dem Fehlen der Nummer bemerkt werden kann. Auf dem ersten Berichtsverzeichnisse eines jeden Jahres ist die letzte Nummer des Vorjahres zu vermerken. Berichtsverzeichnisse sind auch für Einzelsendungen erforderlich.

†) Angabe, ob mit Kurier (Name), Depeschensack (Nummer), Post, Schiff (Name) abgesandt. Gelegenheitskuriere sind anzuweisen, ihre Depeschen nur in dem Hauptbüro des Auswärtigen Amts abzugeben.

A. A. M. u. K. 1305
[illegible]

Geheim 475 3

HPA 900

Im mündlichen und schriftlichen Verkehr mit Privaten soll der Handelspolitische Ausschuß nicht erwähnt und auf seine Ent= scheidungen nicht Bezug genommen werden.

S i t z u n g
des Handelspolitischen Ausschusses
vom 14. Februar 1944.

Nr. 7

Anwesend:

Auswärtiges Amt	Ministerialdirektor Wiehl Ministerialdirektor Clodius Stv. Ministerialdirigent VLR. Ripken Gesandter Benzler (vorübergehend) Gesandter Martius " Gesandtschaftsrat Eberl " Legationsrat Schlitter " Legationssekretär Pamperrien"
Reichswirtschaftsministe= rium	Hauptabteilungsleiter Kirchfeld Min. Dirigent Schultze-Schlutius Reichsbankrat Tüngeler
Reichsministerium für Er= nährung u. Landwirtschaft	Ministerialdirektor Walter Ministerialdirigent Schefold
Reichsfinanzministerium	Ministerialdirigent Litter Ministerialrat Scherer Ministerialrat Breyhan
Reichsverkehrsministerium	Ministerialdirektor Baur Oberregierungsrat Billing
Vierjahresplan	Ministerialdirektor Gramsch
Oberkommando der Wehrmacht -Sonderstab HWK- -We Wi Stab-	Oberst von Mauch Oberstleutnant Radtke Major Roth
Reichsministerium für Rüstung u. Kriegsproduktion	Dr. von Zaberm
Reichsbankdirektorium	Reichsbankdirektor Heinel
Reichsforstamt	Ministerialrat Wrabec
Reichskommissar für die Preisbildung	Dr. von Hagenow Herr Bendick
Frachtenleitstelle Südost	Direktor Michler

Auswärtiges Amt
Prot.B. 2410 IX 180.

Berlin, den 20. Juni 1939.

Sehr verehrter Herr Cirković!

Einer Verabredung mit Herrn Zvekić ent= sprechend beehre ich mich, Ihnen noch eine Liste von Angehörigen des Auswärtigen Amts, deren Aus= zeichnung aus Anlass des Staatsbesuchs Seiner Königlichen Hoheit des Prinzregenten in Frage kommt, in der Anlage zu überreichen.

Wir würden es dankbar begrüssen, wenn diesen Wünschen entsprochen werden könnte.

Indem ich Ihnen für Ihre liebenswürdige Mühewaltung aufrichtigen Dank sage, bin ich mit den besten Empfehlungen

Ihr sehr ergebener

Herrn
Legationssekretär Dr. Stevan Cirković,
Königlich Jugoslawische
Gesandtschaft.

Reichssicherheits-Dienst.

SS-Obersturmführer Hans Schirmer — Ritterkreuz

(Mohr) 6415

125

DEUTSCHE GESANDTSCHAFT.

Peping, den 14.Dezember 1934.

Nr. 1092.

Aktz, 6415/8290/34.

5 Durchschläge.

Inhalt: Betätigung der Mitglieder der Gesandtschaft in der Ortsgruppe Peping der N.S.D.A.P.

Dem Auswärtigen Amt beehre ich mich zu melden, daß die folgenden Mitglieder der Gesandtschaft als "politische Leiter" in der Ortsgruppe Peping der N.S.D.A.P. tätig und als solche von dem Landesgruppenleiter für China bestätigt worden sind :

Gesandtschaftsrat Dr.Lautenschlager
(Stellvertretender Ortsgruppenleiter),

Legationssekretär Dr.Junker
(Leiter der Wirtschaftsstelle),

Attaché Dr.Mohr
(Leiter der Pressestelle),

Konsulatssekretär Janssen
(Kassenwart),

Konsulatssekretär Hürter
(Zellenobmann)

Konsulatssekretär Wobser ist Mitglied des Uschla.

gez. Trautmann.

An das
Auswärtige Amt,
B e r l i n.

DOCUMENT NO. NG - 2805
CONT'D

(Seite 2 des Originals)

U.St.S.Pol.Nr._155_

Berlin, den 26.Februar 1941.

Gesandtschaftsrat Mohr rief heute in Abwesenheit des Gesandten Bene aus dem Haag an und teilte im Anschluss an dessen gestrige Mitteilung ueber die Lage in den Niederlanden folgendes mit:

Der Anlass zur Abschiebung der 400 Juden aus Amsterdam nach Deutschland sei nicht nur die Niederschlagung eines niederlaendischen Wa[illegible]mannes, sondern auch die Tatsache, dass eine deutsche Patrouille im Amsterdamer Judenviertel mit Giftstoffen bespritzt worden sei.

A.A. eing. 15. FEB 1943 Vm

251

Deutsches Generalkonsulat

Sofia, den 8.Februar 1943.

252

Geheime Reichssache

Auswärtiges Amt:
Pol. IV 355 gRs
Eing. 15. 2. 43.
Anl. (...fach) Bsp. d. Eing

No. 84/43

Betrifft : Amerikanisches Memorandum ueber die Donauraumfrage.

2 Durchschlaege
1 Anlage

Büro des Staatssekretärs

In der Anlage beehre ich mich, Fotokopie eines vom Agenten der Abwehr aus dem Hause eines diplomatischen Mitglieds der hiesigen Amerikanischen Gesandtschaft beschafften Memorandums, betr. die Regelung der Donauraumfrage, vorzulegen.

Naehere Angaben darueber, ob es sich um ein offizielles Memorandum handelt oder wer der Verfasser ist, konnten nicht erlangt werden.

I.V.

Mohr

TABLE 40

RIBBENTROP DIPLOMATS IN THE BONN FOREIGN SERVICE

The Fascist Foreign Office – An Instrument of the Imperialist Policy of Conquest

The diplomats of the Foreign Office headed by nazi Foreign Minister Joachim von Ribbentrop were part of the leading clique of fascist Germany that is to the highest possible degree guilty of crimes against peace, international law and humanity.

Ribbentrop was sentenced to death by the Nuremberg International Military Tribunal and executed. Eight more prominent Ribbentrop diplomats – mainly state secretaries and undersecretaries like Weizsäcker, Woermann, Ritter, Keppler, and others – were tried and sentenced by an American Military Court in the so-called Wilhelmstrasse trial in 1948–49 (i.e., one of the 12 trials following the Nuremberg trial). The other leading members of the Ribbentrop staff, most of whom had in 1945 sought refuge in the parts of Germany occupied by the western powers not only remained unmolested in the West German state but were again given key positions in the Bonn Foreign Office.

The Wilhelmstrasse trial revealed the criminal rôle of the Foreign Office and provided evidence that members of its diplomatic staff had substantially participated in crimes of various kinds. Along with the Reich Security Main Office and the Wehrmacht under the command of the OKW, its supreme command, the Foreign Office served to plan and prepare the major aggressions and crimes of fascist Germany. It was a decisive instrument of imperialist power politics. Its members served as key figures in drawing up and implementing aggressive plans. There is no case known of the Foreign Office or even a group of its members having prevented any crime.

The Nuremberg International Military Tribunal defined as criminal aggressions the attacks on Austria on 12 March 1938, on Czechoslovakia on 1 October 1938 and 15 March 1939, on Poland on 1 September 1939, on Great Britain and France on 3 September 1939, on Denmark and Norway on 9 April 1940, on Belgium, the Netherlands and Luxemburg on 10 May 1940, on Yugoslavia and Greece on 6 April 1941, on the Soviet Union on 22 June 1941, and the United States of America on 11 December 1941. (NG, Case XI, Vol. CCXLI, p. 27,624)

Arriving at its verdict in the Wilhelmstrasse trial the court stated:

"We regard everybody who plans, prepares for, starts and carries out aggressive wars and interventions, and everybody who knowingly, deliberately and guiltily takes part in such actions as a criminal offence against international law who must be brought to court, sentenced and punished for his action." (NG, Case XI, Vol. CCXLI, p. 27,622)

This characterization applies to almost all diplomats employed in the Ribbentrop Foreign Office, since almost every member participated in preparing and carrying out the plans of aggression. It was the activity of nazi diplomats in bringing about the Second World War that was particularly fraught with consequences. The Ribbentrop Office was the main centre of inventing the blackmail and falsification manoeuvres leading to the fascist attack on Poland. It was an essential feature of their rule of conduct to voice slogans proclaiming the "right of self-determination" and a "national community", while actually engaging in preparations for the attack on Poland after the aggression against Czechoslovakia thus starting the Second World War. The procedure was quite similar to that followed in all other attacks and acts of aggression, which would have been unthinkable without the criminal activity of the offenders against international law in the Wilhelmstrasse (location of the Foreign Office).

The Foreign Office, its embassies and departments, moreover, engaged in special activity to extend the Second World War. Attempts were made to increase the number of states already participating in the war and to involve the few remaining neutral states. The Hitler diplomats interfered with the neutral status of these states and attempted to misuse them in favour of Hitler Germany's war.

THEY EXTEND THE WAR...

Plans and direct preparations for conquering the Near East provide a characteristic example of this type of activity. Plans for a military invasion of this region were forced by the Foreign Office at the end of 1941 and in the early months of 1942. At that time the fascist armed forces had occupied almost the whole of Europe. The nazi leadership still indulged in the illusion of being able to defeat the Soviet Union. At that time two special staffs were set up. The OKW formed "special staff F" headed by General Felmy, who was in Greece engaged in preparing military cadres for desert war in the Near East, and the Foreign Office formed the "special staff von Grobba" which was in charge of political and organizational preparations for the occupation of these territories. It selected the "rulers" they intended to place in charge of these states, it established contacts with "suitable circles" and organized a fifth column.

The tasks which this "staff" under Ambassador von Grobba had been charged with are defined in a secret note of the Ribbentrop Office, dated 6 November 1941:

"Its task is the political preparation of the German advance into the Arab region, and after the invasion it will be in charge of carrying out German policy on the spot according to the directions issued by the Foreign Office." (Document Centre, State Archives Administration of the GDR, No. 368,142)

Woermann, at that time under-secretary of state, was still more outspoken when he wrote on 6 November 1941:

"Permanent expulsion of Britain from the Near East and permanent establishment of German influence on Arab oil resources must be our dominant aims." And in another place he said: *"The question of selecting the rulers and other leading personalities will be of particular significance."*

The "special staff von Grobba" was thus an instrument of the Foreign Office to be used in replacing the Anglo-French colonial régime in the Arab states by an undoubtedly still more brutal fascist régime.

There exists a document listing, among other items, the "political members" of this staff:

"The staff of the envoy plenipotentiary of the Foreign Office to Arab countries (Ambassador Dr. Grobba).
(a) Political members:
Counsellor of Legation Dr. Granow, at present delegated to the Felmy staff in Athens (was with me in Bagdad, speaks Arabic); Legation Secretary Mirow, at present stationed with Task Force 280 in Laurion (Greece), (was in Jerusalem); Vice-consul Dr. Seydel, at present at the consulate in Tetuan (was with me in Bagdad, speaks Arabic) . . ." And in another place we find the name of Kurt Munzel.

All the persons mentioned here were and are employed in responsible positions in the diplomatic service of the Federal Republic: Until he retired from the Service in 1963 Dr. Granow was a special envoy for Foreign Ministers Brentano and Schröder. The former Legation Secretary Mirow was employed as a counsellor of legation, first class at the West German embassy in Bagdad until diplomatic relations between Bonn and the Arab states were broken off, and Dr. Seydel was counsellor of legation, first class in the West Department (North Africa) of the Foreign Office. Dr. Munzel had been ambassador of the Federal Republic in Congo (Leopoldville) and then in Lebanon (also until diplomatic relations were broken off).

...AND DIVIDE THE WORLD

Similar plans to those for the occupation of the Arab countries were drawn up by the fascist Foreign Office together with the Reich Colonial Federation whose chairman was Ritter von Epp, and, in part together with the OKW, for a colonial redivision of Africa and Asia. There was a plan in existence proposing a new German colonial empire including not only the former German colonies but the French and Belgian Congo, Uganda, Nigeria, Kenya and Zanzibar as well. (cf. *Von Ribbentrop bis Adenauer* – From Ribbentrop to Adenauer, Berlin, 1961)

In cooperation with officials of the Foreign Office the "Gauleiter z.b.V. (for special disposal)" (!) Korswand stated in a memorandum in June 1940 that two principal German colonial territories would have to be established: in Central Africa and the Far East. The memorandum says on this subject:

"Morocco will be Spanish, thus Spain will then – with the exception of Fernando Po, the Rio Muni region, etc. – come into possession of a larger connected colonial territory, extending from Gibraltar – having become Spanish – to the Rio de Oro region. Algiers with a part of the Sahara region remains (in addition to the French colonies in India, the South Sea, West India and South America) in French hands. In compensation, however, France will have to cede (besides Corsica and Savoy in Europe) Tunis and Djibouti to Italy, she will also cede Senegambia, the French Congo and all French colonies of the Guinea Coast as well as the Mascarenes to Germany and its protected states.

"Britain will lose, apart from Gibraltar (to Spain), the islands of Cyprus, Malta, Crete and Perim (to Italy), all of its African colonial possessions. Thus it will cede

(a) the northern part of the formerly British Sudan, British Somaliland and, possibly, Aden to Italy;

(b) the territory of the former South African Union to a future Boer state absolutely independent of Britain;

(c) all the rest – this would include Gambia, Sierra Leone, the Gold Coast, Nigeria, the southern part of the Sudan, and, of course, the former German colonies stolen from Germany, Kenya, Uganda with the off-shore islands of Zanzibar and Pemba, the Seychelles and Admiralty islands – to Germany and its protected states;

"Egypt with the Suez Canal Zone will, as a nominally independent state, be placed under Italian protection as it has up to now been under British protection ...

"A part of the former Belgian Congo, i.e., the eastern part bordering on German East Africa and Northern Rhodesia together with the Katanga copper

region would, apart from economic reasons to be discussed later, have to be added to the German main colony in view of various other considerations . . . "In view of the fact that the Netherlands will probably also be one of the states that will in future be placed under German protection in one way or another we can conclude that in the region of those islands off the shores of Asia and Australia which formerly belonged either to Germany or to the Netherlands another new and very valuable principal colonial empire is going to become available that might perhaps be classified together as the 'colonial island possessions'." (Document Centre, State Archives Administration of the GDR, No. 368,510)

Several departments of the Foreign Office participated actively in the creation of a so-called Colonial Office. The Foreign Office and its staff members obviously showed remarkable initiative to extend the Second World War, to draw more peoples into the war and to develop programs on how to divide the world under the leadership of German imperialism.

COOPERATED IN THE "FINAL SOLUTION OF THE JEWISH QUESTION"

The Wilhelmstrasse diplomats participated substantially in the murder of millions of Jewish people. Summing up their joint responsibility in these crimes the judgment passed in the Wilhelmstrasse trial states:

"There exists no excuse or justification whatsoever for any person who deliberately and approvingly participated in any single act that went to make up these repulsive and horrible crimes, and it does not matter whether he caused or executed them or only rendered assistance or justified them to the world or aided and abetted the delinquents." (NG, Case XI, Vol. CCXLII, p. 27,827)

The Foreign Office under Ribbentrop played an ominous rôle in organizing, planning and concealing these crimes. In the beginning period of the persecution of the Jewish people, from about 1938 to 1940, when mainly the Jews living in Germany were being expropriated, expelled and eliminated, the Foreign Office was engaged in investigating, together with the Gestapo and the SD (Security Service), the question at what suitable time the Jews of foreign nationality living in Germany might be included in the persecutions. The Foreign Office was also placed in charge of promoting anti-Semitism abroad and covering up the atrocities of the fascists. In this way the truth about the terror wielded over the Jewish people was to be kept secret, and the growing hatred of fascism was to be restrained.

Two documents can be considered typical of the activity of the Foreign Office at that time. One of them is a memorandum of 25 January 1939 drawn up by

Wiehls, at that time head of the Foreign Office Economic Policy Department. It is concerned with the steps for expropriating the Jews and was distributed to all embassies and consulates. The second document is also a memorandum of 25 January 1939; its author is Legation Counsellor Schumburg of the "Special Branch Germany". It is called "The Jewish Question as a factor of foreign policy in 1938" and was also sent to all diplomatic representatives of fascist Germany. In the Schumburg memorandum the Foreign Office advocated such a "radical solution of the Jewish question" that even the Reich Security Main Office considered it to be "premature". (See Table 35)

THE PREPARATION OF THE WANNSEE CONFERENCE

In addition to the Reich Security Main Office the Foreign Office had a decisive part in planning and realizing the "final solution of the Jewish question", and it played an essential rôle when the Wannsee conference of 20 January 1942 was being prepared.

At the end of 1941 the Germany Department drafted the *"views of the Foreign Office on the total solution of the Jewish question"* for a conference with Heydrich. On 4 December 1941 the head of the "Special Branch Germany", Luther, drew up the notorious eight-point program which figured prominently at the Wannsee conference. This program contained, among other demands, a call to expel the Jews of various nationalities from Germany and various European countries and destroy them. Point 8 of this program says: *"These measures to be carried out in full accord with the Gestapo."* (Document Centre, State Archives Administration of the GDR, No. 42,550)

Only a short time later, on 23 December 1941, the legal department of the Foreign Office – also for the preparations for the Wannsee conference – provided an expert opinion. Among other measures it suggested the procedure of concluding bilateral agreements with the states from which the Jews were to be deported. This was the course actually followed. Heydrich, who as the head of the Sipo (security police) and the SD (security service) explained the program of the "final solution", pointed out the new tasks of the Wilhelmstrasse diplomats:

"In the course of this final solution of the European Jewish question there were about 11 million Jews to be considered, of whom only 131,800 lived in the original territory of the German Reich, 43,700 in Austria and 74,200 in the Protectorate of Bohemia and Moravia.

"In the course of the final solution the Jews were to be sent to work in the East under proper supervision and in a suitable way, i.e., in large labour columns with the sexes being separated. Without any doubt a large part of them would be eliminated by natural processes; the survivors would have to be treated accordingly

since they were to be regarded as the germ cells of a Jewish regeneration if they were freed.

"It was also intended to have the Foreign Office contact the competent representatives of the security police and the security service with regard to handling the final solution in the European territories occupied by Germany or subjected to its influence. Heydrich went on to say that the problem no longer presents any great difficulties in Slovakia and Croatia; Rumania had also appointed a special commissioner for Jewish questions, and in order to settle the question in Hungary it would be required in a very short time to force an adviser for Jewish questions upon the Hungarian government. Then Heydrich discussed the problem of the Jewish question in Italy and France." (NG, Case XI, Vol. CCXLII, p. 27,842)

It follows, therefore, that the diplomats of the Foreign Office were commissioned with forcing agreement by the "allied" or vassal states, e.g., Hungary, Rumania, Slovakia, so that Eichmann's SS commandos could deport and liquidate the Jewish people living in these countries. The Foreign Office was to follow a similar line in the occupied territories. The Ribbentrop diplomats were to create the prerequisites for the Gestapo to proceed with the "final solution of the Jewish question" in the various European countries. Without the activity of the Ribbentrop diplomats the criminal ferocity of the SS commandos engaged in deportations and extermination would not have been possible to this extent.

If the participation of nazi diplomats in the "final solution" was often not as conspicuous to the outside world as were the Eichmann commandos this is not because they bore less responsibility but simply because they were assigned different tasks in a division of labour with the Gestapo.

HAND IN HAND WITH EICHMANN

In practice the collaboration between the Gestapo and diplomats often took the form of Eichmann and the Gestapo asking for the "agreement" of the Foreign Office before deportations took place. Thus Eichmann informed the Foreign Office on 9 March 1942 of an impending plan to transport to Auschwitz 1,000 French and stateless Jews who had been arrested in France in 1941. He asked if there were any objections to be considered. On 11 March the Reich Security Main Office again informed the Ribbentrop Office that another 5,000 French Jews were intended to be sent to Auschwitz with this transport. Neither the embassy in Paris nor the Foreign Office, as the reply of 20 March shows, "raised the slightest objection".

Many staff members of the Foreign Office were given precisely outlined tasks in the "final solution". Dr. Ernst-Günther Mohr, for example, as one of the closest assistants of Ambassador Bene participated in the extermination operations against the Jewish people living in the Netherlands. (Mohr is today the ambassador of the Federal Republic in Argentina.)

In Hungary the government had up to 1944 managed to prevent the deportation of Jews. On the instruction of the Foreign Office Ambassador Veesenmayr – who in a special report had submitted appropriate suggestions – thereupon installed a new Hungarian government in March 1944. This government then yielded to German requests. The following collaboration between the Foreign Office and the Reich Security Main Office was particularly close. Group leader Winkelmann, whom Himmler had charged with liquidating the Hungarian Jews, was placed under Veesenmayr. And Eichmann, who was partly directing the forced deportations from Budapest himself, used his influence to prevent Hezinger, then consular secretary first class, who for a time was employed at the German embassy in Budapest, from being transferred to some other post. Hezinger, he stated, was "indispensable" for matters concerning deportations. Of the some 400,000 Hungarian Jews about 200,000 were murdered within a few months. At this point it should be noted that Hezinger, too, entered the Bonn diplomatic service. In 1957, for example, he was employed in the Foreign Office as a consular secretary.

In many cases the Ribbentrop diplomats prevented Jews from saving themselves from the terror. At the end of 1943 Hitler's Wehrmacht occupied the French territory that until then had been placed under Italian rule. Eichmann learned that 15,000 Jews were hiding in the mountains of the Principality of Monaco. The Foreign Office thereupon ordered its consul on 23 September 1943 to find out the hiding places of these Jewish people and secure admittance to this region for the German security police.

When in September 1943 a large group of Greek Jews from Salonika succeeded in crossing the Italian demarcation line the Foreign Office in this case, too, did everything in its power to have them handed over to the SS.

It is a gross falsification of historical truth when some diplomats of the German Foreign Office claimed after the war that the persecution of the Jews had been exclusively in the hands of the "Special Branch Germany" headed by Luther, later by Rademacher, and the so-called "SA ambassadors" – as Ambassadors Killinger (Bucharest), Ludin (Bratislava), Kasche (Croatia) and Beckerle (Sofia), who had entered the diplomatic service as members of the SA leadership, were called. Almost all departments and diplomats of the Ribbentrop Office had been entrusted with the "final solution of the Jewish question":

in the Foreign Office it was the "Germany" Department headed by Luther, later by Rademacher (the department grew out of the "Special Branch Germany" after the Wannsee conference);

the Inland II Group headed by Wagner and von Thadden;

the information centre XIV ("Anti-Jewish Action") headed by Schleier, with

Granow and later with Hezinger acting as general secretary, and with members of the commercial, cultural, radio-political and press departments delegated to it;

the national experts in the Ribbentrop Bureau, e.g., Dr. Strack with Dr. Schwarzmann as his predecessor, for France and the country divisions of the Political Department, e.g., Dr. Heinburg, later Dr. Werkmeister, for South-East Europe, Dr. Grundherr for Scandinavia, etc. All these persons named here placed their experience at the service of the Bonn Foreign Office after 1945: Dr. Strack is still employed as reporting legation counsellor first class, Dr. Schwarzmann heads the "Berlin office". Heinburg, Grundherr and Werkmeister have for years been employed in leading positions of the Bonn Foreign Office – until a short time ago Werkmeister was ambassador in Sweden – although the GDR has for years been publishing documentary evidence against them. After retiring they enjoy high pensions.

Attention must also be drawn to the ambassadors, their deputies, the senior staff of the embassies, the officials in charge of nationality or Jewish affairs who were subordinated to Inland II Group, the police attachés, some of whom, as in Bucharest, were also in charge of Jewish affairs, and there were also the officials in charge of cultural affairs, who worked closely together with those in charge of Jewish affairs and often acted as their deputies in their absence.

Moreover, the separate departments and staff members were given various jobs in the "final solution". Inland II Group, information centre XIV and the department in charge of cultural-political affairs prepared, for example, the notorious Krummhübel conference which was held on 3 and 4 April 1944 by the Reich Security Main Office and the Foreign Office together with all embassy officials in charge of Jewish affairs. Legation Counsellor von Thadden (Inland II Group) and SS Hauptsturmführer Dr. Ballensiefen of the Reich Security Main Office submitted reports on the "state of anti-Jewish executive measures". The third main report was given by the head of the department for cultural-political affairs, ambassador and SS Brigadeführer Dr. Six. Among those who took part in the conference were also the representatives of the departments for commercial policy, radio policy and cultural policy affairs and of the press department.

The legal department of the Foreign Office not only drew up an expert opinion on the "best" possibilities for the "final solution" but also acted in other cases. After, for example, the routine notifications on the death of Dutch Jews in German concentration camps had been sent out to the Netherlands in conspicuous numbers and Sweden as the protective power acting for the Netherlands protested and insisted on an investigation, the legal department took up this "case" and searched for ways out. Following a suggestion of the legal department it was finally decided to stop sending any notifications at all. The result was that Swedish protests, too, came to an end.

The same applies to the Foreign Office department in charge of commercial or economic policy affairs. There was constant activity concerned with settling questions connected with the property of the deported and executed Jewish people of foreign nationality.

INTRIGUE WITH 7,000 JEWISH CHILDREN

There were finally important problems that were at least known to the departments involved or were solved in collaboration. This applies to an abominable play of intrigue with the lives of 7,000 Rumanian Jewish children.

In response to a British offer – and with the consent of the Rumanians – the children were to be given permission to emigrate. In order to defeat this offer but utilize it nevertheless for propaganda purposes Inland II Group, the departments in charge of political, cultural policy and radio policy affairs and the press and legal departments cooperated closely in a combined effort for many weeks with the aim of finding a suitable provocative reply. In collaboration with von Thadden, Wagner, Killinger and Eichmann the following persons participated in this action: Heinburg as the nationality expert of the political department, Henke and von Erdmannsdorf as responsible representatives of the political department, Albrecht from the legal department, von Mirbach as the personal assistant of State Secretary von Steengracht, Rühle from the radio policy department and Sonnleithner from the Ribbentrop Bureau. (Von Mirbach has for years been employed as a special envoy of Federal Foreign Minister Schröder and is to be appointed ambassador in India in the near future!) These proceedings were especially mentioned when judgment was passed in the Wilhelmstrasse trial:

"... the Foreign Office and its state secretary were at least offered one opportunity of employing their advice for good and not for evil; here they might have pointed out that it would contribute to improving Germany's foreign relations and reestablishing its prestige in the world if they allowed at least the children to be saved from extermination. But all the steps taken by the Foreign Office, all the advice given were aimed at defeating the efforts of respected neutral and hostile countries to have the children handed over to them; the work of the good Samaritans was to be frustrated, their offer was to be twisted into nazi propaganda." (NG, Case XI, Vol. CCXLIII, p. 27,893)

DREW UP DEATH LISTS

There is a whole chain of further crimes the Ribbentrop diplomats committed in exercising their rule of terror over the various European peoples, particularly in the temporarily occupied territories. In the system of terror the Foreign Office, its departments and staff members had been assigned clearly defined jobs. They were responsible, above all, for suppressing every patriotic, democratic stir, every resistance to the fascist rule of terror. In this respect, too, the so-called Plenipotentiaries of the Reich, the Foreign Office Representatives (VAA) at the various authorities, for example at the "government of the generalgouvernment" collaborated closely with the commanders of the security police and the security service, the commandos of the Gestapo and with the military commanders.

A clearly defined circle of Foreign Office members was regularly informed on the mass murders committed by the notorious special SD commandos. The lists containing the names of thousands who had been arrested, sent to the concentration camps or murdered were usually drawn up in cooperation between the Gestapo, SD and fascist diplomats. The diplomats were also kept informed on the results of such actions. Dozens of murder lists went through their hands and were passed on to the Ribbentrop Bureau and the competent country departments. (See Table 36)

GESTAPO TERROR WAS TOO MILD FOR THEM

Very often the members of the Foreign Office are found to have acted as instigators. Thus at the end of 1942 Auer, at that time consul in Algeria (West German ambassador in Ceylon until 1964), sent his "personal opinion" to the Foreign Office:

"The military victory over France must still be completed by the moral defeat of the French in the occupied territory. It is only by such coercive measures that the anti-German attitude . . . would be associated with fear; the French authorities would be mentally forced to accept and acknowledge defeat, and only thus the necessary respect for demands and directions of the German authorities . . . would be obtained." (German Central Archive, Potsdam, under Auswärtiges Amt, No. 61, 134)

At a time when the collapse of Hitler Germany was obvious to everybody and the peoples in the liberated territories were bringing traitors to trial in regular courts, the legel department of the Foreign Office, under the direction of Albrecht, and the political department (including the country departments) were trying to have patriots from occupied countries who were still in German custody executed. These reprisals were intended to prevent pro-fascist collaborators and war criminals from being brought to justice.

On 22 December 1944 department Pol II in an express letter signed by Steengracht and sent to the Reich Security Main Office and other fascist authorities asked to start proceedings *"which would have to end with severe sentences"*, against Gaullist prisoners and to revoke the reprieves granted to some French patriots who had been sentenced to death. (See Table 37)

"PURPOSEFUL" AND "TRUSTFUL"

We can only mention some of the more significant of the other forms and methods that developed in – as a record of the "Germany" department dated from 8 August 1940 phrases it – "purposeful, close and trustful collaboration" between the Ribbentrop diplomats, the Gestapo and the SD:

Entire companies of SS officers with "special assignments" were temporarily built into the Foreign Service – usually for espionage and sabotage activities and for setting up fifth columns. In a top secret communication the Foreign Office is informed by the Reich Security Main Office, Department VI, on 6 August 1943 that "developments" require the "increased employment of members" of the Reich Security Main Office in the diplomatic representations, particularly in the "still neutral countries". The communication contains detailed instructions in what diplomatic disguise the SD members were to work at the various representations abroad – e.g., in Bern, Geneva, Milan. SS Sturmbannführer Elling, for example, had been chosen for the German embassy at the Vatican, and SS Sturmbannführer Dr. Haas for the Quirinal.

SS officers were taken into the diplomatic service as scientific assistants (WHA). A large number of them were given permanent jobs after their special tasks had been fulfilled and usually they received the diplomatic rank connected with them. In most cases the SS officers, according to their "merits", were made legation secretaries or legation counsellors.

Many Ribbentrop diplomats sent direct reports to the SD or Gestapo. At the Foreign Office postal bureau in the Wilhelmstrasse there was a daily flow of letters from various diplomats for the "Head of the Sipo and SD", e.g., from Lanwer, at that time consul in Aabenraa (Denmark). (See Table 38) Today Lanwer is head of the Bonn Foreign Office department in charge of development policy.

The staff of a large number of diplomatic representations was increased by so-called police attachés. These people were particularly "reliable" agents of the Reich Security Main Office who were subordinated to Himmler as well as the chef de mission or the Foreign Office. Whole lists are still in existence of SS officers who were employed as police attachés, and they were presented as "diplomats" including the names of, among others, such notorious murderers of the Jewish people as SS Sturmbannführer Adolf Hoffmann and SS Hauptsturmführer Dannecker, Wisliceny and Richter.

There were many actions leading to an institutional, organizational interdependence exceeding the framework of mere close collaboration. Thus SS Brigadeführer Dr. Six, head of Department VI of the Reich Security Main Office was in 1943 put in charge of the cultural policy department of the Foreign Office, with the rank of ambassador. This department was – as has been stated above – one of the co-organizers of the Krummhübel conference in 1944.

UNSCRUPULOUS PLUNDERERS

The Ribbentrop diplomats played a decisive part in the robberies of the oppressed peoples and in the exploitation of forced labourers. They created the prerequisites for the crimes, initiated corresponding steps or at least countenanced them.

The "Commercial Policy Committee" (HPA), that central and interministerial directing body established by the nazis as an instrument of the systematic plundering of foreign peoples – for the last two years even "allied" Italy – was directed by nazi diplomats, i.e., by the head of the Foreign Office department in charge of commercial policy affairs, Wiehl, and his deputy Clodius. For some time the meetings of this HPA were attended by such Ribbentrop diplomats as Eberl (today Bonn's ambassador in Uruguay), Schlitter (today Bonn's ambassador in Greece, until then in charge of contract negotiations in the West German Foreign Office, Commercial Policy Department), Junker (today Bonn's ambassador in South Africa), and Schwarzmann (today head of the "West Berlin office" of the Bonn Foreign Office. (See Table 39)

The delegation in charge of economic questions which was attached to the German armistice commission and which played a special rôle in plundering France, was headed by a representative of the Foreign Office, Hans-Richard Hemmen and other nazi diplomats. A large number of nazi diplomats was, moreover, engaged in executing direct orders of German monopolies to secure for them as large a part of the booty as possible. There was, for example, a prolonged attempt by Legation Secretary Lüders of the commercial policy department to have the Shell plants in the Netherlands made the property of IG-Farben. Today Lüders is a counsellor of the embassy at the West German embassy in India.

An abundance of documentary material clearly proves that the Wilhelmstrasse diplomats had a sinister part in planning, preparing and carrying out imperialist aggressive power politics. The attempt to justify themselves by declaring that only the diplomats of the Foreign Office Germany Department, who had been delegated by the SS and SA, together with the "SA ambassadors", had done the "dirty work" simply does not stand up to reality in any case. Almost all diplomats, departments and representations abroad are responsible either directly as originators or at least as abettors of the crimes committed by the Hitler regime.

It is an aggravating fact that the Ribbentrop diplomats – in drastic contrast to their well-arranged and adapted statements before the Nuremberg Tribunal – were among the best-informed civil servants of the fascist system. They were fully able to grasp the full consequences of their criminal activity, as shown in the Wilhelmstrasse trial. They are *"experienced in evaluating political events and in ascertaining the motives governing the actions of parties, civil servants and entire nations; they are masters in the art of reading between the lines of papers apparently written in innocent, moderate language and to find out their real significance concealed by their phrases."* (NG, Vol. CCXLII, p. 27,829)

Thus the Ribbentrop diplomats met all wishes with regard to the rôle they were expected to play. They made the Wilhelmstrasse Office an instrument of fascist leadership that was ready at all times to plan and carry out criminal programs and actions, and which even went beyond these requirements and searched for and found improved ways of attempting to realize the aims of German imperialism to dominate the world.

The Supporters of the Aggressive Bonn Foreign Policy

In contrast to the unanimous demand of the peoples and the judgment passed in Nuremberg the nazi and war criminals, including the Wilhelmstrasse diplomats, have not been brought to justice in West Germany. On the contrary – to the extent that imperialism and militarism regained their power and directed their policy at reversing the results of the Second World War and preparing a new aggressive war the former nazi diplomats have again been employed in the Foreign Service of the Federal Republic. Step by step they took over the key foreign policy positions. Thus the dangerous and at the same time grotesque state of affairs has been reached in which former nazi diplomats act as representatives of the Federal Republic in those countries whose conquest, oppression and pillage they once helped to plan and bring about.

In the German Democratic Republic not a single nazi diplomat has been installed in the service of the Ministry of Foreign Affairs of the GDR. This institution is under the direction of consistent anti-fascists and democrats. The GDR has repeatedly warned against the re-employment of Ribbentrop diplomats in the Foreign Service of the Bonn government. In March 1959 the Committee for German Unity submitted factual material concerning the fascist past of more than 80 leading West German diplomats. In September 1961 the Ministry of Foreign Affairs of the GDR in a collection of documents "Von Ribbentrop bis Adenauer" proved the re-employment of more than 180 nazi diplomats in the Bonn Foreign Service and verified this monstrous fact with an abundance of documentary material.

520 NAZI DIPLOMATS IN THE FOREIGN OFFICE

Instead of dismissing from the civil service those who are accomplices in the nazi crimes and punishing them justly, the experts of war criminal Ribbentrop were more and more purposely moved into the key positions of the Bonn foreign policy institutions. The archive material that has been studied so far provides records of the activity of more than 520 former nazi diplomats who have again been appointed to leading positions in the Bonn Foreign Office, including faithful officials of the fascist state apparatus. More than 30 former Ribbentrop diplomats or other leading nazis occupy top positions as heads of departments or sections or as their deputies.

One of the most influential people in the Bonn Foreign Office is the former SA Rottenführer Rolf Lahr, at present state secretary. Lahr, a member of the nazi party since April 1933, was a government counsellor in the fascist Reich Ministry of Economic Affairs from 1934 up to the end of the war and played an ignoble rôle in the exploitation of such so-called allied states as Hungary and Italy in favour of fascist war production. In cooperation with the economic policy department of the Ribbentrop Office he forced, for example, the Hungarian government in 1941–42 to supply bauxite needed for the fascist war effort to the nazi Reich at a price comparable only to robbery. (German Central Archive, Potsdam, under Auswärtiges Amt, No. 67, 916). Later he was one of the body of nazi experts who prepared the economic pillage of Iraq in case the planned subjugation and colonization of the Arab states could be carried out. Thus Lahr acquired the "experience" that today makes him the exponent of the neo-colonalist Bonn "development policy". Among these nazi diplomats is also the former state secretary in the Federal Presidential Office, Dr. Hans Herwarth von Bittenfeld, who is now ambassador in Rome. After serving Ribbentrop as a diplomat until 1941 he became a training and supervising officer in the notorious Vlassov army and took part in predatory campaigns in the Soviet Union and in atrocities against members of the Soviet army. He was employed as a government director in the Bavarian State Chancellery after 1945; having been appointed a ministerial director in the Bonn Foreign Office in 1950 he was one of the key persons who organized the nomination of nazi diplomats for the leading positions of this office.

One of the top diplomats of the Bonn Foreign Office is, for example, von Mirbach, special envoy of Federal Foreign Minister Schröder. He was the personal assistant of State Secretary von Steengracht, who was sentenced in the Wilhelmstrasse trial, and is an accomplice to countless crimes. His predecessor – as special envoy at the disposal of the federal minister – was Granow, under Ribbentrop the right-hand man of Ambassador von Grobba in preparing the aggression against the Arab states and for some time also general secretary of information centre XIV ("Anti-Jewish Action"). He retired in 1964.

GESTAPO AGENTS HEAD THE EASTERN DEPARTMENT

Franz Krapf, head of the Eastern Department of the Bonn Foreign Office, was one of the Ribbentrop diplomats who established particularly close collaboration with the SD. He was an SS Untersturmführer. In the files there is a note of an SD agent concerning the expansion of the so-called Railway Publicity Centre and its "branch" in Japan – a camouflage name for the centre which the SD had set up to carry out espionage and "special functions" in Japan – which says about Krapf:

"On 24 March 1941 the undersigned was invited to talks between SS Sturmbannführer Finke, SS Obersturmführer Winter, head of the Railway Publicity Centre and Dr. Jörn Leo, head of the Tokyo branch of the Railway Publicity Centre . . . It is intended to place Dr. Leo in charge of coordinating the intelligence network in Japan . . . Dr. Leo will get into contact with the following persons: SS Untersturmführer Franz Krapf, attaché at the German embassy in Japan. As an unpaid associate of former central department III/1 K. had at one time been introduced to SS Sturmbannführer von Vietinghoff-Scheel but has not yet been asked to cooperate. As his personal record is not kept in our local files it was only now that he attracted the attention of the Referent VI C 3. Krapf will receive a written notification by courier post."

One of the diplomats who initiated the "transfer" of Krapf to Tokyo was Hilmar Bassler, at that time legation secretary and in the Foreign Office Press Department (P VIII) in charge of fascist propaganda in East Asia. On 27 April 1940, he wrote to Krapf: *"Dear Mr. Krapf, A couple of lines to tell you that our plan to send you to Tokyo seems to be successful. Kempe phoned me yesterday and informed me – though still privately – of the intention of the personnel department. My most hearty congratulations! Let's keep this matter between ourselves, however! Ambassador Ott has been informed by me. Heil Hitler! Yours, (signed) Bassler."*

Today Bassler is also one of the key figures in the Bonn Foreign Office East Department, and as the deputy head of the East Asia section he is one of Krapf's closest assistants. Before 1945 he was one of the confidential agents of the SD and of Department IV (Gestapo) in the Reich Security Main Office. The Gestapo turned to him with numerous inquiries and orders. This was also the case in December 1940 when the Reich Security Main Office, Department IV, B 4a, asked for his opinion on enterprises in China. In other cases Bassler acted as "mediator" to establish contact with the Reich Security Main Office:

"Ref. P VIII *Berlin, 3 August 1943*
Bassler
Notice!

In the case of Fräulein Lee there is no chance of a reply at present as general air raid precautions have resulted in the records and files being moved to some unknown place. The competent person is Police Captain Kettenhofer in the Reich Security Main Office, Wrangelstrasse 6/7, Berlin-Steglitz. You are recommended to contact him directly under the catchword 'Schutzhaftsache Lee' ('Protective custody Lee'). This to inform Herr von Studnitz."

Bassler was one of those fanatics who enthusiastically cheered the attack on the Soviet Union. Even when the military defeat of Hitler Germany had already become discernible he was still drivelling about "resoluteness", about "seeing it through", etc. On 9 October 1941 he wrote in a letter to Count von Mirbach, at that time press attaché at the German embassy in Japan:

"At the end of this week I shall go to the Russian front and I am especially happy about it. Here in the homeland our enormous military successes have had a particularly lasting effect, and I can only say that never before have the coherence and unity in our conception on the further course of the war and confidence in the final victory been as distinct and clear as they are just now."

To his former close assistant Breuer, who is at present embassy counsellor in the Bonn embassy in Madrid and had meanwhile – also on the initiative of Bassler – been transferred to Tokyo to work under Mirbach he wrote on 25 November 1942:

"We are in an absolutely determined mood. Everybody knows that the final struggle will be hard but that there is no other way for us than seeing it through whatever the cost. The internal situation in Germany is being completely misjudged by the allies, particularly the Americans. An internal collapse is wholly unthinkable." (German Central Archive, Potsdam, under Auswärtiges Amt, No. 58,320)

In another place Bassler confirms in this letter that he knew the real objective of the so-called Railway Publicity Centre: *"I have not seen the films myself but I hope you will enjoy them. Some of them are from the Railway Publicity Centre."* (op.cit.)

Another key position in the Bonn Foreign Office East Department is occupied by one of those diplomats who once entered the service in Wilhelmstrasse on behalf of the Reich Security Main Office: Hans Schirmer, today head of the "Near East" section, reporting legation counsellor first class, former SS Obersturmführer. Schirmer started work in the Foreign Office in 1939, that is he began, like almost all SS officers who joined on special orders, as a scientific assistant. As a "diplomat" and SS Obersturmführer he was then, on orders of the Reich Security Main Office, employed in Croatia and was decorated with the Knight's Cross for his "services". (See Table 39)

As was usual with SS "diplomats" Schirmer was then permanently admitted into the Ribbentrop Office staff with the rank of legation counsellor. In the radio policy department (Ru VII – Near East) he was one of the circle of persons who had to prepare the "Arab region" politically and ideologically for the forcible colonization by the Hitler regime.

Dr. Bock, legation counsellor first class, and Krafft von Dellmensingen, reporting legation counsellor first class, (section "Poland, Czechoslovakia, Yugoslavia, Hungary", etc.) are other former active nazi diplomats who belong to the leading cadres that decide West Germany's "East Policy" and are among the confidants of Krapf.

The example of this department makes it sufficiently clear that the former nazi diplomats constitute the decisive force in the Bonn Foreign Office. Even the former relations between the individual members, above all the SS and SD agents in the Ribbentrop Office, remained in part unchanged.

They Represent Bonn Abroad

The decisive influence of the Ribbentrop diplomats can be seen even more clearly when the appointments for the representations of the Federal Republic abroad are examined. No less than 60 ambassadors extraordinary and plenipotentiary (and heads of diplomatic missions in international institutions with the rank of ambassador) are former nazi diplomats.

Fifteen out of the 25 foreign representations of the Federal Republic in Asia are headed by ambassadors extraordinary and plenipotentiary who proved their reliability in the service of the Hitler regime, among them Dr. Luitpold Werz, today ambassador in Indonesia, Ferring, today ambassador in South Korea, Dr. Böhling, today ambassador in Malaysia, Dr. Munzel, until now ambassador in Lebanon, and the former SS Untersturmführer Dr. Schmidt-Horix, until now ambassador in Iraq. At the West German embassy in India not only Counsellor of the Embassy Lüders but also the heads of the most important consulates-general – Dr. Heinrich Köhler in Bombay and Elgar von Randow in Calcutta – are former Ribbentrop diplomats.

Sixteen out of the 21 foreign representations in Latin America are headed by former nazi diplomats as ambassadors extraordinary and plenipotentiary. Among them are such an inveterate anti-Semite as the ambassador in Argentina, Dr. Ernst-Günther Mohr, and the ambassador in Peru, Dr. Northe. In 1940 Northe denounced the daughter-in-law of a German diplomat in a written statement to the local nazi party leader Wobser, who today is also employed in the Bonn diplomatic service, because she had made "anti-nazi" remarks. The present ambassador of Bonn in Brazil, Dr. Seelos, was in 1939 consul in Lemberg and engaged in espionage to prepare the Second World War, working in close collaboration with Heyden-Rynsch, at that time head of the Foreign Office Secret Service Branch. The present Bonn ambassador in Chile, Dr. von Nostiz, was for some time employed as the representative of Heyden-Rynsch in the Ribbentrop Office. Former SS Obersturmführer Dr. Georg Vogel is ambassador in Venezuela. Dr. Günter Motz, a man in whose opinion only those "devoted to national socialism may be officials and who was himself employed in the fascist Reich Ministry of the Interior, is today ambassador in Bolivia.

There are – according to the results of investigations up to now – ten former nazi diplomats serving in Africa. Bonn even chooses its representatives at international or supra-national organizations from the group of former Ribbentrop diplomats, for example, Sigismund von Braun at the UN, Dr. Rupprecht von Keller at the UN European Bureau, Dr. Grewe (who before 1945 was actively engaged in "East Research") and Dr. Sahm at the NATO.

If, in addition to the ambassadors the top embassy personnel are also taken into consideration – i.e., the deputy heads of embassies, the most important attachés and the first secretaries – the result is that more than 40 further representations abroad of the West German Federal Republic have former nazi diplomats in leading positions. Of about 120 West German representations abroad there remains scarcely a dozen which are not under the decisive influence of nazi diplomats.

Mohr, E. Günther NAZI PROPAGANDIST AND SPY

today: *Ambassador extraordinary and plenipotentiary in Argentina.*

During his service as a legation secretary in the Peking embassy Dr. Mohr was one of the "political leaders" of the Peping local nazi party group. Here he was extraordinarily active as a nazi propagandist and in distributing anti-Jewish concoctions. Some years later, as a legation counsellor in The Hague (Netherlands), he participated, together with Ambassodor Bene, his superior, in the deportation of Jews. On one action 600 Jews were sent to the concentration camps. Only a few of them survived. (See Table 40)

Mohr was actively engaged in espionage, particularly at the time (1943) when he was stationed at the Tangier consulate. This concerns the "neutral" Tangier Zone occupied by Spain, which became the centre of fascist espionage and sabotage activity in the western Mediterranean region after the fascists had been driven out of North Africa. (See Table 40)

On the basis of this evidence it is small wonder that Mohr was one of those "hold out" propagandists who still went on drivelling of "successful defence", intended "large-scale counterattacks, etc., even only a few weeks before the final defeat of fascism. At that time Mohr had advanced to the position of head of special branch Pol. I M in the Foreign Office, was in cooperation with the attaché department of the OKW (Supreme Command) responsible for the appointment of military attachés, and prescribed the "language regulations" they were to use in describing the military situation.

Schwarzmann Hans RIBBENTROP'S CONFIDANT

today: Head of the West Berlin Bureau of the Bonn Foreign Office.

Dr. Schwarzmann was employed as legation secretary in the Ribbentrop Bureau until 1942. He was in charge of contacts between Ribbentrop and the notorious nazi ambassador in Paris, Abetz. In this capacity he participated in reprisals and the execution of hostages, which the fascists carried out in France at that time.

Schwarzmann, who closely collaborated with the Reich Security Main Office, was also involved in the preparation of measures to deport and liquidate Jews living in France. A memorandum concerning procedure of which Dr. Schwarzmann, Bureau RAM (Reich Foreign Minister Ribbentrop) was in charge:

"3. On the question of establishing a central Jewish Office for France Darlan has indicated that he is prepared to place such an institution under the authority of the French government; he pointed out, however, that there is a great vacillation in the attitude of Marshal Pétain with regard to the Jewish question ... In spite of this attitude of Pétain, which does not justify any expectations of a high degree of activity of a Jewish Office that has been established by the French government it is recommended to have it instituted by the French authorities. The central Jewish Office is thus given a legally valid basis, and it can be activated by German influence in the occupied territory in a way that forces the unoccupied territory to follow suit in the steps taken." (NG, Case XI, Vol. CCXXIII, p. 139)

As an "expert on French problems" Schwarzmann had an active part in the commercial policy department of the Foreign Office in plundering France. This is proved, among other evidence by the minutes kept at a meeting of 29 July 1941:

"WHA 806 — *Strictly confidential!*

In oral and written communication with private people the commercial policy committee is not to be mentioned and its decisions are not to be referred to.

Commercial Policy Committee, meeting of 29 July 1941:
No. 26

Present:	*Ministerial Director Wiehl*
Foreign Office:	*Reporting Legation Counsellor Dumont*
	Reporting Legation Counsellor Sabath
	Legation Secretary Schwarzmann

Commissioner for the Four-year Plan:	*Ministerial Director Gramsch*
Supreme Command of the Wehrmacht, Wehrmacht budget:	*Ministerial Director Tischbein* *Chief Commissary Teichert*
Supreme Command of the Wehrmacht, Armament Economy Office:	*Major General Becker*
Supreme Command of the Wehrmacht, Wehrmacht Administration:	*Government Counsellor Grams*
Reich Ministry of Economic Affairs:	*Ministerial Counsellor Schultze-Schlutius* *Government Counsellor Dr. Joerges"*

One of the subjects of this meeting, which was also attended by representatives of the Reichsbank and the Ministry of Finance, was the theft of Poland's gold deposited in France.

Nüsslein Franz

FAVOURITE OF BORMANN AND HEYDRICH

today: consul-general in Barcelona.

Dr. Nüsslein was one of those nazi hanging judges who because of their brutality in sentencing Czechoslovak patriots enjoyed the special favour of SD chief Heydrich and nazi Reichsleiter Bormann. When Czechoslovakia was occupied he was a public prosecutor first in Brno, then in Prague, and exerted himself to pass a large number of death sentences against Czechoslovak citizens. He very quickly advanced into the circle of hanging judges who possessed the particular confidence of Heydrich, deputy of the Reich protector. Heydrich praised his "capacity of understanding the necessity of determined action" against upright Czechoslovak citizens. Using this reference Bormann, acting from the Führer's Headquarters, took personal care to have Nüsslein promoted to senior public prosecutor as a special favour. (*Von Ribbentrop bis Adenauer*, Berlin, 1961)

Altogether he is guilty of the murder of more than 900 Czechoslovak patriots.

Sentenced to 20 years in jail in Czechoslovakia he was handed over to the Federal Republic in 1955 as a non-amnestied war criminal. His "old friends", who meanwhile had been put in charge of selecting the Bonn Foreign Office staff, provided a spectular career for the Bormann-Heydrich favourite: He was treated as a "Spätheimkehrer" (a term generally used for war criminals handed over to the Federal Republic in the mid-nineteen-fifties) and before being appointed to a post in Spain he was head of a branch of the Bonn Foreign Office personnel department!

Melchers Wilhelm **SPECIALIST ON FIFTH COLUMNS**

until end of 1964: *Ambassador in Greece, since then adviser and pensioner.*

Melchers was one of those Ribbentrop diplomats who were mainly engaged in "deposing and installing" governments in the states of the Near and Middle East. As head of department Pol VII ("Middle East") he developed plans to overthrow the neutral government of Afghanistan – where a German embassy existed – and bring a pro-fascist government to power:

*"Copy
Record:*

*Geheime Reichssache!
(Top secret!)*

1. Operation Afghanistan

It is planned to overthrow the present British-dependent government of Mohamed Hashim Khan and reinstate Amanullah.
Object:
Gaining a base for operations of every kind against India. Binding British armed forces. Support for the insurrection movement in Waziristan.
Execution:
Ghulam Siddi Khan, former foreign minister and closest confidant of Amanullah, draws up the following plan in agreement with the king . . .

2. Operation Tibet

It is planned to send SS Hauptsturmführer Dr. Schäfer, who has already been to Tibet three times and has only in July come back from his last research excursion, to Tibet with a small group of about 30 men and with arms sufficient to equip from 1,000 up to 2,000 men. Using his connections he is to . . ." (German Central Archive, Potsdam, under Auswärtiges Amt, No. 61,179)

As a confidant of the Reich Security Main Office Melchers participated in the creation of fifth columns and assisted in preparing the military occupation and political colonization of the Arab states. A document of 16 September 1943 says: *"Yesterday SS Hauptsturmführer Schuback from Department VI of the Reich Security Main Office and Lieutenant Commander Schüler from counter-intelligence I called on me one after another. The two gentlemen had discussions with me on the situation in Iran. It resulted from the discussions that three German centres of action have been formed in Iran . . ." (op.cit. No. 61,138)*

In another letter Melchers notifies the consulate general in Istanbul of three fascist agents:

"Copy as draft — *Berlin, 2 June 1943*
____schrift 1b (KZ) — *Geheime Reichssache!*
____: LR. Melchers — *(Top secret!)*
Pol VII 1033 gRE
Copy sent to the German consulate general in Istanbul by courier!
for information

The men concerned are three Iranian nationalists living in Berlin who work for OKW (Supreme Command), Counter-intelligence II. The Ghaschgai brothers are, as Captain Leverkuehn informs us, already known to the consulate general.

by direction (signed) Ref. Melchers" (op.cit.)

Melchers was also, together with the "von Grobba special staff" and "special staff F", one of the initiators of setting up the "German Orient Corps", the special unit that was prepared by General Felmy for conquering the "Arab region". (See Table 41)

What Melchers thought of the Arabs can be seen in his note for Woermann, in which Melchers on 16 November 1942 states his opinion of the situation in the Arab states:

"A feature not sufficiently pointed out is the lack of the powers of political judgment that is characteristic of the primitive Arab masses, who, with a very poor desert homeland, have developed, like almost no other people, besides many good qualities some characteristics that repel us, their cunning, greed, their passion for wealth and treasures (Arabian Nights) and the seeking for personal gain, because here wealth means power more than anywhere else. In these masses there is not much room for prospering love devoted to their country. The terms patriotism and nationalism have been imported from Europe. It would, therefore, be quite misleading to claim that the Arab tribes were inspired by their vision of uniting all Arab territories." (German Central Archive, Potsdam, under Auswärtiges Amt, No. 61,124)

Melchers was succeeded as West German ambassador in Greece by another Ribbentrop diplomat – Dr. Oskar Schlitter.

Schlitter Oskar JOINT ORGANIZER OF THE AGGRESSION AGAINST DENMARK

today: *Ambassador extraordinary and plenipotentiary in Greece.*

A few days before the malicious attack of the fascists on Denmark State Secretary v. Weizsäcker had a highly secret meeting with seven especially selected and particularly reliable officers and diplomats. The meeting took place on

6 April 1940 and was concerned with the final preparations for the aggression against neutral Denmark that had been decided for 9 April 1940. And in addition to State Secretary Gaus, Major General Himer, Lieutenant Colonel (general staff) Pohlmann, Lieutenant Colonel Boehme (from the OKW) and two other officials from the Wilhelmstrasse Office there was also Dr. Schlitter, at that time legation secretary, who belonged to this narrowly restricted and carefully checked circle. Travelling to Copenhagen a short time later he not only had the uniform of General Himer in his courier's luggage – Himer had already gone to Copenhagen as a "senior government counsellor" – but, above all, the secret orders of the nazi leadership for the preparation of the aggression.

Schlitter, since 1934 also a member of the nazi party, did not abuse the confidence his fascist superiors had in him. General Himer expressed his opinion that *"the operation had in every respect been exemplarily prepared. Secrecy as the prerequisite of success had been completely guaranteed. Knowledge of the operation had been limited to a group of persons which positively had to be informed." (NG, Case XI, Vol. CCCLXXIX, pp. 225–36)*

Just as he proved his "reliability" in this crime against international law Schlitter, who had been rapidly promoted to legation counsellor, continued his career. As a member of department Pol II he worked closely with Schwarzmann and Abetz, above all in intensifying the fascist terror in France, in the execution of hostages, etc. (German Central Archive, Potsdam, under Auswärtiges Amt, No. 61 113, 147)

It was Schlitter again who with Beckerle, the nazi ambassador in Sofia, took care to have Blondel, at that time French ambassador in Bulgaria, "who was married to a Jewess", removed from his post and replaced "by a reliable, pro-German person". (op.cit., No. 61 133, 115)

Later, as a member of the commercial policy department (for Italy) of the Ribbentrop Office he engaged – particularly within the scope of the commercial policy committee mentioned before – in the active economic pillage of "allied" Italy.

Obviously this was a sufficient motivation for the Bonn government to employ him for years, before he was appointed to go to Greece, as a ministerial director in the Bonn Foreign Office Commercial Policy Department in charge of contract negotiations.

Ferring Franz

GOEBBELS BRAGGART OF THE WORST KIND

today: Ambassador extraordinary and plenipotentiary in South Korea.

The members of the radio policy department of the Ribbentrop Office were among the most docile disciples of the war criminal and nazi propaganda minister. One of the worst swaggerers among them was Dr. Ferring, at that time legation secretary. Since 1941 he had been employed in the radio policy department as the expert for East Asia. He tried in the most primitive way to surpass his master and teacher in attempting to incite the East Asian peoples against the allied powers and glorify the fascist murder regime. Ferring's mentality is clearly shown in some excerpts from radio commentaries which he wrote himself and which have to a large extent been preserved in the files of the fascist Foreign Office.

In a speech on 8 January 1941 he declared:

"It seems that the plutocrats and imperialists of Britain have been afflicted by a failure of their memory caused by the constant pounding the German air force and navy are giving them, otherwise they would not have the impudence to claim they wanted to liberate the workers at a moment when on the one side the Indian workers' are carrying out the most strikes to free themselves from British imperialism and on the other side social ideas and the respect for the worker are in full flourish particularly in Germany and Italy, and when the workers here have been set free from imperialist oppression in the truest sense of the word."

And on 6 February 1941 Ferring announced, among other things:

"The Scottish mountains as the last refuge for the English. The last hour has struck for the British plutocracy and its world empire.

"Everybody who has listened to the speech of the Führer on the occasion of the eighth anniversary of the national socialist rise to power will see quite clearly what the year 1941 is going to bring to the British. May the Britons say whatever they like in their boastful propaganda speeches, which are at one time made for the Indians, another time for the American people, the last hour has struck for Britain."

In a speech on 1 February 1941 Ferring pronounced Hitler to be the "most popular and most powerful man in the world"!

And among other things Ferring declared on 10 February 1941:

"In reply to the epoch-making speech of the great Führer of the German people, Adolf Hitler, the main trespasser of the regime of the British, which is covered with war crimes, Churchill, also felt moved to make a counter speech. When one compares the great statesman-like tasks Hitler set himself with the frightened stammer of Churchill one cannot help thinking, for example, of a wrestling bout in the streets of Bombay, after which the beaten contestant tries to make the best of the lost fight by means of a terrible salvo of invectives. Churchill is frightened. He is quite obviously afraid, as the course of the war has shown with convincing clarity that neither propagandistic rhetoric nor insolent lies can stop Britain's fall.

"The new time with its revolutionary impulse overpowers the satiated plutocracies that have grown old but keep on believing that they can stop the advance.

The new ideas prevelant in economy and technique are expressed in the rise of the German Reich under Adolf Hitler." (German Central Archive, Potsdam, under Auswärtiges Amt, No. 48,007)

Grewe Wilhelm

"EASTERN RESEARCHER" AND "NEW ORDER THEORIST"

today: *Ambassador of the Federal Republic at NATO, Paris.*

Among the people who have had a substantial part in deciding the characteristic features of the Bonn Foreign Office and still continue making their mark on it is Professor Dr. Wilhelm Grewe. Before 1945 Grewe was one of the most important intellectual originators and representatives of the fascist policy of aggression and power. As a continuous contributor to a large number of prominent nazi periodicals he unrestrainedly glorified the violations of international law and the war crimes committed by the nazis.

Thus he wrote in the *Zeitschrift für die gesamte Staatswissenschaft* (Vol. 103):

"There is only one issue to be decided by the struggle, i.e., whether we are about to enter an 'American Century', with the United States taking charge of the world – or whether the resettlement of the world represented by the powers of the three-power pact will prevail."

And in 1940 Grewe issued the following call in the *Zeitschrift für Politik* (p. 233):

"Destruction of all Paris churches, palaces, theatres, hospitals, academies, conservatories, law court buildings, halls, triumphal arches, colonnades, the stock-exchange, the bank, the town hall and the bridges as a consequence of 'realistic thinking'."

The systematic and ruthless violation of all rules of international law was "justified" by Grewe in the *Monatsschriften für Auswärtige Politik* in September 1941:

"This war can no longer be considered to come in the categories of traditional law governing war and neutrality and suited to the national state war."

He extolled the criminal attack on the Soviet Union in the same journal (issue 1941, p. 749) with the following words:

"Nobody will want to assert that the decision of 22 June has not grown out of very real considerations. According to all historical experience the great missions of universal historic significance that develop beyond the stage of Utopian dreams and uncommitted planning have usually commenced in this way."

Although Grewe's intellectual authorship of both the war and nazi crimes of the Hitler Reich has repeatedly been revealed by the GDR (most recently in 1959 and 1961) he is still one of the most distinguished representatives of the Bonn

Foreign Office: In the foreign service since 1951 he directed the legal department from 1953 to 1955, then the political department of the Bonn Foreign Office. After that term of office he was in 1958 appointed West German ambassador in the USA, and in 1964 he finally became Bonn's representative at NATO in Paris. Can the aims and personnel policy of an office be more clearly revealed than by the employment of such a man in such key positions?

Etzdorf Hasso von

ACCOMPLICE OF THE ARMED SS

today: *Until a short time ago ambassador in Great Britain, now retired.*

Hasso von Etzdorf was from the time the war started (September 1939) until 1945 representative of the Foreign Office (VAA) at the Oberkommando des Heeres (Army Supreme Command). These liaison men were characterized by the court in the Wilhelmstrasse Trial:

"The work of a liaison man linking two important government branches like the Foreign Office and the General Staff is generally well known. One of these tasks is the obligation for the liaison man to keep himself informed on the objectives, plans and work of the office he has been assigned to, to advise and inform his superior on all relevant questions, negotiate on his behalf with the official authorities he has been assigned to, settle all difficulties eventually arising, and act on all points according to the directives given by his chief. These are not the duties of an errand-boy or a messenger, they require a high degree of penetration, diligence, intelligence . . . and adroitness." (NG, Case XI, Vol. CCXLIV, p. 28,038)

As a major, SA Obersturmbannführer and reporting legation counsellor von Etzdorf was informed about and participated in all aggressive plans. Von Etzdorf had, for example, knowledge of "Operation Barbarossa", the plan for the attack on the Soviet Union, and of "Operation Marita", the plan for attacking Yugoslavia, earlier than von Weizsäcker, at that time state secretary in the Foreign Office.

In marked contrast to his statements made before the Nuremberg Court that he had never had any influence on the orders and directives issued (NG, Case XI, Vol. XCV, pp. 677–681) he effected in numerous cases decrees of the Foreign Office or orders of the OKH – for example, an order to have representatives of the Foreign Office installed in the armies that took part in the aggression against Yugoslavia and the occupation of the country.

Von Etzdorf also shares responsibility for the activity of the special commando of the armed SS under the command of SS Sturmbannführer von Künsberg. Acting on the directives of the Foreign Office von Künsberg robbed the temporarily occupied territories in both Western and Eastern Europe of archival material and art treasures. In a secret military communication of 7 July 1941 he wrote:

"That is why I, immediately after learning of the difficulties encountered by the separate representatives of the Foreign Office (VAA) as a consequence of the OKH order mentioned, asked the VAA at the OKH, Rittmeister (cavalry captain) von Etzdorf, to effect an order making it clear to the army commands (AOK) that both the scope and the competence of the army commands and the "Künsberg Group" are independent of each other, and that the activity of the representatives (VAA) is not limited by the OKH order mentioned, which regulates the activity of the "Künsberg Group". Beyond that it is necessary, however, in the interest of the work carried out for the Foreign Office by the representatives (VAA) in co-operation with the "Künberg Group", to establish closer collaboration in order to make sure that all the available enemy material that is of interest to the Office is seized . . ."

A note of 26 August 1940 sealed and signed by von Etzdorf as the representative (VAA) with the army commander-in-chief says:

"Handsch. (Written by hand) *Art treasures*

"Abetz has received directions from the RAM (Foreign Minister) to continue, i.e., to go on seizing Jewish and public art possessions. (Transport only after preceding contact with OKH). Lammer's decree does not apply to France, for which Abetz has received specific order of the Führer." (German Central Archive, Potsdam, under Nürnberger Gericht, No. 090)

Another document says:

"For minutes of von Künsberg (special reception Künsberg Group) 'Art Treasures' in Palace Chambon secured. Extent 410 cases, 139 other paintings, 67 bales of tapestry, 216 pieces of furniture. Transport of objects to Berlin possible only on the basis of a written order of the Military Administration in France. A corresponding request has been submitted. It will be given special priority. Our lorries are not suited for the transport. Please consider employing expert enterprise for the execution. Nitsch" (German Central Archive, Potsdam, under Nürnberger Gericht, No. 3662)

The nazi diplomat von Etzdorf retired in May 1964 but only to make room for another Ribbentrop assistant. Nazi diplomat Blankenhorn, member of the nazi party since 1 December 1936, until 1943 employed at foreign representations of the fascist Foreign Office in Athens, Washington and Bern, then as a legation counsellor in the political department of Ribbentrop, became Bonn's ambassador in Great Britain. Another example showing that Bonn cannot manage without nazi diplomats.

Ribbentrop Diplomats in the Foreign Service

The following list names further Ribbentrop diplomats who hold decisive functions in the Bonn Foreign Office and its foreign representations today.

Albers, Dr. Karl
before 1945: attaché to the notorious nazi murderer Frank, the then "generalgouverneur" for Poland in Krakow, 1943 employed in the Ribbentrop Office, 1933 NSDAP (No. 1 764 477)
after 1945: ambassador in Nicaragua (1964)

Allardt, Dr. Helmut
before 1945: employed as a nazi diplomat in Ankara until 1943, later in the Foreign Office
after 1945: ambassador in Spain (1964)

Almsick, Dr. Wilhelm Helmuth von
before 1945: expert in the "Office of the Reich Governor in the Sudeten district", 1943 member of a supply and transport staff in Warsaw
after 1945: ambassador in the Dominican Republic (1964)

Altenburg, Dr. Günter
before 1945: ministerial director and head of the information department of the fascist Foreign Office (1941), afterwards until 1944 minister and "Reich plenipotentiary" in Greece, 1935 NSDAP
after 1945: general secretary of the "German Group of the International Chamber of Commerce"

Altendorf, Johann
before 1945: legation secretary in the nazi embassy in Tokyo, 1935 NSDAP (No. 3 604 855)
after 1945: legation counsellor first class and economic expert in the embassy in South Africa

Andres, Dr. Hans
before 1945: legation counsellor in the Foreign Office, 1940 NSDAP (No. 7 555 940)
after 1945: legation counsellor first class in the Bonn Foreign Office

Arnim, Bernd von
before 1945: representative of IG-Farben in Athens and Bucharest
after 1945: economic expert in the Bonn embassy in Vienna

Auer, Dr. Theodor
before 1945: to the outbreak of the war legation counsellor in the fascist embassy in Paris, afterwards in North Africa, collaborated closely with the fascist espionage apparatus, 1934 NSDAP (No. 3 398 113)
after 1945: until 1964 ambassador in Ceylon, then retired on account of age

Aurich
before 1945: worked in the cultural policy department in the Foreign Office
after 1945: chancellor in Aabenraa, consul in Genoa, Italy (since 1958)

Bargen, Dr. Werner von
before 1945: during the fascist occupation representative of the Foreign Office with the military commander in Belgium, 1944 leader of subdepartment Pol II in the Foreign Office, 1933 NSDAP (No. 2 579 492)
after 1945: Bonn ambassador in Baghdad, 1963 retired on account of age

Bassler, Hilmar
before 1945: legation secretary in the Ribbentrop Ministry, responsible for nazi propaganda in East Asia (department P VIII), confidential agent of the Gestapo and SD
after 1945: deputy head of the East Asia section in the east department of the Bonn Foreign Office

Benzing, Dr. Hans
before 1945: government counsellor in the personnel department of the Foreign Office
after 1945: cultural expert in the consulate-general in Istanbul (1963), 1964 transferred to the provincial service of Rhineland – Palatinate

Betz, Eugen
before 1945: until 1945 vice-consul in Shanghai, 1938 NSDAP
after 1945: consul-general in Chicago (1964)

Beye, Dr. Ludwig
before 1945: section chief in the commercial policy department of the Foreign

Office (1942), 1944 fulfilling "special orders" for the head of the commercial policy department, 1935 NSDAP (No. 2 531 036)
after 1945: Bonn ambassador in Libya (1964)

Bidder, Dr. Hans
before 1945: until 1945 various positions in the nazi embassy in China, 1941 NSDAP
after 1945: Bonn ambassador in Bangkok, now retired on account of age

Bismarck, Otto, Fürst von
before 1945: minister of the "Third Reich" in Rome (1940), afterwards ministerial director in the information department of the Foreign Office until 1944
after 1945: 1963 member of the Consulting Congress of the European Council of the West European Union, member of the council of the "German Foundation for Developing Countries"

Blankenhagen, von
before 1945: consulate secretary in the personnel department of the Foreign Office
after 1945: chancellor of the Bonn trade representation in Helsinki (1963)

Blankenhorn, Herbert
before 1945: head of the economics department of the fascist embassy in Bern (1943), afterwards section chief in the political department of the Foreign Office, 1936 NSDAP (No. 6 977 147)
after 1945: ambassador in Rome, since 1965 in Great Britain

Bock, Dr. Günther
before 1945: embassy counsellor in the office of the "Reich Plenipotentiary" in Italy (1944), 1937 NSDAP
after 1945: legation counsellor first class and deputy sub-section chief of the East department of the Bonn Foreign Office

Böhling, Dr. Horst
before 1945: 1939–1945 in the fascist embassy in China
after 1945: now ambassador in Malaysia

Böhme, Kurt
before 1945: until the outbreak of the war in the fascist consulate in Boston
after 1945: vice-consul in Canada

Boll, Emil
before 1945: 1943 to 1944 consul in Russe/Bulgaria, 1934 NSDAP
after 1945: legation counsellor in the commercial policy department of the Bonn Foreign Office

Boltze, Dr. Erich
before 1945: 1943–1945 minister first class in Japan, 1937 NSDAP (No. 6 017 842)
after 1945: ambassador in Cambodia, now retired on account of age

Bormann, Dr. Hans-Heinrich
before 1945: scientific assistant and legation counsellor in the press department of the Foreign Office
after 1945: consul first class in Bergen, Norway (1964)

Bottler, Dr. Richard
before 1945: 1942–1945 legation counsellor in the commercial policy department of the Foreign Office, 1933 NSDAP
after 1945: ambassador in Rangoon (1964)

Braun, Otto
before 1945: 1935–1939 head of the Bucharest branch office of the so-called "Reich Railway Publicity Centre" (a camouflage for special offices of the security service abroad)
after 1945: consul, head of the selection consulat in Livorno, Italy

Braun, Sigismund, Freiherr von
before 1945: vice-consul in Addis Ababa, afterwards nazi diplomat at the Vatican (until 1945)
after 1945: now Bonn government observer at the United Nations in New York

Breer, Dr. Franz
before 1945: until the fascist attack on the USSR legation secretary in the fascist embassy in Moscow
after 1945: consul-general in San Francisco (1963); was then transferred to the embassy of the Federal Republic in London as ambassador first class

Briest, Eckardt
before 1945: until 1944 legation secretary in information bureau III of the Foreign Office

after 1945: now Bonn ambassador in Paraguay

Broich-Oppert, Dr. Georg von
before 1945: during the annexation of Austria legation secretary in the fascist embassy, afterwards leading position in IG-Farben until 1945
after 1945: ambassador in Ankara, retired on account of age

Brunhoff, Kurt
before 1945: until 1944 legation counsellor in Budapest, 1934 NSDAP (No. 2 870 296)
after 1945: Bonn consul-general in Sydney

Bünger, Dr. Karl
before 1945: employed in the fascist embassy in Shanghai with private contract "for special tasks in the field of propaganda", 1943 decorated with the War Service Cross
after 1945: consul-general in Hongkong (1964)

Clausen
before 1945: consulate secretary in Kovno (1939), afterwards in the Foreign Office in the bureau of Ambassador Ritter (liaison with the Supreme Command of the Wehrmacht)
after 1945: chancellor to the Bonn embassy in the South African Republic (1962)

Curtius, Klaus
before 1945: in the economic policy department of the Foreign Office
after 1945: now Bonn consul-general in New York

Dellmensingen, Dr. Leopold Krafft von
before 1945: legation secretary in the protocol department in the Foreign Office, competent for the affairs of the "representation of foreign countries in the occupied territories"
after 1945: section chief in the East department of the Bonn Foreign Office, reporting legation counsellor first class

Deter, Heinz
before 1945: until the end of the war in the fascist consulate-general in Tientsin
after 1945: chancellor to the Bonn embassy in Colombo (1962)

Deubner, Dr. Otfried
before 1945: scientific assistant in the Foreign Office (1943)
after 1945: second secretary of the Bonn embassy in Karachi (1964)

Dietmar, Dr. Helmuth
before 1945: until the end of the war legation counsellor first class in Lisbon, 1939 NSDAP (No. 7 054 879)
after 1945: consul-general in Bombay, retired on account of age

Döhring, Dr. Karl
before 1945: member of the "Hohenfier" Altherrenschaft (an alumni association), SS Obersturmführer, participated in the attacks on Greece and the USSR
after 1945: now ambassador in Cameroon

Duchow, Willi
before 1945: until 1939 in the fascist embassy in Poland, legation in Copenhagen
after 1945: chancellor to the Bonn embassy in the Sudan

Dumke, Horst
before 1945: 1933 SS, participated in the attacks on Poland, France, Yugoslavia and the USSR, 1937 NSDAP
after 1945: legation counsellor first class in the Bonn Foreign Office, now head of department II in the Federal Ministry for Economic Cooperation

Eberl, Dr. Otto
before 1945: head of section IV c of the commercial policy department in the fascist Foreign Office (1943–44)
after 1945: now Bonn ambassador in Uruguay

Engelen, Gerhard
before 1945: until 1945 chancellor at the consulate in Bergen
after 1945: again in the consulate in Bergen

Erlewein, Josef
before 1945: until 1941 vice-consul in Vladivostok, afterwards to the end of the war at the fascist embassy in Nanking
after 1945: consul first class in Lille, France (1964)

Etzdorf, Hasso von
before 1945: representative of the Foreign Office with the supreme command of the army, major and SA Sturmbannführer
after 1945: Bonn ambassador in Great Britain, since May 1965 retired

Fabian, Georg
before 1945: until the attack on the USSR consulate secretary in Kovno
after 1945: embassy secretary in Beirut (1964)

Federer, Dr. Georg
before 1945: until the outbreak of the war legation secretary in the fascist embassy in London, afterwards legation counsellor at the legation in Bern
after 1945: most recently Bonn ambassador in Cairo

Felchner, Friedrich
before 1945: employed at the embassy in Sofia (1944), 1933 NSDAP
after 1945: 1948 in Bulgaria sentenced to 25 years of hard labour for participation in fascist crimes, employed in the personnel and administrative department of the Bonn Foreign Office (1961)

Ferring, Franz
before 1945: in the radio policy department of the Foreign Office, responsible head of the section for propaganda in East Asia
after 1945: now Bonn ambassador in Seoul, Korea

Fischer, Martin
before 1945: 1943 consul-general in Shanghai, 1935 NSDAP (No. 2 552 786)
after 1945: ambassador in the Bonn Foreign Office

Frank, Eugen
before 1945: consul of the Foreign Office (1940)
after 1945: deputy of the West German observer at the United Nations in New York, reporting legation counsellor first class in the Foreign Office 1963)

Frank, Gottlob
before 1945: at the fascist consulate in Bozen (1940)
after 1945: Bonn embassy chancellor in Ankara (1962)

Friedensburg, Dr. Ferdinand
before 1945: 1944 applied for admission to the judicial service, referring to his positive attitude towards the Hitler state, NSKK (national socialist motorist group) Scharführer
after 1945: Bonn ambassador in Madagascar (1962), then in Caracas

Gaerte, Dr. Felix
before 1945: member of SS Sturm 1/80, during the war SS Untersturmführer in the Reich Security Main Office, 1937 NSDAP (No. 4 910 278)
after 1945: consul first class in Bombay (1962)

Galinsky, Wolfgang
before 1945: 1943–1944 legation secretary in Tokyo
after 1945: consul-general in Osaka, Japan (1964)

Gawlik
before 1945: chief inspector in the "Office of the Reich Protector of Bohemia and Moravia", participated in suppressing Czechoslovakia (1943)
after 1945: legation counsellor first class and section head in the legal department of the Bonn Foreign Office (1963)

Gehner, Heinz
before 1945: assistant in the consulate in Krakow, participated in preparing the attack on Poland
after 1945: consulate secretary first class in Linz (1962)

Geier, Hans-Joachim
before 1945: until the outbreak of the war against the USA consulate secretary in New York
after 1945: embassy chancellor in Montevideo (1962)

Gellbach, Dr. Horst-Heinrich
before 1945: government counsellor in the fascist state apparatus, 1942 NSDAP (No. 8 284 777)
after 1945: embassy counsellor in Stockholm (1964)

Geuther, Fritz
before 1945: 1939 consulate secretary in Bratislava
after 1945: in the legal department of the Bonn Foreign Office (1960)

Giffels, Hubert
before 1945: 1939–1940 consulate secretary first class at the consulate in Bergen, participated in the preparation of the fascist attack on Norway

after 1945: chancellor to the Bonn consulate in Lyon (1962)

Gnodtke, Dr. Günther

before 1945: 1937 in the fascist state apparatus in carrying through the racial laws, 1933 SA
after 1945: now ambassador in Nigeria

Grade, Hans

before 1945: 1939 in the fascist embassy in Rome, 1937 SS (No. 310 959)
after 1945: vice-consul in Canada (1964)

Graeff, Dr. Friedrich

before 1945: economic leader of the "Country Group Italy" of the NSDAP, consul-general in Toulouse (1944), 1933 NSDAP (No. 3 391 375)
after 1945: from 1959 to his retirement for old age consul-general in Genoa

Graevenitz, Dr. Kurt Fritz von

before 1945: in the office of the "Special Plenipotentiary" of the Foreign Office "for the South East" in Athens (1941), afterwards consul-general in Iskenderum, Turkey, 1942 NSDAP (No. 8 735 191)
after 1945: ambassador in Mexico (1963), retired (1964)

Gregor, Dr. Werner

before 1945: consul-general in Toulouse (1943), 1936 NSDAP (No. 3 726 551)
after 1945: Bonn ambassador in Tunisia (1961), retired on account of age

Groeppner, Horst

before 1945: at the embassy in Moscow (1941), until the end of the war head of group II in the protocol department of the Foreign Office, 1933 NSDAP
after 1945: now ambassador in Moscow

Haeften, Gerrit von

before 1945: consul-general in Basel (1943), 1937 NSDAP (No. 3 918 543)
after 1945: ministerial director and head of the legal department of the Bonn Foreign Office (1963); now ministerial director (retired), chairman of the European Conference for Telecommunication through Satellites

Hallstein, Professor Dr. Walter

before 1945: university teacher and active nazi at the Universities of Rostock and Frankfurt-on-Main, participant in the legal negotiations between Hitler Germany and fascist Italy
after 1945: president of the European Economic Commission

Hannig, Dr. Th.

before 1945: local group leader of the NSDAP in Shanghai (1935)
after 1945: press chief in the Bonn consulate-general in Istanbul (1962)

Hardenberg, Bernhard Heinrich Ernst Günther Graf von

before 1945: 1939 legation secretary in Kovno, afterwards at the legation in Bucharest, until the end of the war in the Foreign Office, 1933 NSDAP (No. 2 587 251)
after 1945: now ambassador in Costa Rica

Hardenberg, Dr. Hans Karl Graf von

before 1945: government counsellor in the Reich Ministry of Economic Affairs (1941), 1937 NSDAP (No. 4 377 465), SA Rottenführer
after 1945: Consul in Geneva (1962), then named ministerial director in the Bonn Foreign Office (1964)

Hauthal, Dr. Horst von

before 1945: from 1940 in the Foreign Service, 1937 NSDAP (No. 5 062 619)
after 1945: first secretary of the Bonn embassy in Cairo (1964)

Hecker, Dr. Gottfried von

before 1945: 1943 personnel department, later legal department of the Foreign Office
after 1945: legation counsellor first class in the legal department of the Bonn Foreign Office

Hellenthal, Dr. Walter

before 1945: representative of the Foreign Office in army headquarters 6 (1941), legation counsellor first class and consul-general in Monaco (1943), 1933 NSDAP
after 1945: Bonn ambassador in Lebanon, now retired because of old age

Henschel, Reinhard

before 1945: 1943–1944 at the fascist legation in Ankara, 1937 NSDAP
after 1945: legation counsellor first class in the Bonn Foreign Office (1963)

Hensel, Dr. Herbert

before 1945: 1943 consul-general in Aarhus, 1933 NSDAP (No. 3 286 190)
after 1945: legation counsellor first

class and deputy head of section in the West department of the Bonn Foreign Office (1962)

Herwarth von Bittenfeld, Dr. Hans
before 1945: until 1941 legation counsellor in the embassy in Moscow, afterwards in the occupied Eastern territories and helped in the formation of the notorious Vlassow army
after 1945: Bonn ambassador in London, 1963 state secretary in the Federal Presidential Office, now ambassador in Rome

Hess, Dr. Walter
before 1945: legation counsellor and head of the economic department of the fascist legation in Sofia (1943–1944)
after 1945: now ambassador in Morocco

Heyde, Wilhelm Günther Hermann Detlef von
before 1945: legation secretary in the fascist embassy in Washington (1941), 1934 NSDAP
after 1945: reporting legation counsellor first class in the Bonn Foreign Office

Hezinger, Adolf
before 1945: 1942 after his expulsion from Iran employed in the bureau of Minister Ettel (preparation of aggression against the Arab countries), decorated with the War Service Cross Second Class with Swords, 1944 in the information department of the Foreign Office (Inf. XIV – "Anti-Jewish Action"), participant in the notorious Krummhübel Conference
after 1945: 1957 transferred to the Bonn Foreign Office as consulate secretary

Hilger, Gustav
before 1945: head of section 13 ("Russia Group") in the political department of the Foreign Office, 1944 in Ribbentrop Bureau, liaison man with the notorious General Vlassov
after 1945: from 1953 until his retirement "Consultant on Problems of the East" in the Bonn Foreign Office

Hirsch, Dr. Karl
before 1945: 1943 employed with the Reich governor in Vienna, department 2
after 1945: consul in Izmir, Turkey

Hirschberg, Erich
before 1945: until the attack on Denmark consulate secretary at the fascist legation in Copenhagen
after 1945: chancellor in the Bonn consulate-general in San Francisco (1962)

Hirschfeld, Hans Richard
before 1945: since 1941 legation counsellor in the Deutschland department of the Foreign Office (liaison with the leading organs of the nazi party and its subdivisions), 1936 NSDAP (No. 3 715 319)
after 1945: Bonn ambassador in Iceland (1964), retired (1965)

Hochmuth
before 1945: consulate secretary in the fascist embassy in Rome (1933)
after 1945: chancellor in the Bonn embassy at the Vatican (1962)

Hoffmann, Christoph
before 1945: employed in the office of Ambassador Prüfer "Arab Intelligence Bureau" (1945)
after 1945: chancellor first class in the Bonn consulate-general in Wellington (1958)

Holleben, Dr. Werner
before 1945: expert in the cultural policy department of the Foreign Office
after 1945: embassy counsellor in Luxemburg (1964), then head of the consulate in Cleveland, USA

Holten, Carl von
before 1945: vice-consul in the fascist consulate-general in Kattowitz (Katowice)
after 1945: ambassador in Oslo, 1965 retired

Hoops, Dr. Walter Dietrich
before 1945: legation counsellor in Peking (1943), 1933 NSDAP
after 1945: consul in Vancouver, Canada

Jericho
before 1945: nazi consulate in Mozambique
after 1945: chancellor in the Bonn consulate in Porto-Alegre, Brazil (1962)

John, Herbert
before 1945: consulate secretary in Poland and Belgium
after 1945: chancellor in the Bonn consulate-general in Valparaiso, Chile (1962)

Junker, Dr. Werner
before 1945: press head of the NSDAP organization in China, later employed in

Belgrade with the "Special Plenipotentiary for the South-East" of the Foreign Office (1944–45), 1935 NSDAP
after 1945: now Bonn ambassador in the Republic of South Africa

Karstien, Dr. Hans
before 1945: scientific worker and government counsellor in the Foreign Office, 1933 NSDAP (No. 1 596 620)
after 1945: reporting legation counsellor in the Bonn Foreign Office, head of the code and telecommunications section

Kassler, Dr. Rolf
before 1945: legation counsellor in Copenhagen (1944)
after 1945: embassy counsellor first class in the Bonn diplomatic service

Keller, Dr. Rupprecht von
before 1945: associate in the Foreign Office of Under-Secretary of State Woermann, one of Ribbentrop's confidants, 1933 SA functionary, NSDAP (No. 8 012 248)
after 1945: West German observer in the European Office of the United Nations in Geneva, named ambassador in 1964

Kempff, Günther
before 1945: protocol department of the Foreign Office
after 1945: Bonn consul-general in Helsinki (1964)

Klaiber, Dr. Manfred
before 1945: worked in Belgrade and Vienna on behalf of the Foreign Office from 1943 to 1945
after 1945: now Bonn ambassador in Paris

Knoop, Theodor von
before 1945: commercial policy department of the Foreign Office (1944)
after 1945: head of the economic department of the Bonn consulate-general in San Francisco, now retired because of age

Köhler, Dr. Heinrich
before 1945: head of a section of the cultural policy department of the Foreign Office (1945)
after 1945: Bonn consul-general in Bombay (1964)

Krajewicz, Helmut
before 1945: consulate secretary to the fascist representations in London and The Hague
after 1945: chancellor to the Bonn embassy in Paris (1963)

Krapf, Franz
before 1945: 1940 to the end of the war legation secretary and member of the branch office of the "Railway Publicity Centre" (office of the Security Service abroad) at the fascist embassy in Tokyo, member of department III of the Reich Security Main Office, 1936 NSDAP, SS Untersturmführer
after 1945: ministerial director and head of the East department of the Bonn Foreign Office

Krause-Wichmann, Dr. Georg
before 1945: in the fascist legation in Sofia (1944), 1933 NSDAP (No. 1 547 946)
after 1945: consul-general in Genoa (1964)

Krebs, Dr. Herbert
before 1945: until the outbreak of the war at the consulate in Brazil
after 1945: chancellor in the Bonn embassy in Australia (1963)

Krebs, Dr. Kurt
before 1945: collaborator of the fascist "Special Deputy for Economic Problems" in Rumania, participated in the economic plundering of the country
after 1945: section head for agricultural problems at the Bonn embassy in Paris (1963)

Krumdiek, Oskar
before 1945: consul in the fascist consulate in Peru
after 1945: consul in the West German consulate in Peru

Kuhle, Dr. Herbert
before 1945: scientific assistant in the legal department of the Foreign Office (1943–44)
after 1945: Bonn consul in Kansas City, USA (1964)

Kutscher, Dr. Ernst
before 1945: 1944 in the Foreign Office, information department XIV ("Anti-Jewish Action"), participant in the Krummhübel Conference, 1933 NSDAP
after 1945: embassy counsellor in the Bonn embassy in Paris (1962), since 1964 in the Bonn Foreign Office as reporting legation secretary first class

Lane, Dr. Alexander
before 1945: collaborator of Goebbels in the nazi Propaganda Ministry, radio attaché in Sofia until the end of the war
after 1945: legation counsellor first class, section head in the personnel department of the Bonn Foreign Office (1962), 1964 named reporting legation counsellor first class

Lanwer, Dr. Ewald
before 1945: until 1945 consul in Aabenraa, Denmark, responsible for recruiting "German Volunteers" for the armed SS, and for informing on Danish patriots, 1933 NSDAP
after 1945: section head in the development aid policy department of the Bonn Foreign Office (1963)

Lehr, Bruno
before 1945: collaborator of Göring in the fascist Reich Air Ministry SS, 1941 NSDAP (No. 8739967)
after 1945: second secretary of the Bonn embassy in Tokyo (1963)

Lerchenfeld, Dr. Johannes Graf von
before 1945: confidant of IG-Farben in Berlin, Paris and Sofia
after 1945: head of the economic section in the Bonn embassy in Rome (1962)

Linneborn, Kuno
before 1945: legation in Helsinki, afterwards at the consulate in Aabenraa
after 1945: government agent in the Bonn Foreign Office (1957)

Luedde-Neurath, Kurt
before 1945: legation secretary in the embassy in Tokyo, SA Sturmführer, 1938 NSDAP (No. 4745122)
after 1945: reporting legation counsellor in the Bonn Foreign Office (1963)

Lüders, Karl-Heinz
before 1945: member of the Security Service, 1942–1944 scientific assistant in the commercial policy department of the Foreign Office, 1943 the Security Service installed him in Ankara and Istanbul
after 1945: embassy counsellor in India (1964)

Mackeben, Wilhelm
before 1945: legation counsellor in the political department of the Foreign Office, for a time assigned to special tasks in Ambassador Ritter's office
after 1945: Bonn ambassador in Lima until his retirement for old age

Maenss, Hans Ivar
before 1945: employed in the Foreign Office (1944)
after 1945: deputy section head in the Bonn Foreign Office (1964)

Mair, Kurt Alex
before 1945: head of the Seehaus interception service in the cultural policy department of the Foreign Office (1941)
after 1945: chancellor in the Bonn consulate in Conception, Chile (1962)

Maltzan, Dr. Vollrath Freiherr von
before 1945: in the commercial policy department of the Foreign Office, concerned with "economic and financial problems of the occupied western territories" (1940), afterwards in Shanghai on a "special mission"
after 1945: Bonn ambassador in Paris, retired for health reasons

Mangold, Dr. Hans Joachim
before 1945: war administrative officer of the occupation regime in Paris, 1933 NSDAP (No. 2307799)
after 1945: Bonn ambassador in Damascus (1964)

Marchtaler, Dr. Hans Ulrich
before 1945: legation counsellor in the fascist embassy in Tokyo (1944)
after 1945: Bonn ambassador in Stockholm (1961), now retired for reasons of age

Melchers, Wilhelm
before 1945: head of political department VII ("Near East"), where he worked closely with the Gestapo and SD and especially organized and directed the activity of the "fifth column"
after 1945: until the end of 1964 Bonn ambassador in Greece, since then "adviser" and recipient of a pension

Merfels, Josef
before 1945: consul with the "Reich Plenipotentiary" in Denmark (1945), NSDAP regional group leader in Albania, 1934 NSDAP (No. 3398422)
after 1945: consul first class in Bordeaux (1963), now retired for reasons of age

Metzger, Werner
before 1945: consulate secretary in Madrid (1944)
after 1945: counsellor in the Bonn embassy in Ecuador (1957)

Mirbach, Dietrich Freiherr von
before 1945: 1943–1944 personal assistant to State Secretary Steengracht in the Foreign Office, 1933 NSDAP (No. 2731405)
after 1945: ambassador for special missions in the Bonn Foreign Office, since June 1965 ambassador in India

Mirow, Eduard
before 1945: liaison officer of the "Staff of the Plenipotentiary for the Arab Countries" (Grobba Staff), special staff of General Felmy (1942), 1945 vice-consul of the Foreign Office in Zurich, 1931 NSDAP (No. 549764)
after 1945: most recently legation counsellor first class in the Bonn embassy in Baghdad

Mohr, Dr. Ernst Günther
before 1945: legation counsellor in The Hague, responsible for preparing deportations of Jews 1939–1941, afterwards consul in Tangier, collaborator of the fascist espionage service, in the fascist Foreign Office section head for liaison with the Supreme Command of the Wehrmacht (1945), press man of the NSDAP local group of Peping; 1935 NSDAP (No. 3500174)
after 1945: Bonn ambassador in Buenos Aires (1965)

Mohrmann, Dr. Anton
before 1945: legation counsellor in the fascist legation in Sofia (1944)
after 1945: Bonn ambassador in Colombia (1962), now retired on grounds of age

Moltmann, Dr. Gerhard
before 1945: 1943–1944 at the fascist legation in Bern, NSDAP (No. 7005175)
after 1945: Bonn ambassador in Afghanistan (1964)

Motz, Dr. Günther
before 1945: since 1941 in the fascist Reich Ministry of the Interior
after 1945: now ambassador in Bolivia

Moulin-Eckart, Karl Max Graf von
before 1945: head of section Pol III in the political department of the Foreign Office (1938), 1933 NSDAP
after 1945: Bonn consul in Montpellier, France

Mumm von Schwarzenstein, Dr. Bernd Eugen
before 1945: legation secretary in the Foreign Office
after 1945: head of the Bonn trade representation in Warsaw (1965)

Muschke, Kurt
before 1945: chancellor in the fascist embassy in Sofia (1942)
after 1945: chancellor in the Bonn consulate in Naples

Nostiz-Drczewicki, Gottfried von
before 1945: 1938–1940 deputy head of department Pol IM in the Foreign Office (liaison with the espionage service of the Supreme Command of the Wehrmacht), afterwards legation counsellor in the consulate in Geneva
after 1945: Bonn ambassador in Chile

Nostitz, Siegfried von
before 1945: legation counsellor in the fascist embassy in Sofia (1944), 1933 NSDAP
after 1945: consul-general in San Francisco (1964)

Nüsslein, Dr. Franz
before 1945: as senior public prosecutor in Prague he participated in passing terrorist sentences (1942), 1937 NSDAP (No. 4628997)
after 1945: consul-general in Barcelona (1964)

Obermayer, Dr. Adolf Max
before 1945: press attaché in Sofia (1940)
after 1945: now embassy counsellor in The Hague

Oehlandt, Herwarth
before 1945: consulate secretary in Maastricht, Holland (1939)
after 1945: 1960 government agent in the Bonn Foreign Office

Overbeck, Karl Kuno
before 1945: legation counsellor in Budapest, SA
after 1945: ministerial director in the Bonn Foreign Office (1963)

Pamperrien, Dr. Rudolf
before 1945: 1942 head of a section in the commercial policy department of the Foreign Office
after 1945: ambassador in Ecuador (1957), now retired for reasons of age

Pappenheim, Georg Graf von
before 1945: 1944 in the political department of the Foreign Office, section Pol

IM (liaison with the espionage service of the Supreme Command of the Wehrmacht)
after 1945: ambassador in Ecuador (1964)

Panhorst, Dr. Karl
before 1945: secretary of the committee for the "Ibero and Central American Action", confidant of IG-Farben (1939)
after 1945: Bonn ambassador in Guatemala (1962), retired

Paulig, Richard
before 1945: legation counsellor in the political department of the Foreign Office, shares responsibility for the plundering of Croatia (1944)
after 1945: reporting legation counsellor in the Bonn Foreign Office (1961)

Pfeiffer, Arnold
before 1945: consulate secretary in Kovno (1939), afterwards in Budapest
after 1945: chancellor first class in Bombay, afterwards in the Bonn Foreign Office

Pfeiffer, Dr. Peter
before 1945: consul-general first class in Tirana (1943), 1940 NSDAP (No. 8128180)
after 1945: employed as an inspector of the foreign representations of the Bonn Foreign Office (1958), retired ambassador and president of the Goethe Institute

Pfisterer, Dr. Friedrich
before 1945: in the economic policy department of the Foreign Office
after 1945: first secretary of the Bonn embassy in Brussels 1964

Pirch, Dr. Georg von
before 1945: from 1939 employed in the Foreign Office, 1932 Stahlhelm, 1934 candidate of the SS
after 1945: section head in the Bonn Foreign Office (1964)

Przybill, Willi
before 1945: from 1936 consulate secretary in Bratislava
after 1945: chancellor in the Bonn consulate in Graz (1957)

Puttkamer, Dr. Ellinor von
before 1945: co-worker of the Foreign Office
after 1945: reporting legation counsellor first class in department 3 of the Bonn Foreign Office (1963)

Quiring, Dr. Franz
before 1945: legation counsellor to the fascist consulate-general in Geneva (1939), 1933 NSDAP
after 1945: Bonn minister in Kabul (1954)

Rabes, Dr. Rudolf
before 1945: until 1939 legation secretary in the fascist embassy in Rio de Janeiro
after 1945: consul first class in Curitiba, Brazil (1964)

Ramelow, Thomas
before 1945: vice-consul in the Foreign Office (1942)
after 1945: consul first class in Concepcion, Chile (1964)

Randow, Elgar von
before 1945: until 1945 legation counsellor in China, was charged with the central direction of fascist propaganda, intelligence and espionage activity; for this activity he received the War Service Cross Second Class with Swords; 1925 NSDAP (No. 5189)
after 1945: Bonn consul-general in Calcutta

Reichert, Hans-Joachim Ritter von
before 1945: legation counsellor to the fascist "Reich Plenipotentiary" for Italy
after 1945: Bonn ambassador in Honduras (1964)

Reichhold, Dr. Walter
before 1945: scientific assistant in the personnel department of the Foreign Office (language service), which was particularly concerned with espionage (1943); 1944 at the embassy in Madrid with the task of building up a branch office of the "language service"
after 1945: ambassador in Ghana (1964), then transferred to the embassy in Ottawa

Rensinghoff, Wilhelm
before 1945: 1939 taken over as a member of the fascist legation, agent of the fascist secret service, local group leader of the NSDAP in Port Said
after 1945: head of the West German consulate in Puerto Mont, Chile

Richter, Dr. Herbert
before 1945: until 1945 fascist consul-general in Tetuan
after 1945: Bonn ambassador in Algeria (1964)

Richthofen, Oswald Freiherr von
before 1945: legation counsellor in the nazi legation in Budapest 1944, 1932 NSDAP (No. 1440443)
after 1945: Bonn ambassador in Khartoum, Sudan (1964)

Ringelmann, Dr. Max
before 1945: during the fascist occupation of Yugoslavia representative of the Foreign Office with the military commander in Belgrade (1943), 1934 NSDAP
after 1945: consul-general in Salisbury (1964)

Röhreke, Dr. Heinrich
before 1945: 1944 head of the nazi consulate in Hankow, China. In July 1945 he advocated the secret maintenance of the NSDAP within the "Deutsches Amt in China", 1937 NSDAP, SA
after 1945: legation counsellor first class in the Bonn Foreign Office, 1963 named reporting legation counsellor

Rom, Dr. Horst von
before 1945: employed in the fascist Reich justice service
after 1945: Bonn consul in Atlanta, USA (1964), 1965 ambassador in Bamako, Mali

Ruoff, Herbert
before 1945: scientific assistant in the Foreign Office, among others concerned with the exchange of German civil internees in foreign countries in cooperation with the Security Service
after 1945: deputy West German ambassador in Australia (1962), since then legation counsellor first class in the Foreign Office

Rutkowski, Arthur
before 1945: before the war in the fascist legation in Belgrade
after 1945: economic expert in Vienna (1961)

Sachs, Dr. Hans Georg
before 1945: legation secretary in the Foreign Office (1941)
after 1945: ministerial director in the Bonn Foreign Office, head of department 8, since June 1965 ambassador to the EEC and Euratom

Sautter, Dr. Theodor
before 1945: government counsellor in the fascist Reich Labour Ministry (1939), 1937 NSDAP (No. 5373580), 1933 SS
after 1945: legation counsellor in the Bonn embassy in Italy (1957), since 1963 legation counsellor first class in the Bonn Foreign Office

Schaffarczyk, Dr. Herbert
before 1945: member of the Foreign Office (1939)
after 1945: Bonn ambassador in Lisbon (1964)

Schatton, Willi
before 1945: helped prepare in the fascist embassy in Warsaw the attack on Poland
after 1945: government senior secretary in the Bonn Foreign Office (1956), later in the embassy in Moscow (1960)

Scherpenberg, Dr. Albert Hilger von
before 1945: 1935–1945 in the Foreign Office, head of section 6 of the commercial policy department, responsible for the plundering of Denmark and Norway
after 1945: Bonn ambassador in the Vatican (1964), retired 1965

Scheske, Dr. Ulrich
before 1945: junior government official in the fascist state apparatus (1942), 1933 SS (No. 216977)
after 1945: 1963 reporting legation counsellor first class in department West II of the Bonn Foreign Office

Schilling, Dr. Karl
before 1945: government counsellor in the Foreign Office, 1937 SA
after 1945: second embassy secretary in Tokyo (1963)

Schirmer, Dr. Hans
before 1945: 1939 SS Obersturmführer in the Security Service in the Foreign Office; 1940 to 1942 deputy head of the radio policy department of the Foreign Office, shares main responsibility for building up a network of secret stations controlled by the espionage service
after 1945: reporting legation counsellor first class in the East department of the Bonn Foreign Office (1962)

Schlitter, Oskar
before 1945: 1944 section head in the commercial policy department of the fascist Foreign Office, active participant in the plundering of Northern Italy, 1934 NSDAP (No. 3591227)
after 1945: ambassador in Athens (1965)

Schmidt, Rolf
before 1945: consulate secretary in the fascist consulate-general in Antwerp (1940)
after 1945: chancellor in the consulate-general in Salisbury (1962)

Schott, Wilhelm
before 1945: legation secretary in the nazi consulate-general in Zurich (1941), 1933 NSDAP (No. 1890109), SA
after 1945: legation counsellor in the Bonn Foreign Office (1960)

Schubert, Konrad von
before 1945: legation counsellor first class in the Foreign Office, 1933 NSDAP (No. 3281493)
after 1945: West German ambassador in Ethiopia (1964)

Schütt, Nikolaus
before 1945: nazi consul in Potosi, Bolivia (1939)
after 1945: Bonn consul in Sucre, Bolivia (1964)

Schütt
before 1945: consulate secretary in the fascist legation in Oslo
after 1945: chancellor in the Bonn embassy in Bangkok (1962)

Schwarzmann, Dr. Hans
before 1945: liaison man between Ribbentrop and Abetz, nazi ambassador in Paris; from 1942 in the political department of the Foreign Ministry as specialist on France
after 1945: head of the West Berlin office of the Bonn Foreign Office

Schweinitz, Dr. Hans Ulrich von
before 1945: nazi vice-consul in Iskenderum, Turkey (1943), 1933 NSDAP
after 1945: Bonn ambassador in Thailand (1964)

Schwörbel, Dr. Herbert
before 1945: 1942 to 1945 press attaché to the "Reich Plenipotentiary" in Greece
after 1945: Bonn ambassador in Ceylon (1964)

Seelos, Dr. Gebhardt
before 1945: participated in preparing the attack on Poland as consul in Lemberg and supplied espionage reports to the Foreign Office; afterwards transferred to Copenhagen as legation counsellor
after 1945: ambassador in Brazil (1964)

Seydel, Dr. Hans
before 1945: vice-consul in Tetuan (1942), participated in preparing the military occupation of the Arab countries as a member of the "Grobba Staff"
after 1945: in department West II of the Bonn Foreign Office (1963)

Siegfried, Dr. Herbert
before 1945: reporting legation counsellor and consul-general in Geneva (1944), 1937 NSDAP (No. 4009260)
after 1945: Bonn ambassador in Brussels (1964)

Simonis, Dr. Susanne
before 1945: until 1945 NSDAP functionary in the fascist embassies in Tokyo and Nanking
after 1945: legation counsellor in the cultural department of the Bonn Foreign Office (1963)

Solms-Braunfels, Prinz Alexander zu
before 1945: 1941 legation secretary in the fascist embassy in Bucharest, 1937 NSDAP (No. 4255672)
after 1945: ambassador in Salvador (1964)

Sonnenhol, Dr. Gustav-Adolf
before 1945: 1944 vice-consul in Geneva, 1931 NSDAP (No. 545961), 1930 SA, SS Untersturmführer
after 1945: deputy head of the Bonn representation at the OECD in Paris (1962), embassy counsellor first class, since 1964 ministerial director in the Federal Ministry for Development Aid

Spaeth, Joseph
before 1945: participated in preparing the fascist attack on Poland as member of the consulate-general in Kattowitz (Katowice)
after 1945: chancellor in the Bonn consulate in Zagreb (1962)

Stahlberg, Dr. Gerhard
before 1945: legation counsellor in the fascist Foreign Office (1942), in the legal department he had a considerable share in carrying through the fascist racial laws and in justifying the fascist policy of robbery and terror
after 1945: consul-general in Montreal (1964)

Starke, Dr. Gotthold
before 1945: head of section P5 (USSR and Poland) in the press department

of the Foreign Office (1945), chief editor of the fascist occupation newspaper Deutsche Rundschau in Polen
after 1945: reporting legation counsellor first class, 1962 resigned, since then together with war criminal Kohnert active in the revanchist West Prussia Landsmannschaft

Stechow, Johann Karl von
before 1945: legation counsellor in the political department of the Foreign Office (1944)
after 1945: Bonn ambassador in Manila, Philippines (1964)

Steinbach, Hans-Joachim
before 1945: consulate secretary in the fascist consulate-general in Bern (1944)
after 1945: Bonn ambassador in Rwanda (1964)

Stelzer, Dr. Gerhard
before 1945: legation counsellor first class in Bucharest (1941), 1936 NSDAP
after 1945: head of the consulate-general in Antwerp (1961), retired because of old age

Steuer, Theo
before 1945: collaborator of war criminal Abetz in the fascist embassy in Paris 1940
after 1945: chancellor in the Bonn consulate in Cordoba, Argentina (1962)

Stolzmann, Paulus von
before 1945: head of the liaison office of the representative for information belonging to Ribbentrop's personal staff (1944), 1933 NSDAP (No. 3286389)
after 1945: Bonn ambassador in Luxemburg (1964)

Strachwitz, Rudolf Graf
before 1945: since 1939 legation counsellor first class in the fascist embassies in Paris, Budapest, and Barcelona, 1936 NSDAP (No. 3771577)
after 1945: Bonn ambassador in the Vatican (1961), retired because of old age

Strack, Dr. Hans
before 1945: head of section Pol II in the political department (1943); with others responsible for nazi and war crimes in France (deportations of Jews, executions of hostages); 1943 consul in Klausenburg, Hungary, 1936 NSDAP (No. 3752096), NSKK (national socialist motorist group) Sturmführer
after 1945: ambassador in Santiago de Chile (1964), retired because of old age

Strecker, Hermann
before 1945: consulate secretary and member of Ribbentrop's "Russia Committee" (1941), NSDAP
after 1945: government agent in the commercial policy department of the Bonn Foreign Office (1960)

Struch, Friedrich
before 1945: employed in the fascist embassy in Rome (1939)
after 1945: consul first class in Windhuk, South West Africa (1964)

Tancré, Dr. Hans
before 1945: SS Scharführer, 1939 nazi consulate secretary in Sofia
after 1945: consul for re-appointment (1961)

Tannstein, Dr. Kurt
before 1945: legation secretary in the fascist embassy in the Vatican (1941), 1933 NSDAP (No. 2948420)
after 1945: Bonn ambassador in Tunisia (1964)

Templin, Paul Heinz
before 1945: as a member of the fascist consulate-general in Kattowitz (Katowice) he participated in preparing the attack on Poland
after 1945: government agent in the cultural department of the Bonn Foreign Office (1959)

Theusner, Dr. Hans-Joachim
before 1945: patronizing member of the SS
after 1945: consul first class in Edinburgh, Great Britain

Thomsen, Dr. Henning
before 1945: nazi legation counsellor in Dublin (1943), SS Rottenführer and candidate of the NSDAP (1938)
after 1945: reporting legation counsellor first class in the Bonn Foreign Office, head of the section for the development of foreign trade (1962), since 1965 ambassador to Iceland

Tichy, Dr. Alois
before 1945: legation counsellor in the Foreign Office (1945), 1937 NSDAP
after 1945: employed in the political department of the Bonn Foreign Office

Trützschler, Dr. Heinz, Freiherr von Falkenstein
before 1945: 1944 deputy head of section Pol. XII in the Foreign Office, afterwards consul in Geneva, NSDAP (No. 8183952)
after 1945: ambassador in Ireland (1964)

Ungern-Sternberg, Dr. Reinhold Freiherr von
before 1945: legation counsellor in Helsinki (1944), 1933 NSDAP (No. 2594983), SA Sturm 33
after 1945: until 1964 Bonn ambassador in Iran, then transferred to the embassy in London

Venediger, Dr. Günther
before 1945: 1937 active in the Gestapo (Berlin office), 1933 SA, NSDAP
after 1945: member of the Bonn Foreign Office

Vetter, Wilhelm
before 1945: nazi consulate secretary in Russe, Bulgaria (1944)
after 1945: second secretary in the Bonn embassy in Baghdad (1963)

Vogel, Dr. Georg
before 1945: legation counsellor in the legal department of the Foreign Office (1944), 1937 NSDAP, SS Obersturmführer
after 1945: Bonn ambassador in Venezuela (1964)

Waldheim, Gottfried von
before 1945: nazi legation counsellor in Spain (1945)
after 1945: consul-general in Valparaiso (1964)

Walther, Dr. Gebhard von
before 1945: embassy counsellor in the fascist embassy in Ankara (1943), 1939 candidate of the NSDAP
after 1945: ambassador in Ankara (1964)

Weber, Dr. Walther
before 1945: 1943–1944 head of section Pol I in the political department of the Foreign Office, 1937 NSDAP
after 1945: before Federer Bonn ambassador in the United Arab Republic (1964)

Wehrstedt, Dr. Friedrich-Wilhelm
before 1945: government counsellor in the fascist state apparatus, 1938, 1933 NSDAP (No. 2151075)
after 1945: inspector of the Bonn Foreign Office for diplomatic and consular representations abroad (1964)

Weiz, Dr. Gerhard
before 1945: legation counsellor in Buenos Aires (1944); applied for admission to the SS and in 1934 for service in the Gestapo, 1933 SA
after 1945: consul-general in Sao-Paolo, Brazil (1964)

Welck, Wolfgang Freiherr von
before 1945: 1943 legation counsellor first class in the office of Ambassador Ritter (liaison with the Supreme Command of the Wehrmacht), 1935 NSDAP (No. 2549805)
after 1945: Bonn ambassador in Switzerland (1964)

Wendland, Jork Alexander Freiherr von
before 1945: nazi legation secretary in Batavia (1941), 1933 NSDAP (No. 2948710)
after 1945: Bonn ambassador in Mauretania and Senegal (1964)

Werkmeister, Dr. Karl
before 1945: 1940–1944 legation counsellor first class in Hungary
after 1945: Bonn ambassador in Sweden (1963), retired for old age

Werthern, Charlotte Margot von
before 1945: employed in the information bureau of the Foreign Office (1944)
after 1945: head of the press section of the Bonn embassy in Dakar, Senegal (1962)

Wickert, Dr. Erwin
before 1945: 1940–1941 head of the radio department of the fascist embassy in China, afterwards in Japan
after 1945: head of section in the East department of the Bonn Foreign Office (1964)

Wobser, Herbert
before 1945: 1938–1941 NSDAP local group leader in Peking, 1941 to 1945 consulate secretary in Shanghai, 1934 NSDAP (No. 2873664)
after 1945: counsellor in the commercial policy department of the Bonn Foreign Office (1961)

Wollenweber, Dr. Karl-Gustav
before 1945: during the war member of the personnel department and legal de-

partment of the Foreign Office, 1933 NSDAP (No. 3020707)
after 1945: Bonn ambassador in Malta

Wolschke, Waldemar
before 1945: before his entrance into the Foreign Office police inspector, 1945 consulate secretary in Lisbon
after 1945: chancellor in the Bonn consulate in Liverpool (1962)

Wüstenberg, Dr. Paul
before 1945: senior government counsellor in the fascist state apparatus 1941, 1937 NSDAP (No. 5723204)
after 1945: In the Bonn foreign service in Santiago de Chile (1957)

Wussow, Fritz
before 1945: head of the fascist consulate in Orsova, Rumania 1940, 1934 NSDAP
after 1945: consul first class in Melbourne (1963)

Zapp, Dr. Karl-August
before 1945: 1940 as legation counsellor to the "Reich Commissar for the Occupied Districts of the Netherlands" he had a share in carrying out the fascist occupation policy; legation counsellor in Ankara (1944); 1933 NSDAP (No. 2717559)
after 1945: Bonn ambassador in Algeria (1964)

Zimmermann, Dr. Karl
before 1945: consulate secretary in the Foreign Office (1940)
after 1945: chancellor in the Bonn embassy in Lisbon (1962)

Zimmermann, Dr. Walter
before 1945: after 1942 in the radio policy department of the Foreign Office, 1934 NSDAP
after 1945: Bonn ambassador in Peru (1961), retired for reasons of age

Zinser, Dr. Christian
before 1945: nazi embassy counsellor in Manchuria 1942, 1944 in the fascist embassy in Nanking, 1937 NSDAP (No. 66421), 1928 SA, Sturmbannführer
after 1945: consul first class in Porto, Portugal (1964)

Zintel, Ludwig
before 1945: consulate secretary in the fascist consulate in Szeged, Hungary (1939)
after 1945: chancellor in the Bonn embassy in Tripolis (1963)

HITLER'S FIFTH COLUMN IN BONN'S SERVICE

Revanchism – Official West German State Policy

After the First World War German imperialism did not become reconciled with the fact that Germany had been made smaller through its fault. It aimed at re-establishing the frontiers of 1914 and – starting from this position – making a bid to conquer world domination. Its claim for a revision of existing frontiers and its cry for revenge for the defeat suffered were essential components of the preparations for the Second World War.

In order to condition the German people and the German minorities in other countries for revenge and have them participate in stirring up trouble with neighbouring peoples they set up a system of state, cultural and scientific institutions. Institutions of this type were, among others, the "Verein für das Deutschtum im Ausland" (VDA), Association for Germandom in Foreign Countries, the "Deutsches Auslandsinstitut", German Foreign Institute, Stuttgart, the "Deutsche Akademie" München and many dozens of associations engaged in keeping alive the attachment to the native country, like the "Baltische Arbeitsgemeinschaft", the "Sudetendeutscher Heimatbund", the "Vereinigung der Heimattreuen Ost- und Westpreussen" etc. Their aims were strictly limited to keeping alive the idea of a "mission" Germany had – according to their pretensions – in the "East" and to carry on a vigorous propaganda on the necessity of revising the frontiers, in order to make millions of Germans ready for a new war. Neighbouring peoples were systematically defamed as being inferior.

LEADERS OF GERMAN MINORITIES – SUPPRESSORS AND TORTURERS OF THE HOST PEOPLES

After the establishment of the fascist dictatorship these associations and societies entered a period of prosperity. Their activities were centrally coordinated and uniformly directed at preparing an aggressive war. At the same time state-supported new organizations came into being, like the extremely fascist "Bund deutscher Osten" (Federation of the German East), whose then leader, Theodor Oberländer, became minister for refugees in West Germany after 1945. As active functionaries of the nazi party the leaders of these organizations were in charge of subversive actions against Germany's neighbouring peoples that were part of the preparations for the war of aggression. After the attack they acted as the initiators and reliable tools of the fascist policy of extermination.

Many members of the German minorities living in Germany's neighbouring states were misused by these organizations for subversive activity against their host peoples. They were given the jobs of engaging in espionage, undermining the defensive capacity of these peoples and provoking incidents leading to a military attack by Hitler Germany. They drew up lists of "anti-German" minded persons, divided the population into the "racially valuable" and the "racially inferior" and thus created a prerequisite for the systematic decimation and extermination of the population after the attack by the fascist Wehrmacht.

Documents of the fascist Foreign Office and the SS show how the members of the "German Association", a fascist organization of the German minority in the Polish Warthe region, were used to commit terrorist actions serving as a pretext for the military aggression against Poland. (See Table 42, German Central Archive, Potsdam, under Auswärtiges Amt No. 61,150). Those engaged in revenge politics did not shrink from destroying churches, schools and nurses' homes. The leader of the "German Association" mentioned in the documents was Hans Kohnert, SS Oberführer and hangman of thousands of citizens of Bromberg (Bydgoszcz). Today he is the spokesman of the "Landsmannschaft Westpreussen" (Association of Fellow-countrymen of West Prussia) and a leading functionary in the revanchist organizations in West Germany.

During the occupation of the European countries by the Hitler regime those parts of the German minorities that had succumbed to fascist agitation engaged in oppressing, exploiting and murdering the host peoples.

IN THE GDR NO BASIS FOR REVANCHISM

New frontiers were fixed in the Potsdam Agreement and resettlement measures were taken. It was the aim to end once and for all the imperialist subversive activity in the neighbouring countries of Germany, to compensate these countries for the immense losses they had suffered in the war and to create stable frontiers that can never again be used as a pair of pincers by German imperialism against other countries.

Large parts of the German minorities were resettled in Germany in the four occupation zones of the great powers.

In the Soviet occupation zone of Germany no effort was spared to provide relief for the resettlers, who had so ignominiously been betrayed by Hitler, to give them a new existence and a secure perspective. Resettled farmers, for example, were given land of the Junkers and with public assistance they established new farmsteads. Frank and patient explanations showed them who is to blame for the loss of their homeland, that the German imperialists have forever forfeited the former eastern territories by their policy of war and destruction. The resettlers found a new home in the GDR and became equal citizens of the peaceful German state. Here there are no organizations or newspapers advocating revenge. On the contrary the government of the GDR has recognized the existing frontiers in official treaties. For the first time in German history friendly and peaceful relations were established with the neighbouring peoples in the east and south-east of Europe.

IN WEST GERMANY NEW NAMES – OLD AIMS

German imperialism, however, resurrected in West Germany, presses for a revision of frontiers for the third time in this century. The Federal Republic is the only state in Europe which raises claims to foreign territory, to the "frontiers of 1937". The resettlers living in West Germany are misused to propagate this policy of revenge and assist in carrying it out.

For years the West German government has deliberately omitted to incorporate the resettlers steadily and systematically into social life and give them an established status and secure perspective. For years the resettlers have lived in barrack camps and emergency dwellings. Even today, at a time when most of the resettlers in West Germany have settled down, the illusion they might one day be able to return to their former abodes that are now foreign territory is incessantly nourished in them.

After 1945 the old revenge-seeking associations were reestablished and enjoy the active encouragement of the West German government. They did not lose any time to begin with their pernicious activity, but as the old fascist revenge-seeking organizations had compromised themselves too much their names were changed. Thus the "Deutsche Akademie" was renamed "Goethe-Institut", München, the "Deutsches Auslandsinstitut" turned into the "Institut für Auslandsbeziehungen" (Institute of Foreign Relations), Stuttgart, the "Heimatbünde" (homeland federations) changed into "Landsmannschaften" (associations of fellow-countrymen), and the "Bund der Vertriebenen" (Federation of Expelled Persons) replaced the fascist "Bund deutscher Osten". Two documents dated from 1938 and 1959 provide evidence that the aims have remained unchanged. (See Table 43) "Das Deutschtum im Sudetenraum" (Germandom in the Sudeten Area), the map issued in 1938 by the regional Silesian group (Landesgruppe Schlesien) of the "Bund deutscher Osten", and "Sudetendeutscher Turnerbrief")

127 CENTRAL REVANCHIST ORGANIZATIONS

The resettler organizations existing in West Germany today are part of that system of state and non-state institutions which has been established for the purpose of realizing the policy of revenge. It is intended to win all former resettlers and beyond that the whole West German population, if possible, for the policy of revising the frontiers, the "reconquest" of lost territories and the preparation of a new aggression. This system has been devised essentially according to the following aspects:

(1) Organization of revanchism by the federal government and the provincial (Länder) governments. The most important state authorities are, above all, the "Federal Ministry for Expelled Persons, Refugees and War Injured Persons" (BMVt) with the "Federal Equalization Office", the "Advisory Council" serving the minister, the so-called refugee camps as well as the "Federal Ministry for All-German Questions" (BMG) with its countless, often camouflaged organizations ("Kuratorium unteilbares Deutschland" (Committee for an Indivisible Germany), "Forschungsbeirat" Research Advisory Council, etc.).

Department I in the BMG is especially responsible for implementing and encouraging revanchism. According to official explanations it is concerned with *"matters involving the Soviet occupation zone of Germany and the German eastern territories, encouragement for the all-German idea, measures promoting the re-establishment of German unity (which means unification within the 1937 frontiers – editor)." (Die Bundesrepublik, Teilausgabe Bund,* Carl Heymanns Verlag KG, 1962–63, p. 266)

In the BMVt sections I/3, II/2 and II/3 are in charge of the following activities: "Department I/3: Advisory councils, associations, organizations. Department II/2: . . . Questions of reunification and integration. Department II/3: Cultural affairs (§ 96 BVFG), information concerning the East." (ibid., p. 264)

There exist "refugee ministries" or official authorities performing the same functions in the Bonn representations of the federal provinces and in the federal governments themselves.

(2) Organization in more than 30 "Landsmannschaften", based on former residential regions, with their branches and interest groups.

(3) Organization on the basis of vocation, trade and profession, e.g., "Bauernverband der Vertriebenen e.V." (Expelled Farmers' Association).

(4) Organization in societies engaged in working out the theoretical foundations for revanchist propaganda, e.g., "Nordostdeutscher Kulturrat e.V." (North-East German Cultural Council).

(5) Organization according to religious aspects and charitable work, e.g., "Katholische Arbeitsstelle für Heimatvertriebene" (Catholic Charitable Society for Expelled Persons).

ab 28/11.41.

Generalkommissar in Riga
Abteilung II a.

21

Riga, 20. November 1941.

Tagebuch Nr. 446/41 g

An den
Herrn Reichskommissar
für das Ostland

in R i g a .

Betrifft: Monatlicher Bericht über Einrichtung von Ghettos in jüdischen Arbeitslagern, Arbeitseinsatz und Behandlung der Juden.

Bezug: Dortiges Schreiben vom 18.8.1941 IIa 438/41 geheim.

Mit Ablauf des Monats November sind in der vorläufigen Lösung des Judenproblems in Lettland gute Fortschritte zu verzeichnen.

Die Gebiete Mitau, Wolmar und Riga - Land sind endgültig judenfrei.

In den übrigen Gebieten sind Ghettos eingerichtet worden und zwar in Riga, Libau und Dünaburg. Schwierigkeiten bei der Einrichtung eines Ghettos bestehen nur in Libau. Durch starke Zerstörung der Stadt ist es nicht möglich, ein Ghetto innerhalb oder am Rande der Stadt einzurichten. In Libau hat auch kein eigentliches Judenviertel bestanden, sodass eine Umsiedlung der nichtjüdischen Bevölkerung aus 574 Wohnungen vorgenommen werden müsste. Diese Massnahme kann aber wegen der grossen Wohnungsnot kaum durchgeführt werden. Der Gebietskommissar in Libau führt mit der Marine Verhandlungen wegen einer einige Kilometer ausserhalb Libaus leerstehenden Kasernen. Diese Kasernen würden Raum bieten, um die 3890 in Libau lebenden Juden aufzunehmen.

Das flache Land im ganzen Generalkommissariat Lettland ist judenfrei.

Der Reichskommissar
fuer das Ostland
Abt. I HA.

Riga, den 17. September 1941.

3.1.1.2 u

13.11.41
9/XI
28/XI

An saemtliche Herren Hauptabteilungs- und
Abteilungsleiter sowie
alle Gefolgschaftsmitglieder.

Betrifft: Vorlaeufige Geschaeftsordnung.

Vorlage der Eingaenge:

1) Ministerialdirigent Fruendt. -Spaeter nach besonders ergangener Weisung zuerst dem persoenlichen Referenten des Reichskommissars, Regierungsrat Wichmann-

---

Pressenotiz. 29.11.41. 325

Auf der Rückreise von dem Berliner Staatsakt trafen der finnische Aussenminister Exzellenz W i t t i n g und der Chef des Protokolls im Finnischen Aussenministerium, Minister H a k k a r a i n e n in Begleitung des Deutschen Gesandten in Finnland, Minister von Blücher und Legationssekretär Dr. S a c h s vom Auswärtigen Amt in Berlin zu einem kurzen Zwischenaufenthalt in Riga ein. Zu Ehren der Gäste hatten der Reichskommissar für das Ostland und Frau Lohse einen Empfang veranstaltet, an dem von deutscher Seite General Braemer, der Generalkommissar in Riga, Staatsrat Dr. Drechsler, Ministerialdirigent Fründt, Pressechef Dr. Zimmermann und der persönliche Referent des Reichskommissars Reg.Rat Wichmann teilnahmen.

4054²

TABLE 41

TABLE 42

Auswärtiges Amt
Pol. V 983 g Rs
Eing. 2. Aug 1939

Auswärtiges Amt
Pol. V 8008
eing. 21. AUG 1938

Telegramm (Geh. Ch. V.)

Warschau, den 20. August 1939 14.25 Uhr 193

Ankunft: " " " " 15.40 "

Nr.170 v.20.8. Im Anschluß an Telegr.v.18. Nr.167.

Pol V 9699 Rs

Generalkonsulat Thorn drahtet:

Ortsgruppenleiter Diekmann Straßburg meldet, daß Volksdeutscher Erich Brueschke, Briesen ihn und Volksdeutschen Pfarrer Engel, Wittenburg, zur Teilnahme an bevorstehenden provokatorischen Sprengungen aufgefordert habe. Brueschke, der von Stapo Danzig ausgebildet sein will, hat angeblich von dort Auftrag in kommender Woche nach Stichwort des Senders Danzig Sprengungen in Briesen und Wittenburg auszuführen. In Wittenburg soll Kirche, Pfarrhaus, Schwesternhaus oder Molkerei in Betracht kommen. Sprengmittel sollen mit polnischen Kraftwagen von Danzig geliefert werden. Schluß des Telegramms aus Thorn.

Wühlisch

...in 19 St.
...sind gegangen:
1 an Pol.V (Arb. St.)
2 .. R.A.M.
3 .. St.S.
4 .. Chef A.O.
5 .. B.R.A.M.
6 .. Dir. Pers.
7 .. .. Pol.
8 .. D. Pol.
9 .. Dg. W
10 .. Dg. W
11 .. Dir. Recht
12 .. Dg. ..
13 .. Dir. Kult
14 .. Dg. ..
15 .. D. Presse
16 .. Ast Prot.
17 .. Ref Dtschl.
18 .. Partei
19 .. pers. Stab (Hewel)

Der Reichsführer-SS
und
Chef der Deutschen Polizei
im Reichsministerium des Innern

Berlin SW 11, den 25. August 1939.
Prinz-Albrecht-Straße 8
Fernsprecher 120040

207

S.V.7 Nr.372/39 - 509 - 27 gRs.

Bitte in der Antwort vorstehendes Geschäftszeichen und Datum anzugeben.

~~Geheime Reichssache~~
1 Ausfertigung.

Auswärtiges Amt
Pol. V 1107 g Rs
Eing. 1. Aug. 1939

Geheime Reichssache!

An das

Auswärtige Amt,
z.Hd. von Herrn Legationsrat Frhr.von Heyden-Rynsch
- oder Vertreter im Amt -

Berlin W 8

Wilhelmstr.74/76.

Betrifft: Den Volksdeutschen polnischer Staatsangehörigkeit Erich Brüschke.

Auf das Schreiben ~~vom 22. 8. 1939~~ - Pol. V 999 gRs.

Die Politische Polizei in Danzig hat über Brüschke folgendes berichtet:

"Bei Obengenanntem handelt es sich um den volksdeutschen polnischen Staatsangehörigen Erich Brüschke, geb. am 23.7.1913 zu Rodeck, Kreis Hohensalza, wohnhaft in Briesen, ul.Marszalka Pilsudzkiego 23. Brüschke ist dortselbst Inhaber eines Kolonialwarengeschäfts und Mitglied der Deutschen Vereinigung, OG. Briesen. Im Auftrage und auf Veranlassung des SD-Unterabschnitts Danzig hat Brüschke sich vor einigen Tagen vorübergehend in Danzig aufgehalten. Er ist dann von der SD-Dienststelle, Unterabschnitt Danzig, mit besonderen Aufträgen versehen wieder nach Briesen zurückgekehrt. Die erhaltenen Aufträge bewegen sich in Richtung Unterbringung von Sprengstoffen und Waffen in Polen. Über die Rolle, die Brüschke in diesem Zusammenhang in Polen spielt, ist heute vom SD-Unterabschnitt Danzig ein Bericht nach Berlin, und zwar an SS-Brigadeführer Jost, gesandt worden. Der Bericht wird durch SS-H.Stuf. Zitzmann vom SD-Unterabschnitt Danzig überreicht werden, der mit Flugzeug heute nach Berlin geflogen ist."

Im Auftrage
gez.Dr. Best

Beglaubigt:
Verwaltungssekretär

Deutsche Bücherei

ZA 39304

Postverlagsort Frankfurt am Main

SUDETENDEUTSCHER

Turnerbrief

10. Jahrgang | 1. Hornungs (Februar) 1959 | 1. Folge

Auf die erste Seite der ersten Folge des zehnten Jahrganges unseres Turnerbriefes stellen wir die Karte

Ostgrenze nach dem Selbstbestimmungsrecht,

Zwischen Verniggerung und Bolschewisierung

Als ich die heutige Nummer der „Turnerjugend" erblickte, auf deren Titelseite mich das Bild des Niggers Armstrong beunruhigend anstarrte, glaubte ich einer Sinnestäuschung zu unterliegen. Wären darunter nicht im Widersinn die vier roten Jahnschen F und in gotischer Fraktur die Buchstaben „Turnerjugend" wie zum Hohn gestanden, so hätte ich an eine amerikanische Reklameschrift oder einen albernen Fastnachtsscherz glauben können.

Und liest man dann noch die Innenseiten, einschließlich der pflaumenweichen Betrachtung von Karl Wilhelm Schulte und betrachtet man die widerlichen Bilder, dann meint man ein ganz übles, instinktloses Erzeugnis amerikahöriger Fans vor sich zu haben und nicht unser deutsches Erziehungsorgan der Turnerjugend, das wir bislang mit so viel Freude und Stolz regelmäßig in die Hand nahmen!

Es ist entsetzlich!

Das Ganze ist so furchtbar, daß man nach Worten ringen muß, um es in seinem ganzen Ausmaß richtig zu umfassen. Ist uns denn der letzte Rest an Stolz, an Eigenständigkeit, an Kulturempfinden verlorengegangen?

Sind wir denn noch wert, Deutsche, Europäer, Abendländer, die Erben Goethes, Schillers, Mozarts, Beethovens und Bachs genannt zu werden?

Vergessen denn die „Herausgeber" und „Schriftleiter" solcher Zeitschriftennummern, daß sie damit einen Damm einreißen können, einen Damm, den die Turnerjugend als eine der wenigen Aufrechten innerhalb der deutschen Jugend noch hielt? Diesen Damm empfand ich als den Schutzwall vor der Ueberfremdung, vor den Fluten Afrikas wie Asiens!

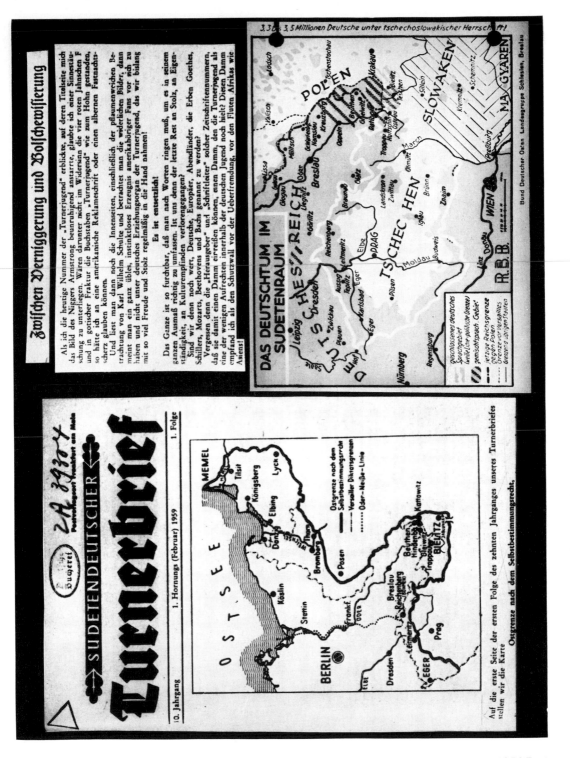

Bund Deutscher Osten Landesgruppe Schlesien, Breslau

Ref. P.Z.(GenKsl.Reinhardt)   Berlin,den 29.Januar 1941

Geheim

Zu den Wahlen im Verein der ausländischen Presse

Bei dem Bericht über die Vorgeschichte der Wahl führt Lemmer ausser den bekannten Tatsachen noch folgendes aus:

Oechsner sei gestern nachmittag (24.1.)/in der amer.Bot. dringend davon abgeraten worden, zu kandidieren, um keinen Konflikt heraufzubeschwören. Es habe dabei wieder "so einen ziemlichen Krach" zwischen Oechsner und Sigrid Schultz (Chicago Tribune) auf der einen Seite und zwischen Enderis (New York Times) und Lochner auf der anderen Seite gegeben. Interessant sei, dass die Entscheidung eigentlich erst in der Botschaft fiel. Für Senatra, so meint Lemmer, haben sie nur den Posten des zweiten Vorsitzenden retten können, da eine derart schlechte Stimmung geherrscht habe. Von verschiedenen Seiten habe man ihnen geraten, einen Neutralen zu nehmen, da sich Italien ja im Kriege befinde. Lemmer spricht sich besonders lobend über den grossen Korpsgeist und die grosse Disziplin der Italiener unter Senatra's Führung aus; man müsse ihre Kampfbereitschaft rühmen.

Ruhmlos sei dagegen das Verhalten der Japaner gewesen, da nicht ein einziger von diesen erschienen war, trotzdem er (Lemmer) einige Tage vorher noch alles mit dem vierten Botschaftssekretär besprochen habe. Das stimme genau mit der Parole überein, so meint Lemmer ironisch, dass sich Oechsner vor allen Dingen auf die Japaner verlassen habe, die versicherten, sie würden ihn wählen. Lemmer meint hierzu, dass da irgend etwas faul sei und er die Sache im Auge behalten werde.

Zum Schluss spricht Lemmer sein Bedauern darüber aus, dass der neue Botschafter Oshima noch nicht da sei; man könne sonst gleich das Nötige veranlassen.

1.) Hn.L.R. Rasche

Dg. P.

2.) Zurück an Ref. PZ

VERTRETER
DES AUSWÄRTIGEN AMTS
BEIM REICHSKOMMISSAR
FÜR DAS OSTLAND

173

Riga, den 13.April 1944
Rosenberg-Ring 12

Nr. 481/44.

Reichskommissar für das Ostland
14. APR 1944
Pressechef

Betr.: Interview-Reise des reichsdeutschen Korrespondenten der Neuen Züricher Zeitung, L e m m e r.

Unter Bezugnahme auf das gestrige Telefonat teile ich ergebenst mit, dass der reichsdeutsche Korrespondent der Neuen Züricher Zeitung auf Anordnung des Auswärtigen Amts und im Einvernehmen mit der Presseabteilung des Reichsostministeriums am 18. ds.Mts. hierher und nach Reval für 3 Tage kommen soll, um von Herrn Landesdirektor M ä e und möglichst auch von SS-Gruppenführer B a n g e r s k i s ein Interview über den Bolschewismus zu erhalten.

Falls die Reisedispositionen eingehalten werden können, soll Herr Lemmer am 18. mit dem Flugzeug hier eintreffen und am 19. nach Reval weiterfliegen.

Windecker

An den
Herrn Reichskommissar
für das Ostland
z.Hd.von
Herrn Pressechef
Z i m m e r m a n n
R i g a

TABLE 44

TRETER
AUSWÄRTIGEN AMTS
REICHSKOMMISSAR
DAS OSTLAND

Riga, den 24.April 1944
Rosenberg-Ring 12

r.481/44

r.: Entsendung eines Korrespondenten der "Neuen Züricher Zeitung."

2 Durchdrucke -

Das Auswärtige Amt hat mir folgendes mitgeteilt:

"Es konnte nunmehr geordnet werden, dass hiesiger Vertreter der Züricher Zeitung Ernst L e m m e r am Donnerstag, den 27. nach Riga für Interview M ä e abfliegt.

Lemmer hat jetzt mehrere Tage für ein auch sonstiges Programm zur Verfügung.

Lemmer ist erfahrener Journalist guten Formats, erscheint geeignet, alle fürs Ausland wirksamen Themen aus dem dortigen Raum zu behandeln. Er ist Reichsdeutscher und auch vertrauenswürdig genug, informatorisch über dortige politische Entwicklung ins Bild gesetzt zu werden. Solche Informationen könnten ihm mittelbar behilflich sein, die Berichte für seine grosse und angesehene Zeitung entsprechend dortiger Orientierung wirksam abzufassen. Es ist Herrn Lemmer gesagt worden, dass er mit diesem ersten Einsatz vielleicht den Vorrang erhält, über die weitere Entwicklung dortiger Dinge im Zusammenhang mit einer späteren neuen Reise berichten zu können. Herr Lemmer wird daher pfleglicher Betreuung empfohlen.

Rückreisetermin bitte ich im Benehmen mit ihm von dort aus festzulegen und Kosten für Rückflug dort zu übernehmen.

Interview-Bericht M ä e , U l u o t s und B a n g e r s k i s und vielleicht sonstige an Ort und Stelle am besten gleich abzufassende Berichte Lemmers für seine Zeitung bitte ich geprüft dem Chef vom Dienst Presseabteilung zwecks sofortiger Weiterleitung an hiesige Vertretung der Zeitung durchzugeben.

gez. Braun von Stumm"

Indem ich diese Weisung des Auswärtigen Amts, die, wie ich erfahre, im Einvernehmen mit dem Reichsministerium für Propaganda und dem Reichsostministerium erfolgt, hiermit weitergebe, wäre ich dankbar, wenn das Notwendige für die Reise Lemmers und die Gewährung

n

skommissar
as Ostland

a

rung der Interviews bei den auch dort geeignscheinenden Personen veranlasst würde.

Zwei weitere Durchdrucke sind beigefügt.

363

ERNST LEMMER
KORRESPONDENT AUSLÄNDISCHER ZEITUNGEN
MITGLIED DES VEREINS
DER AUSLÄNDISCHEN PRESSE, E. V., ZU BERLIN

BERLIN-ZEHLENDORF, 25.4.44
HOHE KIEFER 13
(KLEIN-MACHNOW)
H 4 ZEHLENDORF 3123

An das

Polizeipräsidium II

Berlin

Mggazinstr.

Ich bitte, aufgrund der mir vom Auswärtigen Amt erteilten Anweisung, um Gültigkeitsverlängerung des beigefügten Dienstpasses.

Auf Veranlassung des Auswärtigen Amtes habe ich eine Dienstreise nach Riga und Reval zu unternehmen. Es handelt sich um die Ausführung eines mir erteilten journalistischen Sonderauftrages. Die Abreise ist vorgesehen mit dem Flugzeug für den 27.d.M., Rückreise bis spätestens 10. Mai.

Falls telefonische Rückfrage dortseits gewünscht, steht das Auswärtige Amt zur Auskunft zur Verfügung: entweder die Presseabteilung, Legationsrat Dr. Staudacher, oder die Abteilung R XV.

Heil Hitler!

Lemmer Ernst

381

Auswärtiges Amt
R Pa Lemmer

Berlin W 35, den 26. April 1944.
Am Karlsbad 8

Für den Schriftleiter Ernst L e m m e r war zu Reisen in das Ausland im Auftrage der Reichsregierung anliegender Dienstpass ausgestellt. Da die Voraussetzungen für die Benutzung des Dienstpasses weiterhin vorliegen, wird gebeten, den anliegenden Dienstpass bis zum 26.Juli 44 zu verlängern.

Auswärtiges Amt, Paßstelle
Konsul

An
das Polizeipräsidium, Paßstelle
Berlin C
Magazinstr. 6/8.

TABLE 45

8. April 1936 .

An den

Gauamtsleiter für Kommunalpolitik
Pg. C r u l l ,

S c h w e r i n i/Meckl.
.-.-.-.-.-.-.-.-.-.-.-.-.-.

Adolf Hitlerhaus .

Werter Parteigenosse C r u l l !

Vor einigen Tagen ging in Ribnitz das Gerücht ,dass der frühere Stadtrat Michelsen auf dem Flugplatz Pütnitz Beschäftigung gefunden habe . Ich habe mich sofort um eine Bestätigung bemüht und festgestellt , dass Michelsen tatsächlich als Angestellter bei der Kommandantur des Flugplatzes beschäftigt ist .

[illegible]

Es liegt deswegen meines Erachtens im vordringlichen Interesse der Parteistellen , wenn Michelsen aus diesem Rüstungsbetriebe wieder entfernt wird. Die hiesige Parteileitung und ich halten ihn nicht für politisch so zuverlässig, dass er in dem Betriebe beschäftigt werden könnte.

Ich bitte um Ihre Stellungnahme in dieser Angelegenheit .

Heil Hitler !
Der Bürgermeister .

Nach 1 Woche.
D. 8/4 36.

112/9
Michelsen

3. September 1936 .

Dr. W./Nes.

An die

Mecklenburgische Politische Polizei ,

S c h w e r i n i/Meckl.
.-.-.-.-.-.-.-.-.-.-.-.-.-.

Schelfstraße .

In dem letzten politischen Monatsbericht habe ich absichtlich die Angelegenheit M i c h e l s e n nicht mit aufgeführt , da ich sie in einem besonderen Bericht mitteilen wollte.

Der frühere Stadtrat M i c h e l s e n hat sich wieder ein besonderes Stück geleistet. Wie der Politischen Polizei bekannt ist , ist von den Parteistellen und von mir wiederholt darauf hingewiesen worden , dass eine Beschäftigung des Michelsen in einem Wehrbetriebe im höchsten Grade unerwünscht ist. Michelsen ist , nachdem sein Antrag, bei den Aero-Sportwerken unterzukommen , abgelehnt worden ist , seit einiger Zeit auf dem Fliegerhorst Pütnitz [illegible]

Ich bitte die Politische Polizei , sich in dieser Sache nochmals einzuschalten , damit auf alle Fälle die Entlassung des Michelsen in Pütnitz aufrecht erhalten bleibt .

Der Gauamtsleiter für Kommunalpolitik und der Kreisleiter des Kreises Rostock-Land haben Abschrift dieses Schreibens erhalten .

Sep. 1936

Heil Hitler !
Der Bürgermeister .

Nach 1 Monat.

R.,28.9.36.

Nach 2 Monaten
D. 4/11 36

1.) Michelsen ist in Pütnitz entlassen.
2.) Zu den Akten .

R. 16.1.1937.

TABLE 46

Der Leiter der Berufsvereinigung deutscher Vorgeschichtsforscher.

Königsberg Pr., den 14.2.1934
Theaterplatz 5 B.

Tagebuch-Nr: 425/34

1/16 II - 400/34

Sehr verehrter Herr Minister!

Angesichts der Bedeutung des Falles Herman Wirth für den Nationalsozialismus gestatte ich mir, Ihnen als Nationalsozialist einige Ihnen vielleicht noch unbekannte und meines Dafürhaltens entscheidende Unterlagen über die Beurteilung von Herrn Professor Herman Wirth zu überreichen.

Mit Heil Hitler
ganz ergebenst

Herrn
Minister E n g e l l,
Schwerin i. Mecklenburg,
Regierung.

2. U.

TABLE 47

Berufsvereinigung deutscher Vorgeschichtsforscher.

Königsberg Pr., den 16.1.1934.
Theaterplatz 5b.

A b s c h r i f t!

Sehr verehrter Herr Ministerialrat!

Im Anschluß an unsere Besprechung über den Fall Wirth möchte ich zur Unterrichtung des Herrn Ministers und der Ihrigen Ihnen noch folgendes mitteilen:

Herr Prof. Wirth hat inzwischen in den Hamburger Nachrichten vom 12.1.1934 einen Aufsatz erscheinen lassen, der u.a. scharfe unsachliche Ausfälle gegen Pg. Prof. Neckel enthält. Herr Wirth preist sich dort als alter Marburger Nationalsozialist von 1924. Soweit mir bekannt ist, gehört Prof. H. Wirth noch jetzt wohl der nationalsozialistischen Partei nicht an. Daß er am Beginn des vorigen Jahres noch kein Mitglied war, glaube ich mit voller Bestimmtheit zu wissen. Im Jahre 1929 ereigneten sich die Vorgänge, von denen ich Ihnen schon neulich mündlich Kenntnis gab. Herr Wirth wurde damals von Herrn Schindler-Hamburg unterstützt, den er inzwischen selbst (wohl im Rostocker Anzeiger) als "jüdischer Ölmagnat" bezeichnete. Herr Wirth wandte sich damals mit Hilfe von Herrn Schindler an den Vertreter der jüdischen Hochfinanz, Herrn Warburg, um weitere Unterstützung und ersuchte Herrn Schindler, Herrn Warburg auf die "schöne und wertvolle" Besprechung hinzuweisen, die Wirths Freund Mühlestein in der Frankfurter Zeitung gerade in diesen Tagen hatte erscheinen lassen. Es ist das die Besprechung, die den Wert der Wirth'schen Arbeiten im Kampf gegen die völkische Bewegung und Jugenderziehung besonders unterstreicht. Daß Herr Wirth sich nach diesen Vorgängen als alter Nationalsozialist von 1924 empfiehlt, entspricht der gesamten Eigenart seiner Persönlichkeit. Ein Auszug aus der Mühlestein'schen Besprechung enthält ein von mir diesen Zeilen in Abschrift beigefügter guter Zeitungsaufsatz von H. Urbanek. Näheres hat auch in der Zeitschrift "Der Hammer" 1932, Pg. E. Witte berichtet. Eine Abschrift der damals von Pg. A. Rosenberg an Prof. Wirth gesandten Zeilen lege ich ebenfalls diesem Briefe bei. Ich habe sie s.Z. in meiner Eigenschaft als Dozent an der damaligen nationalsozialistischen Volkshochschule vom Leiter der Fachgruppe für deutsche Vorgeschichte im Kampfbund für deutsche Kultur zur Kenntnis und Verwertung bei der Arbeit gegen Prof. Wirth erhalten.

Über die Beziehungen von Herrn Prof. Wirth zu Freimaurerkreisen im Jahre 1932 könnte Pg. S.A.-Truppführer Prof. Wiegers Berlin-Charlottenburg, Sybelstr. 10, einige Angaben zur Verfügung stellen.

Sehr begrüßt habe ich, daß nach unserer Besprechung am 11. auch im Völkischen Beobachter ein ausführlicher Bericht von Pg. Steche gegen Prof. Wirth's Auswertung der sogenannten Ura-Linda-Chronik erschien. Auch dort ist unterstrichen, daß Wirth kritiklos deutschfeindliche Seiten der sogenannten Ura-Linda-Chronik als wahr ansieht und dementsprechend verwertet. Herr Wirth stellt es in seinem Hamburger oben erwähnten Aufsatz wieder einmal so dar, als ob er sich im Kampf gegen die Liberalisten der Wissenschaft befindet. Das ist erneut eine bewußte Unwahrheit. Herr Wirth weiß genau, daß ihm führend besonders kämpferische Nationalsozialisten gegenüberstehen.

Mit Heil Hitler und deutschem Gruß
Ihr ergebenster

gez. B. Frhr. v. Richthofen.

Herrn
Ministerialrat Sunkel
B e r l i n .

…sche Evangelische Kirche
Kirchliches Außenamt
A 3216/39

Berlin-Charlottenburg 2, den 22. September 39
Jebensstr. 3.

113

An

…as Auswärtige Amt
…urpolitische Abteilung
…s Herrn Vortragenden Legationsrat
Lorenz

Berlin W 8

Der im Kirchlichen Aussenamt beschäftigte Dr. habil. Eugen G e r s t e n m a i e r , geb. 25. August 1906, soll zwecks Abwehr der Propaganda der Westmächte eine informatorische Reise in die nordeuropäischen Länder unternehmen. Dr. Gerstenmaier ist noch nicht zum Militärdienst einberufen, ist aber wehrpflichtig und bedarf für Auslandsreisen eines Urlaubes durch das zuständige Wehrbezirkskommando. Es wird gebeten, Herrn Dr. Gerstenmaier eine Bescheinigung auszustellen, die die Dringlichkeit seiner Reise bezeugt.

Ich bemerke noch, dass Dr. Gerstenmaier Angehöriger des SA Reitersturmes 1/29 ist.

Heckel

…im Reichsministerium des Innern

096

Der Direktor des Instituts für Staatsforschung an der Universität Berlin und sein wissenschaftliches Personal werden von mir laufend zur Bearbeitung staatspolitisch wichtiger Aufgaben herangezogen, die im Zusammenhange mit der Staatsorganisation im Kriege stehen.

Ich bitte daher, bei der Festsetzung des Personal- und Sachetats des Instituts für Staatsforschung an der Universität Berlin für das Rechnungsjahr 1940/41 die Grundsätze anzuwenden, die für gleiche Institute und Anstalten gelten.

Stuckart.

Kult Mob 1628

Berlin, den 23. September 1939.

…f das Schreiben vom 22. September
…39 -A 3216/38 -

Geheim

Heute

Auf das nebenbezeichnete Schreiben wird zur Vorlage bei dem zuständigen Wehrmachtakommando bestätigt, daß die Reise des im Kirchlichen Außenamt tätigen Dr. Eugen Gerstenmaier, geb. 25. August 1906, in die nordeuropäischen Länder im Einvernehmen mit dem Auswärtigen Amt erfolgt und im außenpolitischen Interesse liegt.

Im Auftrag

…errn GK Großkopf Stempel. gez. Großkopf.

…d. Bitte um Vollziehung.

Die Reise erfolgt im Einver…
…en mit Herrn Gesandten von Twar…
…di.

TABLE 48

(6) Youth organizations, e.g., "Deutsche Jugend des Ostens" (DJO), "Aktion Katholischer Landsmannschaftlicher Jugend" im "Bund der Katholischen Jugend".

(7) Organization in groups and sections of the West German political parties, e.g., "Union der Vertriebenen" within the CDU/CSU, the "Exile CDU".

(8) Organization in extremely right-wing radical associations of a semi-fascist character, e.g., "Aktion Oder-Neisse" (AKON) engaged in building up a coordinated front of all ultra-right forces in the various "refugee organizations"; and the "Rat der Ostdeutschen Landesvertretungen", concentrating its subversive activity primarily on Polish and Soviet territory.

(9) There are various committees in the West German parliaments engaged in promoting and encouraging revanchism. The Bundestag alone has five committees, e.g., the "Bundestag Committee for All-German and Berlin Questions".

(10) Three top organizations were set up to coordinate the activity of the various revenge-seeking organizations:

(a) "Bund der Vertriebenen – Vereinigte Landsmannschaften und Landesverbände" (BdV);

(b) "Gesamtverband der Sowjetzonenflüchtlinge" (Association of Soviet Zone Refugees) with the "Vereinigte Landsmannschaften Mitteldeutschlands" (VLM);

(c) "Arbeitsgemeinschaft der West- und Überseevertriebenen" (Working Group of West and Overseas Refugees).

The BdV is in charge of drawing up and coordinating revanchist actions against Germany's eastern and south-eastern neighbours. There are 20 "Landsmannschaften" affiliated to it, and there are a total of eleven regional branches situated in all federal provinces and, contrary to international law, even in the special territory of West Berlin. The "Gesamtverband der Sowjetzonenflüchtlinge" and the VLM with the five "Landsmannschaften" affiliated to them concentrate on subversive activity and instigation against the GDR.

At present there are at least 127 central revenge-seeking organizations in West Germany. They are supported and encouraged by the federal government and represent in various forms the territorial claims of the West German imperialists. This number does not include the militarist, terrorist and anti-Semitic organizations and the neo-fascist political parties.

FINANCED BY THE STATE

The revanchist organizations not only receive every possible intellectual and moral support but also generous financial assistance from the Bonn government. The complete budget of the "Vertriebenenministerium" (Refugee Ministry) rose from 30 million marks in 1955 to 244 million marks in 1963. In the 1964 budget year the contributions for an "intensification of large-scale cultural efforts" of the revanchist organizations alone rose by 250,000 marks compared with 1963.

The organizations also receive large financial contributions from the provincial governments as shown by the example of Hesse, a federal province governed by a social democratic majority. In 1964 alone 2.8 million marks were made available for "Heimatpolitik", (homeland policy), a sum made up of the following:

"There are now the following sums available from provincial sources for the promotion of activity among refugees:
1,150,000 marks for additional social work,
275,000 marks to promote and support meetings arranged by groups of the "Landsmannschaften", and to strenghten all-German consciousness,
370,000 marks for East German questions connected with adult education
460,000 marks for lectures in "Ostkunde"
550,000 marks to promote and support sponsorships concerning East and Central Germany."

(*Ostpreussenblatt*, Hamburg, 27 June 1964)

In 1945 War Criminals – in 1965 Revanchist Leaders

At the head of the West German revenge-seeking associations and ministries are persons who are guilty of having committed serious crimes against peace and humanity.

As high-ranking SS officers and leaders of fifth columns they participated in preparing and triggering off the Second World War and in criminal offences against prisoners of war and the civil population of the countries assaulted by the fascists. Ulitz, spokesman and thus top-ranking functionary of the present "Landsmannschaft Oberschlesien" (Upper Silesia) in West Germany was the leader of the "Deutscher Volksbund für polnisch Oberschlesien", a fascist organization of the German minority in Poland. Ulitz and his "Volksbund" took part in the assault on the Gleiwitz (Gliwice) radio station. The fascists used this provocation as a pretext for the military attack on Poland and thus unleashed the Second World War. Kohnert, at present spokesman of the "Landsmannschaft Westpreussen" (West Prussia), who has already been mentioned, was the leader of the fascist "Deutsche Vereinigung" and in this capacity responsible for the murder of thousands of Polish citizens in Bromberg (Bydgoszcz).

As civil servants working in the fascist occupation authorities leaders of the revenge-seeking organizations participated in plundering, oppressing and exterminating the subjected peoples. This is true, for example, of Dr. Werner Essen, at present ministerial counsellor and official in the "Refugee Ministry". As head of a department in the fascist "Reich Commissariat for the East" he decided who was to be considered "racially inferior" in the fascist occupied Baltic Soviet Republics and the Belorussian SSR. For the people involved this usually meant deportation to a concentration camp and death.

As officials of the fascist authorities in Germany they participated in the persecutions of anti-fascist and Jewish citizens. Thus the former nazi mayor of Ribnitz, Dr. Walter Wegener, today state secretary in the Refugee Ministry of Lower Saxony, exerted all his power to instigate a pogrom against the Jewish citizens living in the town. The citizen Michelsen was, among other people, handed over to the Gestapo by him.

The ranks of the leaders of revenge-seeking organizations in West Germany range from the nazi agent and the fascist general to the fanatical nazi ideologist, from the district chairman to the Gestapo hangman. They have not changed their minds in any way. Their struggle, which again represents the armament monopolies' aims of war, aggression and conquest, is directed against all understanding, against all tendencies towards a realistic policy in relation to the East European countries, and against all relaxation of tension.

Seebohm, spokesman of the "Sudetendeutsche Landsmannschaft" (SL) and a minister in the Erhard government, declared: *"Standing in the foremost frontline we are the pioneers for shaking off the bolshevist colonialism over East Europe." (Der Spiegel,* Hamburg, 17 May 1961) He could have said exactly the same thing under Hitler.

Rumbaur, chairman of the provincial branch of the "Schlesische Landsmannschaft" in Bavaria, called for wider activity to be directed against any attempt to arrive at an international relaxation of tension. *"Let us not fail to come to adequate conclusions regarding the international development that is beginning to take shape. These conclusions can only be ... no yielding, no weakness, no submissiveness." (Der Schlesier,* Recklinghausen, 7 November 1963)

And the *Sudetendeutscher Turnerbrief,* Vol. 8, of 1 August 1957 said: *"The way in which certain newspapers nowadays cultivate tendencies that aim at suppressing the truth is shown by publications in the* Frankfurter Rundschau *or the* Stuttgarter Zeitung *that of all days choose Sudeten German Day to remind us of Lidice. This self-impeachment is disgusting ... Do they not know at least that only the accomplices of paid hirelings were punished in Lidice, who helped to hide murderers?"* (See also Table 43, *Sudetendeutscher Turnerbrief,* 1 April 1956, "Zwischen Verniggerung und Bolschewisierung") This paper is the central organ of the "Work Community of the Sudeten German Gymnasts", whose chairman is the former SA Führer Welwarski.

NAZI INFORMER AND GOEBBELS JOURNALIST

Lemmer Ernst

today: *Minister for "Expelled Persons, Refugees and War Injured Persons"*

Like his predecessors in his office Ernst Lemmer had already proved his reliability as a trustworthy servant of German imperialism and revanchism at the time of fascism. (See also *Ernst Lemmer – Goebbels Journalist, Nazi Informer, Revenge Minister,* National Council of the National Front, Berlin, 1964)

On 24 March 1944 Lemmer as a Reichstag deputy representing the "German Democratic Party" (later "German State Party") voted for Hitler's Enabling Act. He supported the fascist dictatorship in his capacity as general secretary of the "Gewerkschaftsring" (trade union ring). He coordinated this union with the fascist German Labour Front. Stating the position of the "Gewerkschaftsring" Lemmer gave a declaration of loyalty on 14 March 1933:

"The liberal-national trade unions are also willing to place their cooperation at the disposal of the present government which, together with the responsible state power, must shape the destiny of the entire German people." (German Central Archive, Potsdam, under Reichsarbeitsministerium)

The process of coordinating the trade unions culminated when Lemmer instructed all members of the "Gewerkschaftsring" to turn out in full numbers and take part in the May Day demonstration which the fascists were going to misuse for a chauvinist demonstration of power. While thousands of anti-fascists were already being tortured in jails and concentration camps Lemmer wrote in a statement handed to the press: *"The executive board of the Gewerkschaftsring asks its organizations and branches throughout the country to ensure participation of all members of the liberal-national organizations of workers and clerical staff in the May Day events in order to express their appreciation of the social and national state!"*

Consequently Lemmer, who supported Hitler, rose to become a confidant of the nazis. Camouflaged as a journalist working for foreign newspapers he denounced democratic fellow journalists like Schwerdtfeger, staff member of the *Berliner Börsenzeitung.* On 3 March 1964 Professor Herbert Melzig made a statement concerning this case in the Berlin weekly *Wochenpost.* Professor Melzig had been temporarily employed as an interpreter for oriental languages by the press department of the German government or by department IV of the Ministry of Propaganda, until he emigrated in 1938. In his statement he says:

"Looking back to that time I remember that Lemmer acted as an informer for the nazis. Lemmer was one of the informers who denounced the Berlin journalist Schwerdtfeger. Schwerdtfeger had told a foreign news agency of confidential directives which concerned future barbarian actions of the nazis against the Jews and which had been announced to the press by Goebbels at one of the so-called

Reich press conferences. Schwerdtfeger wanted to warn the world. Lemmer did not denounce Schwerdtfeger directly to the Gestapo but to the head of the government press department who then caused Schwerdtfeger to be arrested. He received a life sentence . . ."

These denunciations served as the best recommendations for Lemmer when he started his espionage activities in department VI of the Reich Security Main Office under the direction of SS Brigadeführer Walter Schellenberg, who was sentenced in Nuremberg.

Since 1934 Lemmer worked as a foreign correspondent for several foreign newspapers, among them *Neue Zürcher Zeitung, Pester Lloyd,* the Bern *Bund,* and *l'Indépendance Belge.*

On direct behalf of the Goebbels ministry Lemmer wrote articles that were intended to minimize, justify and propagandistically prepare the persecutions of Jews abroad.

A lawsuit proceeding in 1936 in Switzerland against a Jewish citizen gave publicity to the barbarous treatment of Jews in Germany. The facts caused enraged indignation in foreign countries against the anti-Jewish policy of the nazis.

The Goebbels ministry attempted to intercept this movement and commissioned Lemmer to write a suitable article. On 4 November 1936 the Bern Bund published an article written by Lemmer blaming the Jews themselves for their inhuman treatment and extermination in Germany. On 2 November 1936 Lemmer sent the article to Government Counsellor Diewerge, who was in department VII of the Goebbels ministry in charge of "Jewish affairs" for France, Belgium, Switzerland, Palestine and Egypt. In this letter he said:

"I assume that the final formulation meets our requirements but is at the same time formulated in such a way that it will actually be printed by the liberal Swiss newspaper which I serve . . .

Heil Hitler!

Yours obediently, E. Lemmer"

(German Central Archive, Potsdam, under Propaganda-Ministerium)

In a letter dated 5 November 1936 Diewerge reported to Goebbels that Lemmer had carried out his commission. At the same time Diewerge had this article, which was intended to serve as evidence that the fascist racial policy was being approved, reprinted in the nazi press. The article also met with the full approval of the German embassy in Bern, which wrote to Diewerge on 13 November 1936:

"The article you managed to launch in the Bern Bund has had extraordinarily positive results." (op. cit.)

When the fascists had occupied Belgium the nazis stole the influential Brussels newspaper *Le Soir* and subordinated it to the orders of the German Military Administration. On the initiative of the Foreign Office and in full agreement with the Goebbels ministry Lemmer was appointed "Berlin correspondent" of *Le Soir* and employed as an officious disseminator of nazi propaganda for this paper, too. The character this paper acquired during the fascist occupation is indicated by the following report:

"... one of the most infamous of Goebbels' propaganda sheets, put together by bought subjects, fabricated by traitors to their own country. The tone of the sheet was slavishly pro-Hitler, unscrupulously anti-English and anti-American and, in the field of anti-Semitism, fully adjusted to the jargon of the ignoble Streicher ..." (Telegraf, West Berlin, 4 January 1947)

Desire Denuit, sub-editor of the Brussels *Le Soir* stated in an interview with ADN:

"Not even Goebbels would have been as capable as Lemmer of carrying out nazi propaganda in Belgium under the conditions prevailing at that time! ... With the smart Lemmer they (the nazis – editor) had a man at their disposal who was able to write in a suitably agreeable form, whose correspondence, however, was exactly for that reason the more dangerous in its poisonous effect. Lemmer played Hitler's game." Allgemeiner Deutscher Nachrichtendienst, Berlin, 7 March 1964)

In more than 2,000 articles and reports for foreign newspapers Lemmer glorified Hitler as a man of "genius" and praised fascist justice, the attacks on Czechoslovakia and Poland and the policy of extermination and war pursued by German imperialism.

Some articles in the *Pester Lloyd* written by Lemmer may sufficiently illustrate our point. There he said of the fascist predatory war:

"It is with almost breathless excitement that one follows the description of the individual phases of this war, which after Poland had been subjected and the Scandinavian region threatened by French and British plans for expanding the war had been occupied in an operation that was declared to be unique in German war history by Hitler, finally led on the battlefields of West Europe to a triumph of German arms that had been quite unimaginable and whose dimensions and speed had certainly not been expected by the world." (Pester Lloyd, Budapest, 19 July 1940)

"In the last days the German offensive operations have made significant progress from all sides west of the Volga so that the situation of the Soviet defensive forces grows increasingly difficult and has perhaps already become hopeless. With the capture of important chains of hills south and north of Stalingrad the issue has probably already been settled ..." (op. cit. 4 September 1942)

About the notorious president of the "People's Court" and the terrorist sentences, particularly those passed on people who participated in the attempt on Hitler's life, Lemmer wrote:

"Both of them (Thierack and Freisler – editor) represent the modern national

socialist conception of law . . . The personalities appointed to the leading positions enjoy the reputation of being men of wide legal experience who are energetic and well able to take care of the extended juridical duties of the Reich." (*op. cit.*, 25 August 1942)

"The assassination attempt of 20 July has been speedily avenged with the sentence handed down by the judges of the People's Court . . . That the court decided to inflict this drastic measure is clearly because the crimes of the accused must be regarded as especially infamous . . ." (*op. cit.*, 10 August 1944)

On the occasion of Hitler's fiftieth birthday Lemmer wrote in his article:

"Adolf Hitler – On the occasion of his 50th birthday on 20 April

Berlin, April 1939

"(E.L.) Adolf Hitler has become a historic figure within a bare decade in the view of the world . . . Instinct and intelligence determine the path of the politician. Hitler is creating the Greater German Reich, is assuring its total unity internally and strengthening its power externally in an unprecedented manner . . ." (*op. cit.*, 20 April 1939)

Closely connected with the denunciation of democratic fellow journalists was Lemmer's activity in the "Verein der Auslandspresse" (foreign press club) in Berlin directed at coordinating the work of the foreign journalists. Relevant information is provided by a secret communication of the fascist Foreign Office, (Ref. P. Z.). (See Table 45, German Central Archive, Potsdam, under Auswärtiges Amt, No. 60,526)

How much the fascist authorities appreciated Lemmer's activity is indicated by the following facts:

While listening to foreign radio stations had been generally prohibited by the fascist rulers and hundreds of death sentences had been passed for no other reason Lemmer was given a permit by the Goebbels ministry.

Acting as a confidant of fascist Foreign Minister Ribbentrop Lemmer accompanied the Japanese ambassador in Berlin, Oshima, when he toured South-East Europe in 1942. The journey was directed at bringing about a greater participation by Germany's satellite states in the heavily battered fascist war policy. Lemmer was charged with supervising the trip and sending confidential reports to nazi authorities. Making an entry in his diary Goebbels wrote:

"23 April 1942 (Thursday): The former democratic Reichstag member Lemmer, now a foreign correspondent in Berlin, has left for the South-East with Oshima. He gives a detailed report informing us that Oshima was particularly active in supporting and promoting the axis policy." (*Goebbels-Tagebücher*, Atlantis-Verlag, Zürich, 1948, p. 170)

The "Ostministerium" (ministry in charge of occupied territories in the East), the Foreign Office and the Propaganda Ministry sent Lemmer to those occupied countries where the occupants engaged in particularly cruel terror. Contrary to his claims that he "had fallen into disgrace" the nazi leadership regarded him even in 1944 as the suitable man to go to Riga on special orders in an attempt to silence the indignation rising in foreign countries on account of the fascist crimes, and to glorify the policy of extermination. (See Table 45, German Central Archive, Potsdam, under Auswärtiges Amt, No. 26,106; Latvian Central Archive, Riga, under Reichskommissariat Ostland.)

Krüger Hans ONE OF HITLER'S HANGING JUDGES

today: CDU member of the Bundestag, lawyer, predecessor of Lemmer in office as "refugee minister"

Dr. Hans Krüger was Lemmer's predecessor as minister for "expelled persons, refugees and war injured persons". BdV president for a long time he had carried out CDU orders by engaging in asserting revanchism. Pointing out the influence this man wielded the *Rheinische Post* (CDU) wrote:

"There was scarcely any occasion for a government statement being conceived in Bonn during the last years that had not been taken by the first and up to now only BdV President Krüger as an opportunity for calling at the chancellor's office, usually completely unnoticed by the public, and submitting requests, which were then – more or less distinctly – given expression." (Rheinische Post, Düsseldorf, 18 November 1963)

After a term of office of no more than three months Erhard was forced to sack his "refugee minister" because of the disclosures on Krüger's past as a nazi and his work as a judge in a special court in Konitz (Chojnice, Poland), which the GDR had published. (See *Bonner Revanchistenallianz gegen Entspannung und Abrüstung* – Bonn Revanchist Alliance against Relaxation and Disarmament, National Council of the National Front, Berlin, 1963)

Krüger had declared his allegiance to Hitler as early as 1923 and had, as he stated himself in his personal record, taken part in Hitler's insurrection against the Weimar Republic on 9 November 1923. When the fascists had taken power he immediately became a member of the NSDAP and its organizations, e.g. "NS-Rechtswahrerbund" (Lawyers' Association), "NS-Studentenbund" (Student Union), "Reichskolonialbund" (Reich Colonial Federation) and the VDA. Krüger was particularly active in the extremely fascist organization "Bund deutscher Osten" led by Oberländer.

Immediately after the fascist attack on Poland Krüger was made local nazi party leader and a judge in occupied Konitz (Chojnice). On 5 November 1940 Krüger was appointed senior judge in the lower court in Konitz. In an official interrogation the Polish citizen Pabich said that already in the first weeks of

Krüger's official activity "about 2,000 Polish people from Chojnice were killed, people who had been jailed in Krüger's local prison up to the time they were murdered." As those who survived in Chojnice stated Krüger was "the terror of the prison". The witnesses went on to declare: *"After each visit that Krüger paid to the prison the arrested persons were sorted out and part of them were taken to the place of execution in the 'Valley of Death', where they were murdered." (op. cit.)*

In 1942 he was appointed a "first deputy" at the newly established special court in Konitz. There he developed into a specialist in implementing the fascist policy of extermination that resulted in six million Polish citizens being killed. Even in case of minor offences the special court passed sentences of death or long terms in jail. Only such "absolutely reliable" judges as Krüger were designated special judges.

Giving evidence the Polish citizen Marian Bakowski told the Polish regional public prosecutor:

"Hans Krüger was one of the people who passed sentences at the special court. From the time I was employed as an interpreter I remember very distinctly five death sentences against Polish citizens, among them one against the Polish cadet Jeka."

This information about Krüger's activity at the special court was supplemented by witness Michel Znajdek:

"Hans Krüger did not enjoy a good reputation. He was said to be particularly severe in passing sentences. Even German judiciary officials, like the office clerk Plünner, Chief Inspector Lange, Chief Judicial Inspector Pfeiffer and Judicial Inspector Lehmann said that Krüger had been particularly hostile in his attitude towards the Polish people. They were also afraid of him."

Krüger, hanging special judge, was dismissed as a minister only on account of the storm of protest that swept the world after the exact revelations published by the GDR and the People's Republic of Poland. His political career as a nazi occupation judge was already known in Bonn when he was appointed. As early as 25 November 1963, the Prosecutor General of the GDR offered West German Federal Chancellor Erhard an opportunity to have the original records that revealed one of his ministers as an incriminated nazi inspected.

Now as before, however, Krüger is still a member of the CDU parliamentary group (since 1957!), acts as an adviser to revenge-seeking organizations and carries on his busines as a lawyer, undisturbed.

Oberländer Theodor **THE HANGMAN OF LVOV**

today: CDU member of the Bundestag, one of the most influential revanchist politicians, from 1953 until 1960 – as a predecessor of Krüger and Lemmer – "refugee minister", until 1965 chairman of the "Oder-Neisse" – association in the CDU.

Theodor Oberländer was "refugee minister" from 1953 to 1960. He remained in office although the federal government had known at least since the summer of 1959 that Oberländer was guilty of war crimes and crimes against humanity.

In a public trial before the Supreme Court of the GDR in 1960 Oberländer was sentenced to life imprisonment because of war crimes and crimes against humanity. In spite of the strong resistance put up by the federal government and the revenge-seeking organizations Oberländer had to be dismissed from his post as minister four days after the verdict had been passed. (See *Die Wahrheit über Oberländer* – The Truth about Oberländer, Committe for German Unity, Berlin, 1960)

On 9 November 1923 Oberländer – like Krüger, the hanging judge and his successor in the "Refugee Ministry" – took part in Hitler's insurrection against the Weimar Republic. The great hour came for Oberländer when the fascists rose to power. In rapid succession he climbed up to the highest party offices. On 1 March 1933 he was made director of the Institute for East European Economy in Königsberg and in 1934, at the age of 29, he was appointed professor. He was head of department in the nazi party district office in East Prussia, at first the regional group leader and finally, on the personal request of war criminal Hess, head of the notorious "Bund Deutscher Osten" (BDO), he was also an SA Hauptsturmführer and regional leader of the VDA in East Prussia.

In his capacity as Reich director of the BDO Oberländer participated in a leading position in preparing in theory and practice the aggression against Germany's eastern neighbours. He devoted his attention particularly to the German minorities abroad, who were given the following assignment by him:

"The German was racially superior ... Every German national group can be a Third Reich in miniature and ... fight the Jews." (Kampfblatt für Erzieher, 1939)

This "struggle between the peoples" was to result in the extermination of the Slav people:

"Under the cloak of peace the struggle between the peoples is nothing but the continuation of the war with different means ... A fight protracted over generations with one single aim: Extermination!" (Der neue Weg, 1936)

When the war preparations reached their decisive stage Oberländer joined department II of "counter-intelligence" at the Wehrmacht Supreme Command as an intelligence officer. This department was an espionage and diversionist centre of German fascism. It recruited its agents chiefly among the German minorities in foreign countries.

From May 1939 Oberländer put his experience at the service of the counter-intelligence branch attached to military district VII in Breslau (Wrocław). With some interruptions he remained there until 18 August 1939. Oberländer was one of the group that initiated and organized the faked attack on the Gleiwitz (Gliwice) radio station, which served the fascists as a pretext for the military attack on Poland.

When the fascists had occupied Poland Oberländer placed himself at the head of the extermination fanatics and called for the complete ejection and extermination of the Polish people:

"In any case we must achieve complete Germanization in the eastern territories. Measures effecting complete ejection and resettlement may seem to be hard to those involved ... but severity employed once is better than small-scale warfare carried on for generations ... For this reason, along with many others, an assimilation of the Polish people must be rejected." (*Neues Bauerntum*, April-May 1940)

Before the attack on the Soviet Union Oberländer began to set up and train a special sabotage and diversionist unit for specific operations directed by department "counter-intelligence II" under his political leadership.

This task force was the "Nachtigall" (nightingale) battalion. It consisted of Ukrainian nationalists and fascists together with anti-social and criminal elements. The unit was intended for "special operations" – such as sabotage, diversion, murder and mass executions in the Ukraine. It was the first unit to enter the Soviet Union.

Thus started the most frightful period in Oberländer's career as an "East expert" and "counter-intelligence" officer. The "Nachtigall" battalion reached the Soviet town of Lvov as the first unit of the fascist Wehrmacht on 30 June 1941 and remained there until 7 July 1941. The number of women, children and old people murdered there by the "Nachtigall" battalion during the first six days of the fascist occupation is estimated at 3,000 to 5,000. In Lvov Oberländer began to realize his old plan of exterminating the Polish and Soviet intelligentsia. Among the 3,000 or 5,000 people murdered there were 34 outstanding representatives of intellectual life. Before the aggression against the Soviet Union started their names had already been placed on the death list by the "Institute for German East Activity" in Krakow in cooperation with Oberländer.

But it was not only in Lvov that the "Nachtigall" unit committed massacres among the Soviet population. The battalion, led by Oberländer, perpetrated terrible slaughters among the civil population in the towns of Solochev, Tarnopol, Prokurov, Zhitomir and Vinnitsa.

After a short time as head of the "counter-intelligence II" department with the commander-in-chief of Army Group South Oberländer in the autumn of 1941 accepted the job of setting up a special unit to suppress the Soviet population and fight the partisan movement in the occupied territory. Oberländer pressed members of the Caucasian peoples who had fallen into the hands of the fascists as prisoners of war into this unit.

The "Bergmann" special troop under Oberländer's command was intended to be employed for diversionist actions in the interior of the Soviet Union by the Wehrmacht command. In 1942–43, however, it was mainly engaged in exterminating actions against the civil population and the partisan movement. All these actions were carried out "with the utmost severity". Operation orders were signed by Oberländer. Members of this regiment who refused to take part in the crimes were executed. This was also the case when a part of the regiment began to offer resistance. Oberländer had seven members of the unit court-martialled and executed. After a short operation in the Balkans the regiment, organized and politically formed by Oberländer, distinguished itself in 1944 in the cruel suppression of the "Warsaw insurrection".

At the end of the war he was promoted to the rank of major and placed in charge of training camp "Ostprop.-Abt.z.b.V." (East propaganda, special unit) in Dabendorf near Berlin. This camp served the ideological indoctrination of traitor General Vlassov's army. Faced with the advance of the Soviet army Oberländer fled to Czechoslovakia where he joined a unit of SS war correspondents. On 23 April 1945 he went to the American troops to become a prisoner of war.

Oberländer not only lives in West Germany today without being molested but he continues to represent the CDU in the Bundestag and he exercises great influence on the policy of the West German revanchist organizations, though even the Bonn judiciary, in a vain attempt to clear him of the charges, had to confirm the murderous actions of the "Nachtigall" battalion, led by him, in Lvov.

The appointment of the heavily incriminated nazi and war criminals Oberländer, Krüger and Lemmer as ministers of the federal government is significant of the spirit and the tasks of the Bonn "Refugee Ministry".

Seebohm Hans Chr.

ARYANIZATION PROFITEER

today: spokesman of the "Sudetendeutsche Landsmannschaft" and federal minister of transport

Hans Christoph Seebohm does not miss any opportunity to call for the separation of the Sudeten region from Czechoslovakia. He himself has never been a Sudeten German let alone a Czechoslovak citizen. He was neither born in Czechoslovakia nor did he live and work there for any appreciable period.

When Seebohm speaks of the "right to the Sudeten German homeland" he means coal and profit – means the former monopoly possessions of his family expropriated by the Czechoslovak people, i.e., the former "Britannia-Kohlenwerke AG" in Kralovske-Porice and the "Vereinigten Kohlenwerke AG" in Ervenice.

But Seebohm did not by any means limit himself to exploiting Czechoslovak citizens and mineral wealth, he served his own interest in participating in the fascist policy of Aryanization, i.e., the forcible expropriation of Jewish people, in Czechoslovakia. In 1940 – one year after the fascist annexation of Czechoslovakia – Seebohm was made director of the "Hohenlohe Werke AG". What is behind this career? For decades three members of the Petschek family, a Jewish family of industrialists, had held seats on the board of directors of the Hohenlohe trust. They fell victims to the Aryanization profiteer Seebohm. On his intervention the whole enterprise, in which the Petschek family held a large number of shares, was placed under so-called compulsory management in June 1939. Part of the enterprise was immediately transferred to the "Reichswerke Hermann Göring". Choosing the director of the new company listed again as "Hohenlohe Werke" in the *Handbook of German Joint Stock Companies* from 1941 on, the nazis appointed their man, Dr. Hans Christoph Seebohm.

At the same time Seebohm rid the above-mentioned companies of his family property of Jewish connections simply by having the Jewish capital shares contained in these enterprises expropriated. Three of the leading employees removed by Seebohm were later murdered by the fascists.

Aryanization profiteer Seebohm amalgamated on 28 February 1941 all the enterprises stolen in Czechoslovakia in the "Egerländer Bergbau-Aktiengesellschaft" and appointed himself deputy chairman.

The following excerpt from the *Handbook of German Joint Stock Companies* proves that in the course of the Aryanization process Seebohm not only increased the family property but also, after removing the Petschek family, managed to place himself and his family in the decisive positions of the trust that had been "rid of Jews":

"Egerländer Bergbau-AG – company seat: Königswerth near Falkenau (Egertal)
Founded: 28 February 1941 . . .
Founder: Director Dr. Fritz Rittstieg in Berlin, acting as the alienation trustee of the "Britannia-Kohlenwerke AG" in Königswerth and the "Vereinigte Britannia-Kohlenwerke AG", Seestadt; general manager Kurt Seebohm, Königswerth; Dr. Ing. Hans-Christoph Seebohm, Graupen; Admiral (ret.) Hans Seebohm, Berlin; manager Siegmund Schauberger, Karlsbad.
Chairman: Director General Kurt Seebohm, Königswerth.
Board of Directors: Heinrich Ansmann, lawyer, Berlin, chairman;

Dr. Ing. Hans Christoph Seebohm, mining assessor, Dortmund, deputy chairman; . . ."
(Handbuch der deutschen Aktiengesellschaften, Verlag Hoppenstedt und Co., Berlin, 1942)

The revenge-seeking agitation that Seebohm carries on in West German today is intended to create the conditions for bringing his "Aryanization" profits which he obtained at a time when Czechoslovakia had been occupied by the fascists into his possession again. Yet Seebohm's aims are still higher. When the "Greater German Reich" has been re-established within the frontiers of 1939 he wants to make the rich deposits of fissionable material existing in Czechoslovakia available for the atomic armament potential of West Germany.

"One of the most important – if not actually the most important – deposits of fissionable raw materials for obtaining atomic energy that have so far been opened up on the European continent is in the Sudeten region, i.e., in that part of the provinces of Bohemia and Moravia-Silesia which until 1945–46 had been inhabited by Germans. This fact alone might already justify the call going out to the German public to engage in studying the problems of the region, its people and its relations with its neighbours." (Mitteleuropäische Quellen und Dokumente – Central European Sources and Documents, Munich, Vol. 2, p. 4)

On 9 October 1960 Seebohm announced the plans of the West German revanchists at a meeting of the "Sudetendeutsche Landsmannschaft" in Aschaffenburg:

". . . Czechoslovakia, Poland and the Soviet Union must not entertain the hope that we have written off the land behind the Oder and Neisse. It is a question of the liberation of all peoples in Central and Eastern Europe and the extension of the Christian West throughout Europe. This, however, will have to happen soon . . ." (Strauss und seine Ultras, Materialien des Ausschusses für Deutsche Einheit – Materials of the Committee for German Unity, Berlin, 1961)

Seebohm, federal minister and spokesman of the "Sudetendeutsche Landsmannschaft" wants to resume the march to the Urals relying on the West German imperialists' atomic potential increased by the annexation of Czechoslovak territory.

Wegener Walter GESTAPO TOUT

today: *state secretary in the "Flüchtlingsministerium" (refugee ministry) of Lower Saxony, chairman of the "Landsmannschaft Mecklenburg", chairman of the "Vereinigte Landsmannschaften Mitteldeutschlands", member of the juridical and constitutional committee of the "Conference of German Towns and Municipalities", and member of the mixed personnel committee of the Niedersächsische Spitzenverbände.*

In the nazi party Dr. Wegener was at first "Blockleiter" and "Zellenleiter" (local leader) and from March 1934 until January 1943 he was regional economic adviser. When the fascists rose to power Wegener became mayor of Stavenhagen, and on 12 December 1934 he was appointed mayor of Ribnitz. Wegener initiated the terror against anti-fascists and Jewish citizens in Ribnitz. Documents like those on the "Michelsen" case mark Wegener as a fanatical adherent of Hitler and as a procurer for the Gestapo. (See Table 46, Landeshauptarchiv, Schwerin, under MdI No. 829)

After his "successful" activity in Ribnitz Wegener was in 1944 appointed lower court counsellor by the nazis in the district court of Rostock-Land.

Kohnert Hans

HANGMAN OF BYDGOSZCZ

today: *spokesman of the "Landsmannschaft Westpreussen" (West Prussia) and managing director of the "Verband Deutscher Fleischwarenfabriken" (Association of German Meat-processing Factories)*

In 1935 Dr. Kohnert became chairman of the "Deutsche Vereinigung", the fascist organization of the German minority in the Polish Warthe region. His main methods employed in undermining the Polish state were, besides intensive espionage, the fascist education and military training of young people and the inclusion of as many members of the German minority as possible in the network of the fifth column. Kohnert had close connections with Oberländer and the SS leadership, which provided him with money for his subversive activity.

In 1938 Kohnert began to build up the SS in these regions of Poland. The organization existed under the name of "Selbstschutz" (self-protection) and was employed against the Polish army and population when Poland was attacked. The "Selbstschutz" under the command of Kohnert is responsible for the murder of thousands of citizens of Bromberg (Bydgoszcz). This is what happened in this town, seat of the underground organization under Kohnert's command, on that ill-fated 3 September 1939:

In the morning Kohnert's SS gangs supposing that their hour had arrived opened a strong fire from houses and roof tops on the Polish troops retreating into the interior of the country. The Polish town commandant thereupon gave orders to rid the town of the SS gangs. About 260 assassins of the fascist fifth column were rounded up and executed by the Polish army. These events, which had been provoked by the fascist Kohnert, were taken as a pretext by SS and Gestapo for murdering 10,500 people – among them whole school and high school classes – in Bromberg alone when Poland had been occupied. A further 13,000 people lost their live in deportations.

For these "services" Kohnert was promoted to SS Oberführer in 1939 and became "Landesbauernführer" (regional farmers' leader) in that region of Polish territory known as Netze-Wartheland. Hitler decorated him with the "golden badge of honour of the NSDAP".

Ulitz Otto ORGANIZED THE CRIME OF GLEIWITZ

today: spokesman of the "Landsmannschaft Oberschlesien" (Upper Silesia)

Ulitz was the leader of the "Deutscher Volksbund für polnisch Oberschlesien" since 1921. The great hour of this "Volksbund" struck when Hitler rose to power. Under Ulitz' extremely fascist orientation the hooligan gangs of the "Volksbund" began more and more frequently to provoke violent clashes particularly in 1939. A wave of fascist provocations passed through the Polish land. Their aim was to inject as much tension as possible into the political situation in order to create a suitable pretext for a military attack on Poland.

Ulitz, with his fifth column disguised as "Volksbund" (people's federation), was employed in preparing and carrying out the feigned attack on the Gleiwitz (Gliwice) radio station. In several conferences with the SS leadership Ulitz was entrusted with the following assignments for the plot: he was to act as an adviser to the people who had been selected by the fascist security service (SD) and came to Gleiwitz under the command of the SD man Naujocks, and to acquaint them with the locality. He assisted also in selecting a reliable German of Polish nationality who spoke fluent Polish, who was placed at the disposal of Naujocks. After the feigned "raid" this criminal made an inciting speech in the Polish language, which was transmitted over the Gleiwitz radio station.

The action against the Gleiwitz radio station was carried out on 31 August 1939. The military attack on Poland and the Second World War started the very next day.

In compensation for his various services in preparing the aggression Ulitz was made a ministerial counsellor and head of a department of the government in Kattowitz (Katowice), and on 18 October 1939 he was awarded the "golden badge of honour of the NSDAP".

Richthofen Bolko von A DISHONOURABLE DENOUNCER

today: "federal scientific adviser" and a member of the executive committee of the "Landsmannschaft Schlesien" (Silesia)

Richthofen was one of the anti-Semitic and revenge-seeking professors serving Hitler. In his pseudo-scientific writings he tried to justify the anti-Semitic barbarism of the nazis and the predominance German imperialism sought to establish, particularly over East Europe. Some titles selected from his bibliography may provide ample evidence: *Rasse und Volkstum in der bolschewistischen Wissenschaft* (Race and National Characteristics in Bolshevist Science), *Ursprung der Ostjuden und Chasaren* (Origin of Eastern Jews and Chazars), *Judentum und bolschewistische Kulturpolitik* (The Jews and Bolshevist Cultural Policy).

Richthofen began his political career in the reactionary volunteer forces and the "Schwarze Reichswehr" (i.e., army units continuing to exist contrary to international treaties after the First World War). Later his profoundly reactionary attitude led him into the fascist "Bund Deutscher Osten".

Acting as chairman of the "Berufsvereinigung deutscher Vorgeschichtsforscher" (Professional Association of German Prehistory Research Workers) he denounced Professor Wirth, a scientist who had made statements deviating from fascist racial theories and continued to make friends with Jewish people. There is a large number of documents which cast a significant light on this fanatical representative and defender of the barbarian fascist racial theory and practice. In a letter dated 24 January 1934 he writes to Professor Günther in Jena:

" I do not understand why Wirth should be spared for human and tactical considerations ... Your suggestion to ask the entire body, if possible, of national university teachers to make a statement directed against Wirth appears to me of extraordinary value; it should, however, not be phrased in conciliatory terms but, in my opinion, in penetratingly sharp words." (Also see Table 47, Landeshauptarchiv, Schwerin, under Ministerium für Unterricht, No. 1267)

Professor Wirth was not the only victim of denouncer Richthofen. The scientists Gesemann and Winkler, too, were denounced to the nazi authorities as being "favourably disposed towards Jews and Bolsheviks" by him.

During the Second World War Richthofen worked as expert and "special commissioner" at the Army Supreme Command, "Foreign Armies, East" department, in the espionage system of Reinhard Gehlen, then a lieutenant general and now president of the Federal Intelligence Service. In a letter to Leipzig University Richthofen wrote on 16 October 1944:

"I have mainly made my labour power available to the Wehrmacht and the party, giving lectures on Bolshevism in order to strengthen the will to see this war through." (Archive of the University of Leipzig)

Richthofen also boasted of being a hold-out fanatic in an article in the *Leipziger Neueste Nachrichten*. Among other things, he said there:

"Knowing Europeans, conscious of their responsibility, do not know anything else but to go on fighting to the last against the hell of Bolshevism and its plutocratic associates. Only in this way can our people, Europe and the world be saved." (Leipziger Neueste Nachrichten, 15 November 1944)

Today Richthofen is the leading ideologist of the "Schlesische Landsmannschaft". He is, moreover, one of the organizers and promoters of the right-wing radical and semi-fascist "Aktion Oder-Neisse" (AKON).

He was decorated in 1964 with the Federal Distinguished Service Cross first class by Lübke.

Illing Paul SS TERRORIST

today: federal manager of the "Sudetendeutsche Landsmannschaft" (SL), secretary of the "Bundesversammlung" of the SL, member of the "advisory board" attached to the Lemmer ministry

Illing joined the NSDAP as early as 1 March 1923 in Vienna, where he became "block leader". He joined the SA at the same time. On behalf of the nazi party he went to Czechoslovakia to take part in spreading fascism among the German minority and in subversive actions against the Czechoslovak state. Illing organized the "Volkssport" there, a fascist terrorist organization set up on SS principles and employed against the Czechoslovak population. As a deputy national leader of this organization, which was under the leadership of Hans Krebs, the nazi "Gauleiter" and war criminal, Illing was responsible for the provocations staged by his organization. In bourgeois Czechoslovakia he was therefore sentenced to two years and seven months in prison for activities hostile to the state.

In 1938 Himmler asked him to come to Germany. He was to assist here in preparing the occupation of Czechoslovakia. As an SS Sturmbannführer he was employed as head of two departments in the staff of "SS main sector Elbe". Only one year later he was promoted to SS Obersturmbannführer. Describing his further jobs in the SS Illing wrote in his personal record:

"On 15 March 1939 I was ordered to accompany the Reichsführer SS as a guide and interpreter on the march into Prague. As the leader of the SS recruiting office of the main sector Elbe and as local leader in Prague I was subsequently engaged in building up SS units in the northern protectorate. In December 1939 I was appointed honorary leader of the 103rd SS Standard in Aussig, and since June 1940 I have been honorary district organization leader in Liberec." (Central State Archive of the Czechoslovak Socialist Republic, Prague, under Reichsstatthalter Sudetenland)

Illing was then appointed to the district council in Leitmeritz (Litomerice), one of the largest districts of the Sudeten region. The nazi party, however, was not going to give him up. By order of the "Deputy to the Führer" he joined the NSDAP district leadership in Reichenberg, where he worked as a staff leader. For his active participation in preparing and carrying out the annexation of Czechoslovakia and in organizing the SS terror against the Czech population

Illing was given various decorations, such as the "Totenkopfring" (i.e. a ring enchased with a skull) and the "Ehrendegen des Reichsführers SS" (a sword), the "golden badge of honour of the NSDAP" and the War Service Cross.

Neuwirth Hans ARYANIZATION SPECIALIST

today: *member of the "Sudeten German Council", member of the Adenauer CDU executive, chairman of the legal committee and member of the press committee and the "federal assembly" of the "Sudetendeutsche Landsmannschaft", manager of the "Union der Vertriebenen" (Union of Exiled Persons) within the CDU, and secretary of the "Collegium Carolinum", which is a centre of imperialist East research; he is employed in the Bonn government's Foreign Office.*

Dr. Neuwirth was a deputy of the Sudeten German nazi party from 1935, he became a member of the central leadership and a member of the legal office in 1936. War criminal Henlein called Neuwirth the "political lawyer" of his party. The "Gauleitung" (regional party office) of the NSDAP in Reichenberg characterized him as follows: *"As he had contracted to handle political processes he was paid a fixed salary of RM 1,000 by the VDA. In Nikolsburg he took a strong stand against the influence of the Jewish element apparent in that particular district." (Central State Archive of the Czechoslovak Socialist Republic, Prague, under Gauleitung Reichenberg)*

After the annexation of the Sudeten region by the Hitler fascists Neuwirth concerned himself with plans to exterminate the Czech people. He submitted his suggestions for implementing the fascist policy of extermination to the Ribbentrop Foreign Office in a memorandum of 15 October 1938, under the title "Remarks on the Czechoslovakian question". There he wrote:

"The principal question of what is to be done with the rest of the state is to be urgently decided. There appear to be two possibilities: (A) The Czechs are left to themselves, the remaining state is economically blockaded, the phenomena of economic and social shrinkage are increased to an excessive extent and speed, the aspirations of the Slovaks and Ukrainians to achieve autonomy will thus be encouraged up to the point of political separation, and finally the unavoidable unrest connected with social and economic difficulties serves as the pretext to use the obligation of restoring order, a duty that cannot be shirked, for taking over power in the historical countries and placing them under the direct sovereignty of the Reich. When the regions of the historical countries have been annexed as far as sovereign power is concerned a strictly authoritative administration will have to be set up, which would not be able to do without the sharpest use of police pressure aiming at persecutional displacement. This policy is feasible in principle

but will have to be consistently pursued, however, with all consequences and, if the situation arises, mercilessly ..." (Central State Archive of the Czechoslovak Socialist Republic, Prague, under Auswärtiges Amt, No. D 497,783 ff.)

When the fascists had occupied the remaining regions of Czechoslovakia, too, Neuwirth was commissioned by the notorious war criminal Heydrich with liquidating the Jewish Petschek concern. The Aryanization of the company, which was carried out by the SD in cooperation with Neuwirth, resulted in 12 employees being murdered. The "Aryanized" Petschek undertaking was partly incorporated in the fascist "Hermann-Göring-Konzern". Neuwirth had here proved himself as an expert particularly suited for the theft of Jewish property and was commissioned with "reorganizing" another branch of the Petschek concern, the "Montan- und Industrialwerke AG" in the Falkenau region. After Neuwirth had displaced all Jewish shareholders and handed them over to the Gestapo he joined the managing committee of the "Aryanized" enterprise.

Zoglmann Siegfried

PLEDGED TO THE "FÜHRER"

today: leading functionary of the "Sudetendeutsche Landsmannschaft" and parliamentary secretary of the FDP parliamentary group in the Bonn Bundestag

Zoglmann joined the fascist youth movement in 1928, and in 1931 he started to work as a sub-editor and editor of fascist youth papers, such as *Jungdeutsches Volk, Die Fanfare* and *Deutscher Ostraum.* In 1935 he became Bannführer. War criminal Schirach made him head of the coordination centre in the press and propaganda office of the Reich Youth leader. After the occupation of Czechoslovakia Zoglmann, as a Hauptbannführer and later a Gebietsführer, was appointed head of command centre Bohemia and Moravia of the HJ (Hitler Youth) and head of a department attached to war criminal K. H. Frank, the "Reich protector" in fascist-occupied Prague.

In this capacity he took part in all internal and "militarily supervised" meetings. This circle was accessible for, among others: "Reich protector" K. H. Frank, Oberbannführer Zoglmann, SS Oberführer Stahlecker, leading members of the regional nazi office, among them Konstantin Höss, today a member of the executive committee of the "Witikobund" and formerly regional leader of the NSDAP in Prague (Praha).

The pamphlets for the "political education" of the HJ, published by Zoglmann himself or together with other leading nazis, show him to be a fanatical adherent of the fascist system. In his book *Jugend erlebt Deutschland* (Young People Experience Germany) he wrote, for example: *"Germany lives in the marching columns of the SA and in the steps of the young Wehrmacht"*. And in another place:

"One belief unites them. One will lives in their souls. One flag behind which they march. One "Führer" to whom they have pledged themselves."

In a letter of 20 January 1940 to war criminal Frank Zoglmann asked to be accepted into the SS with a rank corresponding to his position. He referred to a conversation he had with Himmler on 12 January 1940 in Berlin. As a decoration for his part in the occupation of Czechoslovakia Zoglmann received the "golden badge of honour of the HJ". He joined the armed SS in 1943.

Karmasin Franz

HANGMAN OF THE SLOVAK PEOPLE

today: manager of the "Witikobund", the fascist propaganda centre of the "Sudetendeutsche Landsmannschaft", member of the "Sudetendeutscher Rat" and member of the Federal Assembly of the "Sudetendeutsche Landsmannschaft", which is led by Minister Seebohm.

Among the heavily incriminated nazi and war criminals that penetrate the "Sudetendeutsche Landsmannschaft" Karmasin stands out particularly with his atrocious crimes against the Slovak people. In 1962 he went to Slovakia as a functionary of the extremely nationalist "Deutscher Kulturbund" in order to exercise a nationalist influence on the German minorities living there and include them in his subversive activities against Czechoslovakia. It is from this time also that his friendship with war criminal Henlein dates, who on 15 October 1937 appointed him his deputy in the Sudeten-German nazi party and made him his commissioner for Slovakia.

When the German fascists occupied Czechoslovakia they conceded formal independence to Slovakia under the rule of the fascist Tiso, in order to split the will of the Czechoslovak people to resist. In reality this formally independent Slovak state was nothing but a nazi protectorate. Employed in the Tiso government as nazi People's Group leader and state secretary Karmasin was in charge of controlling the Slovak fascists and supervising their obedience to Hitler's orders.

When Slovakia had been separated from Czech territory Karmasin organized the SS, SA and police terror. Among the first victims were 700 members of the German minority who, stamped as anti-social elements, were transported to the extermination camps of the SS. In his letter of 28 July 1942 Karmasin wrote to Himmler:

"Reichsführer!

"I am again moved to thank you, Reichsführer, most heartily for the generous assistance which you have again granted to us by making it possible to expel anti-social elements. The action, which was carried out by Pg. (party member) Lack-

mann of the "Volksdeutsche Mittelstelle" and by Dr. Toth of my office, was completely successful . . . Heil Hitler! Yours, Karmasin." (Archive of the Czechoslovak Ministry of Justice)

To carry out such actions and exterminate the Slovak people Karmasin created the notorious "Freiwillige Schutzstaffel" (FS), a terrorist organization which did not differ in structure, objectives, spirit and leadership from Himmler's SS. In order to prepare the extermination policy and to be able to divide the population into those "racially inferior" and those "racially valuable" Karmasin asked Himmler to send him SS Gruppenführer Pancke, head of the SS Central Racial and Resettlement Office. The SS Gruppenführer described the result of this operation in Slovakia in a report dated 18 June 1940:

"The Jews in Slovakia still enjoy unlimited freedom today . . . Only the actions of the People's Group particularly of the FS (Freiwillige Schutzstaffel) in the towns where there is a greater number of Germans, have resulted in Jews being expelled or forced to emigrate by terrorist measures. When the Jews and Gipsies have been removed and the Magyars and Magyarones have been resettled – involving approximately 500,000 people – this land can, in my opinion, be regained in full for Germandom . . ." (Ibid.)

After the visit of SS Gruppenführer Pancke Karmasin decided that the time had come to fulfil the promise which he and the Slovak fascists Durcansky and Mach had given Göring at a meeting in winter 1938–39, namely, to solve the Jewish proplem in the same way as in Germany. (IMT, Vol. III, p. 171) Karmasin's "Freiwillige Schutzstaffel" had already proved fully reliable in anti-Semitic excesses. It could now be employed on a large scale to deport the Jewish population to the extermination camps:

"Freiwillige Schutzstaffel
FS.-Sturmbann 1

Pressburg, 28 May 1942

To the Home Office, Dept. XIV
c/o Dr. Vasko
Pressburg

Our ref. A/St
Dept. IV-AZ.12a

"Enclosed you will find a list containing the names of FS members who were employed in the auxiliary police service in the safeguarding of Jewish property during the period 7 to 23 May. I request that you take suitable steps to have them compensated for the loss of wages.

Heil Hitler – Nastraz
The adjutant of Sturmbann Asvany"

(Central State Archive of the Czechoslovak Socialist Republic, Prague, under Deutsche Partei)

Sixty thousand of the Slovak Jews deported on Karmasin's order were murdered. In order to make sure that all Jews were really deported to the extermination camps Karmasin insisted even in the summer of 1944 on having all Jews carefully registered:

"Der Führer of the German People's Group in Slovakia

Urgent!!
Pressburg, 2 June 1944

Herrn Minister Alexander Mach

Pressburg

Sir,

"I take the liberty of informing you of the following: Registration forms are being prepared to facilitate carrying out the decree concerning the proper registration and issuing of citizens' legitimation documents. These registration forms lack a column in which to state one's religion so that all Jews thereby have the possibility of concealing themselves. I consider it urgently necessary not only to add such a column but also to inquire about the religion they confessed before 1938 so there can be no doubt.

Heil Hitler! Nastraz!
Karmasin"

(Archive of the Czechoslovak Ministry of Justice)

The reward given to Karmasin for oppressing and exterminating the Czechoslovak people consisted, among other things, in his promotion to SA Brigadeführer and SS Hauptsturmführer.

Himmler, Frank and Henlein evaded the tribunal of the peoples by committing suicide. Karmasin, who carried out their policy in Slovakia, hid after 1945 at first in Austria under the name of Dibak and then he went to West Germany. Although his name is in the list of war criminals issued by Czechoslovakia Karmasin can again bear his proper name in West Germany without risking being arrested and tried for his crimes. And what is more Karmasin is today one of the most influential men in the "Sudetendeutsche Landsmannschaft" around Seebohm and Jaksch.

Hitler's Fifth Column – Bonn Revanchist Leaders

Ammerling, Rudolf

before 1945: SS leader to the commander of the security police in Prague

after 1945: district manager of the "Sudetendeutsche Landsmannschaft" (SL) in Upper Franconia, regional chairman of the SL in Bayreuth and member of the "Witikobund"

Asbach, Hans Adolf

before 1945: 1933 NSDAP, NSDAP Gauwalter of the German Labour front in Stettin (Szczecin), regional prefect in occupied Poland

after 1945: until 1957 social Minister in Schleswig-Holstein, functionary of the BHE in Schleswig-Holstein, member of the party presidium GB/BHE, has long been chairman of the "Pommersche Landsmannschaft"

Aschenbrenner, Dr. Viktor

before 1945: member of the Henlein party, secretary of the "Deutscher Kulturverband" (German Cultural Association) and in 1937 head of the "Sudetendeutsche Stelle", which were both espionage cover organizations. In the Hitler war regional

head of the fascist organization "Kraft durch Freude" (strength through joy)
after 1945: government counsellor in the Hessian provincial government, member of the federal assembly of the "Sudetendeutsche Landsmannschaft", chairman of the "Cultural Committee"

Babenzien, Friedrich
before 1945: 1932 NSDAP, editor of the NSDAP newspaper Westhavelländische Tageszeitung, national socialist regional press official
after 1945: Functionary of the "Landsmannschaft Berlin-Mark-Brandenburg"

Bartl, Ernst
before 1945: functionary of the NSDAP regional headquarters in Eger, second national socialist mayor of Eger
after 1945: editor of Der Egerländer, in the leading staff of the "Arbeitsgemeinschaft sudetendeutscher Turner"

Becher, Dr. Walter
before 1945: SA leader, journalist of the national socialist regional organ Die Zeit (Reichenberg), had a share in the persecution of the Jews in the Sudeten area, PK war correspondent
after 1945: For many years chairman of the "Witikobund", editor of the revanchist Ost- und West-Informationen und Kommentare für Deutschland, general secretary of the "Sudeten German Council", expert on work with the public in the federal executive of the "Sudetendeutsche Landsmannschaft"

Bierschenk, Theodor
before 1945: co-author of a list of Polish journalists from Litzmannstadt (Lodz), who were murdered by the Gestapo at the beginning of November 1939
after 1945: leader of the "Homeland Information Office Poland II" in Lower Saxony and press officer of the "Landsmannschaft Weichsel-Warthe"

Böhm, Dr. Franz
before 1945: secretary of Henlein, chairman of the regional court of the NSDAP Reichenberg regional leadership
after 1945: chairman of the "Sudetendeutsche Landsmannschaft", member of the presidium of the Federation of Expelled Persons

Böhmert, Kurt
before 1945: national socialist lower court counsellor, chairman of the NSDAP regional court Jüterbog-Luckenwalde
after 1945: chairman of the working group of the "homeland regional agents" of the "Landsmannschaft Berlin-Mark-Brandenburg"

Böse, Ossi
before 1945: leader of the "Sudeten German Youth", follower of Henlein
after 1945: federal youth leader of the "German Youth from the East"

Bornemann, Felix
before 1945: regional leader of the NSDAP in Znaim, member of the fascist Reichstag since 1938
after 1945: "homeland regional agent" for all former resettlers from the region of Znaim living in West Germany

Brand, Dr. Walter
before 1945: head of the office and foreign policy expert of Henlein, member of the executive committee of the fascist "Kameradschaftsbund", general expert on Göring's Four Year Plan in the occupied Sudetenland, SA Sturmführer
after 1945: member of the executive committee of the "Witikobund", expert on basic legal problems in the federal executive of the "Sudetendeutsche Landsmannschaft", member of the "Sudetendeutscher Rat" (council)

Brehm, Fritz
before 1945: SS Obersturmbannführer and SS leader with the "Reichskommissar für die Festigung des deutschen Volkstums" (Reich commissioner for the strengthening of German nationality), holder of the "Totenkopfring" (death-head ring) and the "Gold Medal of the NSDAP"
after 1945: member of the executive committee of the "Witikobund" of the "Sudetendeutsche Landsmannschaft"

Breuer, Emil
before 1945: NSDAP group leader in Reichenberg, had a share in the organization of the "Sudetendeutsche Freikorps" of the Henlein SS, 1941 in the management of the savings-bank in Lvov, War Service Cross
after 1945: Sentenced by a Czechoslovak court, economic expert in the federal executive of the "Sudetendeutsche Landsmannschaft"

Christ, Dr. Hans
before 1945: Bannführer of the Hitler Youth in Hungary
after 1945: deputy federal leader and

ideologist of the "German Youth from the East", leader of the federal group "Hungarian-Germans"

David, Dr. Herbert
before 1945: collaborator of Henlein, head of the legal office of the NSDAP regional leadership in Reichenberg, since 1938 member of the fascist Reichstag, national socialist superior provincial court president in Leitmeritz (Litomerice), responsible for the special court there, SS Oberführer
after 1945: member in the provincial executive of the "Sudetendeutsche Landsmannschaft" in Lower Saxony

Delphendahl, Heinrich
before 1945: editor of the nazi press, national socialist mayor of Gotha and Rudolstadt, chairman of the NSDAP regional court in Gotha, head of the NSDAP regional leadership in Thuringia, NSDAP (No. 195 270)
after 1945: chairman of the "Bundeslandsmannschaft Thüringen"

Domabyl, Josef
before 1945: member of the NSDAP leadership in occupied Prague, leading function in the protectorate administration
after 1945: government director in the provincial government of Schleswig-Holstein, expert on finance in the federal executive of the "Sudetendeutsche Landsmannschaft"

Eggert, Dr. Oskar
before 1945: author of "blood and soil pamphlets" on Mecklenburg and Pomerania, army study counsellor in the fascist Wehrmacht
after 1945: co-founder and chairman of the "Pommersche Landsmannschaft", member of the advisory counci in the "Refugee" Ministry

Essen, Dr. Werner
before 1945: member of the fascist Reich Ministry of the Interior, together with Globke participated in drafting and implementing the racial laws, 1941 in the fascist Reich Commissariat for the "East", department head and authoritative "specialist on Germanization"
after 1945: ministerial counsellor and section head in section I/5 of the "Refugee" Ministry and member in the J.G. Herder Research Council", a centre of imperialist research on the East

Föder, Kurt
before 1945: senior administrative inspector in Klingenthal, chief of the local police, sent anti-fascists into concentration camps, after the attack on Poland district governor, 1932 NSDAP
after 1945: chief government inspector in section III/4 of the "Refugee" Ministry

Foltinek, Lothar
before 1945: editor of the nazi regional organ Die Zeit (Reichenberg), employee of the Gestapo
after 1945: chief editor of the Sudetendeutsche Zeitung, member of the federal committee on press and information of the "Sudetendeutsche Landsmannschaft"

Frank, Ernst
before 1945: main regional office head of the NSDAP in Karlsbad, editor of fascist papers and pamphlets in Czechoslovakia, brother of war criminal K.H. Frank
after 1945: editor of the newspaper Wegweiser für Heimatvertriebene and the Sudetendeutscher Turnerbrief, member of the "Witikobund"

Franke, Gotthard
before 1945: district president and political leader of the NSDAP in Gross-Kunetitz and Frywald
after 1945: minister of economic affairs and transport in Hesse, deputy head of the federal executive of the GB/BHE, member of the presidium of the "Witikobund"

Gaksch, Franz
before 1945: NSDAP administrative head in the resettlers' headquarters in Graz of the SS organization "Volksdeutsche Mittelstelle"
after 1945: CSU provincial deputy and administrative head of the Bavarian Provincial Diet, chairman of the "Union der Vertriebenen" (Union of Expelled Persons) in the CSU

Gille, Dr. Alfred
before 1945: national socialist mayor of Lötzen, member of the NSDAP regional leadership in East Prussia
after 1945: chairman of the federal executive of the "Landsmannschaft Ostpreussen", provincial chairman of the "Bund der Vertriebenen" in Schleswig-Holstein, deputy head of the neo-nazi "Gesamtdeutsche Partei"

Gödel, Dr. Johannes
before 1945: 1933 SS, 1941 SS Untersturmführer in the security service
after 1945: government director in the "Refugee" Ministry of Lower Saxony, leader of the central group, chairman of the "Landsmannschaft Schlesien", Hanover group

Götz, Dr. Hermann
before 1945: employee of the fascist secret service in Czechoslovakia; for this activity he was decorated with the "1. October 1938 Memorial Medal"
after 1945: CDU member of the Bundestag, member in the "Sudetendeutscher Rat"

Goldschmidt, Dr. Georg
before 1945: leader of the fascist fifth column in Hungary and chief editor of several nazi newspapers, anti-Semite and racist
after 1945: deputy head of section II/5 of the "Refugee" Ministry

Graebe, Horst
before 1945: active in the fascist fifth column in Poland, the "Deutsche Vereinigung", nazi lower court counsellor in occupied Wrzesnia
after 1945: ministerial counsellor and head of section I/1 of the "Refugee" Ministry

Groeben, Karl von der
before 1945: 1932 NSDAP, political leader, 1936–1943 district president in Insterburg, 1943 transferred to the fascist administration in Lomscha
after 1945: chairman of the Landesgruppe Rhineland-Palatinate of the "Landsmannschaft Westpreussen", until 31 March 1964 senior government counsellor and head of department V (refugee administration and war damage aid) in the Social Ministry of Rhineland-Palatinate

Guthsmuths, Dr. Willi
before 1945: SA Hauptsturmführer, SS Sturmbannführer, managing director of the Sudetendeutsche Bergbau AG in Brüx
after 1945: member of the executive comittee of the "Witikobund", state secretary in the Bavarian Ministry of Economic Affairs and Transport, awarded the grand Federal Distinguished Service Cross of the Order of Merit with shoulder ribbon

Hacker, Gustav
before 1945: founder of the "Bund der deutscher Landjungen" (Association of German Boys) in Czechoslovakia, as a top functionary of the SDP (Sudeten German Party) he led the "Bund der Landwirte" (farmers' association) towards the Henlein Party, employee in the Ministry of Agriculture in occupied Prague (Praha)
after 1945: Hessian minister of agriculture, member of the executive committee of the "Bauernverband der Vertriebenen" Expelled Farmers' Association, member of the presidium of the "Witikobund"

Härtig, Ernst
before 1945: active NSDAP functionary (No. 858977), block leader in Gera-Ost already in 1932
after 1945: business manager of the "Vereinigten Landsmannschaften Mitteldeutschlands", chairman of the Lower Saxon provincial group of the "Landsmannschaft Thüringen"

Hamm, Franz
before 1945: was one of the leaders of the fifth column in Yugoslavia, political deputy of the nazi national group leadership for the South Slavic state, head of the NSDAP parliamentary party in the Hungarian Parliament
after 1945: head of section II/3 in the "Refugee" Ministry

Hanely, Ernst von
before 1945: editor of the nazi regional organ Die Zeit (Reichenberg)
after 1945: chief publisher of the Sudetendeutsche Zeitung

Hergl, Dr. Walter
before 1945: SS Hauptsturmführer in the security police in Prague (Praha)
after 1945: government director, head of the ministerial bureau and the press office in the Bavarian Ministry of Labour (this Ministry is responsible for the promotion of revanchism in Bavaria)

Höller, Franz
before 1945: regional propaganda chief of the NSDAP in the Sudetenland, 1933 SS, head of the Reich propaganda office in the Sudetenland and the provincial chamber of culture
after 1945: chief editor of the Hessian BdV organ (refugee association) Wegweiser für Heimatvertriebene

Höss, Konstantin
before 1945: NSDAP regional leader in occupied Prague (Praha), leader of the fascist "Karpatendeutsche Partei", leader in

the "Sudetendeutsches Freikorps" of the Henlein SS
after 1945: member of the executive committee of the "Witikobund", business manager of the "Verband der heimatvertriebenen Verleger e.V." (Association of Exile Publishers), central organization for 350 revanchist newspapers with a total edition of some two million

Illing, Paul
before 1945: 1923 NSDAP, SA, leading official of the fascist fifth column in Czechoslovakia, organized the formation of the SS in the occupied Sudeten regions, district president in Leitmeritz (Litomerice), staff leader of the NSDAP regional leadership in Reichenberg, SS Obersturmbannführer, decorated with the "golden medal of the NSDAP", "death-head ring" and "sword of honour of the Reichsführer SS"
after 1945: federal business manager of the "Sudetendeutsche Landsmannschaft" and secretary of the "Federal Assembly", member of the advisory council to the "Refugee" Ministry

Jahn, Dr. Hans-Edgar
before 1945: leader of the Hitler Youth and NSDAP, national socialist leading officer
after 1945: member of the executive committee of the "Pommersche Landsmannschaft", editor of militarist pamphlets, president of the "Arbeitsgemeinschaft demokratischer Kreise" (working community of democratic centres), an anti-communist demagogic organization, CDU candidate for the 1965 Bundestag elections

Jahn, Dr. Rudolf
before 1945: national socialist regional leader in the Sudetenland
after 1945: member of the executive committee of the "Witikobund", editor of the Blätter deutscher Gildenschaften

Jaschek, Dr. Felix
before 1945: propagandist of the Henlein party, from 1938 agent of the fascist intelligence service in Czechoslovakia, took part in preparing and carrying through the occupation of Czechoslovakia
after 1945: lawyer in Bremen, member of the Federal Assembly of the "Sudetendeutsche Landsmannschaft"

Jungschaffer, Karl
before 1945: leading official of the Henlein party, editor of the nazi regional organ Die Zeit, Reichenberg
after 1945: publishing director of the Vertriebene Anzeigers and the periodical Wehr und Heimat

Karmasin, Franz
before 1945: from 1926 leading official of the fifth column in Slovakia, 1937 deputy to Henlein, state secretary in the fascist Tiso government in Slovakia and nazi national group leader, SA Brigadeführer, SS Hauptsturmführer
after 1945: business manager of the "Witikobund", member of the "Sudeten German Council", member of the Federal Assembly of the "Sudetendeutsche Landsmannschaft"

Keil, Theo
before 1945: SA Sturmbannführer, leader of the national socialist regional office for education of the regional leadership in Reichenberg, member of the central direction of the "Deutscher Kulturverband" (German Cultural Association), a fifth column in Czechoslovakia, member of the central direction of the fascist "Bund der Deutschen"
after 1945: editor of the Sudetendeutscher Erzieherbrief, leading position in Eastern research

Kiesewetter, Anton
before 1945: treasurer and financial expert of the Henlein party, director of the "Kreditanstalten der Deutschen" in Reichenberg, had a big share in the plundering of Czechoslovakia, official of the "Reich Bank Group" in the Sudetenland
after 1945: economic expert and member of the Federal Assembly of the "Sudetendeutsche Landsmannschaft", pensioner according to the 131-law concerning pensions for nazi activists and national socialist criminals

Köllner, Dr. Fritz
before 1945: close collaborator of Henlein, organization leader of the Sudeten German Nazi Party, 1938 leader of the "Silesia" Group of the "Sudetendeutsches Freikorps" of the Henlein SS, deputy regional leader of the NSDAP in the Sudetenland, SA Brigadeführer, Reich labour trustee for the occupied Sudeten territory, responsible for the deportation of Czechoslovak citizens as slave workers to the fascist armament industry, holder of the "Gold Medal of the NSDAP"
after 1945: senior government counsellor and head of section V/35 in the Bavarian Ministry of Labour

Kohnert, Dr. Hans
before 1945: since 1935 chairman of the "Deutsche Vereinigung", a fascist organization of the German minority in Poland, responsible for provocations on 3 September 1939 (Bromberg bloody Sunday), SS Oberführer, farmers' leader in the Warteland Reich region, bearer of the "golden medal of the NSDAP"
after 1945: spokesman of the Landsmannschaft Westpreussen

Kraft, Waldemar
before 1945: leading functionary in the fascist fifth column in Poland, president of the Agricultural Chamber of Posen (Poznan), employee of the Reich Security Main Office and in the trusteeship administration East, SS honorary Hauptsturmführer
after 1945: 1953–1956 federal minister, since 1953 member of the Bundestag, CDU Eastern expert

Kraus, Silverius
before 1945: nazi lower court counsellor in the Superior Provincial Court of Kattowitz (Katowice), NSDAP block leader, chief instructor, and head of the main educational office
after 1945: senior government counsellor and head of section II/1 of the "Refugee" Ministry

Krautwig, Karl-Ludwig
before 1945: senior military court counsellor, flying army judge, active member of the SA
after 1945: state secretary in the "Federal Ministry for All German Questions, since 1965 representative of the Erhard government in West Berlin, member of the research advisory council of the "All-German" Ministry

Krüger, Hans
before 1945: took part in the Hitler putsch against the Weimar Republic in 1923, active official of the nazi party and various nazi organizations, "deputy in the first line" in the special court in occupied Konitz (Chojnice), sentenced several Polish citizens to death; in the first weeks of his activity 2,000 Poles imprisoned in Krüger's court jail in Konitz were murdered
after 1945: 1958–1963 president of the Association of Expelled Persons, in 1963 named "refugee" minister in the cabinet by Erhard; as a result of GDR disclosures about his nazi past he had to be dismissed after only three months, CDU Bundestag member

Lange, Dr. Heinz
before 1945: Hitler Youth district leader and active NSDAP leader in the Sudetenland
after 1945: chairman of the "Witikobund", member of the "Sudeten German Council" FDP deputy in the North-Rhine Westfalia provincial diet

Lemmer, Ernst
before 1945: voted for Hitler's Enabling Act as a member of the Reichstag; as general secretary of the "Trade Union Ring" he coordinated the policies of this trade union with the German Labour Front; as foreign correspondent he denounced democratic colleagues; close cooperation with the Reich Security Main Office, the Goebbels Ministry and the Foreign Office; glorified fascism's policy of conquest and extermination in more than 2,000 articles; was given special missions by the Goebbels Ministry and the Foreign Office
after 1945: minister in the Adenauer and Erhard governments, since 1963 "refugee" minister

Leukert, Edmund
before 1945: active member of the Henlein party, department head in the regional economic chamber of the Sudetenland
after 1945: chairman of the "Main Committee for Refugees and Exiles" in Bavaria

Maier, Erich
before 1945: editorial head of the nazi organ Die Zeit (Reichenberg)
after 1945: chief editor of the Vertriebenenanzeiger and the Deutscher Anzeiger, editor of the militarist monthly Wehr und Heimat

Maurach, Dr. Bruno
before 1945: 1931 NSDAP, 1933 SS, senior government counsellor and head of the press group in the Goebbels Ministry
after 1945: senior government counsellor and deputy head of section III/5 of the "Refugee" Ministry

Menzel, Wilhelm
before 1945: nazi teacher in the teachers' college in Breslau (Wrocław), NSDAP regional speaker
after 1945: cultural expert of the "Landsmannschaft Schlesien", member of the "Silesian Provincial Assembly"

Metzner, Rudolf
before 1945: regional leader of the NSDAP in Dux (Duchov), head of fascist espionage against Czechoslovakia, regional plenipotentiary for instruction in the German Labour Front
after 1945: member of the presidium of the "Sudetendeutsche Landsmannschaft"

Mühlen, Dr. Heinrich von zur
before 1945: government counsellor in the Foreign Office, close collaborator of the notorious geopolitician and VDA president Karl Haushofer, given special tasks and therefore released from military service
after 1945: employed in section II/3 of the "Refugee" Ministry

Müller-Wurll, Heinz
before 1945: SS officer in the security service of the SS main sector north
after 1945: provincial group chairman of the "Landsmannschaft Berlin-Mark-Brandenburg"

Nehring, Walter
before 1945: fascist tank general; during the attack on the Soviet Union he ordered that no prisoners should be taken; high decorations from Hitler for conducting barbaric warfare
after 1945: deputy chairman of the "Landsmannschaft Westpreussen", chairman of the "Rhein-Ruhr-Club"

Neuwirth, Hans
before 1945: leading official of the Sudeten German nazi party, defended fascist provocateurs as a lawyer, drafted plans for the complete extermination of the Czech people, Aryanized Jewish undertakings and thereby enriched himself
after 1945: member of the Sudeten German Council, chairman of the legal committee and member of the press committee of the Federal Assembly of the "Sudetendeutsche Landsmannschaft", business manager of the "Union of Expelled Persons" in the CSU and secretary of the "Collegium Carolinum", a centre of imperialist eastern research

Niffka, Georg
before 1945: section head in the government of the fascist generalgouvernment in Poland
after 1945: active member of the "Landsmannschaft Oberschlesien" (Upper Silesia), the "Kuratorium unteilbares Deutschland" (Committee for an Indivisible Germany), the propaganda instrument of the Bonn government for the annexation of the GDR and the neo-nazi "Gesamtdeutsche Partei"

Nippe, Eugen
before 1945: major in the Gestapo in Litzmannstadt (Lodz)
after 1945: business manager of the "Landsmannschaft Weichsel-Warthe"

Oberländer, Theodor
before 1945: took part in the Hitler putsch against the Weimar Republic, after 1933 a rapid career as fascist eastern expert; "federal leader" of the BDO, leading ideologist of the fascist fifth column, eastern expansion and the extermination policy against the East European peoples; leader of special mass murder units in Lvov and other Soviet towns
after 1945: 1953–1960 "refugee" minister, convicted of war crimes and crimes against humanity by the Supreme Court of the GDR and sentenced to life imprisonment; forced to resign as a result, he lives unmolestedly in West Germany; member of the CDU group in the Bundestag

Ohmann, Dr. Franz
before 1945: member of the Sudeten German Party and the "Freiwilliger Schutzdienst" (voluntary protective service), a Henlein SS organization, employee of the Gestapo head office in Prague; he was there engaged in persecuting anti-fascists and Jewish citizens
after 1945: deputy chairman of the "Sudetendeutsche Landsmannschaft", member of the Sudeten German Council and of the Federal Assembly of the "Sudetendeutsche Landsmannschaft"

Otto, Egbert
before 1945: nazi provincial farmers' leader, member of fascist Reichstag, member of the "Reich Farmers' Council", head of main department II in the administration office of the Reich Agricultural Board, close collaborator of war criminal Darré
after 1945: executive member of the board of the "Landsmannschaft Ostpreussen" (East Prussia)

Otto, Dr. Hans-Werner
before 1945: 1932 NSDAP, regional office leader, fascist district president in Austria and the occupied eastern territories
after 1945: ministerial director and office head in the "Ministry for Labour, Social Affairs and Expelled Persons" in Schleswig-Holstein

Pfluger, Dr. Karl
before 1945: member of Sudeten German Party, NSDAP, SS, on the staff of the fascist secret service, had a share in the preparation and implementation of the occupation of Czechoslovakia
after 1945: municipal lawyer in Regensburg, member of the Federal Assembly and the presidium of the "Sudetendeutsche Landsmannschaft"

Plette, Dr. Hans
before 1945: SA, NSDAP, as captain of the Todt Organization on active service in the occupied "eastern territories"
after 1945: chairman of the "Bundeslandsmannschaft Thüringen"

Pozorny, Reinhard
before 1945: leading member of the anti-Czech "German Cultural Association", cultural expert in the NSDAP regional leadership in Reichenberg, municipal director in Pilsen, regional NSDAP speaker, Gestapo informer
after 1945: editor of the Sudetendeutsche Zeitung, leading member of the Cultural Committee of the "Sudetendeutsche Landsmannschaft"

Preissler, Dr. Walter
before 1945: NSDAP legal adviser to the "German Labour Front"
after 1945: state secretary in the Ministry of the Interior of Hesse, member of the GB/BHE (Association of Expelled Persons and Those Deprived of Their Rights) and the "Witikobund", presidential member of the "Association of Refugees and Expelled Persons

Richthofen, Bolko von
before 1945: fascist pre-historian, anti-Semite, denounced several scientists to the nazi authorities, special agent in the "Foreign Armies East" espionage service, holdout fanatic
after 1945: "federal scientific adviser" to the "Landsmannschaft Schlesien"

Samulski, Dr. Robert
before 1945: nazi racial and genealogical worker in Silesia
after 1945: leading functionary of the "Landsmannschaft Schlesien" (Silesia) in North Rhineland-Westphalia

Sander, Rudolf
before 1945: SA Standartenführer, member of the chief executive of the Henlein party, regional press chief member of the NSDAP regional leadership in Reichenberg
after 1945: member of the executive committee of the "Witikobund", federal organizational leader of the "Association of Expelled Persons and Those Deprived of Their Rights"

Schellhaus, Erich
before 1945: national socialist mayor of Salzbrunn
after 1945: member of the presidium of the Association of Expelled Persons and Refugees, spokesman of the "Landsmannschaft Schlesien", minister in Lower Saxony

Schlünder, Dr. Ernst
before 1945: chief regional leader of the Hitler Youth, head of the central office in the Reich leadership of German youth
after 1945: member of the executive committee of the "Witikobund", senior government counsellor and personal adviser of Hessian Minister of State Franke

Schubert, Leo
before 1945: one of the first members of the nazi party (No. 87), member of the fascist Reichstag and SS Standartenführer; his services in the preparation of the annexation of the Sudetenland were rewarded by, among other things, the "Sword of Honour of the Reichsführer SS" and the "Golden Medal of the NSDAP"
after 1945: provincial chairman of the "Sudetendeutsche Landsmannschaft" in North Rhine-Westphalia

Schulpig, Hans
before 1945: 1929 NSDAP, 1931 SS, last function SS Standartenführer in the main personnel office of the SS, bearer of the "death-head ring" and the "Sword of Honour of the Reichsführer SS"
after 1945: editorial writer of the central organ of the "Landsmannschaft Schlesien", Der Schlesier (The Silesian)

Schwarz, Sepp
before 1945: nazi regional commissioner for literature in the Sudetenland
after 1945: state secretary in Baden-Württemberg

Sebekovsky, Wilhelm
before 1945: co-founder of the Henlein party, SA Brigadeführer, district president in Karlsbad, associate judge in the "People's Court"

after 1945: co-founder and functionary of the "Witikobund", member of the editorial staff of the Blätter deutscher Gildenschaften

Seebohm, Hans-Christoph
before 1945: took part in the "organization" of Jewish mining enterprises after the occupation of Czechoslovakia, had leading posts in the executives of several "de-Semitized" undertakings
after 1945: oldest federal minister in seniority, spokesman of the "Sudetendeutsche Landsmannnschaft", as former president of the Chamber of Industry and Commerce in Brunswick involved in the embezzlement of 70,000 marks

Seiboth, Frank (formerly Franz)
before 1945: SS Hauptsturmführer, head of regional administration, head of regional indoctrination system, leader of the regional Hitler Youth organization in the Sudetenland, member of the Reichenberg NSDAP regional leadership
after 1945: member of the executive committee of the "Sudetendeutsche Landsmannschaft", chairman of the neo-nazi "Gesamtdeutsche Partei"

Senteck, Rudolf
before 1945: senior government counsellor, SS Unterscharführer, from 1939 in the staff of the SS Central Office for Racial and Settlement Questions
after 1945: ministerial director, head of department IV in the Bonn "Refugee" Ministry, member of the research advisory council of the "All-German" Ministry

Smagon, Albert
before 1945: regional leader of the NSDAP in Czech Teschen, legation counsellor in Bratislava, SS Obersturmbannführer
after 1945: publishing manager of the Ost-West-Kurier, member of the presidium of the "Sudetendeutsche Landsmannschaft" and the "Witikobund"

Springorum, Walter
before 1945: district president in Kattowitz (Katowice), close collaborator of Höss, the commander of the Auschwitz extermination camp
after 1945: active member of the "Landsmannschaft Pommern" (Pomerania) and member of the board of directors of the Hoesch trust

Staffen, Rudolf
before 1945: agent of the Gestapo in Prague, close collaborator of Henlein, member of the NSDAP regional leadership in Reichenberg, regional director for war victims
after 1945: department head in the federal executive of the "Sudetendeutsche Landsmannschaft"

Stain, Walter
before 1945: leader of the Hitler Youth in the Sudetenland, member of the "Sudeten German Volunteer Corps" of the Henlein SS
after 1945: for many years minister of labour in Bavaria, member of the executive of the "Sudetendeutsche Landsmannschaft", top official of the "Witikobund"

Steinbichl, Dr. Wolfgang
before 1945: deputy press chief in the fascist Foreign Office
after 1945: editor of the Wegweiser für Vertriebene, member of the presidium of the "Sudetendeutsche Landsmannschaft"

Sting, Heinz
before 1945: 1927 district and local group leader of the NSDAP, 1933 leading official in the Prussian Ministry of Justice, as mayor of Nordhausen responsible for anti-Semitic outrages, from 1939 on government director in the Brunswick state ministry
after 1945: head of sub-department I/c of the office of the district president in Hanover, government director, chairman of the "Landsmannschaft Provinz Sachsen und Anhalt", member of the executive of the "Vereinigten Landsmannschaften Mitteldeutschlands" (United Associations of Compatriots from Central Germany-VLM), chairman of the VLM provincial group of Lower Saxony

Studentkowski, Dr. Konrad
before 1945: NSDAP regional head of the propaganda centre for Thuringia, received the highest award of the regional leadership of the NSDAP
after 1945: member of the executive and consultant for cultural affairs of the "Landsmannschaft Thüringen" (Thuringia)

Thedieck, Franz
before 1945: senior government counsellor in Cologne, had several Cologne antifascists arrested in June 1933, Reich defence expert, fascist commissioner, was awarded the honorary pin of the VDA (Association

for Germandom in Foreign Countries), medal for special services in the invasion of Austria, adviser to Hitler's military administration in Brussels
after 1945: 1946 sentenced to one year imprisonment for false replies to a questionnaire, 1949 to 1963 state secretary in the "Federal Ministry for All-German Questions"

Tins, Dr. Benno
before 1945: NSDAP regional leader in Asch, had a decisive share in the persecution of Jews in the Sudetenland
after 1945: publisher of the Sudetendeutscher Turnerbrief, editor of the Ascher Rundbrief, member of the Federal Assembly of the "Sudetendeutsche Landsmannschaft", regional homeland adviser for Asch

Trischler, Dr. Josef
before 1945: leader of the 5th column in Yugoslavia and Hungary, leader of a special commando for terrorizing and exterminating the population
after 1945: spokesman for the "Landsmannschaft der deutschen aus Jugoslawien", member of the presidium of the Association of Expelled Persons

Ulitz, Otto
before 1945: from 1921 head of the "Deutsche Volksbund" in Polish Upper Silesia, a fascist 5th column; together with the SS took part in the feigned attack on the Gleiwitz radio station, receiving therefore the "golden medal of honour of the NSDAP" and appointment as ministerial counsellor in Kattowitz (Katowice)
after 1945: spokesman for the "Landsmannschaft Oberschlesien" (Upper Silesia)

Ventzki, Werner
before 1945: regional head of the NSV (national socialist people's welfare), mayor of Litzmannstadt (Lodz), bearer of the "golden badge of the NSDAP", responsible for the deportation of 55,000 Jewish citizens
after 1945: representative of the "Refugee" Ministry in West Berlin, senior government counsellor

Wegener, Walter
before 1945: nazi party functionary, fascist mayor of Ribnitz, Gestapo agent
after 1945: state secretary in the Lower Saxony "Refugee Ministry"

Welwarski, Dr. Wilhelm
before 1945: high SA leader and staff leader under Henlein, leader of the nazi regional gymnastics league in the Sudetenland
after 1945: chairman of the "Sudeten German Gymnastics Group"

Wenzel, Rudolf
before 1945: personal adviser of war criminal Henlein, from 1935 head of the fascist Sudeten German Party, 1938 SS Sturmbannführer and member of fascist Reichstag; for services in the suppression of the Czechoslovak people appointed district president in occupied Teplitz-Schönau; he was awarded the "death-head ring" and the "sword of honour of the Reichsführer SS"
after 1945: co-worker in the federal press committee of the "Sudetendeutsche Landsmannschaft"

Wietersheim, Dr. Hans-Joachim von
before 1945: 1932–1935 full-time personal adviser of Ernst, the notorious chief of the Berlin SA; finally, SA Sturmbannführer, after 1935 employee of the IG-Farben concern
after 1945: senior government counsellor and head of section I/4 in the "Refugee" Ministry

Willinger, Karl
before 1945: regional NSDAP leader and district president in Waldenburg
after 1945: member of the "Silesian Provincial Diet"

Wohak, Dr. Heinz
before 1945: SS Sturmbannführer, decorated by Himmler with the "death-head ring"
after 1945: active member of the "Witikobund", editor of the Handelsblatt

Wolfrum, Dr. Gerhard
before 1945: 1930 Hauptsturmführer, in the Second World War SS Obersturmführer in special commando R of the SS organization "Ethnic-German Centre", publicist in the Schulungsbriefe (indoctrination courses) of the BDO (League of the German East)
after 1945: senior government counsellor and head of section II/5 in the "Refugee" Ministry

Wollf, Ludwig
before 1945: regional NSDAP leader in Litzmannstadt (Lodz), member of the fascist Reichstag, colonel in the country-constabulary, SS Standartenführer in the main office of the "Reich commissioner for the strengthening of German nationality"; for

the suppression and extermination of Polish people awarded the "golden badge of honour of the NSDAP" and the "death-head ring"
after 1945: deputy chairman of the "Landsmannschaft Weichsel-Warthe"

Zawadil, Dr. Walter

before 1945: organizer of the 5th column in Czechoslovakia, regional business manager of the espionage organization "Association of Germans Abroad", chief department head in the regional frontier office, counter-espionage agent of the NSDAP
after 1945: co-founder of the "Witikobund", plays a leading role in the legal committee of the "Sudetendeutsche Landsmannschaft", deputy district president in Bayreuth

Zippelius, Dr. Friedrich

before 1945: district president and SS Standartenführer, member of the regional administration of Reichenberg, close ties with Henlein
after 1945: functionary in the "Witikobund", district president seconded for special duty, Düsseldorf

Zoglmann, Siegfried

before 1945: from 1928 leading role in the fascist youth movement, district leader of the Hitler Youth, department head with war criminal K. H. Frank in occupied Prague (Praha), 1943 armed SS
after 1945: leading functionary of the "Sudetendeutsche Landsmannschaft", parliamentary secretary of the FDP parliamentary group in the Bundestag

THE INTELLECTUAL FATHERS OF GENOCIDE AGAIN POISON PUBLIC OPINION

"Theoreticians" of Nazi Mass Murder – the Intellectual Elite of the Bonn State

The crimes of fascism were possible not least because a part of the German scientists and teachers lowered themselves to the level of assistants and servants of the monopoly masters and their Hitler regime. These representatives of a shamefully raped and abused science in the universities and laboratories, in institutes and class-rooms created the theoretical foundations for the fascist terror, for the racial doctrine, for the extermination of entire national groups, for the wars of conquest and the unconditional subordination to the "Führerstaat" (leader state). Moreover, they participated substantially in carrying out their own murderous theories. Above all they deceived and betrayed – in cooperation with nazi journalists and the authors of books and films – German young people and educated them to be submissive tools of fascism.

The intellectual supporters of fascism, therefore, bear a great part of the responsibility for the murderous war that cost the lives of more than 50 million people.

THE ADORATION OF THE "FÜHRER" PRINCIPLE

Even before Hitler rose to power, but particularly after that time, the fascists and those behind them had to create theories justifying the Hitler regime. A whole staff of pseudo-scientists was busily engaged in recasting injustice, terror, arbitrariness and, finally, murder and genocide into "justice", "legality", "order", "leadership" and conceptions of "valuable and non-valuable nationalities", etc. This "legal conception" gave rise to the murder directives for the fascist bloodstained law courts, which sentenced 80,000 people to death, and for the SS, SD and Gestapo. This "legal conception" also supplied the fascist "right" for the industrialized mass extermination of whole national groups.

The fascist scholars unscrupulously disregarded the most elementary rights of the people. They glorified the "Führer principle" the principle of arbitrariness, of dictatorship. In 1937 Professor Ernst Huber wrote: "*National unity and whole-*

ness require, however, that all political power be combined in the hand of one leader. The supreme will of the leader is manifest in the law. The will of the leader is also manifested in every single decree of the authorities and in all decisions adopted by the courts. The whole political life of the people is determined by the coherent and comprehensive will of the leader." (Professor E. Huber, *Verfassung* – Constitution, Hanseatische Verlagsanstalt, Hamburg, 1937)

The principle of "unconditional adherence" induced German youth to subordinate themselves, almost without any will of their own, to every commanding power, no matter what its content was or what form it took. It was one of the gravest crimes of the intellectual progenitors of fascism when they "scientifically" justified the elimination of independent thought and personal responsibility.

TERROR IS "THEORETICALLY JUSTIFIED"

The nazi professors of public law justified police and Gestapo terror:

"The limitation to the averting of danger will be gradually broken by extending the scope of police duties to include all actions required for incorporating the individual by force into a community." (Professor Th. Maunz, *Deutsches Recht* – German Law, 1935, p. 397)

They called for death sentences against anti-fascists:

"There is a need for forceful leader personalities who do not follow mass instincts and do not succumb to mass suggestions, but pronounce justice out of their original peculiarity, reflecting the national characteristics, and out of their conscience that the right man can only be the expression of the people's conscience." (Professor E. Wolf, *Archiv für Rechts- und Sozialphilosophie* – Archive for Legal and Social Philosophy, No. 3, 1935)

They justified inhumanity and twisted public law to provide the foundations for the occupation regimes in the oppressed countries:

"Radical measures are expected here, some are already in force: Forcible sterilization, the castration of compulsive offenders with hereditary diseases, deprivation of citizenship, protective custody (concentration camp – editor)." (op.cit.)

Another "scholar" wrote:

"In the territories involved we must carry out a policy of conscious depopulation . . . The establishment of institutes to produce abortions should actually be encouraged. Voluntary sterilization is also to be propagated. Infant mortality must not be fought. Mothers must not be instructed on infant hygiene and diseases." (Professor K. Meyer, cited from *New Times*, Moscow, No. 4/1960)

THEY DEMAND THE EXTERMINATION OF "INFERIOR RACES"

Six million Jewish people from almost all European countries were killed by fascism. The Polish people lost six million citizens through the fascist extermination policy. Further millions were shot, beaten to death and hanged in the Soviet Union. In 1939 there were some 233,000 Jews still living in Germany. In 1945 almost all of them had been murdered in the nazi extermination camps.

Barbarians in the garb of science founded the fascist racial doctrine. They knocked a theory together, which taught the "superiority of the Aryan race", and which presented the extermination of "inferior races" like the "Jews and Slavs", as "right and necessary". They called for the physical destruction of entire national groups and trained German young people in this mentality for mass murder:

"The outstanding leadership role of Nordic peoples, tribes and individual persons throughout history is uncontested ... It is only from this point of view that we see the full greatness of the time that pushes open the gates leading to a Reich with wide duties and possibilities of leadership." This is what Professor Karl-Valentin Müller wrote *(Das junge Deutschland* – The Young Germany, 1941)

ANTI-COMMUNISM AS A "HISTORIC TASK"

This barbaric policy and the whole aggressive program of the Hitler regime were declared the "historic mission of the German people":

"National socialism, with its philosophy based on the racial principle, has in the Jewish-Marxist doctrine recognized Bolshevism as its principal adversary, which tries to push forward the world revolution in the military or ideological sphere, having Russia as its base, and which must be regarded as the fiercest enemy of all German and European culture." (Professor H. Ludat, *Polens Stellung in Ost-Europa, in Geschichte und Gegenwart* – Poland's Place in Eastern Europe, in History and in the Present, 1939)

Another concoction says:

"In the world-wide struggle carried on by the German people, united with the congenial fascist Italy, in order to establish a new just settlement of the European territory ..., in this struggle the huge power structure of the Greater German Reich forms the solidly forged core. In the future community of peoples set up on our continent the Reich, however, will have to be conceded a leading position just as it has already accepted responsibility in wide regions." (Professor U. Scheuner, *Deutsches Recht* – German Law, 22 and 29 August 1942)

There is a direct road leading from these hate tirades to the concentration camps in Auschwitz, Maidanek and Theresienstadt, to the mass graves in the Ukraine and the other countries attacked by fascism.

Conscienceless professors and physicians like Kurt Blome, NSDAP Reich office leader Werner Heyde-Sawade, Werner Catel, Siegfried Ruff, Herta Oberhäuser, all members of the medical profession, and others also bear full responsibility for the euthanasia murders and the criminal experiments made on the inmates of concentration camps. More than 100,000 helpless people were declared "not worth living" by them and murdered. The barbarians did not even spare children. Remarks like "Mongoloid wrinkle" in the corner of the eye or "badly-formed ears" were sufficient reason to kill them as "racially valueless creatures".

WAR IS TO THEM THE "FATHER OF ALL THINGS"

The main task set fascist science and its representatives was to work out the theoretical and practical basis for preparing the Second World War and assist in carrying out the policy of suppressing and exterminating the peoples attacked. The nazi ideologists taught:

"War is the best instrument for creating objective historical facts . . ." (Professor P. Jordan, *Physikalisches Denken in der neuen Zeit* – Thinking Physically in the New Age, 1935)

In another place: *"We are not disposed to regard the combination of scientific and military power as an abuse after military power has proved its compelling, constructive force in creating a new Europe."* (Professor P. Jordan, *Die Physik und das Geheimnis des organischen Lebens* – Physics and the Secret of Organic Life, Brunswick, 1941)

"War as the father of all things" – this was the program of these champions of the Hitler dictatorship. With their false doctrines they assisted in militarizing public life in fascist Germany, finding "theoretical" reasons and justifications for the aggressive mania of German imperialism and conditioning youth for the campaigns of conquest planned and carried out by fascism:

"The leading role in the (national) socialist education of the German people must, however, be conceded to the SA and the labour service . . . The school is still burdened with liberal educational aims. In contrast to it the SA and labour service have directly grown out of the struggle of German youth and that generation which fought for national unity." (Professor Th. Wilhelm, *Soziale Erziehung in Deutschland* – Social Education in Germany, in *Internationale Zeitschrift für Erziehung*, 1935)

THEY ACT IN ACCORDANCE WITH THEIR THEORIES

It was primarily after the military attack on Germany's neighbouring peoples that a part of these scientists put their criminal theories into action as civil servants and advisers of fascist authorities. In special units and special staffs of the Wehrmacht, the SS, the espionage services, the fascist occupation authorities or the nazi ministries they participated actively in oppressing, plundering and exterminating foreign peoples.

The economist Professor Otto Schiller drew up the "New Agrarian Order", the plan of the Rosenberg ministry for destroying socialist agriculture in the Soviet Union;
Professor Hermann Raschhofer, expert in international law, acted as a juridical adviser on the extermination policy of war criminal K. H. Frank;
Professor Bolko von Richthofen, expert in research on the East, was responsible as a special leader and espionage officer for fascist crimes committed in Novgorod and Staraya Russa in the Soviet Union.

This enumeration could be continued at will. These pseudo-scientists must not only be considered guilty of intellectual war preparations, they are also responsible for crimes committed during the fascist war.

THE BROWN POISON OF THE GOEBBELS PRESS

While the nazi scientists were engaged in creating the theoretical basis of fascism and justifying the terror, the newspapers, books and films were spreading the nazi poison among the population. Hundreds of thousands of articles, thousands of books and dozens of films served to propagate slavish obedience, race hatred, anti-communism, glorification of war and the policy of seeing the war through in terms "intelligible to the people".

Helmut Sündermann, the journalist and former SS Obersturmbannführer, even wrote as late as 22 December 1944 in the *Völkischer Beobachter*: *"Only a world-wide solution of the Jewish question can bring internal peace back to mankind . . . Ban the Jews from the family of nations, and there will be peace."* (Today Sündermann is the manager of the militarist Druffel Publishing House and a shareholder in the neo-fascist publishing house "Nation Europa".)

Writers like Hans Grimm with his book *Volk ohne Raum* (People without Space), like Erich Dwinger, Werner Beumelburg, Kurt Ziesel, Rudolf Krämer-Badoni, and authors like Felix von Eckardt, who, among other things, wrote the script for the nazi films "Weisse Sklaven" (White Slaves), "Kopf hoch, Johannes" (Head up, Johannes), and "Menschen im Sturm" (Men in the Storm) (all Eckardt films were prohibited by the allied authorities), poisoned the minds of the German people, above all of youth. They made the German people a submissive tool of fascism.

WHERE INTELLECTUAL LIFE HAS BEEN RENEWED

When Hitler fascism had been smashed one of the most important tasks consisted in purifying intellectual life, removing the theoretical pioneers and intellectual assistants of the Hitler regime from their positions, and educating the German people in the spirit of humanism, democracy and peace. The Potsdam Agreement therefore prescribed in its "Political Principles", section 7:

"The educational system in Germany must be so supervised that fascist and militarist doctrines are completely eliminated and a successful development of democratic ideas is made possible."

These prerequisites for a renewal of intellectual life have been created on the territory of the GDR, and especially the entire educational system has been denazified and democratized with all consistency. In 1945–46 out of 37,000 teachers 22,600 former members of the NSDAP were dismissed from the educational service. Their places were taken by scholars and teachers devoting themselves to serving man and distinguished by the courage they had shown in defending the name and honour of German science in the night of fascism. Scientists like the chemist Professor Correns, today president of the National Council of the National Front of Democratic Germany or Professor Brugsch, a medical scientist, have been and are taken as examples by the academic generation growing up in the GDR.

THE OLD IDEOLOGISTS IN BONN'S SERVICE

In contradiction to the decisions of the anti-Hitler coalition the same people who were among the theoretical supporters of fascism mould the intellectual face of the Bonn state. They are all back as dignitaries in high offices, and they rule over the education and training of youth and dominate the mass media for influencing people.

All the nazi professors, journalists and authors mentioned and cited above are again allowed to educate German youth in this spirit, are permitted to fill the newspapers and books with the same ideas. They have not changed. There was no need for them to change, because the Bonn state of the armament monopolies pursues a policy that once again has revanchism, anti-communism, national arrogance and war preparation as its content.

The guilt-laden professors of Hitler and the rising generation of scientists trained by them dominate the scientific advisory boards of the federal government which also draw up the revenge-seeking plans of the Bonn state for the reestablishment of the fascist Reich within the frontiers of 1937 and 1939, and justify them ideologically. One of these boards, for example, is the "Research

Advisory Council for Questions of Reunification in the Federal Ministry for All-German Questions". It is charged with solving all the problems arising in the economic sphere in the case of the planned annexation of the GDR by West German imperialism. Among its leading members are Professors Stadtmüller and Thalheim.

Professor Stadtmüller, during the period of fascism director of the "Südost-Europa-Institut" in Leipzig and a member of the "Institut für deutsche Ostarbeit" in Krakow under the direction of war criminal H. Frank, was one of the nazi experts for South-East Europe. Thalheim, today professor in West Berlin and therefore a member of the West German advisory board only in open contradiction to international law, was, during the period of fascism, a member of the SD and had been the representative for the "Reich Working Group on Space Research" at the Handels-Hochschule in Leipzig, an organization engaged in providing "scientific" foundations for the "living space and big space" theories of fascism.

Professor Erich Kordt is the head of the "Working Circle for East-West Questions" attached to the Bonn Foreign Office. This group is employed with drawing up the features of the revenge-seeking policy pursued by the federal government against the peoples in Eastern and South-Eastern Europe and the Soviet Union, and with producing a pseudo-scientific disguise. Circle leader Kordt was an SS Obersturmbannführer and the confidant of Himmler in the Foreign Office during the nazi period. From 1938 to 1940 he was head of the ministerial office of war criminal Ribbentrop. He played an essential part in the annexation of Czechoslovakia.

The neo-nazi and militarist publishing houses in West Germany, of which there are today well over 100, are almost exclusively under the direction of old incriminated fascists. They flood the West German newspaper and book market with fascist and militarist literature, the basic theme of which is the justification of the Hitler war and the glorification of the nazi regime. Twenty million cheap booklets, describing Hitler's battles in the Second World War in glowing colours, are sold to West German youth every year. Most of the authors are SS generals, Wehrmacht officers and generals who especially distinguished themselves through their barbaric methods of waging war and members of Goebbels' propaganda team.

By re-employing the incriminated fascist scientists, teachers, journalists and authors the West German universities, the educational system, the press, radio and television and sections of literature have again become the centres of dangerous neo-nazism. The West German government bears sole responsibility for this.

They Mould the Intellectual Face of the Bonn State

Gerstenmaier Eugen NAZI PROPAGANDIST ON A SECRET MISSION

today: President of the West German Bundestag, member of the synod of the Evangelical Church of Germany, member of the CDU presidency, president of the German-Africa Society, member of the Council of Europe.

Long before the fascist dictatorship had been established Dr. Gerstenmaier was siding with the nazi movement. Gerstenmaier joined the SA when Hitler made his abortive insurrection against the Weimar Republic in 1923. Since 1931 he had been "office head" in the Reich leadership of the "German Student Body" within the "National Socialist German Student Federation". Gerstenmaier was one of the outstanding advocates of the "leader idea" and of nazism within the Evangelical church.

After the establishment of the fascist dictatorship there were more and more powerful voices of protest rising abroad, not the least among the Christian population, against the policy of extermination and oppression pursued by the nazi leadership. Gerstenmaier, the theologian, became a valuable propagandist of the Hitler regime at that time. He travelled, often in disguise, to the Scandinavian and, above all, to the South-East European countries. Documents from that time prove beyond any doubt that he had been commissioned by the Foreign Office and that his trips served the propaganda of the nazis. (See Table 48, German Central Archive, Potsdam, under Auswärtiges Amt No. 48,050/1)

When after the attack on the Soviet Union the resistance of the Balkan peoples grew stronger and stronger, Gerstenmaier went to these regions on behalf of the fascist Foreign Office commissioned with splitting and smashing the people's movement by making use of the Orthodox church. Giving a report on this journey lasting from 2 to 22 September 1941 Gerstenmaier wrote:

"In agreement with Ambassador Benzler I propose re-establishing a suitable church leadership as soon as possible. Since Metropolitan Jossif, who is at present administering patriarchal affairs without a mandate, has been described to me as being absolutely anti-German . . . I think it . . . advisable to make an attempt with Bishop Nikolai of Zica . . . and employ him for anti-bolshevist propaganda and the support of the Naditsch government." (op.cit. No. 31)

At the end of his report he said: *"Examining the whole situation I think that bigger propaganda actions appear to be necessary again in Bulgaria. Anti-bolshevist propaganda must be intensified there again, through the apparatus of the Orthodox church which reaches into the last village. As far as it has been possible for me in the short time I have created the initial conditions and made preparations." (ibid.)*

Writing fascist propaganda pamphlets chiefly directed against France was another aspect of Gerstenmaier's activity. Thus he participated in the series "Frankreich gegen die Zivilisation" (France against Civilization) writing under a pseudonym. Gerstenmaier wrote booklet No. 12 of this series, under the title "Frankreichs Protestantismus im Kriege" (Protestantism in France in the War). Bishop Heckel, head of the foreign department of the Evangelical church, wrote about this booklet:

"For official considerations the booklet has been published under a pseudonym ... This essay is, like his other work, an example of his faculty of clear judgment and the principled resolute engagement of Gerstenmaier for the Reich." (Spandauer Volksblatt, West Berlin, 20 November 1964)

Gerstenmaier's activity for the nazi leadership also included the denunciation of anti-fascist clergymen, like Professor Siegmund Schultze, known as the pioneer of the ecumenical movement.

Reporting on his Scandinavian trip in 1939 to the Foreign Office Gerstenmaier wrote: *"The contemplated activity of Professor Siegmund Schultze in Zürich, planned to last about three months, must be regarded as an interference with this work that has without any doubt been designed with a pro-German tendency. For the coming year Professor S. Schultze is in possession of the Olaus-Petri-Foundation stipendium and will be engaged in Upsala for a period of about three months ... In view of the negative attitude of the present stipendiary of the Olaus-Petri-Foundation an impediment to every significant German activity is to be expected. I think, therefore, ... that I should submit the confidential request for the Reich to do what can be done to prevent the entry of Professor S. Schultze into Sweden, without it being obvious ..." (Ibid.)*

The Foreign Office reacted promptly. On 30 November it directed the German representations in Copenhagen, Oslo, Stockholm, Bern and Zürich as well as in Geneva to refuse any exit or transit certificate to Professor S. Schultze in Zürich.

On 10 August 1942, Dr. habil. Eugen Gerstenmaier was accepted into ecclesiastical service as a consistorial counsellor for life. During the war he was freed from active service.

Globke Hans-Maria INTELLECTUAL MURDERER OF JEWS

today: *Until July 1963 state secretary in the Office of the Federal Chancellor. Globke had to be relieved of this function because of the documents and other materials of the 1962 trial of Globke before the Supreme Court of the GDR, which were published by the GDR. Nevertheless he receives a high public pension and appears as an expert and witness for the defence in proceedings against of war and nazi criminals.*

From the first to the last day of nazi rule Dr. Globke was employed as a civil servant in the Reich Ministry of the Interior. In this capacity he drew up a large number of laws and decrees that led to the establishment of the fascist dictatorship, resulted in the proscription and separation of the Jewish citizens or were directed at "Germanizing" or exterminating the subjugated population.

On 24 March 1933 the Reichstag passed the Enabling Act, a law delegating unlimited dictatorial power to the Hitler government. In addition the Prussian Ministry of the Interior prepared the "Law to Relieve the Distress of People and Country". This dictatorial law was drafted by Government Counsellor Globke. From his pen also came the law enforcing the dissolution of the Prussian State Council of 10 July 1933 and the Prussian Provincial Council Law of 17 June 1933, which coordinated all parliamentary bodies in Prussia.

As the competent expert of the Reich Ministry of the Interior Globke was the co-author of almost the whole set of laws and decrees directed at persecuting the Jewish people.

He is one of the authors of the Nuremberg Racial Laws, which in the Eichmann trial were characterized as the "basic laws for the final solution of the Jewish question".

He is the man who thought out and introduced the compulsory discrimination against Jewish people by means of the first names "Sara" and Israel" to be added to the original name.

In July 1940 Frick charged his expert Dr. Globke, at that time competent for the occupied western territories, with drafting the conditions for a dictatorial peace treaty with France. In the draft he demanded, among other things, the theft of further French regions, and the deportation of all Jews and Gipsies to the extermination camps.

Globke participated in drafting the 11th decree on the Reich Citizenship Law of 25 November 1941. This decree created the legal basis for the merciless persecution and extermination of all Jewish people.

In the Reich Ministry of the Interior Globke designed the fascist nationality law providing the occupation authorities with the directives for the "Germanization" or the extermination of entire national groups. He caused the mass of the citizens of occupied states to be degraded to the status of "guardianship" or "members of the protectorate". In Poland this was carried out on the strength of the "Decree on the German Folk Lists and German Nationality in the Incorporated Eastern Regions". Globke drafted similar laws for Czechoslovakia, Lithuania, France, Belgium, Luxemburg and Yugoslavia.

In recognition of his services in carrying out the objectives of the nazi state Globke was promoted several times and received high decorations.

The Federal Republic offered this man opportunities to advance to the position of the top-ranking and most powerful civil servant. As the grey eminence in the

Office of the Federal Chancellor he was the man behind the scene pulling the wires whenever and wherever the rights of democratic liberty were being infringed. Making efficient use of Law No. 131 he managed to bring incriminated nazi civil servants – his friends of former times with the same conceptions – into top positions of the Bonn state.

AUTHOR OF FASCIST AGITATION FILMS

Eckardt Felix von

today: *"Plenipotentiary of the federal government" in West Berlin until June 1965 when he was released from this function because of his CDU candidacy for the Bundestag, responsible for press questions in the presidium of the CDU*

Immediately after Hitler came to power in 1933 Felix von Eckardt turned to writing scenarios for feature films. Up to 1945 he was author or co-author of 19 film scenarios. The anti-Soviet film "White Slaves" (armoured cruiser Sebastopol) had its first performance in 1936. The tendency and character of this film, whose co-author von Eckardt was, are indicated in the following critique:

"There is the bang of shots, and unarmed officers and helpless women collapse when the machine gun brought into position on the entrenchment by incited sailors lets fly in a frenzied rage. Quick as lightning the murderous terror of the red revolt races across town and harbour, brutally and unrestrainedly slaughtering everybody who somehow appears to be suspect ... A film whose exciting scenes fascinate to the very last metre, a film well suited to opening the eyes of a lot of disbelievers at home and abroad on the world-wide bolshevist plague." (Potsdamer Tageszeitung, 16–17 January 1937)

The film "Head up, Johannes" had its first performance immediately before the attack on the Soviet Union. It glorified the fascist system of educating youth and aimed at conditioning German youth for the fight against the Soviet Union. Felix von Eckardt was again one of the co-authors of the scenario. The following dialogue is significant for the purpose of this film:

"A new time has arrived, for all of us! Everybody must be ready to answer for Führer and Reich: If one of us should fall the other stands for two, as God gives every fighter a comrade." (Goebbels-Journalisten in Bonner Diensten – Goebbels Journalists in the Service of Bonn, National Council of the National Front, Berlin, 1962)

It was also in 1941 that the film "Men in the Storm" went on the screen. It had the "fate" of the German minority in Yugoslavia as its theme and justified the military assault by Hitler Germany as the "liberation of the German nationals". Two excerpts taken from the book serve to make the intention of the authors – among them Felix von Eckardt – and the producers clear:

"These Serbs, they are not human. These dogs! . . . The Serbs will still drag away all Germans. They will still kill them all. Why? They don't ask why, the dogs! . . . They have already shot the blacksmith . . ." (ibid.) In another place there is the following claim: *"We must demolish all frontiers in Europe!" (ibid.)*

In 1942 Eckardt's film "The Dismissal", glorifying Bismarck's reactionary policy and extolling Hitler as the executor of Bismarck's will, received the distinctive label of "Film of the Nation". This fascist film was re-issued in Bonn in 1961.

After 1945 the allied authorities at first prohibited all films by von Eckardt. The career of this man could not, however, be interrupted. After he had worked as editor of the *Weser-Kurier* for a short time Adenauer made him head of the Press and Information Office of the Federal Government in 1952, with the rank of state secretary. In 1955–56 he was the West German observer in the United Nations but he soon returned to the press and information office. In 1962 Felix von Eckardt received the top West German decoration, the great Federal Distinguished Service Cross with star and shoulder ribbon. When Erhard replaced Adenauer as chancellor in 1963 he sent von Eckardt to West Berlin, the "frontline town". He expected this nazi to direct more closely the federal authorities illegally established in West Berlin and to supervise more efficiently the West Berlin Senate, in order to create the foundations for increased provocations directed against the GDR.

Maunz Theodor LEGALIZED THE GESTAPO TERROR

today: *Has been teaching public law at the University of Munich since 1952, is a member of the executive committee of the Institute of Politics and Public Law; was minister of culture in Bavaria from 1957 to 1964.*

During the nazi period Maunz was professor of public law in Freiburg/Br. In this time he developed into a leading representative of fascist administrative and police law. In 1934 he made a profession of adherence to the nazi state and the fascist conception of law. He wrote: *"the new conception of the state appears with such a claim to exclusiveness that it does not accept the actual conception as the basis for the relevant decision, but only national socialist state thinking." (Neue Grundlagen des Verwaltungsrechts* – New Foundations of Administrative Law, Hamburg, 1934)

And he goes on to say: *"It is not the state which defines the whole complex of the law, but the national system of living grows out of blood and soil." (ibid.)*

In 1937 he declared: *"The principle of the legality of administration proceeds, however, from a completely new definition of law. Law is the executed plan of the Führer and thereby the expression of the national way of living. The executed plan of the Führer is the highest legal commandment."* (*Verwaltung* – Administration, 1937)

Maunz was one of those leading fascist representatives of administrative law who asserted the "racial principle" in this sphere. In October 1936 the fascist Lawyers' Federation held a conference in Berlin on the theme "Jewish Influence in Legal Science". Maunz gave one of the principal lectures entitled "Jewish Influence in Administrative Law". A press report on this lecture said:

"Professor Dr. Maunz ... explained ... primarily the fatal tendency of Jewish representatives of administrative law towards the liberal doctrine of the constitutional state ... Proceeding from the doctrines of the best-known Jewish theorists M. pointed out in detail how the science of administrative law had been emptied of its substance." (*Deutsche Juristenzeitung*, 1936, Col. 1,230)

Maunz devoted particular attention to the legal situation of the fascist police and Gestapo. In 1935 he wrote: *"The limitation to the averting of danger will be gradually broken by extending the scope of police duties to include all actions required for incorporating the individual by force into a community."* (*Deutsches Recht* – German Law, 1935, p. 397)

Maunz said about the Gestapo: *"There is no legal enumeration of the means available to the political police for its preventive activity. Besides the order to fight and intercept all subversive aspirations there is no particular authorization required to apply all the means necessary for the purpose ... it does not make sense for a political police of the national socialist state to distinguish between commission and authorization in the traditional way."* (*Verwaltung*, 1937, pp. 253–54)

In 1943 Maunz gave his opinion on "protective custody" in the concentration camps: *"The Gestapo has the task, in accordance with its essence, of discovering and fighting all subversive endeavours. The deprivation of liberty is one of the means employed in the fight ... The orders for protective custody, their requirements and effects, their content and legality cannot be made the subject of investigations by the courts."* (*Gestalt und Recht der Polizei* – Formation and Law of the Police, 1943)

And he went on to say about the role of the police: *"The German police does not enter the war unprepared. The war and its requirements have made much more clearly visible what work had to be done and has been done by the police in the pre-war time ... After the seizure of power the police has become an outstanding component of the German state."* (*op. cit.*)

With his work on constitutional and administrative law Maunz was one of the prominent supporters of the fascist system in Germany. After 1945 he had and continues to have great influence on the education of the young generation in West Germany, especially in Bavaria.

On 9 July 1964 the Friedrich Schiller University in Jena published specific evidence on the fascist past of Maunz. Only one day later he had to submit his resignation, particularly because the opposition of West German peace forces, too, had become stronger and stronger.

Pölnitz Götz von today:

THE BROWN RECTOR

In November 1964 the Bavarian government appointed Professor Dr. Götz Freiherr von Pölnitz, a historian and writer living in Erlangen, as the founding rector of the Regensburg University that is to be established.

In 1938 Professor von Pölnitz published his pseudo-biographical work *Emir – das tapfere Leben des Freiherrn von Biberstein.* The book, which describes the life of a fanatical fascist and SA rowdy in the style of a wild-west novel, is full of terms like "unmixed race", "Eastern Jewish crowd", or "maintenance of the German national features". The Hitler insurrection against the Weimar Republic is said to be an "action that established law", etc. He wrote in this book on the Weimar Republic that "the young republic . . ." was governed ". . . by immigrated Jews and war service objectors 'commissioned by the people'."

In an essay written for the nazi *Schulungsbrief* in 1940 Pölnitz justified the attack of Hitler Germany on the "hereditary enemy" France by saying that the conquered territory had been transferred *"with the right of blood from the old Franks to the Germans"*. At the end of this article he proclaimed: *"The German people ascend to new power and greatness. The ancient nostalgia of the pan-Germanic idea approaches fulfilment in the Greater German Reich." (Der Schulungsbrief* – the central monthly periodical of the NSDAP, 1940 – the editor of this sheet was the nazi war criminal Robert Ley)

In 1942 a commemorative volume on the history of Munich University was published. In this volume Pölnitz glorified the fascist insurrection of 1923 as he had two years earlier in his *Emir.:*

"Munich students did not refuse the call of the Führer; following the appeal issued by Hermann Göring, they joined the storm troopers and – emulating his overpowering example – participated fervently in the national socialist rising of 1923. Only the use of brute force could put an end to their proud and liberal resistance." (Denkmale und Dokumente zur Geschichte der Ludwig-Maximilians-Universität Ingolstadt – Landshut – Munich, 1942)

Pölnitz praised the subordination of science and its institutions to the objectives of fascism with the words:

"As a force fortified in the philosophical sphere, proved by the research work done, and tried and tested in the conspicuously efficacious proficiency of the army

of its scholars that have emerged from the studies, it (the Munich alma mater – editor) takes it stand – erect, in fighting trim and loyal as in centuries past – in the fight for 'Führer, Volk und Reich' and for a new and better Europe." (op.cit.)

This supporter of Hitler, the anti-Semite and enemy of the French people, Götz von Pölnitz, has been selected by the CDU leadership under nazi leadership officer Strauss as the suitable man to work at the new "East – University" of Regensburg in the service of the revanchist Bonn policy against the neighbouring peoples in the east.

Rauch Georg von

ACTIVE IN HITLER'S FIFTH COLUMN

today: *Member of the "Scientific Examining Board for Teachers in the Higher Schools in Schleswig-Holstein" – this committee decides on the suitability of all teachers for secondary and grammar schools in this federal province; von Rauch is also director of the seminar for East European history and professor in ordinary at the Christian Albrechts University in Kiel, member of the "Johann Gottfried Herder Research Council", the "Baltic Research Institute" in Bonn, the "East Kollegium" of the "Federal Centre for Political Training" and the "Baltic Historical Commission".*

Georg von Rauch comes from a German-Baltic noble family. From 1936 until 1939 he was a lecturer at the philosphical-theological Luther Institute of the Dorpat University. He was one of the "East research workers" there who acted as a fascist fifth column. Von Rauch was a contributor to the newspapers *"Jomsburg* and *Deutsches Archiv für Landes- und Volksforschung.* They were published by the "North and East German Research Association" – a centre of the struggle against Germany's eastern neighbours. In the last years of the war the research association was under the direct control of the Reich Security Main Office. With articles such as "A Polemic on the Jewish Question in Kurland" published in *Jomsburg,* 1941, and "On the Jewish Question in Russia", published in *Deutsche Post aus dem Osten,* No. 11, 1941, von Rauch supported and justified the extermination of the Jewish people by the German fascists.

From 1943 to 1945 he was a lecturer at the "Reich University" in Posen (Poznan). There von Rauch participated actively in the work of the "Reich Foundation for German Eastern Research" and employed all his faculties to justify the extermination campaign against the peoples of the Soviet Union. This is also the spirit in which he wrote his book *Die Universität Dorpat und das Eindringen der frühen Aufklärung in Livland 1690 bis 1710* – Dorpat University and the Probing of the Early Enlightenment in Livland, 1690 to 1710. With "historical" arguments he conjures up a Russian peril and the "culture-destructive character of the Russian neighbourhood".

In 1942 von Rauch wrote in his personnel record: *"After I had taken part in meetings of the NSDAP in the Reich in 1928–29 I joined the national socialist movement in Esthonia and participated in building up the local party group in Dorpat. I was a member of the Dorpat regional leadership and was temporarily – before the movement was allowed to work legally – deputy regional leader in Dorpat . . . As a party candidate I took part in building up the party organization in Posen in 1939 and I am head of the press office of a local party group in Posen. I am also a member of the national socialist Union of Lecturers and the national socialist Altherrenbund (an alumni association) . . . (Archive of the University of Poznan, under Reichsuniversität)*

Wilhelm Theodor

A RACIAL INSTIGATOR

today: Together with Georg von Rauch he is one of the members of the "Scientific Examining Board for Teachers in the Higher Schools in Schleswig-Holstein, professor in ordinary and director of the Pedagogical Institute in the University of Kiel.

Like von Rauch, Wilhelm advocated anti-Semitism and instigated race hatred during the period of fascism. Thus in 1944 he called for *". . . the complete elimination of Jews and freemasonry from national life . . . The fundamental significance of this fact for European intellectual life is obvious. Its importance is underlined by the sinister internal connection between Jewish philosophy and the world system which Bolshevism is trying to establish, a connection which is the more sinister the longer the war lasts." (Die kulturelle Kraft Europas im Kriege* – Europe's Cultural Strength in the War, 1944)

Wilhelm, SA-man and active member of the NSDAP, was in 1934 installed as an editor of the *Internationale Zeitschrift für Erziehung* (Internation Journal of Education) after Professor Friedrich Schneider of Cologne had been removed from this office because of his democratic attitude. Wilhelm was asked to join the staff of the paper by the new editor, Alfred Baeumler.

Baeumler was professor of political education at Berlin University and at the same time Reich office leader with the Führer's commissioner for the entire intellectual and ideological education of the NSDAP. He was the initiator of the fascist burning of books. Wilhelm justified the confidence that "Reich office leader" Baeumler had in him and radically advocated the fascist educational aims in the paper. In 1935 he declared in an article:

"The leading role in the (national) socialist education of the German people must, however, be conceded to the SA and the Labour Service . . . The school is

still burdened with liberal educational aims. In contrast to it the SA and the Labour Service have directly grown out of the struggle of German youth and that generation which fought for national unity." (Internationale Zeitschrift für Erziehung, 1935)

With articles like "The Aims and Results of National Socialist Education" (1939) and "Race as the Fundamental Conception of Educational Science" he exercised a direct influence on the fascist and anti-Semitic education in the schools.

Redecker Martin

ANTI-SEMITE IN ROBES

today: Together with von Rauch and Theodor Wilhelm he is the third nazi ideologist in the "Scientific Examining Board for Teachers in the Higher Schools in Schleswig-Holstein". He is also professor in ordinary and dean of the theological faculty, director of the theological seminar, and director of the Institute of Social Ethics in the University of Kiel.

Redecker, born in Bielefeld, distinguished himself during the nazi period as an anti-Semite in the robes of a priest. He was particularly known for his sermons broadcast over the Goebbels radio stations, in one of which in 1939 he, for example, announced: *"The satanic power of disintegration concentrated in world Jewry and in materialism is only too clearly seen by us." ("Rundfunkpredigten an der Universitätskirche Kiel", 1939)*

Publications like *Germanische Religion und der Religionsunterricht in der Schule* – Germanic Religion and Religious Instruction in the School (1935), too, show the intellectual position of the "theologian" Redecker as an ideologist of the Hitler regime. Together with Professors von Rauch and Wilhelm he has today a decisive influence on the rising generation of teachers and, thus, on the educational system in Schleswig-Holstein.

Buntru Alfred

SS LEADER AND ENEMY OF THE CZECH PEOPLE

today: Professor of hydrography, commercial hydro-engineering and hydraulics at the Technical College in Aachen

Until 1943 Buntru was rector of the Charles University, usurped by the nazis, and until 1945 of the Technical College in Prague. After the German occupants had closed the Czech universities the Charles University and the Technical College were the most important educational institutions in occupied Czechoslovakia.

Buntru had been teaching at the Technical College in Prague since 1928. It was there that he became a confidant of Konrad Henlein, the leader of the fascist fifth column in Czechoslovakia. Henlein chose Buntru, as one of a limited circle of persons, to be initiated into all strategic objects and tactical variations of the fascist movement. When the preparations for the annexation of the Sudeten region had been completed Buntru was called to the "Reich". His services in undermining Czechoslovakia were rewarded by his appointment as rector of the Technical College in Aachen. Himmler made him an SS Untersturmführer.

When the remaining parts of Czechoslovakia had been occupied the fascists could not do without the services of Buntru, the "specialist in Czech affairs". In 1940 he was appointed rector of the German Technical College in Prague, and in 1942 rector of the fascist Charles University. His main task consisted of "Germanizing" these two institutions completely and creating the prerequisites for the liquidation of the Czech intelligentsia. The following judgments about him indicate that he was the right man for this job:

The leader of the Reich Union of Lecturers, SS Brigadeführer Dr. Schultze, wrote in 1939: *"Buntru has, by the way, been known to me for a long time and as an extremely active national socialist." (Central State Archive of the Czechoslovak Socialist Republic, Prague)*

A letter of 16 October 1939 says: *"Buntru enjoys the confidence of Konrad Henlein as well as of Reich leader of the Union of Lecturers SS Brigadeführer Dr. Schultze." (ibid.)*

In 1942 the fascist occupants in Prague began to set up the so-called "Reinhard Heydrich Foundation". The character of this foundation was described by Dr. Beyer, SS Hauptsturmführer and professor at the fascist Charles University in Prague, in a radio lecture: *"In its principal features the new Reich Foundation is a work of the fallen SS Obergruppenführer Reinhard Heydrich ... Obergruppenführer Reinhard Heydrich indicated the tasks, mainly in Bohemia and Moravia, to the Reich Foundation ..." (ibid.)*

This institution, conceived by the notorious Security Service chief, Heydrich, was intended to take part in the "Germanization of the Bohemian-Moravian region" and forever eliminate Czechoslovakia as a state. Buntru was made the head of this foundation, he had meanwhile risen to the rank of SS Standartenführer. (Hauptsturmführer Beyer, cited above, was the personal commissioner of war criminal Frank for setting up the foundation. After 1945 Beyer was a lecturer at the Pedagogical College in Flensburg.)

Buntru's hostility to the Czech people and his anti-Semitism are also revealed in the following documents. The commanding officer of the security police and SD wrote to SS Gruppenführer Frank on 22 June 1942: *" ... I am of the opinion that the board of governors (of the Reinhard Heydrich Foundation – editor) will, of course, have to consist exclusively of the representatives of German authorities.*

Non-German scientific institutions are in the long run unacceptable for Prague . . . I also agree with SS Standartenführer Buntru that the Czechs must be basically eliminated from the boards of all institutions . . ." (ibid.)

On 3 October 1939 Buntru wrote to the "leader of the Reich Union of Lecturers": *"I have always confessed to an attitude of basic rejection of Jewry."* (ibid.)

The influence which this anti-Semite and enemy of the Czech people had in fascist-occupied Prague is indicated by his offices as "regional leader of the Union of Lecturers" and honorary senator of the Charles University, which he held in addition to the two offices as rector and chairman of the "Reinhard Heydrich Foundation". In recognition of his services in the suppression of the Czechoslovak people and in carrying out the "Germanization policy" Buntru had an outstanding career in the SS. In 1938 he was admitted to the SS with the rank of Untersturmführer, seven years later he was an SS Oberführer in the notorious "SS-Leitabschnitt" Prague. This command carried out, among other things, the execution of all leaders of the Czech students in 1939 and had 1,200 Czech students deported to concentration camps.

Gehlen Arnold GLORIFIES THE MARCH INTO THE MASS GRAVE

today: Professor of sociology in the Technical College in Aachen

In 1934 Gehlen, who had been appointed professor in ordinary, was made "office leader" of the body of fascist lecturers at Leipzig University. In his inaugural lecture he glorified the *"national socialist movement that has given this people new impetus in life and new orders of its existence."* (*Der Staat und die Philosophie* – The State and Philosophy, Leipzig, 1935).

The philosophic system of the "élan vital", the passion to risk life, which was developed by Gehlen, was excellently suited for preparing German young people for the march into the mass graves of the Second World War. In this spirit in 1940 he called on the soldiers of the Hitler Wehrmacht to fight valiantly and to risk their lives:

"Valiance is the first of the Germanic virtues, danger is a temptation, and the other virtues, particularly fidelity and self-control, are adapted to it." (*Der Mensch, Seine Natur und Stellung in der Welt* – Man, His Nature and Place in the World, Berlin, 1940)

The aggressive aim of German imperialism, for which the soldiers were expected to fight valiantly and die with passion ("élan vital") was formulated by Gehlen in his pamphlet *Deutschtum und Christentum bei Fichte* (Germandom and Christianity in Fichte) in 1935. There he called for a new "world epoch . . . under German leadership".

Gehlen's principal work in the nazi period, *Der Mensch,* in which he explained his philosophical system of the "élan vital", despising the dignity of man, was republished without any substantial modifications in the Bonn state in 1950, 1955 and 1958.

Mehnert Klaus

RIBBENTROP'S PROPAGANDA SPECIALIST

today: Professor in ordinary and director of the Institute of Political Science in the Technical College in Aachen; member of the "Advisory Council on Development Aid" attached to the "Federal Ministry for Economic Cooperation"; chief editor of the periodicals of the "German Society for East European studies" (a direct successor to the "German Society for the Study of Eastern Europe") – Osteuropa, Osteuropa-Recht, Osteuropa-Naturwissenschaft, Osteuropa-Wirtschaft.

Already before fascism seized power Mehnert was one of the acknowledged "experts on East European affairs". From 1931 to 1933 he was general secretary of the "German Society for the Study of Eastern Europe" and editor of the periodical *Osteuropa.* Mehnert collaborated closely with the Goebbels ministry and the fascist Foreign Office until the end of 1933.

Since Mehnert differed in his conception on some tactical questions of the struggle against socialism and, above all, against the Soviet Union he temporarily incurred the disfavour of the fascist rulers. It did not take him long, however, to become a valuable propagandist for fascist Germany again. A letter of the fascist Foreign Office of 19 February 1942 says:

"Klaus Mehnert ... went abroad in connection with the charges levelled against him. He has worked there for us to a high degree." (German Central Archive, Potsdam, under Botschaft China, No. 2,072)

Mehnert worked as a correspondent for extremely fascist papers like *Angriff* and *Braune Post.* In 1941 he was appointed to the information and propaganda department of the embassy in Shanghai. The Gestapo, too, appreciated his activity for German fascism. Legation Secretary Bassler wrote on 19 February 1942: *"The information department told me that the Geheime Staatspolizei (Gestapo) has not raised any objections to his employment at our mission." (ibid.)*

Mehnert developed more and more into a confidant of the fascist Foreign Office in the Far East. *"As Klaus Mehnert's activity in the information department was directed at countering British and American propaganda and at soliciting for the German point of view ... a person as highly qualified as Klaus Mehnert can be employed much more suitably." (ibid.)*

When the courageous anti-fascist intelligence man Dr. Richard Sorge, correspondent of the *Frankfurter Zeitung,* was arrested in Japan, the top nazi leadership looked for a reliable national-socialist for this post as correspondent – his name was Klaus Mehnert. In April 1942 he was appointed East Asia correspondent of the *Frankfurter Zeitung*, in full agreement with the "Reich press chief" and on the special intercession of the Foreign Office, and at the same time he remained in the position of fascist propaganda specialist in the Shanghai representation of the Ribbentrop Foreign Office.

In recognition of his services as confidant of the fascist Foreign Office and as a Goebbels journalist Mehnert was decorated with the war service cross as late as 5 March 1945, on the proposal of the Reich foreign minister.

Mehnert utilizes today his experience collected in the service of the nazi leadership especially to support the neo-colonialist policy of West German imperialism in the young nation-states of Asia.

Raschhofer Hermann

THE RIGHT HAND OF WAR CRIMINAL FRANK

today: Deputy chairman of the Institute of International Law and International Relations in Würzburg University, and member of the Supreme Court of Bremen; head of the "Law and Political Science Working Group" in the Collegium Carolinum – a centre of imperialist East research and an institution of the "Sudetendeutsche Landsmannschaft".

Raschhofer worked very closely with K. H. Frank, "minister of state for Bohemia and Moravia and Reich protector". Various publications on questions of nationality law and national minorities, mainly concerned with Czechoslovakia and Eastern Europe, which had gained him recognition since the end of the nineteen-twenties, were considered to be the best recommendation for this employment. At that time he became one of the most important propagandists of fascism in Austria and in the Henlein movement in Sudetenland. On the personal request of Frank he was in 1939 appointed to the Charles University and in 1940 was installed as director of the Institute of International Law and Reich Law.

Raschhofer endeavoured in his work to supply Frank with the interpretations of international law that might serve as the basis for destroying the Czechoslovak state and incorporating it finally into fascist Germany. He also wrote essays on international law for the government of the satellite state of Slovakia and for its "President" Tiso.

In August 1941 his intimate friend Frank wrote the following judgment on Raschhofer to justify his decoration with the war service cross: *"Raschhofer distinguishes himself as an expert on international and constitutional law by extensive publishing activity and has supplied valuable contributions to our polemic with enemy propaganda as well as the struggle against the Czechoslovak conception of state and history." (Central State Archive of the Czechoslovak Socialist Republic, Prague)*

In 1942–43 Raschhofer was a member of the notorious "Bergmann" unit, which was led by Oberländer with whom Raschhofer had been acquainted for some time. (About Oberländer see the chapter "Hitler's Fifth Column in Bonn's Service".) This special unit was employed for acts of diversion behind the Soviet front line and for mass executions among the Soviet civil population.

In 1943 Raschhofer was commissioned by Rosenberg with writing a study of the policy pursued by the fascist occupation authorities in the East up till then. In this material Raschhofer proceeded from the view that the increase in "German living space" would have to be ensured. In order to facilitate the interception of the resistance put up by the suppressed peoples Raschhofer recommended that methods of a more demagogical character be observed in occupation policy.

He was then called back by Frank to prepare a propaganda campaign in connection with the fifth anniversary of the Munich Agreement. The two following documents show Raschhofer's importance for the top leaders of the fascist occupation regime, the Reich minister for the occupied eastern territories and war criminal Rosenberg and the hangman of the Czechoslovak people, K. H. Frank:

"Professor Raschhofer — *1 April 1943*
Schwerinstrasse 9
Prague XII
Dear Raschhofer,

"You will find enclosed a copy of my letter to Reichsminister Rosenberg for your information. I hope we shall be successful.

"In the Kaiserhof Herr Hübel showed me a disposition drafted by you and concerned with ideas on the question of how to treat alien nationalities in Europe, contained in two typed pages. I should be grateful if you sent a copy of it to me personally to Prague as soon as possible.

Heil Hitler!
Yours, (signature of Frank)"

(ibid.)

"SS Gruppenführer — *1 April 1943*
1.) Herrn Reichsminister Rosenberg
Kurfürstenstr. 134
Berlin W 35
Sir,

"Your ministry has asked that Professor Dr. Raschhofer, employed here at the German Charles University, be granted a leave of absence to allow him to work on basic legal questions concerning the international order in the occupied East. Professor Raschhofer, who has been working with me for years, has

indicated to me the principal ideas of his work on the occasion of his leave. The work will make use of, among others, the experience gained in legal work concerning nationalities in the Bohemian provinces, for which Raschhofer is regarded as an expert on account of his previous activity, and both the problem set and the solution proposed touch on questions peculiar to my own field of action. I avail myself, therefore, of this opportunity to express to you, sir, my particular interest in the leave of absence being granted, and to ask you to intervene in favour of a quick decision.

Heil Hitler!
Yours truly, (signature of Frank)

(ibid.)

In 1944 Raschhofer went to Slovakia on behalf of the notorious action group H of the SD in order to work out propaganda material to be used in suppressing the popular rebellion of 29 August 1944. For the purpose of preventing the popular rebellion from spreading to other regions of Czechoslovakia Raschhofer recommended granting formal independence to Slovakia and strengthening the pro-German and anti-Soviet elements.

While SS Gruppenführer and "Reichsprotektor" Frank was brought to court and sentenced to death after the defeat of fascism, Raschhofer escaped just punishment. In West Germany he was given the opportunity of working as a university teacher and, faithful to his past, of drawing up the legal justification for the new aggressive program directed against our neighbouring peoples in the East.

Raschhofer has great influence on the "Sudetendeutsche Landsmannschaft". The leadership of this revanchist organization, the people around Federal Minister Seebohm and the president of the "Bund der Vertriebenen", Wenzel Jaksch, member of the Bundestag, call for the annexation of Czechoslovak state territory and a "Greater German Reich" within the frontiers of 1939. These claims are not to the least extent based on the false doctrines of Raschhofer.

v. d. Heydte Friedr. Aug.

DROVE GERMAN SOLDIERS TO THEIR DEATHS

today: Professor in ordinary of public and international law at Würzburg University

Von der Heydte became known as initiator of the police action against the *Spiegel*. On 1 October 1962 von der Heydte, the intimate of Strauss, brought a "private" action against the West German news magazine for "betraying state secrets". Thus he gave the immediate impulse for the "cloak-and-dagger-operation" carried out against this magazine by the Bonn war ministry under the leadership of Strauss. As a reward von der Heydte was promoted to the rank of brigadier on 22 October 1962, the first reserve officer of the Bundeswehr to rise to that rank. In May 1965 even the West German Federal Supreme Court had to acknowledge the complete untenableness of von der Heydte's denunciation.

Von der Heydte had already been a political denouncer during the nazi period. By his radical fascist activity he attracted the attention of the nazi authorities, and he speculated on a great career. In 1936 he signed, for example, a letter to study assessor Pülke, for example, threatening "other measures" in case the central organ of the SS, *Das Schwarze Korps*, was not laid out in the Catholic students' hostel in Münster in the next days.

In 1937 von der Heydte volunteered for the fascist Wehrmacht. As a lieutenant he took part in the attack on France. For his barbarous conduct of war as the commanding officer of a unit of paratroopers Göring decorated him in 1941 with the Knight's Cross, and for his war crimes in the Soviet Union, particularly on the Leningrad front, he received the "German Cross in Gold". The great hour arrived for von der Heydte, who had meanwhile been promoted to lieutenant colonel, in 1944. During the fascist offensive in the Ardennes von der Heydte was in charge of parachute operations. These actions cost, a short time before the war ended, the lives of thousands of German soldiers. He was decorated by Hitler with the oak leaves to the Knight's Cross. Even K. H. Wilhelms, a "dyed-in-the-wool" militarist, today leader of the "Kameradschaft Frankfurt" of the "Union of Former Paratroopers", confirms von der Heydte's barbarous way of handling his command, and admits that the Ardennes offensive was militarily senseless: *"Though he had to recognize clearly before the operation that it would lead to a catastrophe he carried his order out without consideration..." (Frankfurter Neue Presse,* 21 September 1954)

Von der Heydte, who recklessly sent German soldiers to death, brought himself to safety. Although von der Heydte has denied several times that he was a zealous and active member of the SS, this is proved beyond any doubt by the documents in the possession of the Bavarian Ministry of Justice.

Seraphim Peter Heinz

A DESK MURDERER

today: *Director of studies at the "Academy of Administration and Economics of the Industrial District of Bochum", leading economist in the "Schlesische Landsmannschaft"*

Seraphim comes from a family that for generations has engaged in finding a "scientific" justification for the aggressive policy of German imperialism.

In 1937 he was appointed lecturer and deputy director of the Institute for East European Economy in Königsberg. Nominally this institute was part of Königsberg University, in reality, however, it was engaged in espionage and subversive activity in the Eastern European neighbouring countries. In 1941 he was invited to join Greifswald University. In 1943 he was appointed managing director of the "Oder-Donau Institute" which had been founded on his initiative. The institute was in charge of procuring confidential information on the South European economy in order to facilitate improved supplies for the fascist Wehrmacht.

Seraphim supported the fascist racial theory with a large number of essays and books. In 1938 he published a large anti-Semite compilation "Jewry in Eastern Europe". In this book he covers the whole Jewish population in the East European regions of the Soviet Union, Poland, Latvia, Lithuania, Hungary, Rumania and Czechoslovakia. Statistics provide information on the composition of the Jewish population according to age, social group and trade. An extensive provision of maps defined the exact "location" of the Jewish people. Thus Seraphim provided detailed information on the "final solution of the Jewish question". This book qualified him as an expert on "Jewish problems", and he was one of the first to give a lecture on "The Jews in Poland" at the newly-founded "Institute of German Work in the East" in Krakow. He exercised a substantial influence on the character of this institute, whose president was war criminal Hans Frank. When in 1941 the "Institute for Research on Jewish Questions" was being founded by Alfred Rosenberg as an extension of the "Higher School of the NSDAP" in Frankfurt-on-Main, Seraphim, as a corresponding member of this institute, read his theses on the Jewish question at a working meeting (26–28 March 1941). Here he coined the phrase "jüdischer Volkstod" (death of the Jews as a people), and he offered three theses on the implementation of his theory:

(1) Dissimilation without territorial separation from the people they live with.
(2) Internment in ghettos in one part of Europe.
(3) Their removal from Europe by systematic resettlement action.

Elaborating on his theses Seraphim proceeded from the economic consideration that "*in Eastern Europe the Jew will have to be replaced by non-Jews in the towns and at a speed that is feasible according to the availability of qualified non-Jews for this employment, replacement being carried out on the strength of legal and administrative actions.*" (*Weltkampf*, 1941, 1/2, p. 44f.)

All these plans proceeded from the idea of eliminating the Jewish people, and they countenanced their physical extermination.

In 1941 Seraphim, as a senior war administration counsellor at the armament inspection in the Ukraine, participated in the "final solution of the Jewish question". At the same time he was the editor of the periodical *Weltkampf*, the central organ of anti-Semitism in Germany.

Like Globke Seraphim is one of the murderers who operated from their desks and remain unpunished. Up to this day he has not yet disavowed his anti-Semitic theories and practices. In his capacity as director of studies he wields substantial influence on the training of future civil servants of the Bonn state.

Höhn Reinhard

SS LEADER AND HIMMLER'S TOP JURIST

today: *Managing president of the "Academy for Economic Leaders" in Bad Harzburg with an annual salary of 64,000 marks; he is also managing president of the "German Economic Society"*

In the period of fascism Höhn worked very closely with the "Reichsführer SS" and main war criminal Himmler as an expert on constitutional law.

In October 1935 Höhn was appointed director of the Institute of State Research at the Berlin University, and at the same time he was made the head of department 2, branch II of the central SD office in the notorious Reich Security Main Office. In this position he was responsible for the complete spying on all fields of public life in Hitler Germany. Höhn himself described the tasks of the Institute of State Research on 7 June 1939: *"My institute has been commissioned by decisive authorities of the state and party with providing detailed scientific assistance for the practical application of law in the national socialist state." Archiv of the Humboldt University, Berlin)*

One of the tasks of the institute was also to draft constitutional legal principles for the occupation regime in the territories occupied by the fascists. This is revealed by the judgment Höhn wrote about Hofmann, a fellow-worker who, before the attack on the Soviet Union, had worked out "an extensive expert opinion on organization and problems of setting up the administration of the USSR". He said there: *"He (Hofmann – editor) was able to devise excellent solutions of the ways and problems to be encountered by the German military and civil authorities after the military occupation." (ibid.)*

Since 1939 this institute had been working almost exclusively for Himmler. A letter of the "Reichsführung SS" states: *"The director of the Institute of State Research at the Berlin University and his scientific staff have been ordered to serve the Reichsführer SS and chief of the German police during the war within the scope of the scientific tasks of the institute." (ibid.)*

A work report written by Höhn on 22 June 1940 reveals the great importance this institute possessed for the fascist apparatus of terror:

"On the basis of this order the institute has been engaged since 1 September 1939 on a number of tasks set by the Reich minister of the interior and the chief of the security police and the SD. Until now the following have been completed:
1 draft of a law with detailed justification,

3 drafts of decrees with detailed justification,
6 detailed investigations on the system of state organization of foreign states,
20 reports concerning the scope of work of the chief of the security police drawn up on his request,
16 reports concerning the scope of work of the "Reichsführer SS",
12 detailed reports on separate problems of war administration." (*ibid.*)

Höhn was also indispensable for Stuckart, the initiator, author and commentator of the Racial Laws. (See Table 48)

Höhn produced countless publications as a fascist expert in constitutional and administrative law. Describing the essence of the fascist state he wrote: *"People are no longer governed, they are led ... In our state as an organ of the Führer people are ordered and they obey ... parliamentary decisions and votes are outdated as decisions are taken and executed."* (*Die Wandlung im staatsrechtlichen Denken* – The Change in Legal Thinking, Hamburg, 1934)

As late as 1944 he stated his opinion about the oath of loyalty to the Führer: *"The oath of loyalty to the Führer not only expresses the idea that the soldier is, as in a monarchy, subject to a master, but also the obligation to the national socialist idea, the exponent of which is encountered by the soldier in the person of the Führer. As the executor of the political will of his people the soldier takes it upon his oath to the Führer to defend this conception militarily ... Taking an oath to the Führer not only obliges him to allegiance and obedience to the national socialist idea as long as the Führer lives but also beyond his death and, therefore, to the new leader rising out of the movement."* (*Das Reich*, Berlin, 1 October 1944)

Höhn was chairman of the committee for police law at the Academy of German Law founded by war criminal H. Frank. For his "services" Höhn also had a career as an SS man: He was SS Brigadeführer, wore the "honorary sword of the Reichsführer SS" and was in 1945 promoted to the rank of lieutenant general in the armed SS.

Neo-Fascism in Millions of Copies

The neo-fascist and militarist journals, newspapers, books and films as well as radio and television broadcasts gain more and more importance in the process of exercising an ideological influence on the West German population. When Höcherl, jurist in Hitler's service and at present minister of the interior in Bonn, declares that the influence of the neo-fascist propaganda has decreased this is a deliberate deception of the public.

The dangerous influence of these media can not be measured only in the circulation figures reached by some publishing houses. It is clearly visible mainly in the papers published by such "public opinion molding" monopolies as the Springer trust, in radio and television programs and in West German film production. The West German mass media have long since taken over the theories of the neo-nazis. Day after day the West German population is subjected to this flood of chauvinism and revanchism.

The following examples represent only a small selection from the range of more than 100 militarist, fascist and revanchist publishing houses in West Germany.

Some publishing houses and journals have specialized in maintaining and spreading militarist and fascist ideas.

GLORIFIES HITLER'S PREDATORY CAMPAIGNS

The journal *Alte Kameraden* (Old Comrades) is a product of the G. Braun Verlag (publishing house) in Karlsruhe. It is the central organ of about 50 militarist traditional associations and, along with the *Deutsche National-Zeitung und Soldaten-Zeitung*, one of the widest-read militarist papers in West Germany. Editor-in-chief of this paper is Rudolf Böhmler, colonel of the nazi Wehrmacht. The SS organ *Der Freiwillige* certified: *"Rudolf Böhmler . . . as a friend and defender of the rights of the soldiers of the former armed SS has long been intimately known to us." (Der Freiwillige,* Osnabrück, 11/1963)

The journal, which has been published for 13 years, with its supplement *Der deutsche Fallschirmjäger* (The German Paratrooper) presents the extermination campaigns of the fascist Wehrmacht and the assaults on peaceful peoples as examples of soldierly discipline and virtue, and recommends them to the Bundeswehr as exemplary models.

"War adventures" of this type form the greatest part of the publishing program, e.g., Egon Denzel, "Attack on Volkov" (No. 1/60); E. A. Wichers, "Ivan Came Across Lake Ilmen" (No. 6/60); Werner Haupt, "The Clock Showed 3.05. Army Group North on 22 June 1941" (No. 6/61); G. Teschner, "Advance on Bessarabia" (No. 11–12/61).

THE CENTRAL ORGAN OF THE MILITARISTS

The *Deutsche National-Zeitung und Soldaten-Zeitung* (NZ) is the largest militarist and neo-fascist weekly newspaper in West Germany. It is published by Gerhard Frey, neo-fascist and proprietor of the "Deutsche Soldaten-Zeitung Verlags GmbH". This paper is printed in the printing office of Johann Evangelist Kapfinger, intimate and accomplice in the scandals of Strauss, the sacked war minister. The paper has become a central organ of all ultra-right neo-fascist forces in West Germany and defames each and every movement advocating a realistic policy. Thus von der Heydte, SS man and parachute officer of the nazi Wehrmacht, called for long sentences of penal servitude for "renunciation politicians", meaning those forces striving for normal relations with the neighbouring peoples in the east and south-east of Europe.

This paper advocates with peculiar zeal a general amnesty for nazi and war criminals. Hess, main war criminal and former deputy of the Führer, has been called a "prisoner of peace". Under the headline "Justice is not a whore" in No. 5/64 the acquittal of SS Sturmbannführer Erich Deppner, who, among other crimes, had 65 Soviet prisoners of war murdered, is praised as a "turning point in the trials of war criminals".

The "NZ" publishes two supplements with specifically revanchist objectives, the *Schlesische Rundschau* and *Der Sudetendeutsche.* Apart from the continuously growing influence this paper has on the revenge-seeking organizations, it must be noted that readership in the Bundeswehr has increased.

MOUTHPIECE OF THE SS

The central organ of the HIAG, *Der Freiwillige* (The Volunteer), has been published in Osnabrück in a publishing house of the same name since 1955. The HIAG is the organization of the former members of the Waffen SS (armed SS). Decisive influence on the HIAG and its mouthpiece is exercised by SS Generals Felix Steiner, Kurt Meyer, Paul Hausser and Herbert O. Gille.

Der Freiwillige sees its most urgent task in rehabilitating the Waffen SS and justifying its crimes against the peoples of Europe. The paper praises the Waffen SS as the "elite troops" of German fascism and champion of an anti-communist unification of Europe under the rule of German imperialism: *"The name of the Waffen SS will not be wiped off the tablets commemorating soldiers in Europe."* (*Der Freiwillige,* Osnabruck, No. 11/63)

Along with the rehabilitation of the Waffen SS, which has practically been accomplished in the Federal Republic, *Der Freiwillige* sees its task in fighting the "old enemies", the resistance fighters throughout Europe: *"But when our anxiety, our uneasiness about the undoubtedly still uncompleted democracy are responded to by regarding the discussion among ourselves as subversive, when our honourable service in the face of the assault of communist partisan organizations is declared to be dangerous to the state, then justice and freedom of democracy are at stake, and God may have mercy on those who did not shrink from handing us over to the VVN and FIR. (organizations of resistance fighters – editor) to appease their voracity." (op.cit., No. 8/63)*

The hangmen of Lidice, Oradour, Malmedy and the Warsaw Ghetto in the uniform of the Waffen SS present themselves as the champions of democracy and liberty and call the Federal Republic "their" state. Well-known writers and publicists in West Germany, like Blöcker, Böll, Geissler, Gross and Kuby, are targets of mad instigation. The work of these writers was insulted as "progressive literary negligence". *Der Freiwillige* went on to write: *"The accord of real intellect and real genuine principles of leadership in a democracy have been lost. It is in those times that the rats gain power and space." (op.cit., No. 9/61)*

WAR CRIMINALS AS AUTHORS

The program of the Schild Verlag is largely determined by the publication of books on the Waffen SS and the fascist Wehrmacht. Thus this publishing house, which is owned by former NSDAP regional leader Damerau, published, among others, the following books:

The book *Grenadiere*, written by Kurt Meyer, an SS general sentenced to death by the allies and later reprieved; the book *Das goldene Feld* (The Golden Field) on the predatory campaign of German fascism in the Ukraine, written by Kernmayr, former SS Hauptsturmführer and regional press office head in Vienna, published in 1961;

the book *Panzer marsch* (Tank March) written from the papers of the late fascist General Guderian, by Oskar Munzel, tank inspector of the Bundeswehr;

the books *Die Wahrheit über Malmedy* (The Truth about Malmedy), 1958, and *Die Lüge von Marzobotto* (The Lies of Marzobotto), 1959, by former SS Untersturmführer Greil. Both books were intended to justify the horrible blood baths committed by the Waffen SS in these places.

Judicious persons and the heroes of the resistance struggle within the fascist Wehrmacht are defamed as traitors while war criminals are rehabilitated. Thus Peter Strassner published the pamphlet *Verräter – "Nationalkomitee Freies Deutschland" – Keimzelle der "DDR"* (Traitors – "Free Germany" National Committee – Germ Cell of the "GDR".

Since 1953 the Schild Verlag has issued the "Deutscher Soldatenkalender", (German Soldiers' Calendar), which is addressed to the members of the militarist traditional associations, of which there are approximately 600, and to the soldiers and reservists of the Bundeswehr. Contributions and "accompanying remarks" of this calendar are almost exclusively written by generals of the fascist Wehrmacht. Thus Dönitz, Hitler's successor and main war criminal, is the author of the "accompanying remarks" in the 1963 edition.

NAZI IDEOLOGY FOR YOUNG PEOPLE

Of the West German publishing houses which publish militarist and fascist intellectual material, especially directed at young people, in the form of two penny booklets in great number and with a large edition only the Pabel-Verlag in Rastatt/Baden is named here. With 20 different series and a monthly circulation of several million copies it is the largest producer of these booklets in West Germany. The notorious "Landser" series has been published since 1957: "Der Landser", published since 1957 at first fortnightly, since October 1958 weekly. The series reached number 310 in March 1964. "Der Landser-Grossband" (large volume), later called the "Landser-Sonderband" (special volume). There were already 136 issues of this series in March 1964. "Der Landser – Ritterkreuzträger erzählen" (Holders of the Knight's Cross Recount), published monthly since summer 1959 and amounting to 137 issues in March 1964.

During the last years the Pabel-Verlag has also distributed books praising war and the fascist military apparatus. Among the authors are Günther Fraschka, nazi officer, and Count Bossi-Fedrigotti, Austrian fascist leader and cultural expert in the Reich propaganda office.

REVANCHIST DEMANDS AS PUBLISHING PROGRAM

Special publishing houses were set up to propagate the territorial claims of the federal government. The claim for restitution of the "Greater German Reich" determines the content of their publishing program. Some of them are the Heimreiter-Verlag and the Klinger-Verlag.

Head of the Heimreiter-Verlag in Frankfurt-on-Main, is Ernst Frank, a brother of the fascist "Reichsprotektor" of Bohemia and Moravia, sentenced as a main war criminal.

Ernst Frank had a substantial part in preparing the annexation of the Sudeten region and received the "Sudeten medal" as an award in 1938. After the annexation he was national socialist chief editor and regional main office head of the nazi party. Ernst Frank developed the Heimreiter-Verlag into the mouthpiece of the "Witikobund", the propaganda centre of the "Sudetendeutsche Landsmannschaft".

This house publishes, among others, the "Beiträge des Witikobundes zu den Fragen der Zeit" (Contributions of the Witikobund to the Questions of Our Time). Among the authors are such incriminated nazis as Seiboth, NSDAP regional leader at the Reichenberg regional leadership, who today puts up his revanchist claims for territory under the cloak of the right of self-determination. Part of the publishing program is also such revanchist newspapers as the *Sudetendeutscher*

Turnerbrief, whose content is decided by SA leader Welwarski. This paper is produced in the printing office of the former nazi regional leader and anti-Semite Tins.

Prominent book authors are, above all, the SA Sturmbannführer and nazi writer Rudolf Jahn (he published, among others, a book on nazi war criminal Konrad Henlein in 1938) and Ernst Frank. Frank published, among other books, *Heimat ohne Vaterland* (Home without a Fatherland), a novel of present times, *Leidenschaftliches Egerland* (Passionate Egerland), *Grenzen der Freiheit* (Limitations of Liberty), *Gedichte und Szenen* (Poems and Scenes).

LED BY NAZIS

Among the leading men of the Klinger-Verlag in Munich are the active members of the Sudeten German Party and, later, the NSDAP, Karl Jungschaffer and Erich Maier. Prior to 1945 both of them had been employed in the publishing house management or editor's office of the local party paper of the NSDAP Reichenberg regional leadership, *Die Zeit.* In a series of articles in this paper Maier wrote: *"Thus the Jews in the background sullied the honour of the German soldier, thus they managed to shake the courage at home and create the prerequisites for the collapse." (Die Zeit,* Reichenberg, 1939)

An article in the revanchist paper *Vertriebenen-Anzeiger,* published by the Klinger-Verlag, shows that Maier has not changed his views. Under the headline "Wie lange noch 'Kriegsverbrecherprozesse'?" (How much longer will the 'war criminal' trials last?) he called on 1 September 1959 for a general amnesty for all nazi and war criminals.

Among the publications of the Klinger-Verlag is the journal *Wehr und Heimat* subsidized by the Bundeswehr. This paper, published mainly for young people, presents the fascist attack on Poland in the following way: *"1 September 1939: The guns had gone off, the campaign against Poland and, therefore, the Second World War, had started ... It should be noted that there can be no talk of a German attack on Poland ... Command and troops of the Wehrmacht had done their best in this campaign to bring it to an early, victorious end." (Wehr und Heimat,* Munich, No. 9/1959)

The danger of this neo-fascist influence cannot be overlooked; the consequences in the minds of the West German population are already at this time actually frightening. As early as 1958 SPD (Social Democratic Party of Germany) Bundestag member Ulrich Lohmar warned in a session of the Bundestag:

"This aggressive nationalism cannot merely be explained out of itself alone. There is a close connection with an ideology of a western crusade ..." (Brüdigam,

Der Schoss ist fruchtbar noch (The Womb is Fruitful Still), Röderberg-Verlag, Frankfurt-on-Main)

The Bonn state, however, forces this ideology, because it serves its aggressive plans.

Brown Professors and National Socialist Ideologists in West Germany

Aubin, Hermann
before 1945: professor of German medieval and modern history and of East-European history; university professor in Bonn, Giesen and Breslau; was one of Hitler's ideological trail blazers, worked in the executive of the North and East German Research Group – the centre of the struggle against Germany's eastern neighbours
after 1945: Honorarprofessor at Freiburg/Br., president for many years of the "Johann-Gottfried-Herder Research Council", a centre of West German revanchism; Aubin is responsible for the split in the "German Historical Association"

Bartholomeyczik, Horst
before 1945: provincial court counsellor in the special court, Breslau (Wrocław, involved in death sentences
after 1945: superior provincial court counselor in Koblenz until 1963; professor of economic and civil procedure law in the University of Mainz

Berber, Friedrich
before 1945: legal adviser to war criminal Ribbentrop, leading fascist specialist on international law; 1936–1944 deputy director of the Institute of Foreign Policy, Hamburg; 1936 member of the Academy of German Law which was extremely fascist in character and had been founded by Frank; extensive activity as a publicist in conceiving and vindicating fascist foreign policy
after 1945: Since 1954 professor of international law, public law and the philosophy of law; member of the board of the Institute of International Law at Munich University

Bertram, Georg
before 1945: leading member and later managing director of the "Institute for Research on Jewish Influence on Church Life"; published many anti-Semitic writings; 1922–1946 professor of theology in the University of Giessen
after 1945: professor in Frankfurt-on-Main

Boehm, Max Hildebert
before 1945: since 1933 promoting member of the SS; founder of the fascist "sociology of nationhood" and "borderland research", leading ideologist of the fascist 5th column; from 1933 holder of a professorial chair at the Universities of Berlin and Jena
after 1945: lang-time head of the "East German Academy", Lüneburg, an ideological centre of revanchism; president of the revanchist "North-East German Cultural Undertaking"

Bosch, Werner
before 1945: 1942–1943 economic inspection of the fascist army group "Mitte", participated in the economic pillage of Soviet territories, 1943–1945 in the planning office of war criminal and armaments minister Speer as chief department head responsible for the deportation to Germany of the civilian population of the occupied territories to work in Germany as forced labourers, and for putting prisoners of war to work in the fascist armaments industry; 1934 SS, finally SS Untersturmführer
after 1945: professor of political economy at the University of Mainz, member of the research circle of the research advisory council of the "All-German" Ministry

Buntru, Alfred
before 1945: Until 1943 rector of the Charles University and until 1945 rector of the Technical College in Prague, confidant of war criminal Henlein, anti-Semite, SS Oberführer
after 1945: professor at the Aachen Technical College, active in the "Sudetendeutsche Landsmannschaft"

Eckardt, Felix von

before 1945: fascist script author, wrote 19 scenarios for nazi films as author or co-author

after 1945: state secretary in the Press and Information Office of the Bonn government, "plenipotentiary" of the Erhard government in West Berlin, CDU candidate for the 1965 Bundestag elections

Gehlen, Arnold

before 1945: office head of the fascist association of lecturers in Leipzig, glorified the fascist dictatorship and the predatory wars of German imperialism as a philosopher

after 1945: professor of sociology at the Aachen Technical College

Gerstenmaier, Eugen

before 1945: 1923 SA, from 1931 office head in the fascist German Association of Students, exponent of the "Führer idea" in the Evangelical church, on behalf of the Foreign Office made several journeys to neutral or occupied countries for the ideological liquidation of the anti-fascist resistance struggle, denounced the anti-fascist scholar Professor S. Schulze to the nazi authorities; 1942 appointed official for life and excused from military service for the duration of the war

after 1945: president of the West German Bundestag

Globke, Hans-Maria

before 1945: minsterial counsellor in the Reich Ministry of the Interior, responsible for nationality questions and questions of occupied western territories; took part in the liquidation of the Weimar Republic through the working out of dictatorship laws, co-author of the racial laws, thus provided the legal foundations for the extermination of entire groups of people; participated actively in the "final solution of the Jewish question"

after 1945: until July 1963 state secretary in the Office of the Federal Chancellor and most powerful official of the Bonn state; 1962 sentenced to life imprisonment by the Supreme Court of the GDR; had to retire as state secretary because of the incriminating material submitted

Grebe, Hans

before 1945: assistant and pupil of the notorious "racial specialist" Verschuer in Frankfurt-on-Main and at the Kaiser Wilhelm Institute of Anthropology, Human Genetics and Eugenics in Berlin, 1944 reader with a teaching assignment and head of the Institute of the Biology of Heredity and Racial Hygiene at the University of Rostock, influential propagandist of the false racial theories of fascism, head of the scientific department in the "Main Office of World Outlook Education" in the Reich youth leadership, trained Hitler Youth leaders and leading national socialist officers in "heredity and racial hygiene" questions, closely cooperated with the "Race Policy Office" of the NSDAP, took part in "expert opinion examinations" in the notorious Eugen Fischer Institute in Berlin

after 1945: professor with teaching assignment for human genetics at the University of Marburg since 1952, until 1961 president of the German Association of Sport Doctors

Gross, Hermann

before 1945: 1939–1945 head of the department of the Vienna branch of the poison-gas concern IG Farben; explored the possibilities of the economic pillage of the states of South-East Europe; 1933 SA, and since 1936 a member of the fascist German Academy

after 1945: economic specialist for Eastern Europe, professor of politico-economic science at the University of Kiel; since 1962 professor of the economics and society of South-Eastern Europe and since 1964 in the directory of the seminar of the same name at the University of Munich

Grundmann, Günther

before 1945: as a leading fascist art historian he had a share in the stealing of Polish works of art during the Second World War, distinguished himself through anti-Semitic writings

after 1945: president of the "Johann-Gottfried-Herder Research Council", leading West German art historian, 1951–1959 member of the UNESCO "International Committee on Monuments, Artistic and Historical Sites and Archeological Excavations" in Paris; 1959 awarded the Great Federal Distinguished Service Cross of the Order of Merit of the Federal Republic

Heydte, Friedrich-August von der

before 1945: 1937 volunteer of the fascist Wehrmacht, parachute officer, last rank lieutenant-colonel, decorated with the Knight's Cross with Oak-leaves and the "German Cross in Gold" for barbaric warfare, SS after 1945: professor of political science and international law at the University of Würzburg

Höhn, Reinhard

before 1945: 1935 director of the Institute of Political Research at the University of Berlin, 1935–1938 head of department II/2 in the SD main office, close co-worker of Himmler in the field of public law, SS brigadeführer and lieutenant general in the armed SS, distinguished by Himmler with the "Sword of Honour"
after 1945: president of the "Academy of the Leading Forces of the Economy", Bad Harzburg

Hubrich, Georg

before 1945: ministerial director and head of the U department I East in the Reich Ministry of the Interior, co-worker of Globke and Stuchart, author of several laws dealing with Jews, responsible for questions of administration in the occupied eastern territories, especially in fascist-occupied Poland
after 1945: business-manager of the North and West German Radio Union, Hamburg

Jankuhn, Herbert

before 1945: fascist professor of primeval and early history at the University of Rostock, SS Obersturmbannführer in the personal staff of Reichsführer SS Himmler, bearer of the "death-head ring" of the SS
after 1945: professor at the University of Göttingen, member of the "Johann-Gottfried-Herder Research Council"

Jordan, Pascual

before 1945: professor of theoretical physics in Rostock and Berlin, war propagandist, fanatical ideologist of the fascist system
after 1945: since 1947 at the University of Hamburg, 1957–1961 member of the CDU parliamentary group in the Bundestag, advocate of an atomic war

Keyser, Erich

before 1945: historian and state archivist in Danzig, agent of the illegal "North and East German Research Group", helped in the preparation of the occupation of Danzig and Polish territories by German fascism
after 1945: director of the "Johann-Gottfried-Herder Institute"

Köttgen, Arnold

before 1945: teaching activity at the University of Greifswald, since 1939 general police expert and counter intelligence agent of the government, Kattowitz (Katowice); Auschwitz concentration camp whose commandant Höss cooperated closely with the Kattowitz government belonged to the Kattowitz government district; Köttgen was called an indispensable key figure for the construction of the police apparatus of suppression in the occupied Polish territories by District President Walter Springorum; in his works on administrative law he glorified Hitler and the Führer principle in administrative law
after 1945: professor of public, administrative and church law in the legal faculty of the University of Göttingen, director of the juridical seminar, member of the justice examining office of the Superior Provincial Court in Oldenburg and Celle

Kordt, Erich

before 1945: 1938–1940 head of the ministerial office of war criminal and fascist Foreign Minister Ribbentrop, influential in the preparation of the occupation of Czechoslovakia, agent of Himmler in the Foreign Office, SS Obersturmbannführer
after 1945: professor of the history of diplomacy and international law at the University of Cologne, chairman of the committee for East-West problems in the Bonn Foreign Office, head of the ministerial office of the prime minister of North Rhine-Westphalia

Lemberg, Eugen

before 1945: leading nazi educationist and "borderland specialist" in the Sudeten German territory, co-worker on various periodicals of the Sudeten German party, member of the Sudeten German volunteer corps, the Henlein SS, head of the fascist teachers' training college in Reichenberg
after 1945: leading in West Germany in the field of the revanchist influencing of youth in the classroom, for some time president of the "Johann-Gottfried-Herder Research Council", co-editor and author of "Ostkunde im Unterricht" (Eastern Research in the Classroom)

Leverenz, Bernhard

before 1945: senior naval staff judge, 1933 NSDAP
after 1945: minister of justice and deputy prime minister in Schleswig-Holstein, since 1962 presidial member of the "Committee for an Indivisible Germany", the propaganda instrument of the Bonn government for the annexation of the GDR, member of the advisory research council of the "All-German" Ministry

Maunz, Theodor

before 1945: professor of public law in Freiburg/Breisgau, leading fascist specialist on administrative law, introduced the "racial idea" in administrative law and justified the fascist apparatus of extermination and suppression

after 1945: 1952 professor of public law in the University of Munich, 1954–1957 minister of culture in Bavaria, forced to resign on 10 June 1964 after the GDR published material on his nazi past

Maurach, Reinhart

before 1945: fascist specialist in criminal law and head of the Institute of East European Law at the University of Königsberg, department head in the East Europe Institute in Breslau (Wrocław), national-socialist lower court counsellor, distinguished himself by anti-Semitic writings, published articles in Weltkampf, the central organ of anti-Semitism in fascist Germany, active NSDAP official

after 1945: professor and member of the governing body of the Institute of Criminal Law and Criminal Trial Procedures as well as of East European Law at the University of Munich, member of the "Johann-Gottfried-Herder Research Council"

Mehnert, Klaus

before 1945: 1931–1933 general secretary of the "German Society for the Study of Eastern Europe", foreign correspondent of fascist newspapers, propaganda expert in the Shanghai representation of the Foreign Office

after 1945: professor in ordinary and director of the Institute of Political Science at Aachen Technical College, member of the "advisory council for development aid" in the "Federal Ministry for Economic Cooperation", editor-in-chief of the periodicals of the "German Society for Information on Eastern Europe"

Meimberg, Rudolf

before 1945: since 1933 teaching activity at the University of Berlin and the Technical College in Prague, professor at the College of Political Science, fascist economist, active SA leader, deputy SA instructor

after 1945: professor of economics at the University of Mainz, member of the research circle in the advisory research council of the "All-German" Ministry

Meissner, Boris

before 1945: took part in the "ethnic struggle" to undermine the Esthonian state, regional office head of the illegal fascist movement in Esthonia, active member of the SA, attended a special indoctrination course at the leadership school of the highest SA leadership in Dresden, in the Second World War special leader of fascist Esthonian units, decorated with the "medal of valour for the Eastern Peoples in silver" for complicity in crimes committed by these incendiary units, hold-out fanatic

after 1945: for a time in the "East" department of the Bonn Foreign Office, member of the board of the East Faculty of the "Federal Centre for Political Education", member of the managerial committee of the working group for East-West problems in the Bonn Foreign Office, member of the management committee of the "Federal Institute for the Exploration of Marxism-Leninism (Institute of Sovietology)", leading member of the German Society for East European Research, professor of Eastern law at the University of Cologne, since 1965 president of the "Göttinger Working Group", an ideological centre of Bonn revanchism

Meyer, Konrad

before 1945: professor of agrarian science and policy in Jena and Berlin, chairman of the "Reich Work Group for Space Research" controlled by the SS, defender of the "blood and soil policy" and the "people without space" theory, collaborator in the "General Plan East" (the land as far as the Urals was to be transformed into a German colony, and 30 to 50 million people were to be exterminated or displaced), 1939 head of the planning staff of the "Reich commissioner for the strengthening of the German nationality", close collaborator of Himmler and war criminal Darré in "Germanization questions", SS Oberführer

after 1945: professor of rural building and planning at the Hanover Technical College, member of the senate commission for the management of the Academic Foreign Office, member of the select committee, 1957 member of the Academy for Space Research and Rural Planning in Hanover, 1964 emeritus

Mikorey, Maximilian

before 1945: lecturer in psychiatry at the University of Munich, member of the fascist "Academy of German Law", specialist in fascist criminal and court psychology, anti-Semite and propagator of race hatred

after 1945: professor of psychiatry, neurology and medical psychology at the University of Munich, head physician of the Munich neurological clinic

Pölnitz, Götz von
before 1945: since 1936 University of Munich, fascist historian, anti-Semite
after 1945: professor at the Universities of Munich and Erlangen, since 1964 founding rector of the University of Regensburg

Preusker, Victor-Emanuel
before 1945: agent of the Dresdner Bank, worked as "racial specialist" in the "Aryanization" of Viennese banks, SS leader
after 1945: federal minister of housing construction (retired), president of the central association of German real estate owners, member of several boards of directors, member of the advisory research council of the "All-German" Ministry

Rabl, Kurt
before 1945: Henlein's adviser, fascist folk group specialist, 1940 general expert on Polish administrative law in the government of the generalgouvernement, 1941 specialist in the personal staff and head of the legislative department of the "Reich commissioner for the occupied Dutch territories", war criminal Seyss-Inquart, member of the armed SS, had an authoritative part in the introduction and execution of laws on Jews in Slovakia and Holland
after 1945: member of the "federal work group for East German school instruction", collaborator of the periodical Deutsche Ostkunde, member of the board of the Collegium Carolinum, a centre of imperialist eastern research

Raschhofer, Herrmann
before 1945: teaching activity in Göttingen and in the Charles University in Prague, adviser of war criminal K.H. Frank, created the legal justification for the liquidation of the Czechoslovak state
after 1945: professor of international law and international relations at the University of Würzburg

Rauch, Georg von
before 1945: 1936–1939 lecturer at Dorpat University (Esthonia), 1943–1945 lecturer at the Reich University in Posen (Poznan), NSDAP, anti-Semitic east researcher
after 1945: member of the "scientific examing office for higher school teachers in Schleswig-Holstein"

Redecker, Martin
before 1945: theologian in Kiel, appeared in public with anti-Semitic speeches and writings
after 1945: member of the "scientific examining office for higher school teachers in Schleswig-Holstein"

Ruff, Siegfried
before 1945: head of the "Institute for Aeronautical Medicine of the German Air Navigation Experimental Station" in Berlin which carried out inhuman medical experiments for the fascist Luftwaffe on prisoners of Dachau concentration camp
after 1945: since 1952 head of the "Institute for Aeronautical Medicine of the German Air Navigation Experimental Station" in Bad Godesberg, since 1954 supernumerary professor of aeronautical medicine and physiology at the University of Bonn

Schier, Bruno
before 1945: expert on fascist folklore in the staff of the "Reich farmers' leader", war criminal Darré, employee in the office of the murderer of Jews and war criminal Rosenberg and the Reich leader of university lecturers, professor of folklore at the University of Leipzig, executed secret commissions in ethnology for war criminal K.H. Frank, in which he came to the fore as a race-hatred monger, denounced Professor Gesemann of Prague (Praha) as being "friendly to Jews"
after 1945: 1949 University of Marburg, foundation member of the "Johann-Gottfried-Herder Research Council", 1952 University of Münster, director of the folkloristic seminar

Schwidetzky-Roesing, Ilse
before 1945: 1939–1945 lecturer at the University of Breslau (Wrocław), fascist racial theorist, co-editor of the Zeitschrift für Rassenkunde und vergleichende Forschung am Menschen (Journal of Race-lore and Comparative Research on Human Beings)
after 1945: 1950 member of the "Johann-Gottfried-Herder Research Council", 1949 professor in Mainz, 1960 director of the Anthropological Institute at the University of Mainz, 1953 member of the Academy of Demographic Science

Schwinge, Erich
before 1945: 1938 dean of the Faculty of Law at the University of Marburg, 1940 professor in Vienna, specialist in military law, justified the cruel sentences of fascist military courts, wrote comments on the fascist military penal code
after 1945: 1945 professor of criminal law and criminal trial procedures, military

law and the international law of war, 1954 to 1955 rector of the University of Marburg, specialist in West German military penal law, counsel for the defence of SS murderer Simon (he had three citizens of Brettheim/ West Germany executed in April 1945), co-worker in the Neue Zeitschrift für Wehrrecht (New Journal of Military Law)

Seraphim, Peter-Heinz

before 1945: 1937 University of Königsberg (Kaliningrad), 1941 University of Greifswald, there 1943 director of the "Oder-Danube Institute", until 1945 editor-in-chief of the anti-Semitic periodical Weltkampf (World Struggle), member of the "Institute for Research on the Jewish Question" founded by main war criminal Rosenberg
after 1945: study leader and president of the "Administrative and Economic Academy of the Bochum Industrial District"

Taubert, Dr. Eberhard

before 1945: ministerial counsellor in the Ministry of Propaganda, official superior of the notorious "Anti-Komintern", responsible for the whole of fascist propaganda in the occupied eastern territories; initiator of a slander campaign unrivalled so far in form and volume against all anti-fascist forces; 1938 judge on the first panel of the notorious People's Court; in this capacity on 27 November 1942 sent the German anti-fascist Helmut Klotz and on 11 January 1943 the French anti-fascist Marcel Gerbohay to the scaffold
after 1945: chairman and deputy chairman of the "National Association for Peace and Freedom", an anti-communist instigation organization financed by the "All-German" Ministry; on behalf of the Bonn war ministry and NATO works on problems of psychological warfare; close ties with international fascist circles like the "Anti-Komintern-Dienst" in Bad Godesberg

Verschuer, Otmar, Freiherr von

before 1945: 1933 professor of racial hygiene and the biology of heredity, 1933 to 1945 editor of the journal Der Erbarzt, 1935 to 1942 professor and director of the Institute of Heredity and Racial Hygiene in Frankfurt-on-Main, 1937 member of the research department on genetics and race of the extreme fascist "Reich Institute on the History of the New Germany, 1942–1945 director of the notorious Kaiser Wilhelm Institute of Anthropology, Human Genetics and Eugenics
after 1945: 1949 a member of the "Academy of Science and Literature" in Mainz, 1951 professor and director of the Institute of Human Genetics in the University of Münster

Wandschneider, Gerhard

before 1945: nazi district president in Wismar, active NSDAP and SA leader (regional office head, bloc leader, propaganda speaker), shares responsibility for the execution of a Polish worker deported to Germany by the Gestapo on 21 March 1944 in Stove, decorated with the War Merit Cross
after 1945: since 1950 district president in the duchy of Lauenburg, leading member of the "Central Communal Unions" in Cologne, member of the advisory research council of the "All-German" Ministry

Welter, Erich

before 1945: editor of the Frankfurter Zeitung and editor-in-chief of Wirtschaftskurve, 1944 professor of national economics at the University of Mainz, agent of the IG-Farben poison gas trust, investigated the possibilities of plundering the Balkans, confidant of war criminal Kehrl and "Reichsleiter" Ammann
after 1945: since 1951 head of the Research Institute of Economic Policy at the University of Mainz, member of the research circle in the advisory research council of the "All-German" Ministry

Weltz, Georg August

before 1945: doctor in the fascist Luftwaffe, director of the Institute of Aeronautical Medicine at the University of Munich, took part in medical experiments for the fascist Luftwaffe on prisoners of Dachau concentration camp
after 1945: since 1952 supernumerary professor in the University of Munich

Wenke, Hans

before 1945: teaching activity in the University of Erlangen, anti-Semitic educational specialist, glorified the Führer cult in nazi pedagogics and the war of conquest of German imperialism
after 1945: rector of Tübingen University and president of the South West German Conference of Rectors, 1954–1957 senator for education and higher learning in Hamburg, 1958 director of the UNESCO Institute of Education. 1961 chairman of the founding committee of the newly to be founded Bochum University, appointed founding direc-

tor of the Bochum Ruhr University, had to be recalled from this function because of protests against his fascist past

Wilhelm, Theodor

before 1945: anti-Semitic nazi educationist, editor of Internationale Zeitschrift für Erziehung (International Journal of Education)
after 1945: member of the scientific examining office for higher school teachers in Schleswig-Holstein

Wirsing, Giselher

before 1945: employee of the SD, SS Sturmbannführer, influential anti-Semitic nazi journalist, member of the "Institute for the Exploration of the Jewish Problem" (founded by chief war criminal Alfred Rosenberg), editor of the nazi newspaper Tat (renamed Das XX. Jahrhundert in 1939)
after 1945: 1948 founded the West German weekly Christ und Welt, since 1954 its editor-in-chief

APPENDIX-DOCUMENTARY TABLES

TABLE 1

20 November 1932

Your Excellency,
Most Honourable Herr Reich President,

Full of ardent love for the German people and fatherland, like Your Excellency, the undersigned have welcomed with hope the basic change initiated by Your Excellency in the management of the affairs of state. Like Your Excellency we affirm the necessity of a government which is more independent of the parliamentary party system, as is expressed in the idea of a presidial cabinet formulated by Your Excellency.

The result of the Reichstag election of 6 November this year has shown . . .
. . . transformation of the Reich cabinet may take place in a way which brings the greatest possible popular force behind the cabinet.

We confess ourselves to be free from any narrow party political attitude. In the national movement which has seized our people we see the promising beginning of a time which creates the first indispensable basis for an upswing of the German economy by overcoming the antagonisms between classes. We know that this upswing will still demand many sacrifices. We believe that these sacrifices can only be made willingly when the largest group of this national movement will have a leading part in the government.

The transfer of the responsible leadership of a presidial cabinet staffed with the best expert and personal forces to the leader of the largest national group will extirpate the slags and mistakes necessarily inherent in any mass movement and carry along millions of people to affirmative force who today still stand apart.

In full confidence in the wisdom and feeling of national solidarity of Your Excellency we great Your Excellency

with profound respect

Fritz Thyssen

TABLE 2

Berlin, 1 June 1933

Adolf Hitler Donation of the German Economy

I.

To replace the many individual collections of various institutions and associations of the NSDAP, a central collection of all branches of the German economy has come into existence under the name of "Adolf Hitler Donation of the German Economy". This donation is managed by a board of trustees composed of representatives of the participating branches of the economy. Herr Dr. Krupp von Bohlen und Halbach has taken over the chairmanship of this board of trustees (address: Berlin W 35, Königin-Augusta-Strasse 28, Reichsverband der Deutschen Industrie).

The branches of economy have pledged themselves to raise a certain amount in a form suitable for them within one year, in the period from 1 June 1933 to 31 May 1934, and to transmit the collected sums to the board of trustees.

The Reich Association of German Industry and the Association of the German Employers' Federations call upon the associations and firms affiliated to them to support this collection with all means available to them. We expect the active cooperation of all our organizations and enterprises and the personal activity of their leaders. It is a question of acting quickly and generously, carrying out the action simply and economically, avoiding all bureaucratic restrictions.

Current special agreements are to be involved in the general collection.

7. All questions and letters are to be addressed to the business-management of the industrial collection. Copies of this circular are available in any desired amount on request.

For the Reich Association
of German Industry
signed: Krupp von Bohlen
und Halbach

For the Association of
German Employers
signed: Köttgen

Duplicate!

Adolf Hitler Donation of the German Economy

Certificate
D No. 086867

Dresdner Bank
Berlin

takes part in the Adolf Hitler Donation of the German Economy with an amount of one-hundred-and-twenty-thousand Reichsmarks.

Berlin, in June 1934
The Board of Trustees
(signatures)

Collections from the holder of this certificate by all members, authorities and institutions of the NSDAP are forbidden by the party leadership of the NSDAP when the holder of the certificate can produce the corresponding receipts (see collecting prohibition).
Liaison Staff of the NSDAP,
Berlin.

TABLE 5

Deutsche Bank

Board *S. 5/38*

Berlin, 14 January 1938

To the
Directions of our Branch Offices (centres)

Transformation of Non-Aryan Firms

In the recent period we have repeatedly talked with you about the treatment of our non-Aryan engagements and informed you but a few days ago how we judge the future development of these firms. Thereupon we heard from you that you have permanent contacts with these enterprises and have made yourself available in the Aryanization on their request or intend to do so.

Since up to now we have received only a survey of those non-Aryan firms of your branch district which you count among your debtors but have received but little information on your non-Aryan creditors we ask you to send us another list of your non-Aryan debtors and creditors who come into question for Aryanization. Here we are interested in details on the progress of the Aryanization process of the individual enterprises and your active influence on it. The purpose of this list for us is to consider here in the house if we can support your efforts in view of the many requests we receive day after day and the survey thus coming into existence; of course we place great value on having you conduct the direct negotiations in the future, too.

The whole affair must be treated cautiously and prudently and requires much skill so that anger and resentment resulting from incorrect tactics are avoided, which, as we have learned already, have led to consequences concerning the business dealings; this must naturally be avoided.

TABLE 9

Leuna-Werke, 30 March 1941

Report on Visit

Consultation with the Commandant of the Concentration Camp near Auschwitz on 27 March 1941, 3 p.m.

Present: Sturmbannführer Hoess, camp commandant,
Sturmbannführer Kraus, head of the administration of concentration camps, Oranienburg,
Hauptsturmführer Burböck, departmental expert for the employment of prisoners, Berlin-Lichterfelde,
and a few Obersturmführers and Sturmführers as department experts on the special questions dealt with.
Senior engineer Faust, Lu/Dyhernfurth,
Dipl.-Ing. Flöter, Lu/Dyhernfurth,
Ing. Murr, Lu,
Dr. Dürrfeld, Leuna.

Purpose of the consultation:

After the preparatory conference which took place in Berlin on Thursday, 20 March, between Director Dr. Bütefisch and Obergruppenführer Wolf in the presence of Oberführers Glücke – Oranienburg (superintendent of concentrations camps) and Lörner – Berlin (superintendent for the employment of prisoners) now details on the kind of help which can be taken over by the concentration camp in the construction of the works are to be discussed.

General:

It shall be mentioned by way of summary that the conference took place in an extremely matter-of-fact and yet very cordial atmosphere. In all questions the full readiness of the concentration camp to give all possible help in the construction of the works could be stated. The conference was followed by a detailed inspection of the camp with all its installations and workshops.

Agreements:

1) Herr Faust demands some 1,000 unskilled and skilled workers – as far as available – for the current year. This number can be made available by the camp without further preparations.

2) For the year to come a need for some 3,000 prisoners is announced. This number can be made available by the concentration camp when the necessary accommodation in the camps for the increase of the 8,000 prisoners up to now in the camp have been created. At present the camp is building further accommodation but is hampered by the shortage of reinforced steel for the floors and ceilings. We are ready to examine how this can be delivered to the camp more quickly (index and supply question).

3) Making available further workers over the named figure is quite possible since the camp is to be enlarged to accommodate some 30,000 prisoners. Decisive for the speed is the supply of steel and the making available of the necessary number of "Kappos" (foremen and other skilled workers). These Kappos are selected from professional criminals and are to be shifted from other concentration camps to Auschwitz. These actions are in full swing.

4) For the transport of the prisoners to the building site a direct road over the Salo south of Auschwitz to the works area is proposed. For this purpose the concentration camp builds a bridge. Track for a field railway is to be laid over the same line so that the prisoners can be transported in field trains to and from the building site. Both parties care for the supply of the necessary rails.

5) Working hours are determined by the season and are to be fixed at at least 9 hours in the winter and at 10 to 11 hours in the summer. The output is estimated at 75 per cent of that of a normal German worker. Three Reichsmarks are to be paid per prisoner and unskilled worker per day, four Reichsmarks a day for skilled workers. These costs include everything, transport, food, etc. We need pay no costs outside these expenses for the prisoners, except that as a spur small allowances are given (cigarettes etc.).

6) A simultaneous employment of prisoners of war is unsuitable at least in the current year, especially for the reason that the required number of workers can be fully made available by the camp.

Summary:

The entire negotiation was conducted in cordial agreement whereby both sides emphasized their desire to grant all possible mutual aid. Thus, for example, the camp commandant will, if need arises, make available all forces of the camp, camp doctors, ambulances and even means of conveyance until the building site works smoothly. Agreement was reached upon repeating a similar conference when new questions arise. The preparatory building staff under Herr Murr was recommended in particular to turn to Hauptsturmführer Frommhagen, adjutant to the camp commandant, on all questions.

(signed): Dürrfeld

Copy to:
Director Dr. Ambros
Directors Dr. Eymann/Santo
Director Faust
Director Eisfeld } *Lu*
Director Mach
Director Heidebroek

TABLE 11

The General Public Prosecutor
of the Provincial Court

Berlin NW 40, 27 June 1934
Turmstrasse 91
Telephone: C 5 Hansa 7701–7740

Very urgent! *To the* *Mecklenburg Ministry of Agriculture,*
Domains and Forests, Settlement
Department,
Schwerin in Mecklenburg

In the criminal procedure against Lübke and accomplices the immediate sending of the files available to the Schwerin public prosecutor (J. 421/34) against Fritz Lübke because of faithlessness is requested.

In the local criminal procedure 1.Ba.J.53.34 against Heinrich Lübke, director of the Bauernland (farmers' land) Settlement Company, the urgent suspicion has arisen that Heinrich Lübke has received 5,000 marks from the proceeds of realized inventory stock purchases and used them to pay private liabilities.

by direction
Dr. Kaehlig
Court assessor

(the handwritten remarks are only partially legible)

TABLE 12

ATG Machine Building G.m.b.H.
Leipzig – W 32
Central planning – Goele/Qu.

Leipzig, 5 September 1944

17 copies
Secret command matter
4th copy

Conference Protocol

Concerning Leopard
Inspection of all installations in the upper floor, ground floor and living quarters on 4 September 1944
Present: from the Schlempp
Engineering Office – Dipl. Eng. Lübke
Architect Sander
Building Counsellor Rieck
Architect Rössler
Architect Vollmer
Engineer Hill
Of the ATG — Senior Eng. Schmidtke
Senior Eng. Goele
Engineer Steinbach
Engineer Kohlhase

It may be mentioned at the outset that the work is now making visible progress on the broadest front. In the sequence of the inspection held the following points are to be fixed:

1) Leau dwelling camp
It was agreed that the camp will be subdivided for
a) 1,800 male prisoners
b) 1,000 female prisoners
c) 500 foreigners.
A wooden barrack was already set up, three others will be completed in the course of the week, the other barracks are being constructed in masonry and so sped up that the concentration camp prisoners who are now accommodated in a tent come to Leau as quickly as possible since the tent is impossible for the cold season.
80 per cent of the concentration camp prisoners are suffering from serious diarrhoea.
The splinter protective trenches are built outside the dwelling barracks in accordance with our proposal. This requires the acquisition of additional land.

2) Soalberge dwelling camp
Land under lease was inspected. All efforts are being made so that this dwelling camp provided for the accommodation of German prisoners can be occupied after the completation of the first built rooms. In both dwelling camps only dry privies can be installed.

3) Grounds around lift 3
The "...." site plan was submitted and fixed that building 23 (dispatch) will in any case be available in masonry with a length of 60 metres when the work is in process.
To avoid the filling up of the height of the platform, Herr Lübke proposes to create a basement under the building which is to be finished as checkroom and lavatory.
The other buildings and installations are approved and are being carried through as proposed by us.

TABLE 13

Dr. Ludger Westrick
Chairman of the Board of the
Vereinigte Aluminium-Werke
Aktiengesellschaft

Berlin W 8, 4 September 1940
Friedrichstr. 169/170
Tel. 11-74-21

I EM 11 327/40

Herr Lieutenant General von Hanneken
Undersecretary of State in the
Reich Ministry of Economic Affairs
Berlin W 8
Behrenstr. 43

Dear General,

Referring to our telephone talk of yesterday I venture to convey to you the requested details as an enclosure to this letter. I shall be pleased to be at your service should you wish any supplements or changes. The second enclosure is provisionally supplemented to the year 1940–41, whereby the non-German figures for 1941 are only to be assessed as estimates.

I am most obliged to you for the active support you are devoting to this affair.

With my best compliments

Heil Hitler
Yours respectfully
signed (signature)

Enclosures
Handwritten remarks

Not "..." suitable as a basis for a talk Krosigk – Reich Marshal. The achievements of the Reich-owned works must be more accentuated "......."

The whole must be dressed up a little bit. Suitable "......"

Our extension program has met with the demands made on us by the Reich Ministry of Economic Affairs, the Wehrmacht high command and the Office for the Four Year Plan. With regard to the high power consumption of the aluminium works – it amounted to barely 6 thousand million kilowatt hours in 1940 – certain limits were set to this extension planning by the German power situation and the limited possibilities of the timely erection of new power stations.

In the interest of a rapid increase of the aluminium production necessitated by military developments, economic considerations were put aside to a great extent and the new works set up at places where power and steam could be procured in time, taking military policy aspects into consideration. This also explains the regrettable fact that today 78 per cent of aur production is based on coal power and only about 22 per cent is produced with water power, whereas in the entire rest of the world aluminium production is almost completely based on cheap water power . . .

To supply these plants, too, with sufficient raw material, also in case of war, we have since 1933 brought so much bauxite to Germany annually, despite the high financial burden connected with it, that at the beginning of the war we had at our disposal a stock of nearly one million tons, sufficient for a production of 250,000 tons of aluminium.

TABLE 15 (left)

The Reich Commissioner for the East
Finance Department N 1356 – 29 –
Diary no. 1409/42 d *Riga, 27 August 1942*

SECRET

To the General Commissioners
in Riga / Kauen / Minsk

Subject: Administration of Jewish ghettos
Enclosure: . . . Copies for the regional commissioners concerned

Large Jewish ghettos have been set up in Riga, Kauen and Minsk, smaller ones in a few other places (seats of regional commissioners). The administration of the ghettos is not carried out in a uniform way. Especially the financial responsibility is not clarified . . .

2) Accordingly the object of property administration is above all the available personal property. In addition to this is the utilization of the labour power of the Jews which so far is considered as realized property.

The property administration is to be transferred by the Reich minister for the occupied eastern territories to the finance departments which fulfil this task directly or through the municipal and regional commissioners . . .

3) When objects are sold, the proceeds are immediately to be conveyed to the competent cashier's office. The revenues flow to the individual plan of the finance budget administration of the Reich Commissioner. The establishment of special accounts is inadmissible.

4) The utilization of the labour power of Jews takes place in two forms:
a) through hiring out to public or private employers
b) through the operation of workshops (conducted enterprises) . . .

by direction:	*attested*
signed: Dr. Vialon	*signed (signature)*
	government inspector

TABLE 16

The Reich Commissioner for the East	*Department II*
	Administration
	Secret Diary No. (illegible)

Riga, 31 July 1943

SECRET!

Subject: Gathering of Jews in concentration camps – 1 enclosure

On 21 June 1943 the Reichsführer SS ordered that all Jews in the eastern areas still living in ghettos are to be assembled in concentration camps. I enclose a copy of the instruction of the Reichsführer SS of 21 June 1943. It was fixed in repeated talks with the Higher SS and Police Leader that such works the performance of which cannot be shifted to large concentration camps are comprised in small concentration camps. Thus, for example, a small part of the former Riga ghetto will presumably be transformed into a concentration camp in which workshop enterprises fulfil orders of military importance. In addition, the former workshops maintained for the authorities of the General Commissioner and Reich Commissioner, for example, the uniform tailoring, manufacture of black-out devices for official and living quarters, etc., are to be shifted to this concentration camp. The management of this concentration camp which is to be set up is to be taken over by the General Commissioner in Riga, at my request, security police tasks are naturally to be looked after by the police authorities, and the financial proceeds are to flow into my budget, as up to now. Final agreements on this point are not yet available, however.

To the General Commissioner
in Reval

I recommend that you immediately get in touch with the competent authorities of the security police and the SD and, when the occasion arises, carry through similar measures speedily if they are necessary.

I ask you to report to me on the new arrangements by 1 October 1943.

by direction
signed Dr. Vialon
Attested:
Gerlach
Reich employee

TABLE 20 (2nd part)

The Reichsführer SS and
Chief of the German Police
in the Reich Ministry of the Interior
O-Kdo g 2 (O/RV) No. 78 II/43
Please refer to the foregoing
symbols and date in your reply

Berlin NW 7,
5 June 1943,
Unter den Linden 74
Local tel. 120 034
Trunk call 120 037

Express Letter

Subject: Call-up to the military police of the armed SS

I request that First Lieutenant Johannes Rosendahl of the military police be called up according to the decree of 11 February 1942 – O-Kdo. I RV (2) 1 No. 33/42 – for 18 June 1943 for the SS motorized substitute unit in Weimar-Buchenwald.

First Lt. R. is to be informed about his detachment to the H.Dv. 275 and to be instructed that this direction is also valid in its full extent for members of the disciplinary police who are detached to the military police of the armed SS, especially regarding the classification of the subordinate leaders of the disciplinary police in the armed SS in accordance with their police ranks.

by direction
signed: Flade

To the District President
in Merseburg
for information
to the Higher SS and Police Leader Elbe
– Inspector of the Disciplinary Police –
in Dresden

For the Reichsführer
signed: Siekmann Lt.of the Sec.Pol.

TABLE 22

Court of the Wehrmacht
Command in Berlin
A.Z. B/S 14 p/u

Berlin NW 40, 30 May 1944
Lehrter Str. 58

To the supervisory board of the Penitentiary
in Brandenburg-Görden

On Monday, 12 June 1944, at 1.O.p.m., in this prison the death sentences against the following persons will be carried out with the guillotine:
1) former Lance Corporal Alfred Haase,
born 13 July 1923 in Berlin-Weissensee, Evangelical
2) former Gunner Friedrich Mallaschitz,
born 6 March 1921 in Blumau, Vienna-Neustadt region, Catholic
3) former Corporal Helmut Rose,
born 25 March 1921 in Oberhausen, Evangelical
4) former Rifleman Günther Baars,
born 27 November 1921 in Brieg/Breslau, Evangelical
5) former Obertruppführer Wilhelm Klapproth,
born 24 June 1916 in Soest/Westphalia, Evangelical
6) former Scharführer Ignatz Wallner,
born 18 July 1897 in Fisching/Steiermark, Roman Catholic.

Executioner Röttger is charged with carrying out the sentence. This is to be notified to the sentenced there on the same day at 11.0 a.m.

Charged with the supervision of the execution is First Lieutenant Dr. Zellmann who will be attended by Field Inspector of Justice Hilhof.

The sentenced are in the remand prison of the Wehrmacht in Berlin-Tegel, Seidelstrasse 39.

The Police Presidium in Berlin as conveying authority is requested to send the sentenced to Brandenburg on the morning of 12 June 1944. Acceptance is requested.

The local prison doctor is requested to be made available for the execution.

signed Rieder
Senior Miliary Court Counsellor

TABLE 22 (2nd part)

Court of the Navy in Berlin
J III 181/44

(1) Berlin-Charlottenburg,
12 June 1944

To the supervisory board of the Penitentiary
in Brandenburg-Görden

On 19 June 1944, at 1.0 p.m., the death sentence against Seeman IV Horst Henze, born on 22 August 1924 in Berlin, believer in God, will be executed with the guillotine in your prison.

Executioner Röttger of Berlin is charged with carrying out the sentence. The sentenced is to be notified there on the same day at 11.0 a.m.

Senior Naval Staff Judge Dr. Schlegelberger is charged with the supervision; he will be assisted by the document official Naval Inspector of Justice Nothelfer.

The sentenced is in the remand prison of the Wehrmacht in Berlin, Tegel branch, Seidelstrasse 39.

The Police Presidium in Berlin as conveying authority is requested to send the sentenced to Brandenburg on the morning of 19 June 1944.

The local prison doctor is requested to be made available for the execution.

by direction
signed: Schlegelberger
Senior Naval Staff Judge

TABLE 23 (left)

In the Name of the German People!
. . . against Browislawa Ciesielska, née Sluzalek,
. . . owitz, Zellenweg 18, born on 5 June 1896 at the same place, married,
. . . Ottilie Wojcikiewicz, owner of a baker's shop,
. . . zalek from Sosnowitz, born on 8 February 1907 at the same place, married,
because of war economy crimes according to Figure I, section 3 of the Polish criminal law decree of 4 December 1941 § 47 of the Penal Code.

Special Court I in Kattowitz has passed the following verdict in its session on 23 . . . . . 1942 in which took part:
Provincial Court Director Burk as chairman,
Provincial Court Counsellor Dr. Schmidt,
Provincial Court Counsellor Baron Tiesenhausen as assessors,
Public Prosecutor Ottersbach as representative of the Public Prosecutor's Office
Justice employee Matthies as document official of the bureau:
The accused are sentenced to death for damaging the prosperity of the German people, by means of crimes against the war economy, the accused Wojcikiewicz at the same time for charging excess prices, punishable according to Article I section 3 of the Polish criminal law decree . . . .

TABLE 25 (left)

Attested Copy
(Sond. III) 1 PKLs. 35.42 (783,43)

In the Name of the German People!
Criminal procedure
against

the casual labourer Paul Israel Berkheim, born on 10 August 1911 in Berlin, at present held on this matter in the penitentiary in Brandenburg-Görder, single, Jew, on a charge of racial disgrace.

Special Court III of the Provincial Court in Berlin, at the trial on 9 April 1943, in which took part
Provincial Court Director Dr. Böhmert as chairman,
Provincial Court Counsellor Herfurth,
Provincial Court Counsellor Schultz as assessor judges,
Public Prosecutor Dr. Berthold as official of the Public Prosecutor's Office,
Justice Employee Meyer as documentary official of the bureau, returned the following verdict:

The accused is sentenced to death as a dangerous habitual criminal because of racial disgrace in three cases, to the permanent loss of rights according to §§ 32 ff. of the Penal Code, and to the costs of the trial.

Reasons:

The accused was sentenced to a total of seven years in prison and the loss of rights according to §§ 32 ff. of the Penal Code, for five years because of racial disgrace in three cases through the verdict of Special Court V of the Provincial Court in Berlin on 26 September 1942. After the senior Reich public prosecutor lodged a plea of nullity, the Reich Court quashed this verdict on 18 February 1943, including the underlying statements, and remitted the procedure to this extent for a new trial and decision to the Special Court because it has not been examined if the prerequisites of §§ 20 a, section 2, 42 e of the Penal Code and § 1 of the Law on the Change of the Reich Penal Code of 4 September 1941 have been fulfilled.

TABLE 25 (2nd part)

(19) 2 OJS. 110/44 (56/44) *Confidential!*

Verdict

In the Name of the German People!
In the criminal procedure
against

the hewer instructor Max Kyas from Gleiwitz III, Bischofstrasse 53, born on 20 March 1895 in Makoschau, Kattowitz region, Catholic, Reich German, married, previously convicted, at present in prison in Beuthen/Upper Silesia, because of disintegration of the defence strength, the First Penal Senate of the Superior Provincial Court of Kattowitz in Beuthen/Upper Silesia, on the basis of the trial of 15 August 1944, in which took part

Superior Provincial Court President Drendel as chairman,

Superior Provincial Court Counsellor Dr. Zdralek,

Superior Provincial Court Counsellor Burzlaff as assessor judges,

Public Prosecutor Dr. Zienicke as official of the Public Prosecutor's Office,

Junior Barrister Janus as documentary official of the bureau, has returned the following verdict:

The accused has, despite repeated admonitions and warnings, tried to paralyse the will of the German people to military self-assertion through repeated abuses of the German leadership and German soldiers and through the seditious criticizing of military actions and war measures, within the circle of his workmates.

He is therefore punished with death.

He is deprived of civil rights.

TABLE 26 (2nd part)

Government of the Generalgouvernement
Chief Department of Justice

Krakow, 4 January 1944

Ju Per. S. 296/43.

To the
Special Court of the German Court
in Lemberg

Subject: Criminal procedure against Anna Zwarycz
– 4 KLe 46/43 –

I raise

extraordinary protest

against the judgment of 30 July 1943 in accordance with § 32 of the Decree on the German Jurisdiction in the Generalgouvernement of 19 February 1940 (VBl. GG.I S. 57).

According to § 8 of the Decree on the Simplification of Penal Jurisdiction in the Generalgouvernement of 24 October 1942 (VBl.GG. S. 667) I specify the German Superior Court in Krakow as the court which has to make a new decision in this case.

Reasons:

According to the statement of the Special Court the accused has in October 1942 taken over with herself the then 18-months-old child of the Jew Hirsch-Mamut from Brody, cared for and fed it until the beginning of April 1943, although the Jewish child would have had to live in the Jewish residential district set up in Brody from 1 December 1942 at the latest. The Special Court furthermore stated that the accused openly kept the child with herself, known as Jewish to everybody, and even told a woman acquaintance so shortly before her being arrested. The Special Court did not see in this behaviour . . .

. . . the fulfilment of the outward facts of the case on the part of the Jew suffices as prerequisite for the culpability of the person granting shelter. This prerequisite is given in the present case, for the child sheltered by the accused is a Jew who, contrary to a legal prohibition and without an authoritative permit granting exception, that means unauthorizedly (as a matter of fact) . . .

By proxy
signed Dr. Ganser

TABLE 29

Erwin Schüle, assessor
Stuttgart, Am 17
at the present time lieutenant,
field post number 12207 D

In the field,
3 September 1943

Curriculum Vitae

I was born on 2 July 1913 in Stuttgart-Bad Cannstatt as the son of the winegrower Ernst Schüle and his wife Anna Maria née Österle. My father fell in 1916 at Verdun.

I attended the higher technical school in Stuttgart-Bad Cannstatt from 1921 and passed the leaving examination there in the spring of 1933.

After eight terms of study of political science and jurisprudence at the Universities of Tübingen and Königsberg I passed my first juridical state examination in the autumn of 1937. In 1933 I joined the SA and I have been a member of the party since 1935.

On 1 January 1938 I began my preparatory service in the lower court in Waiblingen. I completed my further preparatory service in the district of the Stuttgart Provincial Court. At the end of December 1939 I had to interrupt my preparatory service because I was called up for military service.

On the occasion of my examination leave in January 1941 I passed my great juridical . . .

TABLE 31

14e JAARGANG No 4

Onze Luchtmacht

Vaktijdschrift voor de Luchtmacht
Opgericht 17 september 1948

Secret Command Matter!
Chief = Matter

Airborne Corps
1a No. 38/40 g. Kdos. Chief matter
For commanders only!
This order is to be dealt with
as "secret" during actions!

Berlin, 23 February 1940
53 copies
52nd copy

Order for the operation of the airborne corps in operation "Fortress"

stamp
General Staff of the Air Force
1st Department No. 5683/40 g.K.
Chief matter of 5 April 1940

1) *Intention*
Fortress Holland is to be taken from the back front by surprise by going around the Grebbe Line.
2) *Mission*
The airborne corps (AA div. 7 and 22nd division) has firstly to operate in the Moerdijk-Dordrecht-Rotterdam-Hague area with the mission:
a) *to keep open the bridges near Moerdijk (here centre) and Rotterdam for the following quick troops of the army which advance over Tilburg-Breda (AA div. 7).*
to occupy the capital The Hague and immediately eliminate the crown, government and army leadership there (22nd div.).
3) *Situation of the enemy*
see enclosure 1
4) *Assessment of the situation and general intentions for the conduct of the action*
see enclosure 2
. . . . .

11) Command post of the airborne corps (and of air div. 7) at first Waalhaven airfield
7 enclosures

signed Student
F.d.R.
Trettner
Major, G.S.O.

TABLE 32

3rd enclosure
to 1a No. 38/40 g.Kdos.
53 copies
52nd copy

Individual orders for AA div. 7.

1) Group South (reinforced paratrooper regiment 1) leader Colonel Bräuer
I./paratroopers 1
II./paratroopers
14./paratroopers
paratr. signals platoon 7 (parts)
1./pioneers 22
div. gun battery 7
1st platoon div. AA battery 7 and paratr. medical half-company occupies the two bridges near Moerdijk by surprise – after preceding bomb attack – immediately removes all existing blasting preparations and takes these bridges firmly into its hands. The bridges must be held by all means until the first parts of the army arrive . . .

4th enclosure
to 1a No. 38/40 g.Kdos.
53 copies
52nd copy

Forbidden zone for our own dropping of bombs

For the protection of our own ground troops the following areas are forbidden for the dropping of bombs:
1) From x + 45 min. to x + 150 min. (operation of paratroopers) landing places Katwijk, Ypenburg, Kijkduin, Waalhaven and bridges near Rotterdam and

Dordrecht within a radius of 3 kilometres (from middle of the places or bridges).
The bridges near Moerdijk to a distance of 5 kilometres from the two ends of the bridges.

2) *From x + 150 min. (operation and march movement of the div.). area Katwijk aan Zee (incl.) – Oegstgeest (incl.) – Leiden (excl.) – Benthuizen (incl.) – Moerkapelle (excl.) – Nieuwerkerk (excl.) – Kinderdijk (excl.) – Noord Maas (incl.) – Merwede as far as railway bridge (incl.) – Hooge Zwaluwe (incl.) – Zevenbergschenkhoek (incl.) – Klundert (excl.) – in a straight line to the north-west as far as Maassluis (excl.) – Monster (excl.).*
Attacks on forces of the enemy within this forbidden zone are carried through only on special request and under responsibility of the airborne corps.

signed Student
F.d.R.
Trettner
Major, G.S.O.

... containers are to be saved and secured in order to be able to guarantee a speedy new readiness for action.

signed Student
f.d.R.
Trettner
Major, G.S.O.

TABLE 35 (left)

Copy
Over Legation Counsellor Schumburg
FOREIGN OFFICE
83–26 19/1 *Berlin, 25 January 1939*

Summary:
The Jewish Question as a Factor of Foreign Policy in 1938

1) *The German Jewish policy as a prerequisite and consequence of the foreign policy decisions of 1938*
2) *Aim of the German Jewish policy: emigration*

3) Methods, ways and aims of Jewish emigration
4) The emigrated Jew as best propaganda for the German Jewish policy

It is certainly no accident that the fateful year 1938, along with the realization of the Greater Germany idea, brought the Jewish question nearer solution, for the Jewish policy was the prerequisite as well as the consequence of the events of 1938. Perhaps more than the power political enmity of the former allied hostile powers of the world war did the penetration of Jewish influence and the disintegrating Jewish mental attitude in politics, economy and culture paralyse the strength and will of the German people to rise again. The healing of this illness of the national body was, therefore, one of most important prerequisites for the effort which in 1938 enforced the union of the Greater German Reich against the will of a world.

But the necessity for a radical solution of the Jewish question also becomes evident as a consequence of the foreign policy development . . .
To all diplomatic and professional consular representations abroad

TABLE 35 (2nd part)

Reichsführer SS
Chief of the Reich Security Main Office 286
II 112 o
C 41 13 March 1939
H/Pi SECRET

To the SD Führer of the SS-O.A.
II 112

Subject: "The Jewish Question as a Factor of Foreign Policy in 1938"

Enclosed is a summary of the Foreign Office on the importance of the Jewish question for foreign policy in 1938 for your information.

I point out that although the report correctly demands a radical solution of the Jewish question through emigration – as has been pursued here for years – at the present moment it can not yet be useful to provoke the Jewish question in all European and non-European states since this could greatly hinder the emigration of those Jews still living in Germany. Referring to this shortcoming in the representation of this problem the Reich Ministry of the Interior has already approached the Foreign Office by letter.

The Chief of the Reich Security Main Office
by direction
The Head of Central Department II 1
as a repres. signed Ehrlinger
SS Obersturmbannführer

Handwritten
SS- . . . Eichmann z.K.

TABLE 45 (left)

The Representative of
the Foreign Office
Reich Commissioner for the East — *Riga, 24 April 1944*
No. 481/44 — *Rosenberg-Ring 12*

Sending of a correspondent
of Neue Zürcher Zeitung

2 copies

The Foreign Office has informed me as follows:

"It could now be arranged that the local representative of the Zürcher Zeitung Ernst Lemmer will fly to Riga on 27 March for the interview Mäe.

Lemmer now has several days available for a program which also includes different tasks.

Lemmer is an experienced journalist with good abilities and seems to be suitable for treating all themes of this area of interest for foreign countries. He is a Reich German and also trustworthy enough to be informed about political developments there. Such information could be of direct help to him in writing his reports for his great and distinguished newspaper effectively in accordance with the orientation there. Herr Lemmer has been told that with this first operation he will perhaps be given priority in reporting on the further development of local things on a later second journey. It is therefore recommended that Herr Lemmer be treated carefully.

I ask you to arrange the return date from there in consultation with him and assume the costs for the return flight.

I ask you to pass on interview reports Mäe, Uluots and Bangerskies and perhaps other reports by Lemmer which are to be written on the spot at the best for his newspaper after examination by the head of the press department on duty for the purpose of the immediate passing on to local representatives of the newspaper.

signed Braun von Stumm"

Herewith passing on this instruction of the Foreign Office which, as I learn, is given in agreement with the Reich Ministry for Propaganda and the Reich East Ministry I would be grateful if the necessary steps for Lemmer's journey and the granting of interviews with people who appear to be suitable there, too, are taken.

Two further copies are enclosed.

signed (signature)

To the
Reich Commissioner for the East
in Riga

TABLE 45 (2nd part)

Ernst Lemmer
Correspondent of foreign newspapers
Member of the Union of the Foreign Press e.V. in Berlin

Berlin-Zehlendorf, 25 April 1944
Hohe Kiefer . . . (Klein-Machnow)

To the Police Presidium
Berlin, Magazinstrasse

I ask for the prolongation of the validity of the enclosed service passport by reason of the instruction given to me by the Foreign Office.

I have to make an official trip to Riga and Reval at the suggestion of the Foreign Office in order to carry out a special journalistic mission with which I have been charged. The departure by plane is foreseen for the 27th of this month, return by 10 May at the latest.

Should you wish a telephonic inquiry the Foreign Office will give you information, either the press department, Legation Counsellor Dr. Staudacher, or Department R XV.

Heil Hitler!
signed: Lemmer

Foreign Office
R Pa Lemmer

Berlin W 35, 26 April 1944
Am Karlsbad 8

The enclosed service passport had been made out for editor Ernst Lemmer for travel to foreign countries on behalf of the Reich government. As the prerequisites for the use of the service passport continue to exist, it is requested that the enclosed passport be prolonged until 26 July 1944.

Foreign Office, passport department
signed: (signature)
Consul

To the Police Presidium, passport department
Berlin C
Magazinstrasse 6/8

TABLE 47 (2nd part)

Professional Association of
German Prehistory Research Workers

Königsberg, Prussia, Theaterplatz
5b, 16 January 1934

Copy

To Ministerial Counsellor Sunkel,
Berlin

Dear Sir,

After our talk about the Wirth case I would still like to inform you and His Excellency the Minister about the following:

Meanwhile Professor Wirth has had an essay published in the Hamburger Nachrichten on 12 January 1934 which contains sharp biased attacks on party member Professor Neckel. In it Herr Wirth praises himself as an old Marburg national socialist of 1924. As far as I know Professor H. Wirth does not belong to the National Socialist Party even today. I believe I can say with full certainty that he was not yet a member at the beginning of last year. In 1929 those occurrences happened about which I have already given you oral information recently. Herr Wirth was at that time supported by Herr Schindler of Hamburg, whom he has in the meantime himself called a "Jewish oil magnate" (presumably in the Rostocker Anzeiger). At that time Herr Wirth, with the assistance of Herr Schindler, addressed himself to Herr Warburg, representative of Jewish high finance, to request further support and asked Herr Schindler to direct the attention of Herr Warburg to the "fine and valuable" review which was published by Wirth's friend Mühlestein in the Frankfurter Zeitung in these very days. This is the review which especially emphasizes the value of Wirth's papers in the struggle against the national movement and education of the yong generation.

It corresponds to the entire peculiarity of his personality that Herr Wirth recommends himself as an old national socialist of 1924 after these occurrences. A good newspaper essay by H. Urbanek enclosed with these lines as a copy contains an extract from Mühlestein's review. Party member E. Witte also reported on details in the periodical Der Hammer, 1932. I also enclose with this letter a copy of the lines sent by Party Member A. Rosenberg to Professor Wirth at that time. I received them in my capacity as lecturer at the then National Socialist People's College from the head of the special group for German prehistory in the Militant

Union for German Culture for information and use in the work against Professor Wirth.

Party Member SA Truppenführer Professor Wiegers, Berlin-Charlottenburg, Sybelstr. 10, could make available a few data on Professor Wirth's relations with freemasonry circles in 1932.

I was very glad that after our talk on the 11th a detailed report by Party Member Steche against Professor Wirth's evaluation of the so-called Ura Linda Chronicle was published in the Völkischer Beobachter. There, too, it is stressed that Wirth uncritically considers anti-German sides of the so-called Ura Linda Chronicle as true and uses them accordingly. Herr Wirth again presents things in his above-mentioned Hamburg essay as if he is struggling against liberals in science. This is again a deliberate untruth. Herr Wirth knows very well that he is opposed by leading especially militant national socialists.

Heil Hitler and German greetings
from yours respectfully
signed B. Freiherr von Richthofen

TABLE 48 (left)

German Evangelical Church
Church External Office
A 3216/39

Berlin-Charlottenburg 2,
22 September 1939

To the Foreign Office
Cultural Policy Department
Reporting Legation Counsellor Lorenz
Berlin W 8

SECRET

Dr. habil. Eugen Gerstenmeier, born 25 August 1906, who is employed in the Church External Office, is to undertake an informational journey to the Northern European countries for the purpose of countering the propaganda of the western powers. Dr. Gerstenmeier has not yet been called up for military service, but he is liable for it and needs a leave for trips abroad from the competent district defence command. It is requested that a certificate for Dr. Gerstenmeier showing the urgency of his journey be issued.

I call attention to the fact that Dr. Gerstenmeier is a member of SA Reitersturm 1/29.

signed: (signature)

TABLE 48 (2nd part)

State Secretary Dr. Stuckart
in the Reich Ministry of the Interior

Berlin, 11 December 1939
NW 40, Königsplatz 6
Telephone 110027

The director of the Institute for State Research at Berlin University and his scientific personnel are constantly entrusted by me with tasks of political importance which are connected with state organization in war.

I therefore request that, in fixing the personnel and material budget of the Institute for State Research at Berlin University for the fiscal year 1940–41, those principles are applied which are valid for similar institutes and establishments.

signed: Stuckart

Kult Mob 1628

Berlin, 23 September 1939

In reply to your letter of 22 September 1939 – A 3216/38 –

Today *SECRET*

In reply to the letter referred to it is confirmed for submission to the competent Wehrmacht command that the journey of Dr. Eugen Gerstenmeier, born on 25 August 1906, employed in the Church External Office, to the Northern European countries is agreed to by the Foreign Office and is in the interest of the foreign policy.

by direction
stamp *signed: Grosskopf*

To Herr General Consul Grosskopf
with the request for execution
The journey is approved by Ambassador von Twardowski.

REGISTER OF NAMES

The numbers following the names refer to page numbers and those following the letter „T" refer to the number of the documentary table.

A

B

E

F

G

H

I

J

K

L

M

N

O

P

Q

R

S

T

U

V

W

Z

Verlag Zeit im Bild, 8019 Dresden, Spenerstraße 21
Satz und Bindearbeit: LVZ-Druckerei „Hermann Duncker",
701 Leipzig, Peterssteinweg 19
Druck: Mitteldeutsche Druckerei Freiheit, 402 Halle/Saale
Bildteil: Druckerei Völkerfreundschaft,
8023 Dresden, Riesaer Straße 32
6,60
415/65 (2,3,5) (2)